# CENTRES OF PLANT DIVERSITY

## A Guide and Strategy for their Conservation

# WWF

The World Wide Fund For Nature (WWF) – founded in 1961 – is the largest international, private nature conservation organization in the world. Based in Switzerland, WWF has national affiliates and associate organizations on five continents. WWF works to conserve the natural environment and ecological processes essential to life on Earth.

WWF aims to create awareness of threats to the natural environment, to generate and attract on a worldwide basis the strongest moral and financial support for safeguarding the living world and to convert such support into action based on scientific priorities. Since 1961, WWF has channelled over US$130 million into more than 5000 projects in some 130 countries which have saved animals and plants from extinction and helped to conserve natural areas all over the world. It has served as a catalyst for conservation action, and has brought its influence to bear on critical conservation needs by working with and influencing governments, non-governmental organizations, scientists, industry and the general public.

# IUCN – THE WORLD CONSERVATION UNION

IUCN – The World Conservation Union – founded in 1948, is a membership organization comprising governments, non-governmental organizations, research institutions and conservation agencies in 120 countries. The Union promotes the protection and utilization of living resources.

Several thousand scientists and experts from all continents form part of a network supporting the work of its six Commissions: threatened species, protected areas, ecology, sustainable development, environmental law and environmental education and training. Its thematic programmes include tropical forests, wetlands, marine ecosystems, plants, the Sahel, Antarctica, population and natural resources, and women in conservation. These activities enable IUCN to develop sound policies and programmes for the conservation of biological diversity and sustainable development of natural resources.

# Availability of further information from WCMC

Background data and more general information on the sites documented in this volume have been donated by WWF and IUCN to the World Conservation Monitoring Centre (WCMC), 219 Huntingdon Road, Cambridge CB3 0DL, U.K., where they form part of WCMC's Biodiversity Information Service and where they are available for consultation. Both map and text information are also available from WCMC in electronic format. Readers may be interested to note that the maps (or modified versions of the maps) of Centres of Plant Diversity in this volume can be overlain with other geographic information, such as protected area boundaries and vegetation cover, through the Geographical Information System (Biodiversity Map Library) at WCMC.

# CENTRES OF PLANT DIVERSITY

## A Guide and Strategy for their Conservation

Project Director: V.H. HEYWOOD
Project Coordinator: S.D. DAVIS

## VOLUME 1
## EUROPE, AFRICA, SOUTH WEST ASIA
## and THE MIDDLE EAST

edited by

**S.D. DAVIS, V.H. HEYWOOD AND A.C. HAMILTON**

published by
The World Wide Fund For Nature (WWF)
and IUCN – The World Conservation Union

with financial support from the
European Commission (EC) and the
U.K. Overseas Development Administration (ODA)

## 1994

Citation: WWF and IUCN (1994). Centres of plant diversity. A guide and strategy for their conservation. 3 volumes. IUCN Publications Unit, Cambridge, U.K.

**British Library Cataloguing-in-Publication Data**
A catalogue record for this book is available from the British Library.
ISBN 2-8317-0197-X

Designed and produced by the Nature Conservation Bureau Limited, Newbury, Berkshire, U.K.

Printed by Information Press, Oxford, U.K.

# TABLE OF CONTENTS: VOLUME 1

# CONTENTS OF VOLUMES 2 AND 3

# PREFACE

The balance between people and their environment is being upset. Escalating human numbers and increasing demands for material resources are leading to the transformation and degradation of ecosystems worldwide, with consequent loss of genetic diversity and an inevitable rise in the extinction of species. More and more land is being converted to intensive production of food, timber and other plant products, much of the world's pasture land is overgrazed, and soil erosion and salinization are reducing the fertility of farmlands, especially in semi-arid regions. Wild species are being displaced or overcropped, and wild ecosystems can no longer be taken for granted as reservoirs of genetic diversity and regulators of the cycles of the elements.

Plants are a central component of this threatened nature. The loss of plants is very significant, for they stand at the base of food webs and provide habitats for other organisms. Although people in some modern societies may be mentally distanced from the reality of nature and are unaware of the services it provides, even city inhabitants are part of wider ecosystems, based on wild plants and natural vegetation. For example, genes from the wild can play major roles in the breeding of new varieties of food crops and other cultivated plants. New medicines continue to be derived from wild species. In many countries, natural and semi-natural ecosystems provide many plant products essential for human welfare, including fuelwood, timber, fibre, medicinal plants, fruits and nuts. Forests protect catchments and thus help regulate the flow of water for drinking, hydropower and irrigation. And wild nature – not the least wild plants – contribute to the natural beauty of the world that we rightly cherish.

In Rio de Janeiro in June 1992 over a hundred Heads of States and Governments signed a new International Convention on the Conservation of Biological Diversity – that is, of the world's rich variety of genes, species and ecosystems. They did so not out of altruism, but because they recognized that these resources were economically valuable and important to the future of humanity. Under the Convention – which entered into legal force at the end of 1993 – each country accepts a responsibility to safeguard its own natural diversity and to cooperate internationally, especially to help poorer countries enjoy the benefits of their living resources.

All ecosystems contribute to the biological wealth of the planet, but some have a much higher diversity than others. Tropical forest contains a much richer flora than tundra, and some areas of tropical forest have many more plant species than others. Even agricultural land varies in the diversity it supports, from the richness of traditional agriculture with its many local varieties of crops, to the ecological deserts of industrial farming with high-yielding monocultures. To be effective, conservation of biodiversity must depend in part on surveys to identify how species and ecosystems are distributed and to identify key sites where diversity is greatest.

The three volumes comprising *Centres of Plant Diversity* are the product of information received from hundreds of botanists from many countries. They have worked together to identify some of the most important sites for plants worldwide. These are priority areas for conservation. These volumes are offered to national conservation authorities and to global conservation organizations as an aid in their work, especially in implementing the obligations of States under the Convention.

A publication like this can only be a beginning. Strategies to conserve plant diversity are needed at all geographical levels – global, national and local – and should form an integral part of all land development plans. And strategies have to be turned into action. Many of the sites described in these volumes are subject to threats and pressures and solutions will depend on finding a balance between different interests, site by site. The solutions are likely to be almost as diverse as the sites, since the environmental features of the latter and the nature of the threats to them vary so widely.

People are at the heart of conservation as well as the source of many threats. Virtually all terrestrial ecosystems, even those that appear to be more pristine, have long included people as components. For example, there are very few, if any, areas of tropical forest which do not provide local people with products for their use, and which have not been altered as a result of interaction with the users over the centuries. And, although local people have been components of natural ecosystems, sometimes for tens of thousands of years, their present day interactions with their environment are not necessarily harmonious.

The conservation aim is to conserve the diversity of nature: clearly this must be achieved within the context of cultural diversity. Conservationists must work with local communities, understanding how they use and manage nature, examining whether current practices are sustainable (both for particular species and in terms of wider impacts) and, if necessary, searching for alternative approaches. Moreover, cultures, whether of local people or professionals, including botanists, land managers and legislators, are not static. The search for appropriate practices, which will conserve plant diversity, perhaps while using it and other environmental resources sustainably, will be a continuing process.

It is our hope that these volumes will stimulate such activities throughout the world, not only at the key localities identified here. Without urgent, informed, practical action, the marvellous plant wealth of our planet will not be conserved, and future generations will be the poorer.

Claude Martin, Director General, WWF International (World Wide Fund For Nature).

Martin Holdgate, former Director General, IUCN – The World Conservation Union.

# ACKNOWLEDGEMENTS

The *Centres of Plant Diversity (CPD)* project, a major international collaborative exercise, has involved over 400 botanists, conservationists and resource managers worldwide, together with over 100 collaborating institutions and organizations. Without this enormous amount of help and support, the project would not have been possible. We wish to thank all those who contributed to the text.

A full list of contributors and collaborating organizations is given below, and authors and contributors to individual Data Sheets are given at the end of each sheet. Here, we would like in particular to acknowledge the major contributions to the project provided by Dr Dennis Adams, Dr John R. Akeroyd, Professor Peter S. Ashton, Dr Henk J. Beentje, Dr Robert W. Boden, Professor Loutfy Boulos, Dr David R. Given, Dr Alan C. Hamilton, Professor K. Iwatsuki, Professor R.J. Johns, Dr Ruth Kiew, Professor Valentin A. Krassilov, Dr Domingo Madulid, Dr Robert R. Mill, Dr Tony Miller, Professor P. van Royen, Dr B.D. Sharma, Dr Sy Sohmer, Dr Peter F. Stevens, Dr Wendy Strahm, Professor Wang Xianpu and Professor Yang Zhouhuai, who undertook the preparation of regional texts and/or contributed a number of site Data Sheets, and (with others) helped in the selection of sites for inclusion in the project.

The CPD project has been co-ordinated by the IUCN Plant Conservation Office at Kew, U.K. Throughout this period, the project benefited enormously from the valuable help, advice and information provided by colleagues and staff of the Herbarium of the Royal Botanic Gardens, Kew, as well as from use of Kew's extensive library facilities. We thank all those members of Kew's staff who contributed to individual Data Sheets, in particular Professor Robert J. Johns, who provided extensive help with writing the section on New Guinea, and to Dr John Dransfield for checking sheets for Malaysia and Indonesia. Special thanks are also extended to Milan Svanderlik and colleagues in Media Resources for their help in producing a set of posters on the project which were used throughout the world at CPD Workshops. Particular thanks are extended to the Director, Professor Ghillean Prance, and to the Keeper of the Herbarium, Professor Gren Ll. Lucas, for their support. Indeed, the initial concept of identifying centres of plant diversity and endemism owes much to Gren Lucas and Hugh Synge (then of the IUCN Threatened Plants Unit). Acknowledgement must also be made of the role played by the IUCN/WWF Plant Advisory Group, initially under the chairmanship of Dr Peter Raven, and subsequently Professor Arturo Gómez-Pompa, in planning and developing the CPD project.

Much of the co-ordinating work for the Americas was undertaken by colleagues at the IUCN office at the National Museum of Natural History, Smithsonian Institution, Washington, D.C., U.S.A. In particular, we would like to thank Olga Herrera-MacBryde for her dedication in compiling and writing many of the accounts for South and Central America, and for her part in editing the volume on the Americas (Volume 3 in the series). Additional editors for the Americas volume were Dr Bruce MacBryde, Jane Villa-Lobos, Jane MacKnight and Dr Wayt Thomas.

Sadly, during the latter stages of the project, Dr Alwyn Gentry, who had substantially prepared the Regional Overview for South America, died in a plane crash whilst carrying out a forest survey in Ecuador. The text on South America owes much to the extensive knowledge on the botany of the region which he had accumulated. We acknowledge the help of Dr Carlos B. Villamil in completing the South American overview, and of Jane Villa-Lobos for help with Central America. Shirley L. Maina and Dr Robert A. DeFilipps are thanked for their contributions for North America.

We are indebted to colleagues at the Royal Botanic Garden, Edinburgh, who undertook (with Professor Loutfy Boulos) much of the co-ordinating work for South West Asia and the Middle East. We particularly thank the Deputy Regius Keeper, Dr David G. Mann, and make special mention of the valuable contributions to the project provided by Dr Tony Miller and Dr Robert Mill.

Grateful thanks are also extended to the members of the IUCN Australasian Plant Specialist Group (co-ordinated by Dr Robert W. Boden): John Benson, Stephen Harris, Frank Ingwersen, Dr John Leigh, Dr Ian Lunt, Dr Bob Parsons and Neville Scarlett. Drs Garry Werren, Geoff Tracey, Stephen Goosem and Peter Stanton also provided much valuable advice and contributions for the Australian section. Similarly, we would like to thank the Secretary for the Environment (Government of India), the Botanical Survey of India and the IUCN Plant Specialist Groups for China and Lower Plants.

For Africa, we would particularly like to thank members of AETFAT (the Association pour l'Etude Taxonomique de la Flore d'Afrique Tropicale) for much helpful advice and valuable contributions.

At the World Conservation Monitoring Centre (WCMC), Cambridge, U.K., the following are thanked for their help: Dr Kerry Walter (Threatened Plants Unit) for providing country plant biodiversity tables; Dr Mark Collins, Dr Richard Luxmoore, Mary Edwards and Clare Billington (Habitats Data Unit) for advice on mapwork and for producing regional maps which formed the basis for those used in all three volumes; and to Jerry Harrison, James Paine, Michael Green and Harriet Gillett (Protected Areas Data Unit) for checking protected areas information. Andrew McCarthy provided much valuable assistance with information on Indonesian protected areas. Dr Tim Johnson is thanked for co-ordinating WCMC's input to the project.

CPD benefited from close collaboration with BirdLife International (formerly known as the International Council for Bird Preservation). We would like to make special mention of contributions of bird data provided by Alison Stattersfield, Mike Crosby, Adrian Long and David Wege. The data on birds will be published more fully by BirdLife

International in *A global directory of Endemic Bird Areas* (Stattersfield *et al.*, in prep.) in which the distributions of all restricted-range bird species will be analysed.

Thanks are expressed to colleagues at Botanic Gardens Conservation International (BGCI), with whom the CPD project shared office space and equipment, and benefited from computer and secretarial support. In particular, we would like to thank Diane Wyse Jackson for technical computer support and Nicky Powell, Erika Keiss and Christine Allen for secretarial help and typing manuscripts. Ros Coles, at WWF, is also thanked for her secretarial support. Kevin McPaul (Computer Unit, Royal Botanic Gardens, Kew) provided valuable assistance in converting several incoming computer diskettes into a readable form. For translations, we thank Sally Horan, Doreen Abeledo, Jennifer Moog and Barbara Windisch, and for map drawing Cecilia Andrade-Herrera, Raúl Puente-Martínez, Alice Tangerine, Carlos Bazán, Jeff Edwards and Martin Walters.

Finally, we give particular thanks to the organizations who provided financial support for the CPD project and without which none of this work would have been possible, namely the Commission of the European Communities (EC), the U.K. Overseas Development Administration (ODA), the World Wide Fund For Nature (WWF), IUCN – The World Conservation Union and, in the U.S.A., Conservation International and the Wildcat Foundation. We are most grateful for their support and encouragement throughout the project.

Stephen D. Davis.　　　　Vernon H. Heywood.

The successful completion of this major project has in no small measure been due to the outstanding efforts and commitment of Stephen Davis who has worked unflaggingly and consistently over the whole period of its preparation.

V.H.H.

This work has proved much more difficult to produce than originally envisaged. Credit for formulating the project is due to Professor Vernon Heywood, formerly of IUCN, and Hugh Synge, formerly of WWF. WWF wishes to acknowledge the efforts of the many contributors and especially the dedication of Stephen Davis and Olga Herrera-MacBryde. The assistance of Botanic Gardens Conservation International (BGCI) (Peter Wyse Jackson) and of the Smithsonian Institution for accommodating some of those working on the project is greatfully acknowledged. Here at WWF, Ros Coles has put in monumental efforts, incorporating editorial changes to many of the manuscripts. Also at WWF, I would like to show my appreciation to Clive Wicks, Peter Newborne, Peter Ramshaw and Michael Pimbert for their encouragement and support.

Special thanks are due to the patience, creativity and understanding of the staff of the Nature Conservation Bureau for their task of laying-out and overseeing the printing of the books. Special contributions have been made by Peter Creed, Charlotte Matthews and Joe Little.

Alan Hamilton
Plants Conservation Officer
WWF International.

# LIST OF CONTRIBUTORS

## Regional co-ordinators

### Volume One:
### Europe, Africa, South West Asia and the Middle East

Europe:
Dr John R. Akeroyd and
Professor Vernon H. Heywood
Atlantic Ocean Islands:
Dr Alan C. Hamilton
Africa:
Dr Henk J. Beentje and
Stephen D. Davis
Indian Ocean Islands:
Wendy Strahm
South West Asia and the Middle East:
Professor Loutfy Boulos,
Dr Tony Miller and
Dr Robert R. Mill

### Volume Two:
### Asia, Australasia and the Pacific

Central and Northern Asia:
Professor Valentin A. Krassilov
Indian Subcontinent:
Dr B.D. Sharma,
Mr A.K. Narayanan and
Dr Robert R. Mill
China and East Asia:
Professors Wang Xianpu and Yang Zhouhuai (China),
Professor Kunio Iwatsuki (Japan) and
Dr Vu Van Dung (Vietnam)
South East Asia (Malesia):
Stephen D. Davis
Australia and New Zealand:
Dr Robert W. Boden and
Dr David R. Given
Pacific Ocean Islands:
Professor P. van Royen, Dr Sy Sohmer and
Stephen D. Davis

### Volume Three:
### The Americas

North America:
Dr Robert DeFilipps and
Shirley L. Maina
Middle America:
Olga Herrera-MacBryde
South America:
Olga Herrera-MacBryde
Caribbean Islands:
Dr Dennis Adams

## Major collaborating organizations and institutions

### Africa

Association pour l'Etude Taxonomique de la Flore
d'Afrique Tropicale (AETFAT)

### Argentina

Universidad Nacional de Córdoba, Centro de Ecología y
Recursos Naturales Renovables
Universidad Nacional del Sur, Departamento de Biología

### Australia

A.C.T. Parks and Conservation Service
Australian National Parks and Wildlife Service, New
South Wales
Conservation Commission of the Northern Territory
Queensland Herbarium

### Belgium

Nationale Plantentuin van België, Meise

### Bolivia

Centro de Datos para la Conservación
Centro de Investigaciones de la Capacidad de Uso Mayor
de la Tierra (CUMAT)
Herbario Nacional de Bolivia
Universidad Mayor de San Andrés, Instituto de Ecología

### Brazil

Centro Nacional de Pesquisas de Recursos Genéticos e
Biotecnologia (CENARGEN)
Centro de Pesquisas de Cacau (CEPEC)
Centro de Botânica do Rio de Janeiro
Instituto Brasileiro de Geografia Estadtistica (IBGE)
Instituto Nacional de Pesquisas da Amazônica (INPA)
Jardim Botânico do Rio de Janeiro
Museu Paraense Emilio Goeldi, Departamento de Ecologia
Secretaria de Estado do Meio Ambiente, Instituto de
Botânica
Universidade Federal Rural do Rio de Janeiro
Universidade Estadual de Campinas, Departamento de
Botânica
Universidade Estadual Paulista, Departamento de Botânica
Universidade de São Paulo, Departamento de Botânica

### Chile

Comité Nacional Pro Defensa de la Fauna y Flora (CODEFF)

Corporación Nacional Forestal (CONAF)
Fundación Claudio Gay
Pontificia Universidad Católica de Chile, Departamento de
    Biología Ambiental y de Poblaciones
Universidad de Chile, Departamento de Biología

## China

Commission for Integrated Survey of Natural Resources

## Colombia

Corporación Colombiana para la Amazonia (COA)
Fundación Pro-Sierra Nevada de Santa Marta
Fundación Tropenbos-Colombia
Instituto Nacional de los Recursos Naturales y del Ambiente
    (INDERENA)
Universidad Nacional de Colombia, Instituto de Ciencias
    Naturales

## Costa Rica

Fundación Neotrópica, San José
Instituto Nacional de Biodiversidad de Costa Rica (INBio)
Las Cruces Botanical Garden, Coto Brus
Organization for Tropical Studies, Moravia
Universidad Nacional, Heredia

## Cuba

Jardin Botánico Nacional, La Habana

## Denmark

University of Aarhus, Botanical Institute
University of Copenhagen, Botanical Museum and
    Herbarium

## Ecuador

Fundación Ecuatoriana de Estudios Ecológicos (ECOCIENCIA)
Ministerio de Agricultura y Ganadería, Dirección de
    Desarrollo Forestal
Museo Nacional de Ciencias Naturales, Herbario Nacional
Pontificia Universidad Católica del Ecuador, Instituto de
    Ciencias Naturales
Río Palenque Science Center, Santo Domingo de los Colorados
Universidad de Guayaquil, Facultad de Ciencias Naturales

## France

Centre ORSTOM, Nouméa, New Caledonia
Laboratoire de Phanérogamie, Muséum National d'Histoire
    Naturelle, Paris

## French Guiana

Centre ORSTOM, Cayenne

## Germany

Universität Hamburg, Institut für Allgemeine Botanik
University of Kassel

## Guatemala

Fundación Defensores de la Naturaleza
Universidad de San Carlos, Centro de Estudios
    Conservacionistas (CECON)
Universidad del Valle de Guatemala, Departamento de
    Biología

## Honduras

Mosquitia Pawisa (MOPAWI)
Universidad Nacional Autónoma de Honduras,
    Departamento de Biología

## Hungary

Eszterhazy Teachers' College

## India

Botanical Survey of India
Government of India, Department of Forests

## Indonesia

Southeast Asian Regional Centre for Tropical Biology
    (BIOTROP)
WWF Representation in Indonesia

## Italy

International Board for Plant Genetic Resources (IBPGR)

## Japan

Botanical Gardens, University of Tokyo

## Kuwait

University of Kuwait

## Malaysia

Malaysian Nature Society
Sabah Parks
WWF Malaysia

## Mexico

Centro Interdisciplinario de Investigación para el
    Desarrollo Integral Regional, Instituto Politécnico
    Nacional
Centro de Investigaciones Biológicas de Baja California Sur
Centro Regional del Bajío, Instituto de Ecología
Instituto de Ecología, Centro Regional del Bajío
    Pátzcuaro
Instituto de Ecologia, Xalapa, Veracruz
Instituto Politécnico Nacional
Subsecretaría de Ecología (SEDUE), Dirección de Flora y
    Fauna Silvestres
Universidad Autónoma Agraria Antonio Narro
Universidad de Guadalajara
Universidad Nacional Autónoma de México

## Netherlands

Rijksherbarium, Leiden
University of Amsterdam, Hugo de Vries Laboratorium
Wageningen Agricultural University

## New Zealand

Invermay Agricultural Centre

## Oman

Office for Conservation of the Environment

## Panama

Asociación Nacional para la Conservación de la
    Naturaleza (ANCON)
Universidad de Panamá, Departamento de Botánica

## Paraguay

Centro de Estudios y Colecciones Biológicas para la
    Conservación
Museo Nacional de Historia Natural del Paraguay

## Peru

Fundación Peruana para la Conservación de la Naturaleza
Universidad Mayor de San Marcos
Universidad Nacional Agraria
Universidad Nacional de la Amazonia Peruana

## Portugal

Universidade dos Açores, Depart. Ciencias Agrárias

## Saudi Arabia

National Herbarium, Riyadh

## South Africa

National Botanical Institute, Kirstenbosch
Rhodes University, Department of Botany
University of Cape Town
University of Pretoria

## Spain

Consejo Superior de Investigaciones Científicas
Herbario, Jaca
Jardín Botánico, Universidad de Valencia
Jardín Botánico "Viera y Clavijo", Las Palmas de Gran Canaria
Universidad de Granada

## Sweden

University of Uppsala, Department of Systematic Botany

## Switzerland

Conservatoire et Jardin botaniques, Geneva

## Russia

Institute of Nature Conservation and Reserves
Research Institute of Nature Protection

## Sri Lanka

University of Peradeniya, Department of Botany

## Taiwan

National Taiwan University, Department of Forestry

## Turkey

Istanbul Üniversitesi Eczacilik Fakültesi
Society for the Protection of Nature (DHKD)

## U.K.

BirdLife International
Botanic Gardens Conservation International
Royal Botanic Garden, Edinburgh
Royal Botanic Gardens, Kew
The Natural History Museum
World Conservation Monitoring Centre
WWF U.K.

## U.S.A.

Arizona State University, Department of Botany
California Native Plant Society
Conservation International
Drylands Institute, Arizona
Field Museum of Natural History
Harvard University Herbaria
Louisiana State University, Department of Botany
Missouri Botanical Garden
New York Botanical Garden
Smithsonian Institution, Museum of Natural History
The Nature Conservancy – Latin America Program
University of California, Department of Botany and Plant
    Sciences
University of Colorado, Department of Geography
University of Florida, Department of Wildlife and Range
    Sciences
University of Hawaii at Manoa
University of Maryland of Baltimore County
University of Oregon, Department of Biology
University of South Florida, Department of Biology
U.S. Agency for International Development
U.S. Fish and Wildlife Service
U.S. National Park Service
USDA Agricultural Research Service
WWF U.S.

## Vietnam

Forest Inventory and Planning Institute, Ministry of Forestry

## Zaïre

Association des Botanistes du Zaïre (ASBOZA)

# Individual contributors

The following kindly contributed information to the CPD project:

B. Adams, C.D. Adams, J. Aguirre, D. Aeschimann, M. Ahmedullah, L. Aké Assi, J.R. Akeroyd, R. Alfaro, K. Alpinar, J. Aranda, D.S.D. Araújo, A. Arévalo, G. Argent, H. Arnal, P.S. Ashton, A. de Avila, M.M.J. van Balgooy, J. Balmer, P. Bamps, J. Beaman, J.S. Beard, S. Beck, H.J. Beentje, D. Benson, J. Benson, B.F. Benz, R. Berazaín, J.B. Besong, M. Bingham, J. Black-Maldonado, R.W. Boden, Bo-Myeong Woo, J. Bosser, L. Boulos, D. Bramwell, F.J. Breteler, D. Brummitt, D. Brunner, T.M. Butynski, A. Byfield, J. Cardiel, L.G. Carrasquilla, A.M.V. de Carvalho, H. Centeno, P. Chai, D. Chamberlain, J.D. Chapman, J. Charles, Shankat Chaudhary, A.S. Chauhan, A. Chaverri, J. Chávez-Salas, M. Cheek, Chin See Chung, M. Cifuentes, A. Cleef, A. Contreras, S. Collenette, M. Costa, I. Cordeiro, M. Correa, I. Cowie, R. Cowling, The Earl of Cranbrook, P.J. Cribb, M. Crosby, H. Cuadros, R. Cuevas-Guzmán, A. Cunningham, R. Daly, P. Dávila, S.D. Davis, G.W.H. Davison, R.A. DeFilipps, C. Dendaletche, L.V. Denisova, E. Dias, N. Diego, M.O. Dillon, M.A. Dix, C. Dodson, C. Doumenge, F. Dowsett-Lemaire, J. Dransfield, S.J.M. Droop, G.R.F. Drucker, O.A. Druzhinina, J.F. Duivenvoorden, B. Eastwood, D.S. Edwards, I. Edwards, S. Elliott, J.L. Ellis, J. Estrada, T. Ju. Fedorovskaya, R. Felger, R. Ferreyra, T.S. Filgueiras, P. Fisher, R.M. Fonseca, A. Forbes, E. Forero, F.R. Fosberg, R. Foster, J.E.D. Fox, H. Freitag, F. Friedmann, I. Friis, J. Fuertes, F.M. Galera, S.M. Gan III, C. García-Kirkbride, S. Gartlan, L. Gautier, A.H. Gentry, A.M. Giulietti, D.R. Given, D. Glick, C. Godoy, L.D. Gómez, A. Gómez-Pompa, J.A. González, S. González-Elizondo, R.B. Good, S. Goosem, R. Gopalan, J.-J. de Granville, G. Green, M.J.B. Green, P.S. Green, P. Gregerson, L. Guarino, R. Guedes-Bruni, N. Gunatilleke, R. Guzmán, P.K. Hajra, T. Hallingbäck, S. Halloy, O. Hamann, A.C. Hamilton, B. Hammel, D. Harder, R.M. Harley, S. Harris, He Shan-an, I. Hedberg, O. Hedberg, I. Hedge, A.N. Henry, F.N. Hepper, P. Herlihy, A. Hernández, J. Hernández-Camacho, O. Herrera-MacBryde, H. Hewson, V.H. Heywood, C. Hilton-Taylor, R. Hnatiuk, A. Hoffmann, Horng Jye-Su, V.B. Hosagoudar, R.A. Howard, Huang Shiman, O. Huber, B.J. Huntley, K. Hurlbert, Indraneil Das, F. Ingwersen, S. Iremonger, S. Iversen, K. Iwatsuki, N. Jacobsen, T. Jaffré, D. Janzen, J. Jaramillo, E.J. Jardel-Peláez, C. Jeffrey, J. Jérémie, C. Jermy, V. Jiménez, R.J. Johns, M.C. Johnston, M. Jorgensen, W.S. Judd, N. Jürgens, C. Kabuye, M.T. Kalin Arroyo, M. Kappelle, S. Keel, R. Kiew, T. Killeen, D.J.B. Killick, Kim Yong Shik, J. Kirkbride Jr., K. Kitayama, C. Kofron, J. Kokwaro, V.A. Krassilov, A.N. Kuliev, A. Lamb, M. Lamotte, A. Lara, R. Lara, P.K. Latz, Y. Laumonier, A. Lehnhoff, J. Leigh, H.F. Leitão Filho, A. Leiva, J. Lejoly, D. Lellinger, B. León, J.L. León de la Luz, J. Léonard, Li Zhiji, E. Lleras, M. Lock, G.A. Lomakina, A. Long, F. Lorea, E. Lott, J. Lovett, P.P. Lowry II, L. Lozado, C.A. Lubini, I. Lunt, J. Luteyn, K. MacKinnon, L. Madrigal, D.A. Madulid, G. Maggs, S.L. Maina, B. Makinson, F. Malaisse, T. Maldonado, M.C.H. Mamede, M.A. Mandango, S. Manktelow, M. Marconi, G. Martin, J.F. Maxwell, N.F. McCarten, A.J. McCarthy, W.J.F. McDonald, I. McLeish, J.A. McNeely, R.A. Medellín, W. Meijer, P. Mena, T. Messick, R.R. Mill, A.G. Miller, L.P. de Molas, J. Molero-Mesa, E. Moll, L. Monroy, J. Moore, Ph. Morat, L.P.C. Morellato, J. Morello, S. Mori, H. Moss, M. Mössmer, C. Muñoz, J. Nais, J.C. Navarro, D. Neill, B.W. Nelson, C. Nelson, Ngui Siew Kong, S.V. Nikitina, H.P. Nooteboom, P. Núñez, H. Ohashi, J.C. Okafor, B. Ollgaard, C. Ormazábal, C.I. Orozco, B. Orr, A. Ortega, R. Ortiz-Quijano, J. Paine, G. Palacios, W. Palacios, Pan Borong, B. Parsons, J. Paine, A.L. Peixoto, R. Petocz, Phan Ke Loc, A. Phillipps, P.B. Phillipson, D.J. Pinkava, M.J. Pires-O'Brien, B. Pitts, M. Plotkin, T. Pócs, R. Polhill, D. Poore, G.T. Prance, J.R. Press, J. Proctor, Qiu Xuezhong, N. Quansah, T.P. Ramamoorthy, L. Ramella, O. Rangel-Ch., T. Ravisankar, A. Rebelo, C. Reynel, M. Ríos, D. Roguet, I. Rojas, M. Roos, P. Rosales, L. Rossi, R. Rowe, P. van Royen, J. Russell-Smith, J. Rzedowski, C. Sáenz, N. Salazar, J.G. Saldarriaga, K.A. Salim, Samhan Nyawa, M. Sánchez S., M.J.S. Sands, T. Santisuk, N. Scarlett, C. Schnell, B.D. Sharma, C. Sharpe, D. Sheil, T. Shimizu, P. Silverstone-Sopkin, D.K. Singh, M.W. Skinner, D. Smith, S.H. Sohmer, J. Solomon, V.J. Sosa, J.P. Stanton, A. Stattersfield, P.F. Stevens, J. Steyermark, W. Strahm, T.F. Stuessy, Su Zhixian, W.R Sykes, H. Synge, M. Syphan Ouk, Tae Wook Kim, A. Telesca, D. Thomas, W. Thomas, K. Thomsen, M. Thulin, J. Timberlake, V. Toledo, L. Torres, R. Torres, A. Touw, J.G. Tracey, C. Ulloa, E. Vajravelu, J. Valdés-Reyna, O. Valdéz-Rodas, F.M. Valverde, T. Veblen, J.-M. Veillon, J. Vermuelen, H. Verscheure, J. Vidal, J. Villa-Lobos, L.M. Villarreal de Puga, J.A. Villarreal-Quintanilla, C.B. Villamil, L. Villar, J.-F. Villiers, W. Vink, K. Vollesen, L.I. Vorontsova, Vu Van Dung, D.H. Wagner, W.L. Wagner, K. Walter, Wang Xianpu, D. Wege, T. Wendt, M.J.A. Werger, G.L. Werren, J. Whinam, W.A. Whistler, A. Whitten, J.J.F.E. de Wilde, B. Wilson, P. Windisch, B. Woodley, R.P. Wunderlin, J. Wurdack, A.E. van Wyk, G. Yeoman, Yang Zhouhuai, K.R. Young, D. Yuck Beld, T.A. Zanoni, E. Zardini and Zhou Yilian.

# INTRODUCTION

VERNON H. HEYWOOD AND STEPHEN D. DAVIS

*The primary tactic in conservation must be to locate the world's hot spots and to protect the entire environment they contain.*
Edward O. Wilson, *The Diversity of Life* (1992).

## The importance of plant diversity

The diversity of plant life is an essential underpinning of most of our terrestrial ecosystems. Humans and most other animals are almost totally dependent on plants, directly or indirectly, as a source of energy through their ability to convert the sun's energy through photosynthesis. Worldwide tens of thousands of species of higher plants, and several hundred lower plants, are currently used by humans for a wide diversity of purposes – as food, fuel, fibre, oil, herbs, spices, industrial crops and as forage and fodder for domesticated animals. In the tropics alone it has been estimated that 25,000–30,000 species are in use (Heywood 1992, 1993a) and up to 25,000 species have been used in traditional medicines. In addition, many thousands of species are grown as ornamentals in parks, public and private gardens, as street trees and for shade and shelter.

Very few of these species enter into world trade and only 20–30 of them are staple crops that supply most of human nutrition. A recent study by Prescott-Allen and Prescott-Allen (1990) indicates that 103 species contribute 90% of the national per capita supplies of food plants. The vast majority of the species used by humans do not form part of recorded trade and, therefore, do not appear in official trade statistics. They form a significant part of what is called the hidden economy.

Another important role of plant life is the provision of ecosystem services – the protection of watersheds, stabilization of slopes, improvement of soils, moderation of climate and the provision of a habitat for much of our wild fauna. It is impossible to attach a precise value to such ecosystem services except by counting the costs of failing to maintain them, and of repairing the consequent damage, such as soil erosion and deforestation.

While it is generally accepted today that the conservation of all biodiversity should be our goal, especially through the preservation and sustainable use of natural habitats, this is an ideal that is unlikely to be achieved and there are convincing scientific, economic and sociological reasons for giving priority to the conservation of the major centres of plant diversity throughout the world, especially as this will very often also lead to the conservation of much animal and micro-organism diversity as well.

Recently, BirdLife International (formerly the International Council for Bird Preservation) has published a survey of Endemic Bird Areas (EBAs) as hotspots for biodiversity (ICBP 1992; Stattersfield *et al.*, in prep.) and has suggested that birds can make a unique contribution to determining priorities for the conservation of global biodiversity because (1) they have dispersed to, and diversified in, all regions of the world and (2) they occur in virtually all habitat types and altitudinal zones. These features apply equally well, or with even more force, to plants. However, a third factor, namely that avian taxonomy and geographical distribution of individual bird species are sufficiently well known to permit a comprehensive and rigorous global review and analysis, cannot be claimed for plants. On the other hand, the bird survey covers only 2609 species of birds – those that have had in historical times a global breeding range below 50,000 km² – while there are an estimated 250,000 species of higher plants, the taxonomy and detailed distribution of most of which are poorly known. On the other hand, as we have noted, plants contribute the background habitat for vast numbers of other species, provide many of them with a food source and interact with many of them in pollination and fruit and seed dispersal, so that their significance as determinants of conservation priorities is unrivalled.

## Historical background to the Centres of Plant Diversity project

The idea of preparing a world survey of the centres of plant diversity had its origins in an informal meeting convened by G.Ll. Lucas of botanists from the Threatened Plants Unit of the IUCN Conservation Monitoring Centre and staff from the Herbarium of the Royal Botanic Gardens, Kew in 1982, inspired in part by the work of Haffer (1969) on South American bird species. The suggestion was incorporated into the Plants Programme which was being developed by IUCN and WWF in 1984 and, in the first published draft of this Programme (IUCN/WWF 1984), one of the key themes was "Promoting plant conservation in selected countries". The choice of countries was based on an options paper prepared in 1982 by Hugh Synge based on data from the Threatened Plants Unit of the Conservation Monitoring Centre. The countries were:

**Africa and Madagascar**
  Côte d'Ivoire, Liberia, Madagascar, Mauritius, Morocco, Niger, Tanzania;
**Asia**
  India, Indonesia, Malaysia, Nepal, New Caledonia, Sri Lanka;
**Central and South America**
  Brazil, Chile: Juan Fernández, Costa Rica, Ecuador: Galápagos, Honduras, Peru;
**Europe**
  Atlantic Islands, Greece.

Within each country, project sites for conservation action were proposed, based on biological, operational, political and socio-economic considerations.

As part of the process of plant conservation in selected countries, the Threatened Plants Unit of CMC decided to prepare a "Plant Sites Directory" (Davis 1986), later known as "The Plant Sites Red Data Book" (IUCN 1986), that would include accounts of about 150 areas around the world which botanists consider to be of top priority for plant conservation, building on the areas previously selected as noted above. At a meeting in 1987 the Joint IUCN-WWF Plant Advisory Group (PAG) which had been established in 1984 by the Directors General of IUCN and WWF to advise on the overall content and direction of the Plants Programme gave approval to the preparation of a Plant Sites Red Data Book and agreed the concepts and criteria for site selection.

Subsequently, the PAG made a thorough review of the Plant Sites Red Data Book concept and decided to broaden the concept by not just paying attention to sites whose conservation would ensure the survival of most species, but by aiming at a listing of all the major botanical sites and vegetation types considered to be of international importance for the conservation of plant diversity. It was also envisaged that the work would document the many benefits, economic and scientific, that conservation of those areas would bring, outline the potential of each for sustainable development in line with the principles of the World Conservation Strategy (IUCN 1980) and provide an outline strategy for the effective conservation of each centre. The project was renamed *Centres of Plant Diversity: A Guide and Strategy for their Conservation*. Details were given in a brochure published in 1988 (IUCN 1988).

Although work started on the preparation of the project in 1987 and some sample Data Sheets were prepared, major finance for the project was not received until 1989 when WWF International provided a grant and negotiated an arrangement with the UK Overseas Development Administration (ODA) for matching funding and, subsequently, obtained a grant from the European Commission (EC) to fund the project over a three-year period. WWF contracted IUCN to arrange for the implementation of the project and Professor Vernon Heywood, then IUCN's Chief Scientist, Plant Conservation, was nominated to organize and supervise the work. Stephen Davis, then a member of the Threatened Plants Unit of the World Conservation Monitoring Centre, and who had been closely involved in the development of the project concept, was appointed full-time Project Co-ordinator. Olga Herrera-MacBryde, Smithsonian Institution, Washington, D.C., worked full-time on the Latin American section of the project from 1989 under the IUCN-SI Latin American Plants Project. Networks of regional contributors and advisers were subsequently established.

## The concept of identifying centres of diversity and endemism

The idea of seeking out high concentrations of diversity among plants, animals or both has a long history in biogeography in one form or another. Attention has frequently been paid to the floristic or faunistic richness of certain areas, such as the tropics of Asia, Africa and the Americas, the Mediterranean climatic regions, such as the Cape of Good Hope, and the concentrations of species on islands, such as Madagascar, Cuba and the islands of Indonesia. Particular emphasis has been given to the large numbers of species that are endemic to such areas, most often with an emphasis on animals, particularly large vertebrates. Another focus has been on particular areas that have been identified as the centres of origin and diversity of crop plants – the so-called Vavilov Centres of Crop Genetic Diversity (Hawkes 1983).

More recently, the concept of sites or centres of high diversity has attracted the attention of conservationists, both as a tool for helping determine which areas should receive priority attention, and also as a challenge as to how to undertake the conservation action necessary, especially as the areas of high diversity are most often found in developing countries which usually have limited human and financial resources available for this purpose.

Much attention has also been directed during the past two or three decades at the large numbers of species that are threatened with extinction at some time in the coming decades (Myers 1986, 1988b; Simberloff 1986; Raven 1987, 1990; Wilson 1988, 1992); the World Conservation Strategy (IUCN 1980) suggested giving conservation priority to those areas where a number of threatened species occur together so as to maximize the benefit from conservation efforts and to reduce the risk of losing large numbers of species if particular areas are not conserved.

Such efforts to seek out areas of high priority for conservation have acquired increased urgency in the light of the accelerating losses throughout the world of natural habitats and the biodiversity they contain, as a result of human action and the growth of the world's population. In particular, attention has been directed at the plight of the world's tropical rain forests which are believed to contain the majority of living organisms but which are being destroyed at an alarmingly high rate (FAO 1990a, b; Whitmore and Sayer 1992).

## Determining priority areas for plants

The problem of determining priority areas can be approached at different geographical scales – global, regional, national or local. At a global level, Raven (1987) developed an approach based on analysis of the size of floras that are threatened, and highlighted the fact that about 170,000 of the world's estimated total of 250,000 species of angiosperms grow in tropical regions of the world, with an estimated 85,000 in Latin America, 35,000 in tropical and subtropical Africa (excluding the Cape), and at least 50,000 in tropical and subtropical Asia. He drew attention to the remarkable fact that more than 40,000 plant species – about a quarter of total tropical diversity – occur in Colombia, Ecuador and Peru. Also, the flora of Brazil should be highlighted since it has been estimated to contain between 40,000 and 80,000 species.

Some of these regional figures have been modified subsequently: for example, the count for tropical Africa has been reduced from 35,000 to 21,000 in the light of more accurate assessments (A.L. Stork, pers. comm. to P. Raven 1991) and the figure for tropical Asia appears to have been under-estimated. The total number of single country endemics (excluding Brazil, Paraguay and Papua New Guinea), recorded by the World Conservation Monitoring Centre (see Table 1), and updated by information arising from the present study, is a remarkable 175,976 species, an estimate which casts doubt on the generally accepted global total of about 250,000 species (see also below, p. 7). What is remarkable too is the fact that for many countries of the tropics it is still not possible to provide more than a very rough estimate of the number of species of plants (or of most other groups of organisms) and,

2

for the majority of these countries, the inventory is neither accurate nor complete.

Raven (1987) also singled out areas such as Madagascar, lowland Western Ecuador and the Atlantic forests of Brazil as deserving of critical attention. Each of these areas houses about 10,000 higher plant species and, in each, forest has been reduced to less than 10% of the area which it occupied 50 years ago.

This analysis was developed further by Myers (1988a) who identified 10 tropical forest "hotspots" (defined as areas that feature exceptional concentrations of species with high levels of endemism and face exceptional threats of destruction). Two further hotspots are in the developed world (Hawai'i and Queensland, Australia). Together, these hotspots total about 3.5% of the remaining primary tropical forest, occupy only 0.2% of the land surface of the planet, but contain around 13.8% of the world's plant species. He later extended this analysis by adding another eight areas, four of them in tropical forests and four in Mediterranean type vegetation zones (Myers 1990).

The five areas of Mediterranean-type vegetation – around the Mediterranean itself, in south-western Western Australia, California, central Chile and the Cape region of South Africa – house some 45,000–80,000 higher plant species, depending on how narrowly or widely "Mediterranean" is defined (Heywood 1994b). Of these, an estimated 27,000–35,000 are estimated to be endemic to the areas concerned (data from various sources including Quézel 1985; Cowling *et al.* 1989; Myers 1990; Greuter 1991; Heywood 1991, 1994b). Southern Africa with some 21,000 species of plants (Cowling *et al.* 1989), of which 80% are endemic, presents a special case and has the highest species/area ratio in the world (Huntley 1988). All these areas are subjected to a high degree of human disturbance; consequently, the flora and vegetation are significantly threatened.

## The selection of sites

The analyses of floristic richness and endemism described above, while providing useful general indications as to which areas might be considered for priority action, have severe limitations in that they are based essentially on species richness and endemism in selected areas, irrespective of the nature, relationships and values of the species concerned, the ecological diversity of the areas and socio-economic factors. Nonetheless they give useful pointers.

In the last 10 years, much effort has been put into considering how habitats of conservation importance should be chosen and which of them should be given priority. These problems have been addressed on many occasions, such as the IVth World Congress on National Parks and Protected Areas (McNeely 1993) and they are reviewed in the WRI-IUCN-UNEP *Global Biodiversity Strategy* (WRI, IUCN and UNEP 1992). The Convention on Biological Diversity, which was agreed at the UNCED at Rio de Janeiro in June 1992, and which came into effect in December 1993, also stresses (in Annex I) the importance of identifying ecosystems and habitats containing high diversity, large numbers of endemic or threatened species and those of social, economic, cultural or scientific importance.

Some authors believe that less time should be spent worrying about the persistence of particular species and more time spent on maintaining the nature and diversity of ecosystem processes. Yet it is species that take part in ecosystem processes

and the fact is that species conservation cannot be separated from that of the habitats in which they occur (Heywood 1994a).

A further criticism of the use of ecological or taxonomic hotspots or mega-diversity regions or countries (Mittermeier and Werner 1988; Myers 1988a) to establish priorities to determine the most important areas to conserve comes from authors such as Dinerstein and Wikramanayake (1993), Pressey *et al.* (1993) and Williams, Vane-Wright and Humphries (1993). They regard such methods as arbitrary, unsystematic and lacking a paradigm. Pressey *et al.* (1993) propose three principles for selecting priority regions and regional reserves for the conservation of biodiversity: complementarity, flexibility and irreplaceability and suggest that they can be applied in practice at different scales. At the global level they advocate the use of the WORLDMAP computer program (Vane-Wright, Humphries and Williams 1991) which identifies key regions for conserving the biodiversity of one or more groups at global and national scales. Biodiversity is measured in this case as a combination of the number of species or higher taxa in a region and the taxonomic differences between them, although measures of endemism are also supported. They note that a critical aspect of the system is the implementation of the principle of complementarity which is used to find a priority sequence of regions to represent all taxa by identifying the maximum increment of unrepresented biodiversity possible at each step.

Once a priority region has been identified, there remains the problem of identifying a network of reserves that is able to represent all the features considered as requiring protection. Pressey *et al.* (1993) give examples of the application of the principles of complementarity and flexibility such as the CODA (Conservation Options and Decisions Analysis) procedure (Bedward, Pressey and Keith 1992) which has been applied to the south-eastern forests of New South Wales to find a network of sites which represent a minimum percentage area of all environments as well as occurrences of rare species and other important features.

Dinerstein and Wikramanayake (1993) present a new approach to conservation planning which they call a Conservation Potential/Threat Index. This index forecasts "how deforestation during the coming decade will affect conservation or establishment of forest reserves." It compares biological richness with reserve size, size of protected area, size of remaining forest cover and deforestation rate and is used to identify conservation potentials, threats and strategies for the 23 Indo-Pacific countries.

The above, and other approaches that will undoubtedly be developed, are to be welcomed. They reflect a growing concern that current approaches to biodiversity conservation worldwide are largely serendipitous, poorly co-ordinated, often ineffective and leave many major problems unsolved. What none of them addresses adequately is the great range of perceptions of biodiversity and priorities from a broad array of different interest groups, be they land use planners, conservation biologists, taxonomists, sociologists, economists, genetic resource agencies or politicians. Any top-down approach, no matter how sophisticated the science, is liable to fail unless full cognizance is taken of the detailed needs, perceptions, aspirations and political realities of the countries and regions concerned. As noted below, in the preparation of this book we adopted from the beginning a principle of involving local experts and, wherever possible, national governmental and non-governmental conservation bodies.

002

## TABLE 1. SPECIES RICHNESS AND ENDEMISM

The following table provides a world list of vascular plant floras arranged alphabetically by region. The data are based on those provided by the World Conservation Monitoring Centre (WCMC) and updated with statistics arising from the CPD project. It should be emphasized that many of the figures are estimates. The reader is referred to the Regional Overviews which provide, in many cases, more detailed flora statistics and information sources. Note that the figures given below for the number of vascular plants have been rounded to the nearest 50–100 species for some regions. A note has been added where this is the case.

| | Native vascular plant species | Endemic species | % Species endemism |
|---|---|---|---|
| **AFRICA** | | | |
| Algeria | 3164 | 250 | 7.9 |
| Angola | 5185 | 1260 | 24.3 |
| Benin | 2201 | 0 | 0 |
| Botswana | 2015 | 17 | 0.8 |
| Burkina Faso | >1100 | 0 | 0 |
| Burundi | >2500 | ? | ? |
| Cameroon | 8260 | 156 | 1.9 |
| Central African Republic | >3600 | 100 | 2.8 |
| Chad | >1600 | ? | ? |
| Congo | 6000 | 1200 | 20.0 |
| Côte d'Ivoire | 3660 | 62 | 1.7 |
| Djibouti | 641 | 2 | 0.3 |
| Egypt | 2076 | 70 | 3.4 |
| Equatorial Guinea | 3250 | 66 | 2.0 |
| Ethiopia | >6100 | >600 | >9.8 |
| Gabon | 7151 | 1573 | 22.0 |
| Gambia | 974 | 0 | 0 |
| Ghana | 3725 | 43 | 1.2 |
| Guinea | >3000 | 88 | 2.9 |
| Guinea-Bissau | >1000 | 12 | 1.2 |
| Kenya | 6506 | 265 | 4.1 |
| Lesotho | 1591 | 2 | 0.1 |
| Liberia | >2200 | 103 | 4.7 |
| Libya | 1825 | 134 | 7.3 |
| Malawi | 3765 | 49 | 1.3 |
| Mali | >1741 | 11 | 0.6 |
| Mauritania | 1100 | ? | ? |
| Morocco | 3675 | 625 | 17.0 |
| Mozambique | 5692 | 219 | 3.8 |
| Namibia | 3174 | ? | ? |
| Niger | 1178 | 0 | 0 |
| Nigeria | 4715 | 205 | 4.3 |
| Rwanda | >2288 | 26 | 1.1 |
| São Tomé and Príncipe | 895 | 134[1] | 15.0 |
| Senegal | 2086 | 26 | 1.2 |
| Sierra Leone | >1700 | 74 | 3.5 |
| Somalia | 3028 | 500 | 16.5 |
| South Africa | 23,420 | >16,500 | >70.0 |
| Sudan | >3132 | 50 | 1.6 |
| Swaziland | 2715 | 4 | 0.2 |
| Tanzania | >10,000 | 1122 | 11.2 |
| Togo | 2501 | 0 | 0 |
| Tunisia | 2196 | ? | ? |
| Uganda | 5406 | 30 | 0.6 |
| Western Sahara | >330 | ? | ? |
| Zaïre | 11,000 | 1100 | 10.0 |
| Zambia | 4747 | 211 | 4.4 |
| Zimbabwe | 4440 | 95 | 2.1 |
| **ATLANTIC OCEAN ISLANDS** | | | |
| Ascension | 25 | 11 | 44.0 |
| Azores | 300 | 81 | 27.0 |
| Cape Verde | 740 | 92 | 12.4 |
| Canary Islands | 1200 | 500 | 41.6 |
| Iceland | 378 | 1 | 0.3 |
| Madeira | 1119 | 106 | 9.7 |
| Saint Helena | 60 | 50 | 83.3 |
| Tristan da Cunha | 40 | ? | ? |
| **AUSTRALIA AND NEW ZEALAND** | | | |
| Australia (mainland)[2] | 15,638 | 14,290 | 95.4 |
| Chatham Islands[3] | 320 | 40 | 12.5 |
| Lord Howe Island | 228 | 93 | 40.8 |
| New Zealand | 2400 | 1942 | 80.9 |
| Norfolk Island | 165 | 50 | 30.3 |
| Subantarctic Islands | ? | 35 | ? |
| **CARIBBEAN ISLANDS** | | | |
| Anguilla | 321 | 1 | 3.1 |
| Antigua | 845 | 0 | 0 |

| | Native vascular plant species | Endemic species | % Species endemism |
|---|---|---|---|
| Aruba, Bonaire and Curaçao | 460 | 25 | 5.4 |
| Bahamas | 1129 | 118 | 10.5 |
| Barbados | 572 | 3 | 0.5 |
| Bermuda | 166 | 15 | 9.0 |
| Cayman Islands | 539 | 19 | 3.6 |
| Cuba | 6505 | 3224 | 49.6 |
| Dominica | 1227 | 12 | 1.0 |
| Grenada | 875 | 4 | 0.5 |
| Grenadines | 473 | 0 | 0 |
| Guadeloupe | 1672 | 23 | 1.4 |
| Hispaniola | 5135 | 1445 | 28.1 |
| Jamaica | 3304 | 923 | 27.9 |
| Martinique | 1505 | 24 | 1.6 |
| Montserrat | 670 | 2 | 0.3 |
| Nevis | 260 | 1 | 0.4 |
| Puerto Rico | 2492 | 236 | 9.5 |
| Saint Kitts | 659 | 1 | 0.2 |
| Saint Lucia | 1028 | 11 | 1.1 |
| Saint Vincent | 1134 | 20 | 1.8 |
| Trinidad and Tobago | 2259 | 236 | 10.5 |
| Turks and Caicos | 448 | 9 | 2.0 |
| **CENTRAL AND NORTHERN ASIA** | | | |
| Estimate for whole region, comprising Asiatic part of the former U.S.S.R. | 17,500 | 2500 | 14.3 |
| **CHINA AND EAST ASIA** | | | |
| Cambodia/Laos/Vietnam | >12,800 | ? | ? |
| China | 27,100 | 10,000 | 36.9 |
| Hong Kong | 1984 | 25 | 1.3 |
| Japan (main islands) | 5565 | >222 | >4.0 |
| Korean Peninsula | 2898 | 407 | 14.0 |
| Mongolia | 2272 | 229 | 10.1 |
| Taiwan | 3577 | 1075 | 30.1 |
| Thailand | 12,000 | ? | ? |
| Vietnam | 8000 | >800 | >10.0 |

(Note that the statistics for China and Indochina are very approximate.)

| | Native vascular plant species | Endemic species | % Species endemism |
|---|---|---|---|
| **EUROPE** | | | |
| Albania | 3000 | 24 | 0.8 |
| Austria | 3100 | 35 | 1.1 |
| Belgium | 1550 | 1 | 0.1 |
| Bulgaria | 3600 | 320 | 8.8 |
| Cyprus | 1650 | 88 | 5.3 |
| Czech Republic and Slovakia | 2600 | 62 | 2.4 |
| Denmark | 1450 | 1 | 0.1 |
| Faroes | 250 | 1 | 0.4 |
| Finland | 1045 | ? | ? |
| France | 4650 | 133 | 2.9 |
| Germany | 2700 | 6 | 0.2 |
| Greece | 5000 | 742 | 14.9 |
| Hungary | 2200 | 38 | 1.7 |
| Ireland | 950 | ? | ? |
| Italy | 5600 | 712 | 12.7 |
| Liechtenstein | 1400 | ? | ? |
| Luxembourg | 1200 | 0 | 0 |
| Malta | 914 | 5 | 0.5 |
| Netherlands | 1200 | ? | ? |
| Norway | 1600 | 1 | 0.1 |
| Poland | 2450 | 3 | 0.1 |
| Portugal (mainland) | 2600 | 3 | 0.1 |
| Romania | 3400 | 41 | 1.4 |
| Spain (mainland) | 5050 | 941 | 18.6 |
| Sweden | 1750 | 1 | 0.1 |
| Switzerland | 3000 | 1 | 0.03 |
| United Kingdom | 1550 | 16 | 1.0 |
| Yugoslavia (former territory of) | 5350 | 137 | 2.6 |

(The figures for vascular plants are rounded to the nearest 50 species.)

## TABLE 1. SPECIES RICHNESS AND ENDEMISM ...continued

| | Native vascular plant species | Endemic species | % Species endemism |
|---|---|---|---|
| **INDIAN OCEAN ISLANDS** | | | |
| British Indian Ocean Territory | | | |
| (Chagos Archipelago) | 100 | 0 | 0 |
| Comoros | 416 | 136 | 33.0 |
| Madagascar | 10,000 | 8000 | 80.0 |
| Maldives | 277 | 5 | 1.8 |
| Mauritius[4] | 685 | 311 | 45.4 |
| Réunion[4] | 546 | 189 | 34.6 |
| Rodrigues[4] | 134 | 47 | 35.1 |
| Seychelles | 250 | 87 | 34.8 |
| **INDIAN SUBCONTINENT** | | | |
| Andaman and Nicobar Islands | 2270 | 225 | 9.9 |
| Bangladesh | 5000 | ? | ? |
| Bhutan | 5500 | 100 | 1.8 |
| India | 17,000 | 6800–7650 | 40.0–45.0 |
| Lakshadweep | 348 | 0 | 0 |
| Maldives | 277 | 5 | 1.8 |
| Myanmā (Burma) | 14,000 | 1700 | 12.1 |
| Nepal | 7000 | 350 | 5.0 |
| Pakistan | 5100 | 400 | 7.8 |
| Sri Lanka | 3682 | 902 | 24.5 |
| **MIDDLE AMERICA** | | | |
| Belize | 2600–3100 | 150 | 4.8–5.8 |
| Costa Rica | 11,100–13,100 | 600 | 4.6–5.4 |
| El Salvador | 2900 | 17 | 0.6 |
| Guatemala | 8650 | 1171 | 13.5 |
| Honduras | 5650 | 148 | 2.6 |
| Mexico | >20,000 | >10,000 | ? |
| Nicaragua | 7600 | 30–50 | 0.4–0.7 |
| Panama | 9900 | 1222 | 12.3 |

(The figures for total number of vascular plants are rounded to the nearest 50 species and may vary slightly from those given in the Regional Overview.)

| | Native vascular plant species | Endemic species | % Species endemism |
|---|---|---|---|
| **NORTH AMERICA** | | | |
| Canada | 3270 | 147 | 4.5 |
| Greenland | 497 | 15 | 3.0 |
| U.S.A. (continental)[5] | 20,000 | 4036 | 20.2 |
| **PACIFIC OCEAN ISLANDS** | | | |
| American Samoa | 460 | 17 | 3.7 |
| Bonin (Ogasawara) Islands | 400 | 150 | 37.5 |
| Cook Islands | 284 | 33 | 11.6 |
| Fed. Micronesia | 1194 | 293 | 24.5 |
| Fiji | 1628 | 812 | 49.9 |
| French Polynesia (incl. Marquesas) | 959 | 560 | 58.3 |
| Galápagos | 541 | 224 | 41.4 |
| Guam | 330 | 69 | 20.9 |
| Hawaiian Islands | 1200 | 1000 | 83.3 |
| Juan Fernández | 210 | 127 | 60.4 |
| Kiribati | 22 | 2 | 9.1 |
| Marquesas | 318 | 132 | 41.5 |
| Marshall Islands | 100 | 5 | 5.0 |
| Nauru | 54 | 1 | 1.9 |
| New Caledonia | 3322 | 2551 | 76.8 |
| Niue | 178 | 1 | 0.6 |
| North Marianas | 221 | 81 | 36.7 |
| Palau | 175 | ? | ? |
| Pitcairn Islands | 76 | 14 | 18.4 |
| Tokelau Islands | 32 | 0 | 0 |
| Tonga | 463 | 25 | 5.4 |

| | Native vascular plant species | Endemic species | % Species endemism |
|---|---|---|---|
| Tuvalu | 44 | 0 | 0 |
| Vanuatu | 870 | 150 | 17.2 |
| Wallis and Futuna | 475 | 7 | 1.5 |
| Western Samoa | 894 | 134 | 15.0 |
| **SOUTH AMERICA** | | | |
| Argentina | 9370 | 1100 | 11.7 |
| Bolivia | 17,350 | 4000 | 23.0 |
| Brazil | 56,000 | ? | ? |
| Chile | 4900–5650 | 2698 | 47.8–55.0 |
| Colombia | 51,000 | 1500 | 2.9 |
| Ecuador | 17,600–21,100 | 4000 | 19.0–22.7 |
| French Guiana | 5625 | 144 | 2.6 |
| Guyana | 6400 | ? | ? |
| Paraguay | 7000–8000 | ? | ? |
| Peru | 18,245 | 5356 | 29.4 |
| Suriname | 5000 | ? | ? |
| Uruguay | 2270 | 40 | 1.8 |
| Venezuela | 21,070 | 8000 | 38.0 |

(The figures for total number of vascular plants are rounded to the nearest 50 species and may vary slightly from those given in the Regional Overview.)

| | Native vascular plant species | Endemic species | % Species endemism |
|---|---|---|---|
| **SOUTH EAST ASIA (MALESIA)** | | | |
| Borneo | 20,000–25,000 | 6000–7000 | 30.0 |
| Brunei | 6000 | ? | ? |
| D'Entrecasteaux | >2500 | ? | ? |
| Indonesia (available estimates): | | | |
| Java | 4598 | 230 | 5.0 |
| Sulawesi | 5000 | ? | ? |
| Sumatra | >10,000 | >1200 | >10.0 |
| Louisiade Archipelago | >3000 | ? | ? |
| Malaysia (available estimates): | | | |
| Peninsular Malaysia | >9000 | 2700–4500 | 30.0–50.0 |
| Sabah and Sarawak | >10,000 | ? | ? |
| New Guinea | 15,000–20,000 | 10,500–16,000 | 70.0–80.0 |
| Philippines | 8931 | 3500 | 39.2 |
| Singapore[6] | 1293 | 2 | 0.2 |
| Solomon Islands | 3172 | 30 | 0.9 |
| **SOUTH WEST ASIA AND THE MIDDLE EAST** | | | |
| Afghanistan | 4000 | 800 | 20.0 |
| Bahrain | 248 | 0 | 0 |
| Iran | 8000 | 1400 | 17.5 |
| Iraq | 3000 | 190 | 6.3 |
| Israel | 2225 | 165 | 7.4 |
| Jordan | 2100 | 145 | 7.3 |
| Kuwait | 282 | 0 | 0 |
| Lebanon | 2600 | 311 | 12.0 |
| Oman | 1200 | 73 | 6.1 |
| Qatar | 306 | 0 | 0 |
| Saudi Arabia | 2028 | 34 | 1.7 |
| Syria | 3100 | 395 | 13.0 |
| Turkey | 8650 | 2675 | 30.9 |
| United Arab Emirates | 340 | 0 | 0 |
| Yemen[7] (N) | 1650 | 58 | 3.5 |
| Yemen[7] (S) | 1180 | 77 | 6.5 |
| Socotra (Yemen) | 815 | >230 | >28.2 |
| **[ANTARCTIC, SOUTH ATLANTIC AND SOUTHERN OCEAN]** | | | |
| Antarctic continent | 2 | 0 | 0 |
| Falkland Islands (Malvinas) | 165 | 14 | 8.5 |
| French Southern Territories | 50 | 11 | 22.0 |

(The above region is included here for completeness.)

Notes:

[1] Refers to single-island endemics.
[2] Latest count for Australia, but an estimated 3000–5000 vascular plant taxa yet to be named.
[3] Figures refer to vascular plant taxa (i.e. species, subspecies and varieties).
[4] Figures refer to flowering plant taxa (i.e. species, subspecies and varieties).
[5] Figures refer to flowering plant species.
[6] Figures for gymnosperms and dicots only.
[7] Yemen was unified in 1991; figures for North Yemen (Yemen Arab Republic), South Yemen (People's Democratic Republic of Yemen) and Socotra are kept separate for convenience.

The objectives of the *Centres of Plant Diversity (CPD)* project are:

❖ to identify which areas around the world, if conserved, would safeguard the greatest number of plant species;
❖ to document the many benefits, economic and scientific, that conservation of those areas would bring to society and to outline the potential value of each for sustainable development;
❖ to outline a strategy for the conservation of the areas selected.

These objectives are fully consonant with the *Convention on Biological Diversity*.

As a consequence of the very extensive involvement of local specialists, and well over 100 government and non-governmental agencies and other conservation bodies in the preparation of the project, including the holding of workshops in several parts of the world, we believe that the resultant three volumes comprising *Centres of Plant Diversity* will provide a unique global and regional review of the nature and distribution of the main concentrations of plant diversity in the world, and a guide to the most practical and cost-effective ways of conserving as much of this diversity as possible, together with its sustainable use. It is our aspiration that CPD will provide not only its sponsors, IUCN, WWF, ODA and the EC, but also governments, aid agencies, development banks and conservation organizations, with a considered overview of the status of plant diversity worldwide and clear guidance on which areas are global and regional priorities for its conservation.

Although the original intention was to select between 150 and 200 sites of global priority, the total number finally chosen greatly exceeds these figures. In addition to the 234 priority sites selected for Data Sheet treatment, many more sites are treated in summary paragraphs in the Regional Overviews. By extending the Regional Overviews in this way, we overcame the problem of making an arbitrary selection of a single site where several potential sites occur in a particular area. In some cases, the Regional Overviews also contain a selection of important botanical areas which do not meet the criteria for selection as CPD sites but which are, nonetheless, areas of important conservation concern because, for example, they may contain the best surviving examples of certain vegetation types.

## The criteria and methodology used for selecting sites

The criteria adopted for the selection of sites and vegetation types was based principally on a requirement that each must have one or both of the following two characteristics:

❖ the area is evidently species-rich, even though the number of species present may not be accurately known;
❖ the area is known to contain a large number of species endemic to it.

The following characteristics were also considered in the selection:

❖ the site contains an important genepool of plants of value to humans or that are potentially useful;
❖ the site contains a diverse range of habitat types;

❖ the site contains a significant proportion of species adapted to special edaphic conditions;
❖ the site is threatened or under imminent threat of large-scale devastation.

It has to be stressed that *Centres of Plant Diversity* is concerned with "first order" sites that are of *global* botanical importance. As a consequence some countries have had a number of sites selected, while others have none that qualify for inclusion when viewed on a world basis. If viewed from a national perspective, the selection of sites would have been different. We hope, however, that the publication of these volumes will serve as a stimulus for national programmes aimed at identifying plant sites that are important at a more local level.

The selection process has involved extensive consultations with experts in all the major regions of the world. Networks of individuals and collaborating institutions were established and their advice sought on the listing of sites for the Regional Overviews and for selecting those sites which merit Data Sheet treatment. In Africa, China, India, North America and South America, this involved the holding of workshops within these regions at which data on proposed CPD sites were reviewed and the final selection of Data Sheet sites made. Sometimes this led to some sites being rejected and replaced by others. This is especially true for South America, where the Regional Workshop held in Quito in 1990 to review the site selection led to a total revision of the phytogeographical divisions of South America and to the major revision of the list of sites previously chosen.

To qualify for Data Sheet treatment, most mainland sites have (or are believed to have) in excess of 1000 vascular plant species, of which at least 100 (i.e. 10%) are endemic either to the site (strictly endemic) or to the phytogeographical region in which the site occurs. In many cases, the number of regional endemics is very much higher than 10% of the flora. In all cases the sites have at least some strict endemics.

The criteria for the selection of islands treated as Data Sheets were somewhat different from those used for mainland sites. Many islands have depauperate floras compared with continental areas, but the level of endemism is often very high. For example, Saint Helena has a flora of only 60 vascular plant species but 50 of these are endemic. Clearly, the high concentration of endemics is of considerable conservation importance, and to restrict the selection of sites to those with floras of, or in excess of, 1000 species would lead to the omission of such important areas.

To qualify for Data Sheet treatment, an island flora must contain at least 50 endemic species or at least 10% of the flora must be endemic. Even so, data were not available for some islands that perhaps warranted inclusion. Comoros, in the Indian Ocean, is a good example of such a situation: the only available figures (416 vascular plant species, of which 136 are endemic) are based on an assessment of the flora made in 1917 which is almost certainly incomplete.

For some islands, the Data Sheet covers the whole island (e.g. Socotra) or an archipelago (e.g. the Canary Islands). South East Asia presented a somewhat different problem: practically the whole region is insular and floristically very rich with high levels of endemism on many of the larger islands. In this case, a number of sites and vegetation types were selected throughout the archipelago, with some islands being represented by more than one Data Sheet to cover a range of vegetation and community types.

There was, in some cases, an element of subjectivity involved in the selection process, and other criteria were used (such as degree of threat, diversity of habitats or soil types, presence of scientifically or economically important species) in deciding which out of a number of similar sites, would be chosen as Data Sheets. But the main criteria and principles outlined above were used to make the initial selection, and always with the help and advice of regional and local expertise.

## Content of the Regional Overviews and Data Sheets

Within the constraints imposed by the enormous diversity of the areas covered, a standard format has been adopted for each of the Regional Overviews and Data Sheets. A summary table is provided in each case. There is a certain amount of variation in the headings adopted in the Regional Overviews, but for nearly all the site Data Sheets the following sections are included: Geography, Vegetation, Flora, Useful Plants, Social and Environmental Values, Threats, Conservation and References. An Economic Assessment section is included where data are available.

## Analysis of the information on the sites

### (i) Regional distribution of Data Sheets

A total of 234 sites are selected for Data Sheet treatment. Their general location is shown in the map on page 11. The distribution of the sites in the different regions is given in Table 2.

**TABLE 2. DISTRIBUTION OF DATA SHEETS BY REGION**

| EUROPE, AFRICA, SOUTH WEST ASIA AND THE MIDDLE EAST | |
|---|---|
| Europe | 9 |
| Atlantic Ocean Islands | 4 |
| Africa | 30 |
| Indian Ocean Islands | 3 |
| South West Asia and the Middle East | 11 |
| **Total** | **57** |
| **ASIA, AUSTRALASIA AND THE PACIFIC** | |
| Central and Northern Asia | 5 |
| Indian Subcontinent | 13 |
| China and East Asia | 21 |
| South East Asia (Malesia) | 41 |
| Australia and New Zealand | 14 |
| Pacific Ocean Islands | 8 |
| **Total** | **102** |
| **THE AMERICAS** | |
| North America | 6 |
| Middle America | 20 |
| South America | 46 |
| Caribbean Islands | 3 |
| **Total** | **75** |
| **Grand Total** | **234** |

When considering the figures in Table 2, it must be remembered that the sites vary enormously in size, from extensive mountain systems, such as the Alps, to island complexes, such as the Hawaiian Islands, and to much smaller areas, such as the Sinharaja forest of Sri Lanka. This makes direct comparisons between sites impossible. Attention should also be drawn to the Regional Overviews which place the sites selected in a much wider context and provide a comparative assessment of the biodiversity and conservation status of the different areas within the regions.

### (ii) Floristic diversity

It has proved difficult to obtain accurate data on the number of species in some of the sites and even for some areas. Even estimates for individual countries are imprecise in some instances, such as Bolivia, Indonesia and Thailand. The global figures for species richness and endemism can, however, be summarized as follows:

**TABLE 3. FLORISTIC DIVERSITY AND ENDEMISM BY REGION**

| | Species | Endemics | % Endemism |
|---|---|---|---|
| **EUROPE, AFRICA, SOUTH WEST ASIA AND THE MIDDLE EAST** | | | |
| Europe | 12,500 | 3500 | 28 |
| Atlantic Ocean Islands | 2650 | 785 | 29.5 |
| Africa | 40–45,000 | 35,000 | 77–87.5 |
| Indian Ocean Islands | 11,000 | 9000 | 82 |
| South West Asia and the Middle East | 23,000 | 7100 | 31 |
| **Totals** | **89–94,150** | **55,385** | |
| **ASIA, AUSTRALASIA AND THE PACIFIC** | | | |
| Central and Northern Asia | 17,500 | 2500 | 14 |
| Indian Subcontinent | 25,000 | 12,000 | 48 |
| China and East Asia | 45,000 * | 18,650 * | 41.5* |
| South East Asia (Malesia) | 42–50,000 | 29–40,000 | 70–80 |
| Australia and New Zealand | 17,580 | 16,202 | 90 |
| Pacific Ocean Islands | 11–12,000 | 7000 | 58–63 |
| **Totals** | **156–167,080** | **81–93,352** | |
| **THE AMERICAS** | | | |
| North America | 20,000 | 4198 | 21 |
| Middle America | 30–35,000 | 14–19,000 | 46–54 |
| South America | 70,000 * | 55,000 * | 78.5 |
| Caribbean Islands | 13,000 | 6555 | 50 |
| **Totals** | **133–138,000** | **80–85,000** | |
| **Grand Totals** | **380–399,000** | **216–234,000** | |

* estimate based on available data.

Considerable caution needs to be used in interpreting the figures in this table. It has been exceedingly difficult to obtain accurate figures for many countries. This reflects the relatively poor state of our floristic knowledge, especially in the tropics and subtropics, as has been repeatedly pointed out elsewhere. Effective conservation of biodiversity in the face of such ignorance will be difficult and this is a problem which has to be faced as a matter of urgency. It is notable too that in several regions, such as Africa, Asia, Australia and Latin America, tens of thousands of species are believed still to be undescribed.

The numbers of endemic species given in Table 3 can be totalled meaningfully but the totals of all species in each of the regions, and the sum total of these, are only indicative, as no account is made of the species that are shared between two or more regions. The remarkable total of 227,823 endemic species recorded from the information given in the regional reviews, which themselves reflect the data given in the individual Data Sheets, is surprisingly high when one considers that the *total* number of flowering plants and ferns known today is generally accepted as being around 250,000. It is also substantially higher than the figure of 175,976 endemic species derived from WCMC data (Table 1). The implications are that, if these data can be confirmed, the total number of flowering plant and fern species must be at least of the order of 300,000–350,000 if allowance is made for those species that occur in two or more regions, in more than one continent or are even more widespread.

It is notable too that the total numbers of endemic species (and therefore by implication the total flora) recorded for Asia, Australasia and the Pacific are appreciably higher than those of Latin America and the Caribbean combined. If one takes into account the probability that narrower species concepts are applied in Latin America than in parts, at least, of Asia and the Pacific, as several authors have suggested (e.g. Gentry 1990), the difference will be even greater. This would suggest that conservation agencies might take a closer look at the comparative richness of Latin America/Caribbean and Asia/Pacific in assessing priorities and balance of investment.

If the numbers of Data Sheets for each of the three volumes are compared (Table 4), it will be seen that there is a very broad consistency of treatment.

**TABLE 4. COMPARISON OF FLORISTIC RICHNESS (AS MEASURED BY ENDEMICS) AND NUMBERS OF DATA SHEETS FOR REGIONS IN EACH VOLUME OF CPD**

| Region | Total endemics | Number of Data Sheets |
|---|---|---|
| EUROPE, AFRICA, SOUTH WEST ASIA AND THE MIDDLE EAST | 55,385 | 57 |
| ASIA, AUSTRALASIA AND THE PACIFIC | 93,352 | 102 |
| THE AMERICAS | 79,086 | 75 |

## (iii) Conservation status

As one reads through the paragraphs in the Data Sheets on the conservation status of the sites, two worrying trends may be discerned. On the one hand, many sites are not legally protected, or are only protected in part. On the other hand, a considerable proportion of those sites that are officially protected are not effectively managed, being subject to various forms of degradation, ranging from logging to gathering of fuelwood. This emphasizes the need for extending and strengthening the protected area systems of the countries concerned, if the strategy of protecting biodiversity through setting aside and protecting areas of high floristic and ecological richness is to succeed.

Table 5 gives a breakdown by region of the number of sites included partly or fully within legally designated protected areas. From Table 5 and the information presented in the Summary Table (see final section in Introduction), it is encouraging that many CPD sites are represented (at least in part) in existing protected areas, or are proposed for inclusion. Australia is perhaps the best illustration of this. Here, most CPD sites are well-represented within the National Park system, and some areas have additional protection as World Heritage Sites. Of particular note is the Wet Tropics World Heritage Area which includes virtually all of the remaining tropical rain forest in Australia (see the Data Sheet on the Wet Tropics of Queensland – CPD Site Au10, in Volume 2). In other cases, such as Kakadu-Alligator Rivers region and the Western Tasmanian Wilderness (CPD Sites Au4 and Au9, respectively, also covered in Data Sheets in Volume 2), there are important areas outside the existing reserve boundaries which need to be brought into protection to conserve significant elements of the flora.

Closer examination of the current protection of the CPD sites, reveals that the present coverage of legally protected areas is often inadequate to "capture" the full range of vegetation types and areas of greatest floristic richness within

a region. Worldwide, less than one in four of the Data Sheet sites (21%) are legally protected in full, and only about one-third of the selected sites (35%) have more than 50% of their areas occurring within existing protected areas.

The largest number of totally unprotected sites occurs in Africa (8 sites) and South East Asia (6 sites); many more sites (17) in South East Asia have less than 50% of their areas occurring within legally designated protected areas. Also of significance is the large number of South American sites (32) which have only a relatively small part of their areas covered by any form of legal protection. A priority must be to extend the coverage of the existing network of protected areas in these regions, and particularly to safeguard remaining plant-rich lowland forests.

Better protection of the lowlands is also a priority for areas with Mediterranean-type climates. In the South-West Botanical Province of Western Australia (CPD Site Au7, see Data Sheet in Volume 2), for example, over a third of the state's Rare and Endangered plants are not protected within the existing reserve system. In the California Floristic Province of U.S.A. (CPD Site NA16, see Data Sheet in Volume 3), the lowlands are particularly under-protected. The lowland flora is also under-represented in the present reserve system in the Cape Floristic Province of South Africa (CPD Site Af53, see Data Sheet in Volume 1), which in terms of the number of species per unit area is probably the richest plant area in the world.

In Central and Northern Asia, the Indian Subcontinent, and South West Asia and the Middle East, few CPD sites have more than 50% of their areas protected within existing reserves. In the case of Central and Northern Asia, none of the CPD sites have more than 50% of their areas protected and, of those which are protected in part, the proportion of the area protected is relatively small. Some of the sites in this region are, however, very large. Again, a priority should be to extend the coverage of the reserve system.

In Europe, Australia and New Zealand, and North America, virtually all CPD sites selected for Data Sheet treatment are included (at least in part) within the existing reserve systems of the regions concerned. Mention has already been made of the protection afforded to CPD sites in Australia; in New Zealand the situation is rather different in that all the sites selected for Data Sheet treatment, whilst being partly included within existing reserves, are nevertheless under threat in at least part of their range. One site in Europe (the Massifs of Gudar and Javalambre in Spain – CPD Site Eu7, see Data Sheet in Volume 1) has no current legal protection.

Even when areas are designated for protection, many are nevertheless threatened, some severely so. This can be seen by comparing figures in Table 5 with those in Table 6, which provides a summary of the degree of threat to CPD sites in each region.

Only 33 sites (15% of the total number of Data Sheet sites) are considered to be safe, or reasonably safe, whereas 119 sites (c. 50% of the total) are either threatened or severely threatened. A further 41 sites worldwide are considered to be vulnerable or at risk, and the remainder (40 sites) are partly threatened (for example where encroachment is occurring in part of an area or around its perimeter).

Of particular note is the degree of threat to many sites in the tropics. For example, none of the sites in Middle America are assessed as "safe" or "reasonably safe". Over half the sites in the region are threatened or severely threatened, irrespective of their designation, in whole or in part, as protected areas.

Some of the most seriously threatened floras are those on islands. For example, all of the CPD Data Sheet sites for the Indian Ocean and the Pacific Ocean are assessed as either at risk or threatened. Of the 8 CPD sites selected for Data Sheet treatment for the Pacific, 5 are classified as severely threatened, including the Hawaiian Islands, which include some of the most endangered floras in the world.

In the moist tropics, the main threats to sites are from encroaching agriculture, including slash and burn agriculture, logging and road building. Road building is often followed by unplanned colonization. In Middle and South America, cattle ranching is also a serious threat to a number of sites. An additional threat in some cases is the quest for oil and gas, together with the associated problems of pollution. In South East Asia, many CPD sites are already National Parks, but their protection status is still not secure; most suffer from encroachment from slash and burn cultivators, and from logging or conversion to oil palm plantations. In some cases in the moist tropics, forest clearance has occurred up to the park boundaries.

Almost all the tropical sites which are already protected (at least on paper) suffer from a lack of adequate funding and trained manpower. This affects the security of the areas. Boundaries may not be properly marked or policed, resulting in valuable resources, such as rattans and timber trees, being illegally exploited in an uncontrolled manner, perhaps not sustainable in the long-term. For some areas there are no effective management plans to protect or utilize important genetic resources, and there is mostly no out-reach programme to involve local people in the management and protection of the forests, and to ensure that utilization of plant resources is undertaken on a sustainable basis. In many cases, land zonation within the protected area and its vicinity is needed to ensure that conservation of biodiversity is balanced against other demands on natural resources.

Effective conservation of the CPD sites depends, therefore, on adequate funding and the political will to establish more protected areas where this is necessary and to ensure that all protected areas are effectively managed.

While it is encouraging to note that there are still many opportunities available for protecting and conserving a large proportion of the Earth's wild plant resources *in situ* (supplemented by *ex situ* procedures as necessary), it is alarming that very few of the areas identified as global priorities are assessed as "safe". With the ever-increasing threats to many sites, the opportunities for conservation are disappearing rapidly and the need for emergency action becomes more frequent. There is therefore an urgent need for action from governments, aid agencies and conservation organizations to achieve the conservation of the areas selected as CPD sites before it is too late.

## (iv) Useful plants, social, economic and environmental values

A remarkable diversity of uses of plants is noted in the Regional Overviews, Data Sheets and Summary Tables which follow. Almost all the sites contain important timber trees, fruit trees or medicinal plants. Even in Europe, the native flora contains over 200 crop relatives which represent important genetic resources. For most of the tropical sites detailed information on the uses of plants is not available and a vast amount of research still needs to be undertaken.

### TABLE 5. ANALYSIS OF THE CONSERVATION STATUS OF CPD SITES

| Region | % area of CPD site within protected area(s) | | | | Total no. of sites | % of sites with >50% or 100% protection | |
|---|---|---|---|---|---|---|---|
| | 0 | >0–50 | >50–<100 | 100 | | >50 | 100 |
| Africa | 8 | 7 | 8 | 7 | 30 | 50 | 23 |
| Atlantic Ocean Islands | - | 3 | 1 | - | 4 | 25 | 0 |
| Australia/New Zealand | - | 8 | 4 | 2 | 14 | 43 | 14 |
| Caribbean Islands | 1 | - | 1 | 1 | 3 | 67 | 33 |
| Central and Northern Asia | 1 | 4 | - | - | 5 | 0 | 0 |
| China and East Asia | 1 | 7 | 4 | 9 | 21 | 62 | 43 |
| Europe | 1 | 8 | - | - | 9 | 0 | 0 |
| Indian Ocean Islands | - | 3 | - | - | 3 | 0 | 0 |
| Indian Subcontinent | 2 | 9 | - | 2 | 13 | 15 | 15 |
| Middle America | 3 | 8 | 5 | 4 | 20 | 45 | 20 |
| North America | - | 6 | - | - | 6 | 0 | 0 |
| Pacific | - | 5 | 1 | 2 | 8 | 38 | 25 |
| South America ** | 2 | 32 | 6 | 5 | 45 | 24 | 11 |
| South East Asia | 6 | 17 | 2 | 16 | 41 | 44 | 39 |
| South West Asia and the Middle East | 2 | 8 | - | 1 | 11 | 9 | 9 |
| **Totals** | **27** | **125** | **32** | **49** | **233** | **35** | **21** |

Notes:

** The figures for South America exclude one Data Sheet (SA34), for which data are not available.

For CPD sites having Forest Reserve status, a judgement had to be made whether such a designation confers any degree of protection on the flora. If it is clear from the text of the Data Sheet that no protection is afforded, and especially if the area is under imminent threat of large-scale logging, the percentage area of the CPD site protected has been adjusted accordingly.

### TABLE 6. DEGREE OF THREAT TO CPD SITES

The table shows the number of CPD Data Sheet sites classified under broad categories of threat. For details on each site, see the Summary Table on page 12, and the individual site Data Sheets.

| Region | Safe or reasonably safe | Partly safe but some areas threatened | Vulnerable or at risk | Threatened | Severely threatened |
|---|---|---|---|---|---|
| Africa | 7 | 5 | 7 | 8 | 3 |
| Atlantic Ocean Islands | 1 | - | - | 1 | 2 |
| Australia/ New Zealand | 9 | 2 | 1 | 2 | - |
| Caribbean Islands | - | 1 | 1 | - | 1 |
| Central and Northern Asia | - | - | 4 | 1 | - |
| China and East Asia | 2 | 5 | 5 | 5 | 4 |
| Europe | 2 | 2 | - | 5 | - |
| Indian Ocean Islands | - | - | 1 | 1 | 1 |
| Indian Subcontinent | 2 | 6 | - | 3 | 2 |
| Middle America | - | 5 | 2 | 10 | 3 |
| North America | - | 2 | - | 3 | 1 |
| Pacific | - | - | 1 | 2 | 5 |
| South America ** | 7 | 5 | 3 | 14 | 16 |
| South East Asia | 3 | 7 | 12 | 15 | 4 |
| South West Asia and the Middle East | - | - | 4 | 4 | 3 |
| **Totals** | **33** | **40** | **41** | **74** | **45** |

Notes:

** The figures for South America exclude one Data Sheet (SA34), for which data are not available.

Many of the areas attract large numbers of tourists. Often, it is intact natural vegetation which provides the scenic backdrop, or is the actual focus, for tourism in the areas concerned. If properly planned and controlled to prevent visitor pressure and tourist developments becoming threats to the sites, such visitation could provide substantial long-term financial and employment benefits to the immediate area, as well as to national economies. In a few cases, a partial and preliminary economic assessment of the value of plant resources is given in the Regional Overviews and Data Sheets. This is usually based upon the number of visitors to a protected area, or the amount of wild plant resources gathered from a site.

Mention must also be made of the valuable environmental services provided by the sites, such as the prevention of soil erosion and flooding of downslope agricultural and settled areas, as well as safeguarding watersheds and contributing to climatic stability. It has been impossible to place monetary values on these services within the context of this present work.

The information presented in the Data Sheets and Regional Overviews demonstrates all too clearly the enormous value to humanity of the vast range of riches and economic potential of plant resources. This poses a dramatic challenge to the nations of the world and to the international agencies that are called upon to provide the necessary aid, support, and strategic and practical advice to ensure the survival into the future of this treasure house for humanity.

## Summary information on sites selected for Data Sheet treatment

The Summary Table below includes a world list of the 234 sites which have been selected for detailed treatment as Data Sheets in the three volumes comprising *Centres of Plant Diversity*. Any updates to the information given in the Summary Table will be noted in subsequent volumes.

The following notes indicate the sorts of data presented under each column in the table:

### (i) Type

A letter code categorizing each of the areas selected for Data Sheet treatment. The following codes are used:

S   Site; where the area is a discrete geographical unit, and where the whole area needs to be conserved.
F   Floristic province, often covering a very wide area, or CPD site covering a whole region. Effective conservation of the flora of such areas often requires a network of reserves to be established, as in many cases it would be impractical to protect the entire province or region.
V   Vegetation type. As in "F", effective conservation often requires representative samples to be protected.

### (ii) Area

From information given in the Data Sheets; usually to nearest 1 km² for individual sites, sometimes an estimate to nearest 100 km² or 1000 km² for large regions.

### (iii) Altitude

Altitude range in metres.

### (iv) Flora

Unless otherwise stated, numbers refer to indigenous vascular plant species, or an estimate based on current botanical knowledge of that (or similar) sites, usually to the nearest 100 species, or to nearest 1000 species for some large tropical sites. An asterisk (*) denotes the exact number of plant species present or so far recorded for a site.

taxa – refers to the number of species, subspecies and varieties.
angiosp. – angiosperms.

### (v) Examples of Useful Plants

Important plants or major groups are listed, including names of some commodity groups.

### (vi) Vegetation

The major vegetation formations are listed. Information has been summarized from the Data Sheets. The use of some local names for vegetation types has been retained.

### (vii) Protected Areas

Categories of protected areas are given where a CPD site is fully or partially protected. In most cases, the area of the protected site is given after the category, or a percentage figure is given for that part of the site which is protected. If a site is fully protected, the entry will just show the category of protection.

Abbreviations used:

| | | | |
|---|---|---|---|
| BG | Botanic Garden | PFA | Protected Forest Area |
| BR | Biosphere Reserve | RF | Reserved Forest |
| FoR | Forest Reserve | SF | State Forest |
| GR | Game Reserve | SFoRP | State Forest Park |
| GS | Game Sanctuary | SP | State Park |
| NM | Nature Monument | SpNR | Special Nature Reserve |
| NP | National Park | VJR | Virgin Jungle Reserve |
| NR | Nature/Natural Reserve | WA | Wilderness Area |
| NS | Nature Sanctuary | WHS | World Heritage Site |
| NatM | National Monument | WMA | Wilderness Management Area |
| NatP | Natural Park | | |
| NatS | National Sanctuary | WR | Wildlife Reserve |
| PA | Protected Area | WS | Wildlife Sanctuary |
| PF | Protection/Protected Forest | | |

In many cases, the IUCN Management Category of each protected area is given in the Data Sheet. The definitions of the IUCN Management Categories are given in a separate Appendix.

### (viii) Threats

Only the main threats, with the most important ones first, are listed.

### (ix) Assessment

A summary of the conservation status of the area, including whether the area is safe, reasonably safe, at risk, threatened or severely threatened. An analysis of the threats and conservation status of the CPD sites is given in the Introduction to this volume.

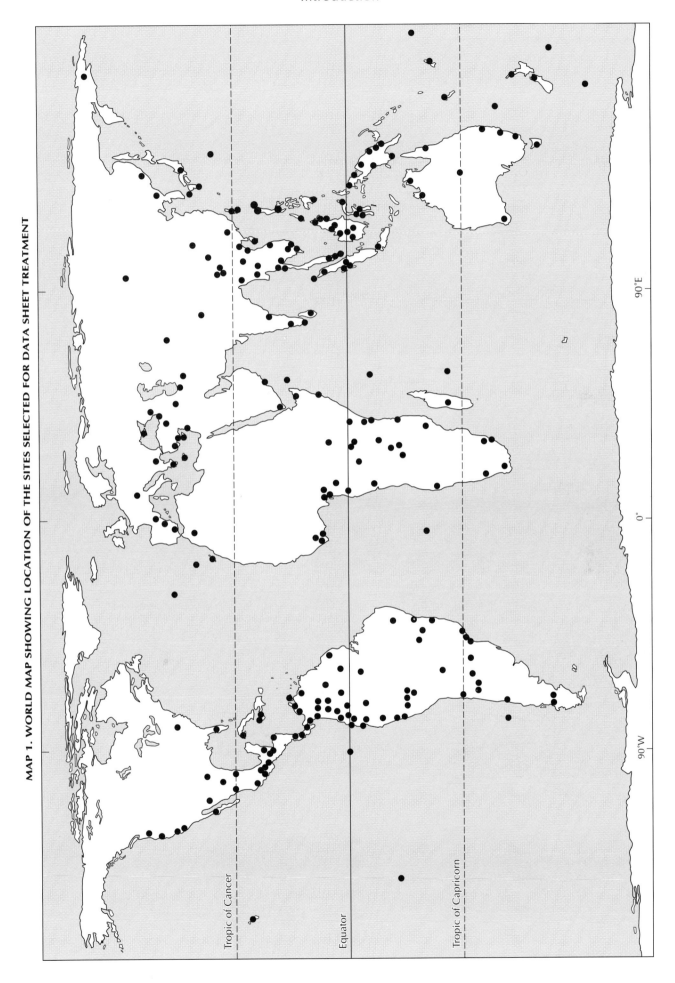

MAP 1. WORLD MAP SHOWING LOCATION OF THE SITES SELECTED FOR DATA SHEET TREATMENT

## CENTRES OF PLANT DIVERSITY: SUMMARY INFORMATION ON SITES SELECTED FOR DATA SHEET TREATMENT

| Code | Site | Type | Size (km²) | Altitude | Flora | Examples of Useful Plants | Vegetation | Protected Areas | Threats | Assessment |
|---|---|---|---|---|---|---|---|---|---|---|
| **AFRICA** | | | | | | | | | | |
| Af81 | Afroalpine region | F | 3500 | 3500–5890 m | 350 | Grazing, browsing, fuel | Moist tree composite woodland, scrub, tussock grassland, bogs | Considerable areas fall within existing NPs and reserves | Overgrazing, fuelwood collection, fire, tourism | Some areas safe, but others severely threatened; management plans needed |
| | **Cameroon** | | | | | | | | | |
| Af11 | Forest zone, River Dja region | S | 8100 | 200–500 m | 2000 | Timber trees, essential oils, medicinal plants | Tropical evergreen rain forest, semi-deciduous forest, swamps, secondary forests | FoR and Fauna Reserve, BR, and proposed NP (5000 km²) | Some encroachment on boundaries from cocoa, coffee and subsistence plots | Reasonably safe; threats not as serious as elsewhere |
| Af12 | Korup NP | S | 1259 | 100–1075 m | 3500 | Medicinal plants, palm canes, chewing sticks, fruit trees | Lowland tropical evergreen rain forest | NP | Over-collecting of bush mango and palm canes, some encroachment | Reasonably secure |
| Af13 | Mount Cameroon | S | 1100 | 0–4095 m | 3500 | Timber trees (especially African mahogany), medicinal plants | Lowland evergreen rain forest to Afromontane forest, scrub, subalpine and montane grasslands, coastal mangroves | 6 FoRs (700 km²), mostly in foothills; proposed Etinde Reserve (360 km²) and Mabeta-Moliwe Reserve (36 km²); Limbe BG. | Agricultural encroachment, fire, logging; potentially grazing | Threatened; most seriously on lower slopes of east and north; montane forest at risk from fire |
| | **Congo/Cabinda/Zaïre** | | | | | | | | | |
| Af16 | Mayombe | S | 2500 | 150–350 m | >1100 | Timber trees, medicinal plants, food plants, plants of cultural value | Tropical lowland semi-evergreen forest, Zambezian savanna, wetlands | Proposed BR | Logging, charcoal production, clearance for agriculture | Threatened |
| | **Côte d'Ivoire** | | | | | | | | | |
| Af2 | Taï NP | S | 3500 | 80–623 m | 1300 | Timber trees, many plants used locally for a variety of purposes | Tropical evergreen rain forest | NP, WHS (all of area), BR (3300 km²) | Logging, agricultural encroachment, gold mining, population pressure | Threatened around perimeter |
| | **Gabon** | | | | | | | | | |
| Af18 | Cristal Mountains | S | 9000 | 0–911 m | >3000 | Timber trees (e.g. okoumé), semi-wild oil palms, raphia, medicinal plants | Mainly tropical lowland and hill rain forest | None | No serious threats at present; logging is a potential threat | Not protected; at risk |
| | **Guinea/Côte d'Ivoire/Liberia** | | | | | | | | | |
| Af4 | Mont Nimba | S | 480 | 450–1752 m | >2000 | Timber trees, oil palm | Lowland and transitional rain forest, grasslands | Strict NR & WHS (Guinea: 130 km², Côte d'Ivoire: 50 km²), BR (Guinea: 171 km²), proposed NR (Liberian part) | Mining of iron ore (Liberia/Guinea), some clearance for agriculture | Liberian and Guinean part greatly damaged by mining and severely threatened |
| | **Kenya** | | | | | | | | | |
| Af62 | Mount Kenya | S | 1500 | 1600–5199 m | 800 | Timber trees, fruit trees, medicinal plants | Montane moist and dry forest, bamboo, woodland, giant heaths, moorland | Above 3100 m, NP (715 km²); BR (718 km²); FoR covers 1421 km² of lower slopes | Logging, monocultures on the lower slopes, visitor pressure at higher altitudes | Lower slopes severely threatened |

| Code | Site | Type | Size (km²) | Altitude | Flora | Examples of Useful Plants | Vegetation | Protected Areas | Threats | Assessment |
|---|---|---|---|---|---|---|---|---|---|---|
| **Liberia** | | | | | | | | | | |
| Af7 | Sapo NP | S | 1307 | 100–400 m | | Timber trees, medicinal plants, wide range of plants used for making artefacts, tools | Lowland tropical rain forest | NP | Potential logging, illegal hunting | At risk |
| **Malawi** | | | | | | | | | | |
| Af64 | Mount Mulanje | S | 500 | 750–3002 m | >800 | Mulanje cedar, Brachystegia, bamboos, fruit trees | Woodland, evergreen forest, montane grassland, high-altitude scrub, rupicolous communities | FoR | Deforestation, illegal logging of cedars, uncontrolled collection of fuelwood, invasive pines | Severely threatened; action urgently needed |
| **Morocco** | | | | | | | | | | |
| Af84 | High Atlas | F | 7000 | 1000–4165 m | 1000 | Timber trees (e.g. walnut, pine, juniper, relict stands of Atlantic cedar), fodder plants | Cedar, juniper, pine and holm oak forests, scrub, alpine meadows, pseudo-steppe, alpine scree communities | 2 NPs (860 km², incl. 1 WS of 8 km²), 1 NR (12 km²); c. 12% of total area | Population pressure leading to clearance for cultivation, overgrazing, fuelwood cutting, timber cutting | Protected area reasonably secure but management needs strengthening; areas outside threatened |
| **Namibia/Angola** | | | | | | | | | | |
| Af50 | Kaokoveld | F | 70,000 | 0–2000 m | 952* | Medicinal plants, plants of cultural value, fodder plants | Desert/escarpment vegetation, mopane savanna | Angola: most in Iona NP (15,150 km²) and a Partial Reserve; Namibia: small area in NP, rest as Game Conservation Area | Timber cutting, overgrazing, over-collecting of food and medicinal plants | Protection needs strengthening; some parts threatened |
| **Nigeria** | | | | | | | | | | |
| Af24 | Cross River NP | S | 4227 | 150–1700 m | >400 trees* | Timber trees, rattans, edible fruits, medicinal plants | Tropical lowland rain forest, freshwater swamp forest, montane forest, grassland | NP | Potential logging, agricultural encroachment | Reasonably secure |
| **Somalia** | | | | | | | | | | |
| Af42 | Cal Madow | S | 9600 | 0–2400 m | 1000 | Frankincense, myrrh, carob relative, timber trees | Dry montane forest, evergreen to deciduous woodland, bushland, semi-desert | Daalo FoR is proposed as NP | Logging, grazing | No protection in practice, but threats to flora probably not severe |
| Af44 | Hobyo | S | 3000 | 0–440 m | <1000 | Medicinal plants, plants used for construction | Deciduous bushland and woodland, dune vegetation | None; proposed GR for part of area | Overgrazing, fuelwood collection | No protection, but threats to flora probably not severe |
| **South Africa** | | | | | | | | | | |
| Af53 | Cape Floristic Region | F | 90,000 | 0–2325 m | 8600 | Ornamentals (e.g. bulbs, succulents, proteas, ericas) | Fynbos, shrubland, Afromontane forest | Montane areas well protected in many reserves; <3% of lowlands protected | Agriculture, urbanization, fire, invasive species, high population growth rate | Most mountain fynbos effectively protected; lowlands much less so; 44% of remaining fynbos area protected |
| **South Africa/Lesotho** | | | | | | | | | | |
| Af82 | Drakensberg Alpine Region | F | 40,000 | 1800–3482 m | >1750 | Forage grasses, grasses and sedges for thatching, rope, hats, fuelwood | Subalpine and alpine grassland and shrubland, scrub, savanna, wetlands | NPs, NRs, WAs cover 2194 km²; Drakensberg/Maluti Ecosystem Conservation Area is a proposed WHS | Overgrazing, soil erosion, arable agriculture, invasive plants | Severely threatened in places; protected areas safe, but coverage inadequate |

| Code | Site | Type | Size (km²) | Altitude | Flora | Examples of Useful Plants | Vegetation | Protected Areas | Threats | Assessment |
|---|---|---|---|---|---|---|---|---|---|---|
| **South Africa/Swaziland/Mozambique** | | | | | | | | | | |
| Af59 | Maputaland-Pondoland Region | F | 201,640 | 0–1800 m | 6000–7000 | Ornamental plants (e.g. *Agapanthus*, *Gladiolus*), cowpea relatives, 900 medicinal plant species | Grassland, Afromontane forest, coastal, sand and swamp forests, valley bushveld, semi-evergreen bushland/thicket, palmveld, aquatic communities | 7.5% in conservation areas, but 93% of conserved area is in northern savanna zone which is not rich in plant endemics | Rapid population growth, slash and burn agriculture, plantation crops, afforestation, urbanization, invasive species, mining | Existing reserve system inadequate to protect plant-rich vegetation types, which remain threatened |
| **South Africa/Namibia** | | | | | | | | | | |
| Af51 | Western Cape Domain (Succulent Karoo) | F | 111,212 | 0–1907 m | 5000 | Ornamentals (e.g. bulbs, succulents), food and medicinal plants | Succulent shrubland (veld) with associated annuals | NP (270 km²) and a few other reserves covering >2% of the region in total | Overgrazing, agriculture, mining, plant collecting, invasive species, urban development | Inadequate coverage of protected areas; threatened |
| **Tanzania** | | | | | | | | | | |
| Af71 | East Usambara Mountains | S | 280 | 150–1506 m | 1921 taxa* | Ornamental plants (incl. African violet, *Streptocarpus*), timber and pole species | Lowland semi-deciduous and evergreen submontane forests | 25 Catchment FoRs, proposed NRs | Logging, pole-cutting, clearance of forest for agriculture, invasive species | Reserves intact; more extensive forest outside threatened and declining |
| Af33 | Mahale-Karobwa Hills | F | 24,000 | 773–2496 m | >2000 | Timber trees, plants used for honey and wax collection | Miombo woodland, riverine, lowland, submontane and montane forests, dambos | Mahale Mountain NP (1613 km²) | Shifting cultivation, influx of refugees, proposed road | Threatened |
| Af57 | Rondo Plateau | F | 250 | 300–700 m | 800 | Timber trees | Dry semi-deciduous lowland forest, woodland and thicket | All remaining forests protected in Rondo FoR | Logging, pole cutting, clearance for farming, burning, inadequate staffing | Threatened |
| **Uganda** | | | | | | | | | | |
| Af25 | Bwindi (Impenetrable) Forest | S | 321 | 1160–2607 m | 1000 | Timber trees, bamboos, medicinal plants | Moist evergreen submontane and montane forests | NP | Logging, over-collection of forest products (e.g. removal of timber and fuelwood) | Isolated forest very threatened despite protection status and conservation projects |
| **Zaïre** | | | | | | | | | | |
| Af49 | Garamba NP and surrounding Domaines de Chasses | S | 56,727 | 710–1061 m | 1000 | Timber trees, papyrus, medicinal plants | Sudanian woodland, savanna, papyrus swamps, riverine forests | NP and WHS (49,200 km²), 3 Domaines de Chasses (7527 km²) | Uncontrolled fires | NP/WHS area safe |
| Af35 | Kundelungu | S | 9000 | 1500–2000 m | | Medicinal plants, timber trees, plants of cultural importance | Miombo woodland, grassland, gallery forest | NP (7600 km²) | Fires, charcoal production, hunting | At risk |
| Af29 | Maiko NP | S | 10,830 | 1000–1200 m | | Timber trees | Tropical evergreen rain forest, Afromontane forest | NP | Minor threats from conversion to savanna, gold mining | Reasonably safe due to difficulties of access, but more management resources needed |
| Af30 | Salonga NP | S | 36,560 | 350–700 m | 1500–2000 | Timber trees, medicinal plants | Tropical evergreen rain forest, swamp and riverine forests, grasslands | NP (whole area), WHS (36,000 km²) | Local population pressure, timber cutting, fuelwood cutting, fire, over-collection of medicinal plants | At risk; inadequate trained staff, infrastructure and management planning |

| Code | Site | Type | Size (km²) | Altitude | Flora | Examples of Useful Plants | Vegetation | Protected Areas | Threats | Assessment |
|------|------|------|-----------|----------|-------|---------------------------|------------|-----------------|---------|------------|
| Af37 | Upemba NP | S | 11,730 | 350–1100 m | >2400 | Fruit trees, fibres, some timber species | Miombo woodland, dry evergreen forest, wooded grassland, swamps | NP | Illegal commercial logging, fire | At risk; inadequate management resources |
| **Zambia** | | | | | | | | | | |
| Af39 | Zambezi Source Area | F | 1700 | 1200–1490 m | >1000 | Timber trees, melliferous plants | Riverine, swamp and dry evergreen forest; miombo woodland, bushland, savanna | 9% gazetted as PFA | Clearance for agriculture, refugees | At risk from inappropriate land management practices |
| **ATLANTIC OCEAN ISLANDS** | | | | | | | | | | |
| AO1 | Azores | F | 2304 | 0–1351 m | 300 | Timber trees (logged out), fodder plants, fruits, dyes, medicinal plants | Evergreen (laurisilva) forest, montane cloud forest, grasslands, seral communities on volcanic rocks | 12 NRs, but only 3 over 10 km². | Clearance for pastures, exotic forestry plantations, invasive plants | Inadequate coverage of protected areas and poor management; threatened |
| AO2 | Canary Islands | F | 7542 | 0–3717 m | 1200 | Ornamental plants, medicinal plants, timber trees, dry zone pasture grasses | Evergreen (laurisilva and pine) forests, montane and coastal scrub, woodland | 4 NPs (273.5 km²), WHS (39.9 km²), BR (5.1 km²), 98 other protected landscapes and parks | Tourist and residential developments, overgrazing, off-road vehicles, invasive plants, fire | Lowlands inadequately protected; seriously threatened |
| AO3 | Madeira/Salvage Islands | F | 728 (M) 3 (S) | 0–1861 m 0–153 m | 1191 | Timber trees (now depleted), medicinal plants, Madeiran bilberry, potential ornamental plants | Dry & humid evergreen forests (incl. laurel forest), coastal herb and shrub communities, cliff vegetation | Madeira: NatP (567 km², incl. 6 fully protected areas), Natural Reserve (14 km², land area); Salvage Is: Natural Reserve (whole area) | Introduced plants, tourism, rats, former clearance for agriculture, fire | Reasonably well protected, but control on tourism and eradication of invasive plants needed |
| AO4 | St Helena | F | 122 | 0–823 m | 60 | Threatened timber trees, incl. endemic ebony, redwood, gumwood | Tree fern thicket, semi-desert, scrub, woodland, severely degraded | c. 10% protected as forest, whole island proposed as BR & WHS | Invasive plants, overgrazing by domestic and feral animals | Rescue and rehabilitation programme underway, but remaining native vegetation still severely threatened |
| **AUSTRALIA/NEW ZEALAND** | | | | | | | | | | |
| **Australia** | | | | | | | | | | |
| Au1 | Australian Alps | F | 30,000 | 200–2228 m | 780 | Timber trees (especially eucalypts) | Grassland, woodland, shrubland, forest, alpine vegetation | NPs and SPs cover 17,000 km² | Tourism, grazing, hydroelectric facilities, fire, feral animals, exotic plants | Generally well protected; reasonably secure |
| Au2 | Border Ranges | F | 600 | 0–1360 m | >1200 | Timber trees (e.g. red cedar, rose mahogany), macadamia nuts, ornamental plants | Various types of rain forest, eucalypt forest, woodland, shrubland, heath | NP (majority of area), SF, WHS (NSW part) | Clearance for grazing, rural development, visitor pressure, fire, invasive plants | Generally well protected; proposal to add Queensland part to WHS will improve protection |
| Au3 | Central Australian Mountain Ranges | F | 168,000 | 500–1531 m | 1300 | Food plants (140 spp. previously used), medicinal plants (70 spp.), timber for artefacts | Hummock grasslands, shrublands, woodlands, open rock and cliff vegetation | 23 NPs and reserves cover 2.2% of area | Increasing tourist pressure, exotic weeds, grazing, mining, fire | More or less intact, but Petermann Ranges degraded by grazing. No reserves in Petermann and Musgrave areas |

| Code | Site | Type | Size (km²) | Altitude | Flora | Examples of Useful Plants | Vegetation | Protected Areas | Threats | Assessment |
|---|---|---|---|---|---|---|---|---|---|---|
| Au4 | Kakadu–Alligator Rivers Region | F | 30,000 | 0–370 m | 1400 | Many plants used by aborigines | Tropical sclerophyll forest, woodland, rain forest, swamp forest, mangrove, saltmarsh, grassland, sedgeland | NP and WHS covers 19,804 km² (c. 66% of region) | Tourism, invasive weeds | WHS area well protected |
| Au5 | Norfolk and Lord Howe Islands | F | 39 (NI) 15 (LH) | 0–319 m 0–875 m | 392* | Ornamental plants (e.g. Kentia palms, Norfolk Island pine, also a timber tree) | Evergreen rain forest, palm forest, "mossy" forest, pine and hardwood forests | WHS covers all Lord Howe; NP of 4.6 km² on Norfolk Island | Tourism, cattle grazing, introduced plants on Norfolk Island; no major threats on Lord Howe | Lord Howe well protected; both areas secure |
| Au6 | North Kimberley Region | F | 99,100 | 0–854 m | 1476* | Pasture grasses, wild fruits and roots formerly eaten by aborigines, medicinal plants | Mostly high-grass savanna woodland, some eucalypt woodland, rain forest patches, mangroves | 13,855 km² as NP and NRs, much of rest is virtual wilderness | Grazing pressure in parts, feral animals including cattle, donkeys | Safe due to remoteness, terrain and small permanent population |
| Au7 | South-west Botanical Province | F | 309,840 | 0–400 m | 5500 | Timber trees, ornamental plants | Eucalypt forest, woodland, mallee, scrub | NPs & NRs cover 25,969 km² (8.4% of area); SForPs cover 17,459 km² (5.6% of area) | Root rot fungus, wild fires | Reserves well protected, but coverage inadequate in agricultural belt |
| Au8 | Sydney Sandstone Region | F | 24,000 | 0–1300 m | 2200 | Australian red cedar and other hardwoods, ornamental plants | Forest, woodland, shrubland, grassland, coastal dune and swamp, mangrove | NPs and reserves cover 11,709 km² (c. 49% of region) | Urban and industrial development, tourism | Generally well protected |
| Au9 | Western Tasmanian Wilderness | F | 14,050 | 0–1617 m | 800 | Timbers, especially Huon pine, King Billy pine, ornamental plants | Cool temperate rain and eucalypt forests, alpine vegetation, sub-alpine scrub, moorland, grassland | WHS (13,800 km²) incl. NPs, BR; most of WHS has NP status | Tourism, fire, Phytophthora root fungus | WHS well protected. North-west forests unprotected and at risk, but recommended as reserve |
| Au10 | Wet Tropics of Queensland | F | 11,000 | 0–1622 m | >3400 | Timber trees, ornamental plants, native food plants, potential medicinal plants | Various types of rain forest, woodlands, shrublands, mangroves | WHS (8990 km²), c. 50 NPs (2073 km²), remainder mainly Crown Land | Tourism, lowland forest clearance, hydro-electric scheme, telecommunication facilities, feral animals, local grazing and logging | Well protected now as WHS, but some areas still at risk, particularly from increasing tourism and illegal clearance |
| **Australia/New Zealand** | | | | | | | | | | |
| Au17 | Subantarctic Islands | F | 949 | 0–668 m | 35 endemic taxa | Macquarie island cabbage, ornamental plants | Grasslands, fellfields and herbaceous communities, wetlands, forests, coastal vegetation | NRs cover all islands, Macquarie Island has BR status | Introduced plants; introduced cats, rabbits and wekas a threat on Macquarie Island | High level of protection; reasonably safe |
| **New Zealand** | | | | | | | | | | |
| Au16 | Chatham Islands | F | 965 | 0–300 m | 320 | Many species used in Maori culture, ornamental plants | Evergreen cool-temperate forest, peatlands, lagoons, coastal communities | Network of reserves, mostly small in size, more recommended | Clearance for agriculture, feral animals, invasive plants, fire | Threatened; degradation persists with many important sites unprotected |
| Au14 | Northland | F | 14,000 | 0–776 m | 620 | Timber trees, ornamental plants, many species used in traditional culture | Moist temperate evergreen lowland forest, swamps, coastal communities | >200 protected areas, incl. Waipoua State Forest Sanctuary (91 km²) | Clearance for agriculture, feral animals, weeds, tourism, plantations | Despite many protected areas, many endemics insufficiently protected and at risk |

| Code | Site | Type | Size (km²) | Altitude | Flora | Examples of Useful Plants | Vegetation | Protected Areas | Threats | Assessment |
|---|---|---|---|---|---|---|---|---|---|---|
| Au15 | North-west Nelson | F | 9500 | 0–1875 m | 1200* angiosp. | Timber trees, ornamental plants, plants used in traditional culture | Moist temperate to montane forest, wetlands, alpine vegetation, grassland | NP (225 km²), >40 reserves, proposed NP for much of Crown Land | Logging, mining, agriculture, introduced plants and animals | Threatened |
| **CARIBBEAN ISLANDS** | | | | | | | | | | |
| **Cuba** | | | | | | | | | | |
| Cb3 | Cajálbana Tableland/Preluda Mountain region | S | 100 | 0–464 m | 330 | Pines (especially *Pinus caribaea*) used as sources of timber and resins, palms used for roofing | Pine forest, xerophytic thorn scrub, riverine forests | Partly in Mil Cumbres Integrated Management Area (166 km²); whole area traditionally managed as "Forestry Patrimony" | Fire, clearance for agriculture, logging, invasive species, tourism | At risk |
| **Jamaica** | | | | | | | | | | |
| Cb10 | Blue and John Crow Mountains | S | 782 | 380–2256 m | >600 | Timber trees, medicinal plants, ornamental plants | Montane rain forests, scrub, savanna, cliff vegetation | NP | Clearance for subsistence farming and commercial crops, fire, invasive species, plant collecting | Southern slopes of Blue Mountains severely threatened; rest of area at risk, regulations need to be enforced |
| Cb11 | Cockpit Country | F | 430 | 300–746 m | 1500 | Few remaining timber trees, potential ornamental plants, yam relatives, several medicinal plants | Evergreen seasonal subtropical forest, mesic limestone forest, scrub thicket | None, although much has FoR status | Clearance for agriculture, fire, road building, illegal timber cutting, fuelwood collection | Severely threatened |
| **CENTRAL AND NORTHERN ASIA** | | | | | | | | | | |
| **Armenia/Azerbaijan/Georgia/Russia** | | | | | | | | | | |
| CA2 | Caucasus | F | 440,000 | 0–5642 m | 6000 | c. 300 food plants, 300 medicinal plants, timber trees, ornamental plants | Broadleaved and coniferous forests, montane steppe, subalpine meadows, semi-desert | 37 NRs cover 8982 km² (c. 2% of region) | Logging, overgrazing, plant collecting, visitor pressure | Inadequate coverage of protected areas; threatened |
| **Kazakhstan/Kirghizia/Tadzhikistan/Turkmenistan/Uzbekistan** | | | | | | | | | | |
| CA3 | Mountains of Middle Asia | F | 550,000 | 100–7495 m | 5500 | c. 1000 species of useful plants, incl. timbers, medicinal plants, fruit and nut trees, ornamentals | Semi-desert, steppes, broadleaved and coniferous forests, juniper and pistachio woodlands, meadows | 18 reserves cover 5720 km² (c. 1% of region) | Industrial/agricultural development in lowlands, overgrazing, tourism, over-collection of medicinal plants | Inadequate coverage of reserves; at risk |
| **Russia** | | | | | | | | | | |
| CA4 | Chukotskiy Peninsula | F | 117,000 | 0–2300 m | 939* | c. 40 species of food and medicinal plants, c. 400 fodder species | Tundra, steppe, shrub communities, rare hot spring communities | Proposed International Ethno-ecological Park to cover c. 50,000 km² | Mining, overgrazing, waste disposal, visitor pressure | Not protected at present; vulnerable |
| CA5 | Primorye | F | 165,900 | 0–1933 m | 1850 | Medicinal plants, honey and food plants, timbers, ornamentals | Mixed coniferous-forest, oak-pine broadleaved montane woodlands, wetlands | 6.5% of region protected in 5 NRs (5299 km²), 8 Refuges (2032 km²), BR (3402 km²) | Logging, pollution, fire, visitor pressure, over-collecting | Some vegetation types and threatened species not included in existing reserves; vulnerable |
| **Russia/Kazakhstan** | | | | | | | | | | |
| CA1 | Altai-Sayan | F | 1,100,000 | 300–4506 m | 2500 | Timber trees, medicinal plants, food plants, ornamentals | Coniferous forests, steppe, subalpine and alpine vegetation, tundra | 1.5% protected in 5 NRs (15,595 km²), c. 300 NMs, small floristic refuges | Forest clearance, fire, overgrazing, plant collecting | Coverage of existing reserves inadequate, more being planned |

| Code | Site | Type | Size (km²) | Altitude | Flora | Examples of Useful Plants | Vegetation | Protected Areas | Threats | Assessment |
|---|---|---|---|---|---|---|---|---|---|---|
| **CHINA AND EAST ASIA** | | | | | | | | | | |
| | **China** | | | | | | | | | |
| EA1 | Changbai Mts region, Jilin | F | 30,000 | 300–2691 m | 2000–2500 | >80 medicinal spp.; timber trees, fruits, fodder plants | Coniferous and broadleaved forests, meadows, tundra, alpine vegetation | NR/BR (1906 km²) | Logging, tourism, over-collection of medicinal plants | Area lacks effective management; at risk |
| EA26 | High Mt and Deep Gorge region – Gaoligong Mts, Nu Jiang River and Biluo Snow Mts, Yunnan | F | 10,000 | 1090–5128 m | 2000 | Timber trees, medicinal plants, ornamental plants | Evergreen broadleaved and sub-alpine coniferous forests, alpine vegetation | 2 NRs (4994 km²) | Clearance for cultivation | Part safe; part severely threatened |
| EA27 | Tropical forests of Hainan Island | V | 33,920 | 0–1867 m | 4200–4500 | >2900 species used locally; timber trees, medicinal plants, rattans, wild litchi | Tropical lowland seasonal rain and monsoon forests, montane seasonal rain forest, mangroves, savanna | 51 NRs cover c. 1500 km² (including marine reserves) | Clearance for cultivation, illegal logging, over-collection of medicinal plants | Severely threatened; reserve coverage adequate, but lack of funds and trained personnel |
| EA40 | High Mountain and Deep Gorge region, Hengduan Mts and Min Jiang River basin, Sichuan | F | 4000 | 600–6250 m | >4000 | Medicinal plants, timber trees, oil and starch plants, bamboos | Evergreen and semi-deciduous broadleaved forests, coniferous forests, alpine scrub and meadows, savanna | BR (2072 km²) including NR (2000 km²) | Logging, visitor pressure, road building, over-collection of medicinal plants | Area lacks effective management; at risk |
| EA31 | Limestone region, Zhuang Autonomous Region | F | 20,000 | 100–1300 m | 2500–3000 | >1000 species used locally; timbers, medicines, bamboo, rattan, ornamentals | Seasonal rain forest, montane evergreen broadleaved and limestone forests | 11 NRs (4000 km²) | Illegal timber cutting, lack of conservation awareness by local people | Protected areas need effective management; severely threatened |
| EA13 | Nanling Mt Range | F | 30,000 | 200–2142 m | >3000 | >800 spp. used locally; medicinal plants, timber trees, fruits, oil, fibres, dyes, wild vegetables | Evergreen broadleaved forest, montane semi-deciduous broadleaved mixed forests | 17 NRs (c. 5000 km²) | Clearance for cultivation, over-collection of medicinal plants | Part safe; part severely threatened |
| EA6 | Taibai Mt region of Qinling Mts, Shaanxi | F | 2779 | 500–3767 m | 1900 | Medicinal plants, oils, fibres, tannins, fodder plants | Broadleaved deciduous and mixed deciduous evergreen forests, sub-alpine coniferous forests, alpine vegetation | NR (540 km²) | Logging, illegal collection of medicinal plants, tourist pressure | Part safe; part severely threatened |
| EA29 | Xishuangbanna region, Yunnan | F | 19,690 | 500–2429 m | 4000–4500 | >800 medicinal species, 128 timber trees, bamboos, rattans, fruits | Tropical lowland and montane seasonal rain forests, evergreen dipterocarp forest, monsoon forest, montane evergreen broadleaved forest | 5 NRs (2416 km²) | Slash and burn agriculture, clearance for plantation crops, illegal logging, colonization | Severely threatened; reserves cover major plant-rich sites, but threats continue and management inadequate |
| | **Japan** | | | | | | | | | |
| EA49 | Mount Hakusan | S | 480 | 1700–2702 m | 1300 | Timber trees, ornamental plants | Montane deciduous forests, subalpine coniferous forests, alpine vegetation | BR (whole area), NP (477 km²) | Tourism, plant collecting, introduced plants | Management needs strengthening; at risk |

| Code | Site | Type | Size (km²) | Altitude | Flora | Examples of Useful Plants | Vegetation | Protected Areas | Threats | Assessment |
|---|---|---|---|---|---|---|---|---|---|---|
| EA50 | Yakushima | S | 503 | 0–1935 m | 1343* | Genetic resources of the timber tree *Cryptomeria japonica* | Evergreen broadleaved and laurel forests, *Cryptomeria* forest, montane scrub | NP covers almost all of island, BR (190 km²) | Tourism | Urgent conservation measures needed; threatened |
| **Korea** | | | | | | | | | | |
| EA44 | Mount Halla (Cheju Do) | S | 151 | 800–1950 m | 1453 | Medicinal plants, fibres, timber trees, ornamental plants | Deciduous broadleaved forest, coniferous forest, scrub, secondary grassland | NP (151 km²), mostly including NR (91 km²) | Visitor pressure, over-collection of medicinal and ornamental plants | Reasonably safe, but summit vegetation at risk from trampling and measures to protect rare species need to be implemented |
| **Taiwan** | | | | | | | | | | |
| EA41 | Kenting NP | S | 177 (land) | 0–526 m | 1350 | Timber trees, medicinal plants, legumes, ornamental plants | Evergreen broadleaved rain forest, semi-deciduous and littoral forests, grassland, scrub | NP | Tourism, grazing, plant collecting, military facilities | Generally well protected, some parts under threat |
| **Thailand** | | | | | | | | | | |
| EA53 | Doi Chiang Dao WS | S | 521 | <800–2175 m | 1200 | Teak (logged out) edible fruits | Lowland mixed evergreen-deciduous and dipterocarp-oak forests, montane forest | WS | Fire | Vulnerable |
| EA55 | Doi Suthep-pui NP | S | 261 | 360–1685 m | 2063* taxa | Timber trees, bamboos, fruit trees, medicinal and ornamental plants, mushrooms | Monsoon forests, incl. lowland dipterocarp-oak and mixed evergreen-deciduous forests, pine forests | NP, BR (whole area) | Encroachment, tourism, road building, tree cutting, fire, over-collecting of ornamental plants | Lack of resources for conservation measures to be implemented fully; threatened |
| EA57 | Khao Yai NP | S | 2168 | 100–1351 m | 2000–2500 | Medicinal plants, rattans | Moist evergreen forest, dry evergreen and mixed deciduous forests, grassland | NP | Encroachment of agriculture, illegal logging, over-collection of forest products, dam construction | Threatened around perimeter; conservation and development programme underway |
| EA59 | Thung Yai-Huai Kha Khaeng WHS | S | 12,000 | 200–1811 m | >2500 | Crop relatives, ornamental plants | Lowland evergreen and deciduous forests, evergreen montane forest | WS/WHS | Encroachment of agriculture, logging, fire, potential dam construction | Management under-resourced; threatened |
| **Vietnam** | | | | | | | | | | |
| EA62 | Bach Ma–Hai Van | S | 600 | 0–1450 m | 2500 | 200 timber trees, 108 medicinals, ornamentals, fibres, rattans, edible fruits | Lowland evergreen forest, tropical montane evergreen forest | NP (220 km²), 2 Environment Protection Forests | High local population density, felling of timber trees, fuelwood cutting | Threatened |
| EA63 | Cat Tien BR | S | 1372 | 60–754 m | 2500 | 200 timber trees, 120 medicinals, rattans, bamboos, orchids | Lowland evergreen and semi-deciduous forests, freshwater swamps, bamboos | BR includes NP (379 km²), Rhino Sanctuary (360 km²) | Illegal logging, over-exploitation of rattans and resins | Reasonably secure |
| EA64 | Cuc Phuong NP | S | 300 | 200–636 m | 1980* | Timber trees, medicinal plants, bamboos, ornamental plants | Lowland evergreen forest, incl. limestone forest, semi-deciduous forest | NP (222 km²) | Illegal felling of timber trees, fuelwood cutting | Reasonably secure |

| Code | Site | Type | Size (km²) | Altitude | Flora | Examples of Useful Plants | Vegetation | Protected Areas | Threats | Assessment |
|---|---|---|---|---|---|---|---|---|---|---|
| EA65 | Langbian-Dalat Highland | S | 4000 | 1400–2289 m | 2000 | 100 medicinal plants, ornamental plants (especially orchids), resin trees, rattans | Pine forest, tropical montane evergreen forest, subtropical montane forest | 3 NRs (535 km²) | Logging, slash and burn cultivation, fire | Severely threatened |
| EA66 | Yok Don NP | S | 650 | 200–482 m | 1500 | 150 timber trees, tannins, resin trees, edible fruits, ornamental plants | Dry dipterocarp forest, lowland semi-evergreen forest, riverine forest | NP (580 km²) | Illegal logging, hunting, forest fires | Threatened |
| **EUROPE** | | | | | | | | | | |
| **Bulgaria/Greece/Serbia** | | | | | | | | | | |
| Eu14 | Balkan and Rhodope Massifs | F | 10,000 | 400–2900 m | 3000 | Medicinal plants, timber trees, ornamental plants | Oak and mixed deciduous forests, fir/spruce forests, shiblyak, grasslands, montane and alpine vegetation | Several NPs; 4 BRs (140 km²) | Tourism, agriculture, overgrazing, fire, political conflicts, changes in land tenure | Extensive and expanding areas under protection; some threats arising from new political order |
| **Cyprus** | | | | | | | | | | |
| Eu18 | Troodos Mts | S | 1800 | 1000–1960 m | 1650 | Timber trees, medicinal herbs, ornamentals | Evergreen scrub, some evergreen oak and coniferous forests, rock and cliff communities | Some areas of forest protected | Tourism and skiing development, road building, fire | Conflict between tourism and conservation, but forests well protected |
| **France/Spain/Andorra** | | | | | | | | | | |
| Eu10 | Pyrenees | F | 30,000 | 0–3404 m | 3500 | c. 20 timber spp., 600 medicinal plant spp., honey and food plants, ornamentals | Evergreen forests, semi-deciduous and deciduous forests, montane and subalpine vegetation, coniferous forests | c. 50 protected areas, including 3 NPs, 7 NatPs, numerous NRs | Tourism, fires, overgrazing leading to soil erosion | Some areas well protected; others threatened |
| **Germany/Austria/France/Italy/Liechtenstein/Slovenia/Switzerland** | | | | | | | | | | |
| Eu11 | Alps | F | 200,000 | 100–4800 m | 5500 | Medicinal plants, food plants, timber trees; 0–20% of the flora is traditionally used | Broadleaved and coniferous forests, meadows, marshes, alpine grasslands, scree/rock vegetation | 9 NPs, many NRs; national and regional legislation | Tourism and associated development, intensive land management, hydroelectric schemes, possibly global warming | Threatened; conflict between tourism and conservation. Legislation needs to be enforced |
| **Greece** | | | | | | | | | | |
| Eu17 | Crete | F | 8700 | 0–2456 m | 1600 | Crop relatives, culinary herbs, ornamentals | Evergreen scrub, fragments of evergreen oak, pine and cypress forest, rock and cliff vegetation | 1 NP (48.5 km²), a few other small reserves | Tourism, agricultural and industrial developments, plant collecting | Protected area coverage inadequate, but threats less acute than in many other areas |
| Eu16 | Mountains of Southern and Central Greece | F | 18,000 | 1000–2495 m | 4000 | Timber trees, culinary herbs, chickpea relative | Coniferous and deciduous forests; rock, cliff and scree vegetation | 4 NPs (173 km²) | Fire, overgrazing, tourism, mining, plant collecting | Threatened |
| **Spain** | | | | | | | | | | |
| Eu4 | Baetic and Sub-Baetic Mts | F | 18,000 | 0–3481 m | >3000 | Lavender, thyme and other perfumes, medicinal plants, pines, cork oak, wild olives, ornamentals | Evergreen oak forest, deciduous/coniferous woodlands, pine-juniper scrub, pastures, scree vegetation | 13 NatPs (7700 km²) | Overgrazing, urbanisation, tourism, fires, agriculture, plant collecting | Threatened: coastal regions particularly by tourism, montane areas by overgrazing |

| Code | Site | Type | Size (km²) | Altitude | Flora | Examples of Useful Plants | Vegetation | Protected Areas | Threats | Assessment |
|---|---|---|---|---|---|---|---|---|---|---|
| Eu7 | Massifs of Gudar and Javalambre | F | 445 | 1200–2020 m | >1500 | Timber trees (especially pines), medicinal plants | Juniper and pine woodlands, grassland, rock communities | None; until recently traditional land management conserved area well | Tourist developments (e.g. ski resorts) | Until recently well conserved; now threatened |
| **Ukraine/Russia** | | | | | | | | | | |
| Eu21 | South Crimean Mountains and Novorossia | F | 80,500 | 0–1200 m | 2200 | Fruits, medicinal plants, aromatic plants, ornamentals | Maquis, shiblyak; oak, pine, pine-beech woodland, grassland | Crimea: 3 Reserves (160.8 km²), Game Preserve (150 km²), 5 Refuges; Novorossia: 15 Refuges for selected biotopes | Forest clearance, pollution, over-collection of ornamental and medicinal plants | Inadequate reserve coverage; threatened |
| **INDIAN OCEAN ISLANDS** | | | | | | | | | | |
| IO1 | Madagascar | F | 587,000 | 0–2876 m | 9345 | Medicinal plants, fibres, timber trees, edible plants, crop relatives, ornamentals | Rain forest, dry deciduous forest, tapia forest, bushland, thicket, mangroves | 38 protected areas covering c. 0.7% of land area, 2 BRs, 1 WHS (1520 km²); protected forests cover 4.6% of land area | Clearance for agriculture, fire, overgrazing, mining, tree felling, plant collecting, invasive species | Many important plant sites included in existing protected areas but level of protection inadequate; threatened |
| **Mauritius/Reunion** | | | | | | | | | | |
| IO2 | Mascarene Islands | F | 4481 | 0–3069 m | >955 angiosp. taxa | Timber trees (e.g. black ebony) virtually exhausted, palm hearts, coffee relatives, ornamentals | Tropical/subtropical coastal and dry lowland forests to moist montane forests, high-altitude heath | Mauritius: NP & numerous NRs cover 2.4% of land area, BR (36 km²); Rodrigues: 3 NRs (58 ha); Réunion: 1 NR (68 ha), more proposed | Invasive plants, introduced animals, development pressure, population pressure | Réunion: inadequate reserve system; Mauritius and Rodrigues: good reserve network but flora severely threatened |
| IO3 | Seychelles (granitic islands) | F | 230 | 0–905 m | 200 angiosp. | Timber trees (over-exploited in past), medicinal plants | Lowland rain forest, hygrophile peak forest, coastal forest, mangroves | 2 NPs (37 km²), 8 NRs, 2 SpNRs (351 km²), 2 PAs, 2 WHS | Invasive plants, tourist pressure | Good reserve coverage, but some important areas not covered, management needed; at risk |
| **INDIAN SUBCONTINENT** | | | | | | | | | | |
| **India** | | | | | | | | | | |
| IS7 | Agastyamalai Hills | F | 2000 | 67–1868 m | 2000 | Medicinal herbs, timber trees, bamboos, rattans, crop relatives | Tropical dry to wet forests | 3 Sanctuaries and a number of RFs protect c. 919 km²; proposed BR | Clearance for hydro-electric projects, plantations, tourism, fire, grazing | Some areas threatened |
| IS17 | Andaman and Nicobar Islands | F | 8249 | 0–726 m | 2270 | Rice and pepper relatives, timber trees, rattans | Tropical evergreen, semi-evergreen and moist deciduous forests, beach forest, bamboo scrub, mangroves | c. 500 km² land protected in 6 parks, 94 Sanctuaries (mostly small islets); part of Great Nicobar proposed as BR, proposed North Andaman BR | Population pressure, logging, hydroelectric schemes, clearance for agriculture | Some areas severely threatened; some areas reasonably safe at present; protected area coverage inadequate |
| IS9 | Nallamalai Hills | F | 7640 | 300–939 m | 758* | Medicinal plants, rice and pepper relatives, bamboos, timbers | Dry and moist deciduous forests, dry evergreen forest, scrub | WS covers 357 km² | Forest clearance, bamboo cutting for paper, fire, fuelwood cutting | Severely threatened |

| Code | Site | Type | Size (km²) | Altitude | Flora | Examples of Useful Plants | Vegetation | Protected Areas | Threats | Assessment |
|---|---|---|---|---|---|---|---|---|---|---|
| IS4 | Namdapha | S | 7000 | 200–4578 m | 5000 | Wild relatives of banana, citrus, pepper; timber trees, ornamental plants | Tropical evergreen and semi-evergreen rain forests, alpine vegetation | NP (1985 km²); whole area proposed as BR with core of c. 2500 km² | Shifting cultivation, refugees and other settlers, illegal timber felling | Core area not threatened; perimeter areas under threat |
| IS2 | Nanda Devi | S | 2000 | 1000–7817 m | 900* angiosp. | Medicinal plants, ornamental plants, edible plants | Coniferous, birch and rhododendron forests, alpine vegetation | NP and WHS (630 km²), proposed as BR | No major threats; potential dam construction | Effectively secure |
| IS8 | Nilgiri Hills | F | 5520 | 250–2000 m | 3240 | Medicinal plants, timber trees, fruit tree relatives | Tropical evergreen rain forest to tropical dry thorn forest, montane shola forest and grassland | Several NPs (incl. Silent Valley NP – 89.5 km²), Sanctuaries and RFs; proposed BR | Forest clearance for timber, plantations, roads, development projects | Some areas threatened |
| **Myanmā (Burma)** | | | | | | | | | | |
| IS14 | Bago (Pegu) Yomas | F | 40,000 | 100–821 m | 2000 | Timber trees (especially teak) | Wet evergreen dipterocarp forest, moist and dry teak forests, bamboo scrub | Proposed NP (146 km²), some RFs | Slash and burn cultivation, road building, dam construction | Protection needs strengthening; threatened |
| IS5 | Natma Taung (Mt Victoria) and Rongklang Range (Chin Hills) | F | 25,000 | 500–3053 m | 2500 | Gingers, peppers, ornamental plants (e.g. orchids) | Tropical and temperate semi-evergreen forests, subtropical evergreen forests, savanna, alpine vegetation | Proposed NP (364 km²) | Slash and burn agriculture | Threatened |
| IS6 | North Myanmā | F | 115,712 | 150–5881 m | 6000 | Medicinal plants, bamboos, rice | Lowland tropical evergreen rain forest to cool temperate rain forest, pine-oak forest, subalpine scrub | GS (705 km²), WS (215 km²); important plant sites not protected | Slash and burn agriculture | Threatened; inadequate coverage of protected areas |
| IS16 | Taninthayi (Tenasserim) | F | 73,845 | 0–2275 m | 3000 | Timber trees (especially teak, rosewood), dyes, vegetables, fibres, medicinal plants | Wet evergreen dipterocarp forests to montane rain forest, bamboo scrub, mangroves | WS (49 km²), GS (139 km²), proposed NR (259 km²) | Logging, resin tapping, fuelwood cutting | Severely threatened in north, inadequate coverage of protected areas |
| **Sri Lanka** | | | | | | | | | | |
| IS11 | Knuckles | S | 182 | 1068–1906 m | >1000 | Timbers, medicinal plants, bamboos, fruit tree relatives, spices, ornamental plants | Lowland dry semi-evergreen to montane evergreen forests, grasslands | No legal protection | Clearance for cardamom, settlements and agriculture, mining, fuelwood cutting | Area below 1200 m under threat |
| IS12 | Peak Wilderness and Horton Plains | S | 224/32 | 700–2238 m/ 1800–2389 m | >1000 | Timbers, medicinal plants, bamboos, fruit tree relatives, spices, ornamental plants | Lowland, submontane and montane wet evergreen forests, montane grassland | Sanctuary (Peak Wilderness), NP (Horton Plains) | Religious tourism, fuelwood and timber cutting, mining, fire, invasive grasses | Reasonably secure, but management plan required; some rich forests in upper regions should also be included in protected areas |
| IS13 | Sinharaja | S | 112 | 210–1170 m | 700 angiosp. | Timber trees, rattans, fruit tree relatives, medicinal plants, ornamentals | Lowland and submontane wet tropical evergreen rain forests, grasslands | National Heritage Wilderness Area and WHS | Population pressure, encroachment of agriculture, over-collection of medicinal plants, potential hydroelectric scheme | Southern part still under threat, otherwise threats declining and reasonably secure |

| Code | Site | Type | Size (km²) | Altitude | Flora | Examples of Useful Plants | Vegetation | Protected Areas | Threats | Assessment |
|---|---|---|---|---|---|---|---|---|---|---|
| **MIDDLE AMERICA** | | | | | | | | | | |
| | **Costa Rica** | | | | | | | | | |
| MA16 | Braulio Carrillo-La Selva region | S | 500 | 35–2906 m | 4000–6000 | Timber trees, ornamental plants (incl. Monstera), vanilla, edible palms | Tropical wet forest to montane rain forests | NP, Biological Station, BR | Ecological isolation, local population pressure, illegal logging, agriculture, grazing | Reasonably secure, but at risk |
| MA18 | Osa Peninsula and Corcovado NP | F | 2330 | 0–745 m | 4000–5000 | Timber trees, medicinal plants, fruit trees, fibres | Mostly tropical wet forest; also premontane and cloud forests, swamp forest, mangroves | NP (572 km²), FoR (819 km²), small Amerindian reserve, regional Conservation Areas | Mining, logging, road building, colonization | Threatened |
| | **Costa Rica/Panama** | | | | | | | | | |
| MA17 | La Amistad region | S | >10,000 | 0–3819 m | 10,000 | Timber trees, medicinal plants, dyes, ornamental plants | Lowland humid forest to subalpine rain forest, páramo | Costa Rica: BR and WHS (6126 km²); Panama: 3 NPs (2345 km²), FoR (200 km²), PF (1250 km²), planned BR | Colonization, agriculture, cattle ranching, fire, oil pipelines, potential mining, road building | Threatened |
| | **Guatemala** | | | | | | | | | |
| MA13 | Petén region and Maya BR | F | 36,000 | 10–800 m | 3000 | Mahogany, edible palms, parlour palms, medicinal plants | Subtropical semi-deciduous moist forest, savanna, wetlands | Maya BR (c. 15,000 km²) | Logging, road building, colonization, grazing, slash and burn agriculture, oil exploration | Region under threat |
| MA14 | Sierra de las Minas region and BR | F | 4374 | 150–3015 m | >2000 | Timber trees (e.g. pines), tree ferns, bamboos, medicinal and edible plants | Tropical dry forest and thorn scrub, tropical wet forest to premontane dry forest | BR (2363 km²) | Clearance for agriculture, colonization, logging, road building | BR reasonably safe, other areas threatened |
| | **Honduras** | | | | | | | | | |
| MA15 | N.E. Honduras and Río Plátano BR | S | 5250 | 0–1500 m | >2000 | Timber trees (especially mahogany and tropical cedar), many plants used locally | Mostly humid tropical and subtropical forests; also mangroves, savanna | BR and WHS (whole area) | Logging, shifting agriculture, cattle grazing, road building, colonization, mining | Threatened |
| | **Mexico** | | | | | | | | | |
| MA5 | Cañón del Zopilote region | F | 4383 | 600–3100 m | >2000 | Softwood and hardwood timber trees, medicinal plants, plants of cultural value | Deciduous tropical forest, oak and coniferous forests, montane forests | Ecological SP (36 km²) | Logging, agricultural encroachment, coffee plantations, colonization, road building | Inadequate coverage of protected areas; threatened |
| MA12 | Central region of Baja California | F | 36,000 | 0–1985 m | >500 | Food and fodder plants, medicinal plants, ornamental plants, fuelwood species | Desert vegetation, lagoon communities | BR covers 15,000 km² (c. 42% of region) | Overgrazing, expansion of agriculture, salinization, road building, mining, oil and gas exploration | Severely threatened |
| MA10 | Cuetras Ciénagas region | F | 2000 | 740–3000 m | 860* | Timber trees, forage plants, medicinal plants | Grasslands, dune communities, desert scrub, oak-pine woodlands, montane coniferous forests | None | Mining, clearance for agriculture, overgrazing, plant collecting (especially of cacti) | Threatened |

| Code | Site | Type | Size (km²) | Altitude | Flora | Examples of Useful Plants | Vegetation | Protected Areas | Threats | Assessment |
|---|---|---|---|---|---|---|---|---|---|---|
| MA9 | Gómez Farías region and El Cielo BR | F | 2400 | 200–2200 m | >1000 | Temperate and tropical timber trees, fibres, medicinal plants, ornamental plants | Tropical dry forest, tropical semi-deciduous forest, cloud forest, oak and pine forests, scrub | El Cielo BR (1445 km²) | Logging, grazing, agriculture (incl. shifting cultivation), fire, expanding settlements | Regulations to protect BR need to be enforced; threatened, although some areas remote and safe |
| MA1 | Lacandon Rain Forest region | F | 6000 | 80–1750 m | 4000 | Timber, fruit and spice trees, chicle gum, ornamental palms | Tropical lowland to montane rain forests, semi-deciduous forest, cloud forest, savanna, seasonally-inundated forest, wetlands | BR (3312 km²), 2 NMs (90 km²), Flora & Fauna Reserve (122 km²) | Road building, logging, colonization, clearance for agriculture, cattle grazing, oil drilling | >50% of forest lost, much of rest going at an accelerating rate; severely threatened |
| MA7 | Pacific lowlands, Jalisco | F | 350 | 0–500 m | 1120* | Valuable timber trees (e.g. rosewood, linum vitae), potential ornamentals | Tropical deciduous and semi-deciduous forests | 1 Biological Station (1.6 km²), 1 Reserve (7 km²) | Clearance for agriculture, resort development, logging | Reserves reasonably safe, but inadequate coverage; no protection of coastal palm forest; threatened |
| MA3 | Sierra de Juárez | F | 1700 | 500–3250 m | 2000 | Medicinal plants, timber trees, ornamental plants | Mainly montane cloud forest; also tropical evergreen forest, pine and pine-oak forests | None | Logging, grazing, colonization, fire, clearance for agriculture, plant collecting, potential dam construction | Severely threatened |
| MA6 | Sierra de Manantlán region and BR | S | 1396 | 400–2860 m | 2800 | >500 spp. have been used traditionally; wild perennial maize, wild beans, oaks, pines | Tropical deciduous and semi-deciduous forests to cloud forest, fir and pine-oak forests | BR | Logging, fire, agriculture, cattle ranching, fuelwood cutting | About 30% in good condition; threatened, although some areas safe |
| MA4 | Tehuacán-Cuicatlán region | F | 9000 | 600–2200 m | 2700 | Cacti and other ornamental plants, medicinal plants, fibres | Sclerophyll scrub, thorn scrub, early-deciduous forest | BG (1 km²) | Agriculture, overgrazing by goats, salinization, plant collecting (especially of cacti) | Threatened |
| MA8 | Upper Mezquital River region, Sierra Madre Occidental | F | 4600 | 800–3350 m | 2900 | >450 species used by local people, including food and medicinal plants; timber trees | Conifer, pine-oak and oak forests, some tropical semi-deciduous forest | BR (700 km²) | Logging, overgrazing, road building | Threatened |
| MA2 | Uxpanapa-Chimalapa region | F | 7700 | 100–2250 m | 3500 | Timber trees (including mahogany), ornamental palms | Evergreen and semi-evergreen rain forest, montane rain forest | None | Logging, colonization, agriculture, grazing, construction of dams and roads | Threatened |
| **Mexico/U.S.A.** | | | | | | | | | | |
| MA11 | Apachian/Madrean region | F | 180,000 | 500–3500 m | 3500–4000 | 60–80 wild relatives of crop plants, >300 food plants, >450 medicinal plants | Coniferous, oak-coniferous and tropical deciduous forests, savanna, chapparal, thorn scrub | <10% of region protected in Mexico; most of region in U.S.A. has some form of protection | Logging, erosion, agricultural encroachment, overgrazing | Part safe, but majority of region not formally protected: areas in northern Mexico severely threatened |
| **Panama** | | | | | | | | | | |
| MA19 | Cerro Azul-Cerro Jefe region | S | 53 | 300–1007 m | 934* | Timber trees, ornamental plants, potential medicinal plants | Tropical premontane wet and rain forests, tropical wet forest | Whole area within Chagres NP | Grazing, agricultural encroachment, fire | At risk |

| Code | Site | Type | Size (km²) | Altitude | Flora | Examples of Useful Plants | Vegetation | Protected Areas | Threats | Assessment |
|---|---|---|---|---|---|---|---|---|---|---|
| MA20 | Darién Province NP | F | 16,671 | 0–1875 m | 2440* | Cativo and other valuable timbers, medicinal plants | Tropical lowland dry, moist and wet forests, swamps, premontane and montane forests, cloud forest | NP (also a WHS and BR) covers 5790 km² | Logging, mining, agriculture, colonization, proposed Pan-American Highway | Threatened |
| **NORTH AMERICA** | | | | | | | | | | |
| **U.S.A.** | | | | | | | | | | |
| NA16 | California Floristic Province | F | 324,000 | 0–4400 m | 3500 | Timber trees and other forest products, wild grape, ornamental plants, medicinal plants | Coniferous and mixed evergreen forests, oak woodlands, chaparral, coastal scrub, grassland | Parks and reserves protect c. 11% of land area, mostly montane | Population pressure, urban and agricultural development, mining, dams, overgrazing, exotic weeds, off-road vehicle recreation | Highlands reasonably well protected; lowland habitats threatened and inadequately protected |
| NA29 | Central Highlands, Florida | F | 10,000 | 20–94 m | 3500 | Few timber trees, food plants, potential insecticides | Xerophytic pine and oak scrub, palmetto flatwoods, wetlands | State, federal and private reserves, state and local parks | Citrus plantations, urban, tourist and recreational developments | Inadequate protected area coverage; threatened |
| NA32 | Edwards Plateau, Texas | F | 100,000 | 100–1000 m | 2300 | Forage species, juniper oil, few timber trees | Semi-arid temperate semi-evergreen forest, grassland, semi-desert scrub | State and municipal parks, several reserves cover <0.05% of region | Clearance for agriculture, grazing, dams, urbanization, introduced species | Protected area coverage very inadequate; threatened |
| NA16c | Klamath-Siskiyou region | F | 55,000 | 0–2750 m | 3500 | Timber trees, beargrass, medicinal plants, including Taxus brevifolia for cancer drug | Coniferous and mixed evergreen forests, prairies, savanna, subalpine meadows | WAs, NatMs, federal, state and private reserves | Logging, agriculture, urbanization, mining, dams, tourism | Most is relatively safe due to remoteness, but logging and mining are considerable threats |
| **U.S.A./Canada** | | | | | | | | | | |
| NA25 | Serpentine flora | V | 4550 | 0–2200 m | >200 | Flax and sunflower relatives adapted to low nutrient soils | Grasslands, chaparral, montane woodland | Frenzel Creek Research Natural Area (2.7 km²), TNC Ring Mountain Preserve (25 ha) | Mining, logging, off-road vehicle recreation, urbanization | Inadequate protected area coverage; threatened |
| **U.S.A./Mexico** | | | | | | | | | | |
| NA16g | Vernal pools (California and Baja California) | V | 20,000 | 0–600 m (–2500 m) | | Limnanthes is potential sperm whale oil substitute, ornamental plants | Annual herbs, wet grassland, aquatics, oak and pine forests | Numerous small pools protected, but more reserves needed | Agriculture, grazing, urban development, mining | Inadequate protected area coverage; severely threatened |
| **PACIFIC OCEAN ISLANDS** | | | | | | | | | | |
| **Chile** | | | | | | | | | | |
| PO4 | Juan Fernández | F | 100 | 0–1319 m | 210* | Some potential horticultural species | Mainly forested | NP | Feral animals, invasive plants | Flora acutely threatened; WWF-sponsored rescue programme underway |
| **Ecuador** | | | | | | | | | | |
| PO2 | Galápagos Islands | F | 7900 | 0–1707 m | 541* | Tomato and cotton relatives, native timber trees | Wide range of generally arid vegetation types, Scalesia forests (much reduced) on higher islands | NP: 7278 km² (96.7% of land area); WHS and BR (7665 km²) | Feral animals, invasive plants, over-exploitation of native woody species, increasing human population, fire | Many plants still at risk despite conservation measures |

| Code | Site | Type | Size (km²) | Altitude | Flora | Examples of Useful Plants | Vegetation | Protected Areas | Threats | Assessment |
|---|---|---|---|---|---|---|---|---|---|---|
| PO1 | **Fiji** | F | 18,270 | 0–1323 m | 1628 | Timber trees, medicinal plants, culturally important plants | Tropical rain, dry and montane forests, grassland, scrub, coastal vegetation | 16 protected areas (65 km²) incl. 8 NRs (62 km², mainly rain forest), 1 NP (2.4 km², coastal), several other small forest parks | Logging, clearance for agriculture, feral animals, invasive plants, population pressure, tourism, mining | Threatened; reserves and funding inadequate, numerous proposals never implemented. Need involvement of local population |
| | **French Polynesia** | | | | | | | | | |
| PO5 | Marquesas | F | 1275 | 0–1260 m | 318* | Ornamental species, food plants | Lowland forest, remnants of dry forest, grasslands, xerophytic scrub | 4 reserves, but inadequate coverage | Overgrazing, introduced species, fire, many species reduced to small populations | Severely threatened |
| | **New Caledonia** | | | | | | | | | |
| PO6 | Grande Terre | F | 16,890 | 0–1628 m | 3322 | Timber trees, ornamental plants, medicinal plants, aromatic plants | Humid evergreen and sclerophyll forests, maquis, mangroves, marshes | 9% covered by protected areas, incl. 14 Special Botanical Reserves (155 km²), 1 of which has Strict Nature Reserve status, and 4 Provincial Parks (105 km²) | Fire, mining, clearance for agriculture and grazing, urbanization, invasive plants | Coverage of protected areas inadequate. Sclerophyll and calcareous forests particularly threatened, along with many point endemics |
| | **Japan** | | | | | | | | | |
| PO7 | Bonin (Ogasawara) Islands | F | 73 | 0–462 m | 456* | Ornamental plants (orchids) | Broadleaved evergreen forest, but mostly destroyed | NP (61 km²) | Population pressure, grazing, introduced plants | NP, but much degraded and highly endangered |
| | **U.S.A.** | | | | | | | | | |
| PO3 | Hawaiian Islands | F | 16,641 | 0–4205 m | 1200 | Native plants used by indigenous people for all their needs; ornamentals, hardwood trees | Wide range of vegetation types: dry to mesic lowland to subalpine forests, shrublands, grasslands, herblands | 2029 km² (12% of land area) protected in many state, federal and private reserves, but not all plant-rich communities covered | Development, introduced plants and animals, fire | Possibly the most endangered island flora in the world; severely threatened |
| | **Western Samoa/American Samoa** | | | | | | | | | |
| PO9 | Samoan Islands | F | 3114 | 0–1860 m | 775 | Timber trees, >100 medicinal plants, incl. possible cancer & AIDS treatments | Coastal, lowland and montane rain forests, cloud forest, upland and volcanic scrub, mangroves, marshes | Proposed NPs on Tutuila and Ta'u, American Samoa; 2 village-level reserves on Western Samoa | Increasing population pressure, shifting cultivation, cash crops, logging, invasive plants, hydroelectric scheme | Severely threatened; lowland forests almost eliminated, montane forests increasingly threatened |
| **SOUTH AMERICA** | | | | | | | | | | |
| | **Argentina** | | | | | | | | | |
| SA35 | Anconquija region | F | 6000 | 400–5550 m | 2000 | Timber trees, crop relatives (e.g. tomato relatives), medicinal and ornamental plants | Amazonian winter-dry rain forest to temperate cloud forest, Andean páramo grassland, spiny shrubland | Several protected areas covering c. 370 km², proposed NP of 3000 km² | Logging, clearance for agriculture, grazing, plant collecting, road building, dams, potential mining | Varying degrees of threat; some protected areas reasonably secure, remote areas self-protected; other areas severely threatened |
| | **Argentina/Chile** | | | | | | | | | |
| SA34 | Altoandina | | | | | (Information not available) | | | | |
| SA46 | Patagonia | F | 600,000 | 0–2000 m | 1200 | Forage plants, many species used traditionally for food and medicine | Steppe shrublands and grasslands | NP (110 km²) | Overgrazing, desertification | Inadequate coverage of protected areas, some areas threatened |

| Code | Site | Type | Size (km²) | Altitude | Flora | Examples of Useful Plants | Vegetation | Protected Areas | Threats | Assessment |
|---|---|---|---|---|---|---|---|---|---|---|
| **Argentina/Paraguay/Bolivia/Brazil** | | | | | | | | | | |
| SA22 | Gran Chaco | F | 1,010,000 | 100–2795 m | 1200 | Timber trees, medicinal plants, ornamentals, fibres | Xerophytic deciduous to semi-evergreen forests, palm woodlands, savanna, steppes, wetlands | 5 NPs & 1 National NR cover 11,720 km² (c. 1%) of region | Logging, agricultural development, oil and gas exploration, road building, colonization, fire | Inadequate protected area coverage, none at all in Bolivian part; some areas threatened |
| **Bolivia** | | | | | | | | | | |
| SA24 | Llanos de Mojos region | F | 270,000 | 130–235 m | 5000 | Forage grasses, legumes, rubber, Brazil nut, palm hearts, pineapple relatives | Mosaic of savanna and various evergreen forest types, wetlands | BR (1350 km²), FoRs, Biological Station, Amerindian territories, regional park, private reserves | Overgrazing, fire, road building, logging | Inadequate protected area coverage; key forest areas severely threatened |
| SA36 | Madidi-Apolo region | F | 30,000 | 250–2000 m | >5000 | Timber trees (e.g. mahogany), quinine, medicinal plants, ornamental plants, palm oils | Mainly humid evergreen tropical montane forest, dry forest, cloud forest, grasslands | Proposed NP (18,000 km²) | Logging, road building, colonization, oil exploration | Mostly intact, but without protection; threatened |
| SA23 | South-eastern Santa Cruz | F | 70,000 | 350–1157 m | 2000–2500 | Timber trees, forage grasses, *Copernicia* palms for telephone poles, forage plants | Dry forest, savanna (cerrado and campo rupestre), wetlands, thorn scrub | National Historical Park (c. 170 km²), 2 proposed NPs (39,000 km²), proposed FoRs, proposed Biological Reserve (6000 km²) | Cattle ranching, agriculture, mining, gas pipeline, road building | Inadequate coverage of protected areas; severely threatened |
| **Brazil** | | | | | | | | | | |
| SA12 | Atlantic moist forest of southern Bahia | V | 3500 | 0–1000 m | | Brazil-wood, rosewood, and other valuable timbers | Tropical Atlantic rain forest, semi- and dry deciduous forests, littoral forest | <300 km² or <0.1% of original wet forests protected in 6 reserves | Logging, clearance for cattle grazing, cash crops and subsistence agriculture, pulpwood plantations | Inadequate coverage of protected areas, even existing reserves inadequately protected; severely threatened |
| SA14 | Cabo Frio region | F | 1500 | 0–500 m | 1500–2200 | Brazil-wood, medicinal plants | Coastal evergreen scrub, xeromorphic forest, mangroves, submontane rain forest | Protected areas cover c. 10% of region | Land development, tourism, clearance for cattle grazing, sugar cane plantations | Inadequate coverage of protected areas, even existing reserves inadequately protected; severely threatened |
| SA19 | Caatinga of north-eastern Brazil | V | 1,000,000 | 0–1000 m | | Forage plants, fruits, timber trees, palms | Xerophytic deciduous forest to sparse scrub, savanna, gallery and montane forests, cerrado, grassland | 3 NPs (1048 km²), 5 Biological Reserves (132 km²), 5 Ecological Stations (13,602 km²), 1 National Forest (383 km²), 2 Environmental Protection Zones | Overgrazing, timber and fuelwood extraction, agriculture, salinization, plant collecting | Inadequate coverage of protected areas; severely threatened |
| SA21 | Distrito Federal | F | 5814 | 750–1336 m | >3000 | Timbers, fruit trees, medicinal plants, ornamental plants | Gallery, mesophytic and cerrado forests, wetlands, savannas | Protected areas cover only 3.2% of region and do not protect full range of vegetation types | Population pressure, fires, invasive species, potential dam construction | Inadequate funding and coverage of existing reserves; threatened |
| SA20 | Espinhaço Range region | F | 7000 | 1000–2107 m | >4000 | Fruit trees, ornamental plants, medicinal plants | Mainly campo rupestre, with cerrado, marshes, montane to dry deciduous forests | 2 NPs (1858 km²), 2 SPs (430 km²), Ecological Station, 3 Environmental Protection Zones | Grazing, erosion, fire, charcoal production, plant collecting, hydroelectric schemes, road building, mining | Inadequate coverage of protected areas; threatened |

| Code | Site | Type | Size (km²) | Altitude | Flora | Examples of Useful Plants | Vegetation | Protected Areas | Threats | Assessment |
|------|------|------|-----------|----------|-------|---------------------------|------------|-----------------|---------|------------|
| SA17 | Juréia-Itatins Ecological Station | S | 792 | 0–800 m | >500 | Timber trees, edible palms, medicinal plants, ornamental plants | Tropical Atlantic rain forest, restinga forest and scrub, littoral forest, mangroves, grassland | Ecological Station | Illegal logging, over-collection of palm hearts | Isolated and relatively secure |
| SA5 | Manaus region | F | 71,000 | 16–130 m | >1000 tree spp. | Timber trees, rosewood, Brazil nut, fruit trees, edible palms | Terra firme rain forest, permanently and seasonally inundated forests, caatinga forest, scrub, grasslands | Numerous protected areas | Clearance for cattle ranching, oil palm plantations, urban expansion, road building | Inadequate reserve coverage, no várzea (inundated) forests protected nearby |
| SA15 | Mountain ranges of Rio de Janeiro | F | 7000 | 60–2800 m | 5000–6000 | Timber trees (e.g. Brazil-wood), palmito palm hearts, medicinal plants, ornamental plants | Tropical Atlantic rain forests, high-altitude meadows | 20 conservation areas cover c. 3220 km² (46%) of region | Clearance for agriculture, settlements, over-collecting of palms and ornamentals, logging | Protected areas lack management plans; forests outside protected areas severely threatened |
| SA16 | Serra do Japi | S | 354 | 800–1300 m | 300* tree spp. | Timber trees, fruit trees, medicinal and ornamental plants | Semi-deciduous forests, semi-arid vegetation on rock outcrops | "Historical patrimony" (191 km²), Environmental Protection Zone, small municipal reserve | Population pressure leading to clearance for settlements, industrial developments, logging, air pollution, fire, mining, tourism | Protection status needs strengthening; severely threatened |
| SA13 | Tabuleiro forests, N. Espírito Santo | V | 484 | 28–90 m | 837* tree spp. | Timber trees, resins, oils, medicinal plants | Tropical Atlantic rain forest, várzea forest, savanna | FoR (220 km²), 2 Biological Reserves (264 km²) | Fire, logging | Protected areas reasonably secure and protect almost all the remaining forests |
| SA4 | Transverse Dry Belt | F | 150,000 | 5–600 m | | Timber trees, Brazil nut, rubber and cocoa relatives, vanilla, curare, rosewood | Lowland (terra firme) semi-deciduous and deciduous forests, permanently and seasonally inundated swamp forests, various savannas | 1 Biological Reserve (38,500 km²), 1 National Forest (3150 km²), 2 Ecological Stations (5771 km²), Amerindian reserves | Mining, pollution, logging | Relatively inaccessible but development beginning; protection status needs strengthening |
| **Brazil/Colombia/Venezuela** | | | | | | | | | | |
| SA6 | Upper Rio Negro region | F | >250,000 | <100–1000 m | >15,000 | Centre of diversity for many useful plants, incl. rubber, rosewood, Brazil nut | Amazon caatinga forest and scrub, flood forest (igapó), submontane forest | Well protected in 7 NPs and reserves (c. 34% of region), Amerindian reserves | None; potential threats: gold mining, cocoa plantations, logging | Relatively safe; further areas proposed as NPs and reserves |
| **Chile** | | | | | | | | | | |
| SA43 | Lomas formations of the Atacama Desert | V | >5000 | 0–1100 m | 550 | Ornamental plants, potential genetic resources | Desert vegetation of annual, short-lived perennial and woody scrub | NP (438 km²), Nature Reserve (30 km²) | Urbanization, mining, fuelwood cutting, grazing | Inadequate coverage of protected areas; threatened |
| SA44 | Mediterranean region and La Campana NP | F | 5000 | 300–2222 m | 2000 | Timber trees (e.g. Nothofagus), fruit trees, Chilean honey palm, dyes, medicinal plants, ornamentals | Nothofagus forest, submontane to alpine vegetation, palm forest, bamboo scrub, matorral | 2 NPs, 5 National Reserves (840 km²), 1 NS (116 km²), proposed reserve (c. 5000 km²) | Agriculture, cattle ranching, urbanization, road building, mining, fire, fuelwood cutting | Partially protected, but areas outside protected areas are severely threatened |
| SA45 | Temperate rain forest | V | 110,000 | 0–2000 m | 450 | Timber trees (e.g. Araucaria, Fitzroya) | Evergreen and deciduous temperate rain forests | 25 NPs, 14 NRs, 1 NatM | Logging, agriculture, grazing, fire, plantation forestry | Coverage and staffing of existing reserves inadequate; severely threatened |

| Code | Site | Type | Size (km²) | Altitude | Flora | Examples of Useful Plants | Vegetation | Protected Areas | Threats | Assessment |
|---|---|---|---|---|---|---|---|---|---|---|
| **Colombia** | | | | | | | | | | |
| SA7 | Chiribiquete-Araracuara-Cahuinarí region | F | 50,000 | 150–700 m | 12,000 | Timber trees, rubber, cocoa and pepper relatives, fruit trees, medicinal plants | Tropical lowland rain forest, evergreen sclerophyllous scrub, grassland | 2 NPs (18,550 km²), 3 Amerindian reserves (3470 km²) | Potential unplanned colonization, burning, road building, mining | Reasonably safe at present due to remoteness; management plan for protected areas yet to be developed |
| SA39 | Colombian Pacific Coast region | F/V | 130,000 | 0–1000 m | 8000–9000 | Timber trees, fruit trees, medicinal plants, ornamentals | Lowland and premontane tropical pluvial to moist forests, mangroves | 4 NPs (2076 km²) | Logging, colonization, agriculture, grazing, mining | Present reserve system inadequate; large areas of forest under threat |
| SA29 | Colombian Central Massif | F | 2000 | 1000–4500 m | 1200 | Medicinal plants, fodder plants | Páramo, montane and mid-altitude forests, tropical deciduous forest | NP (830 km²), private reserve, Amerindian reserves | Mining, road building, cattle ranching, fire, tree felling, draining of wetlands | Inadequate coverage of protected areas; threatened |
| SA28 | Los Nevados Natural National Park region | S | 12,200 | 300–4600 m | 1250 | Medicinal plants, dyes, timbers, edible species | Lowland dry forests, oak and laurel forests, páramo, super-páramo | NP (583 km²), 3 other protected areas (115 km²) | Logging, fire, volcanic eruptions, cattle grazing | Region at mid-altitudes severely threatened |
| SA27 | Páramo de Sumapaz | F | 15,000 | 300–4250 m | | Plants used for medicine, agriculture, construction | Lowland to montane forests, dry forests, páramo | 1 NP (1540 km²) | Road construction, colonization, cattle ranching, logging, mining | Increasingly at risk from population growth and needs; more reserves needed |
| SA25 | Sierra Nevada de Santa Marta | S | 12,232 | 0–5776 m | >1800 | Medicinal plants, dyes, cultural species, edible species, timber trees páramo | Humid tropical forest, montane tropical rain forest, cloud forest, | 2 National Natural Parks (3980 km²), Amerindian reserves | Colonization, erosion, agriculture, cattle ranching | Severely threatened |
| SA26 | Sierra Nevada del Cocuy-Guantiva | F | 4260 | 500–5493 m | | Medicinal plants, spices, plants for construction | Dry xerophytic scrub, Andean forests, páramo | 1 NP (3060 km²), including Amerindian reserve (216 km²) | Excessive sheep grazing, agricultural spread, tourism | Improved regulation; an additional reserve and management plans needed |
| **Colombia/Ecuador** | | | | | | | | | | |
| SA30 | Volcanoes of Nariñense Plateau | F | 1400 | 3000–4500 m | 450 | Medicinal plants, edible plants, ornamental plants | Páramo grassland and peat bogs, scrub, forests with Miconia | Fauna and Flora Sanctuary (176 km²) | Volcanic eruptions, agriculture, cattle ranching, plantation forestry using exotics | Inadequate protection; severely threatened |
| **Ecuador** | | | | | | | | | | |
| SA40 | Ecuadorian Pacific Coast mesic forests | V | 3700 | 0–900 m | 5300 | Timber trees, ivory-nut palm, ornamental plants | Lowland tropical moist, wet and pluvial forests | FoR (1300 km²), Ecological Reserve (2040 km²), several othersmall reserves (c. 5 km²) | Logging, colonization, agriculture, grazing | Threatened; some areas severely threatened |
| SA38 | Gran Sumaco and Upper Napo River region | F | 9000 | 300–3732 m | 6000 | Medicinal plants, crop relatives, culturally important plants | Lowland tropical forest to wet páramo | Biological Station (7 km²); whole area proposed as BR; 2 proposed NPs (1910 km²) | Road building, subsistence agriculture, colonization, cattle ranching, potential mining | Inadequately protected, especially lowlands; threatened |
| SA31 | Páramo and Andean forests of Sangay NP | V/S | 5717 | 1000–5319 m | >3000 | Food, fodder and medicinal plants, fibres, ornamental plants | Páramo, Andean and sub-Andean forests | Included within NP and WHS | Road building, logging, colonization, mining, fire, overgrazing, tourism | Reasonably safe, but management plan needs revision and implementation |

| Code | Site | Type | Size (km²) | Altitude | Flora | Examples of Useful Plants | Vegetation | Protected Areas | Threats | Assessment |
|---|---|---|---|---|---|---|---|---|---|---|
| SA8 | Yasuní NP and Waorani Ethnic Reserve | S | 15,920 | 200–350 m | 4000 | Wild rubber, vegetable ivory palm, valuable hardwoods, medicinal plants | Tropical moist forest | BR: NP (9820 km²), Ethnic Reserve (6100 km²) | Oil exploration, logging, road building, colonization | Severely threatened |
| | **Ecuador/Peru** | | | | | | | | | |
| SA32 | Huancabamba region | F | 29,000 | 1000–4000 m | 2000–2500 | Timber trees, medicinal plants, ornamental plants | Montane cloud forest, dry forest, páramo | NatS (295 km²) | Logging, agriculture; 75% of original humid forest destroyed | Inadequate protection; severely threatened |
| | **French Guiana** | | | | | | | | | |
| SA3 | Saül region | S | >1340 | 200–762 m | 2000 | Timber trees, edible palms, rosewood oil, medicinal plants | Mostly lowland moist forest, swamp forest, montane forest | 2 potential NRs (790 km²) | Slash and burn agriculture, fuelwood cutting, gold mining, potential road | Seriously threatened at present; repeated efforts to protect area since 1975 |
| | **Paraguay** | | | | | | | | | |
| SA18 | Mbaracayú Reserve | F | 600 | 140–450 m | 600 | Valuable timbers, fruit trees, edible palms, Paraguayan tea, medicinal plants | Semi-evergreen subtropical moist forest, savanna, lowland bogs | Private reserve | Agriculture, logging, cultivation of narcotic plants | Inadequately protected; region threatened |
| | **Peru** | | | | | | | | | |
| SA41 | Cerros de Amotape NP region | S | 2314 | 100–1618 m | >500 | Timber trees, forage plants, medicinal plants, ornamental plants, craft plants | Dry forest, matorral | NP (913 km²) forming core area of a BR of 2314 km² | Fuelwood and timber cutting, fire, overgrazing, soil erosion, desertification | At risk |
| SA37 | Eastern slopes of Peruvian Andes | F | 250,000 | 400–3500 m | 7000–10,000 | Timber trees, ornamental plants | Dry, wet and pluvial tropical and subtropical lowland, premontane and montane forests | 3 NPs protect c. 20,000 km²; 2 NatSs, 2 Reserved Zones, 1 PF, 1 National Forest cover 6000 km² | Deforestation from colonization, roads, agriculture, logging, cultivation of narcotics | NPs reasonably safe due to inaccessibility; protection of other reserves inadequate; severe threats in places |
| SA42 | Lomas formations | V | >2000 | 0–1000 m | 600 | Potential genetic resources of crop plants (e.g. tomato) | Desert vegetation of annual, short-lived perennial and woody scrub | 3 National Reserves (1228 km²) | Urbanization, grazing, mining, fuelwood cutting | Coastal areas severely threatened, more protected areas and conservation measures needed |
| SA11 | Lowlands of Manú NP: Cocha Cashu Biological Station | S | 7500 | 300–400 m | 1900 | Spanish cedar, mahogany, cocoa relatives, edible palms and fruits | Mostly evergreen tropical forest | Biological Station (10 km²) within NP of 15,328 km², forming part of a BR of 18,812 km² | Potential road building, oil exploration and mining | Inadequate funding resulting in lack of trained staff; threatened |
| SA33 | Peruvian puna | V | 230,000 | 3300–5000 m | 1000–1500 | Potato relatives, many traditional Andean crops and medicinal plants, spices | Grasslands, scrub, wetlands, tropical alpine vegetation | 9500 km² (4% of area) within 3 NPs, 5 National Reserves, 3 NatSs, 3 Historical Sanctuaries | Overgrazing, fire, soil erosion, mining, fuelwood cutting | Inadequate funding resulting in lack of trained staff; inadequate coverage of protected areas; threatened |
| SA10 | Tambopata region | F | 15,000 | 250–3000 m | 2500–3000 | Timber trees, Brazil nut, rubber, fruit trees | Subtropical premontane/montane wet forests, tropical moist forest, swamp forest, savanna | NS (1021 km²), Reserved Zone (14,000 km²), Tambopata Reserve (5.5 km²) | Cattle ranching, subsistence agriculture, gold mining, local population pressure | Conservation measures need implementing in Reserved Zone; threatened |

| Code | Site | Type | Size (km²) | Altitude | Flora | Examples of Useful Plants | Vegetation | Protected Areas | Threats | Assessment |
|---|---|---|---|---|---|---|---|---|---|---|
| **Peru/Colombia** | | | | | | | | | | |
| SA9 | Iquitos region | F | 80,000 | 105–140 m | >2265 | Timber trees, medicinal plants (incl. curare), fibres, >120 spp. of edible fruits | Evergreen Amazonian moist forests, swamps | Peru: National Reserve (in part), Communal Reserve (3225 km²); Colombia: National Natural Park (1700 km²) | Clearance for settlements and agriculture | Inadequate coverage of protected areas; some habitats threatened |
| **Venezuela** | | | | | | | | | | |
| SA1 | Coastal Cordillera | F | 45,000 | 0–2765 m | 5000 | Quinine and other medicinal plants, quality hardwoods | Montane/submontane semi-deciduous and evergreen forests, hill savanna, cloud forest, coastal and upper montane scrub, mangroves | 11 NPs (6640 km²) and 5 NMs | Population pressure, deforestation, colonization, fire, agriculture, roads | Protected areas reasonably secure, but coverage inadequate |
| SA2 | Pantepui region | S/F | 7000 | 1300–3015 m | 3000 | Ornamentals (e.g. bromeliads, orchids, carnivorous plants), undoubtedly rich in potentially useful species | Montane forests, tepui scrub, pioneer communities on cliffs and rocky areas | NPs and NMs cover entire region | No serious threats, but potential threats from increased tourism and over-collecting | Safe at present but potentially at risk without more effective controls |

## SOUTH EAST ASIA (MALESIA)

| Code | Site | Type | Size (km²) | Altitude | Flora | Examples of Useful Plants | Vegetation | Protected Areas | Threats | Assessment |
|---|---|---|---|---|---|---|---|---|---|---|
| **Brunei Darussalam** | | | | | | | | | | |
| SEA13 | Batu Apoi FoR, Ulu Temburong | S | 488 | 50–1850 m | 3000 | Timber trees (especially dipterocarps, Agathis), medicinal plants, ornamentals | Lowland dipterocarp rain forest, lower and upper montane forests | FoR, planned NP | Logging, potential dam construction | At risk |
| **Indonesia (Irian Jaya)** | | | | | | | | | | |
| SEA68 | Arfak Mountains | F | 2200 | 100–3100 m | 3000–4000 | Timber trees, rattans, fruit tree relatives, ornamental plants (especially rhododendrons) | Lowland, hill and lower montane rain forest, grassland/heath communities, lake vegetation | NR (450 km²); proposal to extend to 653 km² as Nature Conservation Area | Population pressure, resettlement schemes, agriculture and logging, road building | Lowlands threatened in particular |
| SEA69 | Gunung Lorentz | S | 21,500 | 0–4884 m | 3000–4000 | Fruits, vegetables, fibres, building materials | Lowland to montane rain forests, mangroves, bogs, swamps, heaths, grasslands, alpine vegetation | NR; proposals for NP, BR & WHS status | Mining, logging, petroleum exploitation, road building, tourism, colonization | Threatened; high-altitude vegetation vulnerable to trampling |
| SEA70 | Mamberamo-Pegunungan Jayawijaya | F | 23,244 | 0–4640 m | 2000–3000 | Timber trees, especially southern beech, podocarps, conifers | Lowland to montane rain forest, lowland swamp forest, mangroves | Proposed NP/WHS (14,425 km²), GR (8000 km²), proposed GR (819 km²) | Petroleum exploitation, logging at lower altitudes | Lowlands particularly at risk |
| SEA71 | Waigeo | S | 14,784 | 0–999 m | | Timber trees, wild sugar cane | Lowland to lower montane rain forest, riverine forest, mangroves, limestone and ultramafic vegetation | NR (1530 km²), marine reserve covers offshore islets and reefs | Potential nickel mining | At risk if mining goes ahead |

| Code | Site | Type | Size (km²) | Altitude | Flora | Examples of Useful Plants | Vegetation | Protected Areas | Threats | Assessment |
|---|---|---|---|---|---|---|---|---|---|---|
| **Indonesia (Java)** | | | | | | | | | | |
| SEA64 | Gede-Pangrango NP | S | 150 | 1000–3019 m | >1000 | Timber trees, medicinal plants, ornamental plants | Mostly montane and submontane rain forest, grass plains | NP (whole areae), BR (140 km²) | Timber and fuelwood cutting, agricultural encroachment, visitor pressure, plant collecting | Encroachment around boundaries; at risk |
| **Indonesia (Kalimantan)** | | | | | | | | | | |
| SEA15 | Bukit Raya and Bukit Baka | S | 7705 | 100–2278 m | 2000–4000 | Timber trees (especially dipterocarps), fruit trees, illipe nuts, rattans | Lowland tropical rain forest, swamp forest, lower and upper montane forests, ericaceous scrub | NP (1811 km²) | Logging, road construction, shifting cultivation | Encroachment in west; at risk |
| SEA17 | Gunung Palung | S | 900 | 0–1160 m | | Timber trees, fruit trees, ornamental plants | Dipterocarp rain forests, montane forests, swamp forests, beach forest, mangroves | NP | Logging, shifting cultivation | Buffer zones needed; most of area safe, but some parts at risk |
| SEA19 | Sungai Kayan-Sungai Mentarang NR | S | 29,000 | 100–2556 m | 2000 | Timber trees, fruit trees, gingers, rattans | Lowland and hill dipterocarp rain forests, montane forests, riverine, swamp and heath forests | NR (16,000 km²); proposed extensions 13,000 km²) | Logging, mining, shifting cultivation | Boundaries at risk |
| **Indonesia (Sulawesi)** | | | | | | | | | | |
| SEA46 | Dumoga-Bone NP | S | 3000 | 200–1968 m | | Timber trees, rattans | Tropical lowland semi-evergreen rain forest, riverine forest, montane forest, some limestone forest | NP | Over-collection of forest products, shifting cultivation, potential mining, road building | Boundaries threatened but demarcation and zoning being implemented |
| SEA47 | Limestone flora | V | | 150–1000 m | | Sugar palm, fruit tree relatives, plants for degraded land | Forest over limestone, scrub, lithophytic vegetation | c. 70% of all outcrops unprotected | Quarrying, firewood cutting, clearance for agriculture, fire | Threatened |
| SEA50 | Pegunungan Latimojong | S | 580 | 1000–3455 m | | Ornamental plants | Lower and upper montane forests, hill forest, montane grassland, subalpine vegetation | PF; proposed NR | Clearance of lower slopes for agriculture | Lowlands threatened, but most of area not threatened |
| SEA48 | Ultramafic flora | V | 12,000 | | | Plants of potential value for rehabilitating degraded areas | Ultramafic facies of lowland forest, scrub, some montane vegetation | Mostly unprotected | Mostly intact, but agricultural development planned | Threatened |
| **Indonesia (Sumatra)** | | | | | | | | | | |
| SEA41 | Gunung Leuser | S | >9000 | 0–3466 m | 2000–3000 | Timber trees (especially dipterocarps), fruit trees, medicinal plants, ornamentals | Lowland dipterocarp rain forest, montane and subalpine forests, freshwater swamp forest, marshes | NP (7926 km²), BR (9464 km²) | Encroachment of settlements, agriculture, illegal logging, over-collection of rattans | Threatened, especially in the lowlands; inadequate funding |
| SEA42 | Kerinci-Seblat NP | S | 1484 | 200–3805 m | 2000–3000 | Fruit trees, timbers (e.g. dipterocarps, Agathis), medicinal plants, rattans | Lowland and hill dipterocarp rain forests, montane forests, montane swamp forest | NP | Encroachment of settlements, agriculture, illegal logging, over-collection of rattans | Threatened, especially in the lowlands |

| Code | Site | Type | Size (km²) | Altitude | Flora | Examples of Useful Plants | Vegetation | Protected Areas | Threats | Assessment |
|---|---|---|---|---|---|---|---|---|---|---|
| SEA43 | Limestone flora | V | 5000 | 150–1500 m | 1500–2000 | Ornamental plants, fruit tree relatives | Forest over limestone, scrub, lithophytic vegetation | Very few outcrops protected | Quarrying | Threatened |
| SEA45 | Tigapuluh Mountains | S | 2000 | 150–800 m | 2000–3000 | Timber trees | Tropical lowland evergreen and hill dipterocarp rain forests | None | Logging, conversion to forestry and rubber plantations, shifting cultivation | Eastern lowlands severely threatened |
| **Indonesia/Malaysia** | | | | | | | | | | |
| SEA16 | Lanjak Entimau WS, Batang Ai NP, Gunung Bentuang dan Karimun | S | 10,111 | 500–1284 m | | Timber trees, especially dipterocarps, illipe nuts, rattans, fruit tree relatives | Lowland and hill evergreen rain forests, heath, swamp and montane forests | WS (1688 km²), proposed extensions (184 km²), NP (240 km²), NR (8000 km²) | Agricultural encroachment, logging | Boundaries and lower slopes at risk |
| SEA18 | Limestone flora of Borneo | V | | 0–1710 m | | Ornamental plants (especially orchids, gesneriads, begonias, balsams, ferns) | Lowland to upper montane forest on limestone, lithophytic vegetation | Some major areas in Sarawak in NP, few in Sabah in FoRs, proposed NPs in Kalimantan, other sites unprotected | Quarrying, fire, clearance of surrounding forests for agriculture, tourism | Some major areas safe, some relatively safe but unprotected, most others threatened |
| **Malaysia (Peninsular Malaysia)** | | | | | | | | | | |
| SEA2 | Endau-Rompin State Parks | S | 500 | 100–1000 m | | Timber trees (including dipterocarps), rattans, fruit trees, wild banana relative, medicinal herbs | Mainly tropical lowland rain and hill dipterocarp forest, hill swamp forest | FoR; proposed State Parks | Logging, clearance for development schemes, tourist facilities, commercial collection of ornamental plants | Protection needs strengthening; at risk |
| SEA3 | Limestone flora | V | 260 | 0–713 m | >1300 | Ornamental plants, especially orchids, begonias, palms, gesneriads | Limestone forest, scrub, lithophytic vegetation | A few outcrops protected in Taman Negara (NP); some occur in FoRs; some are Temple Reserves (no protection to flora) | Quarrying, mining, encroachment from agriculture, fire, tourism, plant collecting | Many outcrops severely threatened, some at risk, a few safe |
| SEA4 | Montane flora | V | 2180 | 810–2188 m | >3000 | Ornamental plants (especially orchids, pitcher plants, rhododendrons) | Lower and upper montane forests | Most peaks fall within FoRs, G. Tahan is in NP, Cameron Highlands is in WS, G. Kajang is in WR | Large-scale resort development, agriculture/horticulture, road building, plant collecting | Most areas outside NP severely threatened |
| SEA5 | Pulau Tioman | S | 72 | 0–1038 m | 1500 | Ornamental plants, especially slipper orchids, Rafflesia used medicinally | Coastal forest, hill and upper montane forests, some mangroves | WR | Large-scale resort development, airstrip construction, over-collecting of orchids and Rafflesia | Threatened; protected status not enforced |
| SEA8 | Taman Negara | S | 4343 | 75–2188 m | >3000 | Timber and fruit trees, rattans, ornamental plants (e.g. orchids), potential medicinal plants | Lowland, hill and montane rain forests, "padang" vegetation, limestone and quartzite vegetation, riparian communities | NP | Logging, hydroelectric dams, lack of buffer zone, some tourist developments | Safe at present, but frequently threatened |

| Code | Site | Type | Size (km²) | Altitude | Flora | Examples of Useful Plants | Vegetation | Protected Areas | Threats | Assessment |
|---|---|---|---|---|---|---|---|---|---|---|
| SEA10 | Trengganu Hills | S | 150 | 60–920 m | 1500 | Timber trees, rattans, ornamental plants | Lowland and hill rain forest | FoR, 3 small VJRs | Logging, land clearance for cultivation | At risk |
| **Malaysia (Sabah)** | | | | | | | | | | |
| SEA22 | East Sabah lowland/hill dipterocarp forests | V | 20,000 | 0–1298 m | 5000–6000 | Timber trees (seraya, keruing, kapur), rattans, fruit trees, ornamentals | Tropical evergreen lowland and hill dipterocarp rain forests | 4077 km² protected in conservation areas | Conversion to agriculture, human settlement, tree plantations, unsustainable logging | Threatened, some areas seriously threatened; protection of reserves needs strengthening |
| SEA24 | Kinabalu Park | S | 753 | 150–4101 m | 4500 | Timber trees, ornamental plants (e.g. pitcher plants, orchids) | Mostly montane rain forest, some tropical lowland rain forest, ultramafic forest, alpine vegetation | SP | Clearance for cultivation, illegal logging, mining, tourism | Boundaries threatened |
| SEA27 | North-east Borneo ultramafic flora | V | 3500 | 0–3000 m | | Timber trees, potential ornamental plants, nickel- and manganese-tolerant species | Ultramafic facies of tropical lowland evergreen rain forest, lower and upper montane forest | Kinabalu SP only area of formal protection; small areas in Danum Valley Conservation Area; Mt Silam is a protected watershed | Clearance for cultivation and golf course, logging, fire, dam construction, road building | Inadequate coverage of protected areas; threatened |
| **Malaysia (Sarawak)** | | | | | | | | | | |
| SEA34 | Lambir Hills | S | 69 | 30–467 m | 1500 | Timber trees (incl. 69 dipterocarp spp.), mango and durian relatives, rattans | Lowland mixed dipterocarp forest, heath forest, scrub | NP | Logging, clearance for agriculture | Encroachment around boundaries; threatened |
| **Malaysia/Brunei** | | | | | | | | | | |
| SEA33 | Gunung Mulu NP/Medalam PF/Labi Hills/Bukit Teraja/Ulu Ingei/Sungei Ingei | S | 1521 | 30–2376 m | 3500 | Timber trees, especially dipterocarps, fruit and nut trees, sago palm, rattans, medicinal plants | Lowland mixed dipterocarp to montane forests on sandstones, limestones and shales, heath forests, peat swamp forest | Malaysia: NP, PF; Brunei: PF and Conservation Area within FoR | Logging around perimeter of Mulu NP, shifting cultivation along some rivers, potential threat from road construction | Mostly safe at present, but would be at risk if proposed road went ahead; buffer zones to Mulu NP need to be implemented |
| **Papua New Guinea** | | | | | | | | | | |
| SEA89 | Bismarck Falls-Mt Wilhelm-Mt Otto-Schrader Range-Mt Hellwig-Gahavisuka | S | 9754 | 250–4499 m | 5000–6000 | Traditional food and medicinal plants, timbers, fibres, plants of cultural value | Lowland swamp and rain forest, montane forests, alpine vegetation | Proposed NP (Mt Wilhelm), small Provincial Park (Gahavisuka); region proposed as WHS | Population pressure, logging, agriculture, coffee and cardamom plantations | Protected area coverage inadequate; at risk |
| SEA91 | Huon Peninsula (Mt Bangeta-Rawlinson Range; Cromwell Ranges-Sialum Terraces) | S | 3415 | 0–4120 m | 4000–5000 | Fruit trees, vegetables, fibres, potential timber species | Lowland tropical rain forest to subalpine forest, grasslands, mangroves | No formal protection | Logging, road building | At risk |
| SEA98 | Menyamya-Aseki-Amungwiwa-Bowutu Mts-Lasanga Island | F | 6695 | 0–3278 m | 1500–3000 | Fruits, vegetables, fibres, building materials, potential timber species | Lowland rain forests to upper montane forests, ultramafic vegetation | NP (20 km²), local support for conservation area in Bowutu Mts, several reserves throughout region needed | Logging, road building, local population pressure | Severely threatened in places, protected area coverage inadequate |

| Code | Site | Type | Size (km²) | Altitude | Flora | Examples of Useful Plants | Vegetation | Protected Areas | Threats | Assessment |
|---|---|---|---|---|---|---|---|---|---|---|
| SEA86 | Mt Giluwe-Tari Gap-Doma Peaks | S | 3346 | 1000–4368 m | >3000 | Traditional food and medicinal plants, fibres, ornamental plants | Montane and subalpine forests, grasslands, alpine communities | Local reserves in Tari Gap area | Logging, road building, clearance for agricultural plantations, dieback of *Nothofagus* | Protected area coverage inadequate; at risk |
| SEA92 | Southern Fly Platform | F | 18,644 | 0–30 m | >2000 | Edible palms, traditional food and medicinal plants | Monsoon and savanna vegetation, mangroves, lowland swamps, mangroves | Wildlife Management Area (5900 km²) | No major threats, some grazing pressure from introduced deer, potential threat from mining | Reasonably safe, but protected area coverage inadequate |
| **Philippines** | | | | | | | | | | |
| SEA51 | Batan Islands | S | 209 | 0–1008 m | >500 | Timbers, fibres, medicinal plants, food plants | Lowland evergreen to mid-montane rain forest, grassland, secondary vegetation | Proposed as Protected Landscape and 2 "critical watersheds" under National Integrated Protected Area System | Typhoons, clearance for grazing, crops, shifting cultivation, over-collection of forest products | Vulnerable, but growing conservation awareness among local people |
| SEA52 | Mt Apo | S | 769 | 500–2954 m | >800 | Ornamental plants (e.g. orchids, aroids, begonias), timber trees | Lowland rain forest (mostly cleared), montane forests, "elfin woodland", scrub, grassland | NP | Construction of geothermal plant, clearance for agriculture, illegal logging, shifting cultivation | Severely threatened |
| SEA57 | Mt Pulog | S | 115 | 2600–2929 m | 800 | Timber tree provenances (especially pines), ornamental plants | Montane forest, pine forest, grassland | NP | Conversion of forest to vegetable and cut-flower gardens, fire | Threatened |
| SEA59 | Palanan Wilderness Area | S | 2168 | 0–1672 m | 1500 | Timber trees, rattans | Lowland and hill dipterocarp forest, lower montane forest, ultramafic and limestone forests | Wilderness Area; proposed as NP | Illegal logging, shifting cultivation, over-collection of forest products, potential large-scale logging | Mostly safe at present, but could become severely threatened |
| SEA60 | Palawan | F | 14,896 | 0–2085 m | >2000 | Timber trees, rattans, almaciga resin, fruit trees, orchids, nipa palm | Lowland evergreen dipterocarp and semi-deciduous forests, ultramafic and limestone forests, mangroves | BR (11,508 km²), NP (39 km²), various other protected areas covering 3.4% of land area | Logging, mining, shifting cultivation, tourism, over-collection of forest products | Inadequately protected; threatened |
| SEA61 | Sibuyan Island | S | 445 | 0–2052 m | 700 | Timber trees, almaciga resin, ornamental plants | Lowland dipterocarp forest, montane forest, grassland, mangroves | Proposed NR | Logging, slash and burn agriculture, fire, over-exploitation of rattan | Threatened |
| **SOUTH WEST ASIA AND THE MIDDLE EAST** | | | | | | | | | | |
| **Iran** | | | | | | | | | | |
| SWA10 | Touran Protected Area BR | S | 18,604 | 690–2281 m | 1000 | Medicinal herbs, food and fodder plants | Semi-desert, psammophytic and halophytic vegetation | Protected Area divided into WR (5650 km²) and Protected Area (12,954 km²); BR covers 10,000 km² | Overgrazing, fuelwood cutting | At risk; protection measures need to be enforced |
| **Iran/Azerbaijan** | | | | | | | | | | |
| SWA18 | Hyrcanian forests | V | 50,000 | 0–2500 m | | Timber trees, ornamental plants | Broadleaved deciduous forest, shrubland | Several protected areas; no information available on current status | Clearance for agriculture, logging, invasive plants in some coastal areas | Threatened |

| Code | Site | Type | Size (km²) | Altitude | Flora | Examples of Useful Plants | Vegetation | Protected Areas | Threats | Assessment |
|---|---|---|---|---|---|---|---|---|---|---|
| **Oman/Yemen** | | | | | | | | | | |
| SWA1 | Dhofar Fog Oasis | F | 30,000 | 0–2100 m | 900 | Frankincense, traditional food, fibre and medicinal plants | Mainly dry deciduous shrubland, montane evergreen shrubland, semi-desert grassland | 1 small Bird Sanctuary, otherwise none | Population pressure, overgrazing, cutting of wood for fuel and timber | Severely threatened; IUCN proposals for reserves in Oman not yet implemented |
| **Saudi Arabia/Yemen** | | | | | | | | | | |
| SWA5 | Highlands of South-western Arabia | F | 70,000 | 200–3760 m | 2000 | Qat (stimulant), coffee, barley, wheat and sorghum relatives, myrrh | Deciduous and evergreen bushland and thicket, juniper woodland | Asir NP (4150 km²) in Saudi Arabia, proposed areas in Yemen | Uncontrolled cutting of wood for fuel, timber and charcoal; overgrazing, erosion | No effective protection over most of area, remaining woodland severely threatened |
| **Turkey** | | | | | | | | | | |
| SWA12 | Anti-Taurus Mts/ Upper Euphrates | F | 60,000 | 700–3734 m | 3200 | Walnut, medicinal plants, dyes, cereal crop relatives | Oak forest, steppe, montane steppe | NP (428 km²) | Dam construction, re-afforestation projects, rock climbing leading to erosion | Urgent action needed to protect more of the region; threatened |
| SWA15 | Isaurian, Lycaonian and Cilician Taurus | F | 45,120 | 0–3524 m | >2500 | Fig, pomegranate, nuts, dune stabilizers | Cilician fir and cedar forests, scrub, thorn-cushion plants, scree vegetation, dune communities | NP (very small), Bird Sanctuary, GR (30 km²) | Road building, export of wild bulbs, overgrazing, tourism, clearance for agriculture | Many important ecosystems unprotected; threatened |
| SWA19 | N.E. Anatolia | F | 33,200 | 0–3932 m | >2460 | Cherries, hazelnuts, timber trees | Coastal humid subtropical forest to fir forest, rhododendron scrub, scree vegetation | 1 NP | Illegal logging, clearance for agriculture, export of wild bulbs | None of the Little Caucasus is protected; at risk but not as seriously threatened as other areas |
| SWA16 | S.W. Anatolia | F | 75,680 | 0–3070 m | >3365 | Cypress, cedar, oriental sweet gum, medicinal herbs | Mediterranean forest and scrub, cedar forest | Several NPs and Protected Zones, 5 Biogenetic Reserves (264.5 km²) | Tourism, overgrazing by goats, export of wild bulbs | Coastal areas severely threatened |
| **Turkey/Iran/Iraq** | | | | | | | | | | |
| SWA14 | Mountains of S.E. Turkey, N.W. Iran, N. Iraq | F | 147,332 | 1400–4168 m | 2500 | Pears, almonds, hawthorns, gum tragacanth | Oak forest, alpine thorn cushion scrub, montane steppe, alpine grassland, scree vegetation | Iran: NP (4636 km²); Turkey: 1 Forest Recreation Area, 1 GR | Influx of refugees, re-afforestation projects, potential dam and irrigation schemes | Inadequate coverage of reserve system, but threats to flora less severe than elsewhere |
| **Turkey/Syria/Lebanon/Israel/Jordan** | | | | | | | | | | |
| SWA17 | Levantine Uplands | F | 96,675 | 0–3083 m | 4160 | Timber trees (e.g. Cilician fir, cedar of Lebanon), fodder plants, spices, edible oils, root vegetables | Oak, pine, cypress, fir and cedar of Lebanon forests; juniper scrub, maquis, garigue, geophytic communities, alpine vegetation | Israel: 7 small reserves; Syria: 2 Protected Areas (6320 km²) | Logging of remaining forests, clearance for agriculture, tourism, urbanization, over-exploitation of essential oils | Threatened; inadequate coverage of protected areas |
| **Yemen** | | | | | | | | | | |
| SWA4 | Socotra | F | 3625 | 0–1519 m | 815* | Dragon's blood, other resins, gums, aloes | Semi-desert, dry deciduous shrubland, montane semi-evergreen thicket, secondary grassland | None | Overgrazing by goats, fuelwood cutting, potential new development projects | No protection but traditional practices have prevented serious exploitation so far |

# References

Bedward, M., Pressey, R.L. and Keith, D.A. (1992). A new approach for selecting fully representative reserve networks: addressing efficiency, reserve design and land suitability with an iterative analysis. *Biological Conservation* 62: 115–125.

Cowling, R.M., Gibbs Russell, G.E., Hoffman, M.T and Hilton-Taylor, C. (1989). Patterns of species diversity in Southern Africa. In Huntley, B.J. (ed.), *Biotic diversity in Southern Africa: concepts and conservation*. Oxford University Press, Cape Town. Pp. 19–50.

Davis, S. (1986). Plant Sites Directory. *Threatened Plants Newsletter* No. 16: 17.

Dinerstein, E. and Wikramanayake, E.D. (1993). Beyond "hotspots": how to prioritize investments to conserve biodiversity in the Indo-Pacific region. *Conservation Biology* 7: 530–565.

FAO (1990a). *TFAP Independent Review Report 1990. Appendix 3, section 3.3.* FAO, Rome.

FAO (1990b). *Interim report on Forest Resources Assessment 1990 Project.* Committee on Forestry 10th Session. COFO–90/8(a).

Gentry, A.H. (1990). Herbarium taxonomy versus field knowledge. *Flora Malesiana Bulletin Special Volume* 1: 31–35.

Greuter, W. (1991). Botanical diversity, endemism, rarity, and extinction in the Mediterranean area: an analysis based on the published volumes of Med-Checklist. *Bot. Chron.* 10: 63–79.

Haffer, J. (1969). Speciation in Amazonian forest birds. *Science* 165: 131–137.

Hawkes, J.G. (1983). *The diversity of crop plants.* Harvard University Press, Cambridge, Massachusetts.

Heywood, V.H. (1991). Assessment of the state of the flora of the west Mediterranean basin. In Rejdali, M. and Heywood, V.H. (eds), *Conservation des Ressources Végétales*. Actes Editions, Institut Agronomique et Vétérinaire Hassan II, Rabat. Pp. 9–17.

Heywood, V.H. (1992). Conservation of germplasm of wild species. In Sandlund, O.T., Hindar, K. and Brown, A.H.D. (eds), *Conservation of biodiversity for sustainable development*. Scandinavian University Press, Oslo. Pp. 189–203.

Heywood, V.H. (1994a). The measurement of biodiversity and the politics of implementation. In Forey, P.L., Humphries, C.J. and Vane-Wright, R.I. (eds), *Systematics and conservation evaluation*. Oxford University Press. Pp. 15–22.

Heywood, V.H. (1994b). The Mediterranean flora in the context of world biodiversity. In Olivier, L. and Muracciole, M. (eds), *Connaissance et Conservation de la Flore des Iles de la Méditerranée*. (In press.)

Huntley, B. J. (1988). Conserving and monitoring biotic diversity. Some South African examples. In Wilson, E.O. (ed.), *Biodiversity*. National Academy Press, Washington, D.C. Pp. 248–260.

ICBP (1992). *Putting biodiversity on the map: priority areas for global conservation*. International Council for Bird Preservation, Cambridge, U.K. 90 pp.

IUCN (1980). *World Conservation Strategy: living resource conservation for sustainable development*. IUCN, UNEP and WWF, Gland, Switzerland.

IUCN (1986). *The Plant Sites Red Data Book: a botanists' view of the places that matter*. IUCN, Richmond, U.K. 48 pp.

IUCN (1988). *Centres of Plant Diversity. A guide and strategy for their conservation*. IUCN, Richmond, U.K. 40 pp.

IUCN (1990). *Centres of Plant Diversity. An introduction to the project with guidelines for collaborators*. IUCN, Richmond, U.K. 31 pp.

IUCN/WWF (1984). *The IUCN/WWF Plants Conservation Programme 1984–85*. IUCN/WWF, Gland, Switzerland. 29 pp.

McNeely, J.A. (ed.) (1993). *Parks for life*. Report of the IVth World Congress on National Parks and Protected Areas. IUCN, Gland, Switzerland.

Miller, K.R. (1984). Selecting terrestrial habitats for conservation. In Hall, A.V. (ed.), *Conservation of threatened natural habitats*. South African National Scientific Programmes Report No. 92, Pretoria. Pp. 95–108.

Mittermeier, R.A. and Werner, T.B. (1988). Wealth of plants and animals unites "megadiversity" countries. *Tropicus* 4: 1, 4–5.

Myers, N. (1986). Tackling mass extinctions of species: a great creative challenge. The Horace M. Albright Lectureship in Conservation. University of California, Berkeley.

Myers, N. (1988a). Threatened biotas: "hot-spots" in tropical forests. *Environmentalist* 8: 187–208.

Myers, N. (1988b). Tropical forest and their species. Going, going...? In Wilson, E.O. (ed.), *Biodiversity*. National Academy Press, Washington, D.C. Pp. 28–35.

Myers, N. (1990). The biological challenge extended: extended hot-spots analysis. *Environmentalist* 10: 243–256.

Prescott-Allen, R. and Prescott-Allen, C. (1990). How many plants feed the world? *Conservation Biology* 4: 365–374.

Pressey, R.L., Humphries, C.J., Margules, C.R., Vane-Wright, R.I. and Williams, P.H. (1993). Beyond opportunism: key principles for systematic reserve selection. *Trends in Ecology and Evolution* 8: 124–128.

Quézel, P. (1985). Definition of the Mediterranean region and the origin of its flora. In Gómez Campo, C. (ed.), *Plant conservation in the Mediterranean area.* Junk, Dordrecht.

Raven, P.H. (1987). The scope of the plant conservation problem world-wide. In Bramwell, D., Hamann, O., Heywood, V. and Synge, H. (eds), *Botanic gardens and the World Conservation Strategy.* Academic Press, London. Pp. 10–19.

Raven, P.H. (1990). The politics of preserving biodiversity. *BioScience* 40: 769.

Simberloff, D. (1986). Are we on the verge of a mass extinction in tropical rain forests? In Elliott, D.K. (ed.), *Dynamics of extinction.* Wiley, New York. Pp. 165–180.

Stattersfield, A.J., Crosby, M.J., Long, A.J. and Wege, D.C. (in prep.). *A global directory of Endemic Bird Areas.* BirdLife International, Cambridge, U.K.

Vane-Wright, R.I., Humphries, C.J. and Williams, P.H. (1991). What to protect and the agony of choice. *Biological Conservation* 55: 235–254.

Whitmore, T.C. and Sayer, J.A. (eds) (1992). *Tropical deforestation and species extinction.* IUCN, Gland, Switzerland and Cambridge, U.K., and Chapman and Hall, London. 153 pp.

Williams, P.H., Vane-Wright, R.I. and Humphries, C.J. (1993). Measuring biodiversity for choosing conservation areas. In LaSalle, J. and Gauls, I.D. (eds), *Hymenoptera and biodiversity.* CABI. Pp. 309–328.

Wilson, E.O. (1988). The current state of biodiversity. In Wilson, E.O. (ed.), *Biodiversity.* National Academy Press, Washington, D.C. Pp. 3–18.

Wilson, E.O. (1992). The diversity of life. Belknap Press, Harvard University Press, Cambridge, Massachusetts.

WRI, IUCN and UNEP (1992). *Global biodiversity strategy. Guidelines for action to save, study and use the Earth's biotic wealth sustainably and equitably.* WRI, IUCN and UNEP. 244 pp.

# REGIONAL OVERVIEW: EUROPE

JOHN R. AKEROYD AND VERNON H. HEYWOOD

**Total land area:** 10,498,000 km².

**Population:** 682,000,000.

**Maximum altitude:** 4807 m (summit of Mont Blanc).

**Natural vegetation:** Tundra, boreal and montane coniferous forest, deciduous forest, Mediterranean sclerophyll forest and scrub, heathlands, steppic grassland, wetlands, montane vegetation, grasslands, scree communities.

**Number of vascular plants:** 12,500 species[a].

**Number of endemic species:** 3500[b].

**Native vascular plant families:** 169.

**Number of endemic families:** 0.

**Number of native genera:** 1340.

**Number of endemic genera:** 75.

**Largest plant families:** Compositae (1326, not including apomictic taxa), Gramineae (880), Leguminosae (840), Caryophyllaceae (655), Cruciferae (649). (no. of European species in brackets)

Sources of floristic data: [a] J. Akeroyd in World Conservation Monitoring Centre (1992); [b] Webb (1978)

## Introduction

Europe has a temperate, often moist, climate and a vegetation that has been drastically modified by human activity over thousands of years. Vegetation types range from the tundra of northern Scandinavia to the semi-arid scrublands that border the Mediterranean Sea, and the steppes of the south-eastern part of the region. Much of central and southern Europe is mountainous, whilst in the east the continent levels out towards the arid plains of Central Asia. The eastern extremity is traditionally demarcated by the north-south range of the Ural Mountains, with the Caucasus (CPD Site CA2, treated in the Central and Northern Asia region) forming the south-eastern boundary. The Atlantic Ocean that washes the western and northern shores of Europe has an ameliorating effect on the climate, especially in the more western parts. There are few large rivers or lakes, and most of the more extensive wetlands have been drained, although there are still a number of important wetland areas, especially on the coasts. Almost all natural or semi-natural forest cover has been cleared from the lowlands, but there remain substantial stands in the mountains and the north. Much of the natural or semi-natural vegetation cover remaining consists of subseral communities such as various forms of scrub (such as matorral, garrigue and maquis) and grasslands which are maintained through human intervention.

Two factors have had a special influence on Europe's vegetation and flora. Firstly, extensive episodes of glaciation during the Pleistocene gave rise to major migrations and extinctions of plants (Godwin 1975); and secondly, some 10,000 years of agriculture and 3000 years of dominant and expansive Western and Islamic civilizations, notably in the Mediterranean region (Braudel 1974), have modified or destroyed most natural plant communities and have introduced a huge alien flora from other parts of the world. The areas of greatest biodiversity and concentrations of endemic species occur in mountainous regions, especially in the south, and represent relics of the former native vegetation and flora.

## Geology

The oldest part of the present continent is the Baltic Shield of eastern Fennoscandia. This is a Precambrian complex of crystalline schists with igneous intrusions; there are traces of a smaller massif to the south, with fragments in west-central and central Europe. The remainder of the continent falls into two main geological and topographical zones: to the east the monotonous Russian Plain, a shallow saucer of sedimentary strata, including clays and evaporites, that extends from the Baltic southwards to the Black Sea and eastwards to the Urals; and the remarkably varied tectogenic landscapes of western and central Europe, dissected by faulting, folding and widespread igneous intrusion. The geology includes a wide range of sedimentary, intrusive and extrusive igneous, and metamorphic rocks.

Since much of Europe was covered, or influenced by the Pleistocene glaciation, there are also considerable deposits of drift and periglacial features such as loess. These frequently have more influence than underlying rocks on the formation of soils. Large areas of Europe are underlain by granite intrusions, which forms extensive outcrops, both in the Alps and in a belt from Scotland and Ireland, through Brittany and the Massif Central of France to north and central Portugal.

The principal mountain ranges of Europe were folded and uplifted 50–100 million years ago, especially during the Tertiary Era. Topographically, western and central Europe are dominated by the great arc of the Alps, Carpathians and Balkan Mountains, together with the subsidiary range of the Pyrenees on the borders of France and Spain. The Alps, Europe's largest and tallest mountain range, rise to 4807 m on Mont Blanc on the border between France and Switzerland. Further south, the same geological upheaval gave rise to the Baetic Cordillera and the mountains of Aragon in Spain, the Dinaric Alps, the Pindhos of Albania and Greece, the mountains of Corsica and the Apennines that form the backbone of Italy. Associated with this uplift was igneous activity, especially in southern Italy and the Aegean region, which are still regions of active vulcanism.

There are a wide range of soil types: fertile brown earths developed under deciduous forests and black earths or chernozems associated with the grasslands of eastern Europe, both favoured for agriculture; limestone soils, the shallow black rendzinas and terra rossa or red Mediterranean soil of southern Europe; the gley and leached podzols of northern Europe and the Atlantic regions; and the great deposits of peat in the bogs of north-west and northern Europe. A few areas on the coast and in the steppic regions of Spain and central and eastern Europe have saline or gypsaceous soils.

## Climate

Europe has a varied climate, much influenced by the North Atlantic Drift current, which brings warmer waters towards the Arctic region. Western Europe has an oceanic climate, moderated by the presence of the Atlantic Ocean. The mean temperature range between winter and summer is in the order of 11.5°C, rain falls throughout the year and winters are usually mild. In central Europe, the temperature range between winter and summer can be as much as 24°C. The summers are warmer and the winters very cold, often with heavy snowfalls and long periods of low temperature. The Mediterranean region is characterised by summer drought between June and September, but the winters are wet, with Atlantic depressions moving through from west to east. All these regions carry a potential climax vegetation of forest, although most of this has been degraded or cleared at various stages during the last 10,000 years. In eastern Europe, from Hungary through Ukraine to western Kazakhstan, the combination of summer drought and prolonged winter cold precludes the development of forest, which is replaced by steppe. Again, most native steppic vegetation has been destroyed. In the most northerly part of Europe, forest is replaced by peat bog and tundra, with permafrost.

## Vegetation

Little native vegetation remains in Europe, although there are still some sizeable stands of forest and montane communities in the higher mountain ranges. The principal zones of natural and semi-natural vegetation in Europe are more or less correlated with latitude and to some extent altitude. There have been countless phytosociological studies but no overall review of European vegetation, apart from the useful popular account by Polunin and Walters (1985). Major regional studies of vegetation have been carried out in, for example, the Balkan Peninsula (Horvat, Glavac and Ellenberg 1974), Spain (Lorca and Rivas-Martínez 1987) and Britain (Rodwell 1991– ).

## Tundra and alpine vegetation

The most northerly parts of Scandinavia (and the mountains of Norway and Sweden) and Spitzbergen are covered with tundra, grading southwards into open forest-tundra with birch and pine. Much of Fennoscandia and the Baltic region is dominated by forests of Norway spruce (*Picea abies*) and Scots pine (*Pinus sylvestris*), a species which also occur widely in the mountains of central Europe and locally southwards to northern Greece and southern Spain. The mountains of central and south-central Europe also have large stands of silver fir (*Abies alba*) and European larch (*Larix decidua*). At higher altitudes the mountain vegetation is dominated by rocky grassland and heath, with open woodland of dwarf pines (*Pinus mugo, P. uncinata*). These alpine communities are floristically amongst the richest of Europe. Notable montane floras occur in the Alps, the Carpathians, the Pyrenees, the mountains of Spain, the Appennines that form the backbone of Italy, and the mountains of the Balkan Peninsula and Crete. Above 3000 m the vegetation is sparse and there is much snow-cover.

## Deciduous forests and scrublands

Away from the mountains, little European forest has survived the encroachment of agriculture, although semi-natural woodlands or plantations are often intermixed with arable and pastoral cultivation. Table 7 lists the amount of surviving forest in Europe. Most of the lowlands of western and central Europe were formerly covered with mixed deciduous forest, dominated by species of oak (*Quercus*), elm (*Ulmus*), hornbeam (*Carpinus*), beech (*Fagus*) and lime (*Tilia*). In southern Europe, notably in the Balkans and the Crimea, large areas are covered with deciduous scrub (shiblyak), often dominated by shrubby oaks, hop-hornbeam (*Ostrya carpinifolia*) and various rosaceous shrubs, derived over centuries of human management by cutting and grazing.

### TABLE 7. NATURAL AND SEMI-NATURAL FOREST COVER IN EUROPEAN TERRITORIES

| | |
|---|---|
| Finland | 72% |
| Sweden | 55% |
| Czech Republic and Slovakia | 36% |
| Romania | 34% |
| Albania | 27% |
| European former USSR | 26% |
| Germany | 23% |
| Austria | 22% |
| Spain | 22% |
| Portugal | 21% |
| Norway | 19% |
| Switzerland | 19% |
| Former territory of Yugoslavia | 16% |
| France | 16% |
| Bulgaria | 14% |
| Poland | 10% |
| Italy | 6% |
| Greece | 3% |
| Hungary | 2% |

Belgium, Britain, Denmark, Ireland, Luxembourg and Netherlands have little surviving natural forest.

Source: World Conservation Monitoring Centre (1992).

## Grasslands

East of the Carpathians and on the plains of Hungary, the climate is drier and less suitable for the growth of trees; forest vegetation is here replaced by steppe. Smaller areas of steppe-like vegetation are found in dry and saline districts of western Europe, as in south-eastern Spain (Almería Province) and south-eastern France (Le Crau), where they contain endemics as well as more eastern floristic elements. Almost all the European steppes are now under cultivation and, overall, as much as 95% of the natural and semi-natural grasslands in Europe has been destroyed by ploughing, reseeding and the over-application of fertilizer since the end of World War II. Remaining species-rich calcareous (Géhu 1984) and dry (Wolkinger and Plank 1981) grasslands are now particularly at risk, either from destruction by ploughing, overgrazing or, where grazing patterns have changed, encroachment by scrub and trees. Within intensive modern agricultural systems, such as those which dominate in Britain, 10% of the remaining semi-natural grassland disappears each year.

## Mediterranean and sub-Mediterranean forests and scrublands

Around the Mediterranean Sea and on its many islands, and over a large inland portion of Spain, the Peloponnese of southern Greece, and southern Italy, the principal semi-natural vegetation type is a sclerophyllous scrub with some stands of woodland, dominated by holm oak (*Quercus ilex*), *Q. pubescens*, kermes oak (*Q. coccifera*), which rarely forms forests except in parts of the east Mediterranean, and pines, especially Aleppo pine (*P. halepensis*) and Calabrian pine (*P. brutia*), which form extensive forests in Spain, France, Italy and Greece. The maritime pine (*P. pinaster*) and the umbrella or stone pine (*P. pinea*) grow in coastal regions, the latter mainly in Spain. A characteristic tree of parts of western Spain, Portugal and extending east to Corsica, Sardinia, Italy and Sicily, is the cork oak (*Quercus suber*), which is also widely planted for its valuable bark. Locally, for example in the mountains of Cádiz Province and the great sand dune and wetland complex of the Coto de Doñana, it forms apparently relict native stands. Higher in the mountains, black pine (*Pinus nigra*) forms extensive forests, together with oaks and other deciduous and semi-deciduous trees. Above 2000 m, junipers (*Juniperus* spp.) are a significant element of the vegetation and may form woodland, as in parts of central Spain. In Crete and Rhodes, the limestone mountains have stands of cypress (*Cupressus sempervirens*), and on Cyprus there is some cedar (*Cedrus brevifolius*); both genera are more typical of adjacent parts of Asia and North Africa. Relict stands of endemic species of *Abies* occur in the mountains of south-west Spain (*A. pinsapo*), north Sicily (*A. nebrodensis* – about 20 trees) and Greece (*A. cephalonica*).

Human interference has transformed much of the Mediterranean forests of Europe into scrublands variously known as matorral, garrigue, maquis and phrygana. These scrublands include shrubby forms of *Quercus coccifera*, *Q. ilex*, *Olea europaea* and other trees, along with *Pistacia* spp. and *Phillyrea* spp. They are variously dominated by *Cistus* and *Halimium*, *Genista*, *Ulex*, *Cytisus* and other leguminous shrubs, *Rosmarinus*, *Erica arborea* and *Arbutus unedo* (in more humid and sub-humid zones), and in more degraded stages by various shrubby Labiatae, such as *Thymus*, *Satureja*, *Lavandula* and *Salvia*, and by species of *Cistus*, *Helianthemum* and *Helichrysum*. In some coastal regions sclerophyllous shrubby communities probably antedate human interference. Unless excessively degraded, most of the scrublands are capable of regeneration to oak/pine forests.

Fire has always been a major factor in maintaining diversity in the vegetation of southern, especially Mediterranean Europe (Trabaud 1981), a zone of natural vulcanism, but recent years have seen extensive destruction through this agency, mostly in the parts of southern France, Greece and Spain which have been intensively developed for tourism.

## Wetlands and coastal communities

Wetlands have never covered such large areas of Europe as of other continents, but there are some major areas, such as the deltas of larger rivers. The native vegetation of these wetlands has been reduced especially during the last 100 years through drainage schemes and the growth of intensive agriculture. The small remnants that survive are important repositories of truly native vegetation and often retain a rich flora and fauna. Amongst the important coastal wetlands of Europe are the Coto de Doñana at the mouth of the Guadalquiver in south-western Spain, the Camargue at the mouth of the Rhône in southern France, the wetlands of the Gulfs of Arta and Missolonghi in western Greece and the Danube delta in south-eastern Romania. These ecosystems, which are very productive in terms of both plant biomass and potential fishery exploitation, include swamp woodland, reed beds and a range of fresh, brackish and saline marshland communities. The Doñana Biosphere Reserve, covering some 772.6 km², and lying on the exposed Atlantic coast of the estuary of the Río Gualalquivir, contains enormous mobile sand dunes which extend many miles inland which, once stabilized, carry a forest cover of umbrella pine (*Pinus pinea*), which was planted in the 18th and 19th centuries, and cork oak (*Quercus suber*).

Sand dune systems are a feature of the coasts of western Europe. Notable examples occur along the south-western coasts of France, the region known as Les Landes, covered by both native and planted forests of maritime pine (*Pinus pinaster*), and large stretches of the coasts of the North Sea, where they form vital sea defences, especially in the Netherlands. They are almost always floristically rich, and home to a number of endemic taxa. One sand dune community in particular, quite unique to Europe, should be mentioned: *machair* is the name given to the flat or gently undulating, species-rich dune grasslands of western Ireland and north-western Scotland, maintained traditionally by a regime of grazing, haymaking and limited arable cultivation.

## Edaphic and climatic formations

Much of the greatest species diversity in Europe is found in vegetation, such as that of sand dunes, where edaphic or climatic conditions have prevented the development of a full cover of forest or peat since the end of the

Pleistocene glaciations. This includes many montane and steppic areas, together with certain coastal and wetland communities, cliffs, gorges and karstic topography, and especially serpentine rocks and soils, as in Albania, northern Greece and other parts of the western Balkan Peninsula, and locally in Italy, southern Spain, Scandinavia, from where for example many intraspecific taxa have been described (Rune 1953; Edmondson 1992), and Scotland.

Extensive weathered limestone, with underground rivers, solution hollows and limestone pavement (karstic scenery, named after the Karst district of Dalmatia) is associated with open vegetation and floristic richness in different parts of the continent. Notable examples include the Burren region of County Clare in west Ireland, where a mild maritime climate strongly influences the vegetation and flora; the Alvar of the Swedish islands of Öland and Gotland in the Baltic Sea; and extensive areas of the Balkan Peninsula, including the Dinaric Alps and the Karst region itself, the mountains of Southern and Central Greece (CPD Site Eu16, see Data Sheet) and the mountains and gorges of Crete (Eu17, see Data Sheet).

## Endemic plant communities

Some communities are unique to Europe. The heathlands that have developed on poor or leached soils and under wind-exposed conditions, on and near the coasts of north-western Europe from central Portugal to Scandinavia, are similar in vegetation structure to the scrublands of the Mediterranean, but have a more restricted distribution. Dominated by dwarf ericaceous shrubs, they share some genera with the Mediterranean scrublands, such as *Cistus* (sunroses) and the leguminous genera *Cytisus* (brooms) and *Ulex* (gorses). Like the Mediterranean communities, they have been at least partially maintained by human management and are rapidly being eroded by fire, afforestation with exotic species and clearance for building. In northern Europe, especially in south-eastern England, a related community is the vegetation developed on larger shingle beaches, comprising a similar heathland flora.

## Flora

In comparison with other parts of the world, the flora of Europe has received disproportionate study by very large numbers of both professional and amateur botanists during the past two or three centuries (Heywood 1978; Davis *et al.* 1986). One or more comprehensive Floras have been written for most European countries, as well as several detailed regional taxonomic treatments, countless articles, and large numbers of local Floras, especially in Britain, Italy, Germany and more recently, Spain. *Flora Europaea* (Tutin *et al.* 1964–80, 1993) provided a continental synthesis of the often disparate taxonomic treatments published on a national basis, and is regarded as a standard text by most botanists and by many official and legislative bodies. Those works that are regarded by the different countries of Europe as Standard Floras are listed in the introductory section of *Flora Europaea*, together with the major regional Floras (Tutin *et al.* 1993).

The flora of Europe includes at least 11,500 vascular plant species, a figure estimated on the basis of the numbers treated in *Flora Europaea* (Webb 1978). The revision of the first volume of *Flora Europaea* suggested that several hundred more species are present (Akeroyd and Walters 1987), perhaps as much as 10% more than had been estimated, and a figure of up to 12,500 species is more realistic. The flora is not nearly as rich as that of some tropical and subtropical regions, but is very varied and contains significant native populations of economically exploited species.

There are several major centres of diversity, especially in the Mediterranean basin and adjacent mountain ranges. Some 75 genera and 3500 species are endemic to Europe, mostly in the mountains of southern and south-central Europe, but there are no endemic families (Webb 1978). A significant proportion of the important floras and ecosystems of the Mediterranean region lie within the boundaries of Europe.

## Floristic richness of South Europe

Southern Europe, with to a lesser extent the mountains of central Europe, is considerably richer floristically than northern Europe, and contains a higher proportion of endemic species (Favarger 1972). Table 8 gives approximate numbers of species in European territories.

### TABLE 8. ESTIMATED NUMBER OF NATIVE SPECIES OF HIGHER PLANTS IN INDIVIDUAL EUROPEAN TERRITORIES

| | |
|---|---|
| Italy | 5600 |
| Yugoslavia | 5350[a] |
| Spain | 5050 |
| Greece | 5000 |
| France | 4650 |
| European former USSR[b] | 4300[a] |
| Bulgaria | 3600 |
| Romania | 3400[a] |
| Austria | 3100[a] |
| Albania | 3000 |
| Switzerland | 3000 |
| Germany | 2700[a] |
| Czech Republic and Slovakia | 2600 |
| Portugal (excl. Azores) | 2600[a] |
| Poland | 2450[a] |
| Hungary | 2200 |
| Turkey-in-Europe | 2100[a] |
| Sweden | 1750[a] |
| Norway | 1600[a] |
| Belgium | 1550[a] |
| United Kingdom | 1550 |
| Denmark | 1450[a] |
| Luxembourg | 1200 |
| Netherlands | 1200 |
| Finland | 1050 |
| Ireland | 950 |
| Faeroes | 250 |

To nearest 50 species, based on data in World Conservation Monitoring Centre (1992) and updated by consultation with regional experts; [a] based on Webb (1978); [b] Russia, Ukraine, Byelorussia and Baltic Republics.

The Pleistocene glaciations denuded the northern part of the continent of most of its flora. The floras of the great southern peninsulas of Iberia, Italy and the Balkans were enriched as plants migrated southwards, and these areas acted as refugia of more favorable climate for more thermophilous elements. Many of the species and genera in these refugia did not apparently expand out of these refugia with the return to warmer climatic conditions and are today relicts of former distributions (Pawłowski 1970). It is likely that such migrations brought taxa together within refugia, thus promoting episodes of hybridization and subsequent evolutionary radiation and speciation.

Some localities have extraordinarily rich endemic floras: for example, Mount Olympus in north-central Greece, with some 26 endemic species and floristic links with other parts of the Balkans, with the Alps and Anatolia, has a flora of at least 1700 species (Strid 1980). Remote and mountainous parts of southern Europe are even today yielding taxa new to science. The severe degradation of native plant communities since the development of agriculture in the region has also promoted more recent speciation through the diversification of ecological niches, especially in Mediterranean Europe.

Much of the endemism reflects the dissected topography of the high mountains, peninsulas and islands of southern Europe. Some of the islands of the Mediterranean have high levels of endemism (cf. Olivier and Muracciole 1994), especially Crete (CPD Site Eu17, see Data Sheet), and the central Aegean islands to the north of Crete, the Balearic Islands (geographically an extension of the Baetic Mountains of south Spain), and the Tyrrhenian Islands, notably Corsica (a mountainous island that can be said to represent an extension of the Alps, but which also has links with its floristically rich neighbours Sardinia and Sicily).

## Useful plants

In northern and western Europe, little use is now made of native plants, although they were formerly a major resource. For example, the heathlands were once a source of turf and broom for fuel, and native woodlands provided timber and a variety of forest products. An exception is the peatlands, which are still widely exploited in Ireland, Finland and northern Russia for their peat, which is stripped mechanically to be used for domestic and industrial fuel, and also as a growth medium, mulch and compost in a rapidly expanding horticultural industry (Plantlife 1992). Forestry is today dominated by exotic conifers and by eucalypts in parts of the south, although native species of conifers are exploited in Scandinavia and in the mountains of central and southern Europe.

## Mediterranean scrublands and woodland-pasture

In south Europe, and to a lesser extent east Europe, local people still employ native plant products for a variety of uses. Indeed, in parts of the Mediterranean region, especially the more mountainous areas, wild plants contribute significantly to the local economy. Scrubland ecosystems are a source of firewood, charcoal, timber for fencing and building, bark for tanning, natural products such as gums, oils and resins, forage and fodder for animals, herbs and medicines, salads and fruits for food, and the most attractive wild flowers for ornament. Other useful products are game, snails, honey (from bees that feed on native flowers) and edible fungi. These scrublands have provided the poorest

with a livelihood and have sheltered both inhabitants and freedom-fighters in times of war.

The mountains of the Balkan Peninsula are one of the last areas in Europe with extensive woodland-pasture (Pallas 1939; Rackham 1986). Parts of southern Spain have a similar management regime (see Data Sheet on Baetic and Sub-Baetic Mountains, CPD Site Eu4). This ancient system of management, widespread in Eurasia since at least the Mesolithic, involves (in part) the pollarding of trees, mostly oaks, hornbeam and beech, with the young growth being fed to stock. It is an appropriate use of sustainable resources in a wooded region, although at the present day overgrazing damages both trees and pastures, with subsequent degradation of habitats.

## Native crop resources

The number of native plants cultivated in Europe and with wild relatives in the continent is much larger than might be expected. There are several cereals, especially oats (*Avena*) and rye (*Secale*), several food legumes, such as pea (*Pisum*) and vetches (*Vicia*), fruits, such as apple (*Malus*), pear (*Pyrus*), cherries and plums (*Prunus*), and vegetables, such as cabbages and other brassicas (*Brassica*), beet (*Beta*) and artichoke (*Cynara*). All of these have rich wild gene pools native to Europe.

Apart from the rosaceous fruits, those of several other native trees still provide valuable crops over much of the continent: the chestnut (*Castanea sativa*) grown for its nuts since classical times but often doubtfully native, the hazel (cob) (*Corylus avellana*) and filbert (*C. maxima*), the pine-nut (*Pinus pinea*), the beech-mast (*Fagus*) and acorns (*Quercus*) for animal forage. In northern and montane Europe, bilberries (*Vaccinium myrtillus*), cranberries (*V. oxycoccus*), strawberries (*Fragaria moschata*), blackberries (*Rubus fruticosus*) and cloudberries (*R. chamaemorus*) are still collected on at least a semi-commercial basis. In southern Europe, cornelian cherry (*Cornus mas*) and various wild plums and cherries (*Prunus*) are harvested.

Europe also provides several major forestry species, such as the conifers *Abies*, *Picea*, *Pinus* and *Larix*, as well as *Quercus*, *Aesculus*, *Fraxinus* and *Fagus*. Other valuable tree species include the poplars (*Populus tremula*, *P. nigra*) and important Mediterranean food trees are the olive (*Olea europaea*), the carob (*Ceratonia siliqua*) and the fig (*Ficus carica*).

Other native crops include reed (*Phragmites australis*) and formerly saw-sedge (*Cladium mariscus*) for thatching, and in the Mediterranean region, giant reed (*Arundo donax*) for fencing and a whole variety of domestic and horticultural uses, and for the best oboe reeds! Europe also has a rich assemblage of native pot herbs, condiments and ornamentals. It is also rich in fodder plants, both legumes and grasses.

The wild European relatives of these species constitute a significant and valuable gene-pool. Examples of these are listed in Table 9 and a full list, excluding some purely ornamental species, is given in Table 10 (based on Zohary and Heywood 1994).

Apart from the crops of European origin, most of the cultivated plants of Europe, however, derive from species selected in south-west Central Asia (and later in the Americas) and brought into the continent by successive waves of invasion, immigration or trade.

**TABLE 9. CROP SPECIES PARTLY ORIGINATING IN EUROPE, WITH EXTANT WILD RELATIVES, THEIR NATIVE HABITATS AND EXPERIMENTAL OR TAXONOMIC STUDIES**

*Allium porrum*, leek (von Bothmer, *Op.bot.* 34: 1–104, 1974); B. Bonnet, *Saussurea* 7: 121–155, 1976; S. Europe, coasts of W. Ireland and S.W. England (wild plants referred to *A. ampeloprasum* L.)

*Apium graveolens*, celery and celeriac; coastal wetlands.

*Beta vulgaris*, beets (B.V. Ford-Lloyd and J.T. Williams, *Bot. J. Linn. Soc.* 71: 89–102, 1975); S. Europe and coasts.

*Brassica cretica* (S. Snogerup, *Willdenowia*, 1990); limestone cliffs, Crete and S. Greece.

*B. oleracea*, cabbages (N.D. Mitchell and A.J. Richards, *J. Ecol.* 67: 1087–1096, 1982); coasts of S. and W. Europe.

*B. napus*, oil-seed rape; open habitats, mainly N. and W. Europe.

*B. rapa*, turnip (E.H. Oost in B.T. Styles, ed., *Intraspecific classification of wild and cultivated plants*, pp. 309–315, Oxford); open habitats over much of Europe.

*Corylus maxima*, hazel or filbert; woodland, S.E. Europe.

*Daucus carota*, carrot (E. Small, *Can. J. Bot.* 56: 248–276, 1978; V.H. Heywood, *Israel J. Bot.* 32: 51–65, 1983); coasts.

*Ficus carica*, fig; rocks and cliffs, Mediterranean region.

*Foeniculum vulgare*, fennel; open habitats, S. and S.E. Europe and coasts.

*Lactuca sativa*, lettuce (D. Zohary, *Israel J. Bot.* 32: 97–127, 1983); open habitats, S.E. Europe.

*Linum usitatissitum*, flax (D. Zohary and M. Hopf, *Domestication of plants in the Old World*, pp. 114–119, 1988, Oxford); W. and S. Europe.

*Malus sylvestris*, apple; woodland, much of Europe.

*Olea europaea*, olive (J. Pagnol, *L'Olivier.* 2nd Ed. 180 pp., 1979, Avignon); woodland and scrub, S.E. Europe.

*Papaver somniferum*, opium poppy (J.W. Kadereit, *Bot. Jahrb. Syst.* 106: 221–244; 108: 1–16, 1986); open habitats, S.W. Europe.

*Pyrus communis*, pear; woodland and scrub, mostly S.E. and E.C. Europe.

*Prunus* spp., cherries and plums; woodland and scrub, mostly S.E. and C. Europe.

*Raphanus raphanistrum*, radish; open habitats and coasts, S. and W. Europe.

*Trifolium* spp., clovers; grassland, especially S. Europe and in the mountains.

*Vicia* spp., vetches; grassland, especially S. Europe.

*Vitis vinifera*, grape; woodland and scrub, S. Europe.

## Social and environmental values

Public awareness of the significance of Europe's floristic richness and diversity has been growing steadily, especially in the most industrialized parts of the continent. The importance of wild plant resources is increasingly being recognized by the agriculture, forestry, horticulture and plant breeding sectors and attention has been focused on the need to conserve the wild relatives of crop plants as part of Europe's heritage (Council of Europe 1991). In addition, there is an enormous popular enthusiasm and interest amongst a considerable section of the educated public in wildlife and the natural environment. The growth of a vocal, influential and articulate "green" lobby has brought to the fore the political issues raised by pollution of air, water and food, the destruction or drastic modification of traditional landscapes, and other forms of environmental damage, such as deforestation of water catchments and mountain areas prone to avalanches.

For much of Europe the natural environment is a major source of leisure and the leisured class is growing. Millions flock to the coasts and mountains of southern and central Europe for holidays, and the Mediterranean region attracts over 100 million holiday-makers each year (Eber 1992). For countries such as Greece, with limited natural resources, tourism is now the major industry. This is putting more pressure on already over-exploited Natural Parks, Nature Reserves and other areas of biodiversity. Coasts are everywhere threatened by development and, for example, three quarters of the sand dunes between Gibraltar and Sicily have disappeared as a result of human action. Already, roads in mountain parks, such as Gran Paradiso in Aosta Province, north-west Italy, have to be closed on summer weekends to prohibit the entry of excessive numbers of motor vehicles. There is evidence, however, that the tourism industry is concerned at the situation and is taking action to ensure that tourism is sustainable (Eber 1992). Many tourists, for their part, are demanding higher standards and are insisting on environmentally sensitive tourist developments which reduce the amount of inappropriate consumption, promote safe disposal of waste, limit environmental damage, and generally demonstrate a concern for the local population and their environment. At the same time, there is an increase in ecotourism which inevitably puts even more pressure on the more environmentally sensitive areas.

## Factors causing loss of biodiversity

Despite such a long history of human exploitation and damage, the biodiversity represented by Europe's flora and vegetation has never been so threatened. Threats range from land drainage and changes in arable farming regimes, to pollution, industrialisation and urbanisation and a burgeoning tourist industry (Council of Europe 1983; Council of Europe/Cariplo Foundation 1993).

Industrial pollution poses a major threat to European forests and the excessive use of pesticides and herbicides affects the fertility of agricultural soils. Soil contamination is also caused in Europe by acidification through airborne pollution, through toxic substances in groundwater or irrigation water, through improper waste disposal, including slurries, phytosanitary products and radioactive substances.

## TABLE 10. LIST OF WILD RELATIVES OF EUROPEAN CULTIVATED PLANTS THAT ARE NATIVE TO EUROPE

Abies alba
Picea abies
Pinus mugo
Pinus nigra
Pinus pinea
Pinus sylvestris

Aegilops speltoides
Aegilops squarrosa
Allium ampeloprasum
Allium porrum
Allium schoenoprasum
Anemone coronaria
Antirrhinum majus
Apium graveolens
Aquilegia vulgaris
Armoracia rusticana
Artemisia abrotanum
Artemisia absinthium
Artemisia dracunculus
Asparagus officinalis
Atropa bella-donna
Avena canariensis
Avena fatua
Avena murphyi
Avena sativa
Avena sterilis
Avena strigoa
Berberis vulgaris
Beta nana
Beta patellaris
Beta trigyna
Beta vulgaris
Beta webbiana
Brassica bourgeaui
Brassica cretica
Brassica hilarionis
Brassica incana
Brassica insularis
Brassica juncea
Brassica macrocarpa
Brassica napus
Brassica nigra
Brassica oleracea
Brassica rapa
Brassica rupestris
Brassica villosa
Bromus inermis
Calendula officinalis
Camelina sativa
Cannabis sativa
Capparis spinosa
Castanea sativa
Ceratonia siliqua
Chamaecytisus proliferus ssp. palmensis
Chamaemelum fuscatum
Chamaemelum mixtum
Chamaemelum nobile
Cichorium endivia
Cichorium intybus
Consolida ambigua
Consolida orientalis
Convallaria majalis
Corylus avellana
Corylus colurna
Corylus maxima
Crocus angustifolius
Crocus biflorus
Crocus cartwrightianus
Crocus chrysanthus
Crocus etruscus
Crocus flavus
Crocus sativus
Crocus tomasinianus
Crocus vernus
Cyclamen balearicum
Cyclamen coum
Cyclamen creticum

Cyclamen graecum
Cyclamen hederifolium
Cyclamen persicum
Cyclamen purparescens
Cyclamen repandum
Cynara algarbiensis
Cynara baetica
Cynara cardunculus
Cynara cornigera
Cynodon dactylon
Dactylis glomerata
Daucus carota
Delphinium elatum
Dianthus barbatus
Dianthus caryophyllus
Digitalis lanata
Digitalis purpurea
Dipsacus sativus
Eruca vesicaria
Erysimum cheiri
Erysimum scoparium
Festuca arundinacea
Festuca pratensis
Festuca rubra
Ficus carica
Foeniculum vulgare
Galanthus nivalis
Galega officinalis
Gladiolus communis
Glycyrrhiza echinata
Glycyrrhiza glabra
Hedysarum coronarium
Hordeum vulgare
Humulus lupulus
Hyacinthoides hispanica
Hyacinthoides non-scripta
Iberis semperflorens
Iris aphylla
Iris germanica
Iris lutescens
Iris pumila
Lactuca altaica
Lactuca saligna
Lactuca sativa
Lactuca serriola
Lathyrus cicera
Lathyrus odoratus
Lathyrus sativus
Laurus nobilis
Lavandula angustifolia
Leucojum aestivum
Leucojum vernum
Linum bienne
Linum usitatissimum
Lolium multiflorum
Lolium perenne
Lotus berthelotii
Lupinus albus
Lupinus luteus
Malus pumila
Malus sylvestris
Mathiola incana
Medicago sativa
Melissa officinalis
Mentha spicata
Mentha suaveolens
Mespilus germanica
Narcissus jonquilla
Narcissus pseudonarcissus
Narcissus tazetta
Nasturtium officinale
Nigella sativa
Olea europaea
Onobrychis arenaria
Onobrychis montana
Onobrychis viciifolia
Origanum vulgare
Ornithopus sativus
Papaver somniferum

Pastinaca sativa
Pericallis cruenta
Pericallis hybrida
Pericallis lanata
Petroselinum crispum
Phalaris canariensis
Phleum pratense
Phoenix canariensis
Phoenix theophrasti
Pisum sativum
Populus nigra
Populus tremula
Portulaca oleracea
Prunus avium
Prunus brigantina
Prunus cerasifera
Prunus cerasus
Prunus cocomilia
Prunus domestica
Prunus dulcis
Prunus fruticosa
Prunus laurocerasus
Prunus lusitanica
Prunus prostrata
Prunus spinosa
Prunus webbii
Punica granatum
Pyrus communis
Pyrus eleagnifolia
Pyrus nivalis
Pyrus pyraster
Pyrus spinosa
Quercus suber
Raphanus raphanistrum
Raphanus sativus
Ribes nigrum
Ribes rubrum
Ribes spicatum
Rosa gallica
Rosmarinus officinalis
Rubus fruticosus complex
Rubus idaeus
Rumex acetosa
Rumex rugosus
Salvia lavandulifolia
Salvia officinalis
Salvia triloba
Scilla siberica
Secale cereale
Setaria italica
Setaria viridis
Sinapis alba
Sorbus domestica
Spiraea salicifolia
Syringa vulgaris
Tanacetum cinerariifolium
Tanacetum parthenium
Tanacetum vulgare
Thymus glandulosus
Thymus hyemalis
Trifolium ambiguum
Trifolium hybridum
Trifolium incarnatum
Trifolium nigrescens
Trifolium occidentale
Trifolium pratense
Trifolium repens
Trigonella caerulea
Trigonella procumbens
Triticum aestivum
Triticum boeoticum
Triticum turgidum
Vicia sativa
Vicia villosa
Viola altaica
Viola lutea
Viola odorata
Viola tricolor
Vitis vinifera

Large-scale farming has changed the pattern of landscapes and eliminated many of the hedgerows and other linear features that provide reserves of biodiversity and formed migration routes for species, populations. Industrialization, urban expansion and tourist developments, especially in coastal areas, are major causes of habitat loss and threats to species and populations. The fragmentation of habitats has made many of them prone to invasion by thermophilous species, including aliens with weedy characteristics.

The database of the World Conservation Monitoring Centre (WCMC) lists some 2200 European species as falling within the IUCN categories of threat, Endangered, Vulnerable, Rare or Indeterminate, although only 25 are recorded as having become extinct since 1600. Most threats to Europe's plant species relate to a shortage of land in an increasingly affluent and mechanised society.

## Agriculture

Approximately 50% of the land surface area of Europe is occupied by arable land. Many habitats have been lost through expanding and developing more efficient agricultural ecosystems, maintained by ploughing, herbicides, fertilizers and pesticides. Conversely, mechanisation has caused the numbers of people working on the land to fall. In some areas, such as parts of the Mediterranean region, scrub and secondary woodland is encroaching into open, species-rich plant communities (Rackham 1990). A similar process is taking place in the Alps. Terracing in south Europe and the Mediterranean region is being abandoned as people leave the land.

Despite EEC legislation on the environment and biodiversity, the large amounts of regional aid being spent in southern Europe are having a detrimental effect on natural and semi-natural ecosystems, especially through drainage and agricultural expansion. A positive solution to this problem is the creation of Protected Landscapes, allowance for which is made under the terms of the EEC's own Habitats Directive.

Where stocking levels are still high, as in some mountain areas of Spain and the Balkans, overgrazing degrades species-rich grasslands and prevents regeneration of native woodland. The eventual result is increased runoff of water and severe erosion.

## Forestry

The standards of forestry vary considerably in Europe. In some countries, such as France and Germany, mixed deciduous woodlands are well managed following traditional practices, while in others, such as the United Kingdom, much woodland craft has been lost. Much more attention needs to be given to maintaining or developing forestry practices which yield forest products as well as providing other services, including conservation of biodiversity. Europe's forests, especially those in northern Europe, have suffered greatly in recent years from acid rain and there has also been a decline in many associated mycorrhizal fungi.

Despite Europe's excellent native tree resources, large areas are still planted with non-native trees, some of which may be ecologically unsuitable. Extensive areas of Portugal and south Spain, including floristically important sites, have plantations of *Eucalyptus*, which dry out soils, supplant native trees and suppress herb and shrub layers. Conifers have frequently been planted in ancient deciduous woodland in Britain, in parts of Spain and elsewhere, where their inflammable nature poses a fire-risk.

## Fire

Although fire is a major determinant of the drier ecosystems of the Mediterranean region, uncontrolled or deliberately provoked fires destroy large areas each year. The use of pines and *Eucalyptus* in plantations increases this threat, for example in the Serra da Estrêla and elsewhere in Portugal.

## Urbanisation, industrial and tourist development

Although the size of the population of Europe is fairly stable, suburban housing is spreading rapidly in line with increasing affluence. In particular, coastal habitats are threatened, especially where sites are level. New roads destroy great swathes of natural plant communities both in the lowlands and the mountains.

The same sort of sites are favoured by industry and tourism. The coasts of the Mediterranean are largely occupied by an unplanned ribbon development of hotels, suburbs and factories.

Europe's mountains today support a huge tourism infrastructure, based on skiing in winter and various forms of outdoor recreation in summer. This puts pressure on grassland communities, and the ease of access to higher altitudes and remote terrain threatens other alpine plant communities. For example, the ski pistes and associated installations have caused considerable damage to the upper slopes of the Sierra Nevada which house a large percentage of the endemic flora (and fauna) of Spain.

The construction of dams in mountainous areas can destroy large areas of important native vegetation.

## Mineral extraction

Mountainous regions frequently have important ore or other mineral deposits. Bauxite is mined in the mountains of central Greece, even within the bounds of National Parks, as on Mount Iti. The exploitation of metal-bearing deposits is a source of serious ecological damage in many parts of Europe. When the mines are exhausted and abandoned, the surrounding landscape is often left in a devastated condition, with mine waste and polluted watercourses often poisoning the soils and making rehabilitation difficult.

## Horticulture

Horticulture, today a major industry in northern Europe, makes huge demands on the continent's resources of peat (Plantlife 1992). There is evidence that the horticultural trade removes large numbers of bulbs and other plants from the wild (Read 1989), mainly from Turkey but also from south Europe. Collection of wild plants for trade occurs throughout Europe, but the centre of the bulb trade is Holland, whence many bulbs are exported to Britain and Germany. Individual amateur botanists, gardeners and collectors, as well as specialist nurseries, pose a threat to some small populations of rare mountain plants in the Alps and southern Europe.

## Invasive species

This is less a threat in Europe than other parts of the world, although the use of exotics in forestry may have similar effects. Eucalypts have been used extensively in reafforestation and in Spain cover nearly 80% of the area of broadleaves planted and represent nearly 10% of all reafforestation acreage (ICONA 1984). A few areas in Spain and Greece have infestations of prickly-pear cactus (*Opuntia* spp.), and in Ireland and elsewhere in the British Isles, native woodland communities on acid soils have been replaced by *Rhododendron ponticum*. Sycamore (*Acer pseudoplatanus*) is an invader of woodlands in the British Isles, and false acacia (*Robinia pseudacacia*) has replaced native trees in parts of south Europe.

## Local exploitation of plants

The traditional use of plants in some areas has sometimes led to damage to wild populations, for example in southern Spain, Crete and the Crimea (see Data Sheets on CPD Sites Eu4, Eu17, Eu21, respectively). Certain medicinal species, such as *Arnica montana*, may be better exploited in future via cultivation rather than from the wild. *Artemisia granatensis* which is a highly prized medicinal herb from Sierra Nevada, is almost extinct in the wild through over-collection. Several aromatic species of *Thymus*, *Satureja* and *Salvia* are threatened locally though over-collection for the distillation of their essential oils.

## Other factors

Political uncertainty and instability in south-east Europe, in particular in former Yugoslavia, threatens Protected Areas and sites of high biodiversity by direct action and by neglect. Trees have been cut down indiscriminately for much needed firewood in Bosnia-Hercegovina, and there are reports of the destruction of both Nature Reserves and botanic gardens. In other parts of the region, political changes following the collapse of Communism have left National Parks and Nature Reserves with an uncertain financial future, with the threat that their land will be reclaimed by those from whom it was taken after World War II. Several botanic gardens, germplasm collections and herbaria are at risk through political instability and lack of financial suppport.

## Conservation

Europe is fortunate to have a large number of human and institutional resources devoted to conservation of plants and their habitats (Heywood 1993a). Most countries have a comprehensive Flora and in some cases very detailed knowledge of the distribution of plants, although there are still gaps in species-rich parts of southern Europe, especially Greece. On the other hand, detailed biosystematic studies are lacking for most species.

An overall problem is the historical political fragmentation of Europe, which has hindered the development of conservation strategies for the whole continent. However, there have been significant developments in recent years. The Council of Europe drafted a European Conservation Strategy and this was adopted by the 6th European Ministerial Conference on the Environment. The Strategy seeks to ensure that landscape conservation is integrated with other uses such as agriculture, forestry, recreation and urban and industrial development. It proposes measures to ensure both the *ex situ* and *in situ* conservation of plants and animals and emphasizes the need to conserve genetic resources. Also, the first pan-European Conference of Ministers of the Environment was held in 1991 in Prague and a pan-European conference on "An Environment for Europe" took place in Lucerne in 1993 involving the Council, the European Community and the United Nations Economic Commission for Europe.

Both national and international legislation and public education are needed to atack these problems. Europe is fortunate that major instruments of legislation are now in place that should safeguard much of the remaining natural heritage. The Bern Convention on the Conservation of European Wildlife and Habitats, drafted by the Council of Europe, and which came into effect in 1982, currently lists in Appendix 1 over 500 species of plants that require strict protection. The EC's Directive on the Protection of Natural and Semi-natural Habitats of Wild Fauna and Flora (Habitats Directive), requiring EEC member states to legislate for the full protection of the habitats of selected rare species listed on the Directive's Annexes, came into effect in 1992. The principal European agreements on the conservation of biodiversity have been summarised by Synge (1992).

### *In situ* conservation measures

Europe is now covered by a network of National Parks and Nature Reserves, although there are still gaps, especially in the south. Summary accounts of the most significant Nature Reserves are given in Polunin and Walters (1985). As with the distribution of botanists, they are predominantly situated in the more northern countries, although an encouraging number is to be found in the Mediterranean region. Nevertheless, several of the territories around the Mediterranean Sea do not have strong enough legislation to protect fully the plants and animals for which reserves have been established, nor to implement legislation such as the EC Habitats Directive. In a crowded continent, the growth of leisure industries, and competing space for agriculture and industry in the little undeveloped land that is left, have taken their toll of land and habitats in areas of high biodiversity. Much work is needed to protect that which remains.

### *Ex situ* conservation measures

Outside natural habitats, Europe has an important network of botanic gardens, arboreta and gene banks, together with a vast number of private gardens, which cultivate a range of European plants. Botanic gardens, of which there are 538 in Europe, and similar institutes can provide the necessary facilities and expertise for the cultivation, propagation and possible restoration of the threatened plants of Europe. Botanic Gardens Conservation International (BGCI) has outlined the conservation strategies that need to be adopted by botanic gardens and other bodies, has produced guidelines for species reintroductions and is assembling a database of botanic garden holdings of threatened plants in Europe and elsewhere. In France, the Ministry of the Environment has set up a number of Conservatoires Botaniques Nationaux charged with the protection of endangered plant species.

# Centres of plant diversity and endemism

The following areas have been selected mainly on the basis of their large floras which have significant endemic elements.

In line with the comparative richness of the flora of southern Europe, there is a concentration of sites in that part of the region, especially in the three great peninsulas of the Mediterranean region, the Iberian Peninsula, Italy and the Balkan Peninsula.

## TABLE 11. EUROPEAN SITES IDENTIFIED AS CENTRES OF PLANT DIVERSITY AND ENDEMISM

The list of sites is arranged according to the sequence adopted in the Regional Overview. Sites selected for Data Sheet treatment appear in bold.

**IBERIAN PENINSULA**
Eu1.  Peneda-Gêres (Portugal)
Eu2.  Serra da Estrêla (Portugal)
Eu3.  Algarve (Portugal)
Eu4.  **Baetic and Sub-Baetic Mountains** (Spain)
Eu5.  Guadalquiver Estuary and Coto Donaña (Spain)
Eu6.  Sierra de Gredos and Sierra de Guadarrama (Spain)
Eu7.  **Massifs of Gudar and Javalambre** (Spain)
Eu8.  Picos de Europa (Spain)
Eu9.  Islas Baleares (Spain)

**WESTERN AND SOUTHERN CENTRAL EUROPE**
Eu10.  **Pyrenees** (Andorra, France, Spain)
Eu11.  **Alps** (Austria, France, Germany, Italy, Liechtenstein, Slovenia, Switzerland)
Eu12.  Appennini and Alpe Apuane (Italy)
Eu13.  Tyrrhenian Islands: Corsica, Sardinia, Sicily and offshore islands (France, Italy)

**BALKAN PENINSULA, AEGEAN REGION AND CYPRUS**
Eu14.  **Balkan and Rhodope Massifs** (Bulgaria, Greece, Serbia)
Eu15.  Mount Olympus (Thessalian Olympus) (Greece)
Eu16.  **Mountains of Southern and Central Greece**
Eu17.  **Crete** (Greece)
Eu18.  **Troodos Mountains** (Cyprus)

**EASTERN EUROPE**
Eu19.  Danube Delta (Romania)
Eu20.  Carpathians (Czech Republic and Slovakia, Hungary, Poland, Romania, Ukraine)
Eu21.  **South Crimean Mountains and Novorossia** (Russia, Ukraine)

**NORTH-WESTERN EUROPE: BRITISH ISLES, FENNOSCANDIA AND BALTIC REGION**
Eu22.  Burren (Ireland)
Eu23.  Öland and Gotland (Sweden)
Eu24.  Białowieża Forest (Byelorussia, Lithuania, Poland)

The list below is arranged alphabetically by country for purposes of cross-reference. Sites selected for Data Sheet treatment appear in bold.

**ANDORRA**
Eu10.  **Pyrenees**

**AUSTRIA**
Eu11.  **Alps**

**BULGARIA**
Eu14.  **Balkan and Rhodope Mountains**

**BYELORUSSIA**
Eu24.  Białowieża Forest

**CYPRUS**
Eu18.  **Troodos Mountains**

**CZECH REPUBLIC AND SLOVAKIA**
Eu20.  Carpathians

**FRANCE**
Eu10.  **Pyrenees**
Eu11.  **Alps**
Eu13.  Tyrrhenian Islands: Corsica

**GERMANY**
Eu11.  **Alps**

**GREECE**
Eu14.  **Balkan and Rhodope Mountains**
Eu15.  Mount Olympus (Thessalian Olympus)
Eu16.  **Mountains of Southern and Central Greece**
Eu17.  **Crete**

**HUNGARY**
Eu20.  Carpathians

**IRELAND**
Eu22.  Burren

**ITALY**
Eu11.  **Alps**
Eu12.  Appennini and Alpe Apuane
Eu13.  Tyrrhenian Islands: Sardinia, Sicily and offshore islands

**LIECHTENSTEIN**
Eu11.  **Alps**

**LITHUANIA**
Eu24.  Białowieża Forest

**POLAND**
Eu20.  Carpathians
Eu24.  Białowieża Forest

**PORTUGAL**
Eu1.  Peneda-Gêres
Eu2.  Serra da Estrêla
Eu3.  Algarve

**ROMANIA**
Eu19.  Danube Delta
Eu20.  Carpathians

**RUSSIA**
Eu21.  **South Crimean Mountains and Novorossia**

**SERBIA**
Eu14.  **Balkan and Rhodope Mountains**

**SLOVENIA**
Eu11.  **Alps**

**SPAIN**
Eu4.  **Baetic and Sub-Baetic Mountains**
Eu5.  Guadalquiver Estuary and Coto Donaña
Eu6.  Sierra de Gredos and Sierra de Guadarrama
Eu7.  **Massifs of Gudar and Javalambre**
Eu8.  Picos de Europa
Eu9.  Islas Baleares
Eu10.  **Pyrenees**

**SWEDEN**
Eu23.  Öland and Gotland

**SWITZERLAND**
Eu11.  **Alps**

**UKRAINE**
Eu20.  Carpathians
Eu21.  **South Crimean Mountains and Novorossia**

## MAP 2. CENTRES OF PLANT DIVERSITY AND ENDEMISM: EUROPE
The map shows the locations of the CPD Data Sheet sites for Europe

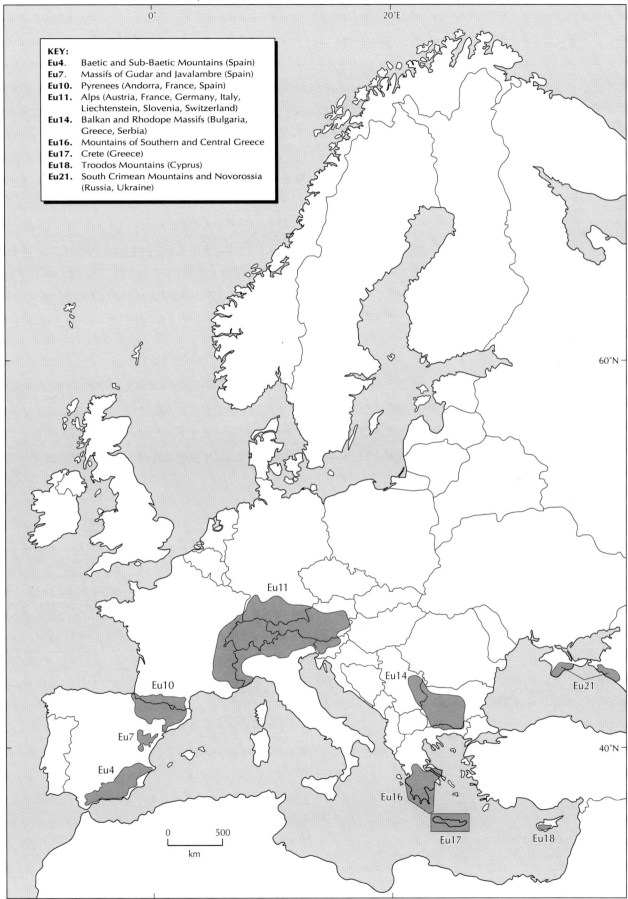

**KEY:**
**Eu4.** Baetic and Sub-Baetic Mountains (Spain)
**Eu7.** Massifs of Gudar and Javalambre (Spain)
**Eu10.** Pyrenees (Andorra, France, Spain)
**Eu11.** Alps (Austria, France, Germany, Italy, Liechtenstein, Slovenia, Switzerland)
**Eu14.** Balkan and Rhodope Massifs (Bulgaria, Greece, Serbia)
**Eu16.** Mountains of Southern and Central Greece
**Eu17.** Crete (Greece)
**Eu18.** Troodos Mountains (Cyprus)
**Eu21.** South Crimean Mountains and Novorossia (Russia, Ukraine)

## IBERIAN PENINSULA

### Portugal

#### Eu1. Peneda-Gerês

Rugged, granite mountains to 1545 m, with high rainfall.
- ❖ Vegetation: Forests of *Quercus pyrenaica* and *Pinus sylvestris*, and good examples of oceanic heaths dominated by *Erica* and *Ulex* species.
- ❖ Flora: 637 taxa, with c. 15% Iberian endemic element (Serra and Carvalho 1989).
- ❖ Conservation: National Park of 600 km² was designated in 1970.

#### Eu2. Serra da Estrêla

Mostly granitic mountains to 1990 m, with high rainfall; the scenery is dominated by glacial features and rounded summits.
- ❖ Vegetation: Forests of *Pinus pinaster, Quercus pyrenaica, Q. robur* and *Castanea sativa*, heaths with species of *Cytisus* and other shrubs, and grasslands.
- ❖ Flora: A number of taxa are endemic (Pinto da Silva and Teles 1980).
- ❖ Threats: The flora and vegetation are threatened by increased visitor pressure.
- ❖ Conservation: National Park of 522 km² has been established.

#### Eu3. Algarve

Mainly schistose hills and, in southern part, limestone coastal promontories forming a plateau, 45–75 m in altitude, at the most south-western extremity of Europe.
- ❖ Vegetation: The coastal vegetation is treeless *Cistus* heath, with several local and many regional endemics. Inland the mountains have acid soil and high rainfall; they were formerly covered with native semi-deciduous oak forest but now mostly replanted with *Eucalyptus*. Heaths and scrub communities are rich in relict and endemic species.
- ❖ Threats: Both protected areas (see below) are threatened by increased pressure from tourism (Woodell 1989).
- ❖ Conservation: There is a Nature Reserve of 60 km² at Ponta de Sagres, and the whole coast, including the more floristically important Cabo de S. Vicente, is now included in a Protected Area.

### Spain

#### Eu4. Baetic and Sub-Baetic Mountains

– see Data Sheet.

#### Eu5. Guadalquiver Estuary, including Coto de Donaña

A wetland area of international importance for vegetation, migratory birds and larger mammals.
- ❖ Vegetation: There are forests of two economically important trees, stone pine (*Pinus pinea*) and cork oak (*Quercus suber*), and extensive Atlantic-Mediterranean heaths, sand dunes and salt and freshwater marshes.
- ❖ Threats: Extensive commercial development along the coast; agricultural development adversely affects the soil water-level.
- ❖ Conservation: Donaña National Park covers 507.2 km²; Donaña Biosphere Reserve covers 772.6 km, but is under pressure.

#### Eu6. Sierra de Gredos and Sierra de Guadarrama

Rugged mountain chain, c. 200 km in length, composed of granite and gneiss, dissected by many streams and springs. Altitude: up to 2600 m.
- ❖ Vegetation: extensive forests of Scots pine (*Pinus sylvestris*) from 1500 m, with fragments of oak (*Quercus pyrenaica, Q. suber*) and chestnut (*Castanea sativa*) forest at lower altitudes.
- ❖ Flora: Rich montane flora with many endemics.
- ❖ Conservation: Nature Reserve of 228 km² has been established in Gredos to conserve the fauna and flora.

#### Eu7. Massifs of Gudar and Javalambre

– see Data Sheet.

#### Eu8. Picos de Europa

The highest part of 240 km chain of Cordillera Cantábrica and a continuation of the Pyrenean flora into north-central Spain. Limestone mountains to 2650 m altitude, with a rich flora, including several endemics, and some of the best preserved, traditionally managed, species-rich hay meadows in Europe.
- ❖ Conservation: A National Park covers 169.3 km².

#### Eu9. Islas Baleares

These islands represent a topographical extension of the Baetic Mountains (CPD Site Eu4, see Data Sheet) and their rich flora. The five principal islands occupy an area of 5014 km².
- ❖ Flora: 1450 vascular plant species, of which 94 are endemic; also species shared with the Tyrrhenian Islands (CPD Site Eu13, see below) to the east.
- ❖ Threats: The islands are increasingly being developed for tourism, although the majority of the endemics occur in the mountains of Mallorca, which rise to 1440 m.

## WESTERN AND SOUTHERN CENTRAL EUROPE

### Andorra, France, Spain

#### Eu10. Pyrenees

– see Data Sheet.

### Austria, France, Germany, Italy, Liechtenstein, Slovenia, Switzerland

#### Eu11. Alps

– see Data Sheet.

## Italy

## Eu12. Appennini and Alpe Apuane

The Alpe Apuane are mainly limestone, and mark a transition between the floras of the Alps and the Appennini. The Abbruzzo Mountains, in the central part of Appennini, have several peaks over 2000 m and a rich alpine flora.

❖ Conservation: A National Park of 400 km² is being expanded and a new park is being set up on Mte Maiella, further south, which has an important flora. Formerly much of the Central and Southern Appennines had National Park status, including major sites such as Monte Pollino in northern Calabria. At the southern extremity of the range, a fragmented Calabria National Park includes the mountains of Sila and Aspromonte, with rich forests of beech (*Fagus sylvatica*) and silver fir (*Abies alba*).

## France, Italy

## Eu13. Tyrrhenian Islands

### Corsica

Mountainous island, 20% of the land being over 2000 m or more, and granitic except for about a third of the area in the east and north. There are more than 40 peaks above 2000 m, the highest rising to 2710 m. There are sea-cliffs on most coasts, but those of the east are flat and contain lagoons.

❖ Vegetation: The island is still well wooded, and is famous for its lush maquis scrub communities, especially in the west.
❖ Flora: Both geology and the montane flora represent a southern extension of the Alps; the flora of 2180 vascular plant species includes 126 endemic taxa, many in alpine communities above 1800 m. Several endemics are shared with the Balearic Islands, including species such as *Naufraga balearica*, believed to be Tertiary or earlier relicts.

### Sardinia

Largely granitic.
❖ Flora: 2100 vascular plant species with a large endemic element, and at least 26 species restricted to the island, although a recent estimate puts the total number of endemic taxa as high as 115, together with 37 endemic species shared with Corsica and Sicily.

### Sicily and offshore islands

❖ Flora: Sicily has a rich flora that has links with south Greece and north-west Africa, with several endemics. The three most floristically important areas are:

*Madonie Mountains* in the north, an area of 500 km²; limestone, sands and clays, with eight peaks of 1800 m or more. There are forests of oak, together with relics of evergreen forest dominated by holly (*Ilex aquifolium*), and the mountains are the most southerly station for a number of northern and central European taxa. At least 10 narrow endemics, notably Sicilian fir (*Abies nebrodensis*), together with significant populations of other Sicilian endemics (Raimondo 1984).

*Mount Etna* in the east, an active volcano (3370 m), with stabilized lava slopes, covering an area of 1500 km².

Endemics include *Astragalus siculus*, *Genista aetnensis* (also on volcanic Lipari Islands) and distinctive variants of several widespread species.

*Egadi Islands*, off the west coast, mostly limestone (up to 680 m); several endemics, including a species of cabbage, *Brassica macrocarpa*.

## BALKAN PENINSULA, AEGEAN REGION AND CYPRUS

An area of high mountains; the most mountainous part of Europe outside the Alps. Principal ranges include the Dinaric Alps (Velebit, Durmitor), the Albanian Alps, the Pindhos Mountains of south Albania and north and central Greece, and the Balkan Mountains of eastern Serbia, Bulgaria and small part of Greece. The predominantly limestone mountain chains run north-west to south-east, swinging eastwards in the southern Aegean region from Crete to Rhodes.

The region is one of crustal instability, with major faulting of rock strata, seismic activity and some relict vulcanism, especially in the southern Aegean. The topography is deeply dissected, with many mountain peaks above 2000 m, rising to over 2900 m at Olympus, Pirin and Rila, valleys and flat basins, and cliffs and a multitude of islands along the Adriatic coast and in the Aegean Sea. Many areas have karstic limestone landscapes, and there are widespread outcrops of serpentine in Albania, Bosnia-Hercegovina and northern Greece.

## Bulgaria, Greece, Serbia

## Eu14. Balkan and Rhodope Massifs

– see Data Sheet.

## Greece

## Eu15. Mount Olympus (Thessalian Olympus)

Probably the finest individual site in the Balkan Peninsula. The massif rises to 2917 m, and includes several peaks over 2500 m.

❖ Flora: 1700 vascular plant species, of which 26 are endemic to the mountain (Strid 1980). Many other species are Balkan endemics and it is a station for several northern and central European plants.
❖ Threats: No immediate threats
❖ Conservation: Mount Olympus National Park covers 40 km².

## Eu16. Mountains of Southern and Central Greece

– see Data Sheet.

## Eu17. Crete

– see Data Sheet.

## Cyprus

### Eu18. Troodos Mountains

– see Data Sheet.

## EASTERN EUROPE

### Romania

### Eu19. Danube Delta

❖ Vegetation: One of the most important wetlands of Europe. Huge reed-beds (*Phragmites communis*), with floating reed islands (*plav*) and swamp forests, make this a major habitat for birds as well as plants.
❖ Threats: An area of c. 400 km² has been damaged previously by drainage. The Danube Delta is now legally protected from further drainage and agricultural development.
❖ Conservation: A Nature Reserve covers 400 km².

### Czech Republic and Slovakia, Hungary, Poland, Romania, Ukraine

### Eu20. Carpathians

A long chain of mountains, some 100 km wide, in eastern Europe, from Poland (Tatra) to Romania and Ukraine. They are a climatic link between western and eastern Europe.
❖ Vegetation: Forests of *Fagus sylvatica*, *Abies alba* and *Picea abies*, with *Quercus robur* at lower altitudes. Extensive areas of grassland and rock communities above 1800 m.
❖ Flora: 2000 vascular plant species are recorded from the Ukrainian Carpathians alone, at least 100 of them endemic to these mountains. Floristic links with the Balkan Mountains (see Data Sheet on the Balkan and Rhodope Mountains, CPD Site Eu14, and the Alps – CPD Site Eu11, see Data Sheet).
❖ Conservation: Retezat National Park in Romania covers 130 km²; in Ukraine, the Carpathian National Park covers 503 km² and the Sinevirska National Park covers 404 km². As in the Alps, an overall coordinated conservation policy by the various territories is required.

### Russia, Ukraine

### Eu21. South Crimean Mountains and Novorossia

– see Data Sheet.

## NORTH-WESTERN EUROPE: BRITISH ISLES, FENNOSCANDIA AND BALTIC REGION

Britain has 9 National Parks and a network of National and Local Nature Reserves, preserving fragments of a landscape often devastatingly altered by human activity (Hywel-Davies and Thom 1984). Some communities are characteristic of these islands, notably lowland heaths, some coastal shingle and cliff communities, and the dune grassland known as *machair*, as are some man-made communities, such as medieval parkland. There is a large bryophyte and lichen flora, with development of bryophyte-dominated communities, especially in the west and north-west.

Scandinavia retains much forest cover (see Table 1) and large areas of mountain and arctic communities. The region has extensive protected areas: Norway has 15 National Parks, covering over 8500 km²; Sweden has 10 National Parks, covering over 6000 km²; Finland has 9 National Parks, covering over 2500 km².

## Ireland

### Eu22. Burren

520 km² of karstic limestone landscape on the western coast of Ireland with an Atlantic climate.
❖ Flora: Includes Mediterranean, Alpine and Arctic-alpine elements.
❖ Threats: Greatly increased visitor pressure and quarrying of the limestone (O'Donoghue 1991).
❖ Conservation: A National Park of 260 km² protects the central part of the habitat.

## Sweden

### Eu23. Öland and Gotland

Alvar, on karstic limestone, with a rich flora and many southern elements at the northern end of their range.

## Byelorussia, Lithuania, Poland

### Eu24. Białowieża Forest

Situated in eastern Poland, on the frontier between Lithuania and Byelorussia.
❖ Vegetation: Ancient, some probably wildwood, forests at low (150–170 m) altitude; swamp woodland and raised bogs.
❖ Flora: Some 70 woody species in pine, Norway spruce, and mixed deciduous forests, with a rich shrub layer.
❖ Conservation: National Park, established in 1921 of 51 km². It has a rich fauna, including European bison.

## References

Akeroyd, J.R. and Synge, H. (1992). Higher plant diversity. In World Conservation Monitoring Centre, *Global Biodiversity: status of the Earth's living resources*. Chapman and Hall, London. Pp. 64–87.

Akeroyd, J.R. and Walters, S.M. (1987). *Flora Europaea*: the background to the revision of volume 1. *Bot. J. Linn. Soc.* 95: 223–226.

Braudel, F. (1973). *The Mediterranean and the Mediterranean world in the age of Philip II.* Vol. 1. Collins. 642 pp.

Council of Europe (1983). *List of rare and threatened endemic plants in Europe.* Council of Europe, Strasbourg.

Council of Europe (1991). *The conservation of the wild progenitors of cultivated plants.* Council of Europe, Strasbourg.

Council of Europe/Cariplo Foundation (1993). *International Conference. The state of the environment in Europe: the scientists take stock of the situation.* Cariplo Foundation for Scientific Research, Milan.

Davis, S.D., Droop, S.J.M., Gregerson, P., Henson, L., Leon, C.J., Villa-Lobos, J.L., Synge, H. and Zantovska, J. (1986). *Plants in danger: what do we know?* IUCN, Gland, Switzerland and Cambridge, U.K. xlv, 461 pp.

Eber, S. (1992). *Beyond the green horizon. A discussion paper on principles for sustainable tourism.* WWF U.K., Godalming.

Edmondson, J.R. (1992). Review of recent taxonomic work on European serpentinicolous phanerogams. In Baker, A.J., Proctor, J. and Reeves, R.D. (eds), *The vegetation of ultramafic (serpentine) soils.* Intercept, Andover. Pp. 435–449.

Favarger, C. (1972). Endemism in the montane floras of Europe. In Valentine, D.H. (ed.), *Taxonomy, phytogeography and evolution.* Academic Press. Pp. 191–204.

Géhu, J.M. (ed). (1984). *La végétation des pelouses calcaires.* Cramer, Vaduz, Liechtenstein.

Godwin, H. (1975). *The history of the British flora.* 2nd Ed. Cambridge University Press, Cambridge.

Heywood, C., Heywood, V.H. and Jackson, P.W. (1990). *International directory of botanical gardens V.* 5th Ed. Koeltz Scientific Books, Koenigstein. 1021 pp.

Heywood, V.H. (1978). European floristics: past, present and future. In Street, H.E. (ed.), *Essays in plant taxonomy.* Academic Press, London. Pp. 275–289.

Heywood, V.H. (1993a). Flora conservation. *Naturopa* 71: 24–25.

Heywood, V.H. (1993b). Coordinating plant conservation action in Europe. In: *International Conference. The State of the Environment in Europe: the scientists take stock of the situation.* Council of Europe and Cariplo Foundation for Scientific Research, Milan. Pp. 215–217.

Horvat, I., Glavac, V. and Ellenberg, H. (1974). *Vegetation Südosteuropas.* Gustav Fischer Verlag, Stuttgart.

Huntley, B. and Birks, H.J.B. (1983). *An atlas of past and present pollen maps for Europe: 0–13000 years ago.* Cambridge University Press, Cambridge, U.K.

Hywel-Davies, J. and Thom, V. (1984). *The Macmillan guide to Britain's nature reserves.* Macmillan, London. 717 pp.

ICONA (1984). *Inventario Forestal Nacional ICONA. Años 1965 a 1974.* ICONA, Madrid.

Lorca, M.P. and Rivas-Martínez, S. (1987). *La vegetación de España.* Universidad de Alcala de Henares. 544 pp.

O'Donoghue, O. (1991). Mullaghmore – a healing wilderness. *Plantlife Newsletter* 4: 4–5.

Olivier, L. and Muracciole, M. (eds) (1994 in press). *Connaissance et Conservation de la Flore des Iles de la Méditerranée.* Colloque International.

Pallas, M. (1939). *Aspects of the vegetation of Europe.* London. 66 pp.

Pawłowski, B. (1970). Remarques sur l'endemisme dans la flore des Alpes et des Carpates. *Vegetatio* 21: 181–243.

Pinto da Silva, A.R. and Teles, A.N. (1980). *A flora e a vegetação da Serra da Estrêla.* Coleção Parques Naturais 7, Lisboa. 52 pp.

Plantlife (1992). *Commission of Enquiry into peat and peatlands.* Plantlife, London.

Polunin, O. and Walters, M. (1985). *A guide to the vegetation of Britain and Europe.* Oxford University Press. 238 pp.

Rackham, O. (1986). *The history of the countryside.* Dent, London. 445 pp.

Rackham, O. (1990). The greening of Myrtos. In Bottema, S., Entjes-Nieborg and Van Zeist, W. (eds), *Man's role in the shaping of the eastern Mediterranean landscape.* Balkema, Rotterdam. Pp. 341–348.

Raimondo, F.M. (1984). On the natural history of the Madonie mountains. *Webbia* 38: 29–52.

Read, M. (1989). *Grown in Holland?* Fauna and Flora Preservation Society, Brighton. 12 pp.

Rodwell, J.S. (ed.) (1991- ). *British plant communities.* (1 – *Woodlands and scrub*; 2 – *Mire and heaths*; 3 – *Grasslands and montane communities*; 5 vols planned in total.)

Rune, O. (1953). Plant life on serpentines and related rocks in the north of Sweden. *Acta Phytogeographica Suecica* 31: 1–139.

Serra, M.L. and Carvalho, M.S. (1989). *A flora e vegetação do Parque Nacional da Peneda-Gêres.* Coleção Natureza e Paisagem 6, Lisboa. 78 pp.

Strid, A. (1980). *Wild flowers of Mount Olympus.* xxviii, 362 pp. Kifisia.

Synge, H. (1992). *Environmental agreements at European level on the conservation of biological diversity.* IUCN Plants Office, Richmond, U.K.

Trabaud, L. (1981). Man and fire: impacts on Mediterranean vegetation. In Di Castri, F., Goodall, D.W. and Specht, R.L. (eds), *Mediterranean-type shrublands.* Elsevier, Amsterdam. Pp. 523–537.

Tutin, T.G. *et al.* (eds) (1964-1980). *Flora Europaea, 1–5.* Cambridge University Press, Cambridge, U.K.

Tutin, T.G. *et al.* (eds) (1993). *Flora Europaea, 1.* 2nd Ed. Cambridge University Press, Cambridge, U.K.

Webb, D.A. (1978). *Flora Europaea* – a retrospect. *Taxon* 27: 3–14.

Wolkinger, F. and Plank, S. (1981). *Dry grasslands of Europe.* Council of Europe, Strasbourg.

Woodell, S.R.J. (1989). Cape St Vincent and the Sagres Peninsula, Portugal: important biological sites under threat. *Environmental Conservation* 16: 33–39.

World Conservation Monitoring Centre (1992). *Global biodiversity: status of the Earth's living resources.* Chapman and Hall, London. xx, 549 pp.

Zohary, D. and Heywood, V.H. (eds) (1994). *A catalogue of the wild relatives of native species that are cultivated in Europe.* (In press.)

# BAETIC AND SUB-BAETIC MOUNTAINS
## Spain

**Location:** Southern Spain, covering much of Andalucía and adjacent parts of Albacete, Murcia and Alicante provinces.

**Area:** 18,000 km².

**Altitude:** 0–3481 m (summit of Mulhacén).

**Vegetation:** Evergreen forests of holm and cork oak; deciduous and semi-deciduous oak woodlands; pine and Spanish fir (*Abies pinsapo*) forests; Mediterranean and montane scrub; steppic and arid communities; alpine grassland, rock and scree communities.

**Flora:** Rich flora of some 3000 vascular plant species, with an important endemic element, especially in the high mountains (80% endemism in some habitats in the Sierra Nevada); in lowlands, many species of disjunct distribution or African affinity.

**Useful plants:** Aromatic and medicinal plants, native timber trees, wild olives, some crop relatives and wild flowers for honey production. Many mountain plants have horticultural potential.

**Other values:** Rich flora and fine landscape attract tourists; conserved areas support rare fauna.

**Threats:** Forest fires, pollution, tourist developments (e.g. ski resorts), road building, overgrazing, over-extraction of water for agriculture.

**Conservation:** Limited until recently, but 13 Natural Parks now established, covering 7700 km².

## Geography

The Baetic and Sub-Baetic Mountains are situated in the southern part of the Iberian Peninsula, covering much of Andalucía and adjacent parts of Albacete, Murcia and Alicante provinces. The topography is very heterogeneous, ranging in altitude from sea-level to 3481 m at the summit of Mulhacén, the highest point in the Sierra Nevada. Much of the land is above 1000 m and elevations close to, or higher than, 2000 m predominate.

Among the most interesting physiographical features are: the coast, which has many high cliffs and small coves, notably mountainous coastal areas such as Lujar, Alhamilla and Cabo de Gata; the inter-montane basins, such as those of Antequera, Guadix-Baza, Vega de Granada and Almeria; the valleys of Lecrín, Guadalfeo, Geníl and Almanzora; the Sub-Baetic sierras of Harana, Mágina, Cazorla and Alcaraz; and the Baetic and peni-Baetic massifs of Tejeda, Almijara, Sierra Nevada, Filabres, Ronda and Gador. The Islas Baleares represent a topographic extension of the Baetic Cordillera.

The mountains form part of the Alpine system in which the predominant tectonic formation is nappe de charriage. There are also depressions of Quaternary origin which have a diverse lithology and varied edaphic conditions. Among the peculiar geological formations of the region are the Sierras of the Campo de Gibraltar which are composed of sandstone grit of extremely pure quartz with almost no cementing material. The Sierra of Cabo de Gata, on the other hand, is volcanic in origin. Erosion of these rocks has resulted in one of the most outstanding landscapes in Andalucía.

The climate (Rivas Martínez 1990) is varied due to the large altitudinal range. The thermomediterranean zone occurs all around the coasts, and extends inland in some places along rivers, ascending to 700 (–800) m in the coastal mountain ranges. The mesomediterranean zone is the broadest, being replaced by the supramediterranean zone at 1300 (–1400) m, depending on the proximity of the coast. The oromediterranean zone begins at 1700 (–1800) m, depending on aspect; it is very localised and only relatively extensive in the Sierra Nevada. The cryoromediterranean zone is restricted to the Sierra Nevada, above 2800 m. Annual rainfall in the lower, semi-arid, area is about 150 mm, but exceeds 1600 mm in the Sierras of Algeciras and Grazalema.

## Vegetation

The biogeographical province of Murcia-Almería, in the south-eastern part of the region, has a characteristic thermomediterranean vegetation, associated with semi-arid to arid regions. Important shrubby seral communities here include those dominated by *Periploca angustifolia*, found on steep, exposed areas where the climate is influenced by the sea, and by jujube (*Ziziphus lotus*). Also present are communities dominated by the fan palm (*Chamaerops humilis*) and lentiscus (*Pistacia lentiscus*), typically with *Rhamnus lycioides*, replaced by Kermes oak (*Quercus coccifera*) with increasing altitude and distance from the coast. These communities occur in the Baetic province in the Guadix-Baza region.

Holm oak (*Quercus ilex* subsp. *rotundifolia*) formations, and their variants, are potentially the most widespread climax communities (Valle 1991). However, due to the high rainfall and the lack of seasonal drought in some places, deciduous vegetation, including maple

(*Acer granatense*) woods, are frequently found on base-rich soils, while Pyrenean oak (*Quercus pyrenaica*) woods occur on more acid soils. These communities are uncommon in the Mediterranean region and are, therefore, of great interest.

On siliceous rocks in sub-humid/humid areas, cork oak woods (*Quercus suber*) are frequent, and on base-rich soils over limestone, dolomite or serpentine in the Serranía de Ronda, there are important forests of the endemic Spanish fir (*Abies pinsapo*). In the south-western part of the Iberian Peninsula, in the Sierra de Algeciras, with a humid climate and siliceous soil, there are woods of the semi-evergreen Andalusian gall oak (*Quercus canariensis*).

The oromediterranean zone constitutes a distinct and remarkable facies, unique in the Mediterranean region, dominated by pines, including Scots pine (*Pinus sylvestris*) and dwarf juniper (*Juniperus communis* subsp. *nana*), together with broom (*Genista* spp.) and thyme (*Thymus* spp.), where the unfavourable ecological conditions (snow in winter, suffocating heat in summer, wind, scarce soil) have given rise to a specialised ecological grouping of species, amongst which are several endemics.

The cryoromediterranean zone of the Sierra Nevada is one of the most unique facies of the Mediterranean region. The characteristic vegetation of these areas is an open, dry grassland. More than 80% of the species, including *Eryngium glaciale* and *Festuca clementei*, are endemic to the Sierra Nevada.

## Flora

The flora of the Baetic and Sub-Baetic Sierras has been well studied, although there has been no regional synthesis. With an area equivalent to 12.5% of the land surface of Spain, the Baetic and Sub-Baetic Sierras are home to more than 3000 vascular plant species, about half of the flora of Spain, and including about half of the country's endemic species. The Baetic and Sub-Baetic region is therefore the richest centre for endemic species in Europe and the western Mediterranean basin.

There are several monotype endemic genera, such as *Euzomodendron bourgaeanum*, *Guiraoa arvensis* and *Lycocarpus fugax* (Cruciferae), and *Rothmaleria granatensis* (Compositae). Diverse, or well represented genera include: *Arenaria* (8 species endemic to the area), *Centaurea* (13 endemic species), *Erodium* (6), *Erysimum* (6), *Helianthemum* (7), *Hormathophylla* (4), *Limonium* (8), *Linaria* (16), *Sarcocapnos* (4), *Saxifraga* (9), *Sideritis* (8), *Teucrium* (9) and *Thymus* (8).

The endemic species are concentrated in the mountains, although they also occur in the lower and drier parts of Almería and Murcia provinces. The Sierra Nevada stands out in importance, having a flora of more than 2000 vascular plant species within an area of 2000 km². They include the largest concentration of endemic species in the Iberian Peninsula (more than 250 endemic species, of which 80 species are restricted to the massif). In the summit areas, 30–40% of the

**MAP 3. THE BAETIC AND SUB-BAETIC MOUNTAINS OF SPAIN (CPD SITE Eu4)**

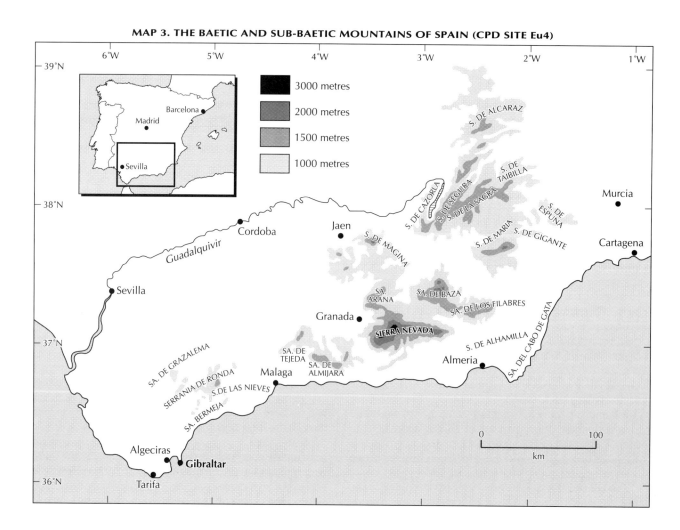

flora is endemic, while in some ecological niches, such as on rocky ground or in gorges, the proportion of endemic species reaches 80%.

There are many species with disjunct distributions. In the siliceous mountains of Algeciras (Cádiz province), a group of ferns can be found that are more characteristic of Macaronesia or subtropical regions, including species such as *Psilotum nudum*, *Pteris incompleta*, *Culcita macrocarpa*, *Christella dentata*, *Diplazium caudatum* and *Davallia canariensis*. There are also species which are more characteristic of areas further north, and which are at their southernmost limit of distribution in the Baetic and Sub-Baetic Sierras, occurring in small or localised populations in mountainous areas (e.g. *Vitaliana primuliflora*, *Saxifraga oppositifolia* and *Ranunculus glacialis*). Many of the endemics are themselves relict or palaeo-endemic species, such as *Arenaria alfacarensis*, *Lavatera oblongifolia*, *Pterocephalus spathulatus*, *Andryala agardhii*, *Rothmaleria granatensis*, *Euzomodendron bourgaeanum*, *Rhododendron ponticum* subsp. *baeticum* and *Viola cazorlensis*.

An important component of the flora is a group of Iberian-North African species that are widespread in the low, arid, south-eastern part of the region. They include *Ammochloa palaestina*, *Anabasis articulata*, *Caralluma europaea*, *Centaurea maroccana*, *Hammada articulata*, *Koelpinia linearis*, *Lapiedra martinezii*, *Lasiopogon muscoides*, *Leysera leyseroides*, *Notoceras bicorne*, *Pteranthus dichotomus*, *Rosmarinus eriocalyx*, *Senecio flavus*, *Tetraclinis articulata* and *Zizyphus lotus*. The majority of these species have their only European stations here.

The Baetic and Sub-Baetic Mountains also share species with the mountains of North Africa. These include *Abies pinsapo*, *Adenocarpus decorticans*, *Alyssum spinosum*, *Arenaria pungens*, *Cochlearia megalosperma*, *Erodium tordylioides*, *Fumaria macrosepala*, *Lonicera arborea*, *Papaver rupifragum*, *Pseudoscabiosa grosii*, *Ranunculus granatensis*, *Rupicapnos africana* and *Thalictrum speciosissimum*.

## Useful plants

The region has many species of aromatic plants which are used extensively in the making of perfumes, in food preparation and in pharmacy. Members of the genera *Thymus*, *Lavandula*, *Ziziphora*, *Salvia*, *Sideritis* and *Ruta*, among others, are collected for these purposes. Many other species are traditionally used in medicine by the inhabitants of the region.

Timber is little exploited today, as native woods of Spanish fir (*Abies pinsapo*), Spanish juniper (*Juniperus thurifera*), deciduous or semi-deciduous oaks (*Quercus canariensis*, *Q. pyrenaica*, *Q. faginea*), holm oak (*Q. ilex* subsp. *rotundifolia*) and pines (*Pinus nigra* subsp. *salzmanni*, *P. sylvestris* var. *nevadensis* and native *P. pinaster*) are protected. Only pines (*P. nigra*, *P. sylvestris*, *P. pinaster* and *P. halepensis*), the majority of which derive from afforestation programmes and which cover wide areas, are exploited for timber.

In the westernmost part of the region, woodland-pastures dominated by cork oak and holm oak are still used for the grazing of semi-wild bulls and Iberian pigs.

The collection and cultivation of caper (*Capparis spinosa* subsp. *spinosa*) is of particular importance in the region,

although the old, widespread crops of Esparto (*Stipa tenacissima*) have practically disappeared. Wild olive (*Olea europaea* var. *sylvestris*) is frequently found at lower altitudes in the mountains, where it locally forms woods. Many species, especially in the mountains, have considerable horticultural potential. Many species are used as sources of honey.

## Social and environmental values

Evidence of human activity dates back to the upper Palaeolithic. Crops have been cultivated in the region since Neolithic times, beginning 8000 years ago (Garcel culture, Almería). Ever since cultivation and domestic animals were introduced the natural vegetation and landscape have been progressively degraded, especially in the east. This process has been exacerbated by increasing aridity. Natural or semi-natural vegetation has been preserved only in the most inaccessible areas of the Baetic and Sub-Baetic Sierras, while the region of Almería-Murcia resembles semi-desert.

The whole of the south-east, from Granada to Murcia, shows evidence of soil erosion. In an attempt to control this process, the LUCDEME programme (Fight Against the Mediterranean Desert Process) is being developed as part of a global study promoted by the Ministry of Agriculture, Fisheries and Food, through ICONA (Nature Conservation Institute).

Large areas of land are taken up by crops. In the fertile coastal plains of Málaga and Motril, sugar cane is being substituted by other subtropical crops, including avocado pear and custard apple, together with extensive greenhouse cultivation of early vegetables. Inland, olive groves occupy large areas. The lower slopes of the Baetic and Sub-Baetic Sierras are one of the most important areas in the world for this crop.

Tourism, the mainstay of the economy of the region, is based on the historical and cultural richness of the region, and benefits from the Mediterranean climate. Until recently, tourism was centred on the coastal fringe of the Costa del Sol, but today it has spread to the ski resorts of the Sierra Nevada and the mountains in general, due to the attraction of the Natural Parks and the relatively unspoiled countryside.

The mountains contain a varied Mediterranean fauna and are an important reserve for the wildlife of the Iberian Peninsula. Pardine lynx, ibex and mongoose survive in the region, together with badger, stone marten, otter, and many bird species (including raptors).

## Threats

The most serious environmental problems of the Baetic and Sub-Baetic Sierras are overgrazing, urbanization, tourism, pollution, fires, expanding agriculture and plant collecting.

Deficient planning has allowed the excessive use of natural pastures for the grazing of herds, especially during the summer.

Urbanization and the tourist developments are most evident in the coastal areas of Málaga province (Costa del Sol), but development is spreading to Granada and Almería provinces. Ironically, areas set aside as Natural Parks and other protected areas are attracting visitors who expect unspoiled landscapes. This demand is itself creating impacts in some areas and needs careful controls which at the moment are lacking.

An extensive network of roads allows access to places of high ecological value using 4-wheel drive vehicles, which can even drive to the highest part of the Iberian Peninsula at Mulhacén. The development of the skiing industry also creates a demand for improved access.

Pollution arises from disposal sites and the contamination of water from these and industrial wastes.

Fire is one of the most serious threats to the vegetation. The incidence of fire is increasing each year, most forest fires being started deliberately. The large-scale planting of pines in afforestation programmes exacerbates the problem. Erosion following the destruction of vegetation cover has created large areas of desert-like landscape in the provinces of Murcia, Almería and Granada.

The expansion of irrigation for agricultural crops is placing excessive demands on water resources. As a result, the water-table is being lowered over wide areas and salination of aquifers is occurring along the coast, especially in Almería province.

Large quantities of wild plants (especially aromatic and medicinal species) are collected for research and private botanical collections, popular festivals and traditional uses.

## Conservation

Legislation to protect the environment in the Baetic and Sub-Baetic Sierras is very recent. At State level, Law 4/1989 of 27 March 1989 on "Conservation of Natural Species and Wild Flora and Fauna" and Royal Decree 439/1990 of 30 March 1990 (BOE [Official State Bulletin] No. 82 of 5 April 1990) on the "Catalogue of Endangered Species" have been proposed. The environmental management of the Baetic and Sub-Baetic Sierras is the responsibility of four Autonomous Communities: Andalucía, Murcia, Castilla-La Mancha and Valencia.

In the Autonomous Community of Andalucía, which includes the greater part of the area, the "Law for the Inventory of Protected Natural Species of Andalucía" was passed by the Andalucian Parliament on 18 July 1989 (BOJA [Official Bulletin of the Andalucian Government] No. 60 of 27 July 89). As a result, 13 Natural Parks were declared in the Baetic and Sub-Baetic Sierras, covering an area of some 7700 km$^2$. The Governing Body of each park controls the use and management of these resources and establishes certain areas as reserves for the protection of threatened animal and plant species.

## References

Blanca, G. (1988). Origen de la flora Nevadense. Especiación Endemismo. *Monogr. Fl. Veg. Béticas* 3: 99–110.

Blanca, G. and Morales, C. (1992). *Flora del Parque Natural de la Sierra de Baza.* Secretariado de Publicaciones de la Universidad de Granada.

Fernández, C., Cruz, M.C., López-Pulido, M., Amezcua, C. and Casado, D. (1991). *Flora de Andalucía. Catálogo bibliográfico de las plantas vasculares.* Jaén.

Gómez-Campo, C. et al. (1987). *Libro rojo de especies vegetales amenazadas de España peninsular e islas Baleares.* ICONA, Madrid.

González-Tejero, M.R. (1990). *Investigaciones Etnobotánicas en la Provincia de Granada.* Secretariado de Publicaciones de la Universidad de Granada. Microfichas. (ISBN 84-338-1218.)

Losa-Quintana, J.M., Molero-Mesa, J. and Casares, M. (1986). *El paisaje vegetal de Sierra Nevada: La cuenca alta del Río Genil.* Secretariado de Publicaciones de la Universidad de Granada. 285 pp.

Molero-Mesa, J. and Pérez-Raya, F. (1987). *La flora de Sierra Nevada. Avance sobre el catálogo florístico nevadense.* Secretariado de Publicaciones de la Universidad de Granada. 396 pp.

Rivas Martínez, S. (1990). Bioclimatic belts of west Europe (relations between bioclimate plants ecosystems). *Folia botanica matritensis* 7: 1–22.

Sagredo, R. (1987). *Flora de Almería. Plantas vasculares de la Provincia.* Instituto de estudios Almerienses, Almería.

Valle, F. (1991). Végétation du soud-est de la péninsule Ibérique. (Rapport présenté pendant le Séminaire préparatoire de la première expedition de l'OPTIMA). *Bocconea* 1: 29–41.

## Acknowledgements

This Data Sheet was prepared by Dr Joaquin Molero-Mesa (Universidad de Granada, Spain).

# MASSIFS OF GUDAR AND JAVALAMBRE
## Spain

**Location:** East-central Spain, between 40°06'N and 1°00'W (Pico de Javalambre) and 40°23'N and 0°38'W (Pico de Peñarroya, Gudar).

**Area:** 445 km² (of which Javalambre covers 350 km²).

**Altitude:** 1200–2020 m.

**Vegetation:** Woodland of juniper, especially Spanish juniper (*Juniperus thurifera*), Scots pine (*Pinus sylvestris*) and mountain pine (*P.* × *uncinata*), also *P.* × *rhaetica*; grassland and rock communities.

**Flora:** Flora of more than 1500 vascular plant species; many endemic species. Phytogeographical relationships between these mountains, the Baetic and Sub-Baetic Mountains, and the Pyrenees (CPD Sites Eu4 and Eu10, respectively; see separate Data Sheets).

**Useful plants:** Excellent forestry resources with extensive stands of pines. The area is also a source of medicinal plants in a region with a great tradition of ethnobotany.

**Other values:** The area is important for ecotourism, with much potential for creating nature trails and parks. The landscape and human settlements are of great cultural and architectural interest.

**Threats:** Unplanned development of tourism, construction of ski resorts.

**Conservation:** There is no special legislation; the region should be declared a Nature Park or Reserve.

## Geography

The Massifs of Gudar and Javalambre form part of the eastern sector of the Systema Ibérico. The area which should be conserved is that containing the two great massifs, separated by the depression of the River Mijares. To the north, Gudar has a maximum altitude of 2019 m at the Pico de Peñarroya; to the south, the Pico de Javalambre reaches 2020 m. The neighbouring sierras of Camarena, Corbalan, Allepuz, Palomita, Ares and Penyagolosa should also be included in the zone to be protected.

The geology is complex, resulting in a wide range of substrates. The most widespread rock formations are Cretaceous and Triassic limestones; there are also base-poor conglomerates and sandstones. In the wetter zones, such as Gudar, leaching of carbonates sometimes occurs on the surface. Siliceous rocks are more frequent towards the east and are in fact most prevalent in the Sierra of Espadán, outside the area of study.

The climate is continental, especially on Javalambre; in Gudar it is more temperate, due to the higher rainfall. Supramediterranean and oromediterranean bioclimatic zones dominate the region. The supramediterranean climate has an average annual temperature of between 8°–13°C; the average lowest temperature of the coldest month is between -1°C and -4°C; the average highest temperature of the coldest month is between 2°–9°C. The oromediterranean climate has more extreme characteristics. The average annual temperatures are between 4°–8°C; the average temperature of the coldest month is between -7° and -4°C; and the average highest temperature of the coldest month is between 0°–2°C. The principal climate is dry with average rainfall of 350–600 mm, although in certain circumstances it may reach 600–1000 mm.

## Vegetation

The vegetation consists of forests of Spanish juniper (*Juniperus thurifera*) which dominate the supramediterranean levels. There are also woodlands of Lusitanian oak (*Quercus faginea*), which are more or less intact in the wetter and most favourable parts; in the less extreme areas they are to be found with juniper or holm oak (*Quercus ilex* subsp. *rotundifolia*). In the oromediterranean zone, Scots pine (*Pinus sylvestris*) is dominant, together with savin (*Juniperus sabina*). In the highlands and around pines, grasslands (pastures) are the main formation. There are snowfalls in the winter.

The junipers represent an ancient, very important vegetation, forming a tree layer dominated by Spanish juniper (*Juniperus thurifera*) and common juniper (*J. communis* subsp. *hemisphaerica*), with *Berberis vulgaris* subsp. *seroi* and *Festuca asperifolia*. This open woodland usually occurs in the upper mesomediterranean and supramediterranean areas, with a dry and subhumid climate. Today, this type of community is degrading to scrub in which species such as *Genista pumila*, *Linum appresum* and *Artemisia lanata*, and grasses, such as *Festuca hystrix*, *Poa ligulata* and *Avenula gonzaloi* can be found.

Lusitanian oak (*Quercus faginea*) is plentiful in the region. The most widespread woodland types are closed formations dominated by deciduous trees: *Q. faginea* is the dominant species, usually accompanied by *Acer granatense*, *Paeonia humilis*, *Cephalanthera longifolia*, *Rosa agrestis* and *Brachypodium phopenicoides* (*Viola-Quercetum fagineae* association). These belong at supramediterranean levels, with deep soils and a climate between subhumid and humid.

Both the *Juniperetum* and the *Violo-Quercetum fagineae* associations are found between 1000 m and 1500 (–1600) m altitude. Above 1500 m there is the oromediterranean zone, with *Pinus sylvestris* and *Juniperus sabina*, which grow up to the summits, often on leached soils (terras fuscas) containing organic material. Grassland at this altitude is very rich in endemic species, such as *Arenaria aggregata* subsp. *microphylla*, *Sideritis glacialis*, *Astragalus muticus*, *Erodium celtibericum* and *Thymus godayanus*.

Pyrenean pine (*Pinus nigra* subsp. *salzmanii*) occurs between 1400–1500 m; mountain pine (*P. uncinata*) occurs on Gudar. On higher ground with pronounced continental climate, there are many areas with special formations of lichens, dominated by *Spaherothalia desertum*.

## Flora

The flora is essentially Mediterranean in character. The floristic significance of the flora lies in the high level of endemism and the occurrence of many relict species. The high endemism is the result of the degree of isolation of these ancient mountains, which have been a migratory route for certain floristic elements migrating southwards from the Pyrenees and northwards from the Baetic Mountains.

Some of the greatest resources of the region are the stands of *Pinus uncinata*, since they represent the only extensive population of this Alpine-Pyrenean species in the Iberian Peninsula, outside the Pyrenees. The presence of *P.* × *rhaetica*, the hybrid between *P. uncinata* and *P. sylvestris*, enhances the value of these stands of conifers. There are ancient forests of Spanish juniper (*Juniperus thurifera*), savin (*J. sabina*) and *Pinus nigra* subsp. *salzmanii* which are important for conservation.

Apart from those plants with centres of distribution in the Baetic Mountains or the Pyrenees, there are many local endemic species, such as *Berberis hispanica* subsp. *seroi*, *Astragalus muticus*, *Erodium celtibericum*, *Dianthus algetanus* subsp. *turolensis*, *Thymus godayanus*, *Erodium celtibericum*, *Sideritis javalambrensis* and *Linum appresum*.

## Useful plants

The pine forests are of regional economic importance, providing a traditional source of timber. Harvesting needs to be regulated to ensure sustainable yields.

The region is notable for the cultivation of aromatic plants, such as *Lavandula pyrenaica*. There is a great local tradition of ethnobotany, with many plants used in popular medicines. These are currently being studied to gain an understanding of their uses and chemical composition.

Of interest too are the fodder plants of Gudar and Javalambre. Special attention should be paid to these fodders, in order to improve and exploit them successfully. Several of the high mountain species are of ornamental value in horticulture.

## Social and environmental values

The region is of great historical interest. Its towns and villages are notable for their architecture and buildings, which are generally well conserved. Folk traditions, fiestas, food and craftwork are also cultural attractions for tourists.

Both the massifs have been well preserved. Mountains, forests, ravines and peaks create landscapes of high scenic value, with enormous potential for walking and other outdoor recreation pursuits. Springs and spas are also an important facet of the natural heritage of the region.

## Threats

Up until very recently, the region was very well conserved, the landscape being dedicated to the traditional activities of livestock raising and forestry. It is now under threat from unchecked development of tourism and urbanisation. The greatest threat is from skiing. This has led to severe damage to some ecosystems. Many unsightly building developments have occurred.

## Conservation

Currently no special measures exist for the conservation of the area. The Autonomous Government of Aragon has plans for developments in the region, such as the construction of ski-slopes and a huge expansion of tourism. This would put at risk the conservation of the area.

Conservation measures should be drawn up to safeguard the environmental and cultural heritage of the Gudar and Javalambre Massifs, which should be declared an area of significant interest for conservation, either as a Nature Park or Reserve.

## References

Costa, M. (1986). *La vegetación del Paris Valenciano*. Cultura Universitaria Popular, Universitat de Valencia. 246 pp.

Costa, M. (1987). El Pais Valenciano. In Peinado Lorca, M. and Rivas Martínez, S. (eds), *La vegetación de España*. Universidad de Alcalá de Henares. Madrid. Pp. 281–307.

Rivas Goday, S. (1955). Los grados de vegetación de la Peninsula Ibérica. *Anales Inst. Bot. Cavanilles* 13: 269–331.

Rivas Goday, S. and Borja, J. Estudio de la vegetación y florula del Macizo de Gudar y Javalambre. *Anales Inst. Bot. Cavanilles* 19: 1–155.

Rivas Goday, S. and Rivas Martínez, S. (1963). Estudio y clasificación de los pastizales españoles. *Pub. Ministerio de Agricultura*. Madrid. 269 pp.

## Acknowledgements

This Data Sheet was written by Professor M. Costa (Jardí Botanic, Universitat de Valencia, Spain).

# PYRENEES
## France, Spain and Andorra

**Location:** The northern half lies in south-west France, the southern half in north-east Spain and Andorra, between latitudes 42°00'–43°00'N and longitudes 2°00'W–3°00'E.

**Area:** 30,000 km².

**Altitude:** 0–3404 m (summit of Aneto).

**Vegetation:** Mediterranean evergreen forests, semi-deciduous submediterranean forests, deciduous Atlantic forests, montane and subalpine coniferous forests, Mediterranean montane scrub, meadows and pastures, rock and scree communities.

**Flora:** c. 3500 vascular plant species, of which about 200 are endemic, numerous distinct communities.

**Useful plants:** c. 20 tree species used for timber; c. 70 tree species with a variety of uses; c. 600 plant species used as sources of medicines, pharmaceuticals, food (including fruit) and honey. Several species used for fodder and ornament.

**Other values:** Phytogeographical, with many mountain species at western or south-western limit, North African-Iberian species at northern limit. Major water resource; hydroelectric power. Considerable tourist attraction.

**Threats:** Growing pressure from tourism, accidental fires, natural and man-made erosion, surface and subterranean contamination of water.

**Conservation:** Many species are protected, both in France and Spain. About 50 protected areas, including 3 National Parks, 7 Nature Parks and numerous Nature Reserves.

## Geography

The Pyrenees extend for over 400 km in a west-east direction, from the Atlantic Ocean to the Mediterranean Sea, with an average width of 80 km. To the west, they border the Basque Valley, to the north, the Aquitaine Plain, to the south, the Ebro Valley, and in the east they descend almost to the sea.

Most of the northern slopes belong to France; the southern slopes belong to Spain and Andorra. The Pyrenean-Iberian catchment contributes to the Ebro Basin, the largest river in Spain, the Bidasoa Basin, to the west, as well as to eastern basins, including Llobregat and Ter. The French territory contributes to Atlantic rivers, including the Adour and Garonne, and to Mediterranean rivers, including the Aude and Tech.

The underlying rocks are mainly Palaeozoic granites, sandstones and schists, uplifted during the Hercynian folding to form an axis culminating in Aneto (3404 m). Mesozoic rocks cover both sides of the axis. They include mainly limestone and chalk, uplifted during the alpine folding at the beginning of the Tertiary, reaching altitudes of up to 3355 m at Monte Perdido. Oligocene and Eogecene conglomerates are less extensive, as are clayey and chalky marls of the Eocene and Miocene. There are also some outcrops of volcanic origin, especially in the eastern Spanish Pyrenees.

Glacial action during the Quaternary shaped the upper contours and left significant deposits of moraine above 600–800 m, as well as river gravels and alluvial terraces. The eastern Pyrenees, from Andorra to the Mediterranean, are predominantly siliceous, while the central Pyrenees, from Pallars-Ariege to Ossau-Tena comprise siliceous and calcareous rocks; limestones dominate to the west.

Ascending from the Mediterranean side, an altitude of 2900 m is reached (Puigmal) after only 70 km; on the Atlantic side, the range rises gradually and reaches 3000 m at Balaitus after 150 km. The highest massifs are in the central region; about 200 summits over 3000 m occur in the Aragón Pyrenees.

Besides the bioclimatic zoning common to all the mountains of southern Europe, the climate of the Pyrenees displays two important divisions:

1. Maritime-continental conditions from west to east.

2. Humidity-drought conditions from north to south.

In the western region and on the northern slopes, from the Basque country up to Neouvielle-Perdido and Ariegea, a maritime climate prevails: overcast skies, rain in every season, although mostly in the winter, mild winters and cool summers. On the central and southern slopes, Mediterranean-continental climatic conditions prevail: clear skies, torrential rain mostly falling in autumn or at the equinoxes, quite pronounced dry summers, temperature variations and very cold winters. Finally, the region adjacent to the Mediterranean, both in France and Spain, exhibits a coastal Mediterranean climate.

From October to June or July the build-up of snow is very prolonged, especially above 2000 m and in the western section, with perpetual snows and glaciers above 2500 m. Between one snow fall and the next, many peaks, particularly Spanish ones in the central and eastern region, have sunny, dry periods. Winter is the driest season. Goriz, in the Monte

61

Perdido massif (Spain) at 2215 m, only registers 16% of the total annual precipitation during this cold period.

The average annual temperature is less than 4°C on the peaks (Nuria, 4.8°C, at an altitude of 1967 m). At this altitude or above, it may freeze or snow throughout the whole year, although this rarely happens in July or August. The average annual temperature increases at lower levels, reaching 13.4°C in Yesa at 491 m altitude, for example. The ice-thaw cycles, with the ensuing periglacial action, are more frequent towards the end of the snow season and in autumn.

Temperature differences between sunny and shaded spots are very large, so that conditions change from oromediterranean to subalpine over short distances. Besides this, in many valleys or enclaves, temperature inversions occur, mainly in autumn and winter. Diurnal and seasonal temperature ranges are greatest in the central part of the mountain range.

In summary, the bioclimatic types in the Pyrenees (Montserrat 1974) from west to east are: the maritime, western, central, eastern and Mediterranean. Rivas-Martínez (1990) distinguishes between the following bioclimatic levels on the southern slopes of the Central Pyrenees: the mesomediterranean (200–600 m), the montane (900–1600 m), the subalpine (1600–2400 m) and the alpine (2400–3400 m) zones. The first of these is not found on the northern slopes, where furthermore a snow-line above 3000 m is found (according to Gruber 1992). Bioclimatic schemes proposed by Vigo and Ninot (1987) and by Saule (1991) are also useful.

## Vegetation

The location of the Pyrenees between two seas, the geological structure of the mountain range, and the east-west and north-south climatic asymmetries, give rise to a rich mosaic of vegetation types. Over a distance of just 150 km, all the phytogeographical elements of western Europe can be found.

The Pyrenees can be divided into two main phytogeographical units:

1. The extensive Euro-Siberian Region, with two provinces – the Pyrenean and the Cantabrian – containing Northern Alpine elements at higher altitudes.

2. The smaller Meditteranean Region, with two provinces – the Aragonese and the Valencian-Catalan-Provencal.

The vegetation of the Pyrenean province (Rivas-Martínez 1990) covers 70% of the region, occurring in both France and Spain. There are two sectors which are strictly Pyrenean (eastern and central) and a north-eastern sector (Cevennene), which has affinities with the vegetation of the Massif Central of France. Altitudes mostly range from 800–1000 m to 3400 m above sea-level.

Cantabrian vegetation covers about 15% of the region, occurring on the slopes towards the Basque Valley and Aquitaine, between 100–2000 m, and occasionally descending to sea-level.

Mediterranean vegetation occurs to the south and east of the main axis of the Cordillera, bordering the Ebro Valley and the Mediterranean, from sea-level to 800–1200 m, covering an area of some 5000 km². Within this area the following sectors can be identified:

1. West and Central (Spain): Castilian-Cantabrian, Riojan-Estelles, Somantano-Aragonese (Province of Aragón).

2. East (France and Spain): Vallesano-Empordanes (Valencian-Catalan-Provencal).

The southern slopes of the Pyrenees are more diverse in species than the northern slopes, because of their larger area and due to the intergradation of Euro-Siberian and Mediterranean vegetation. At least two forest formations, Mediterranean holm oak (*Quercus ilex* subsp. *rotundifolia*) and submediterranean semi-deciduous oaks, do not extend as far as France, although in Aragón they can be found to within a few kilometres of the frontier. Atlantic forests of pedunculate oak (*Quercus robur*) predominate in the Aquitaine foothills, the Basque country and Navarra, but there are a few traces of them in Catalonia also (Bolòs 1987).

In the humid mountain zone, there are various types of beech woodlands (*Fagus sylvatica*), with or without firs; in the dry montane zone there are Scots pine forests (*Pinus sylvestris*), whilst in the subalpine zone there are mountain pine (*Pinus uncinata*) woodlands.

In the alpine zone, there are various types of grasslands (with *Festuca airoidis* and *Carex curvula*), together with species found in areas with late snow cover (e.g. *Cardamine alpina*, *Salix herbacea*), along with rock and scree communities (e.g. *Androsace ciliata*, *Crepis pygmaea*).

## Flora

The Pyrenees are a rich centre of diversity and endemism, with each phytogeographic unit containing its own distinct flora, including many rare species. Many of the massifs can be considered biologically as terrestrial islands containing elements which have long-since disappeared from the surrounding plains as a result of Quaternary glaciation and the development of late to post-glacial forest between 4000–6000 years ago (cf. Jalut 1988).

The total vascular plant flora is estimated at about 3500 species and subspecies (Dupias 1985), of which about 5% are endemic to the Pyrenees or the Pre-Pyrenees. The steep slopes and the peaks above the tree-line harbour the greatest proportion of endemic taxa, mostly chasmophytes and scree species. They total about 200 species belonging to 90 genera and 34 families, of which the Compositae, Scrophulariaceae, Caryophyllaceae, Gramineae, Cruciferae and Saxifragaceae are prominent (Villar and Garcia 1989).

There are two endemic genera, relicts of subtropical affinity (Braun-Blanquet 1958), *Borderea pyrenaica* and *B. chouardii* (Dioscoreaceae) from the central Pyrenees, and the monotypic *Xatardia scabra* (Umbelliferae) from the eastern Pyrenees. Another genus, *Petrocoptis* (Caryophyllaceae), is more or less endemic, given that 6 of its 9 recognised taxa are restricted to the central Pyrenees, with 3 more found in the Cordillera Cantabrica or Iberian Mountains.

The western Pyrenees have many calcicolous endemics, including *Thalictrum macrocarpum*, *Androsace hirtella* and *Saxifraga hariotii*. This sector shares endemics with the Cordillera Cantabrica, for example *Euphorbia chamaebuxus* and *Rumex aquitanicus*. In the eastern Pyrenees, the siliceous soils have many endemics, exemplified by *Senecio leucophyllus* (Compositae). The genus *Ramonda* (Gesneriaceae), which has one species (*R. myconae*) exclusive to the Pyrenees and adjacent north-east Spain, and two species in the Balkans, should also be noted.

Amongst the other phytogeographical elements, the central European is better represented than the Mediterranean. For example, in the Ribes Valley, in the province of Gerona (Spain), from a total of 1428 species more than 50% are Euro-Siberian and Boreal, whilst barely 20% are characteristically Mediterranean; a further 20% are from more than one region and the rest are orophytes and diverse groups.

The Pyrenees represent the last great alpine range in south-western Europe. As a result, many European mountain taxa reach their westernmost limit of distribution. Examples include edelweiss (*Leontopodium alpinum*), alpenrose (*Rhododendron ferrugineum*) and silver fir (*Abies alba*). In addition, many Mediterranean or Iberian taxa reach their northernmost limit in the Pyrenees (e.g. *Silene mellifera*, *Ononis aragonensis* and *Pinus nigra* subsp. *salzmanni*).

## Useful plants

Some 300 species of trees and shrubs occur in the Pyrenees; of these, about 20 are used for timber (Sese 1992). Of note are Scots pine, beech, silver fir and introduced poplar (*Populus*) hybrids. In addition, another 70 woody species have varying uses (e.g. for making brooms, poles and baskets, and hurdles for animals). Charcoal used to be made from holm oak (*Quercus ilex* subsp. *rotundifolia*).

About 600 indigenous species have medicinal uses, of which about 300 are used as home remedies (Villar *et al.* 1992); some are also used as poisons, in perfumery, and as foods. Honey production, a local tradition, has been in decline during the last few decades.

Various Pyrenean species have ornamental value, such as mountain ash (*Sorbus aucuparia*), yew (*Taxus baccata*) and box (*Buxus sempervirens*). Many types of fodder plants (e.g. species of *Fraxinus, Onobrychis, Medicago, Vicia, Dactylis, Arrhenatherum, Festuca*) provide forage or pasture in the Pyrenees, although many pastures are now being abandoned.

There are many species of fruit trees (e.g. *Pyrus, Malus*); however, their use is also declining. Nevertheless, these species are an important potential genetic resource.

## Social and environmental values

Due to the climate, geology, biogeography and social history of the region, the Pyrenees harbour one of the most varied landscapes and natural environments in Western Europe. They are the highest mountains of the Iberian Peninsula. In some of the valleys, traditional lifestyles have maintained a balance between exploitation and conservation until very recently.

The forests are relatively well conserved. Together with the pastures, they serve to protect slopes from erosion, ensure reasonably pure water and preserve a very varied fauna. The latter includes brown bear and bearded vulture. Another important community is the fauna of the karstic massifs.

The main attraction of the Pyrenees is the open and diverse natural landscape, which is sparsely populated and increasingly becoming better linked to the surrounding towns.

## Economic assessment

The Pyrenean economy was traditionally based on cattle raising and forestry. However, socio-economic changes have brought about rural depopulation and a decline in these economic activities. Many dams have been built for hydroelectricity, or as water reserves for low-lying zones.

In the last 20 years, widespread seasonal tourism has become established, with the growth of second homes, ski resorts, mountaineering and walking activities, health resorts, hunting and fishing. Future prospects indicate that the resident population will not increase, and will continue to provide service industries (catering, leisure) and non-polluting quality products, such as organic agricultural produce, wood and crafts.

The region will become increasingly important as a source of water and energy for the urbanised foothills and lowlands. An increasing amount of both state and international funds will be needed to protect the environment.

## Threats

Faced with rural depopulation, the ecological fragility of some Pyrenean landscapes is becoming apparent, although others are returning to a wild state. Although society's attitude towards nature conservation is becoming more responsible, huge problems remain. The main risks for the survival of biodiversity in the Pyrenees are:

1. Soil erosion. This is aggravated by the continental climate of the central Pyrenees and torrential rain, deforested hillsides, significant overgrazing, road building and other developments at all altitudes, and the abandonment of traditional land management.

2. Mass tourism. Residential settlements and sports developments are increasingly affecting the purity of water, and leading to disturbance of the fauna and trampling of the vegetation.

3. Catastrophic fires. These are particularly damaging in dry years. Their origins are both natural and man-made.

Despite these threats, many areas still harbour a rich flora; few species are threatened and almost none have become extinct. There are certain exceptions, such as some of the lower and humid regions. For example, some plant populations have become seriously reduced in the Adour Basin (France), and in some river gorges, such as the Guara Canyons (Spain).

Acid rain affects very few forests, apart from some local areas in the central Pyrenees in France, and in Catalonia.

## Conservation

There are more than 50 protected areas in the region. They are becoming more and more valued as centres of socio-economic regeneration and for education.

The existing network includes 3 National Parks (Ordesa and Aigües Tortes in Spain, and the Western Pyrenees in France), 7 Nature Parks, and many reserves (including Hunting Reserves, Nature Reserves and Biosphere Reserves). Some of these areas fulfil more one than function. In both France and Spain new conservation proposals are currently being drawn up.

There were many fires in 1991 as a result of successive dry years. In Aragón (Spain) in 1992, the lighting of fires in the mountains was prohibited and the use of forest and country paths was restricted. Such controls were already in operation in France. A limit on the number of visitors is being considered in defined areas, such as the National Park of Ordesa and Monte Perdido, which annually welcomes about 600,000 visitors.

# References

Balcells, E. and Gil, E. (1992). Consideraciones fenológicas de las biocenosis de altitud en el Parque Nacional de Ordesa y Monte Perdido, acompañadas y apoyadas mediante estudio preliminar de los datos meteorológicos obtenidos, desde 1981 a 1989, en el observatorio de Góriz. *Lucas Mallada* 4: 71–160.

Bolòs, O. de (1987). Cataluña y la Depresión del Ebro. In Peinado, M. and Rivas-Martínez, S. (eds), *La vegetación de España*. Universidad de Alcalá de Henares. Pp. 309–347.

Braun-Blanquet, J. (1958). Les souches préglaciaires de la flore pyrénéenne. *Collectanea Botanica (Barcelona)* 2(1): 1–23.

Dendaletche, C. (1982). *Guía de los Pirineos. Elementos de Biología, geología y ecología*. Ed. Omega, Barcelona.

Dupias, G. (1985). Végétation des Pyrénées. C.N.R.S., Toulouse.

Gruber, M. (1992). Schéma des séries dynamiques de végétation des Hautes-Pyrénées (Pyrénées centrales françaises). *Botanica Complutensis* 17: 7–21.

Izard, M. (1988). Sur la continentalité dans les Pyrénées et son impact sur la végétation. In Homenaje a Pedro Montserrat, *Monografías del Instituto Pirenaico de Ecología* 4: 597–602.

Jalut, G. (1988). Les principales étapes de l'histoire de la forêt pyrénéenne française depuis 15000 ans. In Homenaje a Pedro Montserrat, *Monografias del Instituto Pirenaico de Ecología* 4: 609–615.

Montserrat, P. (1974). L'exploration floristique des Pyrénées occidentales. *Bol. Soc. Brot. 47(2a ser.) suppl.*: 227–240.

Rivas Martínez, S. (1990). Los pisos subalpino y alpino en los Pirineos y Cordillera Cantábrica. In Botánica pirenaico-cantábrica. *Monografías del Instituto Pirenaico de Ecología* 5: 577–595.

Saule, M. (1991). *La grande flore illustrée des Pyrénées*. Ed. Milan, Toulouse.

Sese, J.A. (1992). *Arboles, arbustos y algunas matas de Aragón*. Gobierno de Aragón, Zaragoza.

Vigo, J. (1983). El poblament vegetal de la Vall de Ribes. *Acta. Bot. Barcinonensia* 35.

Vigo, J. and Ninot, J.M. (1987). Los Pirineos. In Peinado, M. and Rivas-Martínez, S. (eds), *La vegetación de España*. Universidad de Alcalá de Henares. Pp. 349–384.

Villar, L. and Garcia, B. (1989). Vers une banque de données des plantes vasculaires endémiques des Pyrénées. *Acta biol. montana* 9: 261–274.

Villar, L., Palacin, J.M., Calvo, C., Gomez, D. and Montserrat, G. (1992). *Plantas medicinales del Pirineo Aragonés y demás tierras oscenses*. CSIC y Diputación de Huesca. Jaca y Huesca.

# Acknowledgements

This Data Sheet was written by Dr Luis Villar ( Jaca, Spain) and Professor Claude Dendaletche.

# ALPS
# Austria, France, Germany, Italy, Liechtenstein, Slovenia, Switzerland

**Location:** The highest mountain range in central Europe, within a rectangle of 500 × 900 km from Nice to Vienna, between latitudes 44°00'–48°00'N and longitudes 5°00'–16°00'E.

**Area:** 200,000 km².

**Altitude:** 100–4800 m.

**Vegetation:** Broadleaved and conifer forests, marshes, dwarf shrub communities and moorland, alpine grasslands, moraine, scree and rock communities; arable land, meadows and pasture.

**Flora:** c. 5500 species of vascular plants, of which 7% are endemic. Floristic affinities with other mountains of Europe, also Asia and Arctic region. About a third of the species can be classed as Extinct, Endangered, Vulnerable or Rare.

**Useful plants:** c. 10–20% of the flora is traditionally used for timber, crafts, food and medicine; local knowledge of plant uses disappearing; modern commercial methods of harvesting damaging some species.

**Other values:** Wide variety of landscapes; enormous potential for educational tourism, significant forestry resources; largest freshwater reserves in central Europe.

**Threats:** Mass tourism, ski resorts, construction of communication links, hydroelectric dams, decline in traditional agriculture. Global warming and damage from acid rainfall or high ozone levels may also threaten the high-altitude environment.

**Conservation:** 9 National Parks, many Nature Reserves. Regional and national legislation, which will be harmonised within the Alpine Treaty. International Commission for the Protection of the Alps.

## Geography

Situated in the heart of Europe from Nice to Vienna, the Alpine chain, 1200 km in length, falls within a rectangle of 500 × 900 km. The Alps lie between latitudes 44°00'–48°00'N and longitudes 5°00'–16°00'E and have a surface area of nearly 200,000 km². A detailed analysis of the Alps in relation to other European mountain ranges is given in Ozenda (1985). The Alps extend across seven countries: Italy (32% of their area), Austria (30%), France (18%), Switzerland and Liechtenstein (13%), Germany (4%) and Slovenia (4%).

From the Alpes-Maritimes on the Mediterranean coast to Mont Blanc, the altitude ranges from sea-level to 4807 m, with large areas above the tree-line (2000 m). The Alps contribute to four major river basins: the Rhône, which drains into the Western Mediterranean, the Po, which drains into the Adriatic, the Rhine, draining into the North Sea, and the Danube, draining into the Black Sea. From a geological point of view, an obvious assymetry exists between the western and eastern Alps. To the east, the intra-alpine axis consists largely of crystalline rocks, whereas the northern and southern Pre-Alps are sedimentary. However, to the west, the intra-alpine axis is mainly sedimentary, separated from the French sedimentary Pre-Alps by the crystalline Belledonne chain, the Pre-Alps of the Italian foothills being themselves crystalline. The principal soil types are brown soils, podzols, rankers and rendzinas.

The Alps have a mainly temperate climate. The north-western part is influenced by an Atlantic maritime climate, the south by the proximity of the Mediterranean Sea, while the north-east has a continental climate. The contrast between the climate of the pre-alpine belt and the continental climate of the inter-alpine valleys is an important factor to be noted. Precipitation can range from just under 600 mm annually to more than 2000 mm. Ozenda (1985) uses topography, geology and climate to support his argument that the alpine chain should be divided up into two main phytogeographical zones, the pre-alpine zone and the intra-alpine axis.

## Vegetation

In the central Alps, the following zones can be distinguished (Landolt and Aeschimann 1986):

### Colline Zone

Maximum altitude: 700–900 m. Average annual temperature: 8–12°C; growing period at least 250 days. Principal plant formations: hornbeam and oak woodland (*Quercus robur, Q. petraea, Carpinus betulus*), pubescent oak woodland (*Quercus pubescens*), Scots pine forests (*Pinus sylvestris*), hop-hornbeam woodland (*Ostrya carpinifolia*), sweet chestnut woodland (*Castanea sativa*), meadows (steppe-like in the intra-alpine valleys) and cultivated areas.

In the colline zone of the Maritime Alps, two other zones occur (Ozenda 1981): a mesomediterranean zone of holm oak (*Quercus ilex* subsp. *ilex*) and, on the coast, a thermomediterranean zone of carob (*Ceratonia siliqua*).

### Montane Zone

Maximum altitude: 1300–1600 m. Average annual temperature: 4–8°C; growing period at least 200 days.

Principal plant formations: beech woodland (*Fagus sylvatica*) with sycamore (*Acer pseudoplatanus*), silver fir (*Abies alba*) and Scots pine forests (*Pinus sylvestris*), peat bogs, meadows, pastures and cultivated areas.

## Sub-alpine Zone

Maximum altitude: 1800–2400 m. Average annual temperature: 0–4°C; growing period at least 100 days. Principal plant formations: forests of Norway spruce (*Picea abies*) with ericaceous subshrubs (*Vaccinium* spp.), pines (*Pinus uncinata*, *P. sylvestris*), larch (*Larix decidua*) and arolla pine (*Pinus cembra*), rhododendron heaths (*Rhododendron ferrugineum*), green alder (*Alnus viridis*) and dwarf mountain pine (*Pinus mugo*) scrub, tall-herb communities (e.g. *Adenostyles alliariae*, *Cicerbita alpina*), meadows and pastures.

## Alpine Zone

Maximum altitude: 2700–3100 m. Average annual temperature: >0°C; growing period >100 days. Principal plant formations: juniper (*Juniperus communis* subsp. *alpina*) scrub and dwarf ericaceous subshrubs (*Calluna vulgaris*, *Vaccinium* spp., *Empetrum nigrum* subsp. *hermaphroditum*, *Loiseleuria procumbens*), acid grasslands (*Carex curvula*, *Festuca varia*, *Nardus stricta*), neutral grasslands (*Sesleria coerulea*, *Carex sempervirens*, *Festuca violacea*, *Carex ferruginea*, *Carex firma*), snow-hollows on acid soils (with *Salix herbacea*, *Alchemilla pentaphyllea*, *Sibbaldia procumbens*), snow-hollows on calcareous soils (with *Salix reticulata*, *S. retusa*, *Arabis caerulea*), acid scree communities (*Androsace alpina*, *Oxyria digyna*), calcareous scree communities (*Draba hoppeanea*, *Thlaspi repens*, *Leontodon montanus*), acid rock communities (*Androsace vandelli*) and calcareous rock communities (*Androsace helvetica*).

## Nival Zone

Permanent snow-fields at 2700–3100 m; patchy vegetation in locally sheltered areas (e.g. *Ranunculus glacialis*, *Saxifraga biflora*, *Eritrichium nanum*).

## Flora

The Alps have a flora of between 2000–3000 vascular plant species. Ozenda (1985) estimates that the whole chain includes about 5500 species of vascular plants, approximately 43% of the European flora. However, there has been no comprehensive study of the flora throughout the whole Alpine chain (Aeschimann, Küpfer and Spichiger, in press) which would confirm this figure.

According to Pawlowski (1970), about 350 species of vascular plants are endemic to the Alps (c. 3% of Europe's flora and c. 7% of the Alpine flora). No single family is endemic to the Alpine chain, but there are four monotypic genera: *Rhizobotrya alpina* (Cruciferae) and *Physoplexis comosa* (Campanulaceae) in the Dolomites, *Hladnikia pastinacifolia* (Umbelliferae) in Slovenia, and *Berardia subacaulis* (Compositae) in southern French Alps. Genera that are rich in endemics include *Saxifraga*, *Primula*, *Gentiana*, *Campanula* and *Salix*.

Pan-alpine endemic species include *Viola pinnata*, *Saxifraga muscoides*, *S. seguieri*, *S. biflora*, *Daphne striata*, *Androsace alpina*, *Eritrichium nanum*, *Cirsium spinosissimum* and *Artemisia atrata*.

Species endemic to the western Alps include *Saponaria lutea*, *Brassica repanda*, *Coincya richeri*, *Saxifraga diapensioides*, *Viola cenisia*, *Veronica allioni*, *Campanula alpestris*, *Berardia subacaulis* and *Artemisia glacialis*.

Species endemic to the eastern Alps include *Dianthus alpinus*, *Silene elisabethae*, *Rhodothamnus chamaecistus*, *Primula clusiana*, *Pedicularis aspleniifolia*, *Paederota bonarota*, *Carex baldensis*, *Valeriana supina*, *Achillea atrata* and *Achillea oxyloba*.

Three major centres of endemism can be noted: the Maritime Alps, the south-eastern Alps and, to a lesser extent, the north-eastern Alps. Many endemic species occur on extensive moraines produced by Quaternary glaciation. The origin of the distribution patterns of endemic species is often problematical.

Only a few species survive from the Tertiary, amongst them *Juniperus thurifera*, *Berardia subacaulis* and *Wulfenia carinthia*. At the end of the Tertiary the average annual temperature in central Europe was close to that of today, and some temperate species migrated towards central and southern Europe, replacing the ancient subtropical flora. Later, during the height of the Alpine orogeny, certain species facies developed, leading to the evolution of many of the species of the mountains of central and southern Europe that occur there today. During the Quaternary, the glaciers brought about the almost complete destruction of thermophilous elements, the suppression of many species in the periglacial areas and nunataks, and increased floristic exchanges with other mountains and regions, particularly the Arctic. Therefore, according to partial statistics compiled by Jerosch (1903), of 420 species found above 1500 m in the Swiss Alps, it is estimated that a little over 50% are either Alpine or from the mountains of central and southern Europe, whilst more than 40% are Arctic-Alpine or Altaic-Alpine. However, in the absence of complete floristic data for the whole Alpine chain, it is not possible to give exact figures for the affinities of the whole flora of the Alps.

Given the great range of the Alpine chain and its diversity – geographical, ecological, floristic, cultural, and political – it is difficult to draw up a comparable table of rare and endangered species. Degrees of risk vary considerably from one country to the next, even between two adjacent regions, and legislation is heterogeneous. In the Swiss Alps, the percentage of Extinct, Threatened, Vulnerable and Rare species varies between sectors by between 31% and 42%, with a mean of 37% (Landolt 1991). The breakdown for this average figure is: Extinct or disappearing (5.4%); Threatened (13%); Vulnerable (8.6%); and Rare (9.8%). However, most of these species are not endemic to the Alps. It is fair to assume that these figures are comparable for all of the Alps. The compilation of a single list of rare or threatened species for the Alps is the subject of an international floristic project initiated in 1992 (Aeschimann, Küpfer and Spichiger, in press).

## Useful plants

There is a long tradition of human use of the Alpine flora (Lieutaghi 1991). This cultural heritage is still very much alive in isolated regions, whilst it has practically disappeared where there is significant tourist and economic development. In certain regions, notably the southern Alps, Piedmont, the Aoste valley, Valais, central Switzerland, the Grisons, the Austrian Tauern, and Slovenia, rural culture has been relatively less affected by the socio-economic changes of the last 20 years. Here, a wide range of plants are still harvested for a range of products.

Medicinal species, such as masterwort (*Peucedanum ostruthium*) and monks' rhubarb (*Rumex alpinus*) often grow in the vegetable gardens of mountain villages. Docks (*Rumex* spp.), *Urtica dioica, Chenopodium bonus-henricus*, plants that have benefitted from the spread of cultivated areas and pastures, are used in medicines and as wild vegetables. A variety of plants have been used by country people for soups, salads, dyes, bedding and fodder. Often, people would rely on wild vegetables in times of hardship such as war, famine and during cattle disease epidemics. About 10–20% of the flora is, or has been utilized, depending on the area.

During the last 50 years, some species have been commercially exploited. This endangers certain species such as *Artemisia genipi* and *A. glacialis*, and sundews (*Drosera* spp.). This tendency has been partially compensated for by cultivation, e.g. of *Artemisia glacialis*, to respond to the demands of industry. Other species are threatened because of their decorative and/or horticultural value, such as *Lilium martagon, L. bulbiferum, Eryngium alpinum, Androsace* spp. and *Leontopodium alpinum*.

The use of timber, such as that of arolla pine (*Pinus cembra*) and larch (*Larix decidua*) is widespread, but rarely on an intensive scale. The gathering of wild fruits (e.g. *Rubus idaeus, Vaccinium* spp.) is a long-standing tradition; the gathering of mushrooms is more recent. Herbal plants ("teas from the Alps") and medicinal plants, such as *Arnica montana* and *Gentiana lutea* are still regularly used by elderly people. Throughout the Alps, there is a big industry producing liqueurs or eaux-de-vie (Chabert 1895), based on wild plants (e.g. chartreuses, génépis, Krauter and gentiane).

## Social and environmental values

There are five, very different, Alpine cultures: German, Italian, French, Slovene and Rhaeto-Romansh. Over thousands of years, these cultures have served to accentuate the diversity and quality of the landscape which now supports a growing tourist industry.

In the Alps, about half of the forests play a role in protecting against the natural risks of landslides and avalanches. Of the land with agricultural potential, three-quarters is pasture. There is a need to redress the balance between forest and pasture, whilst ensuring that mountain agriculture continues (its abandonment generally brings about erosion and avalanches).

Finally, the alpine chain harbours the largest reserves of fresh water in central Europe.

## Economic assessment

Until the middle of the 19th century, the alpine economy was noted for rural over-population and economic independence. Around the end of the 19th century and the beginning of the 20th century, a fragile balance was achieved, but now, at the end of the 20th century, this has been rapidly destroyed by a growing disparity between the mountains and the plains. Between 1950 and 1970, there was substantial loss of agricultural land: according to Ozenda (1985), 30% in France, 25% in Bavaria, 20% in Italy and 15% in Austria. Only in Switzerland has the position remained relatively stable. In the upper valley of the Durance (France), the amount of cultivated land has decreased from 25% to 1% within a century.

On average, over the whole Alpine chain, the amount of forest cover is about 30%. Many forests, for example larch, have developed as succession from scrub. On the plains and certain inner valleys, intensive agriculture is being developed. There has also been an increase in the polluting electro-chemical industry (e.g. Valais and Maurienne), as a result of the vast hydroelectric resources. However, considerable progress has been made over the last 20 years in waste filtering techniques.

Since the 1950s, mass tourism, especially during the winter season, has been growing. This makes a major contribution to the economy of the Alpine nations.

Several roads and railways follow natural and ancient routes through the Alps to link southern and northern Europe.

## Threats

The Alps are one of the last great natural wildernesses of central Europe. Largely spared until now (especially in the alpine and subalpine zones), their ecosystems have, over the last 30 years, been subject to growing pressures from industrial growth, mass tourism (notably during the winter season, e.g. construction of ski slopes), growth of settlements, transalpine communication links, hydroelectric exploitation, and the alteration of water courses. A significant change in agroforestry systems is also occurring, a change which is accelerating as a result of European integration and growing economic liberalism. There is a marked decline in traditional agriculture in all of the most isolated and unprofitable regions, and intensive methods of land management. In the lowlands, for example, there is an increase in the use of herbicides, while in the montane and subalpine zones considerable areas have been replanted with forests which are relatively poor in species.

There is extensive tree damage in parts of the Alps as a result of air pollution (acid rainfall and/or high ozone levels).

There is the possibility of global climatic warming which could reduce the extent of the Alpine zone and its constituent species (Ozenda and Borel 1991). Results of the "Man and Biosphere" project recently carried out in the upper mountain zones (MAB 6), demonstrate a loss of the ancient balance between people and the natural environment (Brugger and Messerli 1984; Messerli 1989), with two main consequences:

1. Reduction in biodiversity (in certain regions of 30–70%), as a result of the disappearance of traditional land management.

2. A serious increase in natural disasters, particularly avalanches and erosion, in vast areas of abandoned agricultural land.

As a result of this, a qualitative change in methods of exploiting the environment becomes a matter of urgency (Messerli 1989), and a new balance between nature, agriculture and tourism must be sought.

## Conservation

In addition to several Regional Parks and Nature Reserves, there are many National Parks (with other areas currently being evaluated). Existing protected areas are:

Austria:       Hohe Tauern (250 km²)
France:        Ecrins (918 km²), Mercantour (685 km²), Vanoise (528 km²)
Germany:       Berchtesgaden (208 km²)
Italy:         Grand Paradiso (700 km²), Stelvio (1346 km²)
Slovenia:      Triglav (848 km²)
Switzerland:   Basse-Engadine.

Berchtesgaden and Hohe Tauern are in the IUCN Management Category: V (Protected Landscape), the remainder are in IUCN Management Category: II (National Park).

For several decades, legislation has been in operation in different regions of the Alps. Harmonisation is now necessary, particularly with regard to the protection of individual species. The Alpine Treaty signed on 7 November 1991 by several Alpine states, opens the way for such harmonisation. The Treaty's protocol on the protection of nature and maintenance of the countryside is currently being drawn up. Article 13, notably, anticipates that:

1. Contracted parties will agree to take appropriate measures to conserve their indigenous flora and fauna, genetic diversity and sufficient populations, ensuring in particular, that there are enough habitats for them.

2. They will pay particular attention to threatened indigenous species in the alpine region and their habitats.

The measures agreed to in the different regions of the Alps and the signing of the Alpine Treaty, are encouraging. However, enforcement of the Treaty's protocals is needed. National organisations for the protection of nature in the seven Alpine states have been re-organised into one main organisation, CIPRA (International Commission for the Protection of the Alps). It is essential to provide researchers with a quantitative and qualitative analysis of Alpine plant biodiversity; this information should also be standardised (Aeschimann, Küpfer and Spichiger, in press). These studies must provide a range of tools that can be of use to a range of experts and decision makers in the fields of environmental management and legislation.

From an economic viewpoint, the free market requires a large reduction in subsidies to mountain agriculture. To avoid the threats caused when valleys are abandoned, agricultural subsidies will have to be converted into compensation schemes on ecological grounds over the next 20 years, with Alpine farmers becoming "gardeners of the mountain countryside". Ethnobotany should play an important role in defining conservation aims for the various regions, taking into account cultural differences and encouraging active participation of the local inhabitants.

The Alpine chain has been influenced by humans for thousands of years (there are no more than 20 hectares of virgin forest in Switzerland). Despite this, it has only taken two generations to reverse this fragile balance. The protection of the environment in the Alps implies both an understanding of the environment and the close relationship between man and the plant kingdom.

## References

Aeschimann, D. (1985). Etude biosystématique du *Silene vulgaris* s.l. (Caryophyllaceae) dans le domaine alpin. Essai d'interprétation évolutif et propositions taxonomiques. *Candollea* 40: 67–98.

Aeschimann, D. and Burdet, H. (1989). *Flore de la Suisse et des territoires limitrophes. Le nouveau binz.* Griffon, Neuchâtel. liv, 597 pp.

Aeschimann, D., Küpfer, Ph. and Spichiger, R. (in press). Projet pour une Flore des Alpes. In Küpfer, Ph. and Galland, P. (eds), *Actes Congr. Int. Ecol. Biogéogr. Alpines.* La Thuile, 2–6 septembre 1990.

Brugger, E.A. and Messerli, P. (eds) (1984). *Umbruch im Berggebiet.* Haupt, Bern.

Chabert, A. (1895). De l'emploi populaire des plantes sauvages en Savoie. *Bull. Herb. Boissier* 3: 291–343.

Chabert, A. (1897). Noms patois et emploi populaire des plantes de la Savoie. *Bull. Herb. Boissier* 5: 568–578.

Correvon, H. (1923). *Plantes et santé.* 2nd Ed. Delachaux and Niestlé, Neuchâtel.

Dupont, P. (1990). *Atlas partiel de la Flore de France.* Secrétariat de la Faune et de la Flore, Muséum National d'Histoire Naturelle, Paris. 442 pp.

Fenaroli, L. (1971). *Flora delle alpi.* 2nd Ed. Martello, Milan. 429 pp.

Guichonnet, P. et al. (1980). *Histoire et civilisations des Alpes,* 2 vols. Privat and Payot, Toulouse.

Hegi, G. (1906- ). *Illustrierte Flora von Mitteleuropa.* 13 vols.

Jenny-Lips, H. (1948). *Vegetation der Schweizer Alpen.* Büchergilde Gutenberg, Zurich. 240 pp.

Jerosch, M. (1903). *Geschichte und Herkunft der schweizerischen Alpenflora.* Engelmann, Leipzig. 253 pp.

Landolt, E. and Aeschimann, D. (1986). *Notre flore alpine.* 3rd Ed. CAS, Bern. 333 pp.

Landolt, E. (1991). *Plantes vasculaires menacées en Suisse: listes rouges nationale et régionales.* OFEFP, Berne. 183 pp.

Lieutaghi, P. (1986). *L'herbe qui renouvelle: une aspect de la médecine traditionnelle en Haute Provence.* La Maison des Sciences, Paris.

Lieutaghi, P. (1991). La plante compagne, pratique et imaginaire de la flore sauvage en Europe occidentale. *Sér. Doc. Conserv. Jard. Bot. Genève* 28: 220 pp.

Meilleur, B.A. (1985). Gens de montagne, plantes et saisons. Savoirs écologiques de traditions à Termignon (Savoie). *Le monde alpin et rhodanien* 1: 10–78.

Merxmüller, H. (1952). *Untersuchungen zur Sippengliederung und Arealbildung in den Alpen.* München (Ver. Schutze Alpenpflanzen und -Tiere). 105 pp.

Messerli, P. (1989). *Mensch und Natur im alpinen Lebensraum. Risiken, Chancen, Perspektiven. Zentrale Erkenntnisse aus dem schweizerischen MAB-Programm, XII.* Haupt, Bern. 368 pp.

Nicollier, F. and Nicollier, G. (1984). Les plantes dans la vie quotidienne à Bagnes: noms patois et utilisations quotidiennes. *Bull. Murith. Soc. Valais. Sci. Nat.* 102: 129–158.

Ozenda, P. (1981). *Végétation des Alpes sud-occidentales.* CNRS, Paris. 258 pp.

Ozenda, P. (1985). *La végétation de la chaîne alpine dans l'espace montagnard européen.* Masson, Paris. 331 pp.

Ozenda, P. and Borel, J.-L. (1991). *Les conséquences possibles des changements climatiques dans l'Arc alpin.* Rapport FUTURALP no. 1.

Pawlowski, B. (1970). Remarques sur l'endémisme dans la flore des Alpes et des Carpates. *Vegetatio* 21: 181–243.

Pignatti, S. (1982). *Flora d'Italia*, 3 vols. Edagricole, Bologna.

Richard, L. and Pautou, G. (1983). *Végétation des Alpes du nord et du Jura méridional.* CNRS, Paris. 315 pp.

Schaer, J.-P. et al. (1989). *Guide du naturaliste dans les Alpes.* Delachaux and Niestlé, Neuchâtel. 448 pp.

Schönfelder, P. and Bresinsky, A. (1990). *Verbreitungsatlas der Farn- und Blütenpflanzen Bayerns.* Ulmer, Stuttgart. 752 pp.

Schröter, C. (1926). *Das Pflanzenleben der Alpen.* 2nd Ed. Raustein, Zürich. 1288 pp.

Schüle, R. (1975). Les guérisseurs d'Hérémence (Valais). *Gesnerus* 32: 173–181.

Veyret, P. and Veyret, G. (1967). *Au coeur de l'Europe: les Alpes.* Flammarion, Paris. 546 pp.

Vincent, P. (1987). *Les jardins du ciel (cueillette, calendriers, potagers d'altitude).* Arthaud, Paris.

Welten, M. and Sutter, R. (1982). *Atlas de distribution des ptéridophytes et des phanérogames de la Suisse*, 2 vols. Birkhäuser, Basel.

## Acknowledgements

This Data Sheet was written by Dr David Aeschimann and Mr Didier Roguet (Conservatoire et Jardin botaniques, Geneva, Switzerland).

# BALKAN AND RHODOPE MASSIFS
## Bulgaria, Greece and Serbia

**Location:** Central part of Balkan Peninsula between latitudes 41°00'–44°40'N and longitudes 22°00'–28°00'E.

**Area:** 10,000 km².

**Altitude:** 400–2900 m.

**Vegetation:** Oak and mixed deciduous forests; pine, silver fir (*Abies alba*) and Norway spruce (*Picea abies*) forests; woodland-pasture, shiblyak and grasslands; montane and alpine rock and scree communities.

**Flora:** c. 3000 vascular plant species, with a large regional and local endemic element; several relict species with Asiatic links, arctic-alpine elements.

**Useful plants:** Herbs, medicinal plants, timber trees.

**Other values:** Potential for ecotourism.

**Threats:** War between the former constituent republics of Yugoslavia; possible fragmentation of National Parks in Bulgaria following the end of Communist rule; expanding agriculture and tourism; overgrazing and fire.

**Conservation:** Good network of National Parks but with an uncertain future in the current political climate. Important conservation areas include the Balkan Central National Park (732.6 km²), Rila Mountains National Park, Stenato National Park (39 km²), Vitocha National Park (254.9 km², including 97 km² as a Biosphere Reserve). A number of smaller Reserves in Bulgaria are also designated as Biosphere Reserves: Boatine (12.8 km²), Djendema (17.8 km²), Doupkata (12.1 km²).

## Geography

The Balkan and Rhodope Massifs are part of the complex of mountain ranges that dominate the Balkan Peninsula, the most mountainous part of Europe outside the Alps. They lie in the central part of the peninsula, between latitudes 41°00'–44°40'N and longitudes 22°00'–28°00'E.

The mountains were formed mostly during the Alpine orogeny between 100 and 50 million years ago, although locally there are regions of more ancient crystalline rocks. The Balkan region exhibits great crustal instability, reflected in a very dissected topography, major faulting of rock strata, seismic activity and some relictual vulcanism; the mountain chains run predominantly north-west to south-east.

The Balkan Mountains (or Stara Planina) are the main mountain massif of eastern Serbia and Bulgaria. Topographically and geologically the mountains represent a southern extension of the Carpathians (CPD Site Eu20), which extend northwards from the Danube basin which separates them from the Balkan Mountains.

The rocks are mostly Cretaceous limestones, with some igneous and metamorphic rocks in the west and centre. The summits are rounded and there are few peaks above 2000 m. To the north and east are extensive limestone foothills (up to 700 m), which reach the Black Sea coast at Cape Emine north of Varna.

The Rhodope Massif is of more ancient geological origin, with extensive formations of igneous and metamorphic rocks, especially crystalline limestones. The landscape is more rugged and deeply dissected, with many mountain peaks rising to more than 2000 m (60 over 2600 m in Pirin) and up to 2900 m in the Rila and Pirin Mountains, where there is evidence of local Pleistocene glaciation. The southernmost part of the massif (the Rhodope Mountains) forms the frontier between Bulgaria and Greece. The Rhodope Mountains are more rounded with summits up to c. 2000 m, similar to that of the Stara Planina.

The Balkan and Rhodope Massifs have a mostly subcontinental climate. Annual rainfall varies from about 500 mm to 600 mm; average July temperatures are in the region of 22°C. The east-west axis of the mountains separates the Central European climatic zone to the north from the more Mediterranean climate of Thrace to the south. The climate of the mountains is mostly Central European, with a variable amount of rain falling throughout the summer months, grading southwards towards a montane Mediterranean climate with profound summer drought. Over most of the mountains, winter snowfall is heavy and snow can last until July.

## Vegetation

The vegetation of the region is described in detail by Horvat, Glava and Ellenberg (1974). The vegetation of the Balkan Mountains, especially that of the forests and grasslands, is central European in character. Valleys and sheltered slopes have forests dominated by beech (*Fagus sylvatica*) and hornbeam (*Carpinus orientalis* and *C. betulus*), replaced at lower altitudes by mixed oak forest (including *Quercus cerris*, *Q. frainetto* and *Q. polycarpa*). On more shady slopes there are local stands of oriental beech (*Fagus orientalis*) and other eastern elements, such as cherry-laurel (*Prunus laurocerasus*).

On higher ground there are heaths dominated by juniper (*Juniperus communis*) and dwarf ericaceous sub-shrubs, including the Balkan endemic *Bruckenthalia spiculifolia*. Limestone cliffs support a rich flora of Balkan and local endemics. Above 1800(–2000) m, the higher peaks have alpine and arctic-alpine floristic elements (e.g. *Dryas octopetala*).

The Rhodope Massif has a similar central European type of vegetation, with mixed deciduous forests on the slopes and coniferous forests at higher altitudes, with silver fir (*Abies alba*), Norway spruce (*Picea abies*) and Crimean pine (*Pinus nigra* subsp. *pallasiana*). There are important stands of Balkan pine (*Pinus heldreichii*), a species which is restricted to the Balkan Peninsula and a few localities in southern Italy, and Macedonian pine (*P. peuce*), an ancient relict species restricted to the central part of the Balkan Peninsula. Near and above the tree-line, there are extensive montane grassland, cliff and rock communities.

The vegetation of the lower, southern slopes of the Rhodope Massif is sub-Mediterranean, with forests of pubescent oak (*Quercus pubescens*), together with manna ash (*Fraxinus ornus*) and Mediterranean juniper (*Juniperus oxycedrus*). Forests on higher slopes include Balkan pine and Norway spruce. Spruce forest extends south across the Greek frontier, where this mostly boreal tree reaches its southernmost limit in Europe.

To the south-east of the Rhodope Mountains and eastwards from the River Evros, the Istranca Daglari, a range of mountains up to 1000 m that run into European Turkey, have a more Asiatic vegetation and flora. Several taxa reach their westernmost limit here, such as *Prunus laurocerasus*, *Rhododendron ponticum* subsp. *ponticum*, and the fern *Dryopteris caucasica*. These plants are characteristic of the Pontus region of north-eastern Turkey (see Data Sheet on North-east Anatolia – SWA19).

## Flora

It is estimated that the flora of the Balkan and Rhodope Massifs includes about 3000 vascular plant species. Some 30% of the flora of Bulgaria comprises species endemic to the Balkan Peninsula. This rich flora probably derives from the end of the Pleistocene glaciation, when the flora of much of Europe was displaced into sheltered parts of the mountains of southern Europe and was unable to recolonise northward during the post-Glacial period. The Balkan and Rhodope Massifs, as well as having a major proportion of this rich endemic flora, are a meeting place of Central European, Alpine and Mediterranean floristic elements.

Montane grasslands, of great economic importance as pastures, are dominated by central European species of grasses (e.g. *Agrostis* spp., *Festuca* spp., *Nardus stricta* and *Poa* spp.) and perennial clovers (*Trifolium* spp.). The higher mountains hold populations of arctic-alpine species, such as *Oxyria digyna*, *Primula farinosa* and *Salix herbacea*.

The endemic element, both regional (Balkan) and local, is particularly important. The Rhodope Massif has at least 50 endemic species in all, included in a wide range of families and genera. Their major populations are restricted in Bulgaria, but many extend just into northern Greece (e.g. *Lathraea rhodopaea* and *Scabiosa rhodopaea*). A characteristic and widespread endemic of these mountains is *Haberlea rhodopensis* (Gesneriaceae), a Tertiary relic belonging to a mostly tropical family. It extends southwards just into northern Greece. In the same family, *Ramonda*

*serbica* is endemic to the western Balkan Mountains, Albania and the adjacent region. Two endemic species of *Primula*, *P. deorum*, from wet grassland in the Rila, and *P. frondosa*, from shady cliffs in the central Stara Planina, are also thought to be Tertiary relics. These species are prized by horticulturists, as are other local endemics, such as *Arabis ferdinandi-cobergi* (especially a variegated variant), from the Pirin.

Pirin shares some endemics with the important limestone flora of Mount Olympus (CPD Site Eu15), 250 km to the south (e.g. *Brassica nivalis*, of which subsp. *jordanoffii* occurs in Pirin, and *Poa pirinica*; another species, the curious shrubby violet *Viola delphinantha*, occurs on Pirin and Olympus, a few other limestone mountains and on Mount Chelmos in southern Greece – see Data Sheet on the Mountains of Southern and Central Greece, CPD Site Eu16).

In the eastern Balkan Mountains, there is an outlying population of the well-known Balkan endemic tree, the horse-chestnut (*Aesculus hippocastanum*), a Tertiary relic with relatives in North America and East Asia, widely planted in Europe as an ornamental.

## Useful plants

The people of the Balkan and Rhodope Mountains still exploit their native flora for timber, food and pharmaceutical products, as well as for amenity and ornament. As well as the collection of brushwood, culinary herbs, salads and fruits, there are a number of local industries based on plant products. Much material is collected for tisanes, for example members of the mint family (Labiatae), such as *Sideritis scardica* and *Stachys iva*.

As noted above, many of the endemics have horticultural value, and many more have potential in horticulture. *Brassica nivalis* subsp. *jordanoffii* belongs within a major genus of crop plants and might have potential in future breeding programmes.

## Social and environmental values

The mountains of the Balkan Peninsula are one of the last areas in Europe with extensive woodland-pasture (Pallas 1939; Rackham 1986). This system of management, widespread in Europe since at least Mesolithic times, involves (in part) the pollarding of young trees, mostly of oak, hornbeam and beech, the young growths of which are then fed to stock. It is an appropriate use of sustainable resources in a wooded region although, at present, overgrazing damages both trees and pastures, with consequent environmental degradation. The dense shiblyak that covers vast areas of the hills and lower mountain slopes derives partly from this management regime.

Locally, large forests have survived, mostly of coniferous trees. These forests provide timber and protect hillsides from excessive evaporation and run-off. Forest products, such as bark for tanning and brushwood for charcoal, are still valued. The forests themselves are increasingly serving as places of recreation and support surviving populations of large mammals, notably bears, wolves and wild pigs. Hunting is a traditional activity, but requires careful management and strict controls.

The mountainous areas are important for recreation and tourism, which is one of the major industries of Bulgaria. The National Park of Vitocha, for example, just to the south of Sofia, combines nature conservation with a major skiing and outdoor recreation centre.

## Threats

As over much of southern Europe and the Aegean region (see, for example, the Data Sheets for the Baetic and Sub-Baetic Mountains of Spain, and that for Crete, CPD Sites Eu4 and Eu17, respectively), overgrazing is damaging large tracts of grassland, scrub and alpine vegetation.

Increasing pressure of tourism, especially as Bulgaria expands its economy in the post-Communist era, is likely to impinge on the National Parks that are managed both for conservation of biodiversity and for recreation facilities.

A scheme to divert water from the River Mesta threatens the hydrobiological balance of the Pirin region.

A general problem for protected areas in Bulgaria and other former Communist nations is that there is some uncertainty about their future as land may be claimed by those from which it was originally appropriated. Economic problems associated with the change to a market economy may divert resources away from protected areas.

## Conservation

Bulgaria has established several important National Parks and other protected areas in the mountains. The most important of these, mostly in the Rhodope Massif, are the Rila National Park, which includes a representative sample of forests and mountain habitats, Stenato National Park (39 km²), which includes some major forests and karstic landscapes, and Vitocha National Park (254.9 km², including 97 km² as a Biosphere Reserve), which has mixed forests and a range of mountain habitats.

In the Balkan Mountains, the Balkan Central National Park covers 732.6 km². A number of smaller Reserves are also designated as Biosphere Reserves, namely: Boatine (12.8 km²), Djendema (17.8 km²) and Doupkata (12.1 km²).

The forests are managed on a sustainable basis by the Ministry of Forestry, which has set aside particular areas, such as the "Red Wall" near Plovdiv (Polunin 1980), famous for its endemic flora. Although the network of protected areas is good, there is uncertainty with regard to its future in the current political climate.

## References

Horvat, I., Glava, C.V. and Ellenberg, H. (1974). *Vegetation Sudosteuropas.* Gustav Fischer, Stuttgart.

Jordanov, D. (ed.) (1975). *Problems of Balkan flora and vegetation.* Bulgarian Academy of Sciences, Sofia. 441 pp.

Pallas, M. (1939). *The general aspects of the vegetation of Europe.* Taylor and Francis, London.

Polunin, O. (1980). *Wild flowers of Greece and the Balkans.* Oxford University Press, Oxford.

Rackham, O. (1986). *The history of the countryside.* Dent, London. 445 pp.

## Acknowledgements

This Data Sheet was prepared by Dr John R. Akeroyd.

# MOUNTAINS OF SOUTHERN AND CENTRAL GREECE
## Greece

**Location:** Peloponnese and central Greece, between latitudes 36°20'–39°00'N.

**Area:** 18,000 km².

**Altitude:** Reaching 2495 m at the summit of Vardousia; many peaks over 2000 m.

**Vegetation:** Forests of black pine, Greek fir, beech and oak; scrub, rocky grassland, rock, cliff and scree vegetation.

**Flora:** c. 4000 vascular plant species, of which 35% of the montane species are endemic to Greece; 11% of the montane flora are local endemics; some disjunct alpine and Anatolian taxa.

**Useful plants:** The flora includes softwood timber trees and various species utilized on a small-scale by the inhabitants.

**Other values:** Water catchment and erosion protection, hydroelectric energy, tourism; several plants have horticultural significance or potential, others are crop relatives.

**Threats:** Fire, excessive grazing, increased tourism, bauxite mining, over-collecting.

**Conservation:** There are 4 National Parks in, or adjacent to, the region, covering a total of 173 km².

## Geography

The area under consideration includes the mountains of the Peloponnese, one of the largest peninsulas of the Mediterranean region, forming the southern extremity of mainland Greece, and the mountains of central Greece. The two areas are divided by the waters of the Gulf of Corinth, a separation established less than one million years ago. The Peloponnese occupies an area of some 13,370 km². Both regions are mountainous, mainly composed of limestone and dolomite, and can be considered as a single floristic province. The largely limestone and mountainous island of Crete (CPD Site Eu17, see Data Sheet) lies to the south, but has been separated from the Peloponnese for several million years and has its own distinct and rich flora.

Central Greece and the Peloponnese have a rugged and dissected topography, with many promontories and mountains, and several islands off the coast. The main mountain masses of the Peloponnese are the high ranges that lie adjacent to the Gulf, notably Chelmos or Aroania (2340 m) and its neighbour Killini (2375 m). Southwards from this part of the region, the mountains run from north-west to south-east. The western and the largest range is Taygetos (2400 m), which is 100 km long, and which terminates in the rugged Mani Peninsula; to the east is the lower range of Parnon (1935 m). A topographic feature of the Peloponnese is large internally drained basins (poljes) similar to those on Crete, the largest of which is partly occupied by the city of Tripolis. There are few lowland plains, except on coasts, especially on the western and north-western sides of the peninsula.

The most important mountains of southern-central Greece are the mostly limestone range centred on Parnassos at the southern end of the Pindhos Mountains that form the central backbone of mainland Greece. The main peaks are Parnassos (2457 m), Giona (2510 m), Vardousia (2495 m), Iti (2152 m)

and, somewhat to the north, Timfristos (2316 m). The large island of Evvoia to the east, with its summit of Dhirfis (1743 m), belongs within this geographical and floristic unit, as do the smaller mountains that surround Athens.

## Vegetation

The slopes of the mountains are mostly densely clothed with forests of Crimean pine (*Pinus nigra* subsp. *pallasiana*), Greek fir (*Abies cephalonica*, grading into *A. borisii-regis* in central Greece), up to 1800 m (Quézel 1964), and beech (*Fagus sylvatica*), on more sheltered slopes at 1000–1800 m. Drier slopes have woodland of pubescent oak (*Quercus pubescens*). Where forests have been cleared there is scrub, often of a semi-deciduous nature. Locally there are stands of other trees, such as the groves of *Juniperus drupaceus* on Parnon, its only European station, and *J. foetidissima*. The mostly limestone mountains above 1800 m are dominated by rocky grassland, and cliff and scree vegetation. In damper areas, locally there may be closed grassland, but much of the terrain is rocky, with open, species-rich communities.

Especially where there is grazing, around and above the tree-line there develops a low scrub dominated by the "hedgehog" hummocks of spiny *Astragalus* species, together with species such as *Daphne oleoides* and *Acantholimon echinus* or dry, overgrazed, "pseudo-steppe" communities dominated by the tussocky grass *Stipa pennata* (Voliotis 1976). At the highest levels the ground is rocky, with little vegetation cover; there are pockets of alpine vegetation, especially near late snow patches. The flora is rich in endemics, together with a relict Alpine element.

A particularly interesting community of the higher mountains is a short, species-rich "lawn", often on ground that has late snow and is grazed during the summer months. The characteristic species are local or regional endemics:

for example *Herniaria parnassi*, the clovers *Trifolium parnassum*, *T. repens* var. *orphanideum* and *T. noricum* var. *ottonis*. Of particular note is the tiny Greek beet (*Beta nana*). This species, along with others in this community, occur also on Mount Olympus to the north.

## Flora

The flora of the region is rich and justifiably famous. There are no recent figures available for the number of species, either overall or in the mountains, although 30 years ago, and without the benefit of modern floristic exploration, the native flora was estimated to comprise about 3000 species. Floristic exploration by French botanists in the 1960s and by the *Mountain Flora of Greece* project (Strid 1985, 1991) during the 1970s has revealed at least 30% more taxa than were previously recognised in the mountains of central and southern Greece. A figure of approximately 4000 vascular plant species is a reasonable estimate for the size of the flora, i.e. about 80% of the total flora of Greece. Greek endemics are an important element in the flora (c. 35% of the total). Of these, local endemics constitute 11% (Strid 1986).

A remarkable feature of the flora is a group of plants that have their nearest localities in South West Asia. Two mostly Asiatic members of the Boraginaceae, *Macrotomia densiflora* and *Solenanthus stamineus* occur in the Styx Valley of Mount Chelmos; *Aethionema cordatum* occurs in Europe only on Chelmos and Iti; and *Thlaspi kotchyanum*, recently reported from Iti, occurs elsewhere eastwards from Iraq, with one station in central Turkey.

Special mention should be made of the mostly limestone range of Mount Olympus, some 100 km to the north of the main body of the mountains discussed here, but with considerable floristic affinity; it has probably the richest flora of any mountain in Greece, with at least 26 endemic species. Some of these, such as *Jankaea heldreichei*, are very distinct and apparently represent relict elements of a Tertiary flora. The flora of Olympus has been well researched (Strid 1980). The massif is a National Park and its flora is apparently under no threat at present.

## Useful plants

A number of species, such as members of the genera *Thymus*, *Micromeria* and *Sideritis* (Labiatae) are gathered and sold as herbs and tisanes. One scarce endemic species, *Cicer graecum*, endemic to the lower slopes of Chelmos and Killini, is an annual relative of the chickpea and, therefore, represents a potential genetic resource, as do the various clovers. Of particular importance is *Beta nana*, related to the beets of commerce, which is cold-tolerant, an attribute that might be of value for enhancing future crops. Other species have horticultural potential.

## Social and environmental values

The mountains of the region still have considerable stands of pine and fir that are exploited for forestry. The forests are managed apparently on a sustainable basis by the Forestry Service. The forests also protect catchment areas and prevent erosion; this will benefit hydroelectric energy schemes that are being established in the southern Pindhus Mountains. The vegetation is a valuable grazing resource, but the numbers of animals need to be controlled, at least locally.

Local people collect various herbs, medicines and teas, which are sold in mountain villages and in shops in the larger towns of the adjacent lowlands. Increasingly the mountains are a place of recreation for large numbers of people.

Many of the plants, including the endemics, have horticultural value or potential. Several species have potential for future plant breeding programmes.

## Economic assessment

The mountains are becoming an important area for tourism and recreation. If this can be kept within bounds, it will provide a basis for "green" tourism of the type now being expanded in Crete (CPD Site Eu17, see Data Sheet). This will complement the stock-rearing, timber extraction and local gathering of herbs and other plants that at present support the economy of the mountains.

## Threats

Parnassos, in particular, is extensively exploited and developed for tourism. Most seriously, a skiing centre has been expanded, and the associated roads and lifts are both damaging native vegetation and allowing unprecedented numbers of visitors into previously remote and inaccessible areas. Skiing is now also being developed on Chelmos and Killini.

Iti has been established only recently as a National Park, but bauxite mining threatens to destroy native vegetation, directly and indirectly (as a result of road building). Already the local endemic *Veronica oetaea*, restricted to a few tiny meltwater pools, is under threat from the building of roads to within a few metres of its habitats.

The National Park of Parnes lies adjacent to the suburbs of Athens, where visitor pressure is considerable. Fires, some of them started deliberately, are now a constant threat around Athens during the summer months.

The main general threat to the flora of central and southern Greece is overgrazing by sheep and goats. There is also increasing danger to individual species, particularly in well-known and floristically rich sites such as the Styx Valley on Chelmos, from over-collecting. *Biebersteinia orphanidea* was described from Killini in the 19th century but soon afterwards was apparently exterminated, although still present in Anatolia. The flora of Mount Olympus does not appear to be under threat, as large tracts of the mountain are not grazed and much of it is remote and inaccessible to visitors. Visitor pressure is increasing and there has been some damage to habitats, together with over-collecting, on the main route up the mountain, but damage overall is minimal.

## Conservation

There are four National Parks or Reserves in the region, namely: part of the Ionian Island of Cephalonia (29 km²), Mount Iti (72 km²), Mount Parnassos (35 km²) and Mount

Parnes (37 km²). These contain forests, especially of Greek fir, and at higher altitudes areas of rocky ground in which much of the endemic flora occurs. Mount Olympus (40 km²), just outside the region, has extensive forests of fir, pine and beech, and large, remote expanses of rocky grassland, cliffs and screes; conservation is encouraged by an active branch of the Hellenic Alpine Club.

Like Mount Olympus, Mount Parnassos has been a National Park since 1938, but no practical steps have been taken to implement any sort of conservation measures. The growth of skiing and other forms of tourism must therefore be viewed with some alarm.

Similarly, the mining of bauxite on Iti would seem to be incompatible with the mountain's National Park status. All these sites are threatened by the excessive pasturage of sheep and goats, and in summer the flora of Parnassos appears to suffer severely from overgrazing. The Hellenic Society for the Protection of Nature has repeatedly drawn attention to the inadequacy of legislation to protect the plants and animals of Greece.

## References

Polunin, O. (1980). *Wild flowers of Greece and the Balkans.* Oxford University Press, Oxford.

Quézel, P. (1964). Végétation des hautes montagnes de la Grèce méridionale. *Vegetatio* 12: 289–385.

Strid, A. (1980). *Wild flowers of Mt Olympus.* Goulandris Museum, Kifisia. xxviii, 362 pp.

Strid, A. (ed.) (1985, 1991). *The mountain flora of Greece, 1, 2.* (1 – Cambridge University Press; 2 – Edinburgh University Press.)

Strid, A. (1986). The mountain flora of Greece with special reference to the Anatolian element. *Proc. Roy. Soc. Edinb.* 89B: 59–68.

Turrill, W.B. (1958). The evolution of floras with special reference to those of the Balkan peninsula. *Bot. J. Linn. Soc.* 56: 136–152.

Voliotis, D. (1976). Die Geholzvegetation und die Vegetationszonierung des Gebirgszuges Tymphristos-Oeta-Parnassos. *Candollea* 31: 37–51.

## Acknowledgements

This Data Sheet was prepared by Dr John R. Akeroyd.

# CRETE
# Greece

**Location:** South Aegean Sea, between Greece and Libya, between latitudes 34°55'–35°41'N and longitudes 23°31'–26°19'E.

**Area:** 8700 km², including small offshore islands.

**Altitude:** 0–2456 m.

**Vegetation:** Extensively cleared or modified by agricultural management; evergreen scrub, fragments of evergreen oak, pine and cypress forest, montane rock and cliff vegetation.

**Flora:** Rich flora of some 1600 vascular plant species, with a large (10%) endemic element; floristic links with southern Greece and Anatolia. 1 endemic (monotypic) genus.

**Useful plants:** Crop relatives, many wild species utilized by the local population, many species with horticultural potential.

**Other values:** Flora attracts tourists.

**Threats:** Fire, tourism, agricultural and industrial development.

**Conservation:** Only limited practical measures have been taken. Samaria National Park (48.5 km²) includes a number of endemic species; the island of Dia (12 km²) is a Nature Reserve; the largest grove of Cretan date palms (*Phoenix theophrasti*) has been fenced and is monitored by the forestry service; a small Nature Reserve has been established to protect a population of the endemic orchid, *Cephalanthera cucullata*, and is now also a National Monument; some rare endemics are protected by Presidential Decree, but legislation is often ignored.

## Geography

Crete is the fifth largest island in the Mediterranean and forms the most southerly region of Greece. It is a narrow island with an east-west axis 250 km long, but is nowhere more than 56 km in width. The land area is 8700 km², including a number of small offshore islands. The landscape is rugged and mountainous, the main topographic feature being the four distinct mountain ranges of Lefka Ori (up to 2452 m) in the west, Psiloritis or Ida (up to 2456 m) in the centre, and Dhikti (up to 2155 m) and Sitia Ori (up to 1476 m) in the east. The proximity of such high mountains to the sea, to which they are linked by deep gorges, is a factor of major phytogeographical importance. To the south of the central mountain range is a broad, extensively cultivated valley, the Messara. The Geropotamos River that drains this area is the only one of the island's few rivers that continues to flow throughout the summer. Most water-courses are winter torrents with stony beds and alluvial fans near the coast. There are limited areas of marsh, mostly brackish, near the sea and there is one small freshwater lake, Lake Kournas, in the west.

Crete has existed as an island for some 5.5 million years. It represents, together with the smaller islands of Kithira, Antikithira, Karpathos, Kasos and Rodhos, part of an arc of mountains from the Peloponnese to south-western Turkey that was folded in the Tertiary. The dominant geological formations are Jurassic, Cretaceous and Eocene limestones, which have created the islands majestic mountain scenery. These overlay harder metamorphic schists, shales, slates and quartzites of the Triassic, which outcrop mainly in the westernmost part of the island. The erosion of the limestone has created the gorges for which the island is famous, together with other karstic features such as underground streams and poljes, several of which, such as the plateau of Lassithi, are characteristic topographic features of Crete. Softer Tertiary and Quaternary rocks such as chalks, sandstones and conglomerates occur in the lowlands, and there are some small outcrops of Jurassic and Cretaceous intrusive igneous rocks.

Soils are mostly terra rossa and rendzina, although more acid soils are found in the western part of the island, derived from the shales and other metamorphic rocks.

Crete has the mild, wet winters and hot, dry summers of the true Mediterranean climate. The mean January temperature in the lowlands is in the region of 12°C, whereas the mean August temperature is close to 27°C (Naval Intelligence Division 1945). The proximity of the sea somewhat ameliorates the climate and the high mountains attract rainfall from depressions moving across the Mediterranean from the west. In winter the mountains have heavy falls of snow, which persists on higher ground until May (Lefka Ori means "White Mountains"). Most of the annual rainfall occurs between November and January, although heavy downpours are frequent in March and April. The island is drier at the eastern end, the mean annual rainfall varying from about 600 mm to 550 mm west to east. The south coast, with a mean annual rainfall of 400–450 mm and exposed to scorching winds from North Africa, is also dry. The far eastern portion of the island is exposed and windy and in summer is as dry as the south coast.

## Vegetation

The greater part of the native vegetation has been destroyed or profoundly modified by over 5000 years of human activity, and today at least 50% of the land surface is used for the grazing of sheep and goats. Large tracts of land below 1000 m are planted with olives, vines and, more locally, oranges. Where the ground is relatively flat, notably in the Messara, there are important market gardens, mostly now under glass or polythene tunnels.

The dominant vegetation is an evergreen scrub dominated by Kermes oak (*Quercus coccifera*), either maquis up to 5 m tall, or garigue (Zohary and Orshan 1965). There are some surviving stands of native forest, mainly pines, evergreen oaks and cypress. Calabrian pine (*Pinus halepensis* subsp. *brutia*) occupies about 5% of the land surface and is locally more common than 20 years ago (Rackham 1990). Woodland occupies less than 10% of the land surface of Crete.

The most important native forests are those of cypress (*Cupressus sempervirens* var. *sempervirens*), mostly above 500 m in Lefka Ori, Psiloritis and Dhikti. This species frequently grows with the semi-deciduous *Acer sempervirens* and sometimes with the endemic *Zelkova cretica*. There are four main stands and many fragments of once extensive forests of Calabrian pine, mainly at lower altitudes and in the east of the island, and some remarkable stands of mature evergreen Kermes oaks.

There are woods of chestnut (*Castanea sativa*) in the west, some at least probably planted, and also relict woods of evergreen Valonia oak (*Quercus macrolepis*).

At higher altitudes, dwarf spiny shrubs occur, such as *Astragalus* spp. and *Berberis cretica*, together with some endemic species such as *Verbascum spinosum*, which grow as "hedgehog" hummocks that resist grazing. In the mountains and gorges, the cliffs are an important habitat with an open vegetation that includes many of the endemics. The gorges especially form a varied habitat that provides sheltered and equable microclimates, especially during the summer months.

Another specialized habitat is solution hollows or dolines with clayey soils of the limestone mountains, which support endemics such as *Polygonum idaeum*.

## Flora

The varied topography, geology and climate of Crete is reflected in the island's rich flora. A recent checklist of the flora of Crete lists 1586 native vascular plant species (Barclay 1986), including 35 species of pteridophytes and 5 species of gymnosperms. Subsequent floristic exploration has added at least 10 further species of angiosperms (Turland, Chilton and Press 1993), and it is likely that further discoveries will be made.

Western Crete has some floristic affinity with the Peloponnese, whereas the flora of eastern Crete has more affinities with that of Anatolia. An interesting element in the flora is a group of species shared with Cyrenaica and Palestine that are otherwise absent or rare in Europe.

The significant and famous endemic element comprises some 10% of the flora. This large percentage reflects the long isolation of the island, together with the dissected topography giving rise to many distinct habitats. Most of the endemic species are ancient relicts. The majority are to be found in the four principal mountain ranges, including the gorges, and most are plants of cliffs and rocky ground; the largest concentration is in the Lefka Ori. A few are restricted to small offshore islands and some are constituents of phrygana or

dwarf scrub, notably *Ebenus creticus*, which can colour hillsides pale crimson in May. One genus, the monotypic *Petramarula pinnata* (Campanulaceae), is endemic. Several genera appear to have been actively evolving in Crete and adjacent parts of the Aegean islands, for example *Asperula*, *Dianthus*, *Erysimum*, *Linum* and *Muscari*, especially in cliff vegetation communities and on the coast.

Perhaps a third of the contemporary Cretan flora is introduced. Many of these adventive species are weeds or ruderals, and few compete with the endemic flora – although some cliff endemics have readily invaded ruderal habitats such as walls.

## Useful plants

Many species are utilized by local people, although the use of wild species has been declining along with traditional patterns of village life. Nevertheless, wild-collected herbs and salad plants are on sale in markets and restaurants and are widely gathered by individuals. Examples include leaf-rosettes of various species of Compositae for winter and spring salads (radikia tou vounou or "dandelions of the mountain"), flowers of *Tulipa* spp. for ornament, and bulbs of *Muscari comosum* for pickling and eating. In general, these plants represent a renewable resource but the wild populations of at least one species, Cretan dittany (*Origanum dictamnus*), are threatened by over-exploitation.

In the village of Fodele, to the west of Iraklion, local people still collect an aromatic gum from *Cistus incanus* subsp. *creticus*, a practice mentioned by ancient writers.

## Social and environmental values

As noted above, the native flora of Crete includes plants of local economic importance. Tourism is now the island's major industry. Each spring several hundred visitors are attracted to the island especially to see the flowers. Many more tourists show at least some interest in the flora, and increasingly the Cretans are aware of this aspect of tourism. One species in particular, the Cretan date palm (*Phoenix theophrasti*), is recognized on the island for its tourist potential and features, for example, on postcards and as a name for cafés. The main grove is protected by the forestry authorities and is regarded as a significant tourist attraction. The Samaria Gorge National Park, one of the premier assemblages of endemic plants, is now marketed as an important site for walkers and naturalists.

Reforestation is a practical possibility, and the native cypress forests in the higher mountains are an important natural resource. In the past, cypress has been introduced elsewhere and is still planted on roadsides. At low altitudes, Calabrian pine is a feasible species for reforestation. In the westernmost part of the island, chestnut would be particularly suitable.

## Economic assessment

Since ancient times, the pleasant climate, rugged scenery and Minoan antiquities of Crete have brought tourists to the island. Crete is also rich in remains from the Roman and Byzantine eras and from later Venetian and Turkish occupations. Tourism is now the major industry. In recent years tourists have taken an increasing interest in the flora, and the island attracts many "botanical holidays" and student field-courses from other parts of Europe. Several tour operators in Britain that organise holidays in Crete are members of Green Flag International, an organisation that not only avoids environmentally damaging tourist development, but seeks to channel funds in support of local conservation projects. "Green tourism" is expanding in Crete, especially in unspoilt parts of the west, where it has had considerable economic impact and has helped to counteract progressive depopulation of rural villages.

Widespread use of wild plants for food continues, especially during late winter (Akeroyd 1994, in press). If organised on a sustainable basis, the use of wild plants could continue to make a significant contribution to the rural economy of Crete. The major native trees are suitable for forestry.

## Threats

During recent years there has been considerable tourist and light industry development, especially along the north coast. Few sandy and marshy stretches of the coastline have escaped development. Agriculture has also expanded, with increasingly intensive management and the greater use of herbicides and artificial fertilizers. At the western end of the island, some of the moist wooded valleys are being replanted with oranges and avocado pear orchards. Flat, sandy and marshy areas near the sea are particularly threatened by expanding glasshouse cultivation and the building of hotels, villas and apartments.

The lowlands and lower mountain slopes are no longer grazed as heavily as in the past, resulting in the encroachment of scrub and trees into formerly open areas rich in bulbs and other herbaceous species. Trees on Crete are now more abundant than at any time in the last few centuries (Rackham 1990).

Tourists have so far had little impact on the gorges and the endemic flora, which are mostly remote and relatively inaccessible, although there is some commercial development at the head of the Samaria Gorge, with the threat of a large, new hotel on the Omalos Plateau. This would destroy not only a historic agricultural ecosystem, with some rare communities of bulbous plants, but would damage a unique landscape.

A major industry on Crete is the production of concrete, a vital building material in a country with so little timber, from the readily available limestone. Together with road building, this has devastated large areas of land and threatens some local conservation sites.

Plant collecting may be a long-term threat to some endemic species. This needs to be monitored.

## Conservation

Few practical measures have been taken to conserve the flora of Crete. An area of 48.5 km² in and around the Samaria Gorge in the west has been incorporated into a National Park, which includes stands of forest and endemic species, especially chasmophytes. The island of Dia (of area 12 km²) off the north coast is a Nature Reserve, managed mainly for a population of Cretan ibex transferred from the Samaria Gorge. The introduction of ibex has, ironically, been to the detriment of the Dian flora.

The largest grove of Cretan date palms, extending 1 km along a coastal valley at Vai in the north-eastern corner of the island, has been fenced and is monitored by the forestry service.

A small Nature Reserve established to protect a population of the endemic orchid, *Cephalanthera cucullata*, from grazing has been declared a National Monument (Z. Kipriotakis, pers. comm.), and a small coastal marsh at Almeria, to the south of the busy resort of Agios Nikolaos, has recently been established as a reserve. Some of the rarer endemic species are protected by Presidential Decree, but the legislation may often be ignored. Attempts are being made to set up a conservation organization for the island. No further reserves are planned at present.

If conservation measures can be implemented, the protection of the endemic flora must be given priority. Nature Reserves should include the more extensive remaining stands of native forest, a representative sample of the gorges and offshore islands with their chasmophyte flora, and any stretches of flat or sandy coasts not already earmarked for development. Specialized weed communities that include endemic species of tulip (*Tulipa saxatilis*, *T. bakeri* and *T. doerfleri*), characteristic of traditional upland field systems, such as in parts of the Lassithi and Omalos plateaux, require protection before they disappear in the face of modern agricultural practices.

## References

Akeroyd, J.R. (1994, in press). From nature's garden. *Convivium* 1: 7–12.

Barclay, C. (1986). Crete. Checklist of the vascular flora. *Englera* 6: i–xiii, 1–138.

Naval Intelligence Division (1945). *Greece. Volume III. Regional geography.* Cambridge (Naval Intelligence Division Geographical Handbook Series).

Polunin, O. (1980). *Flowers of Greece and the Balkans.* Oxford University Press, Oxford. Pp. 57–76.

Rackham, O. (1990). The greening of Myrtos. In Bottema, S., Entjes-Nieborg and Van Zeist, W. (eds), *Man's role in the shaping of the eastern Mediterranean landscape.* Balkema, Rotterdam. Pp. 341–348.

Strid, A. (ed.) (1985, 1991). *The mountain flora of Greece, 1, 2.* (1 – Cambridge University Press; 2 – Edinburgh University Press.)

Turland, N.J., Chilton, L. and Press, J.R. (1993). Annotated checklist of the Cretan flora. H.M.S.O. and Natural History Museum, London.

Zohary, M. and Orshan, G. (1965). An outline of the geobotany of Crete. *Israel J. Bot.* 14, suppl.: 1–49.

## Acknowledgements

This Data Sheet was prepared by Dr John R. Akeroyd.

# TROODOS MOUNTAINS
## Cyprus

**Location:** Cyprus is situated in the eastern Mediterranean Sea, 60 km from the southern coast of Turkey, between latitudes 34°33'–35°41'N and longitudes 32°17'–34°35'E. The Troodos Mountains are on the western side of the island.

**Area:** 1800 km².

**Altitude:** c. 1000–1960 m (summit of Mount Khionistra, or Olympus).

**Vegetation:** Extensively cleared or modified by agriculture in lowlands; evergreen scrub, evergreen oak, pine, cypress and cedar forest in the mountains; rock and cliff communities.

**Flora:** 1650 native vascular plant species on Cyprus; Troodos Mountains have 62 of the island's 88 endemic species, 36 of them locally endemic.

**Useful plants:** Forests (18% of island's land surface) managed for their timber. The flora is of phytogeographical interest, representing a transition between the floras of Europe and Asia. Several endemics of horticultural value.

**Other values:** The flora is a potential tourist attraction.

**Threats:** Fire, unplanned tourist development, road building.

**Conservation:** The management of the mountain forests includes the protection of the flora.

## Geography

Cyprus is the third largest island in the Mediterranean. It is situated 60 km from the southern coast of Turkey and 120 km from the coast of Syria. The island has a maximum dimension of 225 × 100 km; the land area is 9255 km².

There are two ranges of mountains: the mainly limestone Kyrenia Mountains (to 1025 m), some 80 km from west to east, lie adjacent and parallel to the northern coast, and the mostly igneous and acid Troodos Mountains (to 1960 m) lie in the central western part of the island. The two ranges are separated by a region of low plains, the Mesaorea, much of which is under cultivation. This central plain has the island's longest river, the Pedieos. The other rivers are mostly winter torrents.

Some 50% of the land surface is cultivated. There is a rich mixed agriculture, mainly cereals, potatoes, carob, citrus fruits and tobacco. Grazing by sheep and goats, such a problem in Greece and Crete, is restricted in the forested parts of the mountains. The island's population was estimated in 1986 as 673,100 (Europa Publications 1987).

The principal topographic features of the island are the two mountain ranges, representing a continuation of the Amanus Mountains of southern Turkey. The geology and topography of these two ranges are in marked contrast. The Kyrenia Mountains consist for the greater part of massive beds of hard Cretaceous limestone, with rugged karstic scenery; at lower altitudes there are Tertiary marls, sandstones and conglomerates. The Troodos Mountains, on the other hand, are rounded but higher, with several peaks over 1500 m, and the highest (Mount Khionistra, or Olympus) reaching 1960 m. The Troodos represents a plutonic dome intruded into sedimentary rocks. The mountains cover an area of some 1800 km².

At higher altitudes there are extensive outcrops of gabbro, diabase and serpentine; at lower altitudes there are Cretaceous limestones, clays and marls, together with pillow lavas and Tertiary sandstones. These mountains have deeper soils and more surface streams than those of the limestone Kyrenia range. Metamorphic processes around the intrusion have given rise to deposits of metal ores, especially copper (hence the island's name), chromium and iron.

The island's climate is typically Mediterranean, the rain falling from November to March, but is generally arid, with (at times) extensive periods of drought. The annual rainfall varies from 300 mm in the east to 1000 mm in the Troodos Mountains. There is winter snowfall above 1000 m in the Troodos, which persists until April. The mean January temperature in the capital, Nicosia, near the centre of the island, is 15.7°C; the mean August temperature is 36.9°C (Meikle 1977).

## Vegetation

Much of the lowland vegetation has been replaced by arable agriculture or, where used for grazing, by a low garigue or phrygana scrub. Garigue communities dominated by *Sarcopoterium spinosum* cover the uncultivated lowlands, although locally there are stands of taller maquis dominated by *Pistacia lentiscus* (Zohary 1973). About 19% of the native forest survives (Thirgood 1981), a relatively high proportion for a Mediterranean territory. Native lowland woodlands have been replaced by carob (*Ceratonia siliqua*) and Aleppo pine (*Pinus halepensis*), although stands of Calabrian pine (*Pinus brutia*), representing just over 50% of the island's tree cover (Thirgood 1981), survive throughout the island up to an altitude of 1200 m. Stands of *Quercus infectoria* also survive, mostly below 1500 m in the Troodos Mountains.

There are extensive stands of usually rather open forest, amounting to 31% of the land surface over 300 m (Thirgood 1981). In the Kyrenia Mountains, the forests are dominated by *Pinus brutia* and by native cypress (*Cupressus sempervirens* var. *sempervirens*). In the Troodos Mountains, with a moister climate, more surface water and deeper soils, above 1000 m there are forests of the endemic Cyprus cedar (*Cedrus libani* subsp. *brevifolia*), Balkan pine (*Pinus nigra* subsp. *pallasiana*) and local stands of *Juniperus foetidissima* above 1600 m. At 800–1600 m there are stands of the handsome endemic golden oak (*Quercus alnifolius*). At higher altitudes, cliff and rock communities support the greater part of the island's rich endemic flora.

## Flora

The island has a flora of about 1650 native vascular plants, which includes 20 species of pteridophytes and 12 of gymnosperms. The island has been well explored botanically, but the precise identity and distribution of a number of species require confirmation and additions to the flora will doubtless be made. There are about 350 naturalized adventive species on Cyprus, and there have been many exotic plantings, especially of trees and shrubs.

The number of endemic species is 88, some 5% of the flora. Of these, the greatest number (62 species) occur in the Troodos Mountains. Some island endemics are widespread, but 36 species are restricted, or more or less restricted, to the Troodos range. Several are shared with the Kyrenia range, which itself has 11 endemic or near-endemic species. There are also 15 subspecies and 10 varieties endemic to Cyprus, representing a rich gene-pool of variation.

Two families of major economic importance, Cruciferae and Labiatae, contribute 8 endemic and 16 endemic species, respectively; there is one endemic genus, the grass *Lindbergella sintenisii*. Other, regional, endemic species are shared with southern Turkey and Crete.

Many species of European affinity, including such species as red and white clovers (*Trifolium pratense* and *T. repens*), together with floristic elements from further east (e.g. *Corydalis rutifolia*), are only found in Cyprus in the Troodos Mountains. The flora contains a significant tropical element of some 30 species, including an endemic species of *Bosea* (Zohary 1973). An interesting feature of the island's mountain flora is the apparent segregation of closely related, vicarious endemic populations between the Troodos and the Kyrenia ranges.

## Useful plants

As in other Mediterranean countries, local people use wild plants as a source of salads, herbs and medicines. One species of particular economic potential is a native endemic variant of the culinary and medicinal herb, sweet marjoram (*Origanum marjorana* var. *tenuifolium*), perhaps the wild progenitor of the plant in commerce (Meikle 1985).

Sumach (*Rhus coriaria*) is used for the tanning of Morocco leather, and is protected on Cyprus, as are the aromatic herbs *Salvia fruticosa* and *S. willeana*, the latter endemic to the Troodos Mountains. As elsewhere in the Mediterranean, aromatic plants are gathered extensively from the wild.

The two endemic trees of the Troodos Mountains, the elegant and relatively small cyprus cedar (*Cedrus libani* subsp. *brevifolia*) and golden oak (*Quercus alnifolia*), are cultivated in other parts of Europe as ornamentals. The Cyprus cedar is being used in afforestation schemes. An endemic shrub in the Amaranthaceae, *Bosea cypria*, is utilised as a hedge-plant on Cyprus.

The Cyprus endemic white-flowered cabbage (*Brassica hilarionis*) is restricted to limestone cliffs in the Kyrenia Mountains. This species is a potential genetic resource for plant breeding. It is closely related to *B. cretica* of southern Greece and Crete, and is probably related to the cauliflower of cultivation.

## Social and environmental values

The native tree species of the Troodos Mountains, as elsewhere on the island, are managed for forestry and are a valuable resource. Wild plants are used by local people for a wide range of uses. The flowers of Cyprus are becoming more famous, and the flora has potential to attract more tourists to the island.

Two restricted-range land birds are confined to Cyprus, namely the Cyprus wheatear (*Oenanthe cypriaca*) and Cyprus warbler (*Sylvia melanothorax*); these species are common and widespread throughout Cyprus and occur in the Troodos Mountains which, because of their remaining forest, have the richest bird habitat. The island's location relative to the western Palaearctic and Africa results in an additional 200 species occurring as regular passage migrants.

## Economic assessment

The carefully conserved and managed timber resources of the Troodos Mountains play a major role in the economy of Cyprus. The island's total afforested area comprises just over 1000 km² (Thirgood 1981). As is the case with other Mediterranean islands such as Crete (CPD Site Eu17, see Data Sheet), the flora and vegetation has considerable potential to attract "green tourism", such as via tour operators who are committed not only to avoiding environmental damage but also to supporting local conservation projects.

## Threats

Political partition means that Cyprus is not subject to a single administration or legislation. Unrest between the Greek and Turkish ethnic communities led, in July 1974, to invasion by the Turkish army. Since then, the northern part of the island has been administered by Turkey. About 100 km² of forest in the northern part of the island was burned during the conflicts (Thirgood 1981).

The partition of Cyprus makes an overall conservation policy for the island difficult. The floristically richest area, with its major forest resources, the Troodos Mountains, is under the control of the Cyprus Government. All plants ("forest produce") growing in the forests are under the protection of forest legislation; there is, however, no legislation to protect the wild flora outside the forests (Davis *et al.* 1986).

The greatest threat to the flora is increased tourism, and associated tourist developments and new roads. Cape Akamas, in the north-western part of the island, topographically and floristically an extension of the Troodos range, is under threat from expanding tourist infrastructure (Sfikas 1990). Populations of at least one endemic species (*Origanum cordifolium*) are known to be under threat from road building. In the Troodos Mountains, the development of skiing facilities, which introduces large numbers of visitors to previously inaccessible sites, poses a special threat.

Visitors on a large scale also increase the risk of fire during the dry summer months, especially in forested areas.

## Conservation

Forest Law No. 14 of 1967 protects all the plants ("forest produce") that grow in the forests. This includes much of the special flora of the Troodos Mountains. It has been noted that 40% of the endemics are to be found in the central part of the Troodos in an area of some 5 x 4 km between Prodhromos and Troodos, and thus a small but significant protected area could be established here. The Akrotiri Peninsula in south-western Cyprus, is now a Nature Reserve, although it does not include any of the island's most floristically rich areas.

## References

Davis, S.D., Droop, S.J.M., Gregerson, P., Henson, L., Leon, C.J., Villa-Lobos, J.L., Synge, H. and Zantovska, J. (1986). *Plants in danger: what do we know?* IUCN, Gland, Switzerland and Cambridge, U.K. xlv, 461 pp.

Europa Publications (1987). *The Middle East and North Africa 1988.* 34th edition. Europa, London. Pp. 311–335.

Meikle, R.D. (1977, 1985). *Flora of Cyprus, 1, 2.* Bentham-Moxham Trust, Kew, U.K.

Sfikas, G. (1990). *Wild flowers of Cyprus.* Athens.

Thirgood, J.V. (1981). *Man and the Mediterranean forest. A history of resource depletion.* Academic Press, London.

Zohary, M. (1973). *Geobotanical foundations of the Middle East,* 2 vols. Fischer, Stuttgart, and Swets and Zeitlinger, Amsterdam. 739 pp.

## Acknowledgements

This Data Sheet was prepared by Dr John R. Akeroyd.

# SOUTH CRIMEAN MOUNTAINS AND NOVOROSSIA
## Ukraine, Russia

**Location:** South Crimean Mountains and Caucasian Black Sea coast between Anapa and Tuapse; between latitudes 44°00'–45°00'N and longitudes 33°00'–39°00'E.

**Area:** 80,500 km².

**Altitude:** 0–1200 m.

**Vegetation:** Maquis and shiblyak; oak, pine, pine-beech and juniper woodland; dry grassland.

**Flora:** Enclave of Mediterranean flora on Black Sea coast, with some 2200 vascular plant species, of which some 200 are endemic.

**Useful plants:** Fruits, volatile oil-bearing plants, medicinal plants, ornamental plants.

**Other values:** Recreation and tourism.

**Threats:** Forest clearance, pollution from agriculture, over-collecting of plants.

**Conservation:** In Crimea – 3 Strict Reserves (Zapovedniki) cover 160.8 km², 5 Refuges (Zakazniki) for protection of some biotopes or communities, 1 Game Preserve (150 km²); in Novorossia – 15 refuges for rare plant communities.

## Geography

The South Crimean and North-western Caucasus (Novorossian Botanical Province) represent the major enclave of Mediterranean climate and vegetation in the Black Sea area.

The Crimean Peninsula is transected by the Crimean Mountains (Krymskiye Gory), which run for some 150 km south-west to north-east and reach 1545 m above sea-level. The peaks rise above highland plateaux. Locally, there are karstic features called *yajla*. The southern yajla slopes facing the Black Sea are steep and expose Jurassic limestones underlain by sandy shales. Jurassic volcanic rocks are widespread throughout the South Crimean Mountains and occur as large massifs in some places, e.g. Karadag in the eastern Crimea. Landslides result in large blocks of limestone or volcanic rocks being displaced over shale strata along the coast, forming small offshore islands. Soils are mainly brown earth woodland soils and terra rossa in open areas over calcareous substrates.

South Crimea is shielded by the mountains from cold, northerly winds, and has a Mediterranean climate, with dry summers. The average annual temperature is 11°–14°C, while monthly mean temperatures range from 2°–3.5°C in February to 23°C in July. Annual precipitation varies from 223–557 mm, of which about 60% occurs in winter, causing floods and mudslides. Snow cover is low or absent.

The Novorossian Province (Krasnodar Region) of the north-western Caucasus consists of parallel mountain ranges with an average height of 300–500 m, rising to 600 m above sea-level. The mountains, formed by the folding of carbonate flysh deposits, run in a north-west to south-east direction, grading into the main Caucasus range to the east of Tuapse. (For Data Sheet on the Caucasus, CPD Site CA2, see Central and Northern Asia.)

## Vegetation

The vegetation of central South Crimea is typical of the Mediterranean region, with *Juniperus excelsa*, *Pinus nigra* subsp. *pallasiana*, *Ruscus ponticus*, *Cistus tauricus*, *Rhus coriaria* and *Arbutus andrachne*. Western South Crimea includes steppe vegetation in open areas and in the herb layer of woodlands. The colder winters in eastern South Crimea reduce the number of Mediterranean elements, and their place is taken by steppic and halophytic communities containing many endemic species, e.g. *Anthemis sterilis*, *Astragalus arnacantha* and *Hedysarum candidum* (Maleev 1938, 1948).

Strand, rock and pebble beach communities survive as remnants along the coast. They are floristically poor, but contain some endemics, such as *Asparagus litoralis*, species rare in Crimea, such as *Cladium mariscus*, and Asiatic elements, such as the rare shrub *Nitraria schoberi* (Zygophyllaceae).

Crimean maquis (*shiblyak*) consists of shrubby pubescent oak (*Quercus pubescens*), together with eastern hornbeam (*Carpinus orientalis*), Christ's thorn (*Paliurus spina-christi*), pyracantha (*Pyracantha coccinea*) and a hawthorn (*Crataegus pentagyna*). Shiblyak is a secondary formation, replacing the original Mediterranean oak and (in drier sites) *Pistacia* woodland, and consists of prickly thickets 2–4 m tall. South-facing rocky slopes include remnant patches of *Juniperus excelsa* and woods of pitsunda pine (*Pinus pityusa*, a variant of Calabrian pine, *P. halepensis* subsp. *brutia*), in which individual trees can be 4–8 m tall and between 100–200 years old. Shrubs, such as *Jasminum*, *Spiraea* and *Paliurus*, annual grasses and legumes occur between the trees, giving the vegetation a savanna-like appearance.

*Pinus pityusa* forests occur up to 1000 m. Above 1000 m this tree is replaced by *P. hamata* and eastern beech (*Fagus orientalis*), which forms pure and mixed stands.

On the Caucasian coast, *Quercus pubescens* dominates slopes up to 200 m above sea-level, where it is accompanied by *Fraxinus oxycarpa*, *Pistacia mutica* and *Juniperus oxycedrus*. Pure juniper (*J. excelsa*) woodlands also occur.

Characteristic of both areas are semi-natural landscapes dominated by introduced plants. In South Crimea, the commonest introduced tree is Italian cypress (*Cupressus sempervirens* var. *sempervirens*), first introduced in 1787. Cedar of Lebanon (*Cedrus libani*), holm oak (*Quercus ilex*) and evergreen magnolia (*Magnolia grandiflora*) are semi-naturalized, while Judas tree (*Cercis siliquastrum*) is an invasive pioneer plant of abandoned vineyards.

## Flora

The montane flora of the Crimea includes 2200 vascular plant species in 667 genera and 105 families. Among the most species-rich genera are *Hieracium* (with 47 species), *Carex* (35), *Veronica* (31), *Vicia* (30) and *Centaurea* (30). The flora has evolved as a result of repeated migrations of species from the Mediterranean region and Central Asia during interglacials and warm periods of the Holocene, and the gradual migration of boreal and arctic-alpine elements to higher altitudes (Maleev 1948; Rubtsov and Privalova 1964).

The following phytogeographical elements can be distinguished:

1. Ancient Mediterranean: 750 vascular plant species (c. 34% of the flora), relics of the rich xerothermic flora which once extended along the Tethys coast. Most of the species now have disjunct ranges.

2. Asian: 53 vascular plant species, mostly hemi-xerophytes and mountain xerophytes, together with 17 mesophytic woodland and meadow species.

3. Eurasian: 115 species, including shiblyak dominants (e.g. *Paliurus spina-christi*, *Carpinus orientalis*), some woodland, meadow (e.g. *Crocus speciosus*) and steppe (e.g. *Stipa pontica*) elements, and desert elements (e.g. *Capparis spinosa*).

4. Eastern Mediterranean: mostly evolved *in situ* within the general region of Crimean, West Caucasus, Balkans and Anatolia. 154 species, mostly hemi-xerophytes and montane xerophytes, some woodland and meadow species, steppic grasses and weeds. The major forest dominants, *Fagus orientalis*, *Pinus pallasiana*, *P. hamata* and *Juniperus excelsa* belong in this group.

The 200 or so Crimean endemics mostly appear to be of comparatively recent origin. These include *Veronica taurica*, *Cotoneaster tauricus* and *Tulipa monticula*. No more than 22–33 endemics are considered to be Tertiary relics (Rubtsov 1960); they are supposedly more numerous in the western Caucasus (Maleev 1941).

## Useful plants

The montane forests are a source of wild fruits, such as those of *Pyrus*, *Malus*, *Crataegus* and *Berberis*.

Medicinal plants include *Valeriana officinalis*, *Atropa belladonna* and *Glaucium flavum*, the stocks of which were formerly considerable, but have now been reduced by over-collecting.

The Novorossian flora is outstandingly rich in ornamental plants which are widely used in horticulture.

The Herbarium of Nikitski Botanical Garden (NBG) includes more than 100,000 specimens of Crimean plants, and the garden itself includes a collection of useful plants.

## Social and environmental values

The region is a major recreational resort for both Russia and Ukraine, attracting millions of people during the summer months. Most resorts occur within the 300 m wide strip of land behind the beaches. The maquis of slopes behind the resorts has been cleared for vineyards and other agricultural usage.

The Crimea is a traditional area of the fruit, vine and tobacco industries. Its attraction to tourists is dependent upon the diversity of the landscape and its natural and semi-natural plant communities. The stabilizing effect of vegetation on climate, which in turn is crucial for recreation and health resorts, is important. Vegetated slopes prevent mudslides, which are especially dangerous during the winter rainy season. The diversity of cultivated plants in the region also adds to the beauty of the Crimean landscapes. For example, there are extensive rose plantations – a source of the rose oil – which alternate with fields of lavender and opium poppy.

## Threats

In both South Crimea and the north-western Caucasus (see Data Sheet on the Caucasus, CPD Site CA2, covered in the Central and Northern Asian region) the primary vegetation has been greatly reduced in extent, or has been highly modified, as a result of many years of agricultural and recreation activity. Oak forests have either been completely cleared, as in eastern South Crimea, or else degraded to shrubby thickets. Juniper forests have been cleared except at a few isolated sites. Ancient eastern beech forests are in a critical state because regeneration is hampered by trampling by visitors and browsing by the rapidly increasing Crimean deer populations.

The vegetation of the coastal and lower slopes is under threat from quarrying, the development of tourist resorts and road building. Over-collecting of ornamental and medicinal plants has seriously reduced the numbers of many individual species.

## Conservation

About 85 species are catalogued in the Russian and Ukrainian Red Data Books. About 30 species are protected by local regulations, including *Viola oreades*, *Veronica officinalis*, *Hesperis picnotricha*, *Scilla biflora*, *Pulsatilla taurica*, *Arabis caucasica* and *Tulipa monticula*.

South Crimea has a network of protected areas, including Strict Reserves (Zapovedniki) and Refuges (Zakazniki). The "Mys Martyan" Reserve was established in 1973 on the territory of the Nikitski Botanical Garden. The reserve includes 1.2 km² of oak and juniper forest and adjacent wetlands. It includes about 459 species (20% of the total Crimean flora), of which 13 are Crimean endemics (e.g. *Asperula rumelica*, *Centaurea stankovii* and *Cotoneaster tauricus*).

Yaltinskiy Reserve (145.9 km²), established in 1973, includes forests, stone fields, cliffs and meadows, with representative samples of montane oak, beech and pine forests, as well as yajla karstic communities, which contain many rare species. There are 1367 vascular plant species (about 65% of the Crimean mountain flora), among them 113 endemics, notably in the Rosaceae (24 endemic species), Compositae (21) and Labiatae (16). The endemics include *Adenophora taurica*, *Heracleum pubescens*, *Lamium glaberrimum*, *Ranunculus dissectus* and *Sobolewskia lithophila*.

The Karadagskiy Reserve (13.7 km²), was established in 1979 primarily to protect the landscapes of the Karadag volcanic massif, comprising forested slopes, steppe and scrub communities. The area includes 1040 species, 60 of which are Endangered. Notable amongst the Karadag endemics are *Crambe koktebelica*, *Agropyrum karadaghense* and *Eremurus jungei*.

The Crimean Game Preserve (150 km²) protects an area of mountain forests and high yajlas with herbaceous and creeping pine-juniper communities. It includes 1100 vascular plant species, including 90 endemics.

Five Refuges (Zakazniki) are intended for protection of some selected biotopes or communities, e.g. juniper woodlands (Novyj Svet, Aja Point), pubescent oak forests (Aju-Dagh, Khapkal) and rare orchid species.

The Novorossian area lacks Reserves but there are about 15 Refuges which protect *Pistacia-Juniperus* woodland, pitsunda pine forest, pedunculate oak forest and other rare communities. The most important of these is the Markotkh Range which contains a cluster of no less than 30 endemic species.

## References (Titles have been translated.)

Altukhov, M.D. and Litvinskaya, S.A. (1986). Rare and endangered species in the flora of Krasnodar Region. In *Plant Resources, part 3*. Rostov University Press, Rostov. Pp. 211–238.

Koval, I.P. and Litvinskaya, S.A. (1986). Rare plant communities of the Krasnodar Region. In *Plant Resources, part 3*. Rostov University Press, Rostov. Pp. 57–116.

Maleev, V.P. (1938). Vegetation of the Black Sea countries (Euxine Province of the Mediterranean), its origin and affinities. *Proc. Bot. Inst., Leningrad, ser. 3*, 4: 135–251.

Maleev, V.P. (1941). Tertiary relics in the flora of western Caucasus and major stages of the Quaternary floristic and vegetational evolution. In *Materials on the history of flora and vegetation in the USSR. 1*. Acad. Sci. USSR, Moscow and Leningrad. Pp. 61–144.

Maleev, V.P. (1948). Major evolution stages of vegetation in the Mediterranean and southern USSR montane provinces (Caucasus and Crimea) in the Quaternary time. *Proc. Nikita Bot. Gard.* 25(1–2): 2–28.

Maleev, V.P. (1948). Vegetation of the South Crimea. *Proc. Nikita Bot. Gard.* 25(1–2): 29–48.

Rubtsov, N.I. (1960). Brief review of the Crimean flora endemics. *Proc. Nikita Bot. Gard.* 29: 18–54.

Rubtsov, N.I. and Privalova, L.I. (1964). Crimean flora and its geographical links. In *150 years of the Nikita Botanical Garden*. Kolos, Moscow. Pp. 16–36.

## Acknowledgements

This Data Sheet was written by Drs L.V. Denisova and S.V. Nikitina (Institute of Nature Conservation and Reserves, Moscow.)

# REGIONAL OVERVIEW: ATLANTIC OCEAN ISLANDS

ALAN C. HAMILTON

**Total land area:** Ascension, 94 km²; Azores, 2304 km²; Canary Islands, 7542 km²; Cape Verde, 4033 km²; Iceland, 102,819 km²; Madeira, 731 km²; St Helena, 122 km²; Tristan da Cunha, 159 km².

**Population:** Ascension, 1050; Azores, 259,800; Canary Islands, 1,450,000; Cape Verde, 317,000; Iceland, 239,000; Madeira, 257,692; St Helena, 5564; Tristan da Cunha, 299.

**Maximum altitudes:** Ascension, 859 m; Azores, 1351 m; Canary Islands, 3717 m; Cape Verde, 2829 m; Iceland, 1833 m; Madeira, 1861 m; St Helena, 823 m; Tristan da Cunha, 2160 m.

**Natural vegetation:** Macaronesian islands: originally largely covered in forest; laurisilva (broadleaved evergreen forest with abundant Lauraceae) in wetter areas; dry scrub and dry thermophilous forest in dryer areas (such as at lower altitudes on south Madeira and on the relatively dry Canary Islands). The Cape Verde Islands are said to have once been largely forested. Heath communities at high altitudes.

**Number of vascular plants:** c. 2650 species for region; Macaronesian islands include c. 2300 flowering plant species.

**Number of endemic species:** 881 for region (c. 33% species regional endemism); 779 flowering plant species endemic to Macaronesia (34% species endemism).

**Number of endemic genera:** Endemic to single archipelagos: Azores 1, Madeira and Salvage 3 (possibly 4), Canary Islands 20, St Helena 10.

Land areas and population mainly from Davis *et al.* (1986); data on numbers of vascular and endemic species from Takhtajan (1986) and CPD Data Sheets.

## Geography

There are a number of oceanic islands of volcanic origin scattered through the North Atlantic Ocean. From north to south, these include Iceland, the Azores, Madeira, the Salvage Islands, the Canary Islands and the Cape Verde Islands (the last five island groups comprising the Macaronesian Islands). Ascension Island, St Helena and Tristan da Cunha are among the oceanic islands of the South Atlantic. None of these islands have ever been connected to the continents and the floras are all products of long-distance dispersal of propagules by wind, animals and the sea.

The original vegetation of many of the Macaronesian Islands has been devastated since the arrival of Europeans over the last few hundred years. Native trees were ruthlessly exploited for their timber, while the forests, especially in the lowlands and on mid-slopes, were cleared for settlements and for agriculture, such as the cultivation of sugar cane, bananas and other tropical and subtropical crops. Introduced species of plants and animals are a serious threat to the survival of some native species and ecosystems.

The most characteristic vegetation type of the Macaronesian Islands is laurisilva, an evergreen broadleaved forest which was widespread in the Mediterranean region before the Quaternary ice ages; it has survived in the more benign climate of the Atlantic islands. Many of the tree species on the Macaronesian Islands are single-island or Macaronesian endemics; laurisilva is also the home of many endemic herbaceous species. Other important vegetation types include: grassland (probably encouraged by grazing); dry scrub and *Euphorbia*-rich vegetation in the lowlands of the Canary Islands; and thermophilous forest at relatively low altitudes on the Canary Islands.

Cape Verde comprises 14 islands which were originally largely forested. The islands are drier than the other islands in the region. Virtually all the forest has been cleared and replaced by cultivated areas, or by scrub and eroded bare ground. Grasslands cover most of the interior of the islands. The flora of the mountains includes a number of Macaronesian elements, including the Dragon tree *Dracaena draco*; that of the lowlands includes many African elements.

## Flora

The Azores, Madeira, Salvage Islands, Canary Islands and Cape Verde belong to the Macaronesian Floristic Region, which, according to Takhtajan (1986), extends to southern Morocco and the territory of Western Sahara. More than half of the species occur also in the Mediterranean region. The total flora, according to Takhtajan (1986), includes c. 2300 species of angiosperms, of which about 779 species are endemic to Macaronesia (see Table 12 for updated estimates). There are a considerable number of relict genera and species, some with disjunct distributions.

The numbers of endemic vascular plant species and genera are as follows (Davis *et al.* 1986, with updates from CPD Data Sheets):

### TABLE 12. NUMBER OF ENDEMIC SPECIES AND GENERA ON THE ATLANTIC OCEAN ISLANDS

| | Endemic species | Endemic genera |
|---|---|---|
| Ascension | 11 | 0 |
| Azores | 81 | 1 |
| Canary Islands | 500 | 20 |
| Cape Verde | 92 | 2 |
| Iceland | 1 | 0 |
| Madeira* | 123 | 1 |
| St Helena | 50 | 10 |
| Tristan da Cunha | 40 | - |

*The figure for Madeira refers to species endemic to the Madeiran and Salvage archipelagos.

A characteristic of many of the islands' floras is the presence of woody or shrubby species of genera which are elsewhere herbaceous.

For details of Useful plants, Threats and Conservation, see the individual site Data Sheets.

## Centres of plant diversity and endemism

The following islands are treated as CPD sites:

## AO1. Azores

– see Data Sheet.

## AO2. Canary Islands

– see Data Sheet.

## AO3. Madeira (including the Salvage Islands)

– see Data Sheet.

## AO4. Saint Helena

– see Data Sheet.

## Cape Verde Islands

Although meeting the floristic criteria for selection as a CPD island site, having 92 endemics and a species endemism rate of 14%, the Cape Verde islands were not selected for Data Sheet treatment as much of the original vegetation has been totally destroyed by clearance for agriculture, plantations and by grazing.

## References

Davis, S.D., Droop, S.J.M., Gregerson, P., Henson, L., Leon, C.J., Villa-Lobos, J.L., Synge, H. and Zantovska, J. (1986). *Plants in danger: what do we know?* IUCN, Gland, Switzerland and Cambridge, U.K. xlv, 461 pp.

Takhtajan, A. (1986). *Floristic regions of the world.* University of California Press, Berkeley, California. 522 pp.

# AZORES
## Portugal (Autonomous Region)

**Location:** Mid-way between America and Europe in the North Atlantic; the islands are located between latitudes 36°00'–39°00'N and longitudes 25°00'–31°00'E.

**Area:** 2304 km², distributed over 9 islands.

**Altitude:** 0–1351 m (summit of Mount O'Pico).

**Vegetation:** Laurisilva (very reduced), montane cloud forest, shrubland, grassland, seral communities on volcanics, wetlands, littoral communities.

**Flora:** 300 vascular plant species, of which 81 (27%) are endemic; 1 endemic genus. 400 species of bryophytes (5% endemic). Flora belongs to the Macaronesian Floristic Region.

**Useful plants:** Timber trees (logged out), fodder, fruits, dye plants, medicinal plants.

**Other values:** Watershed protection, genetic resources, tourism.

**Threats:** Development pressures, including conversion of native vegetation to pasture or exotic tree plantations; lack of environmental awareness, lack of official conservation strategy and regulatory bodies, invasive plants.

**Conservation:** 12 Nature Reserves, but only 3 over 10 km². Legally protected areas not properly managed; need for official conservation plan and establishment of well-managed protected areas; research and environmental education needed.

## Geography

The Azores are a volcanic archipelago in the North Atlantic; the archipelago is geologically the most recent of the Macaronesian Islands. There are 9 main islands, all inhabited, distributed over a wide area of the North Atlantic between latitudes 36°00'–39°00'N and longitudes 25°00'–31°00'E. The islands are 1600 km from Newfoundland and 1400 km from Lisbon. The maximum distance between the islands is 615 m. The size of the islands varies greatly, from 746 km² (São Miguel) to 17 km² (Corvo). The 3 largest islands, São Miguel, Terceira and Pico, comprising 69% of the total area of the archipelago.

The islands are geomorphologically varied, the older being dissected by a large number of incised ravines and river valleys and with extensive alluvial and colluvial deposits. Fresh basalt lava flows are found on the youngest islands. Calderas are notable features. Soils are mainly andosols, with lithosols also well-represented. Histosols develop on lava and inceptisols on volcanic ash.

The climate is oceanic, with little variation in temperature. The mean annual temperature at sea-level is c. 17.5°C, the coldest month being February (13.8°C). Frosts occur above 1000 m. The annual rainfall increases westwards, from 710 mm in Ponta Delgada (São Miguel) to 1592 mm in Santa Cruz (Flores). This rainfall gradient significantly influences the nature of lower altitude vegetation. Strong winds, especially from the south to south-west, are ecologically important. The humidity is high, with an annual mean of over 75–80% relative humidity.

## Vegetation

The Azores were uninhabited until the mid-15th century. Much of the original vegetation cover was dense evergreen forest (laurisilva), with special local types of vegetation near coasts, on recent lava flows, in wetlands, on cliffs and at high altitudes (subalpine vegetation: on Pico only). The dominants in the original forest may have been *Laurus azorica*, *Myrica faya* and *Picconia azorica*. No large areas of natural forest survive in the lowlands, having been cleared for agriculture, settlement or having been replaced by exotic plantations of *Acacia*, *Cryptomeria japonica*, *Eucalyptus* and *Pittosporum undulatum*. Native trees can still be found as isolated individuals or, in some cases, forming an understorey within the plantations. The only patch of lowland forest remaining is in south-west Terceira, where there is a small area of *Erica azorica* forest on very poor soils; native trees are also present in the few remaining areas of coastal scrub.

Moderately large areas of natural and semi-natural forest occur above 500 m on Pico, Terceira (which has the best remaining forests) and São Miguel (Mount O'Pico). These are cloud forests, which vary in height from 10 m to only 1 m. So-called "elfin forest" occurs above 1100 m on Pico. The dominant species include *Erica azorica*, *Ilex perado* subsp. *azorica*, *Juniperus brevifolia* and *Laurus azorica*. There are abundant epiphytes (bryophytes, ferns), with a ground layer of large ferns and mosses. A unique type of elfin forest with *Erica*, *Juniperus* and *Daphne laureola* is present on the island of Pico at 1100–1400 m.

Other vegetation types occur on coasts and on recent lava flows. Montane moorland occurs on Mount O'Pico. Montane grasslands on Terceira contain endemic grasses and herbs, such as *Festuca jubata*, *Holcus rigidus* and *Tolpis azorica*.

## Flora

There are 300 native vascular plant species, of which 81 (27%) are archipelago endemics. Eight of the 11 native trees are endemic, 2 others being found elsewhere only on Madeira. There is one endemic vascular plant genus. The flora includes 2 giant species of herbs, namely *Lactuca watsoniana* (Azorian endemic) and *Melanoselinum decipiens* (Macaronesian endemic). There are many introduced species.

The flora belongs to the Macaronesian Floristic Region (Takhtajan 1986).

## Useful plants

At one time *Picconia azorica* was in great demand for its timber.

## Social and environmental values

Denser types of natural vegetation help to protect catchments. An endemic bullfinch is dependent on montane forest.

## Threats

A continuing threat to remaining areas of native vegetation is clearance for agriculture and forestry plantations. Further expansion of plantations of the exotic *Cryptomeria japonica* has reportedly ceased, since plantations of this species are uneconomic (the trees being subject to wind damage). Invasive species, such as *Hedychium gardnerianum*, are a serious problem. The introduced *Pittosporum undulatum* prevents regeneration of native *Myrica faya*.

Coastal development and rubbish dumping are threats to some species and surviving areas of semi-natural coastal vegetation.

## Conservation

Most of the sites with surviving fragments of natural vegetation were once common land, but now come under the control of the Forestry Service. There is a Protection Service, but it has no jurisdiction over the Forestry Service.

The Forestry Service has been responsible for much of the clearance of native forest for pasture or tree plantations. The protected areas system in the Azores is poorly developed, with 12 Nature Reserves listed in 1989. Only three reserves cover more than 10 km² (IUCN 1992). There is a small Botanical Reserve on Pico da Vara (São Miguel). The Garden of Indigenous Azorean Flora was founded in 1988 at Ponta Delgada (São Miguel).

There is an urgent need to protect remaining areas of natural vegetation and to attempt rehabilitation of natural communities. Some specific areas where protection or rehabilitation are recommended are given in Le Grand, Sjögren and Furtado (1982) and Haggar, Westgarth-Smith and Penman (1989).

## References

Le Grand, G., Sjögren, E. and Furtado, D.S. (1982). *Pico da Vara*. Universidade dos Açores, Ponta Delgada.

Haggar, J.P. (1988). The physiognomy and status of cloud forests of Pico Island, the Azores. *Biol. Conserv.* 46: 7–22.

Haggar, J.P., Westgarth-Smith, A.R. and Penman, D. (1989). Threatened flora and forests in the Azores. *Oryx* 23: 155–160.

IUCN (1992). *Protected areas of the world: a review of national systems. Volume 2: Palaearctic.* IUCN, Gland, Switzerland and Cambridge, U.K. xxviii, 556 pp.

Takhtajan, A. (1986). *Floristic regions of the world.* University of California Press, Berkeley, California. 522 pp.

## Acknowledgements

This Data Sheet was prepared by Eduardo Dias (Universidade dos Açores), with additional material from Haggar, Westgarth-Smith and Penman (1989).

# CANARY ISLANDS
## Spain (Autonomous Region)

**Location:** Archipelago with seven principal islands, between latitudes 27°37'–29°23'N and longitudes 13°20'–18°16'W. An autonomous region of Spain.

**Area:** 7542 km² (largest island: Tenerife, 2058 km²).

**Altitude:** 0–3717 m (summit of Pico de Teide, Tenerife).

**Vegetation:** Coastal vegetation, dry lowland zone with scrub (0–600 m); *Euphorbia*-rich vegetation and thermophilous woodland, laurel and montane pine forest (400–1800 m); montane scrub (2000–2500 m).

**Flora:** c. 1200 indigenous vascular species, of which 500 are Canary Island endemics and a further 200 are Macaronesian endemics.

**Useful plants:** Genetic resources for horticultural and crop plants, including dry zone pasture grasses, medicinal plants, timber trees.

**Threats:** Tourist and residential developments, overgrazing, off-road vehicles, invasive plants, fires.

**Conservation:** 4 National Parks (IUCN Management Category: II) covering 273.5 km², Garajonay National Park also a World Heritage Site (39.9 km²), Los Tilos y El Canal Biosphere Reserve covers 5.1 km²; 98 other protected areas. More effective management needed, lowlands inadequately protected. Active integrated *in situ* and *ex situ* work underway.

## Geography

The Canary Islands are situated off the west coast of North Africa between latitudes 27°37'–29°23'N and longitudes 13°20'–18°16'W. The archipelago is formed of seven principal islands (Gran Canaria, Tenerife, Fuerteventura, Lanzarote, La Palma, La Gomera, El Hierro), 4 small islands (Lobos, La Graciosa, Alegranza, Montaña Clara) and 2 islets (Roque del Este, Roque del Oeste). The easternmost point of the islands (Fuerteventura) is separated from Cape Juby on the African coast by almost exactly 100 km.

The total area of the archipelago is 7542 km². The largest island is Tenerife with an area of 2058 km², followed by Fuerteventura (1725 km²) and Gran Canaria (1532 km²). The maximum altitude occurs on Tenerife at the summit of Pico de Teide (3717 m).

The islands are volcanic and vary in age between c. 40 and 2 million years. The islands are still volcanically active and there were major eruptions on Tenerife in 1704, 1706 and 1798 and, on Lanzarote, between 1730 and 1736, when the volcanic mountains now included in the Timanfaya National Park were formed. The most recent eruption took place on the island of La Palma in 1971. The topography is generally rugged, with deep eroded valleys alternating with razor-backed ridges; secondary volcanic cones are frequent and there is a sharp contrast between the north coasts, with steep slopes and high sea-cliffs, and the southern more gentle slopes, with cliffs and sandy beaches.

The islands have been under European influence since the 15th Century and the natural vegetation, especially the forests, has been ruthlessly exploited ever since. The current population is about 1,450,000, the two major islands of Gran Canaria and Tenerife having about 87% of the total inhabitants. Population density ranges from 11 per km² on Fuerteventura to 411 per km² on Gran Canaria. The main industries are tourism and agriculture, with commerce and fishing also important.

## Vegetation

The vegetation of the islands lies in three main zones, the basal zone between sea-level and 600 m, the montane forest zone between 400 and 1800 m and a high mountain zone between 2000 and 2500 m. Though the coastal and lowland communities of the Canaries, including the thermophilous woodland, bear some resemblance to those found in Sous Province of southern Morocco, they are generally so rich in endemic species that they can be considered to be unique. The laurisilva formation is shared by the Canary Islands, Madeira and the Azores, but in each archipelago and, indeed in the Canaries on each island, there are unique elements and local endemic species. This makes all remaining examples important for conservation of biodiversity. *Pinus canariensis* forest is found only in the Canaries and is, therefore, of special conservation value, as are the endemic species-rich high mountain communities.

### Basal zone

This zone has a characteristic hot dry climate with low rainfall and high insolation. On the coast, the vegetation is predominantly halophytic, with such species as *Astydamia latifolia*, *Argyranthemum frutescens* and *Limonium pectinatum*. Coastal dunes are found on the islands of Gran Canaria, Lanzarote and Fuerteventura where local endemics, such as *Androcymbium psammophilum*, and North African plants, such as *Limonium tuberculatum* and *Traganum moquinii*, are found. Inland the vegetation is dominated by xerophytic shrubs, with *Launaea arborscens* and *Plocama pendula* in the driest areas. *Euphorbia* communities

89

(tabaibales and cardonales) are widespread over the rest of the zone.

At the upper limits of the basal zone, a dry thermophilous forest formation with *Olea*, *Pistacia* and *Juniperus phoenicea* was formerly abundant, but is now much reduced by exploitation, mainly for domestic fuel and as a source of energy for the now redundant sugar industry. There are small, impoverished relicts on Gran Canaria, Tenerife and La Gomera.

### Montane forest zone

There are two markedly different ecosystems: humid broadleaved forest and pine forest.

The **evergreen broadleaved forest** (laurisilva) is dominated by four species of the family Lauraceae: *Apollonias barbujana*, *Laurus azorica*, *Ocotea foetens* and *Persea indica*. It is found mainly on the northern slopes of the islands at altitudes bathed by trade wind mists and clouds. In drier areas on northern slopes, a community, locally known as fayal or brezal, predominates: it is a low woodland of *Erica arborea* and *Myrica faya*. The broadleaved forest is of great interest, being a relict of a type of vegetation found throughout the Mediterranean region in the Tertiary, but which became extinct in that region during the ice-ages of the early Quaternary. It survives only in the more sheltered and warmer Macaronesian Islands. Unfortunately, only a small percentage of the original laurel forest still survives in the Canary Islands, though the most complete and natural area, the forests of El Cedro on the island of La Gomera, has recently been given full protection as a National Park and declared a World Heritage Site.

Extensive **pine forests** of *Pinus canariensis* (Canary pine) are found principally on the islands of Tenerife, Gran Canaria, La Palma and El Hierro. There are two types of pine forest: a dry open, savanna-like forest found on southern slopes, with a sparse undergrowth of *Adenocarpus foliolosus*, *Chamaecytisus proliferus*, *Cistus symphytifolius* and various species of Labiatae and Leguminosae, and a more humid, denser forest found in areas of a more northerly orientation where elements of the laurisilva may be found in the undergrowth. Pine forests include a number of local endemics, such as *Micromeria pineolens* on Gran Canaria and *Lactucosonchus webbii* on La Palma, but are generally not as species-rich as other forest communities.

### High mountain zone

The summits of the highest islands (Tenerife, La Palma and Gran Canaria) have a low scrub vegetation above 1800 m. This formation is dominated by leguminous shrubs, such as *Adenocarpus viscosus* and *Spartocytisus supranubius*, and is rich in local endemic species. These include such rarities as *Viola cheiranthifolia*, *Echium auberianum* and *Bencomia exstipulata* on Tenerife, *Echium gentianoides* and *Genista benehoavensis* on La Palma, and *Crambe scoparia* on Gran Canaria.

## Flora

The native flora of the Canary Islands includes c. 1200 vascular plant species, of which c. 500 species are endemic to the islands. The total vascular plant flora (including introduced species) comprises about 2000 species. More than 120 species are shared with the rest of the Macaronesian region. There are no endemic plant families, but some 20

genera are confined to the Canary Islands, including *Bencomia* (4 species), *Dendriopoterium* (2), *Todaroa* (1), *Gonospermum* (5), *Schizogyne* (2), *Allagopappus* (2), *Vieraea* (1), *Sventenia* (1), *Dicheranthus* (1), *Gesnouinia* (1), *Neochamaelea* (1), *Parolina* (4), *Ixanthus* (1), *Spartocytisus* (2), *Plocama* (1), *Kunkeliella* (3), *Normania* (1) and "*Ceballosia*" (1). About 13 further genera are shared with other Macaronesian Islands, including: *Argyranthemum* (22 species), *Picconia* (2), *Marcetella* (2), *Aichryson* (14), *Monanthes* (17), *Cedronella* (1), *Pleiomeris* (1), *Bystropogon* (5), *Phyllis* (2), *Isoplexis* (4), *Visnea* (1), *Drusa* (1) and *Pericallis* (14).

More widespread genera with large endemic sections or subgenera in the Canaries are: *Ceropegia* (6 species), *Descurainia* (7), *Crambe* (10), *Lotus* (18), *Teline* (11), *Aeonium* (32), *Sonchus* (24), *Echium* (24), *Micromeria* (18), *Sideritis* (25), *Cheirolophus* (14) and *Limonium* (17). The high number of species in genera such as *Aeonium*, *Sonchus*, *Argyranthemum* and *Echium* is due to the evolutionary processes of adaptive radiation and inter-insular vicariance. The Canarian flora provides some of the world's best scientific models of both processes in an island context.

Due to the rugged nature of the landscape, the flora is rich in cliff species, especially at sites such as Teno on Tenerife, Anden Verde on Gran Canaria and Sabinosa on El Hierro.

Introduced species form a considerable part of the present day flora and some of them, such as *Eucalyptus* spp. and *Opuntia ficus-indica*, have become prominent features locally in the landscape. *Ageratina adenophora* has become an invasive weed in laurel forests.

## Useful plants

*Pinus canariensis*, *Juniperus cedrus*, *Persea indica*, *Apollonias barbujarra* and *Ocotea foetans* have been traditionally used as timber trees for construction and furniture manufacture, but useful timber is now mostly imported. Of the indigenous species, *Juniperus cedrus* in particular has been reduced almost to extinction and only a few isolated individuals remain on La Palma, Tenerife and Gran Canaria.

A hybrid of *Pericallus lanata* and *P. cruenta*, both endemic to Tenerife, has given rise to the florist's cineraria (*P. hybrida*), which is an important ornamental house-plant worldwide. Other species widely used as ornamentals in parts of the world with a Mediterranean or subtropical climate include *Dracaena draco*, *Phoenix canariensis*, *Echium pininana*, *E. wildpretii*, *Lotus berthelotii*, *Limonium arborescens*, *Nauplius sericeus*, *Argyranthemum frutescens* and *Gonospermum ptarmaciflorum*. Several others, such as *Lotus maculatus*, *Micromeria pineolens*, *Isoplexis isabelliana* and most members of the genera *Aeonium*, *Argyranthemum*, *Echium* and *Limonium* have enormous potential as ornamentals.

Several local endemics are of considerable interest to plant breeders because of disease resistance or for their potential as pasture grasses for dry zones. These include *Avena canariensis*, *Beta webbiana*, *Dactylis smithii*, *Chamaecytisus proliferus* and several endemic species of *Lotus*.

A large number of endemic species have traditional medicinal uses and some are still widely employed. These include *Bystropogon origanifolius*, *Salix canariensis*, *Lavendula buchii*, *Sideritis* spp., *Isoplexis* spp. and *Hypericum canariense*.

## Social and environmental values

The Canary Islands, Madeira and the Salvage Islands form one Endemic Bird Area with 9 restricted-range land birds, of which 5 species are restricted entirely to the Canary Islands. The islands are important for breeding seabirds.

Though legal measures for environmental protection still meet with occasional resistance in some rural communities, this is usually based on the loss of potential for land speculation, though it is sometimes spuriously presented as a threat to traditional rural agriculture or as a brake on local community development. In fact, future development of many such communities depends on their potential for attracting income from environmental protection agencies and particularly from ecotourism. The flora, fauna and landscape values of the islands make them a major factor in the future tourist development of the Canaries and their potential should be maintained without further degradation.

The forests of the Canaries, like those of Madeira, are extremely important in the hydrology of the islands. Dense vegetation cover prevents soil erosion in periods of torrential rainfall and intercepts rain and mist precipitation, contributing to groundwater supplies. In areas where forests have been cleared, soil erosion is now a major factor inhibiting rural development.

## Threats

Land speculation, both for tourism and for local second residences, is the major threat facing large areas of the islands. General urban sprawl and extraction of minerals and building materials are also serious problems, especially in those areas of the coast not dedicated to tourist development. The remaining undamaged natural coastline should be strictly protected. Forest clearance is no longer a major threat, though it is still locally significant in some areas of Tenerife and La Palma, where large areas of forest are still in private hands.

Overgrazing is probably the second most important threat to the natural vegetation in some parts of Gran Canaria and, particularly on the island of Fuerteventura. In those cases the original thermophilous forest landscape has been reduced to desert over the centuries. The little remaining natural vegetation is threatened by the introduced North African ground squirrel (*Atlantoxerus getulus*).

A more recent, and extremely damaging activity is the Jeep Safari using off-road vehicles. This is a threat to plant communities in several parts of the islands, for example, the southern and central regions of Gran Canaria and the dunes of Fuerteventura, especially on the Jandia Peninsula and in the south of Lanzarote at Playa de los Papagayos. Strict measures are needed to control this activity and prevent it becoming even more of a threat to the conservation of important local plant communities.

Introduced plants, such as *Agave americana*, *Opuntia dillentii* and *O. ficus-indica*, are serious invaders of lowland xerophytic communities and often almost completely replace the natural *Euphorbia*-rich vegetation. The excessive development of forest roads in the 1970s has opened up a network of potentially disastrous routes for the entry of weeds and invaders deep into laurel forest communities. The role of disturbed roadside habitats in promoting the spread of non-native species can clearly be seen in the Anaga region of Tenerife, along the forest roads to the east of El Bailadero.

## Conservation

Within the Canarian archipelago numerous protected areas have been designated. These include four National Parks, Timanfaya (51.1 km²) on Lanzarote, El Teide (135.7 km²) on Tenerife, Tabouriente (46.9 km²) on La Palma and Garajony (39.8 km²) on La Gomera. The last named protects one of the most important areas of laurisilva in Macaronesia and has recently been designated a World Heritage Site. The forest area known as Los Tilos y El Canal on La Palma is a MAB Biosphere Reserve (of area 5.1 km²). The Ley de Declaración de Espacios Naturales de Canarias, recently approved by the Canarian Parliament, designates no less than 98 additional protected areas, either as Protected Landscapes or Natural Parks, and current legislation, which is in an advanced stage of preparation, establishes management systems for these areas.

Most of the Endangered plant species are also protected, either by local, national or EEC legislation. However, effective protection has not yet been established and several areas, such as Arinaga on Gran Canaria, continue to be damaged by illegal sand extraction or use for new agricultural developments, despite having legal protection.

As the existing protected areas system in the Canaries does not adequately protect lowland communities, a proposal for a new National Park on the island of Gran Canaria is currently being considered to include a large sector of the *Euphorbia* communities, as well as the important eroded volcanic landscape of the centre of the island which is in need of urgent protection against land speculation and progressive, uncontrolled urbanisation.

## References

Bramwell, D. (1990). Conserving biodiversity in the Canary Islands. *Ann. Missouri Bot. Gard.* 77: 28–37.

Bramwell, D. and Bramwell, Z.I. (1990). *Flores silvestres de las Islas Canarias*. 3rd Ed. Editorial Rueda, Madrid. 376 pp.

González, N., Rodrigo, J. and Suarez, C. (1986). *Flora y vegetación del Archipielago Canario*. Edirca S.L., Las Palmas de Gran Canaria. 335 pp.

Hansen, A. and Sunding, P. (1985). Flora of Macaronesia. Checklist of vascular plants. 3rd revised edition. *Sommerfeltia* 1: 1–167.

Montelongo, V., Rodrigo, J. and Bramwell, D. (1984). Sobre la vegetación de Gran Canaria. *Botánica Macaronésica* 12–13: 17–50.

Synge H. (1991). *Conserving the wild plants of Gran Canaria*. Cabildo Insular de Gran Canaria/WWF/IUCN, Las Palmas de Gran Canaria. 38 pp.

## Acknowledgements

This Data Sheet was written by Dr David Bramwell (Jardín Botánico "Viera y Clavijo", Las Palmas de Gran Canaria, Spain).

# MADEIRA
# (including the Salvage Islands)
# Portugal

**Location:** Madeiran archipelago – between latitudes 33°10'–32°20'N and longitudes 16°10'–17°20'W. Salvage Islands – between 30°00'–30°10'N and 15°50'–16°05'W.

**Area:** Madeiran archipelago – 728 km²; Salvage Islands – 3 km².

**Altitude:** Madeiran archipelago – 0–1861 m (summit of Pico Ruivo, Madeira); Salvage Islands – 0–153 m (Salvagem Grande).

**Vegetation:** The principal vegetation of the Madeira is evergreen forest in which the dominant arboreal species are regional endemics. The remaining islands have been greatly altered by agriculture and exploitation.

**Flora:** 1226 species, with 1163 on Madeira, 448 on Porto Santo, 119 on the Desertas and 105 on the Salvages. The numbers of endemics (to the Madeiran and Salvage archipelagos as a whole) are 123, 113, 29, 30 and 11, repectively for the various geographical entities.

**Useful plants:** Madeiran archipelago: indigenous trees were formerly a major source of timber, fuel and charcoal, and still provide agricultural materials (mainly fencing). Various species have local medicinal and culinary uses. Salvage Islands: mineral-rich herbaceous and shrubby species were formerly burnt for soda-ash.

**Other values:** Madeiran archipelago: watershed protection and augmentation of groundwater supplies (both domestic and agricultural), high landscape quality, numerous endemic birds, tourist attraction.

**Threats:** Madeiran archipelago: competition from introduced plants, tourism, clearance for agriculture, fire. New infrastructure, mainly roads.

**Conservation:** Madeiran archipelago: extensive areas already protected, particularly evergreen forest in the uplands, but lowland vegetation less well protected. Salvage Islands: fully legally protected.

## Geography

The islands of the Madeiran archipelago lie in the eastern Atlantic about 978 km from Lisbon and 630 km off the west coast of Morocco, between latitudes 33°10'–32°20'N and longitudes 16°10'–17°20'W. All the islands are of Tertiary volcanic origin and are estimated to be between 60 and 70 million years old; the rock is mainly basalt. Unlike the Azores and Canary Islands, there has been no recent volcanic activity. The soils have been little studied but are said to be mostly of the pedalfer type, being poor in calcium and potassium, acidic and rich in humus.

Madeira is the largest and highest of the islands. It has an area of 728 km² and reaches 1861 m at its highest point (Pico Ruivo). The terrain is generally rugged and is dissected by deep ravines and gorges. A central ridge running east to west includes all the high peaks of the island, as well as the high plateau of Paúl da Serra. Madeira and Porto Santo are the only permanently inhabited islands in the archipelago. The other islands in the archipelago are Ilhéu Chão, Deserte Grande and Bugio (collectively known as the Desertas), three small islands 24 km off the south-east coast of Madeira.

Lying between Madeira and the Canary Islands are the Salvage Islands, a separate archipelago of very small volcanic islands and sea rocks which have strong biogeographic links with the Canary Islands (180 km to the south). They are just 350 km from Africa and have a land area of less than 3 km². They attain 153 m at Pico Atalaya on Salvagem Grande. There is no permanent water on any of the Salvage Islands.

The climate of the Madeiran archipelago is influenced by the Azores anticyclone and the trade winds which, in Madeira,

are principally from the north and north-east. Coastal fogs affect the southern and northern slopes of Madeira and have considerable influence on the formation of dominant communities, especially the evergreen forest.

In 1991, Madeira had a population of 257,692, of which 126,000 people lived in the capital, Funchal. Other, but very small, population centres are Calheta, Câmara de Lobos, Machico, Ponto do Sol, Ribeira Brava and Santa Cruz on the south and south-east coasts, and Porto do Moniz, Santana, and São Vicente on the north coast. The population of Porto Santo is only 5000, the majority living in the main town, Vila Baleira. Between 1981–1991, the population of Madeira rose by only 1.3%, due to high rates of emigration.

## Vegetation

In Madeira, altitude has a strong influence on the distribution of species and vegetation types. Many species are confined to specific altitudinal bands because of narrow ecological tolerances. There are also marked differences in the occurrence of vegetation types between the northern and southern parts of the island. Local variations occur as a result of variations in relative humidity and temperature, related to aspect and relief.

A herb and shrub community (*Aeonio-Lytanthion* alliance) occurs primarily in coastal regions of the island, rarely being fully developed at altitudes above 300 m in the south and 100 m in the north. Clearance for urban development and intensive cultivation has occurred. The shrub layer is not always present and in some areas the dominant native species (including *Globularia salicina*, *Euphorbia piscatoria* and

*Echium nervosum*) have been replaced by introduced species (e.g. *Opuntia tuna, Ulex europaeus* and *Cytisus scoparius*).

Evergreen forest (or laurisilva) once covered some 60% of Madeira, but is now reduced to 16% (100 km²) on the main island. The four dominant tree species, *Apollonias barbujana, Laurus azorica, Ocotea foetans* and *Persea indica*, are all members of the family Lauraceae and (with the exception of *Laurus azorica*) are endemic to Macaronesia. Evergreen forest develops in conditions of high precipitation, high humidity and mild temperatures, and is especially dependent on coastal fogs. The most crucial factor limiting the altitudinal distribution of forest in Madeira and the Azores is probably mean minimum temperature. The forest is generally described as being a relict of the Tertiary forests that once extended across southern Europe and north-west Africa. However, the present-day Macaronesian forest is much poorer in tree species than those earlier forests, although the shrub and herb layers are species-rich and contain numerous endemics. Bryophyte and lichen communities (especially epiphytic communities) are highly developed and diverse.

Two types of indigenous evergreen forest occur in Madeira. Dry evergreen forest develops where annual precipitation is low – between 350 and 500 mm – and sea fogs are sporadic. Important arboreal species are *Apollonias barbujana, Visnea mocanera* and *Picconia excelsa*. There are few hygrophilous ferns and lianas, and species such as *Ocotea foetans* and *Persea indica* never occur. Little is known about this forest type in Madeira, but it has been suggested that it formerly occupied much of the southern slopes between 300–700 m and also occurred in scattered, drier parts of the northern slopes between 100–400 m. These areas were the earliest and most extensively altered by exploitation and agriculture, and are now occupied by intensively cultivated land and forests of the exotics *Pinus pinaster, Eucalyptus globulus* and *Acacia* spp. No extensive areas of dry evergreen forest remain.

The second type of evergreen forest on Madeira is humid evergreen forest (*Clethro-Laurion* alliance). It occurs in areas receiving 500–1200 mm annual precipitation and where coastal fogs are frequent. The dominant trees are *Laurus azorica, Ocotea foetans* and *Persea indica*. This forest type also contains the endemic tree species, *Clethra arborea*. Humid evergreen forest covers large areas at 300–1300 m on northern slopes and 700–1200 m on southern slopes, and reaches its richest development in deep, extensive ravines such as Ribeiro Frio, Ribeira da Janela and Encumeada. Although the altitudinal limits may have been contracted by the activities of man, the natural limits are probably not more than 100 m above or below those which now exist.

Above the altitudinal limits of evergreen forest, the main communities are widespread *Erica arborea* and *Vaccinium padifolium* scrub, grazed grassland and, in the high peaks, *Erica cinerea* scrub.

Particular mention should be made of the vegetation of cliffs and coastal ravines. The cliffs along much of the north coast and parts of the south coast, such as Cabo Girão, have a striking flora with many chasmophytic and endemic species on vertical faces, e.g. *Sonchus ustulatus, Euphorbia piscatoria* and species of *Aeonium, Aichryson, Andryala* and *Helichrysum*. Some of the southern coastal ravines, especially

**Laurisilva and the mountainous central part of Madeira (CPD Site AO3). Laurisilva is still well preserved in parts of the Natural Park, which covers much of the more rugged higher parts of the island. The forest cover is recognised as essential for conserving supplies of water, used for drinking, agriculture and the production of electricity.** Photo: Alan C. Hamilton.

those close to built-up areas, offer refugia for indigenous vegetation and are often the sites for rare endemics, such as *Chamaemeles coriacea* and *Jasminum azoricum*.

The original vegetation of Porto Santo appears to have had *Juniperus phoenicea* as a dominant species, together with *Dracaena draco*. A thermophilous type of evergreen forest with *Apollonias barbujana* was also present. None of this vegetation remains. The vegetation of the Desertas, Salvage Islands and various islets has been degraded by rabbits and goats, except on Salvagem Pequena and neighbouring Ilhéu de Fora, where grazing animals have never been introduced. However, even here the vegetation is low, open, somewhat monotonous and dominated by a few halophytic species, such as *Suaeda vera*, *Mesembryanthemum nodiflorum*, *M. crystallinum*, *Limonium papillatum*, *Frankenia laevis* and *Senecio incrassatus*. There are a number of rare endemics.

## Flora

The flora belongs to the Macaronesian Floristic Region (Takhtajan 1986) and is relatively well-known, although some inaccessible areas need further investigation.

### TABLE 13. ENDEMISM IN THE MADEIRAN AND SALVAGE ARCHIPELAGOS

| | Number of species | Endemics to the archipelagos | Macaronesian regional endemics |
|---|---|---|---|
| Madeira | 1163 | 113 (10%) | 60 (5%) |
| Porto Santo | 448 | 29 (6%) | 18 (4%) |
| Desertas | 119 | 30 (15%) | 19 (10%) |
| Salvages | 105 | 11 (10%) | 11 (10%) |
| **All islands** | **1226** | **123 (10%)** | **69 (6%)** |

Besides endemic species, there are also many infraspecific taxa which are unique to the archipelagos.

Few of the 134 families represented in the flora of the two archipelagos contain large numbers of species. Important groups with a high proportion of archipelagic and regional endemics combined include the Compositae (132 species, 24 insular and Macaronesian regional endemics), Cruciferae (47, 11), Crassulaceae (229,11), Labiatae (39, 9), Liliaceae (24, 7) and Gramineae (139, 8). The only endemic genera are *Chamaemeles* (Rosaceae, 1 species), *Musschia* (Campanulaceae, 2 species), *Parafestuca* (Gramineae, 1 species) and possibly *Monizia* (Umbelliferae, 1 species). The pteridophyte flora (75 species, 14 insular and Macaronesian regional endemics) is particularly rich in the evergreen forests.

The large number of species introduced to the archipelagos occur mainly in Madeira and Porto Santo. Most are found in the lowlands, but some have also penetrated the higher regions. They often compete with native species and a few have become very invasive.

## Useful plants

Large quantities of native timber were exported from Madeira over a long period of time, beginning shortly after colonisation in the 15th century. The main species involved were *Ocotea foetans* and *Persea indica*, the latter being heavily exploited for its dense, fine-grained timber which was prized for cabinet making. The rare regional endemic *Juniperus cedrus* was formerly exploited for local use. Two introduced species used for reforestation, *Pinus pinaster* and *Eucalyptus globulus*, are widely planted at mid-altitudes.

The evergreen forest has long been a source of fuel. When sugar cane was a major crop, timber was used to power the sugar mills and, in World War I, great quantities of charcoal were produced, mainly from large specimens of *Erica arborea*. Although the forest is still regarded as a legitimate source of fuel, hydroelectricity (which now provides 20% of all electricity and the supply of which is dependent on the existance of the laurisilva) and butane gas have greatly reduced the demand for fuelwood.

Controlled cutting of native hardwoods is allowed for making agricultural materials. *Ilex perado* provides fence poles, while *Erica arborea* provides frames for vines, fence posts, panels and wind-breaks.

The burning of large quantities of *Mesembryanthemum nodiflorum*, *M. crystallinum* and *Suaeda vera* for soda ash (or barrilha) is now discontinued.

Various species are locally gathered for a variety of folk remedies and other uses. As examples, the fruits of the Madeiran bilberry *Vaccinium padifolium* are picked for making conserves, and the green twigs of *Laurus azorica* are used for cooking meat. *Melanoselinum decipiens*, a regional endemic also found in the Azores, is a notable fodder species.

A large number of species are of potential horticultural value, including 5 species of orchids (3 of which are endemic), species of *Argyranthemum* and *Saxifraga*, shrubby species of *Erysimum* and *Echium*, and *Isoplexis sceptrum*. There is a large and flourishing cut-flower industry in Madeira both for the home market and for export. Some wild species are important in local trade, but most are introduced species which often have become semi-naturalised.

## Social and environmental values

Madeira forms one Endemic Bird Area along with the Salvage Islands and the Canary Islands. Nine restricted-range land birds occur in the EBA, of which 1 species is restricted entirely to Madeira. Madeira and the Salvage Islands are important for breeding seabirds. Freira (*Pterodroma madeira*) only survives on Madeira with a population of less than 30 pairs.

The flora of Madeira is a major factor in attracting tourists to the islands – the indigenous forests contribute to the aesthetic and striking beauty of the interior. Tourism provides a major source of income.

The evergreen forest plays a major role in the hydrology of the island, particularly in precipitating droplets of water from the dense fogs which often wreath the upper regions. This contributes considerably to the groundwater supply. At even higher altitudes, *Erica arborea* plays a similar role. Given the topography of Madeira, erosion and the protection of watersheds are serious problems in areas where the cover of vegetation has been removed, especially in the south of the island where felling and overgrazing is most evident. In the more sparsely populated northern half of the island, where more of the original vegetation remains on upper slopes, problems are less severe. As a result, streams in the north flow permanently clear, while many of those in the south are turbid with silt after heavy rains and become almost dry in the summer.

# Threats

Clearance for agriculture and, to a lesser extent, urban development and road building, has reduced the extent of native vegetation in Madeira. Only the less accessible parts of the islands, such as steep coastal cliffs, deep gorges and the higher mountain slopes of the interior, support relatively undisturbed vegetation. Fortunately, the inaccessibilty of these areas provides a large measure of protection from further exploitation and destruction. Grazing and browsing by stock is legally controlled, as is deliberate burning, although the vegetation of the Desertas, the larger Salvage Islands and, in particular, Porto Santo, may be too degraded to recover fully.

A recent threat to the evergreen forest is the black rat (*Rattus rattus*). Adept at climbing, this species voraciously eats berries and new buds of several indigenous trees and can cause considerable damage. The brown rat (*R. norvegicus*) is a lesser threat.

The many trails in Madeira are increasingly popular with visitors who choose to visit the island for its flora and landscapes. A large increase in the number of visitors could be damaging to the flora and native vegetation.

Perhaps the greatest potential threat comes from introduced plants. Invasive species are already a problem at low altitudes, where species of *Acacia*, and *Pittosporum undulatum* (among others) are widespread and increasing. Others, such as *Ageratina adenophora* and *Erigeron karwinskianus*, have penetrated the higher regions. *Hedychium gardnerianum*, a serious problem in the Azores, is also present in Madeira. Eradication programmes have been set up, notably for *Acer pseudoplatanus* in the Ribeiro Frio area, and others may need to be carried out.

# Conservation

The following protected areas have been established: Salvage Islands Natural Reserve (94.5 km², of which only 2.8 km² is terrestrial), Natural Park of Madeira (567 km²) and Desertas Natural Reserve (96.7 km², of which 14.2 km² is terrestrial).

The Natural Park of Madeira contains several categories of reserve which receive different levels of protection. The most important are the 6 Wholly Protected Reserves (total area: 23.2 km²) and 10 Partially Natural Reserves (total area: 64 km²). The former are completely protected areas with access limited to scientific study only. All the remaining virgin evergreen forest occurs within these reserves. Partially Natural Reserves have a lower level of protection and a greater degree of access is allowed. They include those areas of evergreen forest which are still well preserved, despite human interference. Lowland vegetation is less well covered in the protected areas system.

The Natural Park of Madeira is also the title of the authority responsible for advising on, and overseeing, conservation measures in the islands. The primary aims of the Natural Park are: (a) conserving and regenerating the evergreen forest, and (b) protecting and managing the altitudinally sensitive zones. These aims are being achieved by a combination of legal instruments to restrict exploitation and more damaging agricultural practices, and a government policy of acquiring land in the more sensitive areas.

# References

Bravo, T. and Coello, J. (1978). Descripción geográfica del Archipiélago de las Salvajes. In *Contribución al estudio de la Historia Natural de las Islas Selvajes*. Aula de Cultura de Tenerife. Pp. 9–14.

Bravo, T. and Coello, J. (1978). Aportación a la geologia y petrología de las Islas Selvajes. In *Contribución al estudio de la Historia Natural de las Islas Selvajes*. Aula de Cultura de Tenerife. Pp. 15–35.

Costa Neves, H. (1987). A importância da preservação da floresta laurisilva na ilha da Madeira. In *I. Jornadas Atlânticas de Protecção do Meio Ambiente*. Angra do Heroismo. Pp. 260–268.

Hansen, A. and Sunding, P. (1985). Flora of Macaronesia. Checklist of vascular plants, 3. Revised edition. *Sommerfeltia* 1: 167 pp.

Monod, T. (1990). Conspectus Florae Salvagicae. *Bol. Mus. Mun. Funchal*, Suppl. 1: 79 pp.

Perez de Paz, P.L. and Acebes Ginoves, J.R. Las Islas Salvajes: Contribución al conocimiento de su flora y vegetación. In *Contribución al estudio de la Historia Natural de las Islas Selvajes*. Aula de Cultura de Tenerife. Pp. 79–105.

Santos, A. (1990). *Evergreen forests in the Macaronesian region*. Council of Europe Nature and Environment Series, No. 49. 78 pp.

Silva, F.A. and Menezes, C.A. (1946). *Elucidário Madeirense*, 2nd ed. 3 vols. (Facsimile published by Secretaria Regional de Turismo e Cultura, Funchal, 1984.)

Sjögren, E. (1972). Vascular plant communities of Madeira. *Bol. Mus. Mun. Funchal* 26: 45–135.

Takhtajan, A. (1986). *Floristic regions of the world*. University of California Press, Berkeley, California. 522 pp.

Tavares, C.N. (1965). Ilha da Madeira. O meio e a flora. *Revta Fac. Ciên. Univ. Lisb.* 13: 51–174.

# Acknowledgements

This Data Sheet was prepared by J.R. Press (The Natural History Museum, London).

# SAINT HELENA
# British Dependent Territory

**Location:** South Atlantic Ocean, about 1960 km from Africa and 2900 km east of South America, centred on latitude 15°58'S and longitude 5°43'W.

**Area:** 122 km².

**Altitude:** 0–823 m (summit of Diana's Peak).

**Vegetation:** Tree fern thickets, dominated by *Dicksonia arborescens*, once covered the central mountain ridge, but are now only found at High Peak and Diana's Peak; c. 10% of land area is forest (mostly forestry plantations); over 60% of island consists of eroded areas of rock, semi-desert and various introduced scrub communities; cattle pasture and abandoned New Zealand flax (*Phormium tenax*) plantations.

**Flora:** c. 60 vascular plant species, of which 50 (83%) are endemic; 10 endemic genera, 8 of which are monotypic.

**Useful plants:** Timber trees, heavily exploited in the past, such as gumwood (*Commidendrum robustum*), St Helena ebony (*Trochetiopsis melanoxylon*) and St Helena redwood (*Trochetiopsis erythroxylon*).

**Other values:** Replanting of endemic species to prevent soil erosion and flooding, landscape quality, cultural heritage.

**Threats:** Overgrazing by goats, pigs, cattle; invasive plants. "The most devastated of all the tropical islands in the South Atlantic". Grazing animals, timber cutting, collection of firewood and clearance for agriculture have destoyed much of the natural vegetation.

**Conservation:** c. 10% protected as forests. 4 National Forests recognised as category IV protected areas (Managed Nature Reserves): Diana's Peak Forest Reserve (1.3 ha), Hardings and Casons Forest Reserve (24.6 ha), High Peak Forest Reserve (4.9 ha) and Horse Ridge Nature Reserve (7.1 ha). Whole island proposed as Biosphere Reserve and World Heritage Site.

Highly successful St Helena Endemic Plants Propagation Programme, involving the Government of St Helena, the U.K. Foreign and Commonwealth Office, FFPS, IUCN, WWF, ODA, Royal Botanic Gardens, Kew, and the Botany School, Cambridge, set up in 1983 to propagate and re-introduce threatened endemics. Integrated Conservation Plan in preparation.

## Geography

St Helena (15°58'S, 5°43'W) is a British Dependent Territory in the South Atlantic Ocean, about 1960 km from Africa and 2900 km east of South America. The main island is about 15 km long and 10 km wide, and there are a number of tiny offshore islets. It is one of the most isolated islands in the world. The area is 122 km².

The island is the eroded summit of a large shield volcano which rises from the sea-floor at a depth of 4224 m. Eruptions which were later to give rise to the island first began on the mid-Atlantic Ridge about 30 million years ago (Nunn 1983). The island first emerged above sea-level about 15 million years ago, and volcanic eruptions continued until about 7.5 million years ago. The present land surface represents only the top 5% of the volcano, the dimensions of which far exceed those of any continental volcano.

The dominant feature of the island is a high central ridge (highest point: Diana's Peak, 823 m), from which deep gorge-like valleys radiate, incised to depths of up to 300 m. The coastline comprises a series of alternating bays and high cliffs. The main rock type is basalt, but there are also alkali olivine basalt-trachyte-phonolite assemblages interbedded with ash and pyroclastic material, making exposures vulnerable to erosion. (A detailed description of the geology of St Helena can be found in Baker 1968.)

Rainfall varies according to altitude and location. The mean annual rainfall over the last 80 years has been 881 mm, ranging from 325 mm to 925 mm. Coastal areas and the leeward side of the island receive the least amount of rain. Drought conditions prevailed during the early 1970s.

The size of the human population was 5564 in 1988, of which 1516 lived in Jamestown, the island's port (Paxton 1990).

## Vegetation

When discovered in 1502, St Helena was said to contain "fine woods" according to early Portuguese accounts. Since the introduction of goats in the early 16th century, and also other grazing animals, the original forest has disappeared from most of the island, and only a few remnants survive. Over 60% of the island is now covered by eroded areas of rock, or invaded by exotic weeds, such as prickly pear cactus (*Opuntia*) and *Aloe*. Semi-natural forest only occurs in scattered remnants on the central mountain ridge, totalling less than 10% of the land area. It is these remnant tree fern thickets, dominated by *Dicksonia arborescens*, which once covered the central mountain ridge, but which are now only found at High Peak and Diana's Peak. They harbour most of St Helena's endemic plants (Pearce-Kelly and Cronk 1990).

Cattle pasture, forest plantations and abandoned New Zealand flax (*Phormium tenax*) plantations cover most of the uplands at 450–750 m. Dry pastures occur at intermediate elevations of 300–450 m, which would have originally supported gumwood (*Commidendrum robustum*) woodlands.

In the dry lowlands, rocky semi-desert and sparse scrub communities occur, dominated by exotic weeds. These alien communities include *Chrysanthemoides-Diospyros* scrub, *Opuntia* scrub, *Lantana* scrub and "creeper waste" (dominated by mats of *Carpobrotus*). Semi-desert areas support little vegetation, forming the eroded, barren Crown Wastes, which would once have been covered with scrubwood, *Commidendrum rugosum*.

## Flora

Although the total number of native vascular plants is not large (about 60 species), an extraordinary proportion of these (83%, 50 species) is endemic. Furthermore, there are 10 endemic genera, 8 of which are monotypic. This makes the island an important centre of endemism.

### TABLE 14. ENDEMIC GENERA ON ST HELENA

| Name of genus | Common names | Number of species |
|---|---|---|
| Trochetiopsis | redwood, ebony | 2 |
| Nesiota | olive | 1 |
| Nesohedyotis | dogwood | 1 |
| Mellissia | boxwood | 1 (extinct) |
| Commidendrum | scrubwood, gumwoods | 4 |
| Melanodendron | black cabbage tree | 1 |
| Trimeris | lobelia | 1 |
| Lachanodes | she cabbage tree | 1 |
| Pladaroxylon | he cabbage tree | 1 |
| Petrobium | whitewood | 1 |

St Helena has long been famous for its "bizarre" plants, notably the "cabbage trees" (arborescent members of the Compositae belonging to the genera *Lachanodes* and *Pladaroxylon*). These occur in remnant thickets of native vegetation at Diana's Peak and High Peak, along with most of the other endemics.

St Helena's fern flora includes 14 endemic species, but there are no endemic genera. Of note are the two species of *Dryopteris* (*D. cognata* and *D. napoleonis*), which, together with *D. ascensionis* from Ascension, form a distinct group within the genus. Geographical disjunctions occur: *Microstaphyla* is a South American genus, whilst the nearest relatives to *Pseudophegopteris dianae* occur in the Mascarenes Islands, yet are not found in Africa.

Hemsley (1885) records 23 mosses (12 endemic) and 20 liverworts (11 endemic). The high rate of endemism is almost certainly due to under-collecting. The marine flora is impoverished, embracing some 60 algae species, mostly of very wide distribution except for one endemic, *Predaea feldmannii* (illustrated in Boergesen 1950). Fungi are little known. The list of 11 species given in Hemsley (1885), based on Melliss (1875), is almost certainly an under-estimate of the total fungal flora. The list comprises mainly widespread species, but includes two endemics, *Polyporus induratus* and the ascomycete *Xylaria mellissii*, which is

most likely a synonym of a widespread species (Pearce-Kelly and Cronk 1990).

Of the endemic vascular plant species, 7 are now Extinct, 23 are globally Endangered and 17 are globally Rare.

(In addition to the native vascular flora, there are about 260 species of naturalized aliens. Some of these have become aggressive weeds, see Threats below.)

## Useful plants

Timber trees which were also used for firewood include gumwood (*Commidendrum robustum*), St Helena ebony (*Trochetiopsis melanoxylon*) and St Helena redwood (*Trochetiopsis erythroxylon*). All are Endangered, the last being extinct in the wild and only surviving in cultivation.

## Social and environmental values

Apart from the flora, the landscape, geology, fauna and cultural heritage of St Helena are of global importance.

Among the fauna are over 150 endemic insect species (including the world's largest earwig, the St Helena giant earwig *Labidura herculeana*, which is Endangered), endemic landsnails of potential importance for genetic research; and the threatened endemic St Helena wirebird (*Charadrius sanctaehelenae*). A checklist of the recorded fauna of St Helena is given in Brown (1982). The invertebrate fauna is described in Basilewsky (1970).

The island's rich cultural heritage includes a continuous chronology of globally important scientific research from Holly in 1676 to the present day. Among those who have carried out scientific investigations on St Helena are Joseph Banks, Joseph Hooker and Charles Darwin. Napoleon Bonaparte was imprisoned on the island, where he was buried.

The coastline of St Helena contains some of the highest seacliffs in the Southern Hemisphere. Tourism is restricted due to the isolation of the island. A few hundred visitors arrive each year on cruise ships and between 100 and 150 yachts call at the island annually.

## Economic assessment

Until 1966, the manufacture of flax from *Phormium tenax* (introduced from New Zealand in 1870) was one of the mainstays of the economy. Agriculture, livestock rearing and fishing are now the chief economic activities (Oldfield 1987). The island is principally maintained by public revenue from the U.K. In 1985, this amounted to £9.35 million (Oldfield 1987).

The Agriculture and Forestry Department has recently undertaken large-scale replantings of endemic trees as part of the St Helena Endemic Plants Propagation Programme (see Conservation, below). This conservation programme aims to revegetate barren and degraded areas, helping to arrest erosion which causes considerable economic loss at present, and will help to return these areas (which cover about two-thirds of the island) once again to productive uses.

## Threats

St Helena has been described as "the most devastated of all the tropical islands in the South Atlantic". Goats, introduced in 1513, along with pigs and cattle, decimated the natural vegetation which was then invaded by exotic weeds. The first settlers soon exhausted supplies of gumwood which they used for timber and fuel (Janisch 1884) and, by the early 18th century, ebony was also in decline as it was being burned for lime production. More and more land was cleared for agriculture, and the combined effects of tree felling and overgrazing led to the devastation of about two-thirds of the island, causing serious disputes between settlers and the administration, and contributing to severe floods (Janisch 1884).

Major problems today are erosion, changes in local climate (reduced precipitation and decreased mist interception as a result of forest clearance) and the spread of invasive plants, primarily *Acacia* and *Eucalyptus* (Agriculture and Forestry Department of St Helena 1985).

## Conservation

About 10% of St Helena is protected as forest. Productive forest for timber and fuel covers 10 km²; conservation forests, which include areas of natural woodland as well as "productive" woodland being maintained and established to prevent erosion and soil degradation on steep slopes, cover 2 km².

Four National Forests are internationally recognised as category IV protected areas (Managed Nature Reserves). They are: Diana's Peak Forest Reserve (1.3 ha), Hardings and Casons Forest Reserve (24.6 ha), High Peak Forest Reserve (4.9 ha) and Horse Ridge Nature Reserve (7.1 ha). Their boundaries are fenced to prevent grazing, only endemic trees are planted, and exotics such as New Zealand flax are regularly cut (Agriculture and Forestry Department of St Helena 1985). Diana's Peak and High Peak are particularly important in having the last completely undisturbed areas of native forest on St Helena. In addition to these areas, Peak Dale is botanically important as the only intact area of gumwood (*Commidendrum*) forest on St Helena.

There is now growing support for conservation on the island. The main voluntary organisation is The St Helena Society which undertakes planting of endemic trees (Oldfield 1987). A highly successful St Helena Endemic Plants Propagation Programme was set up in 1983, involving the Government of St Helena (particularly the Agriculture and Forestry Department), the U.K. Foreign and Commonwealth Office, FFPS, IUCN, WWF, ODA, Royal Botanic Gardens, Kew, and the Botany School, Cambridge. A commercial-scale nursery was set up on the island and a number of threatened plants successfully propagated and re-introduced. Rescued plants include *Nesiota elliptica*, which was thought to be extinct until rediscovered on a precipitious cliff, and now represented by over 6000 plants raised in cultivation, and *Commidendrum rotundifolium* which was reduced to one plant in the wild, but now with over 1000 seedlings successfully raised in cultivation. Over 8000 plants of 14 species have so far been replanted in the wild. Continued commitment to this highly successful programme will enable further plants to be saved. (For rescue attempts on threatened species see Benjamin *et al.* 1986; Cronk 1983, 1986a, b, c, and 1987b).

The first stage of an Integrated Conservation Plan was initiated in March 1993 under the auspices of the Royal Botanic Gardens, Kew, ODA, the St Helena Working Group and the St Helena Government.

The whole island is proposed as a Biosphere Reserve and World Heritage Site.

## References

Agriculture and Forestry Department of St Helena (1985). *Nomination of Diana's Peak and High Peak, St Helena for inclusion in the World Heritage List.* Submitted by the Secretary of State for Foreign and Commonwealth Affairs, London.

Baker, I. (1968). *The geology of St Helena Island, South Atlantic.* Ph.D. thesis.

Baker, I., Gale, N.H. and Simons J. (1967). Geochronology of the Saint Helena volcanoes. *Nature* 215: 1451–1456.

Basilewsky, P. (1970). La faune Terrestre de L'Ile de Sainte-Hélène (Première partie). *Annales Musée Royal de l'Afrique Centrale* 181.

Benjamin, G.A., Cronk, Q.C.B., MacDonald, D.J. and Holland, M.D. (1986). *The endemic flora of St Helena: a struggle for survival* (ed. M.D. Holland; illus. M.G. Williams, R.L. Gillett). Produced by the Department of Agriculture and Forestry and the Department of Education, Government of St Helena. Government Printer, Jamestown. 44 pp.

Brown, L.C. (1982). *The flora and fauna of St Helena.* ODA Project Record 59. Land Resources Development Centre, ODA, London.

Cronk, Q.C.B. (1981). *Senecio redivivus* and its successful conservation in St Helena. *Environmental Conservation* 8: 125–6.

Cronk, Q.C.B. (1983). The decline of the redwood *Trochetiopsis erythroxylon* on St Helena. *Biological Conservation* 26: 163–174.

Cronk, Q.C.B. (1984). *The historical and evolutionary development of the plant life of St Helena.* Ph.D. thesis, University of Cambridge, Cambridge, U.K.

Cronk, Q.C.B. (1986a). The decline of the St Helena ebony *Trochetiopsis melanoxylon. Biological Conservation* 35: 159–172.

Cronk, Q.C.B. (1986b). The decline of the St Helena gumwood *Commidendrum robustum. Biological Conservation* 35: 173–186.

Cronk, Q.C.B. (1986c). *Conservation of the St Helena endemic flora: priorities for an integrated environmental programme.* Report of WWF (UK) Project No. 118/86. 22 pp.

Cronk, Q.C.B. (1987a). The history of the endemic flora of St Helena: a relictual series. *New Phytologist* 105: 509–520.

Cronk, Q.C.B. (1987b). The plight of the St Helena olive, *Nesiota elliptica. Botanic Gardens Conservation News* 1: 30–32.

Cronk, Q.C.B. (1989). The past and present vegetation of St Helena. *Journal of Biogeography* 16: 47–64.

Cronk, Q.C.B. (in press). St Helena and Ascension Island. In Bramwell, D. (ed.), *The conservation of island floras.* Croom Helm.

Daly, R.A. (1927). *The geology of Saint Helena Island.* American Academy of Arts and Sciences, Proceedings, 62 (2).

Drucker, G., Oldfield, S., Pearce-Kelly, P., Clarke, D., Cronk, Q., et al. (1991). *St Helena.* Document prepared for recognition of the entire island as an international recognised site of nature conservation importance. Preliminary draft. WCMC, Cambridge, U.K. 34 pp.

Goodenough, S. (1983). *Conservation of the endemic flora of St Helena (report).* Royal Botanic Gardens, Kew, U.K.

Goodenough, S. (1985). Ebonies, cabbages and baby's toes. *World Wildlife News* 1984/85: 6–9.

Hemsley, W.B. (1885). Report on the botany of the Bermudas and various other islands of the Atlantic and southern oceans. In C.W. Thompson & J. Murray, *Report on the scientific results of the voyage of H.M.S. Challenger. 1873–76, Botany* 1: 118–122.

Janisch, H. (1884). *St Helena records.* Jamestown, St Helena.

Melliss, J.C. (1875). *St Helena; a physical, historical, and topographical description of the island including its geology, fauna, flora, and meteorology.* London. 426 pp.

Norcliffe, G.B. (1969). The phormium industry in St Helena. *Journal of Tropical Geography* 29: 49–57.

Nunn, P.D. (1983). St Helena's ancient shores. *Geographical Magazine* 55: 252–257.

Oldfield, S. (1987). St Helena. In *Fragments of paradise, a guide for conservation action in the UK Dependent Territories.* British Association of Nature Conservationists/ WWF U.K.

Paxton, J. (ed.) (1990). St Helena. *The statesman's year-book, statistical and historical annual of the states of the world for the year 1990–1991.* Macmillan Press, London and Basingstoke, U.K.

Pearce-Kelly, P. and Cronk, Q.C.B. (eds) (1990). *St Helena natural treasury.* Proceedings of a symposium held at The Zoological Society of London, 9th September 1988. The Zoological Society of London, Regent's Park, London.

Price, J.H., John, D.M. and Lawson, G.W. (1978). Seaweeds of the western coast of tropical Africa and adjacent islands: a critical assessment. II. Phaeophyta. *Bulletin of the British Museum Natural History (Botany)* 6: 87–182.

Price, J.H., John, D.M. and Lawson, G.W. (1986). Seaweeds of the western coast of tropical Africa and adjacent islands: a critical assessment. IV. Rhodophyta (Florideae) I. Genera A–F. *Bulletin of the British Museum Natural History (Botany)* 15: 1–122.

Price, J.H., John, D.M. and Lawson, G.W. (1988). Seaweeds of the western coast of tropical Africa and adjacent islands: a critical assessment. V. Rhodophyta (Florideae) I. Genera G. *Bulletin of the British Museum Natural History (Botany)* 18: 195–273.

## Acknowledgements

This Data Sheet was written by Stephen D. Davis, based primarily on information in the preliminary report prepared by the working group of the NGO Forum for Nature Conservation in the U.K. territories to support St Helena's recognition as a World Heritage Site (Drucker *et al.* 1991), with updates.

# REGIONAL OVERVIEW: AFRICA

HENK J. BEENTJE
WITH BRYAN ADAMS AND STEPHEN D. DAVIS
AND EDITED BY ALAN C. HAMILTON

**Total land area:** 29,057,990 km$^2$.

**Population (1990):** 629,300,000[a].

**Maximum altitude:** 5895 m (summit of Mount Kilimanjaro).

**Natural vegetation:** Extensive woodland and grassland. Tropical moist forests (all types, see note [b]) estimated at c. 2,121,500 km$^2$ (slightly less than one-fifth of the global resource); major blocks of evergreen and semi-evergreen tropical rain forest in West Africa (much depleted) and Central Africa; montane forests occur as "islands", most notably in north-east and East Africa. Dry forest and extensive deciduous and semi-deciduous open woodland, especially in Sudanian and Zambezian regions; bushland, thicket, scrub, grasslands (both edaphic and anthropic), deserts (including the Sahara, the world's largest desert region) and alpine communities including giant lobelias and senecios (Dendrosenecio spp.). Species-rich fynbos (shrublands) in the Cape region; in terms of the number of species per unit area, probably the world's richest plant area.

**Number of vascular plants:** 40–45,000 species[c], but possibly as many as 60,000[d]
North Africa 10,000 species[e]
Tropical Africa 21,000 species[f]
Southern Africa 21,000 species[g]

**Number of endemic species:** c. 35,000 continental endemics.

**Vascular plant families:** 271 (including 31 fern families).

**Number of endemic families:** 27.

**Number of genera:** 3750.

**Number of endemic genera:** c. 224.

**Important plant families:** Leguminosae, Poaceae, Asteraceae, Orchidaceae, Burseraceae, Euphorbiaceae, Ericaceae, Rubiaceae.

Sources:
[a] United Nations Population Division (World Resources Institute 1992).
[b] Sayer, Harcourt and Collins 1992; forest area includes lowland, montane, inland swamp and mangrove forests; FAO (1988a) estimated 2,110,610 km$^2$ of closed tropical broadleaved forest in 1980.
[c] World Conservation Monitoring Centre (1992).
[d] K. Vollesen 1991, pers. comm.
[e] Based on figures for the size of country floras given in Quézel (1985).
[f] A.L. Stork, pers. comm. to P. Raven (1991), World Conservation Monitoring Centre (1992).
[g] Cowling, Gibbs Russell, Hoffman and Hilton-Taylor (1989).

## Geology

Africa is the second largest continent. With the exception of the Atlas Mountains in the north-west and the Cape ranges in the south, it consists of a crystalline shield (mostly of Precambrian age), overlain in places by Precambrian sedimentary rocks, Jurassic/Cretaceous sediments (along the eastern coast), Jurassic basalts (in southern Central Africa), Miocene-Pleistocene volcanics (especially along the Rift Valleys in eastern Africa) and aeolian sands (particularly in the Saharan and Kalahari regions). The oldest rock outcrops form the rugged massifs of Aïr and Ahaggar, the dissected plateaux of the Guinea highlands, the escarpments flanking the Niger basin, the Jos Plateau in Nigeria and the western rim of the continent from the Cristal Mountains to the Orange River.

Following the break-up of Pangaea (c. 200 million years ago), which, at that time, was located near the South Pole,

Africa, together with South America, Antarctica, Madagascar, India and Australia, formed the southern land-mass of Gondwana and started to drift north. Around its margins were deposited the sandstones, shales, limestones and dolomites of the Maghreb, the western Sahara, Tanzania, Mozambique and the Cape. Subsequent earth movements formed the parallel mountain ranges found today along the south coast of Africa, south of the Great Karoo.

Madagascar (see Regional Overview on the Indian Ocean) is believed to have separated from the African mainland about 160 million years ago (Rabinowitz, Cotlin and Falvey 1983). Africa separated from the other components of Gondwana about 135 million years ago and continued to drift north towards the Equator. Until the end of the Oligocene (25 million years ago) the flora and fauna of Africa evolved in relative isolation, giving rise to their distinctive character. At the end of the Oligocene, the African Plate (together with Arabia) abutted Eurasia, creating the Alps and Atlas Mountains, but from about 15 million years ago Africa again became an isolated land mass, as a result of the rifting apart of Africa and Arabia. At the same time, the climate became much drier, resulting in the expansion of grasslands at the expense of forests.

The rifting process has continued to the present day, giving rise to the Great Rift, extending from Turkey to Zimbabwe, with two major rift valleys in East Africa. This region is still volcanically active and includes the highest mountains on the continent – Mt Kilimanjaro (5895 m) and Mt Kenya (5199 m). Meanwhile, successive uplifting created the Great African Plateau, stretching from South Africa to Tanzania and Zaïre, the largest plateau on earth. Most of the plateau is more than 900 m above sea-level, the highest parts being the Drakensberg in Southern Africa (Thabana-Ntlenyana, 3482 m), Mt Rungwe (2691 m) in southern Tanzania, Mt Mulanje (3002 m) in southern Malawi and Mt Moco (2620 m) in Angola.

## Vegetation

Africa has an enormous range of vegetation types including true desert, dry bushland, wooded grassland, rain forest and alpine desert. The continent is predominantly woodland and grassland, containing more than twice as much open woodland as closed canopy forest. Apart from the major geological processes summarized above, erratic variations in the climate and a general trend toward increasing aridity, especially during the last two million years, have had profound effects on the vegetation (see, for example, Hamilton 1982, 1992). Sometimes the climate has been hotter and wetter than today and sometimes cooler and drier. Climatic change has affected the survival and distribution of individual species and whole vegetation types. In particular, the area of moist forest has at times been considerably reduced during the 21 or so ice ages during the last 2–3 million years, whereas grassland and open woodland expanded during these periods. Increasing aridity resulted in further desiccation of the Sahara and caused several forest areas in Central Africa to become isolated from each other, forming forest refugia. Severe forest reduction is thought to have led to many extinctions, as well as resulting in the fragmentation of populations of some species, encouraging divergent evolution within the isolated forests.

Interglacial periods have been wetter, allowing expansion of forests from refugia. There was marked climatic change as recently as 12,000 years ago, at the beginning of the present post-glacial phase. Relative stability of the climate over the last 12,000 years has allowed significant expansion of forest cover (Hamilton 1989).

It is not clear at what time (or times) the isolated and endemic-rich forests near the East African coast were connected with the main Guineo-Congolian forests further west. High levels of endemism in the East African coastal forests (which include fragmented lowland forest patches from Somalia to Mozambique and submontane forest on the Eastern Arc Mountains of Kenya and Tanzania) indicate a long period of isolation. For example, 40% of forest tree species on the East Usambara Mountains (one of the Eastern Arc forests in Tanzania – CPD Site Af71, see Data Sheet) are not found in the main Guineo-Congolian forests (Hamilton

and Bensted Smith 1989). Endemism levels in some other groups of organisms are even higher.

While there have been periods of forest spread as well as contraction, the richness of the flora of African savannas indicates that extensive areas of savanna have been present throughout the recent geological past. There has also been more recent expansion in the area of savanna vegetation as a result of human activities.

Present day African vegetation has been classified by Monod (1957), Troupin (1966), Greenway (1973) and White (1983), upon which the summary paragraphs below are based (see also Map 4).

## Formations of regional extent

### Forest
Continuous stands of trees 10 m to more than 50 m tall, with interlocking crowns; shrub layer normally present. Nearly all the forests of Africa are evergreen or semi-evergreen.

*Tropical rain forest* now covers only about 7% of the land area of Africa, representing slightly less than one-fifth of the total remaining global resource (Sayer, Harcourt and Collins 1992). Evergreen rain forest tends to be found in the wettest areas, especially if dry seasons are not too severe, such as in the central parts of the Zaïre basin (which receives between 2000 and 2500 mm per annum), in wetter places near the Atlantic coast (including on the seaward side of Mt Cameroon which has an excess of 4000 mm per annum) and at higher altitudes on mountains. More than 80% of Africa's rain forest occurs in a central belt, which stretches from Cameroon and Gabon on the Atlantic coast to western parts of Kenya and Tanzania. In West Africa, large-scale deforestation and fragmentation has left important relict blocks of rain forest at Gola (Sierra Leone), Sapo (Liberia) and Taï (Côte d'Ivoire), all of which are identified below as centres of plant diversity and endemism (CPD Sites Af8, Af7 and Af2, respectively).

The most recent comprehensive assessment of the extent of rain forest in Africa is that of Sayer, Harcourt and Collins (1992) to which the reader is referred. This work provides an in-depth country-by-country survey of the coverage of rain forest, with maps compiled from satellite and radar imagery and aerial photography. Table 19 gives figures for the original and remaining extent of closed canopy tropical moist forest and is derived from this study.

*Dry forest* occurs locally in the Zambezian and Sudanian regions, on the dry coastal plain of Ghana and in Madagascar (which is treated in the Regional Overview on the Indian Ocean).

Forests with rapid changes in structure and floristic composition over short distances occur in south-eastern Africa and in montane regions.

### Woodland
Open stands of trees at least 8 m tall, with a canopy cover of 40% or more, with a field layer usually dominated by grasses. Nearly all types are deciduous or semi-deciduous, but most contain at least some evergreen species. Woodlands are widespread in tropical Africa and are especially characteristic of the Sudanian and Zambezian regions, which have continental climates and moderate precipitation falling in the summer.

## Bushland and thicket

Bushland includes open stands of bushes, usually between 3 and 7 m tall and with a canopy cover of 40% or more; in thicket the stands of bushes are closed. Both types are found under a wide range of climatic and edaphic conditions which are unfavourable for tree growth. They are most frequent in areas where annual rainfall is 250–500 mm and of irregular occurrence, or where there are two pronounced dry seasons. Deciduous bushland and thicket is extensively developed in the Somali-Masai region; evergreen and semi-evergreen bushland and thicket is found in the Cape, coastal east and south-east Africa and associated with the drier types of montane forest. Bushland and thicket, dominated by Ericaceae, forms a distinct zone on many African mountains and crowns the summits of a few peaks in the Guineo-Congolian region. Secondary thicket is also widespread as a seral vegetation type.

## Shrubland

Open or closed stands of shrubs up to 2 m tall. The most extensive shrublands are in the Karoo-Namib region and in the Cape (fynbos). Shrublands also occur in montane and Afroalpine regions. In the latter they are typically dwarf and form but one component of a diverse range of communities.

## Grassland

Land covered with grasses and other herbs, either without woody plants or the latter not covering more than 10% of the ground. Edaphic grasslands are widespread throughout Africa and include vast areas in the Serengeti (developed on volcanic deposits and maintained as grassland by grazing), grasslands associated with seasonally or permanently waterlogged soils and also secondary grassland, which has replaced forest or woodland after human intervention (such as burning and cultivation).

## Wooded grassland

Land covered with grasses and other herbs, with woody plants covering between 10 and 40% of the ground. This is the most widespread vegetation in the Sahel and in the Kalahari part of the Kalahari-Highveld zone. It is also common in the Sudanian and the Zambezian regions.

## Deserts and semi-deserts

Arid landscapes with a sparse plant cover, except in depressions where water accumulates. Semi-desert vegetation begins to occur when the mean annual rainfall drops below c. 250 mm, e.g. in parts of the Karoo-Namib, Somali-Masai and the Sahel and on the margins of the Sahara Desert. True deserts include the Sahara, the floristically richer Namib Desert and parts of northern Kenya.

## Afroalpine vegetation

Physiognomically mixed vegetation confined to the highest mountains in Africa where night frosts are liable to occur throughout the year. Nearly half the flowering plant species present exhibit specialized growth forms, including giant rosette plants such as *Dendrosenecio* and *Lobelia* (see Data Sheet on the Afroalpine region of East and North-east Africa, Af81).

# Transitional formations of local extent

## Scrub forest

Intermediate between forest and bushland and thicket and often dominated by tree-like species of *Aloe* and *Euphorbia*.

## Transition woodland

Intermediate between forest and woodland.

## Scrub woodland

Stunted woodland less than 8 m tall or vegetation intermediate between woodland and bushland.

# Edaphic formations

## Mangroves

Open or closed stands of trees or bushes occurring on shores between the high- and low-water marks. Extensive tracts of mangroves occur on the west coast, the tallest being found in the Niger Delta (Nigeria), with trees up to 45 m tall (according to White 1983) and covering an area of 5400 km$^2$ (according to an unpublished report, SECA/CML 1987, quoted in Sayer, Harcourt and Collins 1992). On the east coast, Tanzania has 1155 km$^2$ of mangroves (Semesei 1991).

Other formations include: **herbaceous freshwater swamp and aquatic vegetation** and **halophytic vegetation** (saline and brackish swamp).

# Formation of distinct physiognomy but restricted distribution

## Bamboo

Only 4 species of bamboo are native to Africa. Of these, *Arundinaria tesselata* and *Sinarundinaria alpina* form Afromontane communities; *Oreobambos buchwaldii* also occurs on mountains, while *Oxytenanthera abyssinica* is widespread in the Sudanian and Zambezian regions. (*Bambusa vulgaris* is locally naturalized.)

# Anthropic landscapes

Human activity has dramatically changed the natural vegetation throughout most of Africa. In some areas, such as the Mediterranean region, the margins of the Sahara, densely settled parts of northern Sudan and urban zones, natural vegetation has been completely destroyed or else reduced to small remnants or individual trees.

Africa is thought to be the original home of man and it is likely that his activities have had a considerable impact on non-forest vegetation, such as woodland, for many tens to hundreds of thousands of years (including through burning) and for thousands of years in the case of at least some forests. Some areas of savanna are probably derived from forest as a result of continuous human pressure, compounded by a low availability of seeds for forest regeneration as human influence has destroyed remaining seed sources. In recent years the scale of destruction of semi-arid, woodland and forest ecosystems has assumed major proportions. Indeed, even apparently remote areas have been influenced by past settlement or collection of forest products.

## Areas of exceptional species-richness

Within some of the above vegetation types there are areas which are exceptionally species-rich, most notably in the Cape area and within rain forests. In some cases wide altitudinal ranges increase the number of habitats available. Some of these species-rich areas are believed to have served as refugia for plant species at times of continental droughts. For example, refugia in Cameroon/Gabon and eastern Zaïre are thought to have been the main, though not the only, centres of forest survival during a severely arid period around 18,000 years ago, during the Würm II glaciation (Hamilton 1992). They are not only rich in species and endemics, but also contain many species which are disjunct between them.

Other sites of very high diversity are some of the plateaux in High Shaba, where the woodland on relatively poor soils has many endemics. Diversity in this area is further enhanced by the presence of a whole range of habitats: gallery forest, ravine forest, rupicolous vegetation, swamps and soils rich in heavy-metals.

It is not just the vegetation types of high rainfall areas which are species-rich. For example, the Karoo, an area of semi-desert, contains a wealth of succulents and other xerophytic plants. Similarly, arid areas on the Somalia/Kenya/Ethiopia border and in the rainshadows of the Eastern Arc mountains in Tanzania (see Lovett 1988) exhibit high levels of species endemism. Fynbos, the evergreen bushland and thicket of the Cape region, has the highest concentration of species per unit area in the world (8550 vascular plant species in 89,000 km²) (Goldblatt 1978).

## Flora

| | |
|---|---|
| **Number of vascular plants:** | 40–45,000 species[a], but possibly as many as 60,000[b] |
| | North Africa    10,000 species[c] |
| | Tropical Africa  21,000 species[d] |
| | Southern Africa 21,000 species[e] |
| **Number of endemic species:** | c. 35,000 continental endemics. |
| **% species endemism:** | c. 58–88%. |
| **Vascular plant families:** | 271 (including 31 fern families). |
| **Number of endemic families:** | 27. |
| **% family endemism:** | c. 10%. |
| **Number of genera:** | 3750. |
| **Number of endemic genera:** | c. 224. |
| **% generic endemism:** | c. 6%. |

Sources:

[a] World Conservation Monitoring Centre (1992).
[b] K. Vollesen 1991, pers. comm.
[c] Based on figures for the size of country floras given in Quézel (1985).
[d] A.L. Stork, pers. comm. to P. Raven (1991), World Conservation Monitoring Centre (1992).
[e] Cowling, Gibbs Russell, Hoffman and Hilton-Taylor (1989).

See also statistics for countries (Table 15) and phytochoria (Table 16).

Despite having an extremely diverse flora, which is very distinct at the generic and specific level, Africa has fewer species than either South America or Asia and many species have relatively wide distributions within the continent. It is also relatively poor in representation in a number of plant families, such as Lauraceae and Palmae. For example, there are only 16 genera of palms in the whole of Africa, compared to 97 in Indomalaya. There are also fewer species of epiphytes in Africa compared to South America and Indomalaya.

There is debate about the reasons for the relative poverty of the tropical Africa flora compared with South America and Asia (Richards 1973; Axelrod and Raven 1978), but a drier climate (most areas of rain forest in Africa have at least one month with less than 100 mm of rain), losses due to past climatic fluctuations and long-term human influence have probably contributed.

The flora includes Mediterranean elements in the north and the extraordinarily species-rich Cape flora in the south. Diversity is not evenly distributed over the continent, as already indicated; a vast part of the Sahara, the Ténéré, is home to only 20 vascular plant species in an area spanning 200,000 km², while the fynbos of the Cape region has over 8550 species in 89,000 km².

Of the 27 families endemic to Africa, 14 are endemic to Southern Africa, while only 4 are endemic to tropical Africa. Some families, whilst not being endemic, have a large number of endemic genera (e.g. Annonaceae, Caesalpiniaceae, Sapotaceae).

While sample plots in African rain forests generally do not contain as many species as those in South East Asia and South America, some have proved exceptionally rich. Reitsma (1988) reports 201–211 plant species (all sizes) in a 0.02 ha primary rain forest site in Gabon (Ekobakoba), while 227 species have been recorded in a 0.01 ha site in Cameroon (Letouzey 1968a). These are among the highest species/area counts recorded for any vegetation type on Earth.

Tables 15 and 16 provide species numbers and levels of endemism for individual African countries and phytochoria, respectively, and from a variety of sources as indicated.

Although the vascular flora of Africa as a whole is relatively well-studied, some countries (such as Gabon, Central African Republic and Zaïre) and important areas (such as parts of the Eastern Arc Mountains of Tanzania) remain very poorly collected. See Campbell and Hammond (1989), for an assessment of the status of plant systematics and plant collection in tropical Africa. Not all countries are covered by a reasonably up-to-date Flora and most major floristic projects remain incomplete, with progress on many being slow in comparison with the rate at which the natural vegetation is being destroyed. Completed Floras include:

*Flore Forestière Soudano-Guinéenne* (Aubréville 1950)
*Flore du Sahara* (Ozenda 1977)
*Flora of West Tropical Africa* (Hutchinson and Dalziel 1927–1936, second edition 1954–1978)

Incomplete regional floras include:

*Flore d'Afrique Centrale* (1948– )
*Flora of Southern Africa* (1963– )
*Flora of Tropical East Africa* (1952– )
*Flora Zambesiaca* (1960– )

## TABLE 15. NUMBERS OF VASCULAR PLANT SPECIES AND LEVELS OF ENDEMISM IN AFRICAN COUNTRIES

| Country | Flowering plants | Gymnosperms and ferns | Total vascular plants | Number of endemics | % species endemism |
|---|---|---|---|---|---|
| Algeria | 3100 | 64 | 3164 | 250 | 7.9 |
| Angola | 5000 | 185 | 5185 | 1260 | 24.3 |
| Benin | 2000 | 201 | 2201 | 0 | 0.0 |
| Botswana | 2000 | 15 | 2015 | 17 | 0.8 |
| Burkina Faso | 1100 | - | >1100 | 0 | 0.0 |
| Burundi | 2500 | - | - | - | - |
| Cameroon | 8000 | 260 | 8260 | 156 | 1.9 |
| Central African Republic | 3600 | - | >3600 | 100 | 2.8 |
| Chad | 1600 | - | >1600 | - | - |
| Congo[a] | - | - | 6000 | [1200] | [20] |
| Côte d'Ivoire | 3517 | 143 | 3660 | 62 | 1.7 |
| Djibouti | 635 | 6 | 641 | 2 | 0.3 |
| Egypt | 2066 | 10 | 2076 | 70 | 3.4 |
| Equatorial Guinea | 3000 | 250 | 3250 | 66 | 2.0 |
| Ethiopia | 6000–7000 | 103 | 6103–7103 | 600–1400 | 10–20 |
| Gabon | 7000 | 151 | 7151 | [1573] | [22] |
| Gambia | 966 | 8 | 974 | 0 | 0.0 |
| Ghana | 3600 | 125 | 3725 | 43 | 1.2 |
| Guinea | 3000 | - | >3000 | 88 | 2.9 |
| Guinea-Bissau | 1000 | - | >1000 | 12 | 1.2 |
| Kenya | 6000 | 506 | 6506 | 265 | 4.1 |
| Lesotho | 1576 | 15 | 1591 | 2 | 0.1 |
| Liberia | 2200 | - | >2200 | 103 | 4.7 |
| Libya | 1800 | 25 | 1825 | 134 | 7.3 |
| Malawi | 3600 | 165 | 3765 | 49 | 1.3 |
| Mali | 1741 | - | >1741 | 11 | 0.6 |
| Mauritania | 1100 | - | >1100 | - | - |
| Morocco | 3600 | 75 | 3675 | 600–650 | 17.0 |
| Mozambique | 5500 | 192 | 5692 | 219 | 3.8 |
| Namibia | 3128 | 46 | 3174 | - | - |
| Niger | 1170 | 8 | 1178 | 0 | 0.0 |
| Nigeria | 4614 | 101 | 4715 | 205 | 4.3 |
| Rwanda | 2288 | - | >2288 | 26 | 1.1 |
| São Tomé & Príncipe[b] | 774 | 151 | 895 | 134 | 15.0 |
| Senegal | 2062 | 24 | 2086 | 26 | 1.2 |
| Sierra Leone | 1700–2480 | - | >1700 | 74 | 3.5 |
| Somalia | 3000 | 28 | 3028 | 500 | 16.5 |
| South Africa | 23,000 | 420 | 23,420 | [>16,500] | [70–80] |
| Sudan | 3132 | - | >3132 | 50 | 1.6 |
| Swaziland | 2636 | 79 | 2715 | 4 | 0.2 |
| Tanzania | 10,000 | - | >10,000 | 1122 | 11.2 |
| Togo | 2300 | 201 | 2501 | 0 | 0.0 |
| Tunisia | 2150 | 46 | 2196 | - | - |
| Uganda | 5000 | 406 | 5406 | 30 | 0.6 |
| Western Sahara | 330 | - | >330 | - | - |
| Zaïre[c] | - | - | 11,000 | [1100] | 10.0 |
| Zambia | 4600 | 147 | 4747 | 211 | 4.4 |
| Zimbabwe | 4200 | 240 | 4440 | 95 | 2.1 |

Sources (except below): Stuart and Adams (1990); World Conservation Monitoring Centre (1992).

[a] Source: UICN (1990a).

[b] Source: Jones (1992); number of endemics refers to single-island endemics.

[c] The estimate for the number of vascular plant species in Zaïre is from Lebrun (1976). Brenan (1978) estimated c. 3200 endemic species; however, this was based on only a sample of the *Flore du Congo Belge et du Ruanda-Urundi* (1948–1963). The figure of 11,000 for the total flora may be an over-estimate. F.J. Breteler (1991 pers. comm.) estimates the level of species endemism to be 10%.

Number of endemic species in square brackets is inferred from estimated level of species endemism.

## TABLE 16. FLORISTIC RICHNESS AND ENDEMISM IN AFRICAN PHYTOCHORIA

Data mostly from White (1983), but some figures have been updated, as indicated below. Arrangement is by number of endemic species.

| Phytochorion | Area 10⁶ km² | Total species | Endemic species | % species endemism | Endemic families | Endemic genera |
|---|---|---|---|---|---|---|
| Guineo-Congolian RCE | 2.80 | 12,000[a] | 6400 | 80 | 5? | c.20[a] |
| Cape RCE[b] | 0.09 | 8600 | 5870 | 68 | 7 | 193 |
| Zambezian RCE | 3.70 | 8500 | 4590 | 54 | 0 | few |
| Afromontane RCE | 0.70 | 4000 | 3000 | 75 | 1–2 | 200 |
| Karoo-Namib RCE[c] | 0.66 | (>7000) | <3500 | 35–50 | 1 | 160 |
| Somali-Masai RCE[d] | 1.90 | 4500 | 1250 | 31 | 2 | 50 |
| Maputaland-Pondoland[e] | 0.20 | 7000 | 1220 | >20 | 2 | 58 |
| Sudanian RCE | 3.70 | 2750 | 960 | 35 | 0 | few |
| Mediterranean RCE | 0.33 | 4000 | 800 | 20 | 0 | 0 |
| Zanzibar-Inhambane RM[f] | 0.33 | 3000 | 450 | 15 | 0 | 25 |
| *Regional Transition Zones:* | | | | | | |
| Lake Victoria RM | 0.22 | 3000 | <50 | <3 | ? | ? |
| Kalahari/Highveld | 1.22 | 3000 | <50 | <3 | ? | ? |
| Mediterranean/Sahara | 0.11 | 2500 | <50 | <3 | ? | 0 |
| Guinea-Congolia/Zambezia | 0.70 | 2000 | <50 | <3 | ? | ? |
| Guinea-Congolia/Sudania | 1.16 | 2000 | <50 | <3 | ? | ? |
| Sahara | 7.38 | 1620 | <50 | <3 | 0 | few |
| Sahel | 2.48 | 1200 | <50 | <3 | ? | 0 |

Notes:
RCE Regional Centre of Endemism (White 1983).
RM Regional Mosaic (White 1983).
[a] F.J. Breteler (1991 pers. comm.).
[b] See Data Sheet on Cape Floristic Region (CPD Site Af53).
[c] Updated statistics from C. Hilton-Taylor (1993 pers. comm.). See also Data Sheet on Western Cape Domain (Succulent Karoo) (CPD Site Af51).
[d] Updated statistics from M. Thulin (1992 pers. comm.).
[e] See Data Sheet on Maputaland-Pondoland Region (CPD Site Af59). Figures for endemics refer to endemic and near-endemic species and infraspecific taxa. Note this Region approximates the Tongaland-Pondoland Regional Mosaic of White (1983), excluding the area south of the Great Kei River (Eastern Cape), which constitutes the Albany Centre (CPD Site Af52). Both the Maputaland-Pondoland Region and the Zanzibar-Inhambane RM are treated below in the section headed Indian Ocean Coastal Belt.
[f] Vollesen (1992) for number of endemic genera.
( ) Refers to flowering plant and fern taxa (i.e. includes species, subspecies and varieties).

## Useful plants

Examples of useful plants are listed under accounts of phytochoria and in the site Data Sheets. Some of the more important food and crop plants with origins in Africa are listed in Table 17 (below); the main timber trees are listed in Table 20.

Important strains of wheat, barley and several other important crops are cultivated in Ethiopia, which is one of the world's eight major centres of crop plant diversity.

### TABLE 17. SOME IMPORTANT FOOD AND CROP PLANTS WITH ORIGINS IN AFRICA

*Crop species*

| | |
|---|---|
| *Cajanus cajan* | pigeon pea |
| *Ceiba pentandra* var. *pentandra* | kapok |
| *Citrullus lanatus* | water melon |
| *Coffea arabica, C. robusta* etc. | coffee |
| *Cola acuminata, C. nitida* | cola nut |
| *Corchorus olitorius* | jute |
| *Cucumis anguria* | gherkin |
| *Cucumis melo* | melon |
| *Dioscorea* spp. | yams |
| *Elaeis guineensis* | oil palm |
| *Eleusine coracana* | finger millet |
| *Eragrostis tef* | tef |
| *Gossypium herbaceum* | diploid cotton |
| *Guizotia abyssinica* | niger seed, noog |
| *Hibiscus cannabinus* | kenaf |
| *Hibiscus sabdariffa* | roselle |
| *Oryza glaberrima* | African or red rice |
| *Pennisetum glaucum* | bulrush millet |
| *Raphia* spp. | raffia |
| *Ricinus communis* | castor |
| *Sesamum indicum* | sesame |
| *Sorghum bicolor* | sorghum |
| *Tamarindus indica* | tamarind |
| *Vigna subterranea* | bambara groundnut |
| *Vigna unguiculata* | cowpea |

## Non-timber forest products

The majority of Africa's population relies on non-cultivated plant resources for a wide range of products. In the rain forests of Central Africa alone, there are around 200,000 people, belonging to groups such as the Aka, Asua, Efe and Mbuti, who live primarily by hunting and gathering, also through generally obtaining part of their food requirements from cultivated plants, mostly through exchanges with agriculturalists. Their health care needs are also met almost entirely from use of forest plants. Indeed, throughout Africa, 80% of all people use traditional forms of medicine for the major part of their primary health care needs (Cunningham 1993a). Firewood supplies 95% of heating requirements in rural areas.

Some non-timber forest products are, or were, exported, such as latex from *Funtumia africana* and *Landolphia heudelotii*, from which rubber can be made. *Strophanthus* spp., the seeds of which contain cardiac glycosides and *Rauvolfia vomitoria*, which contains the alkaloids reserpine and rescinnamine, are exported from Cameroon and Zaïre. Generally, however, non-timber forest products have been important for subsistence and local cash economies rather than for export.

Some species have been over-exploited. In the case of *Prunus africana*, bark-stripping to remove the bark for export to Europe for the manufacture of drugs is causing major degradation and destruction of the mountain forests in west Cameroon (Rietbergen 1992; Cunningham and Mbenkum 1993b) and elsewhere.

Approximately 300 forest species are known to provide wild fruit in Ghana (Abbiw 1989). Fruits of *Thaumatococcus daniellii* provide a sweetening agent which is 20,000 times sweeter than sugar. Between 1975 and 1980, 288,800 kg were exported from Ghana (Enti undated).

*Elaeis guineensis* (oil palm) originated in the forests of West Africa. This is now the world's leading oil-producing plant.

## Ornamentals

Widely cultivated ornamentals from Africa include species and hybrids of the genera *Agapanthus, Freesia, Gerbera* (Barberton daisy), *Gladiolus, Pelargonium, Protea, Saintpaulia* (African violet), *Sansevieria* and *Streptocarpus*.

## Factors causing loss of biodiversity

Human influence on Africa's forests has probably been more pervasive and has occurred over a longer period of time than in other moist tropical regions. There is evidence to suggest that even the most remote tracts of supposedly primary forest are, in fact, old secondary growth or have previously been exploited for forest products.

(The paragraphs below summarize the main threats to the flora and vegetation of Africa. Threats relating to particular regions of Africa are included under individual accounts of phytochoria; site-specific threats are given in the Data Sheets.)

## Population growth

Many factors responsible for the loss of plant biodiversity are directly or indirectly related to population growth. Greatly reduced during the days of the slave trade, the population of Africa in 1990 was estimated to have rebounded to 647,500,000 (UN 1989) and is projected to rise to 1,581,000,000 by the year 2025. Africa continues to have high birth rates and falling death rates (see Table 18). Better health care and other factors have resulted in greatly reduced rates of mortality, but these have not been matched by proportional falls in birth rates. The African population increased at an average annual rate of 2.2% in the period 1950–1955, rising to 2.7% in 1970–1975 and 3.0% in 1985–1990 (UN 1989) and is currently increasing more rapidly than that of any other continent.

The majority of Africa's population is rural. For example, the rural proportion of the population is 65% in Nigeria, 66% in Ghana, 76% in Kenya and 90% in Uganda (World Resources Institute 1992).

### TABLE 18. SIZE AND GROWTH OF POPULATION IN AFRICAN COUNTRIES

| Country | Population 1990 (millions) | Population density 1990 (numbers per km²) | Annual population increase (%) (1985–1990) | Likely population in 2025 (millions) |
|---|---|---|---|---|
| Algeria | 24.96 | 10.5 | 2.72 | 51.95 |
| Angola | 10.02 | 8.0 | 2.70 | 24.73 |
| Benin | 4.63 | 41.9 | 3.00 | 12.59 |
| Botswana | 1.30 | 2.3 | 3.71 | 3.40 |
| Burkina Faso | 9.00 | 32.9 | 2.66 | 23.71 |
| Burundi | 5.47 | 213.3 | 2.91 | 12.98 |
| Cameroon | 11.83 | 25.4 | 3.27 | 36.55 |
| Central African Republic | 3.04 | 4.9 | 2.77 | 7.95 |
| Chad | 5.68 | 4.5 | 2.47 | 13.25 |
| Congo | 2.27 | 6.7 | 3.16 | 6.57 |
| Côte d'Ivoire | 2.00 | 37.7 | 3.78 | 39.33 |
| Djibouti | 0.41 | 17.6 | 2.88 | 1.09 |
| Egypt | 52.43 | 52.7 | 2.39 | 90.36 |
| Equatorial Guinea | 0.35 | 12.5 | 2.42 | 0.83 |
| Ethiopia | 49.24 | 44.7 | 2.67 | 126.62 |
| Gabon | 1.17 | 4.5 | 3.47 | 2.88 |
| Gambia | 0.86 | 86.1 | 2.89 | 1.86 |
| Ghana | 15.03 | 65.3 | 3.15 | 35.44 |
| Guinea | 5.76 | 23.4 | 2.86 | 15.27 |
| Guinea-Bissau | 0.96 | 34.3 | 1.99 | 1.92 |
| Kenya | 24.03 | 42.2 | 3.58 | 79.11 |
| Lesotho | 1.77 | 58.5 | 2.85 | 4.43 |
| Liberia | 2.58 | 26.7 | 3.16 | 7.25 |
| Libya | 4.55 | 2.6 | 3.65 | 12.84 |
| Malawi | 8.75 | 93.0 | 3.52 | 24.73 |
| Mali | 9.21 | 7.6 | 3.04 | 24.77 |
| Mauritania | 2.02 | 2.0 | 2.73 | 5.12 |
| Morocco | 25.06 | 56.2 | 2.58 | 45.65 |
| Mozambique | 15.66 | 20.0 | 2.65 | 35.42 |
| Namibia | 1.78 | 2.2 | 3.19 | 4.70 |
| Niger | 7.73 | 6.1 | 3.14 | 21.48 |
| Nigeria | 108.54 | 119.2 | 3.30 | 280.89 |
| Rwanda | 7.24 | 293.4 | 3.41 | 18.85 |
| Senegal | 7.33 | 38.1 | 2.78 | 16.99 |
| Sierra Leone | 4.15 | 58.0 | 2.49 | 10.05 |
| Somalia | 7.50 | 12.0 | 3.26 | 18.70 |
| South Africa | 35.28 | 28.9 | 2.22 | 65.36 |
| Sudan | 25.20 | 10.6 | 2.88 | 59.61 |
| Swaziland | 0.79 | 45.8 | 3.44 | 2.25 |
| Tanzania | 27.32 | 30.8 | 3.66 | 84.92 |
| Togo | 3.53 | 64.9 | 3.07 | 9.84 |
| Tunisia | 8.18 | 52.7 | 2.38 | 13.63 |
| Uganda | 18.79 | 94.2 | 3.67 | 53.14 |
| Zaïre | 35.57 | 15.7 | 3.14 | 99.37 |
| Zambia | 8.45 | 11.4 | 3.75 | 26.26 |
| Zimbabwe | 9.71 | 25.1 | 3.16 | 22.62 |

Source: World Resources Institute (1992).

## Deforestation

Forest clearance for agriculture and to create grazing lands, as well as repeated burning for hunting and other purposes, have all led to degradation (sometimes severe degradation) of the original vegetation and its species content. Species diversity is already greatly depleted in some areas, especially in the lowlands. Montane areas at higher altitudes are generally the least affected.

Annual deforestation rates in Africa's closed canopy forests for the years 1976–1980 were estimated to be about 0.61% of the total closed canopy forest area in 1980 (FAO/UNEP 1981). Moist forest loss is likely to be about 1% per year during the 1990s (FAO 1990). Of Africa's original rain forests, only about one-third remains (Sayer, Harcourt and Collins 1992). West Africa's forests are being lost at a faster rate than those of any other region (2.1% per annum) (see Table 19).

A major contributing factor causing loss of many remaining areas of natural vegetation is growth of the human population. Higher populations lead to clearance of more land for agriculture or increasing intensity of use in areas already under cultivation or grazing. Most agricultural production is based on methods which give low yields per unit area. At low population densities, traditional methods, involving the alternation of cultivation and fallow are sustainable and, in some areas, may have led to increased species diversity through the creation of vegetation mosaics. Typically, the traditional form of shifting cultivation provides 2–4 years of cultivation on a plot (or shorter periods of grazing) after which the land is left fallow for 10–20 years. However, as the land available for subsistence agriculture has become increasingly scarce in most regions (related to population growth or land being used for cultivation of cash crops), the intervals between clearing have become shorter. In some cases, fallow periods have been eliminated entirely and cultivation of the same areas is continuous, giving rise to serious declines in soil fertility and crop yields. This is particularly the case in parts of the Sahel, parts of mountainous East Africa and in the dry belt from the coast of Angola through Botswana, Lesotho and southern Mozambique. Soil degradation or desertification is most acute in Burundi, Ethiopia, Ghana, Kenya, Nigeria, Rwanda and Togo (Cleaver, Schreiber and Ryden 1992).

### TABLE 19. ORIGINAL AND REMAINING EXTENT OF CLOSED CANOPY MOIST FOREST IN AFRICA

| Country | Approximate original extent of closed canopy tropical moist forest cover (km²)[a] | Remaining area of tropical moist forest (km²)[a] | Remaining moist forests as % of original closed canopy forest | Average annual loss 1981–85 (%)[b] |
|---|---|---|---|---|
| **West Africa** | | | | |
| Benin | 16,800 | 424 | 2.5 | 2.6 |
| Côte d'Ivoire | 229,400 | 27,464 | 12.0 | 6.5 |
| Gambia | 4100 | 497 | 12.1 | 3.4 |
| Ghana | 145,000 | 15,842 | 10.9 | 1.3 |
| Guinea | 185,800 | 7655 | 4.1 | 1.8 |
| Guinea-Bissau | 36,100 | 6660* | 18.4 | 2.6 |
| Liberia | 96,000 | 41,238 | 43.0 | 2.3 |
| Nigeria | 421,000 | 38,620 | 9.2 | 5.0 |
| Senegal | 27,700 | 2045 | 7.4 | nd |
| Sierra Leone | 71,700 | 5064 | 7.1 | 0.8 |
| Togo | 18,000 | 1360 | 7.6 | 0.7 |
| **East Africa** | | | | |
| Djibouti | 300 | 10* | 3.0 | nd |
| Ethiopia | 249,300 | 27,500* | 11.0 | 0.2 |
| Kenya | 81,200 | 6900* | 8.5 | 1.7 |
| Somalia | 21,200 | 14,800* | 69.8 | 0.2 |
| Sudan | 27,000 | 6400* | 23.7 | 0.6 |
| Tanzania[c] | 37,576 | 8500–16,185 | 22.6–43.1 | 0.7 |
| Uganda | 103,400 | 7400 | 7.2 | 1.3 |
| **Central Africa** | | | | |
| Burundi | 10,600 | 413 | 3.9 | 2.6 |
| Cameroon | 376,900 | 155,330 | 41.2 | 0.4 |
| Central African Republic | 324,500 | 52,236 | 16.1 | 0.1 |
| Congo | 342,000 | 213,400* | 62.4 | 0.1 |
| Equatorial Guinea | 26,000 | 17,004 | 65.4 | 0.2 |
| Gabon | 258,000 | 227,500 | 88.2 | 0.1 |
| São Tomé & Príncipe | 960 | 299 | 31.1 | nd |
| Rwanda | 9400 | 1554 | 16.5 | 2.6 |
| Zaïre | 1,784,000 | 1,190,737 | 66.7 | 0.2 |
| **Southern Africa** | | | | |
| Angola | 218,200 | 29,000* | 13.3 | 1.5 |
| Malawi | 10,700 | 320 | 3.0 | nd |
| Mozambique | 246,900 | 9350* | 3.9 | 1.1 |
| Zimbabwe | 7700 | 80 | 1.0 | nd |

[a] Source: Sayer, Harcourt and Collins (1992) except figures marked with an asterisk (*) which are from FAO (1988a). Note that the figures include lowland, montane, swamp and mangrove forests.
[b] Source: World Resources Institute (1992). [Rates of loss in many countries have clearly increased since these figures were compiled, though some may have declined in cases where little forest remains to be exploited. Myers (1989) estimated that by 1989 Cameroon was losing 1.2% of its forest annually, Congo 0.8%, Gabon 0.3%, Côte d'Ivoire 15.6%, Nigeria 14.3% and Zaïre 0.4%.]
[c] J. Lovett (1993, in press).
nd No data.

# Logging

Commercial logging continues on a large scale, although in the late 1980s and early 1990s the volume of timber exported from much of Africa, even from regions with abundant timber resources, declined as a result of worldwide economic conditions. Much of Africa's timber production comes from West and Central Africa (Tables 20 and 21). Nearly all of the moist forest in West Africa has been logged over at least once, whereas in Central Africa there are still large areas of forest in remote areas which remain unlogged (Rietbergen 1992).

The number of timber species in trade continues to be small. For example, 70% of timber production in Cameroon is accounted for by about 15 species, out of 300 which are potentially usable; in Congo, about 50 species are traded out of 300 which are potentially marketable (Sawyer, Stoll, Elliot and Burgess 1992). Only about 15 African timber species are well-established in European markets. Table 20 provides a list of the main rain forest timber trees exported to Europe and the quantities of each.

No commercial species of the important timbers are thought to be in danger of extinction through logging, but some are threatened in parts of their range and there is likely to be serious genetic erosion in some populations.

Some countries (e.g. Nigeria and Ghana) have introduced log export bans for selected species in order to conserve stocks and to encourage local processing. However, in 1987 wood exports from Ghana still consisted of 60% logs and only 30% sawn timber because of problems of enforcement of the bans. Bans, together with tax incentives, have also been used to promote lesser known species. For example, in 1979 Côte d'Ivoire exported 1.47 million m³ of timber, of which 53% comprised lesser-known species not exported before 1973 (Sawyer, Stoll, Elliot and Burgess 1992). However, the harvesting of a greater range of species can result in more disturbance to the forest or the re-logging of forests which have previously been logged, thus hampering regeneration.

Although many countries have committed themselves to sustained yield forestry policies, almost all the timber harvested from tropical forests in Africa is derived from forests which are being logged without a management plan or from forests which are being converted to other uses (either planned or unplanned) (Rietbergen 1992).

Evidence suggests that properly managed low intensity logging in natural forests can be compatible with soil and water conservation, supply of non-timber forest products and, to a certain extent, with conservation of biodiversity. However, most methods currently in use do not ensure sustainable yields and result in forest degradation. Many uncut trees are damaged during the logging process because concession agreements often do not insist upon measures (such as directional felling and marking of residual trees) which would cause less damage to trees remaining after logging operations. Poor harvesting techniques and, worse still, clearfelling, result in a rapid decline in soil nutrients and, often, soil erosion. Soil nutrient levels under tropical forest are anyway usually low, with much of the nutrient stock contained within the plant biomass and thus susceptible to irreversible loss if the vegetation cover is degraded or destroyed.

Logging roads allow slash and burn cultivators to gain access to forested areas, which sometimes results in the

### TABLE 20. THE MAIN AFRICAN RAIN FOREST TIMBER SPECIES IN INTERNATIONAL TRADE

(Includes the main species exported in 1989, mainly to Europe but some to Japan. Data from World Conservation Monitoring Centre.)

| Species | Amount exported |
|---|---|
| Okoume (*Aucomea klaineana*) | >400 million kg (80% from Gabon, rest from Congo, Equatorial Guinea) |
| Tiama/Gedu Nohor (*Entandrophragma angolense*) | >300 million kg (40% from Cameroon, 25% from Liberia, 15% from Ghana) |
| Sapele (*Entandrophragma cylindricum*), Iroko (*Milicia*) African Acajou, African Mahogany (*Khaya* spp.) | Compound figures only: >400 million kg (30% from Congo, 25% from Cameroon, 10% from Ghana) |
| Obeche/Ayous/Abachi/Samba (*Triplochiton scleroxylon*) | 175 million kg (70% from Ghana, 30% from Cameroon) |
| Azobe (*Lophira alata*) | >100 million kg (80% from Cameroon) |
| Sipo/Utile (*Entandrophragma utile*) | >80 million kg (25% from Congo, 20% from Zaïre, 15% from Liberia, 15% from Cameroon) |
| Limba/Afara (*Terminalia superba*) | >50 million kg (40% from Côte d'Ivoire, 30% from Cameroon, 25% from Congo) |
| Makore (*Tieghemella* spp.) | 30 million kg (30% from Côte d'Ivoire) |

### TABLE 21. TIMBER SPECIES THREATENED IN PART OF THEIR RANGE

| Species | Area threatened |
|---|---|
| *Cephalosphaera usambarensis** | Eastern Arc forests of Tanzania, where it is endemic (also in Shimba Hills, Kenya). |
| *Entandrophragma angolense* | Parts of West Africa and Nigeria. |
| *Gossweilerodendron balsamiferum* | Ilaro (Nigeria); Cabinda; central Zaïre. |
| *Irvingia gabonensis* | Likely to be in danger of genetic impoverishment throughout its range (Senegal to Zaïre; Angola; Uganda). |
| *Nesogordonia papaverifera* | Outlying populations in Gabon; Central African Republic; Cameroon; Liberia; Sierra Leone. |
| *Pericopsis elata* | Endangered in parts of range and in danger of genetic impoverishment throughout its range (West Africa; Cameroon; Zaïre). |

Source: FAO (1986) except * Lovett (1993 in press).

clearance of any forest remaining after logging operations. In the extensive Central African forests, for example in Zaïre, new roads allow great increases in the harvesting of bushmeat for trade to urban areas. At present rates of degradation and destruction, some countries, such as Côte d'Ivoire, will lose the last of their unprotected forests within the next 10–20 years.

The history and present status of forest management in tropical Africa is reviewed by Rietbergen (1992).

## Plantation agriculture and forestry

Large-scale land clearance for plantations of commodity crops or exotic trees may rapidly exterminate species of restricted distribution. Such plantations, which often result from the efforts of governments to generate export income, are rarely established on existing agricultural land. In West

**TABLE 22. ANNUAL PRODUCTION OF WOOD AND WOOD PRODUCTS IN AFRICAN COUNTRIES (1987–1989)**

| Country | Fuelwood and charcoal ($10^3 m^3$) | Industrial roundwood ($10^3 m^3$) | Sawn and other processed wood ($10^3 m^3$) | Paper ($10^3$ metric tons) |
|---|---|---|---|---|
| Algeria | 1816 | 250 | 63 | 120 |
| Angola | 4217 | 1045 | 7 | 15 |
| Benin | 4591 | 254 | 11 | 0 |
| Botswana | 1197 | 79 | 0 | 0 |
| Burkina Faso | 7925 | 375 | 1 | 0 |
| Burundi | 3921 | 48 | 3 | 0 |
| Cameroon | 9886 | 2730 | 732 | 5 |
| Central African Republic | 3055 | 394 | 56 | 0 |
| Chad | 3294 | 542 | 1 | 0 |
| Congo | 1729 | 1390 | 110 | 0 |
| Côte d'Ivoire | 9437 | 3362 | 1035 | 0 |
| Egypt | 2108 | 103 | 74 | 160 |
| Equatorial Guinea | 447 | 160 | 61 | 0 |
| Ethiopia | 37,100 | 1759 | 54 | 10 |
| Gabon | 2396 | 1222 | 354 | 0 |
| Gambia | 891 | 21 | 1 | 0 |
| Ghana | 15,905 | 1101 | 542 | 0 |
| Guinea | 3924 | 636 | 90 | 0 |
| Guinea-Bissau | 422 | 143 | 16 | 0 |
| Kenya | 32,495 | 1711 | 234 | 99 |
| Lesotho | 579 | 0 | 0 | 0 |
| Liberia | 4736 | 1089 | 416 | 0 |
| Libya | 536 | 104 | 31 | 6 |
| Malawi | 7016 | 351 | 37 | 0 |
| Mali | 5016 | 342 | 12 | 0 |
| Mauritania | 7 | 5 | 0 | 0 |
| Morocco | 1343 | 665 | 214 | 109 |
| Mozambique | 15,022 | 979 | 44 | 2 |
| Niger | 4023 | 264 | 0 | 0 |
| Nigeria | 97,058 | 7868 | 2945 | 81 |
| Rwanda | 5602 | 240 | 15 | 0 |
| Senegal | 3697 | 589 | 11 | 0 |
| Sierra Leone | 2801 | 140 | 12 | 0 |
| Somalia | 6669 | 88 | 15 | 0 |
| South Africa | 7078 | 12,168 | 2225 | 1614 |
| Sudan | 19,554 | 2030 | 15 | 10 |
| Swaziland | 560 | 1663 | 144 | 0 |
| Tanzania | 30,019 | 1947 | 169 | 28 |
| Togo | 662 | 178 | 5 | 0 |
| Tunisia | 2947 | 141 | 107 | 71 |
| Uganda | 12,080 | 1800 | 29 | 2 |
| Zaïre | 31,540 | 2715 | 174 | 2 |
| Zambia | 11,424 | 606 | 76 | 3 |
| Zimbabwe | 6226 | 1530 | 213 | 82 |

Source: World Resources Institute (1992)

African countries, such as Liberia, Ghana and Nigeria, vast areas formerly occupied by species-rich native forest have been replaced by monoculture plantations of rubber, cocoa and oil palm (Campbell 1990). Such plantations are virtually deserts in terms of species diversity.

## Dry land destruction

A large part of the population in the Sahel and Somali-Masai area consists of pastoralists with large numbers of cattle, goats or camels. When rangeland is fenced or nomadic peoples are settled or become more numerous, the local vegetation receives no relief from the attentions of domestic stock. Recent population increases, combined with prolonged droughts and (in some cases) the restriction of the movements of pastoralists between countries, has led to severe overgrazing and resultant erosion in areas around permanent waterholes and wells. The radical depletion of remaining woody vegetation for timber, fuel and charcoal, combined with overgrazing by domestic animals, has had disastrous consequences for the flora, fauna and man himself.

Patches of wetland in otherwise dry areas, which are often rich in species, such as the dambos and vleis of Southern Africa, are particularly favoured for agricultural use and are often much over-utilized.

The deterioration of dry lands may not perhaps be so immediately obvious as forest destruction, but it is nevertheless as serious, both for local inhabitants and for maintenance of plant species diversity. Generally, the best preserved semi-arid and arid vegetation types can now be found only in remote areas or in National Parks, far from any artificial water supplies.

## Fire

Fire is an important ecological factor in African woodlands, wooded grasslands and grasslands. Fire-tolerant life-forms are numerous and are a noteworthy feature of the African flora. Many savanna and fynbos species are, in fact, dependent on fire for their survival in competition with larger life-forms.

Man has employed fire in Africa for at least 150,000 years and the incidence of fire presumably increased along with the human population. Today, fires are started by people, commonly through the use of burning as an adjunct to agriculture, to create pasture for domestic animals or for hunting and sometimes as a result of such activities as collection of wild honey.

Although many fires started for agriculture are carefully controlled, some fires are allowed to spread unchecked. The result is that much of Africa outside the forests, deserts and areas of densest settlement, is burnt regularly. Forests, especially evergreen forests, are usually too moist to burn, but fires occasionally occur within them, especially during particularly arid years and when the forest has been degraded. It is reported that about 50% of the forest area in Ghana was burnt in the 1982–83 drought (ODA 1992a), believed to have been assisted by the opening up of the forests by logging operations and the presence of the flammable invasive shrub *Chromolaena odorata*.

Occasional fires, on the other hand, may actually increase species diversity in some vegetation types, such as in many types of woodland and in the fynbos of the Cape. They are also necessary to enable the germination of some species.

## Urbanization

Although Africa currently has relatively few very large cities, the size of almost all urban areas is increasing very rapidly as a result of the birth rate and a high level of in-migration. Even small urban centres place heavy demands on the wild plant resources of surrounding regions, especially to provide fuelwood, charcoal, building materials and medicinal treatments.

Where cities are located in areas of high species diversity, urban sprawl may easily eliminate taxa of limited distribution. For example, at least five species formerly occurred only in the area now occupied by the suburbs of Cape Town.

The impact on species diversity is rarely considered when roads, railways, dams, airports, canals and power lines are constructed. The construction of dams not only floods large areas, but is often deleterious to wetlands and riverine vegetation as a result of changes to water flows. Construction of the Kariba and Cabora Bassa dams resulted in the inundation of almost 8000 km² of the Zambezi Valley.

## Fuelwood harvesting

Throughout sub-Saharan Africa domestic energy needs are almost universally met through the burning of fuelwood and charcoal, the proportion derived from these sources exceeding 50% of total domestic energy consumption, even in South Africa. In many countries wood supplies most of the total energy consumed – typically 70–90%. Examples are: Uganda, 96% of total energy usage from fuelwood (530,000 m³ wood, 73,000 tons charcoal) (ODA 1992b), Ghana 70% (12 million m³ wood and charcoal) (ODA 1992a) and Zimbabwe 53% (± 5 million tons wood) (ODA 1992c). Some of this wood comes from plantations and woodlots deliberately established for the purpose, but most is cut from natural woodland and forest.

At low population densities, fuelwood cutting tends to be confined to a few favoured species, but, as populations increase, people become less selective. In many areas today the cutting is on such a scale as to be unsustainable and is a major contributor to the general degradation and loss of woody vegetation.

## Collection of building and craft materials

Cutting of building poles is a major activity, is selective as to species and size class and contributes significantly to the degradation of forests and mangrove formations in many areas. Also harvested in considerable quantities are materials for binding (climbers, tree bark etc.), fencing and thatch.

Crafts such as woodcarving and the making of baskets and mats are widely practised in Africa, resulting in increased pressure on certain favoured species, such as the African blackwood (*Dalbergia melanoxylon*).

## Harvesting of medicinal plants

Collection pressure on plants used in traditional medicine is often severe in the vicinity of large urban centres and, in the case of certain species may be considerable over a much wider area, especially if plants are scarce or slow growing (Cunningham 1993). The value of the bark of *Warburgia salutaris* is such that it has been almost eliminated from most of its range in Southern Africa. However, not all such collecting is necessarily for local use. Cunningham and Mbenkum (1993) and Mbenkum and Fisiy (1992) report over-exploitation of *Prunus africana* in Cameroon as a result of an export trade. The same species is also harvested for export in Kenya, Madagascar, Uganda and Zaïre.

## Mining and quarrying

Soils rich in heavy metals and certain minerals often support endemic-rich floras. While the soils of such sites are not usually suitable for agriculture, the vegetation cover is often threatened by mining. Areas of concern include the Shaba area in Zaïre (CPD Site Af34) (rich in copper and cobalt), Mont Nimba (CPD Site Af4) in West Africa (which has high quality iron-ore) (see Data Sheet), the Great Dyke in Zimbabwe (rich in chromite) (CPD Site Af40) and the Pugu Hills (CPD Site Af56) in Tanzania (kaolinite deposits). Large unexploited deposits of bauxite exist on Mt Mulanje in Malawi (CPD Site Af64, see Data Sheet). Outcrops of limestone and their associated floras may be destroyed by quarrying for manufacture of roadstone or cement.

## Settlement schemes and tsetse control

Irrigation and settlement schemes in countries such as Kenya (for example at Bura River and the Shimba Hills) have resulted in translocation of large numbers of people into species-rich areas where there was previously little pressure.

Successful tsetse fly eradication campaigns (e.g. in the Zambezi Valley) have opened up large areas to often uncontrolled settlement. The subsequent influx of people and cattle has sometimes resulted in rapid degradation of the previously almost untouched vegetation. Attempts to control the fly often involve the spraying of vast areas with insecticides, which may have adverse effects on those plants, such as orchids and asclepiads, which have specific insect pollinators.

## Invasive species

Problems posed by the invasive spread of alien species are particularly severe and well documented in South Africa. There, for instance, large areas of fynbos have been invaded by species of *Acacia, Hakea, Pinus* and (in drier areas) *Opuntia*, despite efforts at biological control. Some 8000 km² of the coastal lowlands of Natal have been invaded by *Chromolaena odorata* (Macdonald 1989). This flammable, scrambling shrub, introduced from the New World, is also a problem in some parts of moist West and Central Africa. In Tanzania, the West African tree *Maesopsis eminii* was introduced to the East Usambaras in experimental plantations and its rapid spread through the submontane forest is now a major cause for concern (Binggeli and Hamilton 1990; see also Data Sheet on East Usambara Mountains, CPD Site Af71).

## Domestic animals

Large tracts of Africa are utilised as rangelands. In many of these areas domestic animals have major cultural significance which goes beyond their direct economic value. Large herds of cattle and goats are maintained and their grazing has a major impact in many areas of woodland, wooded grassland, shrubland and grassland. Impacts include the selective removal of more palatable species, soil compaction and promotion of soil erosion. Traditionally, the management of herds of domestic animals has been based on intimate knowledge of the animals and the land, but restrictions on the movement of animals as land has become enclosed or otherwise expropriated, combined with increases in the numbers of domestic animals, have led to severe environmental degradation through overgrazing in some places.

In dry seasons and droughts, evergreen trees may be severely damaged through removal of their branches to provide browse. Over vast areas large native herbivores have been virtually eliminated to make way for grazing of domestic stock.

## Other factors

Some forests and other areas, as well as individual species, formerly protected by taboos, are now threatened by a breakdown of traditional values (Mbenkum and Fisiy 1992).

Other locally important factors include the impact of increasing tourism (as on Mt Kilimanjaro, CPD Site Af75), the commercial harvesting of wild flowers in South Africa and wars. The effects of the last of these vary from place to place. In Uganda, a breakdown in law and order during the 1970s and 1980s resulted in loss of some areas of government Forest Reserves to agriculture (Hamilton 1984), but most of these have subsequently been reclaimed. In contrast, in Mozambique the resulting depopulation of some areas has tended to allow regrowth of vegetation in some areas. Gebre-Michael, Hundessa and Hillman (1992) review the affects of war on protected areas in Ethiopia, including the Bale and Simen Mountains (CPD Sites Af60 and Af61, respectively).

## Conservation

The account in this section focuses on legally protected areas in Africa. In Africa, the existing legally protected areas

system has evolved largely with a focus on large game animals, with hunting and, later, potential for tourism in mind, or else through the setting aside of forest in reserves, principally for timber harvesting. One result of this has been that large areas of savanna and woodland have been conserved, while some of the most biologically rich habitats have received little or no legal protection. As a result, there are still major gaps in the network of protected areas in almost all countries. A review of the Afrotropical protected areas system by MacKinnon and MacKinnon (1986) reveals that considerable extension of the protected area network throughout tropical Africa is needed and, in particular, in the Guineo-Congolian, East Malagasy and montane areas. So far, about 20% of the remaining forest in West Africa is legally protected, as well as 7% of the remaining forest of Central Africa (Sayer, Harcourt and Collins 1992). The relatively high percentage of West African protected forests could give a misleading impression in that it is a reflection of how much forest has been cleared outside of the protected areas. Indeed, only about 11–12% of the original moist forest cover of West Africa has escaped deforestation according to the recent study of forest cover by Sayer, Harcourt and Collins (1992), compared to about 59% of the original forest remaining in Central Africa.

Whereas most African bird species are found within the protected areas system (Sayer and Stuart 1989), the same cannot be said for plants. The present study revealed that many areas of high plant diversity and endemism remain legally unprotected. Gaps in protected area systems have been recognized in some countries and plans have been developed to ensure better representation of forest types, e.g. in Gabon, Congo and Cameroon (Gartlan 1989; UICN 1990a, 1990b). However, it is not only tropical forest which require more legal protection. The exceedingly rich Cape and Karoo-Namib floras (CPD Sites Af50–53) and are also seriously under-protected, as the Data Sheets in this present work reveal.

The conservation of plants has so far not been given prominence, perhaps because plants are not seen to be as exciting or attractive as large herds of animals. Almost 60% of the sites identified below as centres of plant diversity and endemism are not legally protected or are protected very inadequately.

Over the continent as a whole, there are tremendous differences in present levels of conservation activity and awareness. The area or percentage of land which is legally protected (Table 23) and the level of protection afforded vary greatly from country to country. In some, such as Somalia, protected areas are few and the level of protection minimal. In others, such as Zimbabwe, there are extensive areas covered by reserves, at least some of which are very well managed. However, even in such a conservation-minded country as South Africa, the coverage of different vegetation types is very uneven and the extremely species- and endemic-rich lowland fynbos and succulent karoo are still very inadequately protected (see Data Sheets on the Western Cape Domain (Succulent Karoo) (CPD Site Af51) and the Cape Floristic Region (CPD Site Af53).

Likewise, there is, great variation in the possibilities for further conservation initiatives. The very uneven distribution of diversity aside, it is generally in those countries and biogeographical units where the naturally occurring

### TABLE 23. PROTECTED AREA SYSTEMS IN AFRICAN COUNTRIES*

| Country | Land area (km²) | Number of protected sites[a] | Total land area protected (km²)[a] | % of country protected[a] |
|---|---|---|---|---|
| Algeria | 2,381,740 | 18 | 126,953 | 5.33 |
| Angola | 1,246,700 | 6 | 26,412 | 2.12 |
| Benin | 112,622 | 2 | 8435 | 7.49 |
| Botswana | 574,978 | 9 | 100,250 | 17.43 |
| Burkina Faso | 274,200 | 11 | 26,427 | 9.64 |
| Burundi | 27,731 | 3 | 867 | 3.12 |
| Cameroon | 465,054 | 13 | 20,344 | 4.28 |
| Central African Republic | 622,996 | 12 | 58,560 | 9.37 |
| Chad | 1,270,994 | 2 | 4140 | 0.32 |
| Congo | 342,000 | 10 | 13,331 | 3.90 |
| Côte d'Ivoire | 322,462 | 12 | 19,928 | 6.18 |
| Djibouti | 21,699 | 1 | 100 | 0.43 |
| Egypt | 995,450 | 13 | 8004 | 0.80 |
| Equatorial Guinea | 28,051 | 0 | 0 | 0.00 |
| Ethiopia | 1,184,000 | 11 | 25,341 | 2.48 |
| Gabon | 267,667 | 6 | 10,450 | 3.90 |
| Gambia | 10,368 | 3 | 184 | 1.72 |
| Ghana | 238,538 | 8 | 10,746 | 4.51 |
| Guinea | 245,855 | 3 | 1674 | 0.68 |
| Guinea-Bissau | 36,125 | 0 | 0 | 0.00 |
| Kenya | 582,600 | 36 | 34,702 | 5.96 |
| Lesotho | 30,344 | 1 | 68 | 0.22 |
| Liberia | 111,370 | 1 | 1307 | 1.17 |
| Libya | 1,759,540 | 3 | 1550 | 0.09 |
| Malawi | 94,276 | 9 | 10,576 | 11.24 |
| Mali | 1,204,022 | 11 | 40,120 | 3.24 |
| Mauritania | 1,118,604 | 4 | 17,460 | 1.69 |
| Morocco | 446,300 | 10 | 3621 | 0.79 |
| Mozambique | 784,961 | 1 | 20 | 0.00 |
| Namibia | 824,293 | 11 | 103,706 | 12.58 |
| Niger | 1,267,000 | 6 | 96,967 | 8.17 |
| Nigeria | 923,769 | 21 | 28,727 | 3.11 |
| Rwanda | 26,338 | 2 | 3270 | 12.42 |
| São Tomé & Príncipe | 964 | 0 | 0 | 0.00 |
| Senegal | 197,160 | 10 | 21,807 | 11.09 |
| Sierra Leone | 72,326 | 2 | 820 | 1.13 |
| Somalia | 637,539 | 1 | 1800 | 0.29 |
| South Africa | 1,225,100 | 229 | 73,895 | 6.24 |
| Sudan | 2,505,813 | 14 | 93,575 | 3.73 |
| Swaziland | 17,366 | 4 | 459 | 2.64 |
| Tanzania | 930,700 | 28 | 130,000 | 13.83 |
| Togo | 56,500 | 11 | 6469 | 11.39 |
| Tunisia | 155,360 | 7 | 449 | 0.27 |
| Uganda | 236,036 | 32 | 18,708 | 7.91 |
| Zaïre | 2,345,236 | 8 | 85,770 | 3.66 |
| Zambia | 752,617 | 20 | 63,609 | 8.45 |
| Zimbabwe | 389,361 | 25 | 30,678 | 7.86 |

* Note that the figures presented here refer only to those areas which meet the criteria for inclusion in the *1990 United Nations List of National Parks and Protected Areas* (IUCN 1990). The protected sites included are those which cover an area of 10 km² or more, are in IUCN Management Categories I–V and are managed by the highest authority. It is very important to note that, in some cases, this figure includes sites which are only partially protected. Therefore, in some cases, the figures imply a greater area protected than is actually the case. A further important consideration is that many protected areas have been established primarily for their fauna and do not necessarily protect the best areas for plants.

[a] Source: World Conservation Monitoring Centre (1992).

(For a recent review of national systems of protected areas and details of protected area legislation in each country of the Afrotropical Realm, see IUCN 1992.)

vegetation is most diminished that the need for conservation action is greatest, but, at the same time, the scope for the protection of additional areas is least. Some vegetation types in some countries have already been totally extirpated or so degraded that the opportunity to protect even a representative area has already been lost.

Along with the need to expand the protected areas network, there is a need for considerable improvement in the management of many existing reserves. Designation of a protected area does not mean that it is necessarily well-managed. Some so-called National Parks exist largely on paper while, in other countries, areas accorded a lower category are much more effectively managed. Increases in management levels require additional funding and it is understandably difficult to persuade politicians to earmark additional sums for this purpose in some countries, which are among the poorest in the world. In many cases international assistance is clearly necessary and it is encouraging that international donor agencies are showing an increased willingness to support conservation efforts.

For plants in particular, the necessary political will to set aside land for their conservation is often lacking in the face of pressures for other types of utilisation. Conservation efforts are also often hindered by problems with the surveying and demarcation of proposed protected areas. Even some long-established reserves still lack properly defined boundaries. Not only do such activities cost money but, due to inadequate inventories in some areas (as Gabon), the identification of the best areas to protect is sometimes very difficult.

Conservation is made very difficult if there is opposition from the local population. Both governments and the general populace need to be convinced of the need to conserve biodiversity. The emergence of local wildlife clubs in East Africa is a very hopeful sign, with large numbers of young people taking an interest.

With increasing pressures on the land, there will inevitably be restrictions on the ways in which certain areas are utilized. It is vital that land use plans address the needs of conserving biodiversity while also being acceptable to the government, representing the national interest, and to local communities. Such land use plans may contain areas open to harvesting of specific products. Scientists can work together with land managers and local people to devise methods of harvesting which are sustainable in the long run so that resources are not depleted and other environmental values lost.

In some cases, harvesting of wild plant resources cannot be undertaken sustainably due, for instance, to limited abundance of the plants or their demographic characteristics. In such cases there should be a search for alternatives. This can include cultivation in plantations (e.g. plantations of trees to supply timber, poles for fuel, etc.). The cultivation of plants for medicinal products (Nichols 1990) is needed in many places to relieve pressures on wild stocks. Sometimes an alternative can be something surprisingly different. For instance, a recent survey by Dr A.B. Cunningham in Bwindi Forest, Uganda, revealed that supplies of trees for making beer-canoes (hollowed-out trunks used as fermentation chambers) could not be obtained sustainably from the forest. In this case the suggested alternative is concrete-lined pits.

Pressure for land is increasing in all regions of Africa, to such an extent that, if additional areas are not legally protected within the next decade, many areas of botanically interesting vegetation will no longer be available or will be so degraded as to be not worth saving for this purpose. However, the protected areas themselves will not survive unless the needs and aspirations of the people who live in and around them are taken into account. Active local

involvement in planning and management of wildlife resources is essential if protected areas are to continue to provide a refuge for biological diversity and to provide long term economic benefits to the local people. Several projects exist in Africa which attempt to protect critical forest sites while using development assistance to help local communities meet their needs in a sustainable, non-destructive way. They include the WWF Korup Project in Cameroon (see Data Sheet on Korup National Park, CPD Site Af12) and the IUCN East Usambaras Project in Tanzania (see Data Sheet on the East Usambara Mountains, CPD Site Af71).

## Centres of plant diversity and endemism

The most species- and endemic-rich areas for plants are listed below for mainland Africa. The first comprehensive selection of areas of outstanding botanical importance for the African continent was made at the 6th Plenary Meeting of AETFAT (the Association pour l'Etude Taxonomique de la Flore d'Afrique Tropicale) held in Uppsala, Sweden in September 1966 (Hedberg and Hedberg 1968). A list was compiled of 41 sites, regions and vegetation types of scientific interest and in need of urgent protection, in mainland Africa, Madagascar, Socotra and the Azores. Some of the sites were proposed on the basis of protecting individual species, while others included unusual or threatened vegetation types. Some sites were also chosen because of their high species diversity and endemism.

In 1985, the IUCN Threatened Plants Unit (TPU) (now part of the World Conservation Monitoring Centre), concerned at the continuing rate of loss of plant-rich habitats around the world, prepared a candidate list of some 26 top priority African sites in need of conservation. The candidate list was primarily developed from an analysis of the threatened plants database of TPU, together with surveys of the literature; species-richness, endemism and degree of threat were the main selection criteria. The list was presented for discussion at the 11th Plenary Meeting of AETFAT, held at Missouri Botanical Garden in June 1985 (Droop 1988).

The TPU candidate list provided the basis for the expanded and refined list of centres of plant diversity and endemism presented below. Dr Henk J. Beentje (now of the Royal Botanic Gardens, Kew) began work on developing the list in 1990 for presentation at the 13th AETFAT Congress in Zomba, Malawi, in April 1991 (Davis, in press). The final choice of sites to be treated as Data Sheets was agreed at a Workshop on African Centres of Plant Diversity held during the Congress.

Thirty sites have been selected for Data Sheet treatment. They have been selected to represent as broad a range of the diversity of the African flora as possible. The phytochoria recognized by White (1983) (see Map 4) were used as a basis for selecting sites, with species-rich phytochoria being allocated more Data Sheets than species-poor phytochoria.

Each of the sites or vegetation types selected for Data Sheet treatment (Table 24) contains, or is estimated to contain, more than 1000 vascular plant species, of which more than 100 are endemic to that site or phytogeographic region. An exception to this rule is the Afroalpine flora of East and North-east Africa. With only about 300–350 vascular plant species occurring in the Afroalpine communities of East and North-east Africa, this phytochorion is referred to by White (1983) as the Afroalpine Archipelago-like Region of Extreme Floristic Impoverishment. However, the high rate of species endemism (>80% endemism) justifies the selection of the East and North-east African Afroalpine flora (Af81) for Data Sheet treatment. Note that some of the montane sites, selected primarily to represent other phytochoria, contain samples of the Afroalpine flora (e.g. Mt Kenya, CPD Site Af62). The Drakensberg Alpine Region of Southern Africa (Af82) has a rather different floristic composition to the Afroalpine flora further north and has also been selected for Data Sheet treatment.

Where there exist a number of similar sites (e.g. in terms of their species composition, richness, component vegetation types, etc.), only one (or a few examples) have been selected for detailed treatment in Data Sheets. In such cases, the sites chosen for Data Sheet treatment are those which are believed to represent the widest range of plant communities and vegetation types.

The number of Data Sheet sites broadly reflects the diversity of flora and vegetation within each phytogeographic region (see Table 24). Phytogeographical regions with large numbers of species and endemics are allocated proportionately more Data Sheets than those with fewer

species and endemics. There are some exceptions to this, as a result of the inclusion of some sites as representatives of one phytochorion, when they could arguably be included in others. For example, Mount Cameroon (CPD Site Af13) is included under the Guineo-Congolian Regional Centre of Endemism, but it could also have been included to represent the Afromontane flora. The number of Data Sheets per phytochorion is also skewed by the treatment of some phytochoria in their entireties. For example, the endemic-rich regional centres of Southern Africa (e.g. the Cape and Karoo-Namib regions) are treated in their entireties in two Data Sheets. The authors recognize that this arrangement is at variance with the methodology of selecting individual sites for other parts of Africa and it is hoped that the International Conference on Biodiversity (The Conservation and Utilization of Southern African Botanical Resources, convened in September 1993 by the National Botanical Institute, South Africa) will help to refine the selection of CPD sites at the regional and national levels within Southern Africa.

No sites meet the criteria for selection as centres of plant diversity and endemism in the following Regional Mosaics and Transition Zones of White (1983), all of which have fewer than 50 endemic species (see Table 16): Lake Victoria RM, Kalahari/Highveld RTZ, Guinea-Congolia/Zambezia RTZ, Guinea-Congolia/Sudania RTZ, Sahara RTZ and Sahel RTZ. However, several sites of botanical interest are identified in the present account for the Sahara and Sahel zones.

## TABLE 24. NUMBER OF CPD SITES SELECTED FOR EACH PHYTOCHORION

| Phytochorion | Species | Endemics | Species endemism | Number of CPD sites[a] | Number of Data Sheets[b] |
|---|---|---|---|---|---|
| Guineo-Congolian RCE | 12,000 | 6400 | 80% | 30 | 12 |
| Cape RCE | 8600 | 5870 | 68% | * | 1 |
| Zambezian RCE | 8500 | 4590 | 54% | 10 | 4 |
| Karoo-Namib RCE | 7000 [c] | <3500 | 35–50% | * | 2 |
| Afromontane RCE | 4000 | 3000 | 75% | 21 | 3 |
| Somali-Masai RCE | 4000 | 1250 | 31% | 5 | 2 |
| Maputaland-Pondoland Region[e] | 7000 | 1220 [c] | >20% [c] | * | 1 |
| Sudanian RCE | 2750 | 960 | 35% | 4 | 1 |
| Mediterranean RCE | 4000 | 800 | 20% | 1 | 1 |
| Indian Ocean belt: | | | | | |
|    Northern section | 3000 | 450 | 15% | 5 | 1 |
| Afroalpine | | | | | |
|    (East and North-east Africa) | 300–350 | 240–280 | 80% | * | 1 |
| Drakensberg Alpine Region | | | | | |
|    (Southern Africa) | >2000 | ? | 30% [d] | * | 1 |
| Mediterranean/Sahara RTZ[f] | 2500 | <50 | Low | 1 | 0 |

Arrangement here is by number of endemics.

Notes:

| | |
|---|---|
| [a] | Refers to numbered sites listed for each phytochorion. |
| [b] | Refer to previous notes on selection of areas to be treated as Data Sheets. |
| [c] | Refers to vascular plant taxa (i.e. species, subspecies, varieties). |
| [d] | Refers to southern Natal Drakensberg Mountains (Hilliard and Burtt 1987). |
| [e] | Treated in the list of areas under Indian Ocean Coastal Belt. |
| [f] | Treated in the list of areas for North Africa. |
| * | Region treated in its entirety. |
| RCE | Regional Centre of Endemism. |
| RM | Regional Mosaic. |
| RTZ | Regional Transition Zone. |

## TABLE 25. AFRICAN SITES IDENTIFIED AS CENTRES OF PLANT DIVERSITY AND ENDEMISM

The list of sites is arranged according to the sequence adopted in the Regional Overview. Sites selected for Data Sheet treatment appear in bold.

**GUINEO-CONGOLIAN REGIONAL CENTRE OF ENDEMISM**
*a. GUINEAN (WEST AFRICAN) RAIN FOREST UNIT*
Af1.   South-east forest remnants (Côte d'Ivoire)
Af2.   **Taï National Park** (Côte d'Ivoire)
Af3.   South-west Ghana (Ghana)
Af4.   **Mont Nimba** (Guinea, Liberia, Côte d'Ivoire)
Af5.   Cestos-Senkwen River area (Liberia)
Af6.   Loffa-Mano Forest (Liberia)
Af7.   **Sapo National Park** (Liberia)
Af8.   Gola High Forest (Sierra Leone)
Af9.   Loma (Sierra Leone)
*b. CONGOLIAN (CENTRAL AFRICAN) RAIN FOREST UNIT*
Af10.  Campo-Kribi (Cameroon)
Af11.  **Forest zone, River Dja region** (Cameroon)
Af12.  **Korup National Park** (Cameroon)
Af13.  **Mount Cameroon** (Cameroon)
Af14.  Odzala National Park and Biosphere Reserve (Congo)
Af15.  Tsiama or Grand Bangou forest near Kindamba and
       Brazzaville (Congo)
Af16.  **Mayombe** (Congo, Cabinda, Zaïre)
Af17.  Bélinga area and Ipassa-Makokou Forest (Gabon)
Af18.  **Cristal Mountains** (Gabon)
Af19.  Massif de Chaillu (Gabon, Congo)
Af20.  Massif de Doudou (Gabon)
Af21.  Mount Malabo (Bioko)
Af22.  Príncipe
Af23.  São Tomé
Af24.  **Cross River National Park** (Nigeria)
Af25.  **Bwindi (Impenetrable) Forest** (Uganda)
Af26.  Itombwe (Zaïre)
Af27.  Ituri lowland rain forest (Zaïre)
Af28.  Kahuzi-Biega (Zaïre)
Af29.  **Maïko National Park** (Zaïre)
Af30.  **Salonga National Park** (Zaïre)

**ZAMBEZIAN REGIONAL CENTRE OF ENDEMISM**
Af31.  Benguela and Bié Districts (Angola)
Af32.  Itigi thicket (Tanzania)
Af33.  **Mahale-Karobwa Hills** (Tanzania)
Af34.  Haut Shaba (Zaïre)
Af35.  **Kundelungu** (Zaïre)
Af36.  Marungu highlands (Zaïre)
Af37.  **Upemba National Park** (Zaïre)
Af38.  Luangwa Valley (Zambia)
Af39.  **Zambezi source area** (Zambia)
Af40.  Great Dyke (Zimbabwe)

**SOMALI-MASAI REGIONAL CENTRE OF ENDEMISM**
Af41.  Limestone bush/woodland, Ogaden (Ethiopia, Kenya, Somalia)
Af42.  **Cal Madow** (Somalia)
Af43.  Fixed dune vegetation in southern Somalia
Af44.  **Hobyo** (Somalia)
Af45.  Nugaal Valley (Somalia)

**SUDANIAN REGIONAL CENTRE OF ENDEMISM**
Af46.  Adamaoua area (Cameroon)
Af47.  Odienné area (Côte d'Ivoire)
Af48.  Fouta Djallon (Guinea)
Af49.  **Garamba National Park** (Zaïre)

**KAROO-NAMIB REGIONAL CENTRE OF ENDEMISM**
Af50.  **The Kaokoveld** (Angola, Namibia)
Af51.  **Western Cape Domain (Succulent Karoo)** (Namibia,
       South Africa)
Af52.  Albany Centre (South Africa)

**CAPE REGIONAL CENTRE OF ENDEMISM**
Af53.  **Cape Floristic Region** (South Africa)

**INDIAN OCEAN COASTAL BELT**
*a. NORTHERN SECTION*
Af54.  Shimba Hills (Kenya)
Af55.  Msumbugwe (Tanzania)
Af56.  Pugu Hills and Kazimzumbwi Forest Reserves
       (Tanzania)
Af57.  **Rondo Plateau** (Tanzania)
Af58.  Middle Ruvuma River area (Tanzania, Mozambique)
*b. SOUTHERN SECTION:*
Af59.  **Maputaland-Pondoland Region** (South Africa, Swaziland,
       Mozambique)

**AFROMONTANE REGIONAL CENTRE OF ENDEMISM**
Af60.  Bale Mountains (Ethiopia)
Af61.  Simen Mountains (Ethiopia)
Af62.  **Mount Kenya** (Kenya)
Af63.  Mount Elgon (Kenya, Uganda)
Af64.  **Mount Mulanje** (Malawi)
Af65.  Nyika Plateau (Malawi, Zambia)
Af66.  Nyungwe Forest Reserve (Rwanda)
Af67.  Drakensberg Afromontane Regional System (South
       Africa)
Af68.  Imatong Mountains (Sudan)
Af69.  Jebel Marra (Sudan)
Af70.  Taita Hills (Kenya)
Af71.  **East Usambara Mountains** (Tanzania)
Af72.  Nguru Mountains (Tanzania)
Af73.  Uluguru Mountains (Tanzania)
Af74.  Uzungwa Mountains (Tanzania)
Af75.  Kilimanjaro (Tanzania)
Af76.  Kitulo Plateau/Kipengere Mountains (Tanzania)
Af77.  Rwenzori Mountains (Uganda)
Af78.  Virunga National Park (Zaïre)
Af79.  Chimanimani Mountains (Zimbabwe)
Af80.  Nyanga (Zimbabwe)

**AFROALPINE REGIONAL CENTRE OF ENDEMISM**
Af81.  **Afroalpine Region** (East and North-east Africa)

**DRAKENSBERG ALPINE REGION**
Af82.  **Drakensberg Alpine Region** (Lesotho, South Africa)

**NORTH AFRICA**
**(MEDITERRANEAN REGIONAL CENTRE OF ENDEMISM,
MEDITERRANEAN/SAHARA REGIONAL TRANSITION ZONE)**
Af83.  Al Jabal al Akhdar (Libya)
Af84.  **High Atlas** (Morocco)

The list below is arranged alphabetically by country for purposes of cross-reference. Sites selected for Data Sheet treatment appear in bold. Numbers refer to site numbers used in the Regional Overview.

**ANGOLA**
Af31.  Benguela and Bié Districts
Af50.  **The Kaokoveld**

**BIOKO**
Af21.  Mount Malabo

**CABINDA**
Af16.  **Mayombe**

**CAMEROON**
Af10.  Campo-Kribi
Af11.  **Forest zone, River Dja region**
Af12.  **Korup National Park**
Af13.  **Mount Cameroon**
Af46.  Adamaoua area

**CONGO**
Af14.  Odzala National Park and Biosphere Reserve

## TABLE 25 ...continued

Af15. Tsiama or Grand Bangou forest near Kindamba and Brazzaville
Af16. **Mayombe**
Af19. Massif de Chaillu

**CÔTE D'IVOIRE**
Af4. **Mont Nimba**
Af1. South-east forest remnants
Af2. **Taï National Park**
Af47. Odienné area

**(EAST AFRICA)**
Af81. **Afroalpine Region (East and North-east Africa)**

**ETHIOPIA**
Af41. Limestone bush/woodland, Ogaden
Af60. Bale Mountains
Af61. Simen Mountains

**GABON**
Af17. Bélinga area and Ipassa-Makokou Forest
Af18. **Cristal Mountains**
Af19. Massif de Chaillu
Af20. Massif de Doudou

**GHANA**
Af3. South-west Ghana

**GUINEA**
Af4. **Mont Nimba**
Af48. Fouta Djallon

**KENYA**
Af41. Limestone bush/woodland, Ogaden
Af54. Shimba Hills
Af62. **Mount Kenya**
Af63. Mount Elgon
Af70. Taita Hills

**LESOTHO**

Af82. **Drakensberg Alpine Region**

**LIBERIA**
Af4. **Mont Nimba**
Af5. Cestos-Senkwen River area
Af6. Loffa-Mano Forest
Af7. **Sapo National Park**

**LIBYA**
Af83. Al Jabal al Akhdar

**MALAWI**
Af64. **Mount Mulanje**
Af65. Nyika Plateau

**MOROCCO**
Af84. **High Atlas**

**MOZAMBIQUE**
Af58. Middle Ruvuma River area
Af59. **Maputaland-Pondoland Region**

**NAMIBIA**
Af50. **The Kaokoveld**
Af51. **Western Cape Domain (Succulent Karoo)**

**NIGERIA**
Af24. **Cross River National Park**

**(NORTH-EAST AFRICA)**
Af81. **Afroalpine Region (East and North-east Africa)**

**PRÍNCIPE**
Af22. Príncipe

**RWANDA**
Af66. Nyungwe Forest Reserve

**SÃO TOMÉ**
Af23. São Tomé

**SIERRA LEONE**
Af8. Gola High Forest
Af9. Loma

**SOMALIA**
Af41. Limestone bush/woodland, Ogaden
Af42. **Cal Madow**
Af43. Fixed dune vegetation in southern Somalia
Af44. **Hobyo**
Af45. Nugaal Valley

**SOUTH AFRICA**
Af51. **Western Cape Domain (Succulent Karoo)**
Af52. Albany Centre
Af53. **Cape Floristic Region**
Af59. **Maputaland-Pondoland Region**
Af67. Drakensberg Afromontane Regional System
Af82. **Drakensberg Alpine Region (Southern Africa)**

**SUDAN**
Af68. Imatong Mountains
Af69. Jebel Marra

**SWAZILAND**
Af59. **Maputaland-Pondoland Region**

**TANZANIA**
Af32. Itigi thicket
Af33. **Mahale-Karobwa Hills**
Af55. Msumbugwe
Af56. Pugu Hills and Kazimzumbwi Forest Reserves
Af57. **Rondo Plateau**
Af58. Middle Ruvuma River area
Af71. **East Usambara Mountains**
Af72. Nguru Mountains
Af73. Uluguru Mountains
Af74. Uzungwa Mountains
Af75. Kilimanjaro
Af76. Kitulo Plateau/Kipengere Mountains

**UGANDA**
Af25. **Bwindi (Impenetrable) Forest**
Af63. Mount Elgon
Af77. Rwenzori Mountains

**ZAÏRE**
Af16. **Mayombe**
Af26. Itombwe
Af27. Ituri lowland rain forest
Af28. Kahuzi-Biega
Af29. **Maïko National Park**
Af30. **Salonga National Park**
Af34. Haut Shaba
Af35. **Kundelungu**
Af37. **Upemba National Park**
Af36. Marungu highlands
Af49. **Garamba National Park**
Af78. Virunga National Park

**ZAMBIA**
Af38. Luangwa Valley
Af39. **Zambezi source area**
Af65. Nyika Plateau

**ZIMBABWE**
Af40. Great Dyke
Af79. Chimanimani Mountains
Af80. Nyanga

117

## MAP 4. CENTRES OF PLANT DIVERSITY AND ENDEMISM: AFRICA

The map shows the locations of the CPD Data Sheet sites for Africa superimposed on the main phytogeographical areas or phytochoria
(after White, 1983)

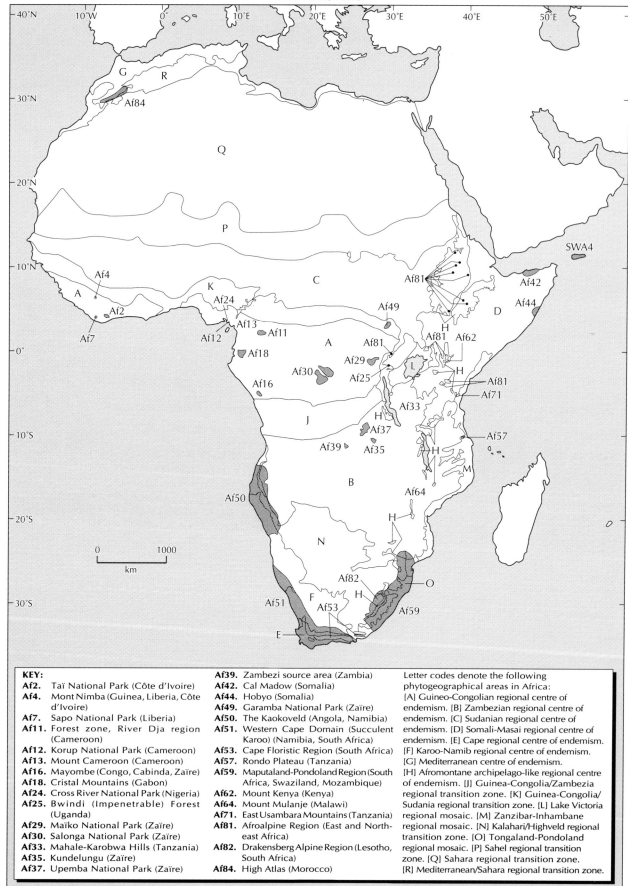

**KEY:**

| | |
|---|---|
| **Af2.** | Taï National Park (Côte d'Ivoire) |
| **Af4.** | Mont Nimba (Guinea, Liberia, Côte d'Ivoire) |
| **Af7.** | Sapo National Park (Liberia) |
| **Af11.** | Forest zone, River Dja region (Cameroon) |
| **Af12.** | Korup National Park (Cameroon) |
| **Af13.** | Mount Cameroon (Cameroon) |
| **Af16.** | Mayombe (Congo, Cabinda, Zaïre) |
| **Af18.** | Cristal Mountains (Gabon) |
| **Af24.** | Cross River National Park (Nigeria) |
| **Af25.** | Bwindi (Impenetrable) Forest (Uganda) |
| **Af29.** | Maïko National Park (Zaïre) |
| **Af30.** | Salonga National Park (Zaïre) |
| **Af33.** | Mahale-Karobwa Hills (Tanzania) |
| **Af35.** | Kundelungu (Zaïre) |
| **Af37.** | Upemba National Park (Zaïre) |

| | |
|---|---|
| **Af39.** | Zambezi source area (Zambia) |
| **Af42.** | Cal Madow (Somalia) |
| **Af44.** | Hobyo (Somalia) |
| **Af49.** | Garamba National Park (Zaïre) |
| **Af50.** | The Kaokoveld (Angola, Namibia) |
| **Af51.** | Western Cape Domain (Succulent Karoo) (Namibia, South Africa) |
| **Af53.** | Cape Floristic Region (South Africa) |
| **Af57.** | Rondo Plateau (Tanzania) |
| **Af59.** | Maputaland-Pondoland Region (South Africa, Swaziland, Mozambique) |
| **Af62.** | Mount Kenya (Kenya) |
| **Af64.** | Mount Mulanje (Malawi) |
| **Af71.** | East Usambara Mountains (Tanzania) |
| **Af81.** | Afroalpine Region (East and North-east Africa) |
| **Af82.** | Drakensberg Alpine Region (Lesotho, South Africa) |
| **Af84.** | High Atlas (Morocco) |

Letter codes denote the following phytogeographical areas in Africa:

[A] Guineo-Congolian regional centre of endemism. [B] Zambezian regional centre of endemism. [C] Sudanian regional centre of endemism. [D] Somali-Masai regional centre of endemism. [E] Cape regional centre of endemism. [F] Karoo-Namib regional centre of endemism. [G] Mediterranean centre of endemism. [H] Afromontane archipelago-like regional centre of endemism. [J] Guinea-Congolia/Zambezia regional transition zone. [K] Guinea-Congolia/Sudania regional transition zone. [L] Lake Victoria regional mosaic. [M] Zanzibar-Inhambane regional mosaic. [N] Kalahari/Highveld regional transition zone. [O] Tongaland-Pondoland regional mosaic. [P] Sahel regional transition zone. [Q] Sahara regional transition zone. [R] Mediterranean/Sahara regional transition zone.

## GUINEO-CONGOLIAN REGIONAL CENTRE OF ENDEMISM

The tropical rain forests of West and Central Africa cover c. 2.8 million km² and consist of two units which are separated by the Dahomey Gap (a region of savanna and woodland). The western unit, the Guinean Rain Forest unit, covers an area of 420,000 km², centred around the forest areas of Guinea, Sierra Leone, Liberia, southern Côte d'Ivoire and Ghana, with a ridge of uplands to the north, stretching from Loma in Sierra Leone to Man in Côte d'Ivoire.

## Climate

Annual rainfall over most of the area is 1600–2000 mm, although in southern Liberia and coastal west Cameroon rainfall can be much higher. Compared to many other major rain forest areas around the world the region is drier and seasonality is more pronounced. In general, there is less seasonality near the Equator (where there is a tendency for two annual rainy periods and a relatively high rainfall) and more pronounced seasonality away from the Equator, where rainfall is less and is mostly concentrated into only part of the year (Hamilton 1989).

## Flora

| Number of species: | <12,000*. |
| Species endemism: | 80% regional endemism. |
| Endemic families: | A few small endemic families. |
| Endemic genera: | c. 20% (mostly small genera)*. |
| Source: White (1983); * F.J. Breteler (1991, pers. comm.). | |

The Guineo-Congolian forests are floristically diverse, sometimes with many species per hectare, most of them woody. Caesalpiniaceae are well-represented, including many endemic genera. Among the few small endemic families in the Guineo-Congolian flora are Dioncophyllaceae (comprising 3 monotypic genera of lianes), Huaceae, Medusandraceae and Scytopetalaceae.

There are some remarkable floristic affinities to the tropical floras of Asia and South America. Thus, the Guineo-Congolian region is the only area in Africa where Ancistrocladaceae and Myristicaceae are found outside of Asia (but one species of the former in East Coast forests). The genus *Gnetum* has two species represented in the Guineo-Congolian flora; it is not found elsewhere in Africa and all other species of the genus are in South East Asia. The links with South America are evident in the occurrence of, for example, Bromeliaceae (one species of *Pitcairnea* being found in Guinea), *Carapa grandiflora* (Meliaceae) (found in South America and the Guineo-Congolian region) and Rapateaceae (one species being found in the Guineo-Congolian region, while the rest of the genus is found in South America and the Caribbean).

The majority of species of the Guinean Rain Forest unit belong to genera also found in the larger Congolian (or Central African) Rain Forest unit. The latter covers 2,380,000 km², centred around the Zaïre basin and bordered by uplands. In the north-west, the unit includes the plateaux and coastal plains of Gabon and Cameroon, as well as forests

in south-east Nigeria. The Congolian lowland forests are the most extensive and species-rich in Africa.

In the Guinean (West African) Rain Forest Unit, endemism is centred around the Liberia/Côte d'Ivoire border.

In the Congolian (Central African) Rain Forest Unit endemism is centred around:

❖ South-east Nigeria and neighbouring south-west Cameroon;
❖ Gabon and adjacent parts of southern Cameroon, Congo and Equatorial Guinea;
❖ Eastern Zaïre, between the Zaïre River and the Albertine Rift Highlands.

The forests of Gabon are probably the richest in endemic species. The Gulf of Guinea islands also have high endemism, especially Bioko (CPD Site Af21) and São Tomé (CPD Site Af23).

## Main vegetation types

Most of the region was once covered by evergreen or semi-deciduous tropical rain forests, but only about 11–12% of the original moist forest cover of West Africa has escaped deforestation, while 59% of the Central African forests remain (Sayer, Harcourt and Collins 1992). Much of the Liberia/Côte d'Ivoire region has been deforested or converted to secondary forest; only remnants of the species-rich forests remain (such as Taï National Park; CPD Site Af2, see Data Sheet). The same is true of Nigeria and parts of Cameroon, where large-scale plantations or agricultural areas now exist in this zone. Congo, Gabon and Zaïre still possess large intact blocks of forest.

Forests dominated virtually by only a single canopy species (often a member of the Caesalpiniaceae) are found from Cameroon to western Uganda. At higher altitudes, wetter types of forest occur, merging into Afromontane forest.

Swamp and riparian forest may be very different in composition from surrounding forests. On inselbergs within the rain forest zone the vegetation can range from shrubby to succulent.

## Species of economic importance

There are a wealth of timber species which have been exploited for many years, mostly for export as rough logs (Table 22). Other important export products include a few species of medicinal plants. Examples of species of economic value include (MacKinnon and MacKinnon 1986):

| | | |
|---|---|---|
| *Aframomum melegueta* | grains of paradise | spice |
| *Ceiba pentandra* | kapok | fibre |
| *Coffea liberica* | Liberian coffee | stimulant |
| *Cola acuminata* | kola | stimulant |
| *Cola nitida* | kola | stimulant |
| *Copaifera, Guibourtia* | copal | resin |
| *Daniellia thurifera* | copal | resin |
| *Dioscorea rotundata* | yam | food |
| *Elaeis guineensis* | oil palm | edible oil |
| *Griffonia simplicifolia* | | medicines |
| *Landolphia* spp. | African rubber | latex |
| *Pausinystalia johimbe* | | medicine |
| *Prunus africana* | | medicine |
| *Pterocarpus erinaceus* | kino | resin/dye |
| *Rauvolfia* spp. | rauvolfia | medicine |
| *Strophanthus hispidus* | strophanthus | medicine |
| *Voacanga* spp. | voacanga | medicine |

## Factors causing loss of biodiversity

The clearance of ever more land to feed burgeoning populations is the most important direct cause of loss of biodiversity, but the degradation of forests through unsustainable commercial logging also continues on a large scale (Tables 19 and 22). Forests formerly protected by their inaccessibility are opened up as logging roads are built. This can result in further forest loss due to slash and burn agriculture and the establishment of permanent settlements. Tracks also open up the forest ecosystems to unregulated commercial hunting for bushmeat.

In some areas, such as West Africa, large areas of forest have been cleared for the cultivation of plantation crops, while uncontrolled fires, mining and charcoal production are important factors in some areas.

Tropical forests could supply a continuous, year-round harvest of forest products, if based on sustainable yield forestry techniques involving careful harvesting methods and the operation of a strict quota system. However, such practices are not in operation over most of the forest belt.

## Conservation

Only 3.6% of the whole phytochorion is currently represented in protected areas, with a further 0.8% proposed. The entire unit is underprotected, particularly in areas of species richness and high endemism (MacKinnon and MacKinnon 1986).

## Centres of plant diversity and endemism

The richest areas for endemism and high species diversity in the Guinean (West African) Rain Forest Unit are along the Liberia/Côte d'Ivoire border. The sites selected for Data Sheet treatment (Taï and Sapo, CPD Sites Af2 and Af7, respectively) are the richest and least disturbed in this region.

For the Congolian (Central African) Rain Forest Unit, there are several areas of high endemism (probably Pleistocene refugia), most notably:

❖ Oban Hills and the Cross River region (CPD Site Af24) of south-east Nigeria, with c. 130 strict endemics;
❖ Mount Cameroon (CPD Site Af13), the main massif of which has 42 strict endemics, about half of which occur in the Guineo-Congolian and foothills forests;
❖ Gabon;
❖ Maiko (CPD Site Af29) and neighbouring lowland and submontane forest on the eastern rim of the Zaïre basin.

Korup (CPD Site Af12, see Data Sheet), typical of the south-east Nigeria/west Cameroon forests and Dja (CPD Site Af11, see Data Sheet), a primary lowland forest representative of the Cameroon-Congolese type, are examples of protected areas in the unit.

Centres of high plant diversity are arranged here by countries in alphabetical sequence.

## GUINEAN (WEST AFRICAN) RAIN FOREST UNIT

### Côte D'Ivoire (Ivory Coast)

Tree-dominated vegetation covers 27,464 km² (or 8.6% of the land area). 13,000 km² of this is lowland rain forest, the rest being dryland, mostly dry savanna woodland (Vooren and Sayer 1992). Deforestation has been at a rate of 2800–3500 km²/year for the past 35 years. Vooren and Sayer (1992) predict that without stringent protective measures, all rain forest will have disappeared by the turn of the century (see also Myers 1989). Taï is the largest remaining tract of undisturbed lowland rain forest in West Africa.

### Af1. South-east forest remnants

Very little forest is left in this area, as a result of population pressure and continued exploitation.

### Af2. Taï National Park

– see Data Sheet.

### Ghana

The two main vegetation types in Ghana are closed forests and savannas. Lowland rain forests cover just 15,839 km² (6.9% of the land area). They are the most species-rich communities in Ghana, two-thirds of which is covered by savannas (Gordon et al. 1992). The two National Parks, below, are treated as one CPD site and probably represent the only areas of Ghana where relatively undisturbed rain forest still exists. Virtually all the extant forest in the country is within Forest Reserves, forest formerly outside these reserves having been converted to cocoa plantations or removed for other reasons (Hawthorne 1990). Over the country as a whole, the greatest threats to remaining forests are agricultural encroachment and fire in drought years. In the 1983 drought, parts of even the wettest forests were severely damaged.

### Af3. South-west Ghana

The important areas are **Bia National Park** (78 km²) and **Nini-Suhien National Park** (106 km²).
❖ Vegetation: Lowland Guinean rain forest, rich in species (Campbell and Hammond 1989).
❖ Flora: 627 vascular plant species recorded so far for Bia, of which 169 are trees. The area is rich in climbers, epiphytic orchids and bryophytes.
❖ Threats: Logging in the Bia Game Production Area; otherwise not known.
❖ Conservation: Bia is partly a National Park (78 km²) and partly a Game Production Area (228 km²). It is proposed to establish Forest Reserves to the south and west of this area. Nini-Suhien is a National Park contiguous, in the south, with the Ankasa Game Production Area (207 km²).

## Guinea, Liberia, Côte D'Ivoire

### Af4. Mont Nimba

– see Data Sheet.

## Liberia

Liberia was originally almost totally covered by tropical moist forest. Today, lowland rain forest covers 41,177 km² (43% of the land area). Mangroves and montane forests cover just c. 0.1% of the land area. Forests are exploited for timber, as well as providing fuelwood and bushmeat. Shifting cultivation accounts for the loss of 2% of the remaining forests each year (Mayers, Anstey and Peal 1992).

### Af5. Cestos-Senkwen River area

An area of coastal lowlands in the centre of the country, including part of the Cestos River basin and the Senkwen River estuary.
- ❖ Vegetation: Littoral forest (possibly the last remnants in West Africa), lowland rain forest and mangroves (Verschuren 1983).
- ❖ Flora: No available figures.
- ❖ Threats: Shifting cultivation is a serious threat along the middle Senkwen and there are some existing logging and mining concessions.
- ❖ Conservation: A 1450 km² area has been proposed as a National Park but is not, as yet, protected.

### Af6. Loffa-Mano Forest

A substantial area of rain forest in the north-west of the country near the Sierra Leone border. Ten years ago the area was reported to be practically uninhabited and difficult of access (Verschuren 1983).
- ❖ Vegetation: Lowland rain forest, probably very similar to that of the adjacent Gola Forest in Sierra Leone.
- ❖ Flora: No available figures.
- ❖ Threats: Logging is apparently proceeding in some areas.
- ❖ Conservation: Not currently protected. An area of 2300 km² has been proposed as a National Park.

### Af7. Sapo National Park

– see Data Sheet.

## Sierra Leone

Over 50% of the country has climatic conditions suitable for tropical rain forest, but less than 5% is still covered with mature, dryland closed forest (Harcourt et al. 1992a). Deforestation is mainly as a result of clearance for agriculture; fuelwood cutting is another major threat. The population was estimated at 4,150,000 in 1990 (World Resources Institute 1992), having increased at an annual rate of nearly 2.5% between 1985 and 1990.

### Af8. Gola High Forest

The last large remnant of near primary rain forest in Sierra Leone; floristically similar to adjacent forests in Liberia. Consists of 3 blocks in the south-east of the country near the Liberian border. Total area: 748 km². The topography is flat to undulating with the highest point being Mt Sangie at 472 m.
- ❖ Vegetation: climax upper Guinean rain forest. Emergent canopy species are of massive size, reaching 60 m.
- ❖ Flora: At least 180 tree species have been recorded, of which one is known to be a site endemic.
- ❖ Threats: Some 40% of the forest has been logged since 1984 and shifting cultivation is affecting the boundaries. It has been proposed that people displaced by hydroelectric schemes be settled around the reserves.
- ❖ Conservation: All three blocks are Forest Reserves in which settlement is prohibited and logging is by concession. Gola East and West have been proposed as a National Park (Davies 1987).

### Af9. Loma

A mountain massif of 500 km² in the north-east of the country.
- ❖ Vegetation: Moist mixed lowland rain forest on the lower slopes, *Parinari* forest from 800 to 1400 m and regularly burnt montane grassland with many geophytes above 1400 m.
- ❖ Flora: 1576 vascular plant species, 11 site endemics (Jaeger 1983).
- ❖ Threats: No information.
- ❖ Conservation: The area is a Forest Reserve.

## CONGOLIAN (CENTRAL AFRICAN) RAIN FOREST UNIT

### Cameroon

Cameroon is one of the most ecologically diverse countries in Africa and includes montane, submontane, lowland evergreen and semi-deciduous forests. There are also extensive areas of mangrove. Closed canopy forests (including lowland, montane, mangrove and swamp forests) cover 155,330 km² (41.2% of the land area), of which lowland forests cover 147,480 km² (31.7% of the land area) (Gartlan et al. 1992).

The richest forests are the evergreen Atlantic (or Biafran) rain forests. They are centres of diversity for such genera as *Cola*, *Diospyros*, *Dorstenia* and *Garcinia* and contain many narrow endemics. They also have some remarkable affinities to the forests of South America (Gartlan et al. 1992), as well as with forests in Upper Guinea. Such affinities are evidence of past connections between these widely separated forests.

At 4095 m, Mount Cameroon is the highest mountain in West Africa and a very important centre of plant diversity (see Data Sheet). Most of its plant biodiversity and endemism occurs below 1500 m; about 300 species of trees have so far been recorded in an area of c. 36 km² at Mabeta-Moliwe in the foothills to the east. However, lowland forests on the west are probably at least as rich, are more extensive and less immediately threatened and, if legally protected, would be valuable additions to the conservation area of Mount Cameroon itself. Rather than including Mount Cameroon as an

Afromontane site, it is selected here for Data Sheet treatment as a site representing the Guineo-Congolian rain forest flora.

Korup has c. 400 tree species and 5–10 strict endemics and is the only National Park in Cameroon within the Atlantic rain forest zone (see Data Sheet). It is contiguous with the Oban Division of Cross River National Park in Nigeria (see Data Sheet), which has c. 130 strict endemics.

Dja belongs to a second type of lowland rain forest, known as Cameroon-Congolese rain forest. Floristic diversity is lower than in the Atlantic forests and the main affinities are with the forests of the Congo basin.

Lowland forests outside of protected areas of high protected status (such as National Parks and Faunal Reserves) are subject to logging; the government recently announced plans to double the current production of industrial wood (currently 2.73 million m³) by the year 2000. It is, therefore, important that further representative samples of both Atlantic and Cameroon-Congolese forest types are included in the protected area system.

## Af10. Campo-Kribi

Area: Coastal, in the south.
- ❖ Vegetation: Lowland rain forest.
- ❖ Flora: No available figures.
- ❖ Threats: Intense logging, hunting.
- ❖ Conservation: None.

## Af11. Forest zone, River Dja region

– see Data Sheet.

## Af12. Korup National Park

– see Data Sheet.

## Af13. Mount Cameroon

– see Data Sheet.

## Congo

To date, over 4000 vascular plant species have been recorded from Congo, but UICN (1990a) estimates that probably as many as 6000 species are present. The floristic richness is a result of varied topography and climate, giving rise to a mixture of forest and savanna vegetation. Up to the 1970s, timber was the main source of export revenue for Congo, but this has now been surpassed by oil.

Congo still has vast areas of inland swamp forest, especially in the Cuvette Congolais, semi-deciduous forest (on the Massif de Chaillu bordering Gabon, comprising 11% of the land area – see CPD Site Af19 – and in the south on the Mayombe Massif – see CPD Site Af16) as well as pockets of evergreen and dry, semi-evergreen forests in the north.

Approximately 213,400 km² (or 40.6% of the land area) are covered by moist forests (FAO 1988a), a figure which includes 33,600 km² of exploited forests.

## Massif de Chaillu

– see CPD Site Af19, under Gabon.

## Mayombe

– see CPD Site Af16, under Congo, Cabinda, Zaïre.

## Af14. Odzala National Park and Biosphere Reserve

Area: National Park – 1266 km²; Biosphere Reserve – 1100 km². Located in the north of Congo, 30 km east of the Gabon border. Altitude: 300–800 m.
- ❖ Vegetation: About 80% covered with dense evergreen forest, partly secondary. Savanna occurs on the hilltops and there are many natural saltpans.
- ❖ Flora: No available figures.
- ❖ Threats: Poaching of large mammals.
- ❖ Conservation: Although a National Park, the boundaries are imprecise and management minimal. Odzala is part of a larger conservation area, with the contiguous reserves of Lekoli-Pandaka and M'boko to the south, covering a total area of 2848 km² (IUCN/UNEP 1987).

## Af15. Tsiama or Grand Bangou forest near Kindamba and Brazzaville

Semi-deciduous forest on sand, with *Hymenocardia ulmoides*, *Pentaclethra* and many lianas. Rich in strict endemics but now severely degraded (Hedberg and Hedberg 1968; Hedberg 1976).

## Congo, Cabinda, Zaïre

## Af16. Mayombe

– see Data Sheet.

## Gabon

Forest still covers about 91% of the country, of which 225,276 km² is lowland forest (87.4% of the land area) (Tutin *et al.* 1992). Of the estimated 7150 vascular plant species, 22% are endemic, but Gabon is poorly known botanically due to lack of road access to extensive areas. Logging is continuing, but selective; most trees removed are of a single species, *Aucoumea klaineana*. There is almost no rural population pressure, so logging operations do not give rise to an influx of settlers and clearances for slash and burn agriculture. Shifting cultivation is the cause of only limited forest loss (IUCN 1988b; Campbell and Hammond 1989; Breteler 1990; Tutin *et al.* 1992).

## Af17. Bélinga area and Ipassa-Makokou Forest

Moist forest in the north-centre of the country (Hallé, Le Thomas and Gazel 1967; Hladik 1986).
- ❖ Vegetation: Dense lowland rain forest, some seasonally flooded. "Elfin thicket" occurs on higher slopes between 900 and 1000 m (White 1983).
- ❖ Flora: Estimated 4000 vascular plant species, with many lianas and epiphytes.
- ❖ Threats: Some encroachment from nearby villages.

❖ Conservation: The Ipassa-Makokou Strict Nature Reserve covers 100 km² and a Biosphere Reserve covers 150 km². The surrounding areas are not protected and there are no buffer zones. Reportedly, management needs strengthening.

## Af18. Cristal Mountains

– see Data Sheet.

## Af19. Massif de Chaillu (also in Congo)

Area: c. 50,000 km², in south-central Gabon, bordering Congo; c. 12,000 km² is in Gabon. Altitude: 600–>1000 m.
❖ Vegetation: Mainly tropical mid-altitude rain forest; some semi-deciduous forest in the Congo part.
❖ Flora: >3000 vascular plant species, with high site endemism (c. 10%) (F.J. Breteler 1991, *in litt.*). Important timber trees include okoume (*Aucoumea klaineana*) and many Caesalpiniaceae. Flora expected to be slightly different to that of the Cristal Mountains (CPD Site Af18, see Data Sheet), but so far insufficiently known.
❖ Threats: Logging, shifting cultivation, hunting.
❖ Conservation: Not protected; threatened.

## Af20. Massif de Doudou

Located in the south-west of Gabon, the Doudou Mountains cover c. 1750 km². There are no permanent settlements. Altitude: 100–800 m.
❖ Vegetation: Lowland Guineo-Congolian and hill rain forest, with an abundance of Caesalpiniaceae. The area may have been a Pleistocene forest refugium. Some inselbergs and steep rock faces are devoid of high forest. The region is bordered by savanna, with pockets of forest to the east.
❖ Flora: Floristically rich, with an estimated >1000 vascular plant species, of which c. 50 species are strict endemics (J. de Wilde 1991, *in litt.*), including *Begonia dewildei*, *Impatiens floretii* and *Trichostephanus gabonensis*.
❖ Threats: Logging; this was on a substantial scale from 1970–1989, but has since been reduced in intensity (J. de Wilde 1991, *in litt.*).
❖ Conservation: The Mougalaba-Dougoua Faunal Reserve (800 km²) includes part of the Massif de Doudou. A proposal exists to link this with the Setté-Cama Reserve to create Gabon's largest protected area (Gamba Reserve). The Doudou Mountains should be included.

## Gulf of Guinea Islands

The Gulf of Guinea include the oceanic islands of Bioko, Príncipe, São Tomé and Annobon. Of 194 vascular plants which are endemic to these islands, only 16 occur on more than one island (Jones 1992).

   **Bioko** (or Fernando Po) still has several hundred km² of forest in the north of the island.

## Af21. Mount Malabo

❖ Vegetation: Lowland rain forest below 900 m (most now destroyed); montane forest between 900 and 2400 m; montane heath to summit at 3008 m.

❖ Flora: >1000 vascular plant species; 49 site endemics (Brenan 1978), including 4 species of *Leptonychia* (Sterculiaceae).
❖ Threats: Agricultural encroachment, particularly coffee plantations.
❖ Conservation: No protection at present.

## Af22. Príncipe

A small island (of area 139 km²) between São Tomé and Bioko. Some 40 km² of lowland and montane rain forest still remain (Jones 1992).
❖ Flora: c. 320 vascular plant species, including 32 single-island endemics and 1 endemic genus (Jones 1992).
❖ Threats: No immediate large-scale threats (IUCN 1988a; Jones 1992).
❖ Conservation: State land, but no protected areas so far designated. The forest is crucial for water production and erosion control.

## Af23. São Tomé

A rugged island (area: 857 km²) of volcanic origin with a number of peaks above 1000 m, the highest rising to 2024 m. Some 240 km² of lowland and montane rain forests still remain (Jones 1992).
❖ Vegetation: Lowland rain forest (mostly cleared, but some still present in the south-west of the island); montane forest above 800 m, very species-rich and with an abundance of lianas, orchids and ferns.
❖ Flora: 601 vascular plant species, including 87 single-island endemics and 1 endemic genus.
❖ Threats: No immediate large-scale threats because most of the forest is on inaccessible steep slopes. Small-scale threats through clearance for subsistence agriculture as the population increases (Hedberg and Hedberg 1968; IUCN 1988a) and from firewood collection in the south-west (Jones 1992).
❖ Conservation: There are no protected areas at present. The forest is crucial for waters production and erosion control.

## Nigeria

Forests cover 38,620 km² of which over a quarter (27%) is mangrove forest. Remaining lowland rain forest on dry land and inland swamp forest cover 28,040 km² (just 3.1% of the land area) and are mostly restricted to Forest Reserves (Lowe, Caldecott, Barnwell and Keay 1992). Major threats result from pressures caused by the increasing population, estimated at 108,540,000 in 1990 (World Resources Institute 1992) and increasing at a rate of 3.3% per annum between 1985–1990.

## Af24. Cross River National Park

– see Data Sheet.

## Uganda

Uganda's forests covered an estimated 12.7% of the land area at the turn of the century, now reduced to 4.4%.

Lowland forests cover 6318 km² (3.2% of Uganda's land area) (Harcourt *et al.* 1992b). There are various types of evergreen and semi-deciduous rain forests (Hamilton 1984). Bwindi (Impenetrable) Forest is exceptionally important in terms of diversity and endemism, being a Pleistocene forest refugium. In addition to lowland forests, montane forests cover 2212 km² (1.1% of the land area) (see Afromontane sites: Mt Elgon and Rwenzori, CPD Sites Af63 and Af77, respectively).

Over the last 50 years the main cause of forest loss has been clearance for agriculture. Uganda had an estimated population of 18,790,000 in 1990 (World Resources Institute 1992), with an annual rate of increase between 1985 and 1990 of 3.7%. About 90% of the population is rural. Today, virtually all surviving forest is in Forest Reserves or other protected areas.

## Af25. Bwindi (Impenetrable) Forest

– see Data Sheet.

## Zaïre

With 1,190,737 km² of forest (of all types), Zaïre contains over half of Africa's tropical moist forests (Sayer *et al.* 1992). The greatest part of Zaïre's forests (most of which are semi-evergreen rain forests) is in the Cuvette Centrale at about 300 m above sea-level. Closed canopy lowland dryland forests cover 919,736 km² (40.6% of the land area); degraded lowland dryland forest covers 86,547 km² (or 3.8% of the land area) (Sayer *et al.* 1992).

Difficulty of access and low market prices have inhibited large-scale logging; deforestation was estimated at 1650 km² between 1967 and 1980 (FAO/UNEP 1981), of which 1350 km² was apparently cleared for shifting cultivation. However, much of this took place in previously logged forest.

Salonga (CPD Site Af30) is the largest rain forest park in the world (see Data Sheet).

## Af26. Itombwe

The Itombwe Mountains run north-south along the Albertine Rift in eastern Zaïre and support the largest area of montane forest along the Western Rift (>6500 km²). Several peaks rise above 3000 m, the highest, Mt Mohi, reaching 3475 m.

❖ Vegetation: Lowland to montane forest, with bamboo and grassland zones.

❖ Flora: No floristic inventories have been made, due to remoteness and, on occasion, political disturbances, but the forest is thought to be one of the richest montane forests in Africa (A.C. Hamilton, pers. comm.).

❖ Threats: The area is under pressure from agriculturists and pastoralists. Cattle are destroying the bamboo belt and increasing in numbers on the high plateaux. Kamituga, just to the north-west, is an important mining centre with a large population.

❖ Conservation: No official protection. The forests on the western side of the mountains are still in good condition (IUCN 1988c).

## Af27. Ituri lowland rain forest

An area of 60,000–70,000 km² in the north-east of the country, inhabited by Mbuti people. Altitude: 600–1500 m.

❖ Vegetation: Tall lowland rain forest, with some savanna patches and forest-savanna mosaic at the margins.

❖ Flora: No available figures, but known to be very rich.

❖ Threats: Logging and intense charcoal production in the east, gold mining, shifting cultivation, in-migration (a road cuts through the centre of the forest) (Hall 1990).

❖ Conservation: Okapi Wildlife Reserve (designated in 1992) covers some 13,000 km². Hunting, new gold mining operations and logging will be prohibited. The remainder of the forest is not protected.

## Af28. Kahuzi-Biega

Area: 6000 km² in eastern Zaïre, 50 km west of Bukavu. Altitude: 900–3400 m (summit of Kahuzi volcano).

❖ Vegetation: Lowland rain forest, transition forest, montane forest intermixed with bamboo, woodland and alpine grassland; some *Cyperus* swamp vegetation and peatbogs (Marius 1976; IUCN 1988c).

❖ Flora: No available figures.

❖ Threats: Mining and population pressure, which is becoming severe. The forest in the area nearest to Bukavu and up to 50 km to the north is being rapidly cleared for agriculture (Collar and Stuart 1988).

❖ Conservation: National Park and World Heritage Site. Management needs more resources, but is reasonably effective in montane areas.

## Af29. Maïko National Park

– see Data Sheet.

## Af30. Salonga National Park

– see Data Sheet.

## ZAMBEZIAN REGIONAL CENTRE OF ENDEMISM

Most of this region is a large plateau (the Great African Plateau), bordered by the Great Escarpment and drained mainly by the Zambezi River, with the northern parts draining into the Zaïre River. In the upper Zambezi basin the aeolian Kalahari Sands, active during the Quaternary Period, may be as much as 150 m deep. On the Great Dyke of Zimbabwe and in the Shaba/Mwinilunga area on the Zaïre/Angola/Zambia border, the soils have high levels of heavy metals (such as chromium, cobalt, copper, manganese and zinc) in very localized areas.

## Flora

| | |
|---|---|
| **Number of species:** | c. 8500. |
| **Species endemism:** | 54%. |
| **Endemic families:** | None. |
| **Endemic genera:** | Few (the characteristic genera *Brachystegia* and *Colophospermum* have their centres of speciation in this region). |
| **Source:** White (1983). | |

Endemism is not very localized, except for areas such as Haut Shaba and the Angolan high escarpment.

## Main vegetation types

This region has a most diverse flora and shows a wide range of vegetation types. Woodland is the most widespread type, especially miombo woodland (with *Brachystegia*, *Isoberlinia*, *Julbernardia*, very common) on dry and shallow plateau soils. Miombo is deciduous or semi-deciduous over most of its area and much of the land has been subject to past cultivation. It is (with exceptions!) not very rich in species, except in the wetter parts near the Zambia/Zaïre border.

Deciduous mopane woodland, dominated by *Colophospermum mopane*, a species highly tolerant of sodic soils, occurs in drier parts of the region (400–800 mm rainfall per annum). Species richness is low. South of the Zambezi another type of woodland occurs, with many species of *Acacia* and *Combretum*, usually on heavy soils. "Chipya" is a type of fire-climax wooded grassland which occurs in Zambia, Malawi and in the Shaba region of Zaïre. Smaller areas are occupied by riparian woodland, dry bushland and thicket, of which the deciduous Itigi thicket on sandy soil in Tanzania is the best example (see CPD Site Af32).

Other vegetation types include dry evergreen forest (remnants only), dry deciduous forest (on deep sandy soils, e.g. the *Baikiaea* forests), associations found on heavy metal-rich soils and dambo grassland in shallow depressions with impeded drainage.

## Species of economic importance

**Important timbers include:**
| | |
|---|---|
| Baikiaea plurijuga | Zambezi teak |
| Dalbergia melanoxylon | mpingo, African ebony |
| Pterocarpus angolensis | bloodwood tree, muninga |

**Other timbers include:**
Guibourtea coleosperma
Ricinodendron rautanenii   (manketti, mugongo)

**Crop species with wild relatives in this area are:**
| | |
|---|---|
| Hibiscus | okra |
| Oryza | African rice |
| Pennisetum | bulrush millet |
| Sorghum | |
| Members of the Cucurbitaceae | |

**Other species of economic importance:**
| | | |
|---|---|---|
| Acacia spp. | | wood, resin |
| Hyphaene petersiana | Ilala palm | basketry, wine |

## Factors causing loss of biodiversity

The main problems are overgrazing, land clearance for agriculture, excessive fuelwood harvesting and inappropriate burning. Logging and mining are locally important.

## Conservation

7.7% of the unit is included within existing protected areas and another 5% is protected within existing game utilisation areas and Forest Reserves (MacKinnon and MacKinnon 1986).

There is a need for an assessment to be made of the whole Zambezian region to identify representative areas for conservation.

## Centres of plant diversity and endemism

The choice of areas to be treated in detail as Data Sheets has focused on the exceptional species richness and high levels of endemism of the Haut Shaba area and adjacent parts in Zambia, of which Kundelungu (see Data Sheet) and the Mwinilunga area (included in the Data Sheet on the Zambezi Source Area) are probably the best examples. The forests of Mahale-Karobwa Hills (see Data Sheet), in the eastern catchment area of Lake Tanganyika, show some affinities to Guineo-Congolian rain forest.

Two areas which were initially considered for inclusion as CPD sites are: **Huila Plateau** (Angola) and the **Okavango-Kwando** region (Angola, Botswana and Namibia). These areas are important for conservation, but are not sufficiently rich in plant species to qualify as centres of plant diversity and endemism. Although containing numerous endemics, the flora of Huila Plateau is relatively poor in species (B.J. Huntley 1992, pers. comm.), whilst the Okavango-Kwando region is a huge inland wetland area of swamps, woodland and savanna. Although being of the utmost importance as a wetland site, its flora is not thought to be of outstanding species-richness, considering the large area involved; it is not expected to contain many endemics.

### *Angola*

## Af31. Benguela and Bié Districts

High escarpment areas in the west of Angola (Lebrun 1960; Exell and Gonçalves 1973; Werger and Coetzee 1978).
❖ Vegetation: High-altitude wooded grassland intermixed with miombo and gallery forests; scrub and thicket at lower altitudes. Very local cloud forest with abundant epiphytes in the north.
❖ Flora: No available figures, but most of Angola's 1260 known endemic vascular plant species are concentrated in the highland and escarpment zones.
❖ Threats: Collection of fuelwood; clearing of the understorey for coffee cultivation.
❖ Conservation: Probably no protection, but status uncertain. The small size of most of the forest patches renders them particularly vulnerable and the lack of security in the country is a major impediment to establishing effective official protection.

### *Tanzania*

## Af32. Itigi thicket

An area of 130 km² with impeded drainage in central Tanzania. Altitude: c. 700 m.

❖ Vegetation: Thicket, dominated by *Baphia*, *Bussea* and *Pseudoprosopis*. Floristically different from other vegetation, but similar to thickets between Lake Mweru Wantipa and Lake Tanganyika in the north of Zambia (Werger and Coetzee 1978).

❖ Flora: No available figures.

❖ Threats: Clearance for agriculture.

❖ Conservation: No official protection.

## Af33. Mahale-Karobwa Hills

– see Data Sheet.

## *Zaïre*

## Af34. Haut Shaba

(See also Data Sheets on **Kundelungu** and **Upemba National Park**, CPD Sites Af35 and Af37).

A series of high and geographically isolated tablelands in the south-east of the country. The plateaux include **Kundelungu** and **Manika**. Soils sandy and mostly nutrient-poor; rich in copper and cobalt. Fires sweep the plateaux annually. Altitude: 1500–2400 m.

❖ Vegetation: Mainly "steppic savannas" dominated by grasses, with many shrubs and bulbous plants. Woodland with *Brachystegia*, *Julbernardia* and *Monotes* occurs on the plateau margins. There are localized swamps, ravine and riparian gallery forests.

❖ Flora: >1450 vascular plant species (Lisowski, Malaisse and Symoens 1971); >300 area endemics (Brenan 1978; Kendrick 1989).

❖ Threats: Mining.

## Af35. Kundelungu

– see Data Sheet.

## Af36. Marungu highlands

Located to the west of the southern half of Lake Tanganyika, these highlands rise to 2460 m at the highest point.

❖ Vegetation: Mainly grassland and bushland, with dense forest in ravines and riparian forest along streams.

❖ Threats: The riparian forest is under severe threat from timber-felling and the erosion of stream banks by cattle.

❖ Conservation: No formal protection although a Marungu Mountains Reserve has been proposed.

## Af37. Upemba National Park

– see Data Sheet.

## *Zambia*

## Af38. Luangwa Valley

A rift valley covering 40,000 km² in the east of Zambia.

❖ Vegetation: The principal vegetation types are: *Acacia-Combretum* woodland, *Acacia tortilis* woodland,

mopane (*Colophospermum*) woodland, *Erythrophloeum* woodland, *Brachystegia* woodland, thickets, some riparian forest and edaphic grasslands.

❖ Flora: 1348 species of vascular plants have been recorded.

❖ Threats: Pressure from human settlements has restricted game migration and has concentrated populations of some animals within the valley, leading to degradation of some habitats. Prospecting, mining and uncontrolled fires are also problems.

❖ Conservation: Most of the valley is covered by a complex of National Parks (3, covering a total area of 13,940 km²) and Game Management Areas. The Luangwa Integrated Resource Development Project aims to reconcile the human use of parts of the area with conservation of biodiversity.

Note: The **mid-Zambezi valley** on the Zambia/Zimbabwe border is less well documented, but might be more diverse in terms of species and vegetation types.

## Af39. Zambezi source area

– see Data Sheet.

## *Zimbabwe*

## Af40. Great Dyke

A 1–11 km wide band of mostly serpentine, with heavy metals, occurring in a band of about 530 km across the centre of the country in a north-south direction.

❖ Vegetation: Serpentine areas (70% of the total area) are covered by short grassland almost devoid of trees. Soils derived from gabbroic rocks and pyroxenite are wooded.

❖ Flora: 322 vascular plant species, with 20 serpentine endemics (Wild 1965).

❖ Threats: The serpentine of the Great Dyke is one of the world's most important sources of chromium ore (chromite). There are also important deposits of platinum, nickel and asbestos, although only the chromite is currently mined. Zimbabwe law places few constraints on mining develop-ment; spoil heaps from numerous small surface mines, as well as large deep mines, now cover extensive areas.

❖ Conservation: A small section of mostly pyroxenite soil is included within the Ngezi Recreational Park (of total area 58 km²). However, none of the botanically important serpentine areas have any protection.

## SOMALI-MASAI REGIONAL CENTRE OF ENDEMISM

A generally low-lying region (mostly below 900 m) in eastern Africa, covering an area of 1,873,000 km², with "islands" of mountains containing Afromontane vegetation.

## Climate

Semi-arid, with a mean annual rainfall of 100–500 mm, but as low as 20 mm in some areas. Rainfall is generally spread over two seasons and varies considerably from year to year.

## Flora

*Acacia, Commiphora, Crotalaria* and *Indigofera* have many species. There are many endemic succulents (e.g. stapeliads) and areas of local endemism on limestone. Endemic families are Cyclocheilaceae (4 species) and Dirachmaceae (*D. socotrana*), the latter being restricted to Somalia and Socotra.

## Main vegetation types

Deciduous bushland, dominated by *Acacia* and *Commiphora*, is the most widespread type and can vary from open bushland 3–4 m tall to almost impenetrable thicket some 10 m tall. A subtype on limestone and gypsum includes many local endemics. Enclaves within this type are riparian forest (along the larger rivers) and semi-evergreen bushland on hills and the lower slopes of mountains. Semi-desert grassland and shrubland occur in low rainfall areas.

## Species of economic importance

| | | |
|---|---|---|
| *Acacia senegal* | gum arabic | resin |
| *Adansonia digitata* | baobab | medicines |
| *Aloe* spp. | aloe | glucosides |
| *Avena abyssinica* | oats | cereal |
| *Boswellia* spp. | frankincense | resin |
| *Citrullus colocynthis* | colocynth | purgative |
| *Commiphora* spp. | | resins, gums |
| *Eleusine coracana* | finger millet | cereal |

A number of commercially important tree species occur, mostly in the montane (Afromontane) areas within the unit.

## Factors causing loss of biodiversity

Overgrazing caused by large-scale herding of animals (cattle, camels, goats) has transformed the original vegetation in many areas. This has become particularly severe in recent years due to increase in population and recurrent droughts. Areas near permanent wells or waterholes are the most affected. Also, over vast areas, the deciduous bushland has been converted to secondary bushed grassland by temporary agriculture or the cutting of fuelwood for charcoal-burning.

## Conservation

4.8% of the unit is included in protected areas (MacKinnon and MacKinnon 1986). Many large National Parks have been established in eastern Africa, mainly for the protection of spectacular concentrations of wildlife in grassland or wooded grassland habitats. Less well covered are the remaining forests, which are the most species-rich communities.

## Centres of plant diversity and endemism

Most species have wide distributions. Somalia is exceptional in having many national endemics (c. 500 vascular plant species out of a total flora of more than 3000 species) and many near-endemics. The chosen areas for Data Sheet treatment have high levels of local endemism, as well as relatively high species diversity.

### *Ethiopia, Kenya, Somalia*

### Af41. Limestone bush/woodland, Ogaden

Deciduous woodland and bushland extending over an area of approximately 200,000 km² in southern Ethiopia, eastern Somalia and a small part of extreme north-eastern Kenya. Altitude: 200–1500 m.
- Flora: Estimated 2000 vascular plant species (I. Friis 1992, *in litt.*), including frankincense (*Boswellia carteri*), myrrh (*Commiphora* spp.) and yeheb nut (*Cordeauxia edulis*).
- Threats: Extremely vulnerable to overgrazing.
- Conservation: None.

### *Somalia*

### Af42. Cal Madow

– see Data Sheet.

### Af43. Fixed dune vegetation in southern Somalia

Large, fixed and vegetated dunes occur in southern Somalia along the Indian Ocean from south of Hobyo to just south of the border with Kenya. These are mostly 10–15 km wide and between 20 and 60 m high and probably were last active under the dry period of the last ice age about 18,000 years ago. Some have been deprived of their vegetation by overgrazing and are moving inland.
- Vegetation: *Acacia* bushland, often dominated by *Acacia tortilis*, with numerous shrubs, annuals and tuberous and rhizomatous perennials.
- Flora: >200 vascular plant species, with over 20 strict endemics (including plants of the sandy beach in front of the dunes). There are also a number of endemic subspecies.
- Threats: The main threats are fuelwood cutting and overgrazing.
- Conservation: Some of this vegetation should be protected by the Lag Badana Bush-bush National Park, but this is apparently not functional (Friis and Vollesen 1989; I. Friis, pers. comm.).

## Af44. Hobyo

– see Data Sheet.

## Af45. Nugaal Valley

An arid area along the Wadi Nugaal, c. 250 km long. The western part consists of massive deposits of gypsum and anhydrites, while the coastal part is mainly limestone.
- Vegetation: Open semi-desert grassland or bushland (M. Thulin, pers. comm.).
- Flora: Numerous succulents and halophytes with a number of local endemics.
- Threats: No information.
- Conservation: Not protected.

(For **Socotra**, CPD Site SWA4, see Data Sheet and Regional Overview on South West Asia and the Middle East.)

## SUDANIAN REGIONAL CENTRE OF ENDEMISM

This region covers an area of 3,731,000 km² across northern Africa from Senegal to the foothills of the Ethiopian Highlands. In general, the area is rather flat or gently undulating, mostly below 750 m. Higher areas occur in northern Nigeria, northern Cameroon and southern Sudan and include the Jos and Mandara plateaux, Jebel Marra (3057 m), the Imatong Mountains (3187 m) and the Dongotona (2623 m) and Didinga (2963 m) ranges, all of which support Afromontane vegetation on their upper slopes.

## Flora

| | |
|---|---|
| **Number of species:** | c. 2750. |
| **Species endemism:** | 35%. |
| **Endemic families:** | None. |
| **Endemic genera:** | Very few. |
| Source: White (1983). | |

## Main vegetation types

Woodland is the most widespread natural vegetation type (typically with *Isoberlinia doka* and *Khaya senegalensis*). *Crotalaria* and *Indigofera* have speciated profusely. Most woody species have wide distributions. Much smaller areas are occupied by wooded grassland, rocky inselberg vegetation and riparian forest. There are also small patches of upland dry or semi-evergreen forest (e.g. in ravines in Mali) and extensive wetlands (Sudd swamps of southern Sudan and part of the inland delta of the Niger River in Mali). Human activities have resulted in much of the region being under secondary vegetation (often secondary scrub or bushland) and there are large tracts of farmland in the moister areas.

## Species of economic importance

| Native species: | | |
|---|---|---|
| *Acacia senegal* | gum arabic | resin |
| *Borassus aethiopicum* | African fan palm | edible fruit, thatch |
| *Butyrospermum parkii* | shea butter | fat |
| *Ceiba pentandra* | silk cotton | kapok |
| *Daniellia ogea* | copal | resin |
| *Faidherbia (Acacia) albida* | African rubber | agroforestry |
| *Landolphia* spp. | aramenena | latex |
| *Urena lobata* | | fibre |

| Food plants native to the region and probably originally domesticated there: | | |
|---|---|---|
| *Digitaria exilis* | fonio | cereal |
| *Digitaria iburua* | black fonio | cereal |
| *Dioscorea rotundata* | yam | edible root |
| *Eleusine coracana* | finger millet | cereal |
| *Macrotyloma geocarpum* | groundnuts | edible nuts |
| *Pennisetum glaucum* | bulrush millet | cereal |
| *Sorghum bicolor* | sorghum | cereal |
| *Vigna subterranea* | groundnuts | edible nuts |

## Factors causing loss of biodiversity

Over large areas the native vegetation has been severely degraded by shifting cultivation or almost totally replaced by permanent agriculture. Overgrazing, especially by goats, and early burning, either for hunting purposes or to encourage grass regrowth for grazing, have caused widespread and serious deterioration. Fuelwood collection has eliminated woody vegetation around major towns.

## Conservation

4.5% of the unit is included within protected areas (mostly woodland and woodland/grassland transitions). A further 4.6% is proposed or falls within resource reserves and multiple-use reserves (MacKinnon and MacKinnon 1986). There are large National Parks in countries such as Côte d'Ivoire (Comoe – 11,500 km²), Senegal (Niokolo-Koba – 9130 km²), Central African Republic (Manovo – 17,400 km²), Cameroon (Faro – 3300 km²) and Nigeria (Kainji Lake – 5341 km²) and these protect important areas of natural vegetation.

## Centres of plant diversity and endemism

### Cameroon

## Af46. Adamaoua area

The Adamaoua Plateau lies in an east-west direction across the centre of Cameroon.
- Vegetation: Wooded grassland with inselbergs ("bowal", as at Le Sabal Haléo); rock vegetation, as at Foui (Letouzey 1968a).
- Flora: No available figures, but known to be a centre of endemism.
- Threats: Surviving areas of natural habitat on the plateau are now severely fragmented.
- Conservation: Not protected.

## Côte D'Ivoire (Ivory Coast)

### Af47. Odienné area

An area with numerous inselbergs in the north-west of Ivory Coast.
- ❖ Vegetation: Wooded grassland (Adjanohoun 1964).
- ❖ Flora: No figures available, but known to be species-rich.
- ❖ Threats: Overgrazing and conversion of land to agriculture.
- ❖ Conservation: No official protection.

## Guinea

### Af48. Fouta Djallon

A rugged mountainous area in the south-east of Guinea. Rainfall is higher than in the surrounding region. Altitude: 500–1387 m.
- ❖ Vegetation: Relict forests with *Erythrophloeum* and *Parinari*. Also rupicolous vegetation and wooded grassland (Schnell 1968).
- ❖ Flora: No figures available, but known to be a centre of endemism.
- ❖ Threats: Pressures resulting from considerable human population within the reserve; timber extraction is permitted in the buffer zone.
- ❖ Conservation: Partially protected by the Massif du Ziama Biosphere Reserve (which has a total area of 1162 km²). A core area of 600 km² with strict protection is surrounded by a buffer zone in which hunting is prohibited.

## Zaïre

### Af49. Garamba National Park

– see Data Sheet.

## SAHEL REGIONAL TRANSITION ZONE

The Sahel covers an area of 2,482,000 km² on the southern fringes of the Sahara Desert. It is characterised by low annual rainfall (150–500 mm) with prolonged droughts, which can, at times, be very severe, lasting for several years. Jebel Marra, a volcanic massif which rises to over 3000 m, receives more than 1000 mm of rainfall. Most of the rest of the Sahel consists of a flat or gently undulating landscape below 600 m.

## Flora

| | |
|---|---|
| Number of species: | c.1200. |
| Species endemism: | >3%. |
| Endemic families: | None. |
| Endemic genera: | None. |
| Source: White (1983). | |

Most species are widespread.

## Main vegetation types

Wooded grassland is widespread in the higher rainfall areas. Nearer the Sahara this is replaced by semi-desert grassland. Deciduous bushland and scrub forest occur on rocky slopes with higher rainfall.

## Species of economic importance

The Sahel contains several species of economic interest, including *Pennisetum glaucum* (bulrush millet) and *Sorghum bicolor* (sorghum), both of which are staple African food crops. The Aïr and Ténéré region includes the rare wild olive *Olea laperrinei*.

## Factors causing loss of biodiversity

A large part of the population consists of pastoralists. As in the Somali-Masai region, recent population increases, combined with prolonged droughts, have led to severe overgrazing and resultant environmental degradation, especially in areas with permanent waterholes and wells. With energy consumption being more than 90% wood-based, the ever growing need for firewood and charcoal has had disastrous consequences for the woody flora.

## Areas of botanical interest

The following areas are of botanical interest, but there are insufficient data to support their designation as CPD sites. Considering the relative poverty and low endemism of the flora of the Sahel region, the sites are not expected to match the diversity of other sites selected for Africa, but they do, nevertheless, contain a good representative sample of the Sahel flora. The Aïr and Ténéré region has a few local endemics.

## Egypt, Sudan

### Jebel Elba

Area: 4800 km²; a mountain region bordering the Red Sea and a disputed international border (Anon. 1986a). The area is inhabited by the Bischarin, a Bedouin people who continue to practice their traditional nomadic lifestyle. Altitude: 0–1549 m (summit of Jebel Elba).
- ❖ Vegetation: Desert, with "mist oases" in the higher areas. Rare ombet (*Dracaena ombet*) forest occurs on the north face of Jebel Elba (Anon. 1986b); mangroves occur along the Red Sea coast.
- ❖ Flora: The area is transitional between Afrotropical and Palaearctic biogeographic realms (Anon. 1986a) and has an estimated three to four times as many plant species as other desert regions further north (Anon. 1986a).
- ❖ Threats: A road constructed along the Red Sea coast threatens to change the traditional lifestyle of the Bischarin and provides easy access for hunting.

❖ Conservation: The Jebel Elba Nature Conservation Area (of 4800 km²) has been formally proposed by the government (Rodgers, Robertson and Sayer 1992; see also Goodman 1985).

## Mauritania

### Atar area

A sand and limestone area in the Adrar region of Mauritania. Vegetation: Varied, ranging from mobile dunes to rock vegetation.

## Niger

### Aïr and Ténéré region

A mountainous area in the north of Niger, up to 1998 m, providing a diversity of habitats.
❖ Vegetation: Sahelian mountain and basin vegetation.
❖ Flora: 430 vascular plant species, including 6 area endemics (Quézel 1965; Ozenda 1977).
❖ Threats: Overgrazing and excessive browsing of trees by livestock. There has also been an influx of outsiders who reportedly have little respect for those Tuareg traditions which formerly protected certain plants and areas.
❖ Conservation: The Aïr and Ténéré National Nature Reserve covers 77,360 km² (c. 6.5% of the country).

## KAROO-NAMIB REGIONAL CENTRE OF ENDEMISM

This region covers an area of 661,000 km² in central, northern and north-western Cape Province, extending along the Namibian coast into south-west Angola (White 1983). The Namib Desert occupies the coastal plain, receiving a mean annual rainfall of 10–100 mm, supplemented by sea mist close to the coast. The Karoo-Namib has been subdivided into five separate phytochoria by Werger (1978), namely: the Namib, Namaland, Karoo, Western Cape and the Southern Kalahari Subdomain.

The Karoo and Namaland Domain receive from less than 250 mm to about 400 mm of rain annually, mostly in summer. More to the south, the Western Cape Domain receives its rainfall in winter and is extremely rich in succulent species; see Data Sheet on the Western Cape Domain (Succulent Karoo) (CPD Site Af51).

## Flora

| | |
|---|---|
| Number of species: | c.7000 taxa*. |
| Species endemism: | 35–50%*. |
| Endemic families: | 1 (Welwitschiaceae; monotypic). |
| Endemic genera: | up to 160. |

Source: White (1983); * C. Hilton-Taylor – see Data Sheet on Western Cape Domain (Succulent Karoo).

The Aizoaceae *sensu lato* includes 95 endemic genera and 1500 endemic species (White 1983). Other groups with large numbers of endemics include the families Asclepiadaceae, Asteraceae, Cassulaceae and Iridaceae and the genera *Aloe* and *Euphorbia*. The west and south of the region, both winter rainfall areas, are especially rich in succulents and have a very high level of endemism (Goldblatt 1978). Petaloid monocotyledons are very numerous. The mass flowering displays of annuals and geophytes in spring are well known.

## Main vegetation types

Dwarf shrubland is the commonest type and stretches over vast areas, especially in the Karoo and in the Western Cape. Bushy shrubland, with many succulents, is typical of Namaqualand and the Little Karoo, particularly the coastal plain of Namaqualand, which has <200 mm of winter rainfall but regular sea mist. Desert vegetation occurs in the Namib Desert, which receives 10–100 mm rainfall. Rainfall in the Namib is erratic, especially in the drier parts, but fog occurs regularly at least up to 50 km inland. Local variations in vegetation arise from the presence of salty, gypsum-rich or chalky soils, depressions or shallow channels, and local occurrences of rock or sand and wet patches related to the presence of underground rivers.

## Species of economic importance

Many native plants of the region are used as food plants by local people and as grazing for livestock; see the Data Sheets on the Kaokoveld and Western Cape Domain (Succulent Karoo) (CPD Sites Af 50 and Af51, respectively).

## Factors causing loss of biodiversity

Overgrazing, especially by goats, is the main cause of habitat destruction. Mining has caused considerable disturbance in some parts and there is extensive dry-land agriculture in the wetter parts of the Karoo. Other problems are invasive alien plant species and the rapacity of succulent collectors.

## Conservation

4.6% of the unit lies within protected areas (MacKinnon and MacKinnon 1986), but the main centres of plant diversity remain unprotected (C. Hilton-Taylor 1993, pers. comm.). More than 10% of the Namib Desert is included within such National Parks, such as Iona (Angola) (see Data Sheet on the Kaokoveld, CPD Site Af50) and Namib/Naukluft (Namibia).

## Centres of plant diversity and endemism

### Angola, Namibia

#### Af50. The Kaokoveld

– see Data Sheet.

## Namibia, South Africa

### Af51. Western Cape Domain (Succulent Karoo)

– see Data Sheet.

A relatively small but species-rich area with several centres of endemism. These are all described in the Data Sheet.

## South Africa

### Af52. Albany Centre

A transitional centre of endemism for genera centred in the Maputaland-Pondoland, Cape and Karoo-Namib regions (for which see Data Sheets).

Low-lying river valleys and basins in south-eastern Cape Province, bounded in the north by the Sneeuberg-Winterberge Mountains (c. 32°30'S), in the south by the Indian Ocean, in the west by the Gamtoos-Groot River Basin (c. 25°00'E) and in the east by the Kei River Basin (c. 28°00'E). Altitude: c. 0–600 m.

❖ Vegetation: Subtropical succulent and semi-succulent thicket (valley bushveld) and allied vegetation cover an area of c. 22,500 km² (c. 30–35% of the whole Albany Centre).

❖ Flora: Estimated 600 vascular plant species, of which c. 10% are endemic. No endemic genera or families, but many succulent genera are centred in the region, both in terms of species numbers and endemics. Most endemics are succulent shrubs (*Euphorbia*, *Haworthia*, Asclepiadaceae, Mesembryanthemaceae). The Albany Centre contains many Cape elements, along with Karoo-Namib and Maputaland-Pondoland elements. South-eastern Cape subtropical thicket includes 125 threatened plant taxa (Cowling 1983; Hoffman and Cowling 1991). Among the important indigenous fodder plants which are vital to the livestock industry is *Portulacaria afra* ("spekboom" or bacon tree), which is severely overgrazed.

❖ Threats: Annual clearance of mesic (Kaffrarian) thicket (in areas receiving >500 mm annual rainfall) probably amounts to 5–10% of all thicket; clearance for agriculture is the biggest threat. Drier thicket is severely overgrazed in most areas. Invasive plants (e.g. *Opuntia*) and urbanization (Algoa Region) are also major threats.

❖ Conservation: Very inadequate. About 1.2% of the thicket was protected in 1985. Existing reserves which include thicket are:
Addo Elephant National Park (Sundays Rive Valley);
Zuurberg National Park (Sundays River Valley);
Andries Vosloos Kudu Reserve (Fish River Valley);
Lennox Sebe Reserve (Fish River Valley).

Several small reserves south of Grahamstown also contain thicket. There are proposals to extend Addo as well as to secure conservation areas near Coega, on the coastal margin of the Sundays River Basin.
(Source: R.M. Cowling 1993, *in litt.*)

## CAPE REGIONAL CENTRE OF ENDEMISM

The Cape Regional Centre of Endemism covers an area of 90,000 km² in south-western and southern Cape Province of South Africa. There are several roughly parallel mountain ranges running from north to south and from west to east. The climate is of the Mediterranean type, with annual rainfall between 100 and 2500 mm, depending on altitude and degree of exposure to the moist sea winds. Winters are mild, with infrequent frosts affecting higher areas. The western part of the area receives most rain in winter, but, towards the east, rainfall is more evenly distributed.

### Flora

In terms of the number of species per unit area, this is probably the richest plant area on the planet.

| | |
|---|---|
| Number of species: | 8600. |
| Species endemism: | 68%. |
| Endemic families: | 6. |
| Endemic genera: | 193. |

Source: A. Rebelo (see Data Sheet).

Families like the Ericaceae, Proteaceae and Restionaceae have their main centres of diversity in the fynbos; there are 600 species of *Erica* alone. Restionaceae are typical and Ericaceae are dominant over very large areas, as are Asteraceae in drier parts. Rutaceae and Thymelaeaceae are also important and there are 20 endemic genera of Papilionaceae. There are many petaloid monocotyledons.

### Main vegetation types

– see Data Sheet.

The main vegetation type is fynbos (or macchia), which is a type of evergreen sclerophyllous shrubland, mostly on sandstone. This is not a fire climax, although occasional fires appear to be necessary for its healthy maintenance and the regeneration of certain taxa.

Fynbos is differentiated into mountain and lowland forms, with the latter being the most species-rich.

### Species of economic importance

– see Data Sheet.

### Factors causing loss of biodiversity

So much of the exceptionally species-rich lowland fynbos has been converted to agricultural land or swallowed up by urban and other development that only about 15% of the original vegetation now remains. Serious threats are grazing and browsing, fires, large scale flower picking, plant collecting and invasive species. The latter include (in the lowland fynbos) *Acacia cyclops*, *A. saligna* and *Leptospermum laevigatum* and (in the mountain fynbos) *Acacia* spp., *Hakea sericea* and *Pinus pinaster*. The spread of these introduced species seriously threatens the native flora (Jarman 1986).

## Conservation

The Cape flora is in danger. Of the higher altitude fynbos (Veld Types 69 and 70), 15–20% is under the Cape Nature Conservation Department and is protected as wilderness or water catchment. Of the lowland fynbos (Veld Types 46 and 47), only some 2% is protected and it is here that there is an urgent need to protect much more in medium-sized reserves.

1430 vascular plants (17% of the flora) are threatened (A. Rebelo 1993, see Data Sheet). Some 26 species have probably become Extinct in recent years and another 103 are Endangered (Hall and Veldhuis 1985).

## Centres of plant diversity and endemism

Since the flora of the Cape region is exceptionally rich and there are many areas of local endemicity, the whole region is treated here as one CPD site.

### South Africa

### Af53. Cape Floristic Region

– see Data Sheet.

## INDIAN OCEAN COASTAL BELT

The northern section of this unit corresponds to the Zanzibar-Inhambane Regional Mosaic of White (1983). This stretches from southern Somalia (c. 1°00'N) to the mouth of the Limpopo River (c. 25°00'S) in Mozambique. White (1983) refers to the southern section, from the Limpopo River south to Port Elizabeth (c. 34°00'S) in South Africa, as the Tongaland-Pondoland Regional Mosaic. This is redefined here as the Maputaland-Pondoland Region (see Data Sheet on Maputaland-Pondoland Region – CPD Site Af59).

Although they are part of the same continuum, the northern and southern sections are very distinct floristically. The coastal belt is generally low in altitude, but in southern Kenya, northern and southern Tanzania and in northern Mozambique, there are hills and small mountains. The Drakensberg range rises to the south of the Limpopo.

The Eastern Arc Mountains are in the Afromontane Regional Centre of Endemism, following the classification of White (1983), although they are really better regarded as belonging to the Indian Ocean Coastal Belt. They contain a range of forest types, including sometimes lowland, submontane and montane forests intergrading altitudinally.

## Climate

The average annual rainfall is 800–1200 mm per year, but occasionally as high as 2000 mm, with one or two dry seasons. Even in the dry season, humidity is generally high, realted to the proximity of the sea.

## Flora

### Northern section (Zanzibar-Inhambane Regional Mosaic)

| | |
|---|---|
| **Number of species:** | c. 3000. |
| **Species endemism:** | c. 15%. |
| **Endemic families:** | None. |
| **Endemic genera:** | 25. |

Source: White (1983); Vollesen (1992).

The lowland coastal vegetation of Kenya and Tanzania (including Zanzibar) has around 100 endemic vascular plant species and 25 endemic genera (Vollesen 1992). Examples of woody endemic genera are: *Streptosiphon*, *Trichaulax* (Acanthaceae); *Asteranthe*, *Cleistochlamys*, *Dielsiothamnus*, *Lettowianthus*, *Mkilua*, *Ophrypetalum* (Annonaceae); *Vismianthus* (Connaraceae); *Paranecepsia*, *Zimmermannia* (Euphorbiaceae); *Burttdavya*, *Cladoceras*, *Lamprothamnus*, *Phellocalyx* (Rubiaceae); and *Inhambanella* (Sapotaceae).

Species diversity and endemism appear to be concentrated in isolated hill forests in southern Kenya and northern Tanzania, but further exploration of similar areas to the south will probably show that these are also rich in endemics. The high level of endemism and near-endemism is believed to be due to the isolation of the coastal forests from other African forests for a long time (perhaps 30–40 million years) and possibly the fragmentation of the forests during more recent arid episodes. Floristic affinities are mainly with the Guineo-Congolian region; however, many of the widespread genera of the Congolian forest are absent from the East African coastal forests.

### Southern section (Maputaland-Pondoland)

| | |
|---|---|
| **Number of species:** | 6000–7000. |
| **Species endemism:** | >20% (endemic/near endemic taxa). |
| **Endemic families:** | 2. |
| **Endemic genera:** | 58 (endemic/near endemic). |

Source: A.E. van Wyk (Data Sheet on Maputaland-Pondoland Region, CPD Site Af59).

*Encephalartos* and arborescent species of *Aloe* and *Euphorbia* are well-represented. Affinities are with the Afromontane, Zambezian and Cape floras.

## Main vegetation types

Moist or dry coastal forest used to be the most widespread vegetation type, with many different types occurring in both north and south. Richest in species are the moist evergreen and semi-deciduous forests and the extensive areas of valley bushveld and grasslands of the Maputaland-Pondoland Region. There are also areas of littoral evergreen thicket, swamp forest, mangroves and palm veld.

Giant heaths (*Erica* spp.) dominate some communities on sand on Mafia and Pemba Islands and on the Mozambique coast.

Due to human activities, natural vegetation in many places has been mostly removed and now occupies a few pockets surrounded by secondary bushland, cultivation, grassland and wooded grassland. Important remnant forest patches, though geographically isolated and heterogeneous, are all close to the coast (i.e. mostly below an altitude of 500 m).

## Species of economic importance

The following economically valuable species occur:

| | | |
|---|---|---|
| Adansonia digitata | baobab | medicines, food |
| Maytenus buchananii | | anti-cancer drugs |
| Carissa grandiflora | Natal plum | edible fruit |
| Dioscorea sylvatica | wild yam | drug, food |
| Sorghum caffrorum | grain sorghum | cereal |
| Vigna spp. | cowpea | legume |

## Factors causing loss of biodiversity

The Indian Ocean coastal zone is one of the most densely populated parts of Africa; the remaining forests are under great pressure. Continued clearance for agriculture, fuelwood collection, charcoal burning and pole cutting threaten to destroy the little original forest that remains. Tourism, especially the development of tourist facilities along the coast, is causing habitat destruction in Kenya. Salt mining (increasing the need for fuelwood) and mining of sand dunes for heavy metals are serious threats. Only in southern Tanzania and northern Mozambique are the pressures relatively low, although an increasing amount of selective felling of "semi-precious" timber for export is taking place in these areas, with resultant deterioration of forests.

## Conservation

In Kenya, some of the smaller forest areas are fully legally protected. Other areas in both Kenya and Tanzania are Forest Reserves. There is an urgent need to designate some of the larger forests as fully protected reserves.

Although there are some very large conservation areas protecting savanna vegetation in the northern Maputaland-Pondoland Region, such as the Kruger National Park (c. 20,000 km²), the endemic-rich grasslands of the central and southern parts of the Region are inadequately protected (see Data Sheet on the Maputaland-Pondoland Region).

## Centres of plant diversity and endemism

Forest remains in small scattered remnants. Some of these, such as the "kayas" in Kenya, are sacred forests, often on limestone, surrounded by agriculture and often containing a very rich flora with numerous rare species and endemics, such as *Saintpaulia rupicola*. A survey carried out by the National Museums, Kenya in 1986/1987 listed about 35 kayas and important sacred groves, the largest being c. 1.5 km². Nearly all kayas in Kilifi and Kwale Districts have since been declared National Monuments and are administered by their elders and the National Museums of Kenya.

There is a scarcity of information about the middle part of this belt (southern Tanzania, northern Mozambique).

## NORTHERN SECTION

### Kenya

### Af54. Shimba Hills

A range of low, mostly sandstone, hills running parallel to the southern coastline about 20 km inland. Altitude: 120–450 m.
- Vegetation: Mosaic of moist forest (including riverine forest), wooded grassland, open grassland, scrub and coastal bushland.
- Flora: High species diversity with numerous endemics.
- Threats: Timber exploitation, conversion to softwood plantations, uncontrolled fires, fuelwood collection, quarrying for roadstone.
- Conservation: An area of 192.5 km² is managed as a National Reserve (IUCN Management Category: II – National Park) and is located within a slightly larger area designated as a Forest Reserve. There are no buffer zones; the hills are surrounded by farmland (IUCN/UNEP 1987).

Also of considerable importance in Kenya is the **Arabuko-Sokoke Forest Reserve** (area 418 km², within which 43 km² has been designated as a Nature Reserve and 6 km² as a National Park). It is East Africa's only surviving lowland coastal forest of any appreciable size, but is surrounded by settlement and is under heavy pressure. Proposals exist to establish the whole of the Arabuko-Sokoke Forest Reserve as a National Park.

### Tanzania

### Af55. Msumbugwe

A forest of about 15 km² located some 15 km from the Indian Ocean and some 24 km south-west of the town of Pangani. Altitude: up to 200 m.
- Vegetation: Evergreen forest on marine clays, mudstones and limestones.
- Flora: No figures available. The forest contains the monotypic genus *Stuhlmannia*, an evergreen tree which is endemic to the forests of this area.
- Threats: Fires, logging, pole cutting, charcoal burning. The forest has been considerably reduced and disturbed by these activities, but largely undamaged areas still exist.
- Conservation: The forest falls entirely within the Msumbugwe Forest Reserve (Burgess, Mwasumbi, Hawthorne, Dickinson and Doggett 1992).

Note: Several other Tanzanian coastal forest remnants are, as yet, insufficiently known, but could be CPD sites, e.g. **Kiwengoma** and **Zaraninge** (Burgess et al. 1992).

### Af56. Pugu Hills and Kazimzumbwi Forest Reserves

Pugu Hills Forest Reserve covers about 10 km² (22 km² in 1970) on a dissected range of hills, 25 km SSW of Dar es Salaam in Kisarawe District. A narrow strip of cleared land separates it from the Kazimzumbwi Forest Reserve, a further 12 km² of forest vegetation on the Pugu Hills. The floras of the two areas are thought to be similar and are treated here as one CPD site.

❖ Vegetation: Dry and moist evergreen forest on kaolinitic sandstones.

❖ Flora: No figures available. 15 site endemics or near-endemics on Pugu Hills.

❖ Threats: Logging, pole cutting, charcoal burning, cutting of fuelwood for brick and tile-making industries, planting of exotic trees and mining (the latter for Pugu Hills).

❖ Conservation: The forests fall entirely within the two Forest Reserves. Kazimzumbwi Forest Reserve is, in some parts, better preserved than Pugu Hills Forest Reserve (Burgess *et al.* 1992).

## Af57. Rondo Plateau

– see Data Sheet.

### Tanzania, Mozambique

## Af58. Middle Ruvuma River area

The Ruvuma River forms the border between southern Tanzania and northern Mozambique. 140 vascular plant species are recorded as endemic to this area (Brenan 1978), but other information is lacking.

## SOUTHERN SECTION

### South Africa, Swaziland, Mozambique

## Af59. Maputaland-Pondoland Region

– see Data Sheet. (Includes the Lake St Lucia area.)

## AFROMONTANE REGIONAL CENTRE OF ENDEMISM

White (1983) referred to this region as the Afromontane Archipelago-like Regional Centre of Endemism. The montane areas are widely scattered and stretch from the Knysna forests in southern South Africa, via the Drakensberg range (see CPD Sites Af59, Af67 and Af82), Mt Mulanje (CPD Site Af64, see Data Sheet) and Kilimanjaro (CPD Site Af75), to the Ethiopian massifs. Further montane areas are associated with the Western Rift, including Virunga (CPD Site Af78) and Rwenzori (CPD Site Af77). Outliers include Jebel Marra (CPD Site Af69) and Mt Cameroon (CPD Site Af13, see Data Sheet).

The Afromontane region consists of scattered "islands" of very distinctive flora surrounded by other vegetation types. The lower altitude limit is usually about 1500 m, but, in the south (Cape region), this can be as low as 300 m.

Soil parent materials vary from ancient Precambrian rocks, through crystalline basement (e.g. Chimanimani) and basalts (e.g. Simen, Drakensberg), to relatively recent volcanics (e.g. Kilimanjaro, Mt Cameroon).

## Climate

Climate is extremely varied (even on a single mountain), depending on geographical position, altitude and prevailing winds. It can vary from rain forest conditions on some moist lower slopes to almost desert conditions in peak areas.

## Flora

| | |
|---|---|
| **Number of species:** | c. 4000. |
| **Species endemism:** | 75% (3000 endemic species). |
| **Endemic families:** | 1–2. |
| **Endemic genera:** | c.200. |

## Main vegetation types

Vegetation on the mountains of sub-Saharan Africa is zoned, related to moisture and temperature (Hedberg 1951). Taken together, the flora of the "archipelago" shows a remarkable continuity and uniformity, its composition changing rather regularly with increasing altitude. The lowermost forests on wetter aspects intergrade into submontane and then montane forests. The arbitrary lower limit of montane forest is often taken to be c. 1500–2000 m (lower away from the Equator). At the lower limit, especially in wetter areas, the montane forest zone has proved highly attractive to agriculturalists and often supports a high rural population.

Conifers are rare in Africa, but those that occur typically do so in Afromontane forest. *Podocarpus* is the most widespread genus, *Juniperus* is found in drier forests of eastern and north-eastern Africa and is encouraged by moderate burning, while *Widdringtonia* is found from Malawi southwards.

On moist slopes, a bamboo zone is often found between 2500 and 3000 m (near the Equator). Above this, there is often a further forest zone with *Hagenia* and then an ericaceous belt or shrubland. On the highest mountains, Afroalpine vegetation occurs, including shrubland or tussock grassland, with giant groundsels (*Dendrosenecio* spp.) and giant lobelias (*Lobelia* spp.). The highest peaks below the ice on Kilimanjaro carry high-altitude semi-desert (see Afroalpine Regional Centre of Endemism). Valleys and ridges, bogs, soil pockets and rock outcrops provide local variations, giving rise to a vegetation mosaic.

## Species of economic importance

Montane forests provide a number of valuable timber trees, such as *Juniperus procera* (pencil cedar) *Podocarpus* spp. (podo) and *Ocotea usambarensis* (East African camphor wood). In addition, the Ethiopian highlands were an early centre for food production and several crops which are still grown in the area were probably domesticated there from indigenous plants. These include:

| | | |
|---|---|---|
| *Coffea arabica* | coffee | beverage |
| *Eleusine coracana* | finger millet | cereal |
| *Eragrostis tef* | tef | cereal |
| *Guizotia abyssinica* | Niger seed, noog | oil seed |
| *Ensete ventricosa* | Abyssinian banana | starchy stems, fibre |

## Conservation

4.5% of this unit is included within protected areas (MacKinnon and MacKinnon 1986).

## Factors causing loss of biodiversity

Even in drier areas, the windward slopes of mountains are often wet enough to carry forest. Inevitably, these moist conditions, when coupled with tillable slopes, attract agriculturalists. The mountains also form an important dry-season grazing area for pastoralists. Almost everywhere the original vegetation, especially of the lower slopes, has been degraded or destroyed. More than 37% of the unit's original vegetation had been transformed by 1986, much of which was accounted for by forest clearance on lower mountain slopes for timber production and agriculture (MacKinnon and MacKinnon 1986). Severe erosion may follow degradation of the vegetation on some mountains.

In many highland areas, large tracts of forest and ericaceous bushland have been replaced by fire-induced grassland or by large-scale plantations of exotic commercial species.

## Centres of plant diversity and endemism

Floristically, the Cameroon Highlands and adjacent highland areas of eastern Nigeria are of considerable importance. Some 130 species are believed to be endemic to montane areas of eastern Nigeria and over 150 to north-western Cameroon (Brenan 1978). Most of these are non-forest species. Mount Cameroon itself has floristically very rich forests. The main massif has c. 42 strict site endemic species, about half of which occur above 1500 m (Thomas and Cheek 1992).

The Albertine Rift Highlands of eastern Zaïre, Rwanda, Burundi and western Uganda is the richest montane area for forest plant species in Africa (A.C. Hamilton 1992, pers. comm.). The area around Lakes Edward and Kivu in Zaïre has at least 62 endemic vascular plant species and a further 26 species are apparently endemic to Rwanda and Burundi (Jenkins and Hamilton 1992).

The Eastern Arc Mountains of Tanzania and neighbouring Kenya are included here. The forests on these mountains range in altitude from near sea-level to 2800 m and include types which may be classified as lowland, submontane and montane. The lowland and submontane forests are particularly rich in endemics, but higher altitude forests may be regarded as equivalent to montane forests elsewhere in Africa are not so rich in endemics, at least regarding their tree floras (A.C. Hamilton 1993, in litt.).

The sites selected for detailed Data Sheet treatment are those which are believed to be most representative for their part of the region. However, every mountain or range encompasses many vegetation types, as well as its own range of endemics and near-endemics. Sites with significant Afromontane vegetation treated in other phytochoria include: Bwindi (CPD Site Af25, see Data Sheet), Itombwe (CPD Site Af26), Kahuzi-Biega (CPD Site Af28) and Mont Nimba (CPD Site Af4, see Data Sheet) in the Guineo-Congolian region, Fouta Djallon (CPD Site Af48) in the Sudanian region and

the high Angolan escarpments (see CPD Site Af31) in the Zambezian region.

## *Ethiopia*

## Af60. Bale Mountains

The Bale Mountains form the core of the south-eastern highlands of Ethiopia and cover an area in excess of 4000 km². Some 2500 people live in the National Park. Altitude: c. 1500–4377 m (summit of Tullu Deemtu). A large part of the massif is accounted for by the Sanetti Plateau, which stretches for vast distances at altitudes between 3500 and 4000 m.
- ❖ Vegetation: Afroalpine (3400–4377 m), subalpine (3100–3400 m) and Afromontane (1500–3100 m) zones represented. Woodland and grassland at lower altitudes, with swamps and bogs in valleys. Ericaceous forest, thicket and bamboo thicket at higher altitudes. The Sanetti Plateau contains the largest expanse of Afroalpine vegetation in Africa.
- ❖ Flora: About 950 vascular plant species, including *Coffea arabica*; at least 15 site endemics (I. Friis 1991, in litt.). The families Compositae and Crassulaceae are particularly rich in site endemics (I. Friis, pers. comm; K. Vollesen, pers. comm.). The bryoflora contains northern temperate, East African and Afromontane species and, although there is no comprehensive account, scattered records suggest a relatively high species diversity among bryophytes, including numerous endemics (T. Pócs 1993, in litt.).
- ❖ Threats: Some activities associated with livestock grazing need to be regulated. Moorlands are burned in dry years to improve grazing. The area has been affected by recent civil war (Gebre-Michael, Hundessa and Hillman 1992).
- ❖ Conservation: The core of the mountains is protected as the Bale Mountains National Park, covering 2471 km².

## Af61. Simen Mountains

A highly dissected basaltic mountain massif in the north of the country. An area of great scenic beauty, with steep escarpments and deep valleys, in Africa only paralleled in the Drakensberg range. Altitude: 1000–4543 m (summit of Ras Dashen, Ethiopia's highest mountain). Areas above 3000 m cover more than 1350 km².
- ❖ Vegetation: Forest and woodland and, above that, bamboo thicket, ericaceous forest, bushland and Afroalpine vegetation. There are also areas of grassland.
- ❖ Flora: Total number of species unknown. 5–10 site endemic species (I. Friis 1991, in litt.).
- ❖ Threats: Clearance for agriculture is the most serious problem with cultivation encroaching even into the Afroalpine zone. Other threats are overgrazing, burning, fuelwood collection and soil erosion.
- ❖ Conservation: Simen Mountains National Park covers 179 km²; this is also a World Heritage Site. Some of the farmers previously living in the park have been relocated. Management and park infrastructure has been severely affected by civil war (Gebre-Michael, Hundessa and Hillman 1992).

## Kenya

### Af62. Mount Kenya

– see Data Sheet.

## Kenya, Uganda

### Af63. Mount Elgon

A large extinct volcano rising to 4315 m on the Uganda/Kenya border.

❖ Vegetation: Mixed moist to dry montane forest below 2500 m, bamboo and *Hagenia-Rapanea* forest between 2400–3300 m, montane heath moorland at 3000–3500 m and Afroalpine communities above 3500 m.

❖ Flora: Total number of species unknown; a preliminary list includes 112 tree species, but this is believed to be incomplete (Howard 1991). Endemism more or less restricted to the moorlands (16 site endemics), but regional endemism of Afromontane species is comparable to that of Mt Kenya. Mount Elgon is not well explored bryologically. 148 moss species (Kis 1985) and c. 50 liverwort species have been recorded so far (T. Pócs 1993, *in litt.*).

❖ Threats: Agricultural encroachment, logging, cutting of bamboo for building poles and replacement of forest with conifer plantations.

❖ Conservation: 169 km² on the Kenyan side is protected as the Mount Elgon National Park. A further 733 km² on the same side and 860 km² on the Ugandan side are covered by Forest Reserves (see Howard 1991).

## Malawi

### Af64. Mount Mulanje

– see Data Sheet.

## Malawi, Zambia

### Af65. Nyika Plateau

A roughly ovoid plateau with 1800 km² above the 1800 m contour. Mostly in northern Malawi, but with about 70 km² in north-eastern Zambia.

❖ Vegetation: 90% of the plateau is covered with short open grassland, but there are also small patches of submontane evergreen forest (including *Juniperus procera* forest, here at its southernmost limit) in valleys and hollows. Dry *Brachystegia* woodland occurs on the western slopes (Dowsett-Lemaire 1985, 1989; IUCN/UNEP 1987; Seyani, Chikuni and Kamundi 1991).

❖ Flora: 1200 vascular plant species have been recorded so far (Seyani, Chikuni and Kamundi 1991). Endemism is relatively high, particularly among grassland species. There is a rich terrestrial orchid flora.

❖ Threats: The remaining forest patches are greatly threatened by dry season fires. There is also agricultural encroachment.

❖ Conservation: The plateau itself on the Malawi side is protected within the 3134 km² Nyika National Park; the contiguous Nyika National Park (Zambia) covers 80 km².

## Rwanda

### Af66. Nyungwe Forest Reserve

Area: 970 km², situated in the south-west of Rwanda and contiguous with the Kibira National Park (area 379 km²) in Burundi. Altitude: 1550–2950 m.

❖ Vegetation: Several types of lower to upper montane forest, bamboo thickets, extensive marsh complexes.

❖ Flora: >100 tree species in the lower montane forest, which remains intact down to 1650 m. Very rich in endemics; over 50 woody species are thought to be site endemics (Collar and Stuart 1988).

❖ Threats: Land clearance around the margins, cutting for fuelwood, charcoal and timber (especially along water courses), gold mining, fires, hunting of large mammals.

❖ Conservation: A Forest Reserve, but needs improved protection. A National Park covering at least 232 km² has been proposed. The area is visited by over 4000 tourists each year as a result of the Nyungwe Forest Conservation Project, financed by USAID and sponsored by Wildlife Conservation International. The area provides local people with a range of forest products and medicinal plants (Offutt 1992).

## South Africa

### Af67. Drakensberg Afromontane Regional System

A series of Afromontane "islands", of total area c. 84,500 km² in Southern Africa (mainly South Africa) situated between 22°50'–34°30'S and 18°20'–31°40'E. Altitude: almost sea-level to c. 2000 m.

❖ Vegetation: Undifferentiated Afromontane forest, bushland, thicket and grassland. The lower altitude forests are regarded floristically as of Afromontane type.

❖ Flora: Number of species not known, but species endemism high. A number of distinct centres are recognised, including (from north to south) the Soutpansberg Centre, Wolkberg Centre (with c. 110 endemic/near-endemic species and infraspecific taxa) (Matthews, Van Wyk and Bredenkamp 1993), Barberton Centre, Afromontane region of the Natal/Transkei Midlands, southern Drakensberg Mountains of Natal and north-eastern Cape (included in the Maputaland-Pondoland Region; CPD Site Af59, see Data Sheet). The Amatola Mountains and the Outeniqua Mountains are Afromontane outliers in the south.

❖ Threats: Fire, bark-stripping of medicinal trees, cattle-grazing, afforestation with exotic trees, firewood collection, invasive plants.

❖ Conservation: The area of montane forest biome conserved in South Africa is estimated at 1610 km² (c. 6.8% of the whole country). The total area of mountain catchment under the management of the

Directorate of Forestry is 8198 km² (or 34.9% of the total land area). However, not all of this lies within the Afromontane region.

(Source: D. Killick 1993, *in litt.*).

## Sudan

### Af68. Imatong Mountains

A group of dome-shaped granitic mountains on the border between southern Sudan and Uganda. Individually known as the Acholi Mountains, Imatong Mountains, Dongotona Mountains and Didinga Hills, they cover an area of about 2000 km², including some of the surrounding lowlands and valleys. Altitude ranges from 500 m (Nile Valley plains surrounding the mountains) to 3187 m (Mt Kinyeti).

❖ Vegetation: To the west, Sudanian woodland; to the east, *Acacia-Commiphora* bushland; in pockets at the base of the mountains, semi-deciduous Guineo-Congolian forest. On the mountains themselves there is a mosaic of Afromontane forest, upland grassland and bamboo thicket, with a very small representation of Afroalpine vegetation at the top of Mt Kinyeti.

❖ Flora: 1400 vascular plant species (nearly half the total flora of Sudan), 12 site endemics (Friis, undated; Friis and Vollesen 1982, unpublished; H. Sommerlatte, pers. comm.).

❖ Threats: Conversion to tea and forestry plantations (currently not progressing due to civil war), regular burning of montane grassland, fuelwood collection (I. Friis 1991, *in litt.*).

❖ Conservation: Part of the largest mountain massif is covered by the Imatong Mountains Central Forest Reserve, although war has made it impossible to enforce the restrictions associated with its status. No other protection, but the proposed Imatong Mountains Nature Conservation Area has been formally proposed by the government and will cover an area of 1000 km².

See also: Jackson (1956); ODA (1977); Noordwijk (1984); Sommerlatte and Sommerlatte (1988); Rodgers, Robertson and Sayer (1992).

### Af69. Jebel Marra

An isolated volcanic massif near the border with Chad, covering approximately 30,750 km². There is a high plateau at between 2300 and 2600 m. Peaks rise to over 3000 m. Annual rainfall is much higher than in surrounding areas (>1000 mm in some parts) and falls almost entirely within the summer months.

❖ Vegetation: Woodland, savanna woodland and thicket in lower areas; riparian forest, woodland, savanna, swamps and montane grassland on the massif proper.

❖ Flora: 932 species of flowering plants, including 11 site endemics (Wickens 1976).

❖ Threats: Agriculture, collection of fuelwood and building materials, overgrazing, forestry plantations and uncontrolled fires which annually sweep most of the montane grassland. In some parts, destruction of the natural vegetation has led to severe erosion.

❖ Conservation: No legal protection, but the Jebel Marra Massif Nature Conservation Area is formally proposed by the government. This will cover 1500 km².

## Tanzania, Kenya

### Eastern Arc Mountains (includes CPD Sites Af70–Af74)

The Eastern Arc Mountains extend in an arc from south-east Kenya through eastern Tanzania. The forests are developed on ancient crystalline rocks and are supported by rain from the Indian Ocean monsoons and by local convectional rain in the proximity of Lake Nyasa (Lake Malawi) (Lovett 1990). The mountains extend in a block from south-eastern Kenya through eastern Tanzania, from north to south: the Taita Hills (in Kenya), Upare, Usambara, Ukaguru, Uluguru, Nguru, Rubeho, Malundwe, Uzungwa and Mahenge (in Tanzania).

The region has a high rural population density (e.g. >300 people/km² in the Usambaras). The forests are under increasing threat of clearance for agriculture.

The flora is rich in endemics: 25–30% of the c. 2000 Eastern Arc plant species are endemic (Lovett 1988), including 67 tree species, 48 epiphytic orchids and 27 species of the genus *Impatiens*. 16 genera are endemic or near-endemic to the forest and forest edge. Endemism is high in lowland, submontane and montane forests.

The East Usambara Mountains have been selected for Data Sheet treatment as a representative Eastern Arc site.

### Af70. Taita Hills

A range of hills which rise abruptly from the plains in the Taita-Taveta District of Coast Province.

❖ Vegetation: Most of the hills are intensively cultivated and little of the original vegetation remains, but about 2.5 km² of moist to semi-dry submontane forest still survives in several patches between 1200 and 2228 m, mostly on hilltops. This forest has many affinities with other Eastern Arc forests.

❖ Flora: 453 forest species of vascular plants. At least 13 site endemics, including species of *Coffea* and *Saintpaulia teitensis* (Beentje 1988a). Among bryophytes, there are several disjunct taxa, with Madagascan affinities, as is typical of the Eastern Arc crystalline mountains, e.g. *Drepanolejeunea madagascariensis* and *Macromitrium rufescens* (T. Pócs 1993, *in litt.*).

❖ Threats: Population pressure. Although there is local interest in preserving the remaining forests, they are still under considerable threat from uncontrolled fires, agricultural encroachment, fuelwood collection, illegal logging and conversion to plantations of exotic species.

❖ Conservation: The forests are under the jurisdiction of the Forestry Department, but have not yet been gazetted.

### Af71. East Usambara Mountains

– see Data Sheet.

## Af72. Nguru Mountains

A massif of four major groups of mountains separated by deep rocky valleys, located in Morogoro District. Area: <265 km² (Polhill 1968). Altitude: 400–2400 m.
- ❖ Vegetation: Lowland moist and dry forest, grading into moist montane forest, with elfin forest, heaths, much rock vegetation and, at the highest altitudes, bamboo thickets.
- ❖ Flora: Total vascular flora c. 2000 species (S. Manktelow 1992, *in litt.*). 26 endemics listed by Pócs, Temu and Minja (1990), including the monotypic orchid genus *Thulinia*. Many Eastern Arc near-endemics. The bryophyte flora of the forests between 1800–2200 m is particularly rich (T. Pócs 1993, *in litt.*).
- ❖ Threats: The surrounding area is densely populated. The forests are threatened by agricultural encroachment, uncontrolled fires, logging (both licensed and unlicensed), fuelwood collection and pole extraction. Several villages are established inside Forest Reserves. Most areas formerly occupied by lowland moist forest have already been cleared, though higher altitude forests are still largely undisturbed.
- ❖ Conservation: 374 km² of catchment forest in 3 reserves; under government control, but management needs further resources. Forests of the rather isolated Mt Kanga are largely undisturbed, being afforded traditional protection.

## Af73. Uluguru Mountains

Located in Morogoro District, just to the south of Morogoro town. The southern part, the steeply scarped Lukwangule Plateau, is the highest area, rising to 2668 m at Kimhandu. Forest covers about 120 km² (Collar and Stuart 1988; Pócs 1976).
- ❖ Vegetation: Moist lowland forest, grading into moist submontane and montane forest with many epiphytes. There is also montane mossy forest, broadleaved elfin forest and bamboo thicket. High-altitude grassland with many Afroalpine species occurs on the Lukwangule Plateau.
- ❖ Flora: Total number of species not known; Polhill (1968) lists 100 woody species. There are many Eastern Arc endemics, including three species of *Saintpaulia*. The bryoflora includes c. 500 species, of which 10 are strict endemics. A further 11 species of mosses are near-endemic (occurring on other mountains of the Eastern Arc). More than 40 species of bryophytes are "Lemurian" species (i.e. they have disjunct distributions, being found also on Madagascar or other neighbouring Indian Ocean islands); other Uluguru species are found elsewhere only in West Africa (T. Pócs 1993, *in litt.*). The genus *Pseudotimmiella* is endemic to the Ulugurus.
- ❖ Threats: Human population density in the lower parts of the mountains is very high, with the result that lower altitude forests are being rapidly cleared for cultivation or degraded through the extraction of timber, building poles and fuelwood.
- ❖ Conservation: Most of the forested area is included within Forest Reserves. The higher forests are on precipitous terrain and not immediately threatened.

## Af74. Uzungwa Mountains

Located partly in Iringa and partly in Kilombero Districts, some 300 km from the Tanzanian coast and notable for a steep south-east facing scarp, behind which is an undulating upland with peaks to 2800 m.
- ❖ Vegetation: Miombo woodland and lowland moist forest, grading into moist montane forest and grassland.
- ❖ Flora: Total number of species not known. One of only two known localities for the commercially important ornamental *Saintpaulia ionantha* (African violet).
- ❖ Threats: Extraction of building poles, fuelwood and timber. Probably also fires and agricultural encroachment, including clearance for tea planting. Much of the lower altitude forest has been mechanically logged (Lovett 1985; Lovett and Congdon 1989), although this has now stopped (Lovett and Pócs 1992).
- ❖ Conservation: Presently some of the area is included in two Catchment Forest Reserves. A National Park of 1000 km², including parts of these reserves, was gazetted in 1992. WWF has started a tree planting project among communities neat the lower boundary of the National Park.

## Af75. Kilimanjaro

A very large, isolated volcanic mountain near the Tanzania/ Kenya border. At 5895 m, Kibo Peak is the highest point in Africa.
- ❖ Vegetation: Moist and dry montane forest and Afromontane/Afroalpine vegetation. Montane forest occurs between 1800 and 3100 m. There is no bamboo zone.
- ❖ Flora: >1800 species of vascular plants. Low species endemism in the woody flora of the forests. About 600 species of bryophytes (of which 415 are mosses and 185 are liverworts). Of these, 12 are strict endemics. The richest belt for bryophytes is between 2100–4100 m. The genus *Pocsiella* is endemic to Kilimanjaro (Pócs 1991, 1993 in press).
- ❖ Threats: The human population of the mountain slopes has more than tripled in the last 40 years and continues to increase rapidly, placing pressures on all of the mountain's natural resources (Newmark 1991). The area of montane forest is declining due to agricultural encroachment and conversion to softwood plantations and much of that remaining is significantly disturbed. Specific threats are uncontrolled fires, illegal logging, collection of fuelwood and building materials and the effects of increasing tourism.
- ❖ Conservation: All the area above the tree line and six corridors through the montane forest belt are protected as the Kilimanjaro National Park, an area of 756 km². Surrounding the park is a Forest Reserve of 1079 km² which includes the remainder of the montane forest. Kilimanjaro National Park was inscribed on the World Heritage list in 1987.

## Af76. Kitulo Plateau/Kipengere Mountains

Undulating highlands in the western Kipengere Mountains in southern Tanzania; the plateau connects the Kipengeres and the Livingstone Mountains, which form the rift wall on the eastern shore of northern Lake Nyasa (Lake Malawi). Area: c. 300 km². Altitude: 2500–2830 m (plateau) with peaks to 2923 m (Chaluhangi) and 2960 m (Mtwori).

- ❖ Vegetation: Floristically-rich high-altitude grassland, montane forest.
- ❖ Flora: 309 native vascular plant species so far recorded (Lovett, Gereau and Sidwell, undated), with a significant endemic or near-endemic component in both the grassland and forest. For example, *Impatiens leedalii* is known only from the Ndumbi forest; *Moraea callista* is found also on the Ulugurus and the Livingstone Mountains. This seems to suggest that Kitulo is not so much a centre of endemism in itself, but is part of a larger southern Tanzanian centre of endemism for high-altitude grassland species (Lovett, Gereau and Sidwell, undated).
- ❖ Threats: Grazing of livestock, introduced pasture grasses, clearance for cultivation.
- ❖ Conservation: None. An urgent priority is the establishment of a significant part of the plateau as a nature reserve. Lovett, Gereau and Sidwell (undated) recommend that this should include the upper catchment area of the Ndumbi River, Mtorwi Peak and the Ndumbi forest.

## Uganda

### Af77. Rwenzori Mountains

A large mountain range (90 km by 40 km at the 2000 m contour) on the Uganda/Zaïre border. The fabled "Mountains of the Moon" of Ptolemy, with ice-clad peaks up to 5110 m.

- ❖ Vegetation: Montane forest to 2400 m; bamboo forest; high rainfall/mist ericaceous forest, rich in bryophytes and lichens, to 3800 m; Afroalpine vegetation above 3800 m, including extensive *Helichrysum* scrub and *Dendrosenecio* vegetation; many small post-glacial lakes and *Carex* bogs providing some of the headwaters of the Nile.
- ❖ Flora: 14 local endemics in the alpine zone. Regional endemism much higher, but unquantified. Equatorial Afroalpine gigantism is found on a scale surpassing that on any of the other East African mountains; genera showing gigantism include *Dendrosenecio*, *Erica*, *Lobelia*, *Hypericum* and *Peucedanum*.
- ❖ Threats: Agricultural encroachment, bamboo cutting.
- ❖ Conservation: Part of Rwenzori in Zaïre is in the Virunga National Park and is a World Heritage Site (7800 km²) (see CPD Site Af78). The Ugandan side has recently been made a National Park and is now the site of a WWF integrated conservation and development project. See Howard (1991); G. Yeoman (1992, *in litt.*).

## Zaïre

### Af78. Virunga National Park

An area of 7800 km² in the north-east of the country, on the border with Uganda and Rwanda and contiguous with Mgahinga National Park (area c. 29 km²) in the former and

the Volcanoes National Park (150 km²) in the latter. The boundaries include part of the Rwenzori Mountains (CPD Site Af77), hot springs and active volcanoes. Altitude: 800–5119 m.

- ❖ Vegetation: Rain forest and various types of savanna at low altitude, bamboo thicket, ericaceous forest, thicket and alpine forests of giant *Dendrosenecio* and *Lobelia* at higher altitudes; also swamps and bogs.
- ❖ Flora: No available figures, but very rich in regional endemics. Most local endemics are at higher altitudes. The flora is described by Robyns (1945, 1947, 1955).
- ❖ Threats: Deforestation, particularly at mid-elevations on Mt Tshiamberimu (Collar and Stuart 1988), fires and the proposed construction of the Semliki and Rutshuru dams. 8000 people live in the fishing village of Vitshumbi (IUCN/UNEP 1987).
- ❖ Conservation: Virunga National Park was established in 1925 as part of the former Albert National Park. Virunga was inscribed on the World Heritage list in 1979.

## Zimbabwe

### Af79. Chimanimani Mountains

A rugged range of mountains at the southern end of the Eastern Highlands. They are composed of quartzite and rise to 2440 m at their highest point.

- ❖ Vegetation: Montane and submontane grassland, with patches of woodland and forest, including some low-altitude rain forest.
- ❖ Flora: 859 vascular plant species above 1200 m. There are 42 strict endemics, including 5 species of *Aloe* (Wild 1964; Friis 1983).
- ❖ Threats: The small forest patches are threatened by fires spreading from surrounding areas. Some are also subject to fuelwood extraction.
- ❖ Conservation: An area of 171 km², which includes the main massif of the mountains, has been a National Park since 1953.

### Af80. Nyanga

An area of 289 km² at the northern end of the Eastern Highlands, dominated by Mt Inyangani which, at 2592 m, is the highest mountain in Zimbabwe. Most of the terrain consists of rolling downlands at altitudes of between 2000 and 2300 m.

- ❖ Vegetation: Mostly submontane grassland maintained by fire. Also patches of stunted *Brachystegia* woodland and submontane forest. There are a number of pine plantations within the park.
- ❖ Flora: One of the richest areas in Zimbabwe, but total number of species unknown.
- ❖ Threats: Wattle (*Acacia* spp.) is now spreading within the Park from plantations outside. There is much conversion of highland areas outside the park to agriculture and softwood plantations.
- ❖ Conservation: One of Zimbabwe's first National Parks, the area has been protected since 1902. Nyanga National Park is administered jointly with Mtarazi Falls National Park (25 km²), which adjoins its southern boundary.

## AFROALPINE REGIONAL CENTRE OF ENDEMISM

Afroalpine vegetation is physiognomically very varied. It is characterized, in East Africa, by the occurrence of giant senecios (*Dendrosenecio* spp.) and giant lobelias (*Lobelia* spp.). Only the latter genus is present in Ethiopia.

Afroalpine communities are found on the highest mountains of tropical Africa (those which reach altitudes above c.3800 m), namely: the Rwenzori Mountains (CPD Site Af77), the Virunga Volcanoes (CPD Site Af78), Mt Elgon (CPD Site Af63), the Aberdare Mountains, Mt Kenya (CPD Site Af62, see Data Sheet), Mt Kilimanjaro (CPD Site Af75), Mt Meru and, in Ethiopia, the Simen Mountains (CPD Site Af61), the Bale Mountains (CPD Site Af60), Mt Guna, Mt Guge, Mt Abune Yosef, Mt Kaka, Choke Mountains, Mangestu Mountains, Mt Bada and Mt Abuye Meda. The Sanetti Plateau, on Bale Mountains, contains the largest expanse of Afroalpine vegetation in Africa (see CPD Site Af60).

The term "Afroalpine" was first coined by Hauman (1933) for the flora characterized by giant life-forms occurring on the higher parts of the East African mountains. It is characterized not only by low mean temperature associated with altitude but also by a pronounced diurnal climate with "summer every day and winter every night". This climate has resulted in striking ecological adaptations (Hedberg 1957, 1964a, 1964b, 1986). The typical flora is restricted to high mountains between 13°N and 4°S. White (1983) referred to the Afroalpine as the Afroalpine Archipelago-like Regional of Extreme Floristic Impoverishment. Although the total number of species is relatively small, endemism is high.

### Af81. Afroalpine region (East and North-east Africa)

– see Data Sheet.

## DRAKENSBERG ALPINE REGION

On the high mountains of Lesotho and South Africa there occurs another cold-adapted, high-altitude type of vegetation termed by White (1983) "altimontane". Other terms applied are "Austro-afroalpine region" of Van Zinderen Bakker and Werger (1974), "Austral Domain of the Afroalpine Region" (by Werger) and "Afroalpine Region" (Killick 1978).

Although the alpine region of Southern Africa may experience equally low mean temperatures, its climate is seasonal and the ecological conditions are somewhat different from those associated with the Afroalpine flora in East and North-east Africa. Floristically it is also very different. It has only about 20 vascular plant species in common with the Afroalpine flora of East and North-east Africa (Hedberg 1986) and lacks the conspicuous tropical-alpine life-forms which are so characteristic of both the Afroalpine vegetation of East and North-east Africa, with morphological parallels also in the páramo of the Andes (see, for example, Hedberg and Hedberg 1979; Hedberg 1992).

For these reasons, the Drakensberg alpine flora is treated separately from the East and North-east African Afroalpine flora in this present study.

### Af82. Drakensberg Alpine Region (Southern Africa)

– see Data Sheet.

## SAHARA REGIONAL TRANSITION ZONE

The Sahara is the largest desert in the world, covering an area of 7,387,000 km². There are some high mountains in the central Sahara, but most of this huge desert consists of basins without outlets, covered by erg (sand sea), reg (gravel plains) and hammada (stony waste).

### Climate

Mean annual rainfall is less than 100 mm, with some areas of the central region (Libyan Desert) being virtually rainless.

### Flora

**Number of species:** 1620 (Quezel 1965).

**Species endemism:** Low (12; 31 according to a more doubtful estimate).

All endemics occur in the mountains.

The figure for the number of species is probably too high. Although endemism was once thought to be relatively high (Quézel 1965; Ozenda 1977), recent revisions give much lower estimates (Lebrun 1983).

### Main vegetation types

Large expanses of erg and reg may be devoid of any visible plant life but, after rain, vegetation cover may reach 50% on sand dunes and 20% on gravel plains. Stone pavements are relatively rich in species, but these are confined to depressions and crevices. Oases, wadis and montane areas support *Tamarix* and *Acacia* woodlands. Swamp vegetation of oases includes doum palm (*Hyphaene thebaica*), but most natural vegetation of oases is now completely replaced by date palm (*Phoenix dactylifera*) and other cultivated plants.

### Species of economic importance

*Tamarix "articulata"*, which is found in the larger sandy wadis, is resistant to browsing by camels and goats and provides the only joinery timber locally available. Tannin is obtained from its galls (White 1983).

*Hyphaene thebaica* (Doum palm) plays an important part in the local economy, providing fibres for ropes, edible fruits, and trunks used for construction purposes.

## Factors causing loss of biodiversity

Overgrazing, particularly in areas with semi-permanent water, fuelwood collection, clearance for cultivation of date palms and other crops.

## Areas of botanical interest

The following areas are of botanical interest, but there is insufficient data to support their designation as CPD sites. Considering the relative poverty and low endemism of the flora of the Sahara region, the sites are not expected to match the diversity of other sites selected for Africa, but they do, nevertheless, contain a good representative sample of the Saharan flora. Tibesti (Chad) is a local centre of endemism.

### *Algeria*

### Tassili d'Ajjer

A highland area covering 90,000 km². 340 vascular plant species have been recorded, including several near-endemics and 1 strict endemic, *Cupressus dupreziana*, which occurs in ravines. Some of the larger trees of this species are among the world's oldest living organisms.

### *Chad*

### Tibesti

A large massif covering 250,000 km² in the north of the country. 350 vascular plant species, including 8 near-endemics, have been recorded. There is no official protection.

## NORTH AFRICA (MEDITERRANEAN REGIONAL CENTRE OF ENDEMISM, MEDITERRANEAN/SAHARA REGIONAL TRANSITION ZONE)

The Mediterranean Regional Centre of Endemism encircles the Mediterranean Sea, but the part treated here is the Maghreb, covering 330,000 km². It is a region of folded mountains, dominated by the Atlas Mountains which stretch for 3000 km from Morocco, via Algeria, to Tunisia. The wettest slopes are the western ones. The main peaks are in Morocco, culminating in the High Atlas (see Data Sheet), with Jebel Toubkal reaching 4165 m. Many of these peaks have snow for most of the year.

## Climate

Summers are hot and dry, while winters are wet, with frost occurring over several months on the higher mountains and plateaux. In the transition zone, mean annual rainfall over most of the area is 100–250 mm, but rainfall on the wetter slopes of the High Atlas can be as high as 1000 mm.

## Flora

| Number of species: | c. 4000 (Maghreb). |
|---|---|
| Species endemism: | 20%. |
| Endemic families: | None. |
| Endemic genera: | None, but c. 250 have their greatest concentrations here. |

Characteristic Mediterranean endemics include: *Cedrus atlantica*, *Laurus nobilis*, *Nerium oleander* and *Quercus suber*.

Families with large numbers of endemics in the area are (Quézel 1978):

Compositae (231 endemic spp.)
Cruciferae (12 endemic genera)
Leguminosae (105 endemic spp.)
Labiatae (99 endemic spp.)

The Mediterranean/Sahara Regional Transition Zone has some 2500 species. There are very few endemics and these are mostly concentrated in south-west Morocco, on the Atlantic coastal plain and on Al Jabal al Akhdar in Libya (CPD Site Af83).

## Main vegetation types

On the mountains there is mainly secondary Mediterranean sclerophyllous forest or scrubland (macchia, maquis, garrigue) with *Arbutus*, *Cistus*, *Erica* and *Genista*, or bushland with *Olea europaea* and *Pistacia lentiscus*. Montane oak forests, with *Quercus ilex* or *Q. suber* as the dominant species, are also widespread, as are coniferous forests with, for example, *Pinus halepensis* and *Cedrus atlantica* (much depleted) at higher altitudes. Thorn cushion vegetation (e.g. with *Vella*) also occurs at higher altitudes.

Vegetation in coastal Egypt and Libya is much degraded to sparse grassland. In the Maghreb, secondary tussock grassland is very common and so too, to a lesser degree, is shrubland. Saline depressions have halophytic vegetation. On the Atlantic coast of Morocco there is succulent shrubland and scrub forest dominated by *Argania* and *Euphorbia*. Much of the vegetation is secondary and influenced, or even designed, by humans, but in parts of the High Atlas the original vegetation is still relatively intact.

## Species of economic importance

Economically important timber trees include *Cedrus atlantica* (Atlantic cedar), *Juniperus thurifera* and *Quercus suber* (cork oak).

## Factors causing loss of biodiversity

Grazing, especially by goats, is a principal cause. In moister areas, especially at lower altitudes, high population pressure results in clearances for cultivation and grazing.

## Centres of plant diversity and endemism

The High Atlas is by far the most species-rich area in the region and is selected for Data Sheet treatment.

### Libya

### Af83. Al Jabal al Akhdar

A mountain to 878 m on the north coast near Benghazi. The flora is mainly of an Eastern Mediterranean character (Drar 1963; Boulos 1972; Bartolo *et al.* 1977) and comprises 1000 vascular plant species, with about 50 site endemics (L. Boulos, pers. comm.). The Kouf National Park covers 1000 km² in this area.

### Morocco

### Af84. High Atlas

– see Data Sheet.

## Areas of botanical interest

The following areas are of botanical interest, but there is insufficient data to support their designation as CPD sites. They contain good representative samples of the North African flora; the Babor Mountains are a local centre of endemism.

### Algeria

### Babor Mountains in Petit Kabylie

Herb-rich deciduous forests with 8 endemics or near-endemics (Knapp 1973).

### Morocco

### Coastal area near Agadir and to south

Many succulents, with *Argania spinosa* and *Euphorbia* spp. (White 1983).

## References

Abbiw, D.K. (1989). Non-wood forest products (minor forest products). *Ghana Forest Inventory Project Proceedings.* Forestry Department, Accra, Ghana. Pp. 79–88.

Adjanohoun, E. (1964). *Végétation des savanes et des rochers découverts en Côte d'Ivoire centrale.* ORSTOM, Paris.

Anon. (1986a). A desert heritage in danger. *WWF News* (Jan./Feb. 1986) 39: 2–3.

Anon. (1986b). Mist oases in a desert region. *WWF Monthly Report* (March 1986): 73–74.

Aubréville, A. (1950). *Flore Forestière Soudano-Guinneéne.* Societé d'Editions Géographiques Maritimes et Coloniales, Paris. (Reprinted in 1975 by Centre Techniques de Forestier Tropical, Nogent-sur-Marne.) 523 pp.

Axelrod, D.I. and Raven, P.H. (1978). Late Cretaceous and Tertiary vegetation history of Africa. In Werger, M.J.A. (ed.), *Biogeography and ecology of Southern Africa.* Junk, The Hague. Pp. 77–130.

Bartolo, G., Brullo, S., Guglielmo, A. and Scalia, C. (1977). Considerazioni fitogeografice sugli endemismi della Cirenaica settentrionale. *Arch. Bot. Biogeogr. Ital.* 53: 131–154.

Beentje, H.J. (1988a). An ecological and floristical study of the forests of the Taita Hills, Kenya. *Utafiti* 1: 23–46.

Beentje, H.J. (1988b). Atlas of the rare trees of Kenya. *Utafiti* 1: 71–123.

Binggeli, P. and Hamilton, A.C. (1990). Tree species invasions and sustainable forestry in the East Usambaras. In Hedberg, I. and Persson, E. (eds), *Research for conservation of Tanzanian catchment forests.* University of Uppsala, Sweden. Pp. 39–47.

Boulos, L. (1972). Our present knowledge of the flora and vegetation of Libya. *Webbia* 26: 365–400.

Brenan, J.P.M. (1978). Some aspects of the phytogeography of tropical Africa. *Ann. Missouri Bot. Gard.* 65: 437–478.

Breteler, F.J. (1989). Gabon. In Campbell, D.G. and Hammond, H.D. (eds.), *Floristic inventory of tropical countries: the status of plant systematics, collections, and vegetation, plus recommendations for the future.* New York Botanical Garden, New York. Pp. 198–202.

Breteler, F.J. (1990). Gabon's evergreen forest: the present status and its future. *Mitt. Inst. Allg. Bot. Hamburg* 23a: 219–224.

Burgess, N.D., Mwasumbi, L.B., Hawthorne, W.J., Dickinson, A. and Doggett, R.A. (1992). Preliminary assessment of the distribution, status and biological importance of coastal forests in Tanzania. *Biological Conservation* 62: 205–218.

Burkill, H.M. (1985). *The useful plants of West Tropical Africa, Vol. 1.* Royal Botanic Gardens, Kew.

Campbell, D.G. (1990). Rates of botanical exploration in Asia and Latin America; similarities and dissimilarities with Africa. *Mitt. Inst. Allg. Bot. Hamburg* 23a: 155–167.

Campbell, D.G. and Hammond, H.D. (eds) (1989). *Floristic inventory of tropical countries: the status of plant systematics, collections, and vegetation, plus recommendations for the future.* New York Botanical Garden, New York. 545 pp.

Chapman, J.D. (1962). *The vegetation of Mlanje Mountains, Nyasaland*. Govt Printer, Zomba.

Cleaver, K., Schreiber, G. and Ryden, P. (1992). Population, environment and agriculture. In Sayer, J.A., Harcourt, C.S. and Collins, N.M. (eds), *The conservation atlas of tropical forests: Africa*. Macmillan. Pp. 49–55.

Cody, M.L. (1986). Diversity, rarity and conservation in Mediterranean-climate regions. In Soulé, M.E. (ed.), *Conservation biology*. Sinauer, Sunderland, Massachusetts. Pp. 122–125.

Collar, N.J. and Stuart, S.N. (1988). *Key forests for threatened birds in Africa*. ICPB Monograph No. 3. International Council for Bird Preservation, Cambridge in collaboration with the IUCN Species Survival Commission, Gland, Switzerland. 102 pp.

Cowling, R.M. (1983). Phytochorology and vegetation history in the south eastern Cape, South Africa. *Journal of Biogeography* 10: 292–419.

Cowling, R.M., Gibbs Russell, G.E., Hoffman, M.T. and Hilton-Taylor, C. (1989). Patterns of plant species diversity in Southern Africa. In Huntley, B.J. (ed.), *Biotic diversity in Southern Africa: concepts and conservation*. Oxford University Press, Cape Town. Pp. 19–50.

Cunningham, A.B. (1993). *African medicinal plants: setting priorities at the interface between conservation and primary healthcare*. UNESCO, Paris.

Cunningham, A.B. and Mbenkum, F.T. (1993). *Sustainability of harvesting Prunus africana bark in Cameroon*. UNESCO, Paris.

Davies, A.G. (1987). *The Gola Forest Reserves, Sierra Leone: wildlife conservation and forest management*. IUCN, Gland, Switzerland and Cambridge, U.K. 126 pp.

Davis, S.D. (in press). Identifying globally important sites for conserving plant diversity: the Centres of Plant Diversity project. In Seyani, J.H. (ed.), *Proceedings of the XIIIth AETFAT Congress, Zomba, Malawi, April 1991*.

Dowsett-Lemaire, F. (1985). The forest vegetation of the Nyika Plateau (Malawi-Zambia): ecological and phenological studies. *Bull. Jard. Bot. Nat. Belg.* 55: 301–392.

Dowsett-Lemaire, F. (1988). The forest vegetation of Mt Mulanje (Malawi). *Bull. Jard. Bot. Nat. Belg.* 58: 77–107.

Dowsett-Lemaire, F. (1989). The flora and phytogeography of the evergreen forests of Malawi 1: Afromontane and mid-altitude forests. *Bull. Jard. Bot. Nat. Belg.* 59: 3–131.

Drar, M. (1963). Flora of Africa north of the Sahara. In Rev. Nat. Resourc. Afr. Continent. *Natural Resources Research* 1: 249–261.

Droop, S.J.M. (1988). The work of the IUCN Conservation Monitoring Centre at Kew and the forthcoming *Centres of Plant Diversity* book. *Monogr. Syst. Bot. Missouri Bot. Gard.* 25: 465–469.

Enti, A.A. (undated). *International trade in non-traditional forest produce*. Forestry Department, Accra, Ghana. (Unpublished.)

Exell, A.W. and Gonçalves, M.L. (1973). A statistical analysis of a sample of the flora of Angola. *Garcia de Orta, sér bot.* 1: 105–128.

FAO (1986). *Databook on endangered tree and shrub species and provenances*. FAO Forestry Paper No. 77. FAO, Rome. 524 pp.

FAO (1988a). *An interim report on the state of forest resources in the developing countries*. FAO, Rome.

FAO (1988b). *Yearbook of forest products*. FAO, Rome.

FAO (1990). *Second interim report on the state of tropical forests*. Report to the 10th World Forestry Congress, Paris. Forest Resources Assessment Project. FAO, Rome. 2 pp.

FAO/UNEP (1981). *Forest resources of tropical Africa. Part 1: Regional synthesis*. FAO, Rome.

Friis, I. (1983). Phytogeography of the tropical north-east African mountains. *Bothalia* 14: 525–532.

Friis, I. (undated). Further studies of the flora of the Imatong Mountains, southern Sudan: report of the botanical field work 1982. Cyclostyled report, University of Copenhagen.

Friis, I. and Vollesen, K. (1982). New taxa from the Imatong Mountains, southern Sudan. *Kew Bulletin* 37: 465–479.

Friis, I. and Vollesen, K. (1989). Notes on the vegetation of southernmost Somalia, with some additions to the flora. *Willdenowia* 18: 455–477.

Friis, I. and Vollesen, K. (unpublished). A check-list of the plants of the Imatong Mts, southern Sudan, including the Dongotona Mts, the Didinga Hills and parts of the Imatong Mts which extend into Uganda.

Gartlan, S. (1989). *La conservation des ecosystèmes forestiers du Cameroun*. IUCN, Gland, Switzerland and Cambridge, U.K. 186 pp.

Gartlan, S. et al. (1992). Cameroon. In Sayer, J.A., Harcourt, C.S. and Collins, N.M. (eds), *The conservation atlas of tropical forests: Africa*. Macmillan. Pp. 110–118.

Gebre-Michael, T., Hundessa, J. and Hillman, J.C. (1992). The effects of war on World Heritage Sites and protected areas in Ethiopia. In Thorsell, J. and Sawyer, J. (eds), *World Heritage twenty years later*. IUCN, Gland, Switzerland and Cambridge, U.K. Pp. 143–150.

Gibbs Russell, G.E. (1985). Analysis of the size and composition of the Southern African flora. *Bothalia* 15: 613–629.

Goldblatt, P. (1978). An analysis of the flora of Southern Africa: its characteristics, relationships and origins. *Ann. Missouri Bot. Gard.* 65: 369–436.

Goodman, S.M. (1985). Natural resources and management considerations, Gebel Elba conservation area. Report for WWF/IUCN Project 3612.

Gordon, D., *et al.* (1992). Ghana. In Sayer, J.A., Harcourt, C.S. and Collins, N.M. (eds), *The conservation atlas of tropical forests: Africa*. Macmillan. Pp. 183–192.

Greenway, P.J. (1973). A classification of the vegetation of East Africa. *Kirkia* 9: 1–68.

Hall, J. (1990). Conservation politics in Zaïre – the protection of the Ituri Forest. *WWF Reports* (April/May 1990): 3–4.

Hall, A.V. and Veldhuis, H.A. (1985). *South African Red Data Book: plants – fynbos and Karoo biomes.* South African National Scientific Programmes Report 117. CSIR, Pretoria.

Hallé, N., Le Thomas, A. and Gazel, M. (1967). Trois rélevés botaniques dans les forêts de Bélinga (N.-E. du Gabon). *Biol. Gabon.* 3: 3–14.

Hamilton, A.C. (1982). *Environmental history of East Africa: a study of the Quaternary.* Academic Press, London. 328 pp.

Hamilton, A.C. (1984). *Deforestation in Uganda.* Oxford University Press, Nairobi, Kenya.

Hamilton, A.C. (1989). African forests. In Lieth, H. and Werger, M.J.A. (eds.), *Tropical rain forest ecosystems.* Elsevier, Amsterdam. Pp. 155–182.

Hamilton, A.C. (1992). History of forests and climate. In Sayer, J.A., Harcourt, C.S. and Collins, N.M. (eds), *The conservation atlas of tropical forests: Africa.* Macmillan. Pp. 17–25.

Hamilton, A.C. and Bensted Smith, R. (eds) (1989). *Forest conservation in the East Usambara Mountains, Tanzania.* IUCN, Gland, Switzerland and Cambridge, U.K. 392 pp.

Harcourt, C. *et al.* (1992a). Sierra Leone. In Sayer, J.A., Harcourt, C.S. and Collins, N.M. (eds), *The conservation atlas of tropical forests: Africa.* Macmillan. Pp. 244–250.

Harcourt, C. *et al.* (1992b). Uganda. In Sayer, J.A., Harcourt, C.S. and Collins, N.M. (eds), *The conservation atlas of tropical forests: Africa.* Macmillan. Pp. 262–269.

Hauman, L. (1933). Esquisse de la végétation des hautes altitudes sur le Ruwenzori. *Bull. Acad. Belg. Cl. Sci. sér. 5,* 19: 602–616, 702–717, 900–917.

Hawthorne, W.D. (1990). Knowledge of plant species in the forest zone of Ghana. *Mitt. Inst. Allg. Bot. Hamburg* 23a: 177–185.

Hedberg, I. (1976). Follow-up of the AETFAT meeting at Uppsala in 1966 on "Conservation of vegetation in Africa south of the Sahara". *Boissiera* 24: 437–441.

Hedberg, I. and Hedberg, O. (eds) (1968). Conservation of vegetation in Africa south of the Sahara. *Acta Phytogeographica Suecica* 54: 1–320.

Hedberg, I. and Hedberg, O. (1979). Tropical-alpine life-forms of vascular plants. *Oikos* 33: 297–307.

Hedberg, O. (1951). Vegetation belts of the East African mountains. *Svensk. Bot. Tidskr.* 45: 140–202.

Hedberg, O. (1957). Afroalpine vascular plants. A taxonomic revision. *Symb. Bot. Upsal.* 15: 1–411.

Hedberg, O. (1964a). Etudes écologiques de la flore afroalpine. *Bull. Soc. Roy. Bot. Belgique* 97: 5–18.

Hedberg, O. (1964b). Features of Afroalpine plant ecology. *Acta Phytogeographica Suecica* 49: 1–144.

Hedberg, O. (1986). Origins of the Afroalpine flora. In Vuilleumier, F. and Monansterio, M. (eds), *High altitude tropical biogeography.* Oxford University Press, Oxford. Pp. 443–468.

Hedberg, O. (1992). Afroalpine vegetation compared to páramo: convergent adaptations and divergent differentiation. In Balslev, H. and Luteyn, J.L. (eds), *Páramo.* Academic Press, London. Pp. 15–29.

Hilliard, O.M. and Burtt, B.L. (1987). *The botany of the southern Natal Drakensberg.* National Botanic Gardens, Cape Town. 253 pp.

Hladik, A. (1986). Données comparatives sur la richesse spécifique et les structures des peuplements des forêts tropicales d'Afrique et d'Amerique. In Gasc., J.P. (ed.), *Vertébrés et forêts tropicales humides d'Afrique et d'Amerique.* Muséum National d'Histoire Naturelle, Paris.

Hoffman, M.T. and Cowling, R.M. (1991). Phytochorology and endemism along aridity and grazing gradients in the lower Sundays River Valley, South Africa. *Journal of Biogeography* 8: 189–201.

Howard, P.C. (1991). *Nature conservation in Uganda's tropical forest reserves.* IUCN, Gland, Switzerland and Cambridge, U.K. 313 pp.

Hutchinson, J. and Dalziel, J.M. (1927-1936). *Flora of West Tropical Africa,* 2nd Ed. 2 Vols. (Vol. 1 revised by R.W.J. Keay, 1954; vols 2 and 3 [parts 1 and 2] revised by F.N. Hepper, 1963, 1968, 1978; pteridophytes by A.H.G. Alston, 1959). Crown Agents, London.

IUCN (1988a). *Conservation et utilisation rationelle des ecosystèmes forestiers en Afrique Centrale. Rapport national: São Tomé et Príncipe.* IUCN, Gland, Switzerland and Cambridge, U.K.

IUCN (1988b). *Conservation et utilisation rationelle des ecosystèmes forestiers en Afrique Centrale. Rapport national: Cameroun.* IUCN, Gland, Switzerland and Cambridge, U.K.

IUCN (1988c). *Conservation et utilisation rationelle des ecosystèmes forestiers en Afrique Centrale. Rapport national: Zaire.* IUCN, Gland, Switzerland and Cambridge, U.K.

IUCN (1990). *1990 United Nations list of national parks and protected areas.* IUCN, Gland, Switzerland and Cambridge, U.K. 284 pp.

IUCN (1992). *Protected areas of the world: a review of national systems. Volume 3: Afrotropical.* IUCN, Gland, Switzerland and Cambridge, U.K. 360 pp. (Prepared by the World Conservation Monitoring Centre.)

IUCN/UNEP (1987). *IUCN directory of Afrotropical protected areas.* IUCN, Gland, Switzerland and Cambridge, U.K. xix, 1034 pp.

Jackson, J.K. (1956). The vegetation of the Imatong Mountains, Sudan. *Sudan J. Ecol.* 44: 341–374.

Jaeger, P. (1983). Le recensement des plantes vasculaires et les originalités du peuplement végétal des monts Loma en Sierra Leone (Afrique Occidentale). *Bothalia* 14: 539–542.

Jarman, M. L. (1986). Conservation priorities in lowland regions of the fynbos biome. *S.A. Nat. Scient. Programme Report* 87: 1–53.

Jenkins, M. and Hamilton, A. (1992). Biological diversity. In Sayer, J.A., Harcourt, C.S. and Collins, N.M. (eds), *The conservation atlas of tropical forests: Africa.* Macmillan. Pp. 26–32.

Jones, P. (1992). São Tomé and Príncipe. In Sayer, J.A., Harcourt, C.S. and Collins, N.M. (eds), *The conservation atlas of tropical forests: Africa.* Macmillan. Pp. 240–243.

Kabuye, C.H.S. (1988). East African plants used in basketry. In Goldblatt, P. and Lowry, P.P. (eds), *Modern systematic studies in African botany. Proceedings of AETFAT Congress, 1985.* Missouri Botanical Garden Monographs in Systematic Botany. Pp. 351–362.

Keay, R.W.J. (1955). Montane vegetation and flora in the British Cameroun. *Proc. Linn. Soc. Lond.* 165: 140–143.

Kendrick, K. (1989). Equatorial Africa. In Campbell, D.G. and Hammond, H.D. (eds), *Floristic inventory of tropical countries: the status of plant systematics, collections, and vegetation, plus recommendations for the future.* New York Botanical Garden, New York. Pp. 203–216.

Killick, D.J.B. (1978). The afro-alpine region. In Werger, M.J. (ed.), *Biogeography and ecology of Southern Africa.* Junk, The Hague. Pp. 515–542.

Kis, G. (1985). *Mosses of south-east tropical Africa. An annotated list with distributional data.* Inst. Ecol. Bot. Hungary Acad. Sci. Vacratot. 170 pp.

Knapp, R. (1973). *Die Vegetation von Afrika.* Gustav Fischer, Stuttgart.

Lebrun, J. (1960). Sur la richesse de flore de divers territoires africains. *Bull. Acad. Roy. Soc. Outre-mer* 4: 669–690.

Lebrun, J.P. (1976). Richesses spécifiques de la flore vasculaire des divers pays ou régions d'Afrique. *Candollea* 31: 11–15.

Lebrun, J.P. (1983). La flore des massifs Sahariens: espèces illusoires et endémiques vraies. *Bothalia* 14: 511–515.

Letouzey, R. (1968a). Cameroun. In Hedberg, I. and Hedberg, O. (eds), Conservation of vegetation in Africa south of the Sahara. *Acta Phytogeographica Suecica* 54: 115–121.

Letouzey, R. (1968b). *Etude phytogéographique du Cameroun.* Editions Paul Lechevalier, Paris. 508 pp.

Lisowski, S., Malaisse, F. and Symoens, J.J. (1971). Une flore des hauts plateaux du Katanga. *Mitt. Bot. Staatssamml. München* 10: 51–56.

Lovett, J.C. (1985). Moist forests of eastern Tanzania. *Swara* 8: 8–9.

Lovett, J.C. (1988). Endemism and affinities of the Tanzanian montane forest flora. In Goldblatt, P. and Lowry, P. (eds), *Modern systematic studies in African botany.* Missouri Botanical Garden, St Louis. Pp. 591–598.

Lovett, J.C. (1989). Tanzania. In Campbell, D.G. and Hammond, H.D. (eds), *Floristic inventory of tropical countries: the status of plant systematics, collections, and vegetation, plus recommendations for the future.* New York Botanical Garden, New York. Pp. 232–235.

Lovett, J.C. (1990). Classification and status of the moist forests of Tanzania. In Proceedings of the Twelfth Plenary Meeting of AETFAT, Hamburg, 4–10 September 1988. *Mitt. Inst. Allg. Bot. Hamburg* 23a: 287–300.

Lovett, J.C. (1993). Eastern Arc moist forest flora. In Lovett, J.C. and Wasser, S.K. (eds), *Biogeography and ecology of the rain forests of eastern Africa.* Cambridge University Press.

Lovett, J.C. and Congdon, T.C.E. (1989). Notes on the Ihanga forest and Luhega forest near Uhafiwa Uzungwa Mountains, Tanzania. *East Africa Natural History Society Bulletin* 19: 30–31.

Lovett, J.C., Gereau, R.E. and Sidwell, K.J. (undated). Vegetation and phytogeography of the Kitulo Plateau, southern Tanzania. 9 pp. (Typescript.)

Lovett, J.C. and Pócs, T. (1992). *Assessment of the condition of the Catchment Forest Reserves*. Forest and Beekeeping Division, Ministry of Natural Resources, Tourism and Environment, Dar es Salaam, Tanzania.

Lowe, R., Caldecott, J., Barnwell, R. and Keay, R. (1992). Nigeria. In Sayer, J.A., Harcourt, C.S. and Collins, N.M. (eds), *The conservation atlas of tropical forests: Africa*. Macmillan. Pp. 230–239.

Macdonald, I.A.W. (1989). Man's role in changing the face of Southern Africa. In Huntley, B.J. (ed.), *Biotic diversity in Southern Africa: concepts and conservation*. Oxford University Press, Capetown. Pp. 51–77.

MacKinnon, J. and MacKinnon, K. (1986). *Review of the protected areas system in the Afrotropical Realm*. IUCN, Gland, Switzerland, in collaboration with UNEP. 259 pp.

Mayers, J., Anstey, S. and Peal, A. (1992). Liberia. In Sayer, J.A., Harcourt, C.S. and Collins, N.M. (eds), *The conservation atlas of tropical forests: Africa*. Macmillan. Pp. 214–220.

Marius, C. (1976). Toelichting bij een vegetatiekartering van de Birunga vulkanen en van Kahuzi-Biega. *Roneo*. 42 pp.

Matthews, W.S., Van Wyk, A.E. and Bredenkamp, G.J. (1993). Endemic flora of the north-eastern Transvaal Escarpment, South Africa. *Biological Conservation* 63: 83–94.

Mbenkum, F.T. and Fisiy, C.F. (1992). *Ethnobotanical survey of Kilum Mountain Forest (Project 4510, Cameroon)*. WWF, Switzerland.

Monod, T. (1957). *Les grandes divisions chorologiques de l'Afrique*. CCTA Publication No. 24. London.

Morton, J.K. (1986). Montane vegetation. In Lawson, G.W. (ed.), *Plant ecology in West Africa*. Wiley, Chichester.

Myers, N. (1989). *Deforestation rates in tropical forests and their climatic implications*. Friends of the Earth, London.

Newby, J.E. and Jones, D.M. (1981). *An ecological study of the Takolokouzet Massif and surrounding area in the eastern Aïr Mountains, Republic of Niger*. Government of Niger, Zoological Society of London, IUCN, Quest 80 and the Fauna and Flora Preservation Society.

Newmark, W.D. (1991). *The conservation of Mount Kilimanjaro*. IUCN, Gland, Switzerland and Cambridge, U.K.

Nichols, G.R. (1990). Making the medicine plants renewable: a conservation strategy in the Durban city parks department. *Mitt. Inst. Allg. Bot. Hamburg* 23a: 25–30.

Noordwijk, M. van (1984). *Ecology textbook for the Sudan*. Khartoum University.

ODA (1977). *Forestry development prospects in the Imatong Central Forest Reserve, southern Sudan*. 1–3. Land Resources Division, U.K.

ODA (1992a). *Environmental synopsis of Ghana*. International Institute for Environment and Development, London.

ODA (1992b). *Environmental synopsis of Uganda*. International Institute for Environment and Development, London.

ODA (1992c). *Environmental synopsis of Zimbabwe*. International Institute for Environment and Development, London.

Offutt, K. (1992). Tourism as a conservation strategy in the Nyungwe forest, Rwanda. In Sayer, J.A., Harcourt, C.S. and Collins, N.M. (eds), *The conservation atlas of tropical forests: Africa*. Macmillan. Pp. 77.

Ozenda, P. (1977). *Flore du Sahara*, 2nd Ed. Editions du CNRS, Paris. 622 pp.

Pócs, T. (1976). Vegetation mapping in the Uluguru Mountains (Tanzania, East Africa). *Boissiera* 24: 477–498.

Pócs, T. (1991). The significance of lower plants in the conservation of Mount Kilimanjaro. In Newark, W.D. (ed.), *The conservation of Mount Kilimanjaro*. IUCN, Gland, Switzerland. Pp. 21–33.

Pócs, T. (1993, in press). The altitudinal distribution of Kilimanjaro bryophytes. In Seyani, J.H. (ed.), *Proceedings of the XIIIth AETFAT Congress, Zomba, Malawi, 2–11 April 1993*.

Pócs, T, Temu, R.-A.P.C. and Minja, T.R.A. (1990). Survey of the natural vegetation and flora of the Nguru Mountains. In Hedberg, I. and Persson, E. (eds), *Research for conservation of Tanzanian catchment forests*. University of Uppsala, Sweden. Pp. 135–149.

Polhill, R.M. (1968). Tanzania. In Hedberg, I. and Hedberg, O. (eds), Conservation of vegetation in Africa south of the Sahara. *Acta Phytogeographica Suecica* 166–178.

Quézel, P. (1965). *La végétation du Sahara: du Tchad a la Mauritanie*. Gustav Fischer, Stuttgart.

Quézel, P. (1978). Analysis of the flora of Mediterranean and Saharan Africa. *Ann. Missouri Bot. Gard.* 479–534.

Quézel, P. (1985). Definition of the Mediterranean region and the origin of its flora. In Gómez-Campo, C. (ed.), *Plant conservation in the Mediterranean area*. Junk, The Hague. Pp. 17.

Rabinowitz, P.D., Cotlin, M.F. and Falvey, D. (1983). The separation of Madagascar and Africa. *Science* 220: 67–69.

Reitsma, J.M. (1988). *Végétation forestière du Gabon/Forest vegetation of Gabon*. Tropenbos Foundation, Ede, The Netherlands.

Richards, P.W. (1973). Africa, the "odd man out". In Meggers, B.J., Ayensu, E.S. and Duckworth, D. (eds), *Tropical forest ecosystems in Africa and South America*. Smithsonian Institution Press, Washington, D.C.

Rietbergen, S. (1992). Forest management. In Sayer, J.A., Harcourt, C.S. and Collins, N.M. (eds), *The conservation atlas of tropical forests: Africa*. Macmillan. Pp. 62–68.

Robertson, S.A. and Luke, W.R.Q. (1993). Kenya coastal forests. World Wide Fund for Nature, Nairobi.

Robyns, W. (1945, 1947, 1955). *Flore des Spermatophytes du Parc National Albert, Vols I–III*. Inst. des Parcs Nat. du Congo Belge, Brussels.

Rodgers, A., Robertson, A. and Sayer, J. (1992). Eastern Africa. In Sayer, J.A., Harcourt, C.S. and Collins, N.M. (eds), *The conservation atlas of tropical forests: Africa*. Macmillan. Pp. 143–160.

Sawyer, J., Stoll, H., Elliot, C. and Burgess, P. (1992). Timber trade. In Sayer, J.A., Harcourt, C.S. and Collins, N.M. (eds), *The conservation atlas of tropical forests: Africa*. Macmillan. Pp. 56–61.

Sayer, J. *et al.* (1992). Zaïre. In Sayer, J.A., Harcourt, C.S. and Collins, N.M. (eds), *The conservation atlas of tropical forests: Africa*. Macmillan. Pp. 272–282.

Sayer, J.A., Harcourt, C.S. and Collins, N.M. (eds) (1992). *The conservation atlas of tropical forests: Africa*. Macmillan. 288 pp.

Sayer, J.A. and Stuart, S.N. (1989). Biological diversity and tropical forests. *Environmental Conservation* 15: 193–194.

Schnell, R. (1968). Guinée. In Hedberg, I. and Hedberg, O. (eds), Conservation of vegetation in Africa south of the Sahara. *Acta Phytogeographica Suecica* 54: 69–72.

SECA/CML (1987). *Mangroves of Africa and Madagascar: the mangroves of Nigeria*. Société d'Eco-aménagement, Marseilles, France and Centre for Environmental Studies, University of Leiden, The Netherlands. (Unpublished report to the European Commission, Brussels.)

Semesei, A.K. (1991). *Management plan for the mangrove ecosystem of mainland Tanzania*. Forest and Beekeeping Division, Ministry of Natural Resources, Tourism and Environment, Dar es Salaam, Tanzania.

Seyani, J.H., Chikuni, A.C. and Kamundi, D.A. (1991). A preliminary survey of the centres of plant diversity in Malawi. 1. Highland areas. (Paper presented at the XIIIth AETFAT Congress, Zomba, Malawi, April 1991.)

Sommerlatte, H. and Sommerlatte M. (1988). A field guide to the trees and shrubs of the Imatong Mountains, southern Sudan. (Cyclostyled.)

Stuart, S.N. and Adams, R.J. (1990). *Biodiversity in sub-Saharan Africa and its islands: conservation, management and sustainable use*. Occasional Papers of the IUCN Species Survival Commission No 6. IUCN, Gland, Switzerland. 242 pp.

Takhtajan, A. (1986). *Floristic regions of the world*. University of California Press, Berkeley. 522 pp.

Taylor, H. C. (1978). Capensis. In Werger, M.J.A. (ed.), *Biogeography and ecology of Southern Africa*. Junk, The Hague. Pp. 171–229.

Thomas, D.W. and Cheek, M. (1992). *Vegetation and plant species on the south side of Mount Cameroon in the proposed Etinde Reserve*. Royal Botanic Gardens, Kew.

Troupin, G. (1966). *Etude phytocénologique du Parc National de l'Akagera et du Rwanda oriental. Recherche d'une méthode d'analyse appropriée à la végétation d'Afrique intertropicale, thèse d'agrégation, Liège*. 293 pp.

Tutin, C. et al. (1992). Gabon. In Sayer, J.A., Harcourt, C.S. and Collins, N.M. (eds), *The conservation atlas of tropical forests: Africa*. Macmillan. Pp. 168–174.

UICN (1990a). *La conservation de ecosystèmes forestiers du Congo*. IUCN Gland, Switzerland and Cambridge, U.K. 187 pp.

UICN (1990b). *La conservation de ecosystèmes forestiers du Gabon*. IUCN Gland, Switzerland and Cambridge, U.K. 215 pp.

UN Department of International Economic and Social Affairs (1989). *World population prospects*. United Nations, New York.

Van Zinderen Bakker, E.M. (sr.) and Werger, M.J. (1974). Environment, vegetation and phytogeography of the high-altitude bogs of Lesotho. *Vegetatio* 29: 37–49.

Verschuren, J. (1983). *Conservation of tropical rain forest in Liberia: recommendations for wildlife conservation and national parks*. IUCN, Gland, Switzerland.

Vollesen, K. (1992). *Trichaulax* (Acanthaceae: Justicieae). A new genus from East Africa. *Kew Bulletin* 47: 613–619.

Vooren, F. and Sayer, J. (1992). Côte d'Ivoire. In Sayer, J.A., Harcourt, C.S. and Collins, N.M. (eds), *The conservation atlas of tropical forests: Africa*. Macmillan. Pp. 133–142.

Werger, M.J.A. (1978). The Karoo-Namib region. In Werger, M. J.A. (ed.), *Biogeography and ecology of Southern Africa*. Junk, The Hague. Pp. 231–299.

Werger, M.J.A. and Coetzee, B.J. (1978). The Sudano-Zambezian Region. In Werger, M.J.A. (ed.), *Biogeography and ecology of Southern Africa*. Junk, The Hague. Pp. 301–462.

White, F. (1983). *The vegetation of Africa: a descriptive memoir to accompany the Unesco/AETFAT/UNSO vegetation map of Africa*. Natural Resources Research XX. Unesco, Paris. 356 pp.

Wickens, G.E. (1976). *The flora of Jebel Marra (Sudan Republic) and its geographical affinities*. Kew Bulletin Additional Series V. HMSO, London.

Wild, H. (1964). The endemic species of the Chimanimani Mountains and their significance. *Kirkia* 4: 125–157.

Wild, H. (1965). The flora of the Great Dyke of Southern Rhodesia with special reference to the serpentine soils. *Kirkia* 5: 49–86.

World Conservation Monitoring Centre (1992). *Global biodiversity: status of the Earth's living resources.* Chapman and Hall, London. 594 pp.

World Resources Institute (1992). *World resources 1992–93: a guide to the global environment.* Oxford University Press, New York. 385 pp. (Prepared in collaboration with UNEP and UNDP.)

## Acknowledgements

The preparation of this text has involved contributions from a large number of individuals. Dr Henk J. Beentje (Royal Botanic Gardens, Kew) prepared the original draft which was presented at the XIIIth AETFAT Congress in Zomba, Malawi, April 1991. Additional information for the introduction and on individual sites was incorporated by Bryan Adams and Stephen D. Davis. Dr Alan C. Hamilton (WWF) offered much advice throughout and provided many contributions to the text, which he also edited.

Special thanks are also extended to the participants of the Workshop on African Centres of Plant Diversity held during the XIIIth AETFAT Congress and to other AETFAT members who have advised on site selection and made contributions to the text. In particular, the authors would like to thank the following:

Professor Paul Bamps (Jardin Botanique National de Belgique), Dr F.J. Breteler (Agricultural University, Wageningen, The Netherlands), Dr Dick Brummitt (Royal Botanic Gardens, Kew, U.K.), Dr Martin Cheek (Royal Botanic Gardens, Kew, U.K.), Professor Richard Cowling (University of Cape Town, South Africa), Dr Tony Cunningham (University of Natal, South Africa), Charles Doumenge (IUCN, Switzerland), Dr F. Dowsett-Lemaire (Jupille, Belgium), Dr Alex Forbes (IUCN Regional Office for Eastern Africa, Nairobi, Kenya), Dr Ib Friis (University of Copenhagen, Denmark), Dan Harder (Missouri Botanical Garden, St Louis, U.S.A.), Professor Olov Hedberg and Dr Inga Hedberg (University of Uppsala, Sweden), Craig Hilton-Taylor (National Botanical Institute, Kirstenbosch, South Africa), Professor Brian J. Huntley (National Botanical Institute, Kirstenbosch, South Africa), Dr D.J.B. Killick (Pretoria, South Africa), Dr Michael Lock (Royal Botanic Gardens, Kew, U.K.), Dr Jon Lovett (University of Copenhagen, Denmark), Professor Francois Malaisse (Université Gembloux, Belgium), Stephen Manktelow (University of Uppsala, Sweden), Professor Eugene Moll (now of University of Queensland, Australia), Helen Moss (formerly of IBPGR, Zimbabwe), Dr J.C. Okafor (Nigeria), Professor Tamás Pócs (Eszterhazy Teachers' College, Eger, Hungary), Dr Roger Polhill (Royal Botanic Gardens, Kew, U.K.), Dr Tony Rebelo (National Botanical Institute, Kirstenbosch, South Africa), Dr Mats Thulin (University of Uppsala, Sweden), Jonathon Timberlake (Zimbabwe), Dr Kaj Vollesen (Royal Botanic Gardens, Kew, U.K.), Professor M.J.A. Werger (Rijksuniversiteit Utrecht, The Netherlands), Dr J.J.F.E. de Wilde (Wageningen Agricultural University, The Netherlands), Professor A.E. van Wyk (University of Pretoria, South Africa) and Guy Yeoman (Sheffield, U.K.).

GUINEO-CONGOLIAN REGIONAL CENTRE OF ENDEMISM: CPD SITE AF2

# TAÏ NATIONAL PARK
## Côte d'Ivoire

**Location:** South-west Côte d'Ivoire (Ivory Coast), between latitudes 5°15'–6°07'N and longitudes 7°25'–7°54'W.

**Area:** 3500 km².

**Altitude:** 80–623 m.

**Vegetation:** Evergreen rain forest of the Guinea zone.

**Flora:** 1300 vascular plant species, 150 endemic to the Taï region.

**Useful plants:** Many locally used species.

**Threats:** Logging, agricultural encroachment, hunting, gold-mining.

**Conservation:** National Park (IUCN Management Category: II) and World Heritage Site covers 3500 km²; core and buffer zone concept; Biosphere Reserve covers 3300 km². WWF Project since 1988.

## Geography

Taï National Park lies in south-west Côte d'Ivoire (Ivory Coast) between latitudes 5°15'–6°07'N and longitudes 7°25'–7°54'W, about 100 km from the coast, in the districts of Guiglo and Sassandra, between the Cavally River on the west (the river marks the border with Liberia) and the Sassandra River on the east (IUCN/UNEP 1987). The area of Taï National Park and World Heritage Site is 3500 km². Taï Biosphere Reserve covers 3300 km².

The park comprises an ancient sloping granitic peneplain (c. 80–200 m altitude), with a number of inselbergs, most notably the Niénkoué Hills (623 m) in the south-west. There are schists in the south. Soils are mostly infertile; more fertile soils are developed over shales. Mean annual rainfall ranges from 2200 mm in the south to 1700 mm in the north, with a dry season from December to February. The park is drained by the Hana, Méno and other rivers which flow westwards.

An extensive bibliography on Taï is in the course of preparation by the Tropenbos Foundation (Hazeu and Sloot, in prep.).

## Vegetation

Taï is the largest remaining area of West African Guinea rain forest and should be one of the world's prime foci for conservation activities. The vegetation and flora have been described by Mangenot (1955), Aubréville (1957–1958), Guillaumet (1967), Guillaumet and Adjanohoun (1971), Aké Assi and Pfeffer (1975), and Huttel and Bernard-Reversat (1975).

The forest is largely evergreen. The tallest trees (40–60 m) include *Gymnostemon zaizou*, *Klainedoxa gabonensis* and *Piptadeniastrum africanum*; the second storey (20–30 m) includes *Chrysophyllum perpulchrum* and *Tarrietia utilis*; shrubs and small trees include species of *Diospyros*, *Garcinia* and Rubiaceae; epiphytes can be abundant. Secondary forest includes *Anthocleista nobilis*, *Musanga cecropioides* and *Pycnanthus angolensis*.

There is a south-north floristic gradient corresponding to a decrease in rainfall, but also perhaps partly due to the presence of schistose soils in the south. The southern forests are the richest in species and endemics, especially Leguminosae (Forêt à *Diospyros* spp. et *Mapania* spp.). Tall species characteristic of this forest type include *Deinbollia cuneifolia*, *Tarrietia utilis* and *Trichoscypha beguei*. Species characteristic of the more northern forest type (Forêts à *Eremospatha macrocarpa* et *Diospyros mannii*) include *Chrysophyllum pruniforme*, *Diospyros mannii* and *Ixora laxiflora*.

There are several forest types of more limited distribution, including forest dominated by *Plagiosiphon emarginatus* on alluvium and various types on wet soils, with *Gilbertiodendron splendidum*, *G. robynsianum*, *Hymenostegia afzelii* and *Mitragyna ciliata*. Thickets of tall Marantaceae are also found.

## Flora

Taï lies within the Guinea zone of the Guineo-Congolian Regional Centre of Endemism. 1300 vascular plant species have been recorded from the park, of which 54% are confined to the Guinea zone (IUCN/UNEP 1987). There is a high level of endemism, with over 150 species endemic to the Taï region. The families Caesalpiniaceae and Rubiaceae are well-represented among the endemics.

## Useful plants

Many species have local uses. Populations of a number of timber and other species are important as genetic resources.

## Social and environmental values

This is a very important area for Guinea zone forest animals, containing 47 of the 54 species of large mammals in this zone, including 5 threatened species. Noteworthy species include pygmy hippopotamus, golden cat, forest elephant (much reduced in numbers), chimpanzee and duikers (including Jentink's duiker and banded duiker).

The Upper Guinea lowland rain forests support 12 endemic and 9 near-endemic bird species (Allport 1991), of which 8 are globally threatened (Collar and Andrew 1988) and 6 have restricted-ranges (Stattersfield *et al.*, in prep.). 230 species of bird are recorded from Taï, including all but two of the endemic and near-endemic species (Allport 1991). This site is considered to be a "key forest for threatened birds" (Collar and Stuart 1988).

Mount Niénokoué has local religious significance.

There has been large-scale timber harvesting near Taï National Park, especially of *Afzelia bella* (doussié), *Khaya ivorensis* (Acajou blanc), *Lovoa trichilioides* (Dibetou), *Tarrieta utilis* (Niangon), *Terminalia ivorensis* (Framiré) and *Turraeanthus africanus* (Avodiré). Having largely depleted the most favoured species, the lumber industry is now turning its attention to other species.

## Threats

Côte d'Ivoire has suffered very serious erosion of its forest estate over the last 30 years (GTZ 1979; Marshall 1990; Seneviratne 1990). There is little forestry management and logging concessions are often followed by agricultural settlement based on the cultivation of subsistence crops, coffee and cocoa. There are logging concessions close to Taï, with some illegal logging in the park.

The north and south borders are believed to be more secure than those on the east and west. There is a particular problem on the west, where at least 36,000 refugees from Liberia have settled close to the park boundary. There are also immigrants from Burkino Faso, Guinea and Mali which have settled in the region. There is some poaching in the park (mainly of duikers and monkeys). The local population of forest elephants has declined drastically over the last 30 years, the immigrants being said to be largely responsible. There is some illegal gold mining (Marshall 1990).

## Conservation

Taï National Park (area: 3500 km²) was created in 1972 and declared a World Heritage Site in 1982 (IUCN/UNEP 1987; Marshall 1990; Seneviratne 1990). There is a management plan, with a buffer zone recognised on the park periphery. Taï Biosphere Reserve covers 3300 km². The Reserve de Faune de N'zo lies to the north.

In 1988, farmers in the buffer zone were given 3 years to resettle, but this has met with some resistance. Since 1988, WWF has been involved in a project at Taï, aspects of the work including aerial and ground surveys, park boundary demarcation, strengthening the management capacity of the park and educational and awareness programmes in villages.

## References

Aké Assi, L. and Pfeffer, P. (1975). *Parc national de Taï: inventaire de la flore et de la faune.* Secrétariat d'Etat aux Parcs Nationaux, Rép. de Côte d'Ivoire. 57 pp.

Allport, G. (1991). The status and conservation of threatened birds in the Upper Guinea Forest. *Bird Cons. Int.* 1: 53–74.

Aubréville, A. (1957-1958). A la recherche de la forêt en Côte d'Ivoire. *Bois forêts Trop.* 56: 17–32; 57: 12–27.

Collar, N.J. and Andrew, P. (1988). *Birds to watch: the ICBP world checklist of threatened birds.* Technical Publication No. 8. International Council for Bird Preservation, Cambridge, U.K.

Collar, N.J. and Stuart, S.N. (1985). *Threatened birds of Africa and related islands.* The ICBP/IUCN Red Data Book, part 1. 3rd edition. ICBP/IUCN, Cambridge, U.K. 797 pp.

Collar, N.J. and Stuart, S.N. (1988). *Key forests for threatened birds in Africa.* ICPB Monograph No. 3. International Council for Bird Preservation, Cambridge in collaboration with the IUCN Species Survival Commission, Gland, Switzerland. 102 pp.

Davey, S. (1991). World Heritage natural sites under threat. *WWF News* 72.

GTZ (1979). *Parc national de Taï.* Etat actuel des Parcs Nationaux de la Comoé et de Taï ainsi que de la Réserve d'Azagny et propositions visant à leur développement aux fins de promotion du tourime, Vol 3. GTZ, Eschborn, Germany.

Guillaumet, J.L. (1967). Recherches sur la végétation et la flore de la région du Bas-Cavally (Côte d'Ivoire). *Mém. Orstom* 20: 1–247.

Guillaumet, J.L. and Adjanohoun, E. (1971). La végétation. In *Le milieu naturel de la Côte d'Ivoire. Mém. Orstom* 50: 157–263.

Hazeu, G.W. and Sloot, P.H.M. (in prep.). *Bibliographie de la region de Taï, sud-ouest de la Côte d'Ivoire.* Tropenbos Foundation, Wageningen, The Netherlands.

Huttel, C. and Bernhard-Reversat, F. (1975). Recherches dur l'écosystème de la forêt subéquatoriale de basse Côte d'Ivoire, 5. *La Terre et la Vie* 2: 203–228.

IUCN/UNEP (1987). *IUCN directory of Afrotropical protected areas.* IUCN, Gland, Switzerland and Cambridge, U.K. 1034 pp.

Mangenot, G. (1955). Etude sur les forêts des plaines et plateaux de la Côte d'Ivoire. *Etud. Eburn.:* 4, 5–61.

Marshall, P. (1990). Optimistic outlook for Taï National Park. *WWF Reports:* June–July (1990).

Seneviratne, G. (1990). Taï: a National Park under threat. *WWF News* 68.

Stattersfield, A.J., Crosby, M.J., Long, A.J. and Wege, D.C. (in prep.). *A global directory of Endemic Bird Areas.* BirdLife International, Cambridge, U.K.

## Acknowledgements

This Data Sheet was prepared by Dr Alan C. Hamilton (WWF).

# MONT NIMBA
## Guinea, Côte d'Ivoire and Liberia

**Location:** The Nimba massif is situated on the border between Guinea, Côte d'Ivoire and Liberia, centred on latitude 7°39'N and longitude 8°30'W.

**Area:** c. 480 km².

**Altitude:** 450–1752 m (summit of Mont Richard Molard).

**Vegetation:** Lowland and transitional rain forest, grasslands.

**Flora:** >2000 vascular plant species so far recorded, c. 13 species endemic; a number of species shared with other mountains of West Africa.

**Useful plants:** Gene pool of timber trees (e.g. *Heritiera*, *Triplochiton*) and oil palm (*Elaeis guineensis*).

**Other values:** Watershed protection, rich fauna. Identified by ICBP as a "Key Forest for Threatened Birds".

**Threats:** Mining of iron ore, some clearance for agriculture, poaching of animals.

**Conservation:** Guinea: Strict Nature Reserve (130 km²), Biosphere Reserve (171 km²). Côte d'Ivoire: Strict Nature Reserve (50 km²). Both reserves form a World Heritage Site. Liberia: proposed Nature Reserve.

## Geography

Mont Nimba is a spectacular mountainous ridge of quartzite rich in iron ore, straddling the border between Liberia, Côte d'Ivoire and Guinea. It forms part of the "Guinean Backbone", along with the Loma Mountains in Sierra Leone, the Simandou and Ziama Mountains in Guinea and the Man Massif in the Côte d'Ivoire. Mont Nimba rises abruptly from the gentle slopes of the surrounding piedmont and reaches an altitude of 1752 m at the summit (Mont Richard Molard). The striking topography of Mont Nimba is due to a large ridge of hard iron-bearing quartzites, approximately 40 km long and with a maximum width of 12 km (in Guinea), exposed after erosion of the surrounding softer schists and granito-gneiss. These quartzites carry very poor skeletal soils, supporting summit grasslands and a belt of savanna vegetation at 500–550 m. The topography is very varied, with deep valleys, high plateaux, rounded hilltops, rocky peaks, abrupt cliffs and exposed granite blocks. The Nimba massif contains the sources of the rivers Cavally and Ya (which forms the Mami River of Liberia).

The mean annual temperature is 25°C at 550 m falling to 20°C at the summit (1752 m). The distribution of rainfall on the mountain is dictated mostly by the characteristics of the south-west monsoon, which reaches the Liberian part of the mountain first. Precipitation also increases with altitude. The combined result is a double rainfall gradient along and up the mountain, with concomitant variations in vegetation. Rainfall figures for September 1947 are as follows (Schnell 1952): 342 mm at the north-east foot of the mountain; a little more than 700 mm at 1700 m at the north-east end of the ridge; and 1200 mm at 1250 m at the south-west end of the ridge. At the summit, the mean annual rainfall is over 3000 mm. Interestingly, the rainy season is less prolonged at the summit than lower down, even though total rain is higher: this is because the summit stands above the cloud belt during the rainy season storms.

It is probable that there has never been any village settlements on the mountain proper, but there are 10 villages in the immediate vicinity, with several thousand inhabitants who are mainly agriculturalists (IUCN/UNEP 1987). The town of Lola is 20 km distant.

## Vegetation

The lowlands and foothills up to about 900–1200 m are mostly covered by Guineo-Congolian rain forest, Nimba being located within the Guinea (West African) Rain Forest unit. Dominant trees include *Heritiera Tarrietia) utilis*, *Lophira alata*, *Milicia regia* (=*Chlorophora regia*), *Morus mesozygia*, *Terminalia ivorensis* and *Triplochiton scleroxylon*. Drier mid-altitude forests are found at the northern end of the massif and include *Parkia bicolor*, *Piptadeniastrum africanum* and *Triplochiton scleroxylon*. Most of the surviving forests are found in Guinea.

At mid-altitudes above 1000 m, forests are dominated by *Parinari excelsa*. These forests are often covered by cloud resulting in a lush growth of epiphytes. This forest type has been referred to as a "mist forest" (Coe and Curry-Lindahl 1965; Colston and Curry-Lindahl 1986). There are extensive grasslands above the forest in the north-east part of the Nimba massif. Gallery forest extends into the grassland only in sheltered ravines and gullies between 1000 and 1600 m. Most of the summit area is covered by high altitude grassland dominated by *Loudetia kagerensis*, with *Protea occidentalis* on slopes. Forest at high altitude occurs in the southern part of the ridge, which are in the direct path of the south-west monsoon. High-altitude forests include Myrtaceae. The tree fern *Cyathea cylindrica* var. *mannii* occurs in ravines.

See Adam (1966, 1970, 1971) and Jaeger and Adam (1975) for details of the vegetation.

## Flora

The flora of Mont Nimba is rich, with over 2000 species of vascular plants recorded (Adam 1971–1984). Of these, about 16 were previously thought to be endemic to the mountain; however, a number of these species have since been reduced to synonymy or have been found elsewhere. Thus, *Blaeria nimbana* is now *Blaeria mannii* (also found in Cameroon), while *Dolichos nimbaensis* is now known also to occur in Sierra Leone. *Asplenium schnellii* could be endemic, but has not been refound. Several other species are near-endemics, re-occurring on mountains elsewhere in West Africa. The floristic importance of Mont Nimba is due mainly to its geographical isolation, varied relief and altitudinal range and the presence of a variety of soil types. The forests are the most species-rich of the communities, while the higher altitude woodlands and grassland have relatively few species. The following floristic elements are present (Schnell 1952): endemic element c. 1%; West African montane endemic element 5%; West African non-forest element 6%; West African forest element 15%; Equatorial African forest element 30%; Afrotropical element 25%; Palaeotropical element 2.5%; and Pantropical element 4%.

## Useful plants

Mont Nimba contains gene pools of timber trees such as *Heritiera utilis* (niangon) and *Triplochiton scleroxylon* (samba). *Elaeis guineensis* (oil palm) is very abundant in secondary vegetation.

## Social and environmental values

Mont Nimba has a rich fauna, today much depleted numerically through uncontrolled hunting by mine workers (F.N. Hepper 1993, *in litt.*). More than 500 species have been described or reported, including several mammals (such as the lesser otter shrew (*Micropotamogale lamottei*), (a primitive insectivore which represents a monotypic genus), more than 10 amphibians and reptiles, several fish, arthropods and molluscs. Mammals present include leopard (*P. pardus*), golden cat (*Felis aurata*), African civet (*Civetticus civetta*), several species of genet (*Genetta* spp.), colobus monkeys (*Colobus polykomos* and *C. badius*), diana monkey (*Cercopithecus diana*), chimpanzee (*Pan troglodytes*) and potto (*Perodicticus potto*). The viviparous toad (*Nectophrynoides occidentalis*, Vulnerable on a world scale) occurs in montane grasslands at 1200–1600 m and is the only tail-less amphibian in the world that is totally viviparous (IUCN/UNEP 1987). Over 20 species of invertebrates are endemic (Lamotte 1983).

The Upper Guinea lowland rain forests support 12 endemic and 9 near-endemic bird species (Allport 1991), of which 8 are globally threatened (Collar and Andrew 1988) and 6 have restricted-ranges (Stattersfield *et al.*, in prep.). All but two of these species have been recorded on Mont Nimba, almost all associated with the Guineo-Congolian rain forest in the lowlands and foothills. The white-eyed prinia (*Prinia leontica*), the only bird species endemic to the West African montane habitats of the "Guinean Backbone", is found on the higher parts of Mont Nimba.

This site is considered to be a "key forest for threatened birds" (Collar and Stuart 1988).

Mont Nimba was "discovered" in 1899, with scientific exploration of the plants beginning in 1909 by A. Chevalier. A Flora was completed in 1984 (Adam 1971–1984). Zoological and geological inventories have also been made. The scientific value of Mont Nimba has been enhanced by research on high altitude grassland phytosociology, primate studies and meteorological recording. With appropriate facilities, Nimba could become a site for tropical ecology of international importance (IUCN/UNEP 1987).

Mont Nimba is an important water catchment area, containing the sources of the Cavally and Ya rivers (the latter becoming the Mami River in Liberia).

## Threats

The major threat is mining of iron ore in the Liberia and Guinean. Massive deposits of high-grade iron-ore (c. 72% pure iron) were discovered in 1955. Exploitation began in 1963 and continues today, along with the working of alluvial diamond deposits. 8 million tonnes of iron ore had been extracted by 1985 and preliminary studies indicated that more than 300 million tonnes of high-quality ore remain to be exploited in the northern Guinean portion alone (Lamotte 1983). About 60 km$^2$ of the mountain are threatened (IUCN/UNEP 1987). Mining has already devastated large areas of vegetation in the Liberian section. Roads, wells and mineshafts have been built and workshops and townships established in an area within the Strict Nature Reserve in Guinea. In Liberia, huge quantities of rock have been removed from large areas of the mountain and many streams are polluted with heavy metals. The Liberian portion of the mountain has been severely damaged, both as a result of excavation and the dumping of capping waste. This has resulted in siltation of rivers and the death of riverine vegetation. Plans were well advanced in 1992 to commence exploiting ores from the Guinean part of Mont Nimba (Anon. 1992). The project, if it proceeds, will create 600 jobs and generate US$ 20,000,000 per annum. The main obstacle to the project is the security situation in Liberia, which prevents the efficient functioning of the railway line along which the ore will reach the coast. The railway through Guinea may be extended to Nimba in order to carry the Guinean ore with greater security.

The influx of probably over 200,000 people to the area has resulted in pressure on the use of land for agriculture and poaching of the local fauna for bush-meat. Forests have been extensively cleared. In Liberia, virtually all of the forests have already been destroyed, except along the River Iti where anyway, there is no protection (Collar and Stuart 1988); in Côte d'Ivoire, some relict patches of forest still remain; in Guinea, the forests are generally intact, but there is little foothill forest, since the northern foothills lie within the forest/savanna ecotone (Collar and Stuart 1988). Enforcement of conservation legislation has proved inadequate.

Some timber concessions have been granted for commercial exploitation of the forests (Verschuren 1983).

In 1991, the World Heritage Committee requested the Guinea to place Mont Nimba on the "World Heritage in Danger" list, pending resolution of the mining threat.

## Conservation

Côte d'Ivoire established the Réserve Naturelle Intégrale de Mont Nimba (IUCN Management Category: I – Strict Nature Reserve) in 1943. It is designated as a "forêt classée" and is under national ownership, managed by the State Forestry Service. It covers an area of 50 km².

In Guinea, the Réserve Naturelle Intégrale de Mont Nimba (IUCN Management Category: I – Strict Nature Reserve) covers 130 km². It was established in 1944. However, prospecting for minerals and sport-hunting are allowed in the reserve. In the case of the Côte d'Ivoire, tourism is prohibited. Both reserves form a World Heritage Site, gazetted in 1981 (Guinea) and 1982 (Côte d'Ivoire). The Mont Nimba Biosphere Reserve was established in 1980 and covers an area of 171 km² in Guinea. It includes a core zone of 100 km².

Unesco has initiated discussion towards formation of a multinational park, but, until this has been accepted by all three countries, it is imperative that as much effort as possible is made by the individual countries to protect their own portions. Rehabilitation of the degraded parts of the mountain would help to create a buffer zone for the World Heritage Site. Some conservationists believe the resources generated by mining could pay for a comprehensive conservation programme for the region (Anon. 1992).

## References

Adam, J.G. (1966). La végétation du Mont Nimba au Libéria et sa protection. *Notes Africaines* 112: 113–122.

Adam, J.G. (1970). Flore descriptive des Monts Nimba. *Mém. Mus. Hist. Nat. Paris* Ser. B. 20: 5–528.

Adam, J.G. (1971-1984). *Flore descriptive des Monts Nimba (Côte d'Ivoire, Guinée, Libéria).* Editions CNRS, Paris. 6 vols. 2181 pp. Vols. 1–4 published in *Mém. Mus. Hist. Nat. Paris* Ser.B. 20 (1971); 22 (1971); 24 (1974); 25 (1975).

Allport, G. (1991). The status and conservation of threatened birds in the Upper Guinea Forest. *Bird Cons. Int.* 1: 53–74.

Anon. (1992). Iron ore mining on Mount Nimba, Guinea. *IUCN Forest Conservation Programme Newsletter* 12: 8.

Coe, M. and Curry-Lindahl, K. (1965). Ecology of a mountain: first report on Liberian Nimba. *Oryx* 8: 177–184.

Collar, N.J. and Andrew, P. (1988). *Birds to watch: the ICBP world checklist of threatened birds.* Technical Publication No. 8. International Council for Bird Preservation, Cambridge, U.K.

Collar, N.J. and Stuart, S.N. (1988). *Key forests for threatened birds in Africa.* ICPB Monograph No. 3. International Council for Bird Preservation, Cambridge in collaboration with the IUCN Species Survival Commission, Gland, Switzerland. 102 pp.

Colston, P.R. and Curry-Lindahl, K. (1986). *The birds of Mount Nimba, Liberia.* British Museum (Natural History), London, U.K.

IUCN/UNEP (1987). *The IUCN directory of Afrotropical protected areas.* IUCN, Gland, Switzerland and Cambridge, U.K. xix, 1034 pp.

Jaeger, P. and Adam, J.G. (1975). Les fôrets de l'étage culminal du Nimba Libérien. *Adansonia* 2: 177–188.

Lamotte, M. (1983). The undermining of Mount Nimba. *Ambio* 12: 174–179.

Schnell, R. (1952). Végétation et flore de la région montagneuse du Nimba (Afrique occidentale française). *Mémoire de l'Institut Fondamental d'Afrique Noire* 22: 598 pp.

Stattersfield, A.J., Crosby, M.J., Long, A.J. and Wege, D.C. (in prep.). *A global directory of Endemic Bird Areas.* BirdLife International, Cambridge, U.K.

Verschuren, J. (1983). Conservation of tropical rain forest in Liberia: recommendations for wildlife conservation and national parks. IUCN/WWF, Gland, Switzerland. (Unpublished.)

## Acknowledgements

The text of this Data Sheet is based upon a preliminary draft prepared by Stephen J.M. Droop (Royal Botanic Gardens, Edinburgh, U.K.). Professor Maxime Lamotte (Paris, France), Laurent Gautier (Conservatoire et Jardin botaniques, Geneva, Switzerland) and F. Nigel Hepper (Royal Botanic Gardens, Kew, U.K.) provided helpful comments and additional data.

# SAPO NATIONAL PARK
## Liberia

**Location:** Eastern Liberia, between latitudes 5°15'–5°40'N and longitudes 8°10'–8°50'E.
**Area:** 1307 km².
**Altitude:** Mostly c. 100–400 m, rising to c. 1400 m at the summit of Mount Putu.
**Vegetation:** Lowland rain forest.
**Flora:** Upper Guinea phytogeographical zone of the Guineo-Congolian region.
**Useful plants:** Many plants used locally.
**Other values:** Important faunal reserve, catchment protection.
**Threats:** Potentially logging; extent of hunting unknown, but could be a threat.
**Conservation:** National Park (IUCN Management Category: II) created in 1983 but under-resourced.

## Geography

Sapo National Park (area: 1307 km²), established in 1983, is the largest remaining block of rain forest in Liberia. It lies in eastern Liberia, 70 km north of the coastal city of Greenville, between latitudes 5°15'–5°40'N and longitudes 8°10'–8°50'E. The Sinoe River forms the long northern boundary of the park.

The park is mostly topographically subdued at c. 100 m altitude, rising in the east to c.1400 m (Mt Putu), where there are steep ridges and many rivers and streams. There are considerable areas of swamp. The rock is of Precambrian gneiss and the soils are acidic.

The mean annual temperature is c.25.5°C (value at Monrovia, at some distance); a temperature range of 22°–28°C has been recorded within the park (Andersen, Williamson and Carter 1983). Annual rainfall at the coast (Greenville) is 4100 mm, but being inland Sapo is drier. An annual mean of 2596 mm has been recorded at Basintown (4 km west of the park, in the direction of the coast) over 5 years of measurement (Carter 1987).

## Vegetation

Although Liberia is the most forested country in West Africa (c. 40% of Liberia still having forest cover), there is very little information on the forests (Anstey 1991). At the time of writing, Carter (1987), reports that there had been only three research projects in Sapo National Park, one on chimpanzees (Andersen, Williamson and Carter 1983), one concerned with park establishment and his own (on birds).

Sapo is covered by lowland rain forest. Andersen, Williamson and Carter (1983) estimated the relative cover of different forest types as: primary and mature secondary forest (63%), young secondary forest (11%), seasonally inundated forest (13%) and swamp forest (13%). The canopy averages 25 m in height (range 12–32 m) (Carter 1987). There are some abandoned farms.

## Flora

Floristically, Sapo belongs to the Upper Guinea zone of the Guineo-Congolian Regional Centre of Endemism. Verschuren (1983) lists the following trees as occurring in Sapo: *Brachystegia leonsis*, *Herrietia* sp. and *Tetraberlinia tubmaniana*. White (1983) lists some trees characteristic of the Upper Guinea forests generally, including *Coula edulis*, *Gluema ivorensis*, *Olfieldia africana*, *Soyauxia grandifolia* and, among Caesalpiniaceae, *Brachystegia leonensis*, *Cynometra ananta*, *C. leonensis*, *Gilbertiodendron preussii* and *Monopetalanthus compactus*. There are fewer species of gregarious Caesalpiniaceae than in the forests east of the Dahomey Gap. In addition to various endemic Upper Guinea forest species, there are also many others which are widely distributed in African lowland rain forests.

## Useful plants

Stephens (1988) reports that forest plants are used by local people for many purposes, including as sources of materials for building, household utensils, rattan products and medicines. From a survey, she reports that most people use, and prefer, traditional medicine, turning to western medicine only as a second choice.

## Social and environmental values

The park is uninhabited, but people are settled all around the boundaries at a low population density. Nearly all these people are subsistence farmers, their main crop being dryland rice grown as part of a system of shifting cultivation. A socio-economic and health survey by Stephens (1988) revealed that many local people are highly dependent on bushmeat for protein.

Sapo is one of the richest forests in West Africa for forest animals (IUCN/UNEP 1987). Among the species present, those with very restricted distributions outside Liberia include Jentink's duiker, zebra duiker, western red colobus, Diana monkey, pygmy hippopotamus and Liberian mongoose (Anstey 1991). A survey of primates and duikers in Liberia seems not to have sampled in Sapo (Dunn 1991).

The Upper Guinea lowland rain forests support 12 endemic and 9 near-endemic bird species (Allport 1991), of which 8 are globally threatened (Collar and Andrew 1985) and 6 have restricted-ranges (Stattersfield *et al.*, in prep.). 114 species of birds are recorded from Sapo, including seven of the species endemic to the Upper Guinea forest and 3 threatened species (Carter 1987, Collar and Stuart 1985). It is believed that the actual species total could be over 200, and that most of the endemic and near-endemic species are likely to occur (Carter 1987; Allport 1991). This site is considered to be a "key forest for threatened birds" (Collar and Stuart 1988).

The forest protects catchments of the Rivers Sinoe and Dugbe.

## Threats

Logging showed a massive increase in Liberia during the 1970s and 1980s (Dunn 1991) and is a serious potential threat to Sapo. There has been one encroachment into the park by a logging company (in 1985); this was stopped by the Forestry Development Authority (Carter 1987).

The extent of (illegal) hunting in the park has not been determined, but hunting must be regarded as a major potential threat given the great contribution of bushmeat to people's diets.

There is some alluvial mining near the park.

## Conservation

Sapo National Park was declared in 1983; formerly, it was part of Sapo National Forest Reserve. Subsequently, park development has concentrated on building an infrastructure, boundary demarcation, conservation education and promotion of tourism. A management plan was produced in 1986; this recognises a buffer zone about one mile wide around the park, in which certain sustainable activities, including harvesting of wildlife, are permitted. The park is said to be under-resourced (IUCN/UNEP 1987). A WWF project started in 1989 was forced to close in 1990, following a breakdown in national security.

Remarks in Stephens (1988) suggest that some local people show a degree of antagonism towards the park. She suggests that this could be greatly reduced if destruction of crops by wildlife could be prevented.

## References

Allport, G. (1991). The status and conservation of threatened birds in the Upper Guinea Forest. *Bird Cons. Int.* 1: 53–74.

Andersen, J.R., Williamson, E.A. and Carter, J. (1983). Chimpanzees of Sapo Forest, Liberia: density, tools and meat-eating. *Primates* 24: 594–601.

Anstey, S. (1991). *Conservation and management of Sapo National Park*. Final report of WWF Project 3216. WWF, Gland, Switzerland.

Carter, M.F. (1987). *Initial avifaunal survey of Sapo National Park, Liberia*. Report to WWF. WWF, Gland, Switzerland.

Collar, N.J. and Andrew, P. (1988). *Birds to watch: the ICBP world checklist of threatened birds*. Technical Publication No. 8. International Council for Bird Preservation, Cambridge, U.K.

Collar, N.J. and Stuart, S.N. (1985). *Threatened birds of Africa and related islands*. The ICBP/IUCN Red Data Book, part 1. 3rd edition. ICBP/IUCN, Cambridge, U.K. 797 pp.

Collar, N.J. and Stuart, S.N. (1988). *Key forests for threatened birds in Africa*. ICPB Monograph No. 3. International Council for Bird Preservation, Cambridge in collaboration with the IUCN Species Survival Commission, Gland, Switzerland. 102 pp.

Dunn, A. (1991). *A study of the relative abundance of primate and duiker populations in Liberia*. WWF/FDA wildlife survey. WWF, Gland, Switzerland. 89 pp.

FDA/IUCN (1991). *Integrated management and development plan for Sapo National Park and surrounding areas in Liberia*. IUCN, Gland, Switzerland. 66 pp.

IUCN/UNEP (1987). *IUCN directory of Afrotropical protected areas*. IUCN, Gland, Switzerland and Cambridge, U.K. 1034 pp.

Stattersfield, A.J., Crosby, M.J., Long, A.J. and Wege, D.C. (in prep.). *A global directory of Endemic Bird Areas*. BirdLife International, Cambridge, U.K.

Stephens, C. (1988). *Environmental and nutrition survey, Sapo National Park*. Report for WWF. WWF, Gland, Switzerland.

Verschuren, J. (1983). *Conservation of tropical rain forest in Liberia. Recommendations for wildlife conservation and National Parks*. IUCN/WWF Project 1567. Report to the Government of Liberia. Gland, Switzerland.

White, F. (1983). *The vegetation of Africa: a descriptive memoir to accompany the Unesco/AETFAT/UNSO vegetation map of Africa*. Natural Resources Research XX. Unesco, Paris. 356 pp.

## Acknowledgements

This Data Sheet was prepared by Dr Alan C. Hamilton (WWF).

# FOREST ZONE, RIVER DJA REGION
## Cameroon

**Location:** East of Zoatélé-Bengbis and west of Lomié, between 2°45'–3°25'N and 12°30'–13°22'E.
**Area:** c. 8100 km².
**Altitude:** 200–500 m.
**Vegetation:** Dense Guineo-Congolian tropical evergreen rain forest of the type found in the Cameroon-Congo area, swamp vegetation, secondary forests.
**Flora:** c. 2000 vascular plants species. Typical of evergreen forests of the Cameroon-Congo area, with stands of *Gilbertiodendron dewevrei*.
**Useful plants:** Timber trees, plants producing essential oils, a few medicinal plants.
**Other values:** Forest resources used by forest peoples, rich fauna.
**Threats:** Cocoa, coffee and subsistence plots encroach on reserve; poaching of animals.
**Conservation:** Dja Réserve de Faune covers 5260 km². Accepted as a Biosphere Reserve in 1981. Proposed as a National Park.

## Geography

The forested massif of the Dja loop is geographically very well defined. It lies completely within the strip of land which is bounded to the north by the River Dja, flowing from east to west, and to the south by the same river, flowing west to east. It is situated to the east of the Zoatele-Bengbis boundary and to the west of Lomie, between 2°45'–3°25'N and 12°30'–13°22'E, 243 km. It is south-east of Yaoundé.

The average altitude is low, between 200 and 500 m, without any marked relief. The substratum consists of schists and quartzites of the Mbalmayo-Bengbis series, ranging in age from Precambrian to Cambrian. These rocks give rise to soils of average to very high clay content (typically pure red earths).

The area has an equatorial Guinean-type climate with four seasons: two dry seasons and two rainy seasons. The average annual rainfall is between 1500 and 2000 mm. Rainfall peaks are in May and September. The average annual temperature is 25°C. August is the coolest month, with a mean monthly minimum of 18°C and a maximum of 27°C. April is the hottest month, with a mean minimum temperature of 19°C and a maximum of 30°C.

Population density is low; a few Pygmies live within the reserve. There are a few urban settlements in the immediate surroundings. A few main roads pass close by the area; some run through a tiny part of the northern section, where there are a few small settlements.

## Vegetation

The forested massif of the Dja loop is part of the Cameroon-Congo evergreen forest zone (Letouzey 1985) of the Guinean-Congolian rain forest region. Physiognomically, it is characterized by tall evergreen trees, sometimes reaching 60 m. Emergent trees are normally quite scattered in the forest and their crowns are often tabular. Smaller trees tend to have straight stems and are evergreen. Shrubs of the undergrowth also tend to be single-stemmed.

The forest abounds in cauliflorous trees, epiphytes and lianas. The stems of the lianas often grow to very large diameters. Generally speaking, the herb layer is sparse limited to light spots.

Some general floristic characteristics which differentiate this forest from formations elsewhere in Cameroon include an absence of semi-deciduous plants, including among understorey Acanthaceae, virtual absence of gregarious Caesalpiniaceae (with the exception of *Gilbertiodendron dewevrei*), abundance of rattans and common stands of *Uapaca paludosa* (Euphorbiaceae) along riverbanks.

## Flora

Knowledge of the flora is still incomplete, but it is estimated that there are c. 2000 vascular plant species. Characteristic trees of this region include: *Afrostyrax lepidophyllus* (garlic tree), *Anthonota ferruginea, Baphia pubescens, Beilschmiedia louisii, Cryptosepalum congolanum, Drypetes paxii, Entandrophragma congoense, Erismadelphus exsul* var. *platyphyllus, Fernandoa ferdinandii, Heisteria trillesiana, Irvingia excelsa, I. robur, Lebruniodendron leptanthum, Licania elaeosperma, Manilkara letouzeyi, Millettia laurentii, Oddoniodendron micranthum, Oldfieldia africana, Omphalocarpum procerum, Pentaclethra eetveldeana, Pericopsis elata, Pseudospondias microcarpa* var. *longifolia, Tessmannia africana, T. lescrauwaetii* and *Vincentella* sp. *Gilbertiodendron dewevrei* forms almost pure stands in valleys with sandy or sandy-clay soils, as well as on valley slopes with red clay soils.

Typical small and large shrubs include many species of *Drypetes*, such as *D. calvescens, D. capillipes, D. chevalieri, D. cinnabarina, D. gracilis* and *D. inaequalis*. Other typical shrubs include *Alchornea floribunda, Beilschmiedia corbisieri,*

*Bertiera bicarpellata, B. globiceps, B. iturensis, Cassipourea congoensis, Cavacoa quintasii, Diospyros hoyleana, D. iturensis, Ficus natalensis, Irvingia smithii, Lepidobotrys staudtii, Magnistipula cupheiflora, Oriciopsis glaberrima, Oxystigma buchholzii, Scytopetalum pierreanum, Synsepalum letouzeyi, S. stipulatum, Vepris louisii* and *Warneckea fosteri.*

Among the lianas there are large populations of rattans belonging to the following genera: *Ancistrophyllum, Eremospatha, Oncocalamus* and, more rarely, *Calamus. Millettia duchesnei* is a very characteristic liana; *Tetracera* spp. are also very common. In the undergrowth on dry terrain there are large patches of the acaulescent palm *Raphia regalis. Uapaca paludosa* is typical of riverbanks, where it forms very extensive stands. *Baillonella toxisperma* (a large member of the Sapotaceaee) spreads over a vast area in the Guinean region and is relatively abundant in the Dja forest where it does not, however, appear to be regenerating.

Finally, it is worth noting the abundance of Raphia palms, which are found in a number of valleys: *Raphia cf. monbuttorum* is very common, but there are other species which await taxonomic study.

Other types of vegetation includes swamp vegetation, old secondary forest around villages (abandoned in 1946) and recently abandoned cocoa and coffee plantations.

## Useful plants

The local people, especially the Pygmies, use a wide range of plant resources for many purposes. Potentially commercial species include those yielding timber and essential oils. The more valuable timber species occur at low densities. The seeds of *Baillonella toxisperma* yield a valuable vegetable oil.

## Social and environmental values

The forest provides important biological resources for local people. Traditional hunting is legally permitted. On the other hand, commercial hunting for sale of bushmeat is regarded as a major threat to the integrity of the forest ecosystem. However, it is very difficult to distinguish between the two types of hunting in practice.

The fauna includes a wide range of primates. These include lowland gorilla (*Gorilla gorilla gorilla*), great white-nosed guenon (*Cercopithecus nicitans*), moustached guenon (*C. cephus*), crowned guenon (*C. pogonias*), talapoin (*Miopithecus talapoin*), white-collared mangabey (*Cercocebus torquatus*), white-cheeked mangabey (*C. albigena*), agile mangabey (*C. geleritus*), mandrill (*Mandrillus sphinx*), Angolan black and white colobus monkey (*Colobus angolensis*) and chimpanzee (*Pan troglodytes*). Other mammals include elephant (*Loxodonta africana*), buffalo (*Syncerus caffer*) and leopard (*Panthera pardus*).

Six restricted-range bird species occur in the lowlands between south-east Nigeria and Gabon, of which 5 are found in Guineo-Congolian rain forest. Several of these are likely to occur in the forests of the River Dja region, and the restricted-range Dja River scrub-warbler (*Bradypterus grandis*) may occur in more open areas, but this is an ornithologically poorly-known region and none have yet been recorded there. However, this site is considered to be a "key forest for threatened birds" (Collar and Stuart 1988).

## Threats

The forest of the proposed National Park has not suffered any serious damage because of its isolated location away from large built-up areas and main roads. However, this situation could change, since commercial logging activities are taking place close to the reserve boundary. There is also some encroachment through the establishment of plots for cocoa, coffee and subsistence agriculture. The rapid population increase is likely to place more pressure on the forests.

## Conservation

Dja Réserve de Faune (5260 km²) was established in 1950 and was accepted as a Biosphere Reserve in 1981. The area is proposed as a National Park. Dja is the focus of an IUCN/ WWF project, with the objective of conserving the forest, including through a programme of education in conservation. An EEC-funded buffer zone project will promote agro-forestry and sustained yield charcoal production around Dja Biosphere Reserve (Sayer, Harcourt and Collins 1992).

## References

Collar, N.J. and Stuart, S.N. (1988). *Key forests for threatened birds in Africa.* ICPB Monograph No. 3. International Council for Bird Preservation, Cambridge in collaboration with the IUCN Species Survival Commission, Gland, Switzerland. 102 pp.

Gartlan, S. (1989). *La conservation des ecosystèmes forestiers du Cameroun.* IUCN, Gland, Switzerland and Cambridge, U.K. 186 pp.

IUCN/UNEP (1987). *The IUCN directory of Afrotropical protected areas.* IUCN, Gland, Switzerland and Cambridge, U.K. xix, 1034 pp.

Letouzey, R. (1968). *Etude phytogéographique du Cameroun.* Editions P. Lechevalier, Paris. 508 pp.

Letouzey, R. (1985). *Notice de la carte phytogéographique du Cameroun au 1:500,000.* Fasc. 4: 95–107.

Mildbraed, J. (1922). *Wissenschaftliche Ergebnisse der Zweiten deutschen Zentral-Afrika Expedition 1910–11.* Band 2, Botanik. Leipzig. 202 pp.

Sayer, J.A., Harcourt, C.S. and Collins, N.M. (eds) (1992). *The conservation atlas of tropical forests: Africa.* Macmillan, London. 288 pp.

## Acknowledgements

This Data Sheet was prepared by Dr J.F. Villiers (Laboratoire de Phanérogamie, Musée National d'Histoire Naturelle, Paris). Dr F.J. Breteler (Agricultural University, Wageningen, The Netherlands) provided valuable comments on an earlier draft.

GUINEO-CONGOLIAN REGIONAL CENTRE OF ENDEMISM: CPD SITE AF12

# KORUP NATIONAL PARK
## Cameroon

**Location:** Between latitudes 4°53'–5°28'N and longitudes 8°42'–9°16'E in Ndian Division, South-West Province. It shares c. 25 km of its western boundary with Nigeria along the Akpa Korup river, between latitudes 5°02'–5°11'N. It lies c. 50 km inland from the coast.

**Area:** 1259 km².

**Altitude:** Only 1% of the park lies above 850 m, including the highest point, Ekundukundu Mountain (1075 m); 17% of the park is below 120 m elevation.

**Vegetation:** Lowland Guineo-Congolian evergreen rain forest, including riverine forest; some secondary forest, rock communities; swamps.

**Flora:** c. 3500 vascular plant species. 836 vascular plant species described so far; c. 400 tree species so far recorded. As many as 5% narrowly endemic species. Korup is a centre of diversity for several tree genera.

**Useful plants:** Medicinal plants, palm canes, chewing sticks, *Raphia* palm, oil palm, bush mango, other fruit trees.

**Other values:** Traditional hunting grounds, diverse fauna, watershed protection, tourism.

**Threats:** Some encroachment along Nigerian border; unsustainable levels of harvesting of bush mango, chewing sticks and palm canes; illegal hunting.

**Conservation:** National Park; totally protected by Presidential Decree No. 86/1283 of October 1986.

## Geography

Korup National Park lies between latitudes 4°53'–5°28'N and longitudes 8°42'–9°16'E in the Ndian Division of South-West Province, Republic of Cameroon. It shares c. 25 km of its western boundary with Nigeria along the Akpa Korup river, between latitudes 5°02'–5°11'N, and is contiguous (in part) with Cross River National Park (CPD Site Af24 – see Data Sheet) in south-east Nigeria. It lies c. 50 km inland from the coast in the Bight of Biafra.

The topography is flat to hilly and mountainous. There are many streams and rivers and three main drainage basins. The soils are poor, acidic and infertile; some are very sandy.

There is a single dry season and a single wet season. The wettest months are July to September and the driest months are December, January and February. The southern part of the park receives about 5 m of rain annually; the north receives about half this amount. There are, on average, only 1023 hours of sunshine per year in the coastal plain (an average of 2.8 hours/day).

The human population occurs at very low densities of less than 2 persons/km² within the park.

## Vegetation

Korup lies within the Biafran rain forest block (Letouzey 1968) of the Guineo-Congolian Regional Centre of Endemism. The Biafran forest is a lowland evergreen association, covering, in total, about 65,200 km² in wet coastal areas with a protracted rainy seasons. It extends from between the Niger and Cross Rivers of eastern Nigeria, south towards the Congo River and east towards the Sangha River. The floral and faunal diversity of this zone is very high and there are

many endemics. This zone is extremely important in terms of conservation priorities and is highly endangered from logging and other human population pressures. Korup is therefore a highly significant protected area in this forest zone.

Although the forests of Korup contain many gregarious Caesalpiniaceae, a characteristic of the Biafran forest is that the most dominant family (in terms of numbers of trees) is the Scytopetalaceae (endemic to Africa), mainly represented by *Oubanguia alata*. As with other lowland rain forests around the Gulf of Guinea, from Oban (south-east Nigeria) to Gabon, the forests of Korup show remarkable affinities with the forests of South America (as noted under the Flora section).

The ecological and biological characteristics of Korup are largely the result of past climatic change. Africa has had a chequered climatic history, with numerous warm, wet phases interspersed with periods of cool, dry climate. The present climate of Africa is relatively benign, with the extent of the rain forest close to its Quaternary maximum. In contrast, as recently as 12,000 years ago the climate was much cooler and drier and the rain forest biome was much reduced. Present evidence seems to indicate that the forests along the coast, including Korup, have persisted even during periods of cool, dry climate. The result is that Korup possesses exceptionally high biological diversity.

## Flora

A total of 836 vascular plant species has so far been described from Korup, about 400 of these being trees. As many as 5% of species are narrowly endemics. It is estimated that the park includes some 3500 vascular plant species

(S. Gartlan 1991, personal estimate). A study by Gentry (pers. comm. 1988) counted over 200 species of woody plants in a sample site of 0.1 ha, a level of plant diversity comparable with the highest in the world. Korup is a centre of diversity for several tree genera. The most important families (in terms of species numbers) are Rubiaceae, Caesalpiniaceae, Euphorbiaceae, Sterculiaceae and Annonaceae.

The forests of Korup show some remarkable affinities with those of South America. Among the trees, *Erismadelphus exsul* (Vochysiaceae) and *Saccoglottis gabonensis* (Humiriaceae) belong to families poorly represented in Africa, but which are abundant in South America. *Andira inermis* (Papilionaceae), which has a very local distribution in the Biafran forest zone, is also found in South America.

**MAP 5. KORUP NATIONAL PARK (CPD SITE Af12) AND CROSS RIVER NATIONAL PARK (CPD SITE Af24)**

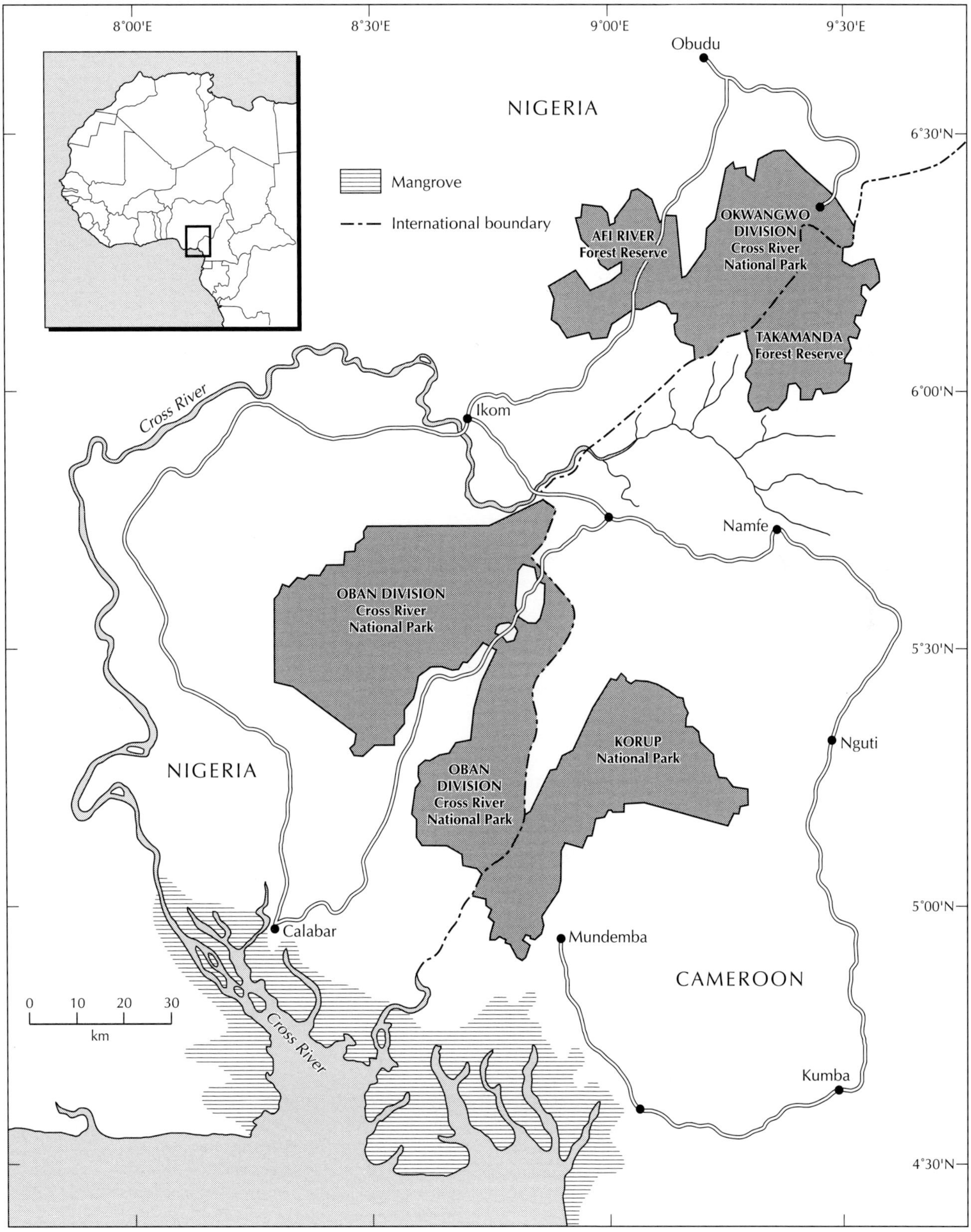

**A new road being pushed through the forest close to Korup National Park (CPD Site Af12).**
Photo: Alan C. Hamilton.

Korup is a centre of diversity for the genera *Cola* (Sterculiaceae), *Diospyros* (Ebenaceae), *Dorstenia* (Moraceae) and *Garcinia* (Guttiferae). Many narrow endemics occur in the forest, including: *Camplyospermum (Ouratea) dusenii* (Ochnaceae), *Deinbollia angustifolia, D. saligna* (Sapindaceae), *Hymenostegia bakeri* (Caesalpiniaceae), *Medusandra* sp. (probably *M. mpomiana*) (Medusandraceae) and *Soyauxia talbotii* (Medusandraceae). However, not all of these are strictly endemic to Korup.

The forest zone in which Korup is situated exhibits strong affinities with forests in other African regions, suggesting past connections. For example, there are common species shared with the Ituri Forest of eastern Zaïre (CPD Site Af27) (e.g. *Diospyros gravilescens*), with the forests of the Congo basin (e.g. *Afzelia bipindensis, Dichostemma glaucescens, Diospyros bipindensis, D. crassiflora, D. hoyleana, Enantia chlorantha* and *Strombosiopsis tetrandra*, and with the forests of Upper Guinea (e.g. *Diospyros kamerounesis* and *D. piscatoria*).

Caesalpiniaceae are common at Korup (about two thirds of the 140 Cameroonian species are restricted to the coastal forests): many species are gregarious.

The northern sector of the Biafran forest in which Korup lies represents the southern and eastern limit of distribution of some tree species characteristic of West Africa, including *Microberlina bisulcata, Monopetalanthus hedinii, Terminalia ivorensis* and *Tetraberlinia polyphylla.*

A shrub community along the Ndian and nearby rivers includes some species known only from the type collections (e.g. *Camplyospermum dusenii, Deinbollia angustifolia, D. saligna* and *Eugenia dusenii*). Another distinct type of forest occurs along the banks of the larger rivers and streams. This riverine forest includes *Fagara* sp. (Rutaceae), *Lecomtedoxa klaineana* (Sapotaceae) and *Vitex rivularis* (Verbenaceae). This forest is of great significance for Korup's endemic red colobus monkey.

Old secondary forests appear to be more important for tree species of commercial value than the primary forests, which are mainly dominated by Caesalpiniaceae. The north-east part of the park could, therefore, provide genetic resource material for species of commercial interest, such as *Afzelia pachyloba, Guarea cedrata, Lophira alata, Microberlinia bisulcata, Milicia (Chlorophora) excelsa, Terminalia superba* and *T. ivorensis.*

## Useful plants

Oil palm (*Elaeis guineensis*), the world's premier oil-producing plant, is found native in Korup, as is its major and most effective pollinator, the weevil *Elaeidobius kamerunicus*, which was exported to South East Asia in 1981 resulting in a rise in production of almost 20% within one or two years, vastly increasing profits.

A WWF nursery at Korup growing seedlings of the climber *Ancistrocladus korupensis*, a species of possible value for development of a pharmaceutical drug. It is vital that local people and the National Park receive some benefits if a new drug is developed, to give them added incentives to conserve the forest and to raise their technical capacities to do so. Photo: Alan C. Hamilton.

There are several species of known medicinal importance at Korup, including *Ancistrocladus korupensis* (Ancistrocladaceae), *Erythroxylum mannii* (Erythroxylaceae) and *Pausinystalia johimbe* (Rubiaceae), the alkaloids of the former being active against the HIV virus *in vitro*. *Thaumatococcus leons* (Marantaceae) has also been collected from Korup. This has potential commercial value as a non-nutritive sweetener.

Species which may be of potential importance for genetic resource conservation include several species of Rubiaceae, tentatively identified as species of *Coffea*. *Diospyros crassiflora* (ebony) also occurs in Korup.

Cane used in basket and furniture weaving is an important product of the Korup forest. It is principally produced from species of the palm genera *Ancistrophyllum*, *Eremospatha* and *Oncocalamus*. Chewing sticks (*Garcinia* spp.) are an important economic product, as is *Irvingia gabonensis*, the bush-mango. Palm wine is produced from *Raphia* sp. and this is distilled into illicit gin.

## Social and environmental values

The Korup forest is the traditional hunting area of the Korup people, to whom it has great cultural and social significance.

The park contains most of the mammalian species endemic to the Niger-Sanaga Pleistocene refuge, such as *Arctocebus calabarensis*, *Cerocebus torquatus*, *Colobus pennanti preussi* (red colobus), *Mandrillus leucophaeus* and *Potamogale velox*. The fauna also includes species of wider distribution in the Guinea-Congolian forest, such as forest elephant (*Loxodonta africana cyclotis*), forest buffalo (*Syncerus caffer nanus*), red river hog (*Potamochoerus porcus pictus*) and chimpanzee (*Pan troglodytes*). Korup is particularly important for its primate fauna, one of the richest and most diverse in Africa. Cameroon possesses about half of Africa's total of some 52 primate species and Korup shelters about one quarter of Cameroon's primate species.

Six restricted-range bird species occur in the lowlands between south-east Nigeria and Gabon, of which 5 are found in Guineo-Congolian rain forest. Four of these have been recorded in or near to Korup National Park, including the globally threatened yellow-footed honeyguide (*Melignomon eisentrauti*), grey-necked rockfowl (*Picathartes oreas*) and Bates's weaver (*Ploceus batesi*). This site is considered to be a "key forest for threatened birds" (Collar and Stuart 1988). A total of 314 bird species has been observed in Korup and its immediate vicinity.

The forest protects the water catchment of the Rio del Rey, a valuable offshore fishery. It also has potential for development of ecotourism.

## Threats

There is some encroachment from Nigeria. Bush mango, chewing stick and palm canes are collected from the forest and are traded with villages in Nigeria. Chewing stick and cane are probably being harvested unsustainably. There is illegal hunting and trapping around the villages located within the park and from the town of Mundemba and an adjacent oil palm plantation. Poaching of elephants for ivory and for meat is a continuing problem.

## Conservation

Korup National Park receives the highest category of legal protection possible in Cameroon. It is totally protected by Presidential Decree No. 86/1283 of 30 October 1986.

## References

Cleaver, K., Munasinghe, M., Dyson, M., Egli, N., Peuker, A. and Wencellius, F. (eds) (1992). *Conservation of west and central African rainforests*. World Bank Environmental Paper No. 1. World Bank, Washington, D.C. 354 pp.

Cloutier, A. and Dufresne, A., (1986). *Plan de Gestion, Parc National de Korup, Cameroun*. Parcs Canada, Québec, Canada. 59 pp.

Collar, N.J. and Stuart, S.N. (1988). *Key forests for threatened birds in Africa*. ICPB Monograph No. 3. International Council for Bird Preservation, Cambridge in collaboration with the IUCN Species Survival Commission, Gland, Switzerland. 102 pp.

Gartlan, J.S., Newbery, D.Mc.C., Thomas, D.W. and Waterman, P.G. (1986). The influence of topography and soil phosphorus on the vegetation of the Korup Forest Reserve, Cameroun. *Vegetatio* 65: 131–148.

Gartlan, S. (1985). *The Korup regional management plan: conservation and development in the Ndian Division of Cameroon*. WWF, Switzerland. 170 pp.

Gartlan, S. and Macleod, H. (eds) (1986). *Proceedings of the Workshop on Korup National Park, Mundemba, Ndian Division, South-West Province, Republic of Cameroon*. WWF, Switzerland. 117 pp.

Gartlan, S. and Momo, D. (1986). A new approach to conservation. *IUCN Bulletin* 17 (1–3): 27.

Gartlan, S. et al. (1992). Cameroon. In Sayer, J.A., Harcourt, C.S., and Collins, N.M. (eds), *The conservation atlas of tropical forests: Africa*. Macmillan. Pp. 110–118.

Letouzey, R. (1968). *Etude phytogéographique du Cameroun*. Editions Paul Lechevalier, Paris. 508 pp.

UNDP (1992). *Environment and sustainable development for Cameroon*. Republic of Cameroon, Ministry of Environment and Forests. Report of Multi-Disciplinary and Multi-Institutional Mission on the Environment, Yaounde. 73 pp.

## Acknowledgements

This Data Sheet was prepared by Dr Stephen Gartlan (WWF Representative, Cameroon). Dr Martin Cheek (Royal Botanic Gardens, Kew) offered helpful comments on an earlier draft.

# MOUNT CAMEROON
## Cameroon

**Location:** South-west Cameroon, on the coast of the Gulf of Guinea. The main peak is at 4°7'N, 9°10'E.

**Area:** Main massif with long axis running SW to NE, about 45 km long and 30 km wide.

**Altitude:** 0–4095 m.

**Vegetation:** Lowland evergreen forest, patches of coastal mangroves and swamp forest, stream vegetation in foothills, submontane forest (two types), montane forest, montane and subalpine prairies. Lava-flow communities at various stages of recolonization at all altitudes. Within the lowland and submontane belts, the forest is interspersed or replaced by meadows or scrub in places.

**Flora:** Estimated 3500 vascular plant species in South-West Province (in which Mount Cameroon lies). Main massif with c. 42 strictly endemics, c. 50 nearly endemic species (occurring also on Fernando Po, Bamenda Highlands or Mt Oku). Foothills poorly known, but also with high endemism: 4 strictly endemic genera.

**Useful plants:** Timber trees, medicinal and food plants, many species in international trade.

**Other values:** Tourism (guided tours to summit and ecotourism).

**Threats:** Timber poaching, clearance for agriculture, fire.

**Conservation:** Protected areas: Bambuko Forest Reserve (266.8 km²); in the foothills, mostly in a band c. 20 km wide around the main massif: Meme River Forest Reserve (51.8 km²), Mokoko River Forest Reserve (90.7 km²), Mouyouka-Kompina Forest Reserve (50 km², but only 20 km² still intact), Mungo River Forest Reserve (46.6 km²), Southern Bakundu Forest Reserve (194.3 km²). Proposed protected areas: Etinde Reserve (c. 360 km²), Mabeta-Moliwe Reserve (c. 36 km²).

## Geography

Mount Cameroon (4095 m) is the highest peak in West Africa. It is an active volcano, erupting about every 20 years. There are no really abrupt peaks apart from the subsidiary and older, non-active Mount Etinde (c. 1700 m) in the south-east part of the main massif. Soils are mostly on young volcanic rocks, very fertile and free draining; there are virtually no streams and extremely few springs on the main massif. The surrounding foothills are up to c. 400 m high, mostly of older volcanic rock, less fertile and sometimes with abrupt ridges; their valleys are drained by numerous streams.

Rainfall varies from over 10 m per annum in the south-west, at Debundscha (one of the world's three wettest places), to 2 m per annum in the mountain's rainshadow in the north-east (Hawkins and Brunt 1965).

## Vegetation

The vegetation of the southern part of the main massif (the proposed Etinde Reserve) has been described by Thomas and Cheek (1992), on which this account is based. Previous descriptions of the vegetation include Maitland (1932), Boughey (1955), Keay (1955), Richards (1963a), Guillaume (1968), Hall (1973) and Thomas (1985). Nine vegetation types in four belts can be recognized (Thomas and Cheek 1992), on a system based on those of Letouzey (1968a, 1985) and Hedberg (1951).

The lowland evergreen belt extends from sea-level to c. 800 m. *Hypselodelphys* forms a species-poor scrub, with tall herbs such as *Aframomum*, covering large areas on the west and south-west slopes, to the exclusion of lowland forest. Moving from west to east along the southern slopes, the forest cover gradually increases until, on the south-eastern slopes, the scrub becomes patchy. The scattered trees include *Macaranga monandra*, *Neoboutonia glabrescens*, *Tabernaemontana crassa* and *Zanthoxylum gilletii*.

Lowland forest is the most species-rich vegetation type, but most on the east and south-east slopes has been cleared. At sea-level along the southern slopes a belt of oil-palm plantations replaces forest up to 200 m. Some forest remains on the surrounding foothills and is extremely varied in composition. The best known sites botanically are Southern Bakundu (Richards 1963b) and Mabeta-Moliwe (Cheek 1992a). The latter is about 36 km² in extent, contains at least 250 species of tree and has patches of mangrove and swamp forest. Frequent emergents are *Ceiba pentandra* and *Desbordesia glaucescens*. The most abundant trees are *Tapura africana*, three species of *Schefflera* and several species of Myristicaceae.

The submontane belt extends from c. 800–1700 m altitude. Three vegetation types can be recognized: meadows, closed canopy forest and discontinuous canopy forest.

Meadows have a dense layer of erect and climbing herbs c. 1 m high, dominated by Commelinaceae, Compositae, Labiatae, Marantaceae, *Aframomum*, and *Piper*. Scattered trees of *Macaranga occidentalis*, *Neoboutonia mannii* and *Vernonia insignis* occur.

Closed canopy forest is mostly restricted to the older, volcanically inert Mount Etinde. It is more species-rich, with a higher proportion of Guineo-Congolian and Afromontane species than the discontinuous canopy forest. It is notably rich in Sapotaceae (*Afrosersalisia* sp., *Aningeria robusta*, *Englerophytum* (*Bequaertiodendron*) sp., *Gambeya* (*Chrysophyllum*) spp., with *Garcinia smeathmannii* being locally dominant, especially on ridge tops. Other common tree species include *Beilschmeidia* sp., *Bersama abyssinica*, *Camptostylis ovalis*, *Cephaelis peduncularis*, *Cola verticillata*, *Cyathea mannii*, *Dasylepis racemosa*, *Dicranolepis vestititus*, *Drypetes* sp., *Guarea glomerulata*, *Ixora foliosa*, *Leptaulus daphnoides*, *Peddiea* sp., *Placodiscus* sp., *Pseudagrostistachys africanus*, *Psychotria camptopus*, *Symphonia globulifera*, *Trichilia prieureana*, *Trichoscypha* sp. and *Uvariodendron* sp.

Discontinuous canopy forest is very open in structure, with large areas of meadow. Common tree species are *Harungana madagascariensis*, *Kigelia africana*, *Macaranga monandra*, *M. occidentalis*, *Neoboutonia mannii* and *Polyscias fulva*. Stands of monocarpic Acanthaceae occur in the understorey.

**The montane belt** extends from c. 1700–2800 m with three vegetation types: montane forest, montane scrub and prairie.

Montane forest has a wider range of species than montane scrub. The main species are *Agauria salicifolia*, *Allophylus bullatus*, *Clausena anisata*, *Hypericum lanceolatum*, *Ilex mitis*, *Lasiosiphon glaucus*, *Maesa lanceolata*, *Myrica arborea*, *Nuxia congesta*, *Pittosporum mannii*, *Prunus africana*, *Rapanea melanophloeos*, *Schlefflera abyssinica*, *S. mannii*, *Syzygium staudtii* and *Xylamos monospora*. The understorey is often dominated by large herbs of Acanthaceae and Labiatae exhibiting synchronous flowering, e.g. *Mimulopsis solmsii*, *Oreacanthus mannii* and *Plectranthus insignis*.

Montane scrub occurs above the forest, forming a narrow band between the forest and prairie, with outliers in gullies and on lava outcrops extending up into the subalpine belt. Scrub apparently acts as a buffer against fire invading the forest. The principal trees found in montane scrub are *Agauria salicifolia*, *Hypericum lanceolatum*, *Lasiosiphon glaucus*, *Maesa lanceolata*, *Myrica arborea* and *Pittosporum mannii;* this scrub is 5–15 m high and the trees are usually well laden with lichens and other epiphytes, particularly ferns and orchids. *Clematis simensis* and *Stephania abyssinica* are common climbers. *Vernonia calvoana*, *V. insignis* and *Crassocephalum mannii* are treelets commonly found in previously burned areas. Shrubs include *Blaeria mannii* and *Phillipia (Erica) mannii*. The herb layer is diverse and dense, especially in formerly burnt areas. Notable species are *Cynoglossum amplifolium*, *Galium simense*, *Geranium ocellatum*, *G. simense*, *Pteridium aquilinum*, *Rumex abyssinicus*, *Rumex bequartii* and numerous Compositae, notably species of *Anisopappus*, *Dichrocephala*, *Senecio*, *Sonchus* and *Vernonia*. In the dryer season, montane scrub is often invaded by fire spreading from the prairie above.

Montane prairie occurs at the upper edge of the montane belt and is characterized by a dense sward of grasses often dominated by *Loudetia camerunensis*; *Andropogon lima* and *Pennisetum monostigma* are also common. Herbs which are particularly common include *Cyanotis barbata* and *Trifolium simense*. Giant *Senecio* and *Lobelia* species, characteristic of East African mountains, are notably absent, although *Lobelia columnaris* reaches c. 3 m tall and pachycaul species of *Helichrysum* can be found.

On old lava outcrops and steep slopes where grass is sparser, terrestrial orchids are found, e.g. *Brownleea parviflora*, *Habenaria* spp. and *Holothrix tridentata*. Other common herbs are *Coreopsis monticola*, *Crassula alba*, *Hesperanthera alpina*, *Hypoxis camerooniana*, *Romulea camerooniana*, *Swertia* spp. and *Umbilicus* sp.

Seasonally wet areas sometimes occur between the grass clumps, species present include *Commelina africana* var. *mannii*, *Holothrix tridentata*, *Radiola linoides*, *Utricularia livida* and *Wahlenbergia* sp.

**The subalpine belt**, with prairie vegetation, occurs above c. 2800 m and is dominated by scattered tussocks of grasses and sedges, particularly *Andropogon amethystinus*, *A. distachyus*, *A. lima*, *A. mannii*, *Bulbostylis erratica*, *B. capillaris*, *Deschampsia mildbraedii*, *Festuca abyssinica*, *Koeleria cristata*, *Sporobolus montanus* and *Tripogon major*. Herbs include *Crepis cameroonica*, *Galium thunbergianum*, *Silene biafrae*, *Veronica mannii* and *Wahlenbergia*. The occasional shrubs include *Adenocarpus mannii* and *Blaeria spicata*. With increasing altitude the vegetation becomes sparser and poorer in species.

## Flora

The main massif has about 42 strictly endemic species (i.e. only occurring on Mount Cameroon) and 50 near endemic species, (i.e. species also occurring in one or two places nearby) (Thomas and Cheek 1992). 29 of the 50 near endemic species also occur on Fernando Po (Bioko) about 30 km to the south in the Gulf of Guinea; others occur in the Bamenda highlands to the north.

A high proportion of the endemic species of the main massif occur in the grassland above the forest or at the forest/grassland boundary. 19 out of the 42 strict endemics and 19 out of the 50 near-endemic species occur in these areas. The majority of the high-altitude endemic species are neoendemics, i.e. suspected to be of relatively recent origin.

Palaeoendemic species, as exemplified by monotypic genera, seem to be richest in the foothills. Examples are *Neoschumannia kamerunensis* (Asclepiadaceae: Man O'War Bay), *Oxygyne triandra* (Burmanniaceae: Moliwe), *Ossiculum* (Orchidaceae: Mungo) and two species of *Medusandra* (Medusandraceae: S. Bakundu, Kumba, N. Korup to Mamfe). *Batesanthus purpureus* (Asclepiadaceae) occurs on Mount Cameroon, but is comparatively widespread, occurring also in Nigeria, Bamenda and Mabeta-Moliwe.

The apparent paucity of palaeoendemic species on the main massif of Mount Cameroon compared to the foothills and surrounding forests, where they are more common, is probably due to the relatively recent origin of Mount Cameroon, even though the general area is believed to be an important Pleistocene refuge. The mountain erupts at intervals of c. 20 years, with lava flows sometimes extending down to the sea. This probably explains why the foothill areas, secure from lava, are richer in palaeoendemic species than the main massif.

The foothill forests have attracted less botanical attention than the main massif, but are just as important for endemic species. A recent investigation of one such area, Mabeta-Moliwe, resulted in many new records for the forest. Among the interesting species present are *Afrothismia pachyantha*, *Afrothismia winkleri*, *Oxygyne triandra* and several rare species of forest *Burmannia*.

Frequent volcanic activity may be linked to the curious absence on Mount Cameroon of montane taxa occurring in highland areas nearby. Examples are the conspicuous mountain bamboo (possibly *Sinarundinaria alpina* (known from Bamenda and widespread in Africa), *Podocarpus latifolius* (known from Mt Oku, Bamenda and widespread elsewhere in Africa) and *Protea elliottii* (Bamenda and widespread in West Africa).

## Useful plants

Timber extraction occurs from sea-level to c. 1200 m. The most valuable timber trees are *Diospyros gracilis*, *Entandophragma* spp., *Khaya* spp. (these last two genera being African mahoganies), *Lophira alata*, *Milicia excelsa* (Iroko), *Piptadeniastrum africanum* and *Pterocarpus soyauxii*.

No exhaustive survey of non-timber forest products has been completed, though an initial study was made by Burford (1990). Wild plants are important sources of food (*Dacryodes edulis*, *Elaeis guineensis*, *Gnetum africanum*, *Irvingia gabonensis* (bush mango), *Solanum* spp. and *Treculia africana*). Spices are obtained from *Aframomum* spp., *Afrostyrax camerunensis*, *Monodora* spp., *Piper guineense* and *Xylopia aethiopicum*. Medicinal plants include *Eremomastax* spp., *Mucuna flagellipes*, *Prunus africana*, *Rauvolfia* spp. and *Salacia* spp. Snacks come from *Cola ficifolia*, *Lavigeria macrocarpa*, *Myrianthus arboreus* and *Thaumatococcus daniellii*. Tools are made from *Carpolobia alba*. *Garcinia mannii* is a good source of chewing sticks. Building materials are obtained from *Culcasia* spp., *Cyathea mannii* and *Triumfetta* spp. *Canarium schweinfurthii* is a source of insect repellants and illumination and craft materials for cane furniture and basket production are obtained from *Laccospermum opacum*, *Pandanus* spp. and *Raphia farinifera*.

Horticulturally important plants with potential in international and local trade are the numerous and colourful species (several endemic) of *Impatiens* and *Begonia*. Gesneriaceae and Orchidaceae also have potential. Some species, e.g. *Ficus lyrata* and *Platycerium stemaria*, are already in trade, but, despite the presence of a botanic garden at Limbe, plant nurseries in the area mostly grow exotic species.

## Social and environmental values

Mount Cameroon is the home of the Bakweri people, who cultivate up to c. 1200 m altitude on the main massif and also utilise a wide variety of wild plants (see above). Wild animals are also hunted, providing important sources of protein and income. In the forest, cane rat, porcupine and monkey are hunted; in the grassland prairie, antelope and elephant. Bushmeat is sold far afield as a gourmet item. Chimpanzee, traditionally taboo, are numerous but declining taboos breaks down (Gadsby and Jenkins, pers. comm.). Butterfly collection is also a source of income for the local people.

Although permanent streams are absent on the main mountain, numerous springs and rivers arise at its foot and supply local villages and towns, e.g. Limbe, with unusually clear water.

Mount Etinde is regarded as sacred and libations are performed by Bakweri elders on climbing the peak.

Tourism is increasing on Mount Cameroon. Climbing to the peak from Buea has become a well-organized affair and a "thing-to-do" on the overland route across Africa. Three huts for shelter have been built on the path. An international mountain race, sponsored by Guinness Cameroon, attracts television coverage and is the single most important sporting event in the region.

Limbe, at the foot of the mountain, is one of the two top coastal resorts in Cameroon, attracting crowds each weekend from Douala, the biggest city, drawn by the spectacular scenery and cool breezes associated with the mountain.

The submontane and montane habitats on Mount Cameroon are part of the Cameroon Mountains Endemic Bird Area (EBA), which includes the mountains of Bioko and the mountain chain which follows the border between Cameroon and Nigeria. Twenty of the 28 restricted-range bird species of the EBA have been recorded on Mount Cameroon, including Cameroon francolin (*Francolinus camerunensis*) and Cameroon speirops (*Speirops melanocephalus*) which are endemic to the mountain. The Guineo-Congolian rain forests at the base of the mountain are part of the Cameroon and Gabon lowlands EBA, which extends from south-east Nigeria to Gabon. Four of the six restricted-range bird species of this EBA have been recorded here, including the threatened grey-necked rockfowl (*Picathartes oreas*) and Bates's weaver (*Ploceus batesi*). This site is considered to be a "key forest for threatened birds" (Collar and Stuart 1988).

## Threats

Timber poaching is well organized in the area. The east and south-east side of Mount Cameroon formerly supported large populations of important timber trees, such as *Aningeria robusta*, *Entandrophragma angolensis* and *Milicia excelsa*, but these are now severely depleted. There have been no legal logging concessions proposed recently, although the granting of such is a possibility.

Clearing for agriculture by small scale farmers, often following in the wake of loggers, is a threat. Encroachment has led to the conversion of large areas of lowland and submontane forest and natural scrubland to agriculture.

*Prunus africanus* bark has been extensively harvested from montane forest on the south-east side of the mountain, sometimes with considerable damage to the trees. A recent concession has been granted for harvesting for the whole of the montane belt.

Long term studies are needed to assess whether annual burning of the montane prairie is a threat to endemic or rare plant species.

## Conservation

The following protected areas have been established:

❖ Bambuko Forest Reserve, covering an area of 266.8 km² on the west side of the massif, and, in the foothills, mostly in a band c. 20 km wide around the main massif:

- ❖ Meme River Forest Reserve, covering 51.8 km² of the foothills to the north;
- ❖ Mokoko River Forest Reserve covering 90.7 km² of the foothills to the north-west;
- ❖ Mungo River Forest Reserve, covering 46.6 km²;
- ❖ Southern Bakundu Forest Reserve, covering 194.3 km² of the foothills to the north-east; Mouyouka-Kompina Forest Reserve (50 km², of which 20 km² are still intact) almost adjoining southern Bakundu to the east.

The following protected areas are proposed by the Limbe Project (see below):

- ❖ Etinde Reserve (c. 360 km², at the southern end of the massif);
- ❖ Mabeta-Moliwe Reserve (c. 36 km², in the south-eastern foothills).

Unfortunately, much of the Southern Bakundu Forest Reserve was reportedly clear-felled in the 1960s. It was high in biodiversity and contained a species of a new discovered Medusandraceae (*Medusandra richardsiana*), which may now be extinct there (F.N. Hepper 1993, *in litt.*). The proposed Mabeta-Moliwe Reserve has been demarcated, but the proposed Etinde Reserve has not yet been completely demarcated.

The "Limbe Project" was started in 1988, jointly supported and staffed by the Forestry Department, Cameroon, and the O.D.A., U.K., advised and supported by the Royal Botanic Gardens, Kew (Cheek 1992b). This project actively patrols the proposed Etinde and Mabeta-Moliwe reserves. It also co-ordinates scientific research and has conducted detailed plant species inventories. The project is based at the Limbe Botanic Garden (established in 1892) which functions as a regional education centre in rain forest conservation and houses a herbarium of c. 5000 named specimens from the Mt Cameroon area.

# References

Boughey, A.S. (1955). The vegetation of the mountains of Biafra. *Proc. Linn. Soc. Lond.* 165: 144–150.

Burford, N. (1990). *Kpe-Mboko ethnobotanical investigations and survey.* Compiled for the Limbe Botanic Garden Rainforest and Genetic Conservation Project.

Cheek, M. (1992a). *Botanical survey of the proposed Mabeta-Moliwe Forest Reserve.* Report on the Limbe Gardens Conservation Project. Royal Botanic Gardens, Kew. 112 pp.

Cheek, M. (1992b). The Limbe Botanic Garden and Genetic Resources Project (Kew/O.D.A./Govt. of Cameroon). *AETFAT Bulletin* 39: 72.

Collar, N.J. and Stuart, S.N. (1988). *Key forests for threatened birds in Africa.* ICPB Monograph No. 3. International Council for Bird Preservation, Cambridge in collaboration with the IUCN Species Survival Commission, Gland, Switzerland. 102 pp.

Gartlan, J.S. (1989). *La conservation des ecosystèmes forestiers du Cameroun.* IUCN Tropical Forest Programme. IUCN, Gland, Switzerland and Cambridge, U.K. 196 pp.

Guillaume, G.M.D. (1968). Quelques considérations sur les biotypes forestiers de la Province de Victoria en relation avec les facteurs du milieu. *Bull. IFAN ser. A* 30(3): 896–910.

Hall, J.B. (1973). Vegetational zones on the southern slopes of Mount Cameroon. *Vegetatio* 27: 49–69.

Hawkins, P. and Brunt, M. (1965). *Soils and ecology of West Cameroon.* FAO, Rome.

Hedberg, O. (1951). Vegetation belts of the East African mountains. *Svensk. Bot. Tidskr.* 45: 140–202.

Keay, R.W.J. (1955). Montane vegetation and flora in the British Cameroon. *Proc. Linn. Soc. Lond.* 165: 140–143.

Letouzey, R. (1968a). *Etude phytogéographique du Cameroun.* Editions P. Lechevalier, Paris.

Letouzey, R. (1968b). Les botanistes au Cameroun. *Flore du Cameroun* vol. 7. Museum National d'Histoire Naturelle, Paris.

Letouzey, R. (1985). *Notice de la carte phytogeographique du Cameroun.* 2 – Revision afromontanarde et étage submontagnard (pp. 27–62); 4 – Domaine de la forêt dense humide toujours verte (pp. 95–142). Centre des Cartes de Végétation, Toulouse.

Maitland, T.D. (1932). The grassland vegetation of the Cameroons Mountain. *Kew Bull.* 9: 417–425.

Richards, P.W. (1963a). Ecological notes on West African vegetation 3. The upland forests of Cameroons Mountain. *Journal of Ecology* 51: 529–554.

Richards, P.W. (1963b). Ecological notes on West African vegetation 2. The lowland forest of the Southern Bakundu Forest Reserve. *Journal of Ecology* 51: 123–149.

Thomas, D.W. (1985). Vegetation in the montane forests of Cameroon. In Stuart, S.N. (ed.), *Montane forests of Cameroon.* International Council for Bird Preservation, Cambridge.

Thomas, D.W. and Cheek, M. (1992). *Vegetation and plant species on the south side of Mount Cameroon in the proposed Etinde Reserve.* Royal Botanic Gardens, Kew. 37 pp.

# Acknowledgements

This sheet was written by Dr Martin Cheek (Royal Botanic Gardens, Kew, U.K.) and Dr Duncan Thomas (Department of Forest Products, Oregon State University). Joseph B. Besong (Forestry Department, Cameroon), Dr Stephen Gartlan (WWF, Cameroon) and F. Nigel Hepper (Royal Botanic Gardens, Kew, U.K.) provided additional material.

# MAYOMBE
## Congo, Cabinda, Zaïre

**Location:** Extreme western Zaïre, between latitudes 5°00'–6°00'S and longitudes 12°00'–13°00'E (as described in this Data Sheet, but in a wider sense the CPD site extends northwards into Cabinda and western Congo).
**Area:** 2500 km² (proposed Biosphere Reserve).
**Altitude:** 150–350 m.
**Vegetation:** Lowland semi-evergreen forest, Zambezian savanna, wetlands.
**Flora:** >1100 vascular plant species. The forest is of Guineo-Congolian type, with some gregarious Caesalpiniaceae.
**Useful plants:** Timber trees; many locally used species.
**Threats:** Logging, charcoal production, encroaching agriculture.
**Conservation:** Proposed Biosphere Reserve.

Note: This centre of plant diversity extends from Zaïre northwards into Cabinda and Congo, but due to shortage of information this account deals only with that part lying within Zaïre.

## Geography

Mayombe (also spelt Maiombe and Mayumbe) is a part of Zaïre lying close to the sea (within 150 km), to the north of the River Zaïre, between latitudes 5°00'–6°00'S and longitudes 12°00'–13°00'E. It is part of a geomorphological unit based on an Appalachian-type mountain chain close to, and parallel with, the Atlantic coastline and running from Zaïre northwards through Cabinda, Congo and on into Gabon. The mountain chain is composed of Precambrian metamorphic rocks, such as schists, amphibolites, quartzites and gneiss. Soils on these Precambrian rocks are acidic and have a clay content of 1–26%. Alluvial soils also occur.

The climate of Mayombe and neighbouring Cabinda is of a humid tropical type. There is a strong maritime influence and the weather can change rapidly during the day. There is a rainy season from October to April, with a short dry break in January and February, and a long dry season from May to September. Annual precipitation is variable from year to year, averaging between 1155 and 1818 mm (Monteiro 1962; Lubini 1990). Atmospheric humidity is high throughout the year (averaging between 78 and 89%), including during the dry season, when it can be even more humid than during the rains. The mean annual temperature is 24.3°C at Luki (max. 33°C; min. 18°C). There are microclimatic differences between valleys and ridges, the former being more humid.

Mayombe and neighbouring Cabinda are densely populated, with an average of 65 inhabitants/km² in Zaïre and 10–50/km² in Cabinda. The people are mainly farmers, growing bananas, cassava, beans, rice, peanuts and taro for domestic consumption, and palm oil, coffee and cocoa for the market.

## Vegetation

Physiognomically, there are three main vegetation types of note within the area considered suitable for a Biosphere Reserve (see Conservation). The first of these is Guineo-Congolian semi-evergreen rain forest. This has been greatly reduced in extent by agriculture and logging. Gregarious Caesalpinaceae occur. Various successional post-cultivation vegetation stages can be seen. The second main vegetation type is savanna, containing Zambesian floristic elements. This is found in the plains. Finally, there is swamp vegetation, including, in the south, extensive areas of papyrus and other herbaceous plants.

## Flora

According to Robyns (1948), the forest is of Guineo-Congolian type, while the savanna contains Zambesian floristic elements. According to observations by Lubini (1990), the area of the proposed Biosphere Reserve (see Conservation) contains over 1100 vascular plant species, sub-species and varieties, belonging to 622 genera and 128 families. Well-represented families include the Apocynaceae, Caesalpiniaceae, Euphorbiaceae, Papilionaceae and Rubiaceae.

The following species have been noted, some of which appear to be endemic to Mayombe: *Aidia ochroleuca, Amphimas ferrigineus, Aningeria superba, Autranella congolensis, Begonia comperei, Beilschmiedia mayumbensis, Campylospermum cabrae, C. lecomtei, Cola brevipes, Croynanthe paniculata, Dalbergia gilbertii, Deinbollia acuminata, Desbordesia glaucescens, Diospyros piscatoria, D. viridicans, D. wagemansii* (and many other species of *Diospyros*), *Entandrophragma* spp., *Erythrophleum suaveolens, Gambeya lacourtiana, Ganophylum giganteum, Gilletiodendron kisantuense, Gossweilerodendron balsamiferum, Hunteria mayumbensis, Hymenostegia floribunda, Isolona dewevrei, Isomacrolobium isopetalum, Julbernardia brieyi, Leptonychia mayumbensis, L. wagemansii, Lovoa trichiloides, Manilkara microphylla, Mocquerysia epipetiola, Nesogordonia kabingaensis, Staudtia stipitata, Terminalia superba, Xylopia chrysophylla* and *X. toussaintii.* Rubiaceae are abundant in the understorey.

Species characteristically found in colonizing forest following agricultural clearance and in secondary forest include: *Anthocleista schweinfurthii, Caloncoba welwitschii, Canarium schweinfurthii, Funtumia* spp., *Harungana madagascariensis, Maesopsis eminii, Milicia excelsa, Musanga cecropioides, Myrianthus arboreus, Pycnanthus angolensis, Terminalia superba, Trema orientalis* and *Zanthoxylum gilletii.*

Savanna species include: *Adansonia digitata, Albizia versicolor, Anarcardium occidentale, Combretum camporum, Digitaria milanjana, Heteropogon contortus, Hyparrhenia filipendula, H. ruprechtii, Hyphaene guineensis, Sarcocephalus latifolia* and *Strychnos henningsii.*

In the northern marshes are found: *Brillantaisia patula, Macaranga saccifera, Mitragyna stipulosa, Scleria racemosa, Rhynchospora corymbosa, Thalia welwitschii* and *Trychyphrynium braunianum.* The aquatic prairie found in the southern marshes contains: *Cyperus papyrus, Echinochloa pyramidalis, E. stagnina, Phragmites mauritianus* and *Typha angustifolia.*

## Useful plants

Wild plants are used locally for many purposes, including for food, medicine, fuel, construction, craftwork and timber. Many species are over-harvested.

## Economic assessment

The main economic activity is logging which started in 1930. The principal timber species exported are *Aucoumea klaineana, Entandrophragma* spp., *Gossweilerodendron balsamiferum, Milicia excelsa* and *Terminalia superba.* Thirty-five per cent of Mayombe was under logging concessions in 1980. Tall trees are very rare today, except in places inaccessible to heavy vehicles. Charcoal production is also a significant industry, in this case for local markets. In time, cutting of trees for the charcoal industry is likely to result in complete destruction of some forest pockets (Vangu *et al.* 1982).

## Threats

Logging and charcoal production are the major causes of environmental degradation and tree loss throughout Mayombe. The growth of demand for charcoal for the towns of Boma, Moanda and Lukula will in future place even greater pressure on the remaining forests. Unless action is taken, a serious shortage of fuel will occur. An additional cause of forest destruction is clearance for agriculture.

## Conservation

There is a need for international coordination for the planning of the conservation of the vegetation and flora of the Atlantic forests of Zaïre and neighbouring countries. The creation of the Dimonika Biosphere Reserve in Congo, with an area of 1360 km$^2$, represents an important first step. Differences in the vegetation and flora further south suggest the advisability of creating an additional Biosphere Reserve, even if this is small. A challenge is the high population density in Cabinda and in this part of Zaïre. It is suggested that the following narrow area in Zaïre, abutting on the Cabinda border, would be suitable; it is an area of relatively low population density. The geographical coordinates are 12°30' to 13°00'E and 4°50' to 5°00'S. The altitude ranges from 150 to 350 m. In greater detail, the boundaries are: the River Lukula in the north (this is a tributary of the River Schiloanga); the River Lukunga to the east (this is a tributary of the River Zaïre); the River Zaïre or the Boma-Moanda road to the south; the Cabinda border to the west. The area is about 2500 km$^2$.

In fact, a regional development scheme based on the Biosphere Reserve concept was proposed for this region of Zaïre (Bas-Zaïre) in 1987. This invoked the core and buffer zone concept as follows: (1) a central core zone designated for total protection (this would include forests with abundant *Gilletiodendron kisantuense* and mature secondary forests near the Cabinda border); (2) an intermediate zone for agroforestry, based, for example, on the growing of bananas in combination with *Terminalia superba*; (3) an outer zone for cattle-raising and rice cultivation in marshy areas.

## References

Duvigneaud, P. (1949). La flore et la végétation du Congo méridional. *Lejeunia* 16: 95–124.

Lubini, C.A. (1990). La flore de la Réserve forestière de Luki (Bas-Zaïre). *Mitt. Inst. Allg. Bot. Hamburg* 23b: 135–154.

Monteiro, R.F.R. (1962). La massif forestier du Mayombe angolais. *Bois For. Trop.* 82: 3–17.

Robyns, W. (1948). Les territoires phytogéographiques du Congo belge et du Ruanda-Urundi. In *Atlas général du Congo Belge.* Inst. Roy. Col. Belge, Bruxelles.

Vangu, L., Elumesaku, D.J., Mabiala, M.K., Malele, M. and Nkiama, M. (1982). *Profil socio-économique du secteur forestier du Bas-Fleuve (Bas-Zaïre).* Publ. Serv. Permanent pour l'Inventoire Agricole et Forestier (S.P.I.A.F.). Départ. Env. Conserv. Nat. et Tour., Kinshasa (Zaïre).

## Acknowledgements

This Data Sheet was compiled by Professor C.A. Lubini (Laboratoire de Biologie, Gombe, Zaïre).

# CRISTAL MOUNTAINS
## Gabon

**Location:** Between latitudes 1°00'N (along the border with Equatorial Guinea) and the Equator (approximately along the line of the "Transgabonais" railway between Libreville and Franceville) and between longitudes 10°00'–11°00'E.
**Area:** c. 9000 km².
**Altitude:** c. 0–911 m.
**Vegetation:** Wet evergreen coastal Guineo-Congolian rain forest.
**Flora:** Estimated >3000 vascular plant species, including >100 strict endemic species.
**Useful plants:** Timber trees, especially *Aucoumea klaineana*, the most important timber tree of Gabon.
**Other values:** Watershed protection for hydroelectric dams and power stations. Potential for tourism.
**Threats:** Excessive hunting, potentially renewed logging.
**Conservation:** None.

## Geography

The Cristal Mountains comprise the north-eastern part of Estuaire Province, Gabon and are located between latitude 1°00'N (along the border with Equatorial Guinea) and the Equator (approximately along the line of the "Transgabonais" railway between Libreville and Franceville) and between longitudes 10°00'E and 11°00'E (along the course of the Abanga River). The central part of the area is drained by the Komo River and its major tributary, the Mbé River. The eastern part falls within the drainage of the Abanga River and its western affluents.

The Cristal Mountains are part of the Cameroon-Gabon plateau of the Precambrian African basement and consist mainly of granite, gneiss, migmatite, quartzite and amphibolite. Inselbergs occur in the north-east. The Precambrian rocks are deeply weathered into yellowish or red ferralsols rich in kaolinite. The terrain is rugged. Altitudes range from almost sea-level (where the Komo River drains into the Gabon Estuary) to around 900 m on several of the numerous mountain tops. The highest point is 911 m.

The climate is influenced by monsoon winds and rainfall is high. The north-west receives more than 3200 mm of rain per year, while the east receives 2000 mm. There is a marked dry season from June to September and a less pronounced dry spell in January to February. During dry periods, skies are very often cloud-covered and temperatures are somewhat reduced. Air humidity is high and drizzle is a common feature in the afternoons. The region is the wettest part of Gabon, with about 200 rainy days per year. The average annual temperature is 26°C, extremes of temperature being c. 14°C and 35°C.

## Vegetation

The wet coastal evergreen rain forest of the Cristal Mountains is within the wettest variant of the Guinea-Congolian regional centre of endemism of White (1983). Outside of Gabon, this forest type, though floristically slightly different, occurs in coastal Cameroon (EDICEF 1983).

The forest contains many species of trees belonging to the Caesalpiniaceae, many of which grow gregariously. Annonaceae, Burseraceae, Euphorbiaceae and Olacaceae are also well-represented in the tree flora. *Aucoumea klaineana* (Burseraceae), Gabon's most important timber tree, has been exploited during past logging activities.

According to Reitsma (1988), the forest does not exhibit distinct stratification. Although some emergent trees reach a height of c. 60 m, the majority of trees do not exceed 30 m. Lianas are common and include species of *Agelaea* and *Rourea* (Connaraceae). *Raphia* swamps occur in the forest but do not cover large areas. Huge acaulous *Raphia regalis* palms are found in the understorey of moist slope forests, but are never found growing on inundated soils.

Epiphytes (including lichens, hepatics, mosses, ferns, orchids and *Begonia*) cover the trunks and branches of trees at higher altitudes. In places, the shrub layer is well developed and floristically very rich, most notably including many species of Rubiaceae. Herbaceous vegetation is often luxuriant along creeks which often have steep banks. Acanthaceae, Araceae, Balsaminaceae and particularly Begoniaceae are well-represented in these areas.

Young secondary forest is dominated by *Musanga*.

## Flora

It is estimated that more than 3000 species of vascular plants occur in the Cristal Mountains (de Wilde 1991, personal estimate). This is nearly half the total vascular flora of Gabon (estimated at 7000 species, of which over 22% are endemic to Gabon according to Brenan, 1978). It is estimated that more than 100 species are endemic to the Cristal Mountains (de Wilde 1991, personal estimate).

Monographic study of the African Begoniaceae reveals that 49 out of a total of 114 species occur in Gabon. Among these, 18 are endemic to Gabon; most have very restricted ranges. *Begonia aggeloptera*, *B. anisosepala*, *B. erectocaulis*, *B. erectotricha* and *B. peperomioides* are known only from the Cristal Mountains.

In a sample plot of 1 ha, located in the eastern drier slopes of the mountains, Reitsma (1988) found 131 species of trees and lianas (>10 cm dbh), belonging to 95 genera and 32 families. A total of 160 species of flowering plants was counted in two subplots of 10 ´ 10 m. Included were 24 species of trees belonging to at least 13 genera of the Caesalpiniaceae. There were many individuals of the genera *Dialium*, *Gilletiodendron*, *Julbernardia* and *Monopetalanthus*.

Recently, several authors (e.g. Sosef 1992; Wilks 1990) have suggested that the Cristal Mountains were a Pleistocene forest refugium, along with the Chaillu Mountains and probably one or two smaller mountainous areas in Gabon. The flora and vegetation of the inselbergs are considered refugia for xerophytes and orophytes and indicate drier and cooler climates in the Pleistocene (Reitsma *et al.* 1992).

The Cristal Mountains are, therefore, of paramount importance as a centre of plant diversity.

## Useful plants

*Aucoumea klaineana* (okoumé) is by far the most important timber tree in the region. The boles are used in making high quality plywood; this species accounts for c. 90% of all Gabonese timber exports. About 15–20 other species are exploited for their timber.

The local population (which is small in numbers) uses *Raphia* for roofing and semi-wild oil palms for making palm wine and palm oil. Rattans of the genera *Ancistrophyllum*, *Eremospatha* and *Oncocalamus* are frequently used for construction purposes.

Numerous barks, resins, leaves and fruits of wild forest species are of great importance in the preparation of food and herbal medicines. Extracts of the leaves and bark of *Tabernanthe iboga* are rich in alkaloids and used in ceremonies. Attempts have been made to introduce *Tabernanthe* into western medicine (Bisset 1989).

## Social and environmental values

Six restricted-range bird species occur in the lowlands between south-east Nigeria and Gabon, of which five are found in Guineo-Congolian rain forest. At least one of these species has been recorded in the Cristal Mountains area, and a second may possibly occur.

Generation of hydroelectric power in the Mbé River basin supplies the capital, Libreville, with power. For this reason alone, maintenance of the vegetation in the water-catchment is of utmost importance.

The Cristal Mountains have potential for the development of ecotourism, being situated within a three-hours drive of Libreville. However, at present the mountains are almost inaccessible due to the poor condition of the roads following earlier logging operations.

## Threats

Logging ceased in the late 1980s and today there seems to be no serious threats to the flora and vegetation of the area. Renewed logging activity is a potential threat.

Illegal hunting eliminated most of a formerly dense elephant population. The fauna is continuously under threat from illegal hunting.

## Conservation

The Cristal Mountains have no protection and, so far as is known, there are no plans by government to establish any reserves in the area. An official plan for conservation is urgently needed to protect one of the very last more or less intact wet coastal evergreen rain forest areas in Africa.

## References

Bisset, N.G. (1989). *Tabernanthe*: uses, phytochemistry and pharmacology. *Wageningen Agricultural University Papers* 89: 19–26.

Brenan, J.P.M. (1978). Some aspects of the phytogeography of tropical Africa. *Annals of the Missouri Botanical Garden* 65: 437–478.

EDICEF (1983). *Géographie et cartographie du Gabon*. EDICEF, Paris.

Letouzey, R. (1968). *Etude phytogéographique du Cameroun. (Encyclopédie Biologique 69)*. Editions Paul Lechevalier, Paris.

Reitsma, J.M. (1988). *Forest vegetation of Gabon*. Tropenbos Technical Series 1. Tropenbos Foundation, Ede, The Netherlands.

Reitsma, J.M. *et al.* (1992). Flore et végétation des inselbergs et dalles rocheuses: première étude au Gabon. *Bulletin Museum National Histoire Naturelle, sect. B. Adansonia* 1: 73–97.

Saint-Aubin, G. de (1963). *La forêt du Gabon*. CTFT, Nogent-sur-Marne, France.

Sosef, M.S.M. (1992). New species of *Begonia* in Africa and their relevance to the study of glacial rain forest refuges. *Wageningen Agricultural University Papers* 91: 117–151.

White, F. (1983). *The vegetation of Africa: a descriptive memoir to accompany the Unesco/AETFAT/UNSO vegetation map of Africa*. Natural Resources Research XX. Unesco, Paris. 356 pp.

Wilks, Ch. (1990). *La conservation des ecosystèmes forestier du Gabon*. UICN, Gland, Switzerland and Cambridge, U.K. 215 pp.

## Acknowledgements

This Data Sheet was written by Dr J.J.F.E. de Wilde (Department of Plant Taxonomy, Wageningen Agricultural University, The Netherlands).

GUINEO-CONGOLIAN REGIONAL CENTRE OF ENDEMISM: CPD SITE AF24

# CROSS RIVER NATIONAL PARK
## Nigeria

---

**Location:** South-eastern Nigeria.

**Area:** 4227 km².

**Altitude:** 150–1700 m.

**Vegetation:** Lowland rain forest, freshwater swamp forest, montane forest (the latter is of very restricted occurrence in West Africa); grassland on the Obudu Plateau.

**Flora:** The lowland forest has the richest forest flora in Nigeria; there are numerous species of Annonaceae, *Diospyros* and *Cola*. Oban Hills includes c. 130 strict endemics.

**Useful plants:** Timber species, rattans, edible fruits and leaves, medicinal plants.

**Other values:** Rich forest fauna, water catchment area, tourist potential.

**Threats:** Unregulated hunting, possible threats from agricultural encroachment and logging, fires (northern part).

**Conservation:** National Park created in 1991.

---

## Geography

Cross River National Park in south-eastern Nigeria was created in 1991 by a decree of the Federal Government of Nigeria. The park lies within the latitudes of c. 5°00'–6°30'N and the longitudes c. 8°15'–9°30'E. In places, the park runs along the border with Cameroon, one section being contiguous with Korup National Park (CPD Site Af12, see separate Data Sheet and Map 5) in Cameroon. There are two divisions: the southern Oban Hills Division and the northern Okwangwo Division, separated by the Cross River and an intervening belt of land 50 km wide, carrying a mixed cover of forest and agriculture.

The Oban Division has an area of about 3000 km², with maximum dimensions of about 80 km from north to south and 65 km from west to east; the only significant road within the park runs north-east from Calabar to Ekang, dividing the park into western and eastern sections. This road has attracted ribbon development. The eastern sector of the Oban Division is contiguous with Korup National Park. The Okwangwo Division is about 50 km from north to south and 45 km from west to east. It is contiguous with the Takamanda Forest Reserve in Cameroon.

The terrain in the Oban Division is typically fairly steep, rising to over 1000 m on either sides of the Calabar-Ekang road. Land within the Okwangwo Division rises northwards and eastwards from the surrounding lowlands, from about 150 m to over 1700 m on the Obudu Plateau in the north-east. The topography is extremely complex with many ridge systems, isolated peaks and outcrops.

Drainage in the Oban Division is to the Cross River to the north and the Calabar, Kwa and Oban Rivers to the south. Drainage in the Okwangwo Division is mainly to the Cross River via the Oyi, Okon and Afi Rivers.

The rocks are metamorphic; soils tend to be sandy and infertile, becoming stony and shallow on steeper slopes.

Rainfall in Oban Division decreases from south to north, but also increases with altitude. The central part of this Division receives over 3500 mm per year, with a rainfall peak between July and September and a major dry season from November to February or March. Rainfall in Okwangwo Division decreases from north-east to south-west and, although detailed rainfall measurements are lacking, the maximum rainfall is probably c. 4500 mm per year in the north-east and the minimum, in the south-west, only 2000–2500 mm per year. The dry season lasts about 3–4 months.

## Vegetation

Lowland rain forest occurs in the Oban and Okwangwo Divisions; the Okwango Division also contains montane forest. The altitudinal range (150–1700 m) of forest in Okwango is unusual for Africa. The northern part of Okwangwo Division is close to the natural forest-savanna ecotone in Nigeria, with a complex pattern of forest, savanna woodland and other vegetation types dependent on soil, climate, other physical factors and human actions. The Obudu Plateau of Okwangwo is predominantly grassland, which is frequently burnt; there are patches of montane forest in valleys.

The lowland Oban forests belong to the species-rich Biafran forest type (Letouzey 1968). A brief description of the Oban forests is given by Okali (1989), as follows: "At the low and medium altitudes of the Oban region, natural vegetation is dominated by moist evergreen forest, in which such economic genera as *Entandrophragma, Lovoa, Khaya, Guarea, Piptadeniastrum, Parkia, Erythrophleum, Berlinia, Brachystegia, Terminalia, Poga, Panda, Pycnanthus* and *Mimusops* are abundant. Deciduous elements, such as species in the Sterculiacae and *Milicia excelsa* increase in abundance towards the north, while low-lying and seasonally flooded sites by rivers are occupied by freshwater swamp forests. Common trees in the latter include *Mitragyna ciliata, Lophira alata, Alstonia boonei, Nauclea gilletii,*

*Spondianthus preusii, Carapa procera, Grewia coriacea, Uapaca* spp. and *Garcinia* spp."

## Flora

The lowland forests are part of the Guineo-Congolian Region and the montane forests (Okwangwo) are part of the Afromontane Region (White 1983).

There has been no complete inventory of the park, but it is known that the lowland forest is rich in species in comparison with many other lowland rain forests in Africa. Even before widespread clearance of forest elsewhere in Nigeria, the forests of the Cross River area were probably the most species-rich in the country. The lowland forests are similar to those in nearby Korup National Park (Cameroon). Over 400 species of trees have been recorded so far. A list of species known or believed (on the basis of nearby records) to occur in the Oban Division is given by Reid (1989). Well-represented families are: Annonaceae, Apocynaceae, Euphorbiaceae, Leguminosae, Orchidaceae, Rubiaceae and Sterculiaceae. Well-represented genera include *Cola, Memecylon, Ouratea, Psychotria, Trichoscypha* and *Xylopia*. Tree species typical of montane forests include *Ilex mitis, Nuxia congesta* and *Podocarpus latifolius*.

There are c. 130 strict endemics in the Oban Hills and it is likely that there are many species which are confined to Cross River National Park or occur only there and in the immediate neighbourhood, including in nearby forests in Cameroon. A species list for the Okwangwo Division has been prepared by White (1990), who comments: "Cross River National Park [is] the largest, most diverse protected area in West Africa." His list is itself partly based on records in Keay (1960), who has listed species for Afi River (contiguous with Okwangwo). Thomas and Thomas (1988) have listed species for Takamanda Forest Reserve (Cameroon) (also contiguous with Okwangwo). See also Medler and Hall (1975) for the flora of Obudu Plateau.

## Useful plants

The park is mostly uninhabited, but there are a number of villages on its periphery. Traditionally, plant and animal resources within the present park boundaries have been utilized by the local population. In the past, timber was extracted from parts of the present National Park and logging continues in surrounding areas. Plant products which continue to be extracted from the park's forests for local and commercial use include rattans (at least 5 species, including *Eremospatha* sp. and *Laccosperma secundiflora*), chewing sticks (especially *Garcinia* spp. and *Massularia acuminata*), two varieties of bush mangoe (*Irvingia gabonensis* var. *excelsa* and var. *gabonensis*), "afan" (*Gnetum* leaves, used for soups) and medicinal plants.

Oil is obtained for local use from the seeds of *Panda oleosa* and *Poga oleosa* and; spices come from *Monodora myristica, Piper guineense, Tetrapleura tetraptera* and *Xylopia* spp.; *Ricinodendron heudelotii* is used as a source of condiments. Fish poisons are made from the fruits of *Omphalocarpum*, the stems of *Adenia lobata*, the twigs of *Olax gambecola* and the bark of *Erythrophleum* spp.

## Social and environmental values

The Cross River National Park represents the only significant protected forest in the rain forest zone of Nigeria, where more than 90% of the original forest cover has been lost. It represents a very significant contribution to conservation of genetic resources, including of species used for timber, fruits, canes and medicines.

Both divisions of the park are important water catchment areas. Important fisheries are protected by the presence of the forest, which is also believed to serve a valuable role in moderating the local climate.

Cross River National Park has a diverse and important fauna, although populations of some species have been severely reduced by hunting. The park is rich in primates; for example, Okwangwo Division contains no fewer than 17 species of primates, nearly a third of Africa's total. These primates include the most westerly African population of gorilla (*Gorilla gorilla*), chimpanzee (*Pan troglodytes*), drill (*Mandrillus laucophaeus*), putty-nosed guenon (*Cercopithecus nictitans*) and mona guenon (*Cercopithecus mona*). Elephant and buffalo also occur. Other interesting animals include the pigmy squirrel (*Nyosciurus pumilio*) and the giant otter shrew (*Potamogale velox*).

The Guineo-Congolian rain forests in this area support at least two of the six restricted-range bird species of the Cameroon and Gabon lowlands Endemic Bird Area (EBA) (which includes the lowlands between south-east Nigeria and Gabon), and another two possibly occur. The montane habitats of the Obudu Plateau are included in the Cameroon Mountains EBA. Seventeen of the 28 restricted-range species of this EBA have been recorded here, including several threatened species. The majority of these birds are found in montane forest, and the Obudu Plateau is considered to be a "key forest for threatened birds" (Collar and Stuart 1988).

Hunting in these eastern Nigerian forests is a traditional pursuit, though now legally prohibited within the National Park. The most commonly hunted animals are porcupine, duiker, bushbuck, monkey and bush pigs. There is some hunting of elephant.

## Economic assessment

There is considerable potential for the development of tourism (perhaps especially in the Okwangwo Division) and associated industries (hotels, transport, crafts).

It may prove possible to develop industries based on sustainable extraction of plant resources (e.g. based on rattans, chewing sticks) within the park, once appropriate management methods have been determined.

## Threats

Unregulated hunting of bushmeat, including for sale to urban markets, is a major problem in the park. Nigeria has a large and rapidly growing population and there is considerable pressure elsewhere in the country to clear forest for agriculture; the park could come under the same pressure in the future. There are also pressures to establish new areas of plantations, including of rubber, *Gmelina* (used for making paper pulp), teak, oil palm and bananas (the latter especially around the

Okwangwo Division). Logging is not allowed in the National Park, but might be a future threat – very little logging in Nigeria is carried out following sustainable management principles. The construction of logging tracks has elsewhere helped to cause an influx of farmers into forested areas.

Fires are a threat in parts of the Okwangwo Division, especially on the Obudu Plateau where many forest patches in the valleys show signs of fire damage.

## Conservation

Cross National River Park was created in 1991 by a decree of the Federal Government of Nigeria. There are two divisions, the southern Oban Hills Division and the northern Okwangwo Division. Much of the land of the new National Park was formerly gazetted as Forest Reserves; some additional land was added when the National Park was created, bringing the total area protected to 4227 km².

Since 1988, the World Wide Fund for Nature (WWF) and the Nigerian Conservation Foundation (NCF) have been involved in assisting the Federal National Parks Service to establish the park. WWF has helped to prepare master plans for both divisions and has two projects on the ground, one in each division. These projects support the work of the Federal National Parks Service and relevant departments of the Government of Cross River State in areas of public awareness, conservation education, park boundary demarcation, anti-poaching assistance and biological surveys (mainly, to date, assessment of the status of the gorilla). A credit fund has been established for rural development at Okwangwo, with assistance from the Ford Foundation. Assistance has been received from Shell Nigeria to enhance protection of the gorillas.

This conservation programme is based on the view that the physical integrity of the park is very vulnerable to the actions of the people living in and around it. The concept of a "support zone" has therefore been adopted. This emphasises mutual dependency between the park and nearby communities; ways are sought of making the park benefit local people, as far as this is possible.

## References

Collar, N.J. and Stuart, S.N. (1988). *Key forests for threatened birds in Africa.* ICPB Monograph No. 3. International Council for Bird Preservation, Cambridge in collaboration with the IUCN Species Survival Commission, Gland, Switzerland. 102 pp.

Cross River National Park (Oban Division) (1989). Plan for developing the park and its support zone. World Wide Fund for Nature (U.K.) and Overseas Development Natural Resources Institute (U.K.).

Cross River National Park (Okwangwo Division) (1990). Plan for developing the park and its support zone. World Wide Fund for Nature (U.K.) and Overseas Development Natural Resources Institute (U.K.).

Keay, R.W.J. (1960). A botanical study of the Obudu Plateau and Sonkwala Mountains. *The Nigeria Field* 44: 106–119.

Letouzey, R. (1968). *Etude phytogéographique du Cameroun.* Editions Paul Lechevalier, Paris. 508 pp.

Medler, J.A. and Hall, J.B. (1975). The flora of the Obudu Plateau and associated highlands: an annotated species list. *Ife University Herbarium Bulletin 9.*

Okali, D.U.U. (1989). Forestry studies in conjunction with the soil survey and land evaluation of the Oban Division of the proposed Cross River State National Park. Report prepared for the World Wide Fund for Nature (U.K.).

Reid, J.C. (1989). Floral and faunal richness of the Oban Division of Cross River National Park. Report prepared for the World Wide Fund for Nature (U.K.).

Thomas, D.W. and Thomas J. (1988). Status and conservation of Takamanda gorillas (Cameroon). Report for World Wide Fund for Nature (U.K.).

White, D. (1990). Cross River National Park, Okwangwo Division: species list. Report for World Wide Fund for Nature (U.K.).

White, F. (1983). *The vegetation of Africa: a descriptive memoir to accompany the Unesco/AETFAT/UNSO vegetation map of Africa.* Natural Resources Research XX. Unesco, Paris. 356 pp.

## Acknowledgements

This Data Sheet was prepared by Dr Alan C. Hamilton (WWF).

GUINEO-CONGOLIAN REGIONAL CENTRE OF ENDEMISM: CPD SITE AF25
# BWINDI (IMPENETRABLE) FOREST
## Uganda

---

**Location:** South-west Uganda near the borders of Rwanda and Zaïre; between latitudes 0°53'–0°8'S and longitudes 29°35–29°50'E.

**Area:** 321 km².

**Altitude:** 1160–2607 m.

**Vegetation:** Moist evergreen submontane and montane forest; a small area of mountain bamboo.

**Flora:** Estimated 1000 vascular plant species. Possibly the richest forest for its altitude in numbers of tree species in East Africa; some central African taxa at easternmost limits of their ranges.

**Useful plants:** Timber species, poles, bamboo, ropes and twine, medicinal plants.

**Other values:** Watershed protection (Nile catchment); very rich fauna, including over half the global total of mountain gorillas and 58% of Africa's montane bird species; tourist attraction; honey-producing forest.

**Threats:** Logging, over-collection of a few other plant resources, poaching, gold-mining.

**Conservation:** National Park. Site of WWF/USAID sponsored project since 1986, with building of a field station and other support to conservation; development project started in 1988 by CARE/USAID – mainly biological inventories, community education, tree planting. The Impenetrable Forest Tourism Development Plan has been accepted by the Uganda Government.

---

## Geography

Bwindi Forest is located in south-west Uganda, in the Rukiga Highlands of the eastern edge of the Western Rift Valley. It lies within Rubanda and Bufumbira Counties of Kabale District and Kinkizi County of Rukungiri District. In 1992, the forest attained National Park status (previously it was a Forest Reserve, administered by the Forest Department, and an Animal Sanctuary, with the same boundaries as the Forest Reserve, administered by the Game Department). Very little forest now lies outside the National Park. The forest is very approximately oval in shape (the South Sector) with a northern extension (the North Sector sometimes known as Kayonza Forest), attached by a narrow forest neck.

The forest lies on shales and phyllites, with quartzite bands, belonging to the Precambrian Karagwe-Ankolean System. The soils of the forest are classified into the Mafuga and Ntendule Series (Harrop 1960). They are ferralitic clay loams and silt clay loams, of poor structure, moderately to very acidic (pH 2.9–5.2) (Chenery 1960) and very deficient in bases (Leggat and Osmaston 1961). They are very liable to erosion when the vegetation cover is removed.

The topography is extremely rugged and much dissected, especially in the higher South Sector. Elevation is highest in the south-east (Rwamanyanyi: 2607 m), descending to 1160 m in the North Sector, resulting in a broad altitudinal range for forest, which is probably unique in East Africa. There is one extensive (1 km²) swamp, Omubwindi (2070 m), situated in the South Sector. The forest is a major catchment at the headwaters of the River Nile.

There is little variation (<2°C) in mean monthly temperature, the coolest season being June–July. Mean annual temperature is 16°C at Ruhizha (2300 m) with mean daily minima and maxima of 13°C and 18°C. Temperatures elsewhere can be calculated from the normal East African lapse rate of 1.98°C per 1000 m (J.A. Channon in Hamilton 1969), though temperature inversion occurs in valleys at night. Rainfall is monsoonal, with peaks in March–April and September–November; the June–August dry season is the longer and more severe.

## Vegetation

Virtually all of Bwindi (Impenetrable) National Park is still covered by evergreen submontane to (moist lower) montane forest, with a few deciduous canopy trees at lower altitudes. There is much variation associated with altitude, topographic position and soil depth (Leggat and Osmaston 1961, which includes data on timber species from an inventory). A forest type map prepared from aerial photographs is given by Cahusac (1958) and descriptions of the vegetation by Hamilton (1969) and Lind and Morrison (1974). Additional aerial photographs were taken in 1989. However, despite this work, knowledge of the vegetation and flora is very incomplete. Hopefully, detailed work at present being carried out by the Impenetrable Forest Conservation Project and the Development Through Conservation Project will help to rectify this situation. The following description of the forest is based on Leggat and Osmaston (1961), which is written from the traditional forester's point of view with an emphasis on timber trees:

### North Sector

This area is dominated by stands (probably climax) of *Parinari excelsa* at c. 1350 m elevation along the valleys of the Rivers Ishasha and Hihizo. *Entandrophragma excelsum* occurs above this elevation, in valleys with better soils, and is often associated with *Aningeria adolfi-friederici, Newtonia buchananii* and *Symphonia globulifera*. Good stands of *Ocotea usambarensis* occur infrequently in swampy areas. On the higher ridges *Podocarpus* has established itself. Along the perimeter of the forest are *Albizia, Canthium* and *Milletia*, which are replaced as one moves into higher grade forest by such species as *Ficalhoa laurifolia, Hagenia abyssinica, Polyscias fulva, Nuxia* sp., and, in some areas, stands of *Maesopsis eminii*.

### South Sector

The most abundant species are *Chrysophyllum* spp. (including *C. gorungosanum*), associated with *Entandrophragma, Newtonia* and *Prunus africana*. Smaller areas dominated by *Parinari* occur in some of the valley bottoms. *Podocarpus latifolius*, previously common on all ridges, has now largely been cut out from all accessible areas; *P. falcatus* is, however, still found along swamp edges.

The understory in both sectors consists of *Allophylus, Myrianthus holstii, Teclea nobilis* and *Xymalos monospora*.

Caternary variation in vegetation near Ruhizha in the south-east has been described by Hamilton (1969). On hilltops and ridges (2300–2450 m), common trees in the 10–20 m tall canopy include *Faurea saligna, Macaranga kilimandscharica* and *Olea hochstetteri*. The 25 m tall canopy in hillslope forest contains *Chrysophyllum gorungosanum* and *Olea*, with a second tree layer c. 18 m tall with *Allophylus* sp., *Cassipourea ruwensorensis* and *Drypetes* sp. aff. *gerrardii*; Rubiaceae are common in the understory. Valley forest (2000 m) reaches 30 m and contains abundant *Newtonia buchananii* and *Symphonia globulifera*, with smaller *Croton macrostachyus* and *Tabernaemontana holstii*. Two common large climbers are *Sericostachys tomentosa* and *Urera hypselodendron*, the former exhibiting periodic mass flowering.

In addition to evergreen forest, there is a small patch (0.4 km²) of mountain bamboo, *Sinarundinaria alpina*, at high altitude in the south-east. Omubwindi Swamp is of considerable importance as an example of natural swamp vegetation, most of the numerous swamps in the region outside the forest having been drained and cleared for agriculture. The vegetation, which is dominated by Cyperaceae and which contains some swamp forest with *Anthocleista*, is described briefly by Hamilton (1969).

An outstanding feature of Bwindi Forest is its altitudinal range extending from near the upper boundary of lowland forest to well within the montane forest belt. It is very important for investigations of altitudinal variations in forest ecosystems in equatorial Africa.

**CPD Site Af25: Bwindi (Impenetrable) Forest; view at c. 2300 m, showing the evergreen forest and rugged topography.** Photo: Alan C. Hamilton.

## Flora

No complete check-list of the plants of Bwindi Forest has been prepared, but there is no doubt that it is one of the most floristically rich forests in East Africa.

The forest can be placed within the Guineo-Congolian and Afromontane phytochoria of White (1983). Lower altitude forest, floristically related to lowland forests in Zaïre, occurs in East Africa only in Uganda and extreme western Tanzania and Kenya (Kakamega Forest). The Uganda forests become increasingly rich floristically towards the south-west of the country, the area which includes Bwindi Forest (Hamilton 1974). Eight tree species are known in East Africa only from Bwindi Forest, namely *Allanblackia kimbiliensis*, *Brazzeia longipedicellata*, *Chrysophyllum pruniforme*, *Croton bukobensis*, *Grewia mildbraedii*, *Leplaea mayombensis*, *Maesobotrya purseglovei*, *Melchiora schliebenii*, *Strombosiopsis tetrandra* and *Xylopia staudtii*. A further 10 tree species are only known from Bwindi and scattered localities elsewhere in south-west Uganda. For most of these species Bwindi represents their easternmost ranges in Africa.

It is known that tropical Africa has witnessed periods of greater aridity during the Quaternary Period, most of the c. 20 major world ice ages being dry episodes (Hamilton 1988). The last world ice maximum (21,000–12,000 BP) is the best known of these dry phases. At that time Lake Victoria was more or less dry (Kendall 1969; Livingstone 1975), the White Nile was much reduced or dry and pollen evidence show more or less complete absence of forest both in the northern Lake Victoria hinterland (Kendall 1969) and on Mt Elgon (Hamilton 1987), both forest areas today.

The above evidence, combined with analysis of the modern distribution of forest trees in Uganda (Hamilton 1974), shows that many forest trees have expanded their ranges eastwards across Uganda after the climate became moister at 12,000 BP. Distributional evidence indicates that the main central African refugium for lowland and moist montane forest trees during the last glacial period lay in Eastern Zaïre (Hamilton 1982). This has raised the possibility that Bwindi Forest itself many have formed a forest refuge area, although it can also be argued that the richness of its flora is due to its proximity to the main forest refugium in Zaïre. There is, in fact, excellent pollen-analytical evidence from very close to Bwindi Forest (5–10 km) to show that vegetation zones were depressed by about 1000 m during the last glacial maximum and that the climate was considerably drier than now (Taylor 1990). By extrapolation, there seems no doubt that most of Bwindi Forest would not have carried forest of the present type, but rather high altitude grassland and ericaceous communities, with some upper montane trees such as *Hagenia abyssinica*. There is, however, a possibility that some montane forest of relatively low altitude types might have survived at the lowermost altitudinal extremities, notably near the Ishasha River. The

**CPD Site Af25: Bwindi (Impenetrable) Forest. This is the frontline for conservation of biodiversity in Africa, as intensive agriculture abutts directly onto one of the biologically richest submontane and montane forests in Africa.**
Photo: Alan C. Hamilton.

North Sector forests in the Ishasha vicinity are quite remarkable in Uganda for their rich flora, producing one "surprising" species after another, in a way not encountered in any other forested locality in the country.

## Useful plants

The forest contains genepools of a number of valuable timber species, such as *Entandrophragma excelsum*, *Maesopsis eminii*, *Newtonia buchananii*, *Podocarpus falcatus* and *P. latifolius*. Poles and firewood have been collected from the forest in sufficient quantities to cause structural degradation to the forest near the boundaries, while bamboo stems are collected for a number of purposes by local people. A survey of the use of forest products by the local people has shown that some uses seem sustainable, considering quantities taken and growth rates of the plants, while others are not (A.B. Cunningham, pers. comm.). For example, most collection of medicinal plants causes little impact, while the very large scale harvesting of poles for climbing beans will result in significant forest degradation if it continues. Discussions are

**Alfred Tsekeli, forest botanist, with a cultivated plant of *Rytigynia kigeziensis*. This plant is used to treat internal parasites. Some local people have expressed the view that they will die if they do not have access to this plant, which grows in Bwindi. Yet, according to National Park regulations, collection of this and other medicinal plants is not allowed. This and other issues of access to the plant resources in the forest are currently under review. Photo: Alan C. Hamilton.**

currently being held with local people and natural park staff to determine measures which might be taken to manage the resources sustainably or, where necessary, to seek alternatives.

## Social and environmental values

The forest is of great value for catchment protection, climate amelioration and for its fauna. Information given here is largely from Butynski (1984a).

Bwindi has undoubtedly one of the richest mammalian faunas in Africa. The forest is known to contain 97 species of mammals and a further 49 are likely to occur. There are seven diurnal primates, the most notable of which are the mountain gorilla (*Gorilla gorilla beringei*) and chimpanzee (*Pan troglodytes*); this is the only place where these two primates are sympatric. On-going census work has now revealed that there are at least 300 individuals of mountain gorilla in Bwindi Forest (T.M. Butynski, pers. comm.), representing more than half of the total world wild population. Gorilla are confined to the South Sector and avoid areas of high human activity; they are therefore largely absent from near the forest boundary.

Other large mammals in the park include elephant (*Loxodonta africana*), giant forest hog (*Hylochoerus meinertzhageni*), bushpig (*Potamochoerus porcus*), golden cat (*Profelis aurata*) and at least three species of duiker. Many of these have suffered severely from poaching; for example elephants are reduced to probably fewer than 30 animals confined to the south-east (Butynski 1984b). Two species, buffalo (*Syncerus caffer*) and leopard (*Panthera pardus*), have become extinct recently through man's actions.

The montane habitats of the Albertine Rift Mountains constitute an Endemic Bird Area (EBA), with 39 restricted-range bird species, of which 38 are endemic. Of these, 26 have been recorded in Bwindi Forest. The majority are montane forest birds, but the threatened Grauer's scrub-warbler (*Bradypterus graueri*) is confined to swamp vegetation. It is thought that Bwindi Forest probably holds the richest forest avifauna (presumably for its size) in Africa (Moreau 1966; Keith *et al.* 1969; Friedmann and Williams 1970), with a particularly rich and important montane forest avifauna. There are at least 334 species of birds, of which at least 184 are true forest species (Keith *et al.* 1969; Friedmann and Williams 1970; Butynski 1984a; Butynski and Kalina 1989, and in press). It holds at least 70 montane forest species, about 90% of all montane forest species in the Albertine Rift Mountains, and 58% of the 120 montane forest species in the whole of Africa. This site is considered to be a "key forest for threatened birds" (Collar and Stuart 1988).

Bwindi Forest has considerable potential for tourism, because of its rugged beauty, fascinating forest, extremely diverse avifauna and the presence of mountain gorilla. Tourists could make an important contribution to the local economy and thus help to ensure that the forest survives. However, tourism will have to be developed carefully to avoid disruption to the natural ecosystem of this small and vulnerable forest.

## Threats

Bwindi Forest represents the conservation frontline in Africa. This small isolated forest of outstanding biological richness lies in an agricultural landscape which supports one of the highest rural population densities in tropical Africa. The extent of forest on Public Land outside the National Park has retreated from c. 120 km² in 1954, to 42 km² in 1972, to virtually none at the present time (Butynski 1984a). The boundary of the forest is today amazingly abrupt, with a line of dead or damaged cypress trees (attacked by an aphid) forming a thin line separating the forest from agricultural land, which here consists of a patchwork of tiny fields used for maize, millet, sorghum, beans, sweet potatoes, Irish potatoes and other crops, with scattered small plantations of eucalyptus in some areas. The immediate question is, therefore, whether pressure from the impoverished rural community will result in further forest loss, In fact, to date there have been virtually no agricultural incursions into the National Park.

Despite this, the forest nevertheless faces on-going major threats which can easily result in major ecosystem degradation. Controls over illegal activities in the forest tended to breakdown during the 1970s and 1980s, related to political turmoil in Uganda. The critical situation in 1983/4 was investigated in detail by Butynski (1984a). He found that large quantities of pit-sawn timber were being collected from all over the forest, including from within two small nature reserves which had been established by the Forest Department. In 1983/4 there were 73 licensed pit-sawyers and an estimated 140–200 illegal pit-sawyers; about 80% of trees were thought to be felled illegally. In addition, considerable quantities of fuelwood, poles and bamboo were being collected without the stipulated permits. Livestock was being grazed illegally, especially in the North Sector. Butynski also found that there was a very high level of hunting (all illegal) in Bwindi Forest, with an estimated 10 traps/km² in the South Sector and 1 trap/km² in the North Sector (where few animals remained anyway). A further threat was illegal gold-mining, involving digging of pits in alluvial sediments; this was regarded as the main law enforcement problem by the Forest Department.

## Conservation

Bwindi (Impenetrable) Forest was, until 1992, a Forest Reserve and Animal Sanctuary in which a range of laws and regulations were designed to control forest exploitation. In 1992, Bwindi Forest was upgraded to National Park status (Hamilton, Baranga and Tindigarukayo 1990).

In 1986 a conservation project, the Impenetrable Forest Conservation Project (IFCP), was launched with funding from WWF and USAID. This Project has worked predominantly through the Game Department and has been remarkably successful in controlling some illegal activities, although little improvement was reported during the early years of the Project regarding illegal timber extraction. The most notable achievements were the near total elimination of poaching and illegal mining by 1990 and the attainment of National Park status for the forest. In addition to these successes, the Project has also constructed a biological field station and has begun to train Ugandan postgraduates. In 1991 the field station became established as Mbarara University's Institute of Tropical Forest Management and Conservation.

Following initial out-reach activities by IFCP, a large community-based development project "Development Through Conservation" was started in 1988 by WWF, subcontracted to CARE and funded by USAID. This project is now run by CARE. The project aims to reach 9600 farm families in a two-parish wide band around the forest and employs 58 Conservation Extension Agents, two in each parish. The main areas of activity are promotion of community forestry, soil conservation and sustainable agriculture; biological inventories are undertaken in the forest.

In 1992, an ethnobotanical survey was carried out under the CARE project, involving surveys of the uses of plants and other products collected in the forest and the effects of this harvesting on the forest ecosystem. One result has been the granting of collecting licences to local hive owners – the first time that a group using natural resources has been allowed to harvest products within a natural park in Uganda (A.B. Cunningham, pers. comm.). Further arrangements to permit collection of certain forest products in controlled ways are expected to follow.

## References

Butynski, T.M. (1984a). *Ecological survey of the Impenetrable Forest, Uganda, and recommendations for its conservation and management.* (Mimeo.)

Butynski, T.M. (1984b). Status of elephants in the Impenetrable (Bwindi) Forest, Uganda. *African Journal of Ecology* 24: 189–193.

Butynski, T.M. and Kalina, J. (1989). Additions to the known avifauna of the Impenetrable (Bwindi) Forest, south western Uganda. *Scopus* 12: 73–78.

Butynski, T.M. and Kalina, J. (in press). Additions to the known avifauna of the Impenetrable (Bwindi) Forest, south western Uganda (1989–1991). *Scopus*.

Cahusac, A.B. (1958). *Impenetrable C.F.R. forest types (Interpretation Report No. 6). Reference map no. KI/45.* Appendix G in Working Plan for the Impenetrable C.F.R. by G.J. Leggat and H.A. Osmaston (1961). Uganda Forest Department, Entebbe, Uganda.

Chenery, E.M. (1960). *An introduction to the soils of the Uganda Protectorate.* Mem. Res. Div. Series 1, No 1. Department of Agriculture, Uganda.

Collar, N.J. and Stuart, S.N. (1988). *Key forests for threatened birds in Africa.* ICPB Monograph No. 3. International Council for Bird Preservation, Cambridge, in collaboration with the IUCN Species Survival Commission, Gland, Switzerland. 102 pp.

Friedmann, H. and Williams, J.G. (1970). *Additions to the known avifauna of the Bugoma, Kibale and Impenetrable Forests, West Uganda.* Contrib. Sci. No. 198, Los Angeles County Museum.

Hamilton, A.C. (1974). Distribution patterns of forest trees in Uganda and their historical significance. *Vegetatio* 29: 21–35.

Hamilton, A.C. (1969). The vegetation of south-west Kigezi. *Uganda Journal* 33: 175–199.

Hamilton, A.C. (1975). A quantitative analysis of altitudinal zonation in Uganda forests. *Vegetatio* 30: 99–106.

Hamilton, A.C. (1982). *Environmental history of East Africa*. Academic Press, London and New York. 328 pp.

Hamilton, A.C. (1987). Vegetation and climate of Mt Elgon during the late Pleistocene and Holocene. *Palaeoecology of Africa*. 18: 121–176.

Hamilton, A.C. (1988). Guenon evolution and forest history. In Gautier-Hion, A., Bourliere, F., Gautier, J.P. and Kingdon, J. (eds), *A primate radiation: evolutionary history of the African Guenons*. Cambridge University Press, Cambridge. Pp. 113–24.

Hamilton, A.C., Baranga, J. and Tindigarukayo, J. (1990). *Proposed Bwindi (Impenetrable) Forest National Park: results of public inquiry and recommendations for establishment*. (Mimeo.)

Harcourt, A.H. (1981). Can Uganda's gorillas survive? – A survey of the Bwindi Forest Reserve. *Biological Conservation* 19: 269–282.

Harrop, J.R. (1960). *The soils of the Western Province of Uganda*. Mem. Res. Div. Series 1, No 6. Department of Agriculture, Uganda. (Mimeo.)

Keith, S., Twomey, A., Friedmann, H. and Williams, J. (1969). The avifauna of the Impenetrable Forest, Uganda. *Am. Mus. Novit* 2389: 1–14.

Kendall, R.L. (1969). An ecological history of Lake Victoria. *Ecological Monographs 39*: 121–176.

Kingdon, J. (1973). Endemic mammals and birds of western Uganda: measuring Uganda's biological wealth and a plea for supra-economic values. *Uganda Journal* 37: 1–8.

Leggat, G.J. and Osmaston, H.A. (1961). *Working plan for the Impenetrable Central Forest Reserve, Kigezi District, Western Province, Uganda*. Uganda Forest Department, Entebbe. (Mimeo.)

Lind, E.M. and Morrison, M.E.S. (1974). *East African vegetation*. Longman, London. 257 pp.

Livingstone, D.A. (1975). Late Quaternary climatic change in Africa. *Annual Review of Ecology and Systematics* 6: 249–280.

Moreau, R.E. (1966). *The bird faunas of Africa and its islands*. Academic Press, London.

Taylor, D. (1990). Late Quaternary pollen records from two Ugandan mires: evidence for environmental change in the Rukiga Highlands of southwest Uganda. *Palaeogeography Palaeoclimatology Palaeoecology* 80: 283–300.

White, F. (1983). *The vegetation of Africa: a descriptive memoir to accompany the Unesco/AETFAT/UNSO vegetation map of Africa*. Natural Resources Research XX. Unesco, Paris. 356 pp.

## Acknowledgements

This Data Sheet was compiled by Dr Alan C. Hamilton (WWF) with grateful thanks to Dr Thomas M. Butynski (Impenetrable Forest Conservation Project, Kampala, Uganda) and Dr Anthony Cunningham (Perth, Australia) for additional information.

# MAIKO NATIONAL PARK
## Zaïre

**Location:** Situated in Haut-Zaïre and Kivu Provinces of Zaïre, between latitudes 0°00'–1°00'S and longitudes 26°00'–28°30'E.

**Area:** 10,830 km².

**Altitude:** c. 1000–1200 m.

**Vegetation:** Guineo-Congolian rain forest; some Afromontane forest in the east.

**Flora:** Little explored, but known to be rich.

**Useful plants:** Rich in genetic resources of timber trees.

**Other values:** Rich fauna, tourism.

**Threats:** Conversion of forest to savanna by people living within the park, small-scale gold mining, hunting.

**Conservation:** National Park (IUCN Management Category: II) since 1970; no existing management plan; priority need is for research on the flora and fauna.

## Geography

Maïko National Park is situated in the provinces of Haut-Zaïre and Kivu, Zaïre, between latitudes 0°00'–1°00'S and longitudes 26°00'–28°30'E. It was created in 1970, replacing an earlier hunting area (Réserve de Chasse) declared in 1938, and comprises a vast forested area of some 10,830 km². The park is traversed by numerous rivers, including the Maïko, Loya, Lubero, Lubutu and Osso. The flat western part of the park lies at about 1000 m, rising to 1200 m in the east.

The climate is equatorial, hot and humid throughout the year, and without a true dry season. There is heavy annual precipitation, with a peak in October–November and a minimum in July–August. Annual rainfall at Lubutu was recorded at 2277 mm in 1987 and 1843 mm in 1988. The mean annual temperature is about 25°C.

## Vegetation

Most of the park consists of dense rain forest. Preliminary research on the flora and vegetation by J. Lejoly in January and June 1977 resulted in the collection of a number of plant specimens. These have been deposited in the herbarium of the Université Libre de Bruxelles. There has been no further botanical prospecting.

Forest types on drier soils include mixed forest and forest dominated by single species of Caesalpiniaceae (*Cynometra alexandri, Gilbertiodendron dewevrei*). There are also swamp forests, with *Uapaca guineensis*, and secondary forests associated with tree falls and regeneration after agriculture.

## Flora

Tall trees in mixed forest include *Anthonotha macrophylla, Brazzeia congensis, Canarium schweinfurthii, Cynometra hankei, Desplatsia chrysochlamys, Monopetalanthus microphyllus, Panda oleosa* and *Piptadeniastrum africanum*. The shrub layer includes *Campylospermum claessensi, C. elongatum, C. reticulatum, Garcinia ovalifolia, Rhabdophyllum bracteolatum, Sclerosperma mannii, Thomandersia hensii* and *Whitfieldia arnoldiana*. The undergrowth comprises shrubs 0.5–1 m tall, giving an unusual structure: species include *Ardisia lisowskii, A. staudtii, A. uragaensis, Ixora nana, Phyllobotryum maioense* and *Pycnocoma chevalleri.*

Several species collected in 1977 proved to be new to science, including *Ardisia lisowskii, Ixora nana* and *Phyllobotryum maikoense*. Further botanical studies are required.

## Social and environmental values

Settlements are scattered throughout the interior of the park, but the total number of inhabitants is very small. People are concentrated along the roads (Lubutu-Walikale, Lubutu-Pene Aluta, Opienge-Loya, Manguredjipa-Etaïto), as well as between the rivers Lubero and Lindi. There is little cultivation, hunting being the predominant form of subsistence. Temporary groups of up to 50 people are engaged in gold mining.

The rich fauna includes chimpanzee, okapi and elephant, with gorilla in the east. The Guineo-Congolian rain forests of the lowlands of eastern Zaïre are an EBA, with 6 endemic restricted-range bird species (Stattersfield *et al.*, in prep.). None of these have yet been recorded in Maiko National Park, but several are likely to occur as there is suitable habitat present (Prigogine 1985). The threatened Congo peacock (*Afropavo congensis*) is known from the park.

Access to the park is difficult and tourism is not feasible at present. However, it is possible that eventually the natural salt-licks in the park, where concentrations of animals can be seen more easily, could be developed as tourist attractions. A paved road passes south of the park, connecting Kisangani and Lubutu; this is at present being extended and will eventually facilitate exploration of the park. Rivers in the region are often only navigable over short distances due to numerous waterfalls.

## Threats

The area is rather inaccessible and not under great pressure at present. However, hunting may be causing significant ecosystem change. Gold mining and conversion of forest to savanna are minor threats.

## Conservation

Maïko National Park was created in 1970, replacing an earlier Hunting Reserve (Réserve de Chasse). The park is the responsibility of the Institut Zaïrois pour la Conservation de la Nature (IZCN) (Doumenge 1990). There is no management plan at present. Management difficulties include insufficient human and material resources, and difficulties of access to some areas.

There is a need for research on the flora and fauna, as well as on the distribution and ways of life of the local people. After these studies, a management plan should be drawn up to provide better possibilities of controlling activities in the park.

## References

Bamps, P. and Lejoly, J. (1981). Une nouvelle espèce de *Phyllobotryum* (Flacourtiaceae) en Afrique centrale. *Bull. Jard. Bot. Nat. Belg.* 51: 423–426.

Doumenge, C. (1990). *La conservation des écosystèmes forestiers du Zaïre*. IUCN, Gland, Switzerland and Cambridge, U.K. 254 pp.

Prigogine, A. (1985). Conservation of the avifauna of the forests of the Albertine Rift. In Diamond, A.W. and Lovejoy, T.E (eds), *Conservation of tropical forest birds*. Technical Publication 4. International Council for Bird Preservation. Cambridge, U.K. Pp. 277–296.

Robbrecht, E. and Lejoly, J. (1982). Une nouvelle espèce d'*Ixora* (Rubiaceae-Coffeeae) du Zaïre. *Bull. Jard. Nat. Belg.* 52: 487–489.

Taton, A. and Lejoly, J. (1990). Une espèce nouvelle d'*Ardisia* (Myrsinaceae) du Zaïre. *Bull. Jard. Nat. Belg.* 50: 461–463.

## Acknowledgements

This Data Sheet was prepared by Professor Jean Lejoly (Université Libre de Bruxelles, Belgium).

# SALONGA NATIONAL PARK
## Zaïre

**Location:** Southern part of the Equateur region of the Central Zaïre basin, between latitudes 1°00'–3°20'S and longitudes 20°–22°30'E.

**Area:** 36,560 km².

**Altitude:** 350–700 m.

**Vegetation:** Tropical evergreen Guineo-Congolian rain forest, swamp and riverine forest, secondary vegetation, grasslands.

**Flora:** Estimated 1500–2000 vascular plant species, of which c. 10% are endemic.

**Useful plants:** Timber trees, medicinal plants.

**Other values:** Rich fauna.

**Threats:** Local population pressure in surrounding areas, fire, tree cutting for firewood, hunting, lack of sufficient management infrastructure.

**Conservation:** National Park (36,560 km²) and World Heritage Site (36,000 km²).

## Geography

Salonga National Park (Parc National de la Salonga) is located in the southern part of the Equateur region in the central basin of the Zaïre River between latitudes 1°00'–3°20'S and longitudes 20°–22°30'E. The park is divided into two sectors of approximately equal size, separated by about 45 km. Its elevation is between 350–700 m, but most of the area is low-lying swampy ground below 500 m. There are three main landforms: river terraces, low plateaux and high plateaux, the higher ground being in the east. In the north sector, rivers are large and meandering and have marshy banks. In the south sector, rivers occupy deeper valleys with cliffs up to 80 m high. The south sector includes the watershed of the Luilaka, Likoro and Lukenje rivers. The soil consists of a thin humus layer above Kalahari sands. "Dry-land soils" belong to the "hygrokaolisol" group, while alluvial soils are often waterlogged.

The climate is continental equatorial, with a mean annual rainfall of 2000 mm. There is a season with less rain between June and August. The mean annual temperature is 25.5°C.

## Vegetation

Tropical evergreen Guineo-Congolian rain forest covers most of the area; and most of this is still intact. Dry-land forests on plateaux are dominated by *Brachystegia laurentii* in association with *Panda oleosa, Polyalthia suaveolens, Schotia romii* and *Staudtia stipitata*. Wet valley forests are dominated by *Gilbertiodendron dewevrei* in association with *Cleistanthus mildbraedii, Garcinia kola* and *Pterocarpus ledermannii*.

Various types of inundated swamp forests occur. They include: forests of *Guibourtia demeusei* and *Oubanguia africana*, in association with *Aframomum meleguetta, Cercestis congensis, Diospyros alboflavescens, Scytopetalum pierreanum* and *Vitex rivularis; Lasiodiscus mannii* forests, in association

with *Aphanocalyx cynometroides, Cleistanthus bipendensis, Monopetalanthus microphyllus, Pseudomacrolobium mengei* and *Sorindeia befalensis*; and *Rothmannia megalostigma* forests, with *Afromomum sanguineum, Cleistanthus zenkeri, Klaineanthus gaboniae* and *Newtonia aubrevillei*. Forests which are inundated for long periods belong to three associations: *Coelocaryon botryodes* forest association; *Uapaca guineensis/Mitragyna stipulosa* forest association; and *Mitragyna stipulosa/Pycnanthus marchalianus* forest association.

Old secondary forests contain *Albizia gummifera, Canarium schweinfurthii, Milicia excelsa, Ricinodendron heudelotii, Sterculia bequaertii, Zanthoxylum gilletii* and others.

A small area (0.5% of the total park area) of grassland occurs in the north sector; it is locally known as "botoka-djoku" or "the elephant's bath" (IUCN/UNEP 1987).

## Flora

There have been no detailed studies of the flora of Salonga (but see Jongen and Jamagne 1966, and Evrard 1968). It is estimated that there are between 1500–2000 vascular plant species (Mandango 1992, personal estimate), of which about 10% are endemic. The flora belongs to the centro-Guineo-Congolian phytochorion of White (1983). Notable species include *Coelocaryon botryoides, Entandrophragma* spp., *Eremospatha* spp., *Guarea* spp., *Khaya anthotheca* and *Staudtia gabonensis*. Two of the main families present are Leguminosae and Rubiaceae.

## Useful plants

Salonga contains a wealth of timber trees and medicinal plants. Among the timber trees utilised for building are *Afzelia bipindensis*, *Autranella congolensis* (mukulungu), *Entandrophragma candollei*, *Khaya anthotheca*, *Milicia excelsa* (iroko), *Millettia laurentii* (wenge), *Nauclea diderrichii* (bilinga), *Pericopsis elata* (afrormosia) and *Pterocarpus soyauxii* (padouk). *Diospyros crassifolia* (ebene) is used for local craft materials. Usually only the smaller trees are exploited, which means that much of the forest remains intact. Trees are also cut for firewood.

Medicinal plants include *Allophylus africanus* and *Piptadeniastrum africanum*.

## Social and environmental values

The forests are the home of some Pygmy groups (IUCN/UNEP 1987). Most of the local population live in the relatively small area of land between the two sectors of the park. The forests supply firewood, building materials, medicinal plants and food (both plants and animals).

No systematic faunal survey has been carried out (IUCN/UNEP 1987). Among the mammals reported are bonobo (*Pan paniscus*), endemic to Zaïre, monkeys (*Colobus polykomos angolensis*, *Cercopithecus badius* and other species), long-tailed pangolin (*Manis tetradactyla*), giant ground pangolin (*M. gigantea*) and both subspecies of the African elephant (*Loxodonta africana africana* and *L. africana cyclotis*). Birds include the endemic Zaïre peacock (*Afropavo congensis*).

## Economic assessment

There are no figures or estimates available for the quantities or economic values of timber and medicinal species harvested. Long-term studies are needed.

## Threats

The main threat is from encroachment and disturbance to the forest in areas close to the settlements between the north and south sectors of the park. There is some disturbance locally as a result of tree cutting, poaching of animals, collection of firewood and medicinal plants, and honey gathering. More serious, perhaps, is the lack of sufficient management infrastructure and trained staff (IUCN/UNEP 1987).

## Conservation

Salonga was declared a National Park in 1970 (of area 36,560 km²) and is defined in law as "une Réserve Naturelle Intégrale". 36,000 km² was inscribed as a World Heritage Site in 1984. An IUCN and WWF team who visited the area in 1985 suggested that increased effort should be given to making the local population more aware of the park and, if possible, involving them in management activities. It was also recommended that information on the relationship between local population and the park should be collected, for example through ethnobotanical studies, and that a research station should be built (IUCN/UNEP 1987).

## References

Doumenge, C. (1990). *La conservation des ecosytèmes forestiers du Zaïre*. IUCN, Gland, Switzerland and Cambridge, U.K. 242 pp.

Evrard, C. (1968). Recherches écologiques sur le peuplement forestier des sols hydromorphes de la Cuvette centrale congolaise. *Publ. INEAC, Ser. Scient.* 10: 1–295.

IUCN/UNEP (1987). *The IUCN directory of Afrotropical protected areas*. IUCN, Gland, Switzerland and Cambridge, U.K. 1034 pp.

Jongen, P. and Jamagne, M. (1966). *Carte des sols et de la végétation du Congo, du Rwanda et du Burundi. 20 – Région Tshuape-Equateur*. INEAC, Brussels. 82 pp.

White, F. (1983). *The vegetation of Africa*. Natural Resources Research 20. Unesco, Paris. (Map in 3 sheets; Memoir, 356 pp.)

## Acknowledgements

This Data Sheet was written by Professor M.A. Mandango (Chairman, Association des Botanistes du Zaïre, Kinshasa, Zaïre). Professor Paul Bamps (Jardin Botanique National de Belgique, Meise, Belgium) kindly provided additional material.

ZAMBEZIAN REGIONAL CENTRE OF ENDEMISM: CPD SITE AF33

# MAHALE-KAROBWA HILLS
## Tanzania

**Location:** Hilly and mountainous country east of Lake Tanganyika in the Kigoma and Rukwa administrative regions, between latitudes 5°20'–6°40'S and longitudes 29°43'E–31°00'E.
**Area:** c.120 by 200 km; 150 km² of forest.
**Altitude:** 773–2496 m (summit of Mfitwa).
**Vegetation:** Forest of Guineo-Congolian affinities, Zambezian woodland, grassland, swamp.
**Flora:** Estimated > 2000 vascular plant species.
**Useful plants:** Timber trees (e.g. Pterocarpus angolensis). Plants useful for honey and wax production.
**Other values:** Many endemic or rare butterflies. Populations of chimpanzees and monkeys. Tourist potential.
**Threats:** Shifting cultivation, settlement.
**Conservation:** Mahale Mountain National Park (IUCN Management Category: II) covers 1613 km².

## Geography

The mountainous Mahale peninsular and Karobwa area is located in western Tanzania, on the central eastern shore of Lake Tanganyika (Kano 1972; JICA 1980; Collins and McGrew 1988; Nishida 1990). The area consists of a complex series of hills, ridges and valleys, between the lake shore at an altitude of 773 m and the Uvinza to Mpanda road on the Ugalla Hills at 1200–1500 m. The Mahale Mountains extend out into Lake Tanganyika on a peninsula which forms the Mahale Mountain National Park. There are a series of peaks, of which six are higher than 2000 m, including the highest are, Mfitwa (2496 m) and Nkungwe (2460 m). Further east is another series of mountains (the Karobwa) which actually consist of two ranges either side of the Luegele River. The south-western range consists of the Kakungu Mountains in the north and the Karobwa Mountains in the south, connecting with Mweze Mountain. The north-eastern range is a 80 km long sandstone ridge, running south-east from Kapalagulu Mountain near the lake to Sombwe Mountain, peaking at Sifuta Mountain (2075 m) and covering 600–700 km². North of Kapalagulu Mountain, between the Lugufu River basin and the lake shore, is the Kararumpeta ridge (1500–1600 m) and the Mukuyu Hills (which peak at 1530 m). The whole area drains westward into Lake Tanganyika.

Geologically the area is part of the western rift. To the north, the Malagarasi Depression may be tectonically old, but has recently been rejuvenated. To the south, the Karema Gap is an old rift valley, older than the Lake Tanganyika rift, with its western end represented by the Lukuga Gap at Kalémié in Zaïre. The Mahale Hills are formed mainly of gneiss. Soils vary, but are often shallow and infertile on hills, with more fertile alluvial soils in valley bottoms. The rainfall is 1500–2500 mm per annum on uplands near the lake. Eastwards, towards the Mpanda road, the rainfall is 1000–1500 mm per annum. Cloud and mist occur at higher altitudes. The dry season is from May to October and the rainy season from November to May.

## Vegetation

The vegetation is primarily woodland or wooded savanna, with patches of riverine, lowland, submontane and montane forest (Kano 1972; Nishida and Uehara 1981, 1983; Collins and McGrew 1988). The area is well drained, but there are occasional swamps and dambos. Grasslands occur on mountain ridges and plateaux as well as in formerly cultivated areas. Many areas of grassland are secondary, following cultivation and fire.

### Forest

Forests are Guineo-Congolian and cover approximately 150 km² (Rodgers *et al.* 1985). They occur in two main situations: riverine and montane.

Riverine forest is confined to river banks and tends to be in long narrow belts 5–20 m wide (exceptionally 100 m) of evergreen and deciduous trees, mainly at altitudes of 1500–1800 m (in mountainous areas), but also extending to the lake shore. Narrow belts of riverine forests may be the remnants of more extensive forest areas, possibly reduced by fire and shifting cultivation.

Lowland forest (740–1300 m) includes *Albizia glaberrima*, *Canarium schweinfurthii*, *Cynometra alexandri*, *Harungana madagascariensis*, *Julbernardia seretti*, *Khaya anthotheca*, *Milicia excelsa*, *Newtonia buchananii*, *Parkia filicoideaa*, *Pseudospondias microcarpa*, *Pycnanthus angolensis*, *Trichilia prieuriana* and *Xylopia parviflora*. Small forest clumps are sometimes found in depressions in short grassland or covering the lower mountain slopes; as example can be seen at Karoge and there was formerly another at Helembe.

Submontane forest (1300–1800 m) includes *Anthocleista schweinfurthii*, *Anthonotha noldeae*, *Bridelia micrantha*, *Carapa procera*, *Croton megalocarpus*, *Erythrophleum suaveolens*, *Maesa lanceolata*, *Parinari excelsa* and *Synsepalum cerasiferum*.

Montane forest occurs as evergreen patches between 1700–2350 m and includes *Anthonotha noldeae*, *Bersama abyssinica*, *Cyathea* sp., *Ficalhoa laurifolia*, *Ficus thonningii*, *Macaranga kilimandscharica*, *Nuxia congesta*, *Parinari excelsa*, *Phoenix reclinata*, *Podocarpus* sp., *Polyscias fulva*, *Psychotria mahonii* and *Rapanea melanophloeos*. There are patches of mountain bamboo, *Sinarundinaria (= Arundinaria) alpina*, on the Mahale Mountains.

## Woodland

Closed woodland, dominated by *Brachystegia* covers more than 80% of the land between 900 and 1800 m. Open woodland forms an ecotone between this closed woodland and grassland, and also occurs above 1800 m.

Open woodland, below 1800 m, includes *Annona senegalensis*, *Bauhinia petersiana*, *Diplorhynchus condylocarpon*, *Combretum* spp., *Markhamia obtusifolia* and *Vitex doniana*.

Closed woodland is dominated by *Brachystegia* spp. with stands of *Uapaca kirkiana* and *Monotes*. Other species include: *Afzelia quanzensis*, *Julbernardia paniculata*, *J. globiflora* and *Pterocarpus angolensis*.

**MAP 6. MAHALE-KAROBWA HILLS (CPD SITE Af33)**

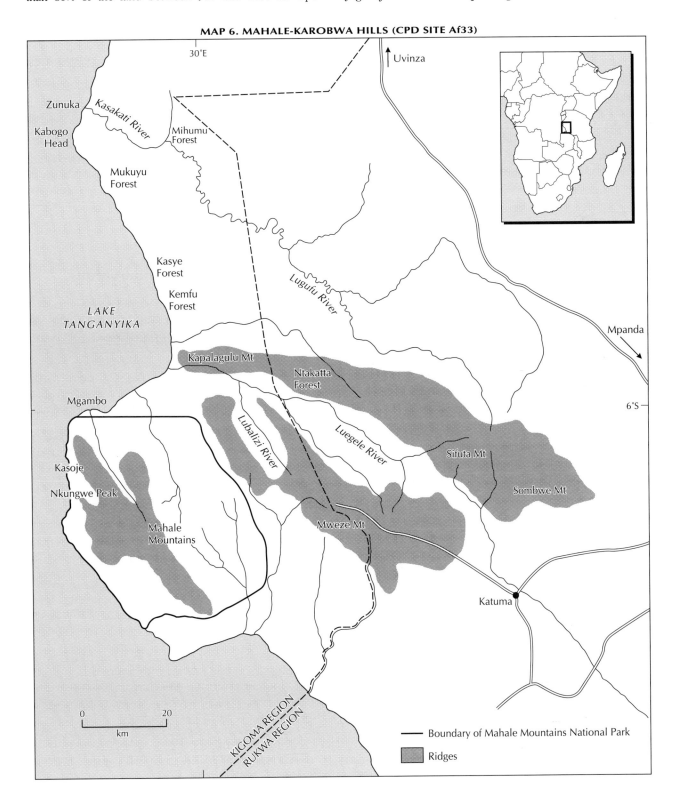

185

High-altitude woodland, above 1800 m, includes *Erythrina abyssinica*, *Parinari curatellifolia*, *Protea* spp. and *Terminalia mollis*.

### Grassland

There are two main types of grassland, tall grassland (up to 3 m), surrounding riverine forest in valleys and high-altitude montane grassland (1 m tall). In addition, there are papyrus swamps in shallow rivers and marshes (up to several kilometres wide along the Malagarasi River), seasonally-inundated mbuga grassland with scattered shrubs and trees in low basins and valley bottoms, and bamboo scrub consisting of *Oxytenanthera abyssinica*, which can form thick pure stands 7–10 m tall.

### Important forest areas

On the Mahale Mountains (6°00'–6°25'S, 29°47'–30°03'E) damp air blowing in from Lake Tanganyika results in mist and cloud which supports extensive montane forest above 1800 m. Submontane forests at lower altitudes give way to semi-evergreen lowland forests (Kasoge Forest 6°07'S, 29°44'E) at the north-western foot of the mountain from 780–1300 m. The latter stretch for 7 km, from the Myako Valley to the Lubulungu River. Eastern sides of the mountains are rather drier and are covered by *Brachystegia* woodlands. Lowland riverine forests have been the main site of shifting cultivation and are now mostly secondary, with the exception of the "isigo lyetabami" burial area.

On the Kapalagulu-Sombwe sandstone ridge, the vegetation is primarily *Brachystegia* and *Uapaca* woodland, with areas of open grassland (for example on Mt Kapalagulu). Forest occurs at Ntakatta (6°10'S, 30°20'E) where submontane and montane forests cover a wide valley with an area of 30–40 km², from an altitude of 1200 to 1700 m (Kielland and Congdon 1990).

Other forest areas of interest are Kasye and Mihumu (Kielland and Congdon 1990). Kasye Forest (5°50'S, 29°55'E), with an area of about 20 km², covers hills and valleys at 800–1000 m near the Kasye River where it runs into Lake Tanganyika. Mihumu Forest (5°30'S, 29°55'S) is in the basin of the Kasakati River, about 20 km from Kabogo Head on Lake Tanganyika and about 70 km south-south-east of Kigoma, at 900–1000 m altitude.

## Flora

The flora consists of both Zambesian and Guineo-Congolian elements, the total in these two categories probably being in excess of 2000 vascular plant species (J. Lovett 1993, personal estimate, based on the wide range of habitats and altitudes). The area is poorly known botanically, with extensive collections only from the Mahale Mountains. There are expected to be numerous rare plants.

The woodlands are Zambesian and are composed mainly of relatively widespread species, though some species of restricted distribution also occur. The forests are Guineo-Congolian and are likely to contain more species of restricted distribution; they are known to be rich in unusual butterflies, with 58 species endemic to the area. In particular the Ntakatta, Kasye and Mihumu forests are of importance.

Examples of species endemic to western Tanzania include the following: in riverine forest – *Impatiens*

*percordata* subsp. *percordata*, *Julbernardia unijugata*, *Keetia procteri*; in woodland and thicket – *Fadogia verdcourtii*, *Keetia ferruginea*; in swamps – *Anchomanes boehmii*.

Examples of species endemic to western Tanzania and adjacent areas in Zambia and Zaïre include:

in riverine forest – *Monopetalanthus richardsiae*, *Tessmannia burttii*; in woodland – *Brachystegia angustistipulata*, *Lannea asymmetrica*.

Apart from a few bryological records from material collected by an Oxford University Exploration Club Expedition in 1959, the only publication on the bryoflora of the Mahale Mountains is Ochyra and Pócs (1986), with a list of 44 species. The bryophyte flora seems to be transitional between West-Central and East African.

## Useful plants

Forests near settlements supply building poles and timber for boat building. In woodlands, Mninga (*Pterocarpus angolensis*) is a valuable timber. Observations of the use of medicinal plants by chimpanzees at Mahale has led to the discovery of antibiotic and antischistosomal compounds (Sears 1990; Ohigashi *et al*. 1991; Jisaka *et al*. 1992; Page *et al*. 1992).

## Social and environmental values

The forests protect catchment areas and river banks. The Mahale Mountain National Park, with its scenic beauty and chimpanzee populations is attracting tourists. Traditional honey collecting is a sustainable use of forest resources.

The submontane and montane forests of these hills are included in the Albertine Rift Mountains EBA. Two of the 39 restricted-range bird species of this EBA have been recorded here, including the threatened Kungwe apalis (*Apalis argentea*).

The butterfly fauna is known to be rich in endemics; 58 species are restricted to the area (Kielland 1978, 1990; Kielland and Congdon 1990).

## Threats

The main threat to the forests is shifting cultivation. Many forest patches have been destroyed in the last 20 years. Recently, there has been an influx of refugees from Zaïre, Rwanda and Burundi, resulting in large sprawling settlements. The refugees have settled along the Lake Tanganyika shoreline, at the point where the Mpanda road approaches the Lugufu River at Mishamo, and around Mweze Mountain.

There are plans to construct a road from Kigoma to Mgambo village close to Mahale Mountain, which would lead to an influx of people into currently uninhabited or sparsely-settled areas and increase pressure on the remaining forest patches.

Kemfu and Mukuyu Forests, north of Helembe, have been cut down recently for shifting agriculture and a large patch of lowland forest (900 m altitude) at Helembe has been severely reduced.

## Conservation

Mahale Mountain National Park was gazetted in June 1985 and covers 1613 km² of the Mahale Mountains on a peninsular jutting out into Lake Tanganyika. It was gazetted primarily to conserve chimpanzees. People living in the area were moved to villages outside the park in 1975. Chimpanzees are also found in the north-east part of the Mahale-Karobwa area, where they co-exist stably with current levels of selective logging and honey collection. This low density savanna population is regarded as being of unique scientific interest (Moore 1992).

Although the wide altitudinal range of forests and woodlands covered by the Mahale Mountain National Park is of botanical importance, the presence of many rare butterflies indicates that the botanically poorly known Ntakatta, Kasye and Mihumu forests are also of interest. Currently these forests are not protected.

## References

Collins, D.A. and McGrew, W.C. (1988). Habitats of three groups of chimpanzees (*Pan troglodytes*) in western Tanzania. *Journal of Human Evolution* 17: 553–574.

JICA (1980). *Study for the proposed Mahale Mountains National Park. Final Report, May 1980*. Japan Int. Coop. Agency.

Jisaka, M., Kawanaka, M., Sugiyama, H. and Takegawa, K. (1992). Antischistosomal activities of sesquiterpene lactones and steroid glucosides from *Vernonia amygdalina*, possibly used by wild chimpanzees against parasite-related diseases. *Bioscience Biotechnology and Biochemistry* 56: 845–846.

Kano, T. (1972). Distribution and adaptation of the chimpanzee on the eastern shore of Lake Tanganyika. *Kyoto Univ, African Studies* 7: 37–129.

Kielland, J. (1978). A provisional checklist of the *Rhopalocera* of the eastern side of Lake Tanganyika. *Tijdschrift voor entomologie* 121: 147–237.

Kielland, J. (1990). *Butterflies of Tanzania*. Hill House, London.

Kielland, J. and Congdon, T.C.E. (1990). A report on forests in Tanzania which are greatly in need of protection. (Unpublished MS.)

Moore, J. (1992). "Savanna" chimpanzees. In Nishida, T., McGrew, W.C., Marler, P., Pickford, M. and Waal, F.B.M. de (eds), *Topics in primatology. Vol 1: Human origins.* University of Tokyo Press, Tokyo. Pp. 99–118.

Nishida, T. (ed.) (1990). *The chimpanzees of the Mahale Mountains. Sexual and life history strategies*. University of Tokyo Press, Tokyo.

Nishida, T. and Uehara, S. (1981). Kitongwe name of plants: a preliminary listing. *African Study Monographs* 1: 109–131.

Nishida, T. and Uehara, S. (1983). Natural diet of chimpanzees (*Pan troglodytes schweinfurthii*): long-term record from the Mahale Mountains, Tanzania. *African Study Monographs* 3: 109–130.

Ochyra, R. and Pócs, T. (1986). East African bryophytes, X.K. Norikoshi's collection from the Mahale Mountains National Park, western Tanzania. *Hikobia* 9: 387–394.

Ohigashi, H., Jisaka, M., Takagaki, T. and Nozaki, H. (1991). Bitter principle and a related steroid glucoside from *Vernonia amygdalina*, a possible medicinal plant for wild chimpanzees. *Agricultural and Biological Chemistry* 55: 1201–1203.

Page J.E., Balza, F., Nishida, T. and Towers, G.H.N. (1992). Biologically active diterpenes from *Aspilia mossambicensis*, a chimpanzee medicinal plant. *Phytochemistry* 31: 3439.

Rodgers, W.A., Mziray W. and Shishira, E.K. (1985). *The extent of forest cover in Tanzania using satellite imagery.* Institute of Resource Assessment, University of Dar es Salaam. Research Paper No. 12.

Sears, C. (1990). The chimpanzees' medicine chest. *New Scientist* 127: 42–44.

## Acknowledgements

This Data Sheet was compiled by Jon Lovett (The Botanical Museum, University of Copenhagen, Denmark) from published and unpublished literature. Additional information on bryophytes was kindly supplied by Professor Tamás Pócs (Eszterhazy Teachers' College, Eger, Hungary) and on chimpanzees by Jim Moore.

ZAMBEZIAN REGIONAL CENTRE OF ENDEMISM: CPD SITE AF35

# KUNDELUNGU
## Zaïre

**Location:** Shaba Province, south-east Zaïre, between latitudes 9°00'–11°00'S and longitudes 27°30'–28°15'E.
**Area:** c. 9000 km².
**Altitude:** c. 1500–2000 m.
**Vegetation:** Miombo woodland, grassland, gallery forest.
**Flora:** Zambezian flora, with endemics on the plateaux.
**Useful plants:** Numerous local uses.
**Threats:** Fires (destroying forest patches), tree cutting for charcoal production, hunting.
**Conservation:** Kundelungu National Park (IUCN Management Category: II) covers 7600 km².

## Geography

Kundelungu is a mountain chain in Shaba Province, south-east Zaïre. It contains a National Park, created in 1970. It is botanically important especially for the vegetation and flora of its high plateaux, themselves part of a larger area of high plateaux in Shaba Province. The park lies to the north of the town of Lubumbashi, between latitudes 9°00'–11°00'S and longitudes 27°30'–28°15'E. The mountains cover an area of c. 9000 km², of which 7600 km² are protected within the National Park. The bedrock is mainly sandstone schist. Kalahari Sands of relatively recent geological age are extensive on the plateaux. The soils of Kundelungu have not been investigated, but, judging by a study carried out in the vicinity (Bourguignon, Streel and Calembert 1963), the plateaux soils are sandy and include red latosols, while alluvial soils occur in the plains.

The mountains are drained to the west by the Lufira, a tributary of the Lualaba (itself a tributary of the River Zaïre), while drainage to the east is by various rivers flowing into Lake Mweru. The most prominent tributary of the Lufira within the park itself is the Lofoi. Water-flow in the Lofoi varies from calm to torrential. A waterfall on the Lofoi is the highest in Africa, at 347 m.

The climate is of a humid tropical type, with a long dry season from May to September. Rains are concentrated in November to March. The mean annual temperature is about 20°C, with pronounced diurnal variation during the dry season (Devred 1960).

Population density is very low, with, for example, only 1.26 inhabitants per square kilometre in Kambove Region (Bourguignon, Streel and Calembert 1963). There is probably a concentration of settlements along the Likasi-Mituaba road to the west of the park. Agriculture is the dominant economic activity, crops including maize, cassava and sorghum. Hunting is practised on the plateaux.

## Vegetation

The vegetation consists mainly of wetter Zambezian miombo woodland and grasslands, with small pockets of gallery forest of Guineo-Congolian type.

Common trees in the miombo woodlands are *Balanites aegyptiaca*, *Bauhinia tomentosa*, *Brachstegia boehmii*, *B. bussei*, *B. longifolia*, *B. stipulata*, *B. taxifolia*, *B. utilis*, *Julbernardia paniculata* and *Monotes katangensis*. Open forests with *Berlinia giorgii*, *Brachystegia spiciformis* var. *latifoliolata* and *Marquesia macroura* occur on the driest, poorest and shallowest soils.

The grasslands have been classified as belonging to the phytosociological unit *Ctenio-Loudetietea simplicis* by Duvigneaud (1949). They can be found both on soils developed from Kalahari Sands on the plateaux and also in seasonally inundated sites in valleys. Plateau grasslands include the following species: *Bulbostylis laniceps*, *Elionurus argenteus*, *E. hensii*, *Loudetia simplex*, *Microchloa caffra*, *Monocymbium ceresiiforme* and *Trachypogon plumosus*. Woody plants include: *Annona stenophylla*, *Lannea edulis*, *Parinari capensis* and *Syzygium guineense*.

Dambos (seasonally inundated valley grasslands) contain *Loudetia simplex*, *Monocymbium ceresiiforme* and *Tristachya thollonii* and various species of Cyperaceae, Eriocaulaceae, Melastomataceae, Scrophulariaceae and Xyridaceae. Peat bogs with *Drosera*, *Lycopodium*, *Sphagnum* and Xyridaceae are found on the plateaux.

Gallery forests are often dominated by *Syzygium*, older individuals of which carry abundant semi-parasites (Loranthaceae). Other genera present include *Antidesma*, *Bersama*, *Tricalysia* and *Uapaca*. Pioneer vegetation along rivers includes the palm *Raphia* and also *Ficus* and *Zanthoxylum*.

Shrubland is found in areas of better drainage on the plateaux. Plants present include *Parinari*, *Philippia benguelensis*, *P. pallidiflora*, *Protea* sp. and *Uapaca robynsi*.

## Flora

There has been no systematic study, but collections have been made by Duvigneaud (1949), Malaisse (1979) and Schmitz (1952, 1971). As elsewhere in Katanga, the geographical isolation of the plateaux of Kundelungu has led to a certain degree of local endemism. Examples include *Ochna katangensis* and *Protea lemairei* (both on deep sands with poor drainage) and various varieties of *Brachystegia spiciformis* (*latifoliata, mpalensis, schmitzeii*). Other noteworthy species include: *Crotalaria argenteotomentosa, C. exelliana, C. florida* var. *monosperma, C. kundelungensis, C. oxyphylla, Cyphia brachyandra, Lobelia baumarnnii, L. kundelungensis* and *Triglochin bulbosa* subsp. *bulbosa*. The flora includes both Afromontane and Southern African elements, the former including *Agauria salicifolia, Juniperus procera, Philippia benguelensis, P. pallidiflora* and *Podocarpus* sp. and the latter various species of *Limeum* and *Psamorapha*.

## Useful plants

Plants are used locally for construction, firewood, charcoal, medicines and craftwork. Various plants also have cultural significance, for instance in terms of helping to define ethnic identities.

## Social and environmental values

The Kundelungu plateaux are of limited use for cultivation due to the unproductive sandy nature of the soils. Cattle raising is a significant economic activity. There is considerable potential for tourism, including viewing of the impressive waterfall on the River Lofoi. The fauna includes eland, hippopotamus, leopard, rowan antelope and zebra.

## Threats

The main threats are considered to be fires, hunting and tree cutting for charcoal production. Fires are believed to be a threat to the survival of small forest patches. Hunting is intense and could lead to disappearance of species such as the leopard.

## Conservation

Kundelungu National Park was created in 1970. There is a need to take active steps to conserve the small remaining pockets of forest and to control fires. Additionally, park boundaries should be defined and land zones designated for different uses.

## References

Bourguignon, P., Streel, M. and Calembert, J. (1963). Prospection pédobotanique des plaines superiéures de la Lufira. *Problèmes Sociaux Congolais, C.E.P.S.I.*: 60.

Devred, R. (1960). La cartographie de la végétation au Congo belge. *Bull. agr. C. B.* 51: 529–541.

Duvigneaud, P. (1949). La flore et la végétation du Congo méridional. *Lejeunia* 16: 95–124.

Malaisse, F. (1979). L'écosystème miombo. In *Ecosystèmes forestiers tropicaux*. Unesco, Paris. Pp. 64–659.

Schmitz, A. (1950). Principaux types de végétation forestière dans le Haut-Katanga. *C.R. congr. scient. Elisabethville, Comm.* 51, IV, 2: 276–304.

Schmitz, A. (1952). Essai sur la délimitation des régions naturelles dans le Haut-Katanga. *Bull. agr. C. b.* 43: 697–733.

Schmitz, A. (1960). Aperçu sur les groupements végétaux du Katanga. *Bull. Soc. Roy. Bot. Belg.* 96(2): 233–447.

Schmitz, A. (1971). Végétation de la plaine de Lubumbashi (Haut-Katanga). *INEAC, ser. scient.* 113. Bruxelles. 388 pp.

## Acknowledgements

This Data Sheet was prepared by Professor C.A. Lubini (Laboratoire de Biologie, Gombe, Zaïre).

# UPEMBA NATIONAL PARK
## Zaïre

**Location:** Shaba Province, south-east Zaïre, between latitudes 26°12'–27°10'E and longitudes 8°00'–10°00'S.

**Area:** 11,730 km².

**Altitude:** 350–1100 m.

**Vegetation:** Miombo woodland, dry evergreen forest (muhulu), wooded *Acacia*, grassland, aquatic and swamp communities, some riparian Guineo-Congolian forest.

**Flora:** Very poorly known; probably over 2400 vascular plant species; species on poor plateaux soils probably of special interest.

**Useful plants:** Many locally useful plants; some timber trees.

**Other values:** Tourism, catchment protection.

**Threats:** Tree-felling, poaching, fires.

**Conservation:** National Park established 1939; needs further management resources.

## Geography

Upemba National Park, created in 1939, is situated in the Province of Shaba in south-east Zaïre, between latitudes 26°12'–27°10'E and longitudes 8°00'–10°00'S. It lies to the west of Kundelungu National Park (see Data Sheet on Kundelungu, CPD Site Af35). The altitude ranges from 350 to 1100 m. The area is 11,730 km².

The park is in the centre of the high plateau region of Katanga. The park itself contains an extensive area of low-lying country to the west, containing Lake Upemba and numerous swamps. The east of the park is higher, with the very extensive, deeply dissected, plateaux of Mt Kibara, consisting of Precambrian basalt. The Kamalondo Rift and Mts Bia and Hakansson lie to the south. Drainage is mainly into the River Lualaba. There are diverse soil types, especially ferrallitic latosols (some highly leached) and alluvium.

The climate is hot and humid, with a dry season of 120–150 days (May–September, with no rain in June–August). Annual precipitation is c. 1300 mm. The mean annual temperature is c. 25°C.

Population density is low, at c. 5–20 people/km². The extent of cultivated land is very low, perhaps c. 1 ha/km² (Abdel Kader and Fatma 1978). Crops include cassava, maize and sorghum. There is illegal hunting of antelopes, elephants and monkeys in the park.

## Vegetation

The park is in the zone of contact between Guineo-Congolian rain forest and Zambezian woodland. There is much variation related to topography and soils. There are extensive areas of wooded grassland on alluvial soils, as well as of aquatic and semi-aquatic vegetation.

There are two types of woodland or forest on the Kibara plateaux. One of these is open miombo woodland (Schmitz 1963, 1971), which contains *Anisophyllea boehmii*, *Brachystegia boehmii*, *B. bussei*, *B. floribunda*, *B. microphylla*, *B. spiciformis*, *B taxifolia*, *B. utilis*, *Daniella alsteeniana*, *Erythrophleum africanum*, *Julbernardia paniculata*, *Marquesia macroura*, *Monotes angolensis*, *M. katangensis*, *Protea bequaertii*, *P. homblei*, *Pterocarpus angolensis*, *Uapaca nitida* and *U. pilosa*. This woodland type is regarded as originating through degradation of the other tree-dominated vegetation type, known as "muhulu". The latter is a dry evergreen type of forest, with numerous lianes, containing *Anthocleista schweinfurthii*, *Diospyros hoyleana*, *Entandrophragma delevoyi*, *Erythrophleum suaveolens* and *Parinari excelsa*.

There are strips of Guineo-Congolian forest along rivers, containing *Garcinia polyantha*, *Khaya nyasica*, *Phoenix reclinata*, *Syzygium cordatum* and *Treculia africana*.

Wooded grassland occurs on alluvial soils. Trees include *Acacia polyacantha* subsp. *campylacantha*, *A. seyal*, *A. sieberiana*, *Borassus flabellifer*, *Kigelia aethiopicum*, *Markhamia obtusifolia* and *Terminalia mollis*. Grasses include *Beckeropsis uniseta*, *Hyparrhenia cymbaria*, *Imperata cylindricum*, *Pennisetum purpureum* and *Themeda triandra*.

Papyrus (*Cyperus papyrus*) swamps are very extensive. Other species recorded from swamps include *Echinochloa crus-pavonis*, *Eleocharis dulcis*, *Leersia hexandra*, *Ludwigia abyssinica*, *L. stolonifera*, *Phragmites mauritianus*, *Polygonum salicifolium*, *Rhus anchietae* and *Typha angustifolium*. Temporarily inundated soils contain grassland of *Sporobolus festivus*, accompanied by *Desmodium hirtum* subsp. *delicatum*. Aquatic plants include *Azolla pinnata*, *Ceratophyllum demersum*, *Lemna perpusilla*, *Marsilea diffusa*, *Nymphaea lotus*, *Ottelia uivifolia* and *Ruppia maritima*.

## Flora

The flora of the park has never been properly studied. Some information is given by Bourguigon, Streel and Calembert (1963), and by Schmitz (1971). The flora contains both

Guineo-Congolian and Zambesian elements and there are also some Afromontane elements (e.g *Agauria, Philippia*) on the plateaux. Duvigneaud (1949) divided the park into two phytogeographical units (West Katanga and the High Plateaux of Katanga). Robyns (1948) included a part of the park in his floristic District du Bas-Katanga.

The diversity of habitats is associated with a diverse flora. Schmitz (1971) has recorded the following numbers of taxa from the Lubumbashi Plain near the park: gymnosperms – 1 species; dicotyledons – 115 families, 567 genera, 1707 subgeneric taxa; monocotyledons – 26 families, 188 genera, 690 subgeneric taxa. Well-represented genera include *Brachystegia, Crotalaria* and *Vernonia*. Noteworthy species on the plateaux include *Cyphia brachyandra* var. *witteana, Lobelia lasiosalycina* and *L. molleri*.

## Useful plants

Plants are used for many purposes, including as sources of fruits (*Aframomum albo-violaceum, Annona sengalensis, Saba florida*) and for manufacture of mats (*Cyprus papyrus*).

## Social and environmental values

Upemba National Park provides the local people a number of useful resources, such as fuelwood, game and fish. Fish are traded to Lubidi, Bakama, Malemba-Nkulu and Manono. There is tourist potential on the lake and in the plateaux area. The park also serves a protective function for catchments. The fauna includes Cape eland, elephant and numerous zebra, as well as several rare species of monkeys. Among the avifauna, the threatened black-lored waxbill (*Estrilda nigriloris*) is endemic to the area around the Lualaba River and Lake Upemba, where it is found in level grassy plains with tall grass and bushes (Collar and Stuart 1985).

## Threats

These include illicit commercial tree-felling and poaching. Burning might result in retreat of forest.

## Conservation

Upemba National Park was established in 1939. The management needs strengthening. Study of the flora and fauna is a top priority for formulation of management plans.

## References

Abdel Kader, F. and Fatma (1978). La végétation. In Laclavère, G. (ed.), *Atlas de la République du Zaïre*. Jeune Afrique: 20–21.

Bourguignon, P., Streel, M. and Calembert, J. (1963). Prospection pédobotanique des plaines supérieures de la Lufira. *Problèmes Sociaux Congolais, C.E.P.S.I.* 60.

Collar, N.J. and Stuart, S.N. (1985). *Threatened birds of Africa and related islands*. The ICBP/IUCN Red Data Book, part 1. 3rd edition. ICBP/IUCN, Cambridge, U.K. 797 pp.

Duvigneaud, P. (1949). La flore et la vegetation du Congo meridional. *Lejeunia* 16: 95–124.

Robyns, W. (1948). Les territoires phytogéographiques du Congo Belge et du Ruanda-Urundi. In *Atlas Général du Congo Belge*. Inst. Roy. Col. Belge, Bruxelles.

Schmitz, A. (1963). Aperçu sur les groupements végétaux du Katanga. *Bull. Soc. Roy. Bot. Belg.* 96: 233–447.

Schmitz, A. (1971). La végétation de la Plaine de Lubumbashi (Haut-Katanca). *Publ. INEAC sér scient.* No. 113. Bruxelles. 388 pp.

## Acknowledgements

This Data Sheet was prepared by Professor C.A. Lubini (Laboratoire de Biologie, Gombe, Zaïre).

# ZAMBEZI SOURCE AREA
## Zambia

**Location:** The Ikelenge "pedicle" of the Mwinilunga District in North-Western Province, Zambia; between latitudes 10°53'–11°24'S and at longitude c. 24°23'E.

**Area:** c. 1700 km².

**Altitude:** c. 1200–1490 m.

**Vegetation:** Riverine and swamp forest, dry evergreen forest, chipya woodland, miombo woodland, orchard bushland, scrub, suffrutex savanna, dambo grassland.

**Flora:** Forest trees and orchids of Guineo-Congolian affinities, rich higher-rainfall miombo and Kalahari Sand communities; woody flora is between 950–1000 species.

**Useful plants:** Timber trees (e.g. *Pterocarpus angolensis*), plants used for honey and wax production.

**Other values:** Watershed protection; refuge for wildlife (small mammals, birds, reptiles, insects), tourist potential.

**Threats:** Shifting cultivation.

**Conservation:** 9 Protected Forest Areas, in which settlement and cultivation are prohibited. Legislation prohibits riverine clearing, but implementation of the law is ineffective. 2.6 km² designated as National Forest and National Monument.

## Geography

The Ikelenge pedicle of Mwinilunga District is situated in the North-Western Province of Zambia, bordering on Angola and Zaïre. The international border with Zaïre is the watershed between the Zambezi and Zaïre (Congo) river system. Apart from the headwaters of the Luakera, in the neck of the pedicle, the whole area drains into the Zambezi, which itself flows westward into Angola.

The area lies within the higher rainfall miombo zone and experiences a narrower range of temperature extremes than the rest of Zambia. The annual rainfall is about 1400 mm. Virtually all the rain falls between November and April. Mean July temperatures are above 20°C for the whole area, which is the warmest in the country, with maximum temperatures in October.

There is a diversity of soil types reflecting a variety of parent materials. Some flat interfluves carry remnants of a mantle of aeolian sand, known as Kalahari Sand, which covers much of the western part of Africa south of the Equator. The greater relief of the Mwinilunga District has resulted in erosion of the sand from the slopes and a greater mixing of the sand with finer material derived from exposed underlying rock.

The flat Kalahari Sand-capped interfluves vary from well-drained to seasonally waterlogged, the waterlogging being caused by rainwater stagnation over an impervious substrate. The well drained areas carry evergreen forest or woodland and the areas with seasonally waterlogged subsoil support a suffrutex savanna vegetation, which is one of the well known features of the area.

Interfluves with soils other than Kalahari Sand carry miombo woodland, as do the valley slopes. Riverine forest occurs along most permanent rivers and streams.

## Vegetation

The vegetation types occurring in the area are: forest (including seepage, or swamp forest, riverine forest and dry-evergreen forest), woodland (open forest), including miombo woodland and chipya woodland, scrub, termite mound vegetation, savanna (including orchard bushland and suffrutex savanna), grassland and dambo grassland.

The term woodland, as used by locally, is generally applied to any wooded vegetation which carries a more or less continuous ground cover of grasses or other flammable material and is, therefore, subjected to annual fires. Forests, on the other hand, are not flammable. The seepage and riverine fringing forests of Mwinilunga are the richest in Zambia and certainly contain species as yet unrecorded. They have strong Guinea-Congolian affinities. In the past, the riverine forests were left undisturbed, but, more recently, the Lunda people have cleared areas to grow sugarcane, bananas and vegetables.

Dry evergreen forest (chipya) survives only as relicts in secondary woodland. There are two types of chipya: Lake Basin Chipya, which refers to the type of evergreen thicket associated with the Bangweulu lake basin of north-eastern Zambia, and Kalahari Chipya, which is derived from *Cryptosepalum* forest on Kalahari Sand. Whether the Mwinilunga "lake basin" soils have a lacustrine origin is doubtful and it seems advisable to adopt the term "muhulu", used in Zaïre. *Cryptosepalum* forest, dominated by *C. exfoliatum* subsp. *pseudotaxus*, which occurs abundantly further south in Zambia, stops short just south of the pedicle.

Kalahari chipya woodland is derived from *Cryptosepalum* forest after partial clearance for cultivation and the introduction of a fire regime. The canopy remain more or less intact.

Miombo woodland is the main vegetation type of well-drained interfluves. It is dominated by species of *Brachystegia* and *Isoberlinia angolensis*. Interfluve soils of higher clay content have many termite mounds, with vegetation distinct from that of any of the local woodland or forest types, but with affinities to thicket types occurring in areas of drier climate.

Orchard bushland is an open savanna with small trees, many of them bearing edible fruits and occupying the areas bordering the watershed plains, where the ground begins to slope off. On steeper slopes it gives way to miombo woodland on the lower side. Pineapples are grown on the fringes of suffrutex savanna, but the natural vegetation of most of the area is not threatened.

Seepage dambos are permanently wet bogs of mucky peat. They are rich in orchids and other interesting herbs. Other dambos are riverine grasslands which are seasonally waterlogged.

Scrub (degraded woodland) occurs on land abandoned after cultivation. Annual fires prevent or delay the regeneration of woodland.

## Flora

The Mwinilunga District Forest Reserve contains between 950–1000 woody species (Fanshawe undated). This is the highest count of wood species of any District in the area which he considered. Fanshawe lists 53 "endemic" species, many of these being Guineo-Congolian endemics. The fact that Mwinilunga is on the border between two countries means that there are probably no species endemic to Zambia alone, although little appears to be known of the adjacent areas of Angola and Zaïre. Since the Angolan area has been a war zone since the 1970s, there has been little opportunity for exploration.

## Useful plants

The most important timber tree species is *Pterocarpus angolensis*. A number of species are used for honey and wax production. The woodlands supply firewood, herbal medicines and edible fungi.

## Social and environmental values

The total population of the Mwinilunga District is c. 82,000 (1990 census), with a density of 3.9 km². The density of the Ikelenge pedicle is probably 3–4 times as high as the District average, giving an estimated population of between 5000–7000 (M. Bingham, personal estimate). This could be an under-estimate.

There are 5500 traditional beekeepers in Mwinilunga District and, of these, about 1000–2000 are in the predicle. The whole western part of the North-Western Province was a major source of exported beeswax before Zambian independence and beeswax is still one of the major sources of income. Recently, the industry has been supported with financial and technical aid and honey and wax are now exported to Europe. Most of the honey is from bark hives, but it is also foraged from the woodlands. Bark-hive beekeeping has been criticized for the destruction of trees from which the hives are made, but those involved in supporting the industry point out that it is preferable to shifting agriculture, which is more destructive.

There is only one viable commercial farm in the Ikelenge pedicle (Hillwood Farm) which supports cattle and sheep.

Small-scale farming mainly occurs along access roads. Poor road maintenance may result in migration towards the commercial centres or even out of the area altogether.

## Threats

The Lunda still practice a form of shifting cultivation, the main crops being cassava which is cultivated on mounds made by heaping up soil after clearing and burning the woodlands, maize and finger millet (*Eleusine*). Restricted marketing facilities have kept production at subsistence levels. Most of the interfluves have been cleared, but the settled areas along the roads are much more heavily utilised. Other crops which have been introduced to the area include pineapples, bananas, citrus fruits and oil palm. Inroads by UNITA soldiers from Angola have forced people to move away from the border areas.

Extraction of commercial hardwood timber is virtually restricted to one species, *Pterocarpus angolensis*, locally known as mukwa. The wood is used for furniture making. Some of the wood is exported (to South Africa), but the export of wood is restricted to finished products. As only the larger trees are harvested, the species itself is not threatened. More serious is the loss of habitat by woodland clearing for cultivation.

## Conservation

Approximately 9% (154 km²) of Mwinilunga is gazetted as Protected Forest Areas (PFAs), in which settlement and cultivation are excluded. These PFAs are of two categories: National Forest and Local Forest. The National Forest Estate was established mainly to protect river catchments and forested areas of particular interest. Of the nine PFAs in the pedicle, only the Zambezi Source Area (2.6 km²) is a National Forest. This is also a National Monument and is, therefore, totally protected. The Local Forests are reserves for local exploitation, to supply building materials and other forest products.

## References

Edmonds, A.C.R. (comp.) (1976). *Vegetation map of Zambia. 1:500,000*. Survey Department, Lusaka.

Fanshawe, D.B. (1971). *The vegetation of Zambia*. Division of Forest Research, Kitwe.

Fanshawe, D.B. (undated). *The vegetation of Mwinilunga District*. Forest Research Pamphlet No. 27.

Wen Tin-tiang (1987). *The soils of North-Western Province. 1:1,000,000 soil map and accompanying memoir*. Soil Survey Unit, Department of Agriculture.

## Acknowledgements

This Data Sheet was prepared by M. Bingham (Lusaka, Zambia). P. Fisher (Ikelenge) provided information on settlement and agriculture.

SOMALI-MASAI REGIONAL CENTRE OF ENDEMISM: CPD SITE AF42

# CAL MADOW
## Somalia

**Location:** North and north-east Cerigaabo (Erigavo) in the Sanaag Region of northern Somalia; between latitudes 10°40'–11°08'N and longitudes 47°05'–49°05'E.

**Area:** c. 9600 km².

**Altitude:** 0–2400 m.

**Vegetation:** Dry montane forest; evergreen, semi-evergreen and deciduous bushland and woodland; semi-desert vegetation.

**Flora:** Estimated 1000 vascular plant species; high species endemism, many disjunct taxa.

**Useful plants:** Frankincense, myrrh trees, carob relative, timber trees.

**Other values:** Rich fauna.

**Threats:** Logging, overgrazing.

**Conservation:** Daalo Forest Reserve proposed as a National Park. Threats to flora not so severe as in some other areas of Somalia.

## Geography

Cal Madow (Al Medu) is situated in a part of northern Somalia consisting of two physiographic regions: a coastal plain bordering the Gulf of Aden, locally known as the "Guban", and an uplifted limestone plateau lying to the south and dipping to the south-east. The plateau scarp reaches 2416 m at Shimbiris (the highest point in Somalia), to the north-west of Ceerigaabo.

The Cal Madow area as defined here includes parts of the coastal plain near Maydh (Mait), a hilly subcoastal zone of varying width running along the coastline, a continuous block of steep escarpment, about 200 km long, and a part of the neighbouring plateau which contains areas of gypsum.

The climate is influenced by monsoon winds. Annual rainfall in the coastal and subcoastal zone is less than 100 mm and is very variable. The upper part of the escarpment is the wettest area in Somalia, receiving a mean rainfall over 700 mm per annum. A major part probably falls during winter months, during the north-east monsoon, when mists are also frequent. The plateau itself is in a rain-shadow and receives considerably less rain. Rain falling on the escarpment is drained to the north and many seasonal streams run across the coastal plain.

Temperatures vary from a mean maximum of well over 40°C on the coastal plain during the summer months, when hot, dry winds from the west and south-west are frequent, to occasional frosts on the plateau scarp in winter.

## Vegetation

The vegetation varies greatly according to altitude and rainfall. The coastal plain near Maydh is desert or semi-desert, with little or no vegetation, while the subcoastal zone has sparse to dense vegetation dominated by woody species in genera such as *Acacia*, *Commiphora* and *Boswellia*. At intermediate altitudes, the slopes of the escarpment are largely covered by a macchia-like evergreen or semi-evergreen scrub with, for example, *Buxus hildebrandtii*, *Cadia purpurea*, *Dracaena schizantha* and *Pistacia aethiopica*. The upper zone of the evergreen scrub grades into remnants of *Juniperus* forest along the scarp.

To the south of the escarpment open woodlands, dominated by *Acacia etbaica*, have been severely degraded as a result of overgrazing and tree cutting. Very few trees remain.

## Flora

Botanical exploration of Cal Madow began in the 1870s; numerous Somali plants were first described from this area. There have been many collections in the west, north of Ceerigaabo, and in the east, around Galgalo, but most parts of Cal Madow remain inaccessible and unexplored. The total number of vascular plant species is estimated at about 1000.

Phytogeographically, the area belongs to the Somali-Masai Region, but it contains many disjunct elements linking it also with, for example, the Mediterranean, Macaronesian and Afromontane regions. It is clear that the area has served as a refugium for arid and semi-arid relictual elements. Some examples of phytogeographically interesting species present in Cal Madow are: *Aeonium leucoblepharum*, *Anemone somaliensis*, *Ceratonia oreothauma*, *Conocarpus lancifolius*, *Drusa glandulosa*, *Euphorbia balsamifera*, *Helianthemum* (4 endemic species), *Kissenia arabica*, *Livistona carinensis*, *Securigera somaliensis* and *Thamnosma* (2 species, 1 of which is endemic).

The families Barbeyaceae, Cyclocheilaceae and Wellstediaceae, endemic or near-endemic in the Somali-

Masai Region, are all represented in Cal Madow; the isolated monotypic genus *Renschia* is a strict endemic of Cal Madow.

Endemic elements include several succulent species of *Euphorbia*, many species confined to limestone rocks and species restricted to gypsum substrates, such as *Reseda sessilifolia*. Among endemics restricted to northern Somali escarpments, it is estimated that well over 10 are present in Cal Madow.

## Useful plants

Of particular importance are frankincense trees (*Boswellia frereana* and *B. sacra*), which occur on cliff faces and in rocky gullies in the subcoastal zone. The area is one of the major frankincense producing areas in Somalia and Maydh has been one of the centres for export of frankincense since ancient times. *Commiphora myrrha* (myrrh) is also found in Cal Madow, and the area has a large proportion of the remaining *Juniperus* forests of Somalia.

*Conocarpus lancifolius* is a large tree which has valuable wood; it is also a popular street tree in Somalia. It is restricted to northern Somalia and found in the subcoastal zone of Cal Madow.

*Ceratonia oreothauma* is the only close relative of the carob tree, *C. siliqua*.

## Social and environmental values

Cal Madow has a rich fauna, including the Beira gazelle. The Cal Madow region lies within the North Somalia mountains EBA. All of the three restricted-range bird species which are endemic to this EBA occur at Cal Madow. Two of these are found in open, rocky areas, including the threatened Somali pigeon (*Columba oliviae*), and the threatened Warsangli linnet (*Carduelis johannis*) also occurs in evergreen scrub and *Juniperus* forest.

With its varied and dramatic topography and interesting flora and fauna, the area has potential for ecotourism.

## Threats

*Juniperus* forests have been severely degraded by logging, particularly near Ceerigaabo. *Acacia* woodlands on the plateau have almost disappeared over large areas as a result of overgrazing and fuelwood collecting.

The most interesting vegetation along the escarpment is still largely intact and threats to the flora are not particularly severe at present.

## Conservation

Daalo Forest Reserve, to the north of Ceerigabo, and the surrounding mountain area have been proposed for protection as a National Park. However, at present, there are no functioning nature reserves in Somalia.

## References

Hemming, C.F. (1966). The vegetation of the northern region of the Somali Republic. *Proc. Linn. Soc.* 17: 173–249.

Lavranos, J.J. (1978). On the Mediterranean and western Asiatic floral element in the area of the Gulf of Aden. *Bot. Jahrb. Syst.* 99: 152–167.

Thulin, M. (in press). Aspects of disjunct distributions and endemism in the arid parts of the Horn of Africa, particularly Somalia.

Thulin, M. and Warfa, A.M. (1987). The frankincense trees (*Boswellia* spp., Burseraceae) of northern Somalia and southern Arabia. *Kew Bulletin* 42: 487–500.

## Acknowledgements

This Data Sheet was prepared by Dr Mats Thulin (Department of Systematic Botany, Uppsala University, Sweden).

# HOBYO
# Somalia

**Location:** Around Hobyo (Obbia) in the Mudug Region of central Somalia; between latitudes 5°00'–6°00'N and longitudes 48°00'–48°57'E.

**Area:** c. 3000 km².

**Altitude:** 0–440 m.

**Vegetation:** Deciduous bushland and woodland, dune vegetation.

**Flora:** No reliable estimate for the number of vascular plants can be given, but suspected to be <1000 species; high species endemism.

**Useful plants:** Medicinal plants; some plants used locally for building materials.

**Other values:** Rich fauna, including oryx.

**Threats:** Overgrazing, fuelwood collection.

**Conservation:** None; part of the area is proposed as a Game Reserve.

## Geography

The Hobyo area as defined here includes: (a) the coastal plain around Hobyo with dunes of white or orange sand and areas of limestone pavement, particularly in the north; (b) a low limestone escarpment running more or less parallel to the coastline; and (c) a more or less flat, low plateau further inland.

The limestone escarpment reaches about 440 m southwest of Hobyo. It is dissected by deep gorges which run approximately east to west. The gorges contain seasonal streams.

Rainfall is very variable and probably amounts to c. 200 mm; it is bimodal, with peaks during spring and autumn. Temperatures vary little over the year. Mean monthly maxima are 30°–36°C; mean minima are 19°–23°C.

## Vegetation

The coastal plain is open and treeless with a low vegetation of grasses, herbs and shrublets. One of the most common shrublets is the Somali endemic *Indigofera sparteola*. Small-scale planting of exotic woody species took place on some mobile dunes during the 1980s in an attempt at dune stabilization.

The limestone escarpment is covered with species-rich *Acacia-Commiphora* bushland. The gorges have a mesic element in their flora. The inland plateau has bushland and woodland dominated by species of *Acacia* and *Commiphora*.

## Flora

Botanical exploration of the Hobyo area started at the end of the 19th century and there have been several subsequent visits by collectors. The area is still relatively inaccessible; even when visited by botanists, it can prove impossible to study the flora given the unpredictable rainfall, with its controlling influence over phenology. During a brief visit by M. Thulin and A.M. Dahir in 1989, about 80 (selective) collections were made, of which 25 proved to be undescribed species. No reliable estimates of the total number of species or number of endemics can be made at present, although it is suspected that the area contains less than 1000 species of vascular plants.

Phytogeographically, the area belongs to the Somali-Masai Region. Of special interest is the occurrence of the enigmatic family Dirachmaceae, endemic to this region. *Dirachma somalensis*, one of the two species in the family (both of which are endangered) has its richest known locality in the limestone gorges west of Hobyo. Also of phytogeographical interest is the disjunct mesic element present in these gorges, including species such as *Buxus hildebrandtii*, *Maytenus undata* and *Vepris eugeniifolia*.

Examples of interesting endemics in the area are *Lochia parvibracta* (the two other species of *Lochia* are found on Socotra, Abd-al-Kuri and in Oman) and *Amphiasma gracilicaulis*. Many of the endemics are cushion-plants shaped by the sand-carrying winds. Succulents are also frequent. The monotypic genus *Puntia* has its only known locality just north of the area, as here defined, but probably also occurs within it.

## Useful plants

Many species are used locally as medicines and for building. Many woody species are utilized as fuelwood. The area supports grazing animals.

## Social and environmental values

The wildlife of the Hobyo area is still relatively rich and includes dibatag, oryx and Soemmering's gazelle. The

Hobyo area lies in the northern part of the Central Somalia coast EBA, which extends southwards to near Mogadishu. Two bird species are endemic to this EBA, occurring in arid grassland and desert. Only one of these has been recorded around Hobyo, but it is speculated that the second, the threatened Ash's lark (*Mirafra ashi*), may also range into this area (Collar and Stuart 1985). Extensive beaches occur along the coast.

## Threats

Threats to the flora are not particularly severe at present, although the effects of overgrazing and cutting of woody vegetation for fuelwood are damaging in some places. Fortunately, the most botanically interesting vegetation, that of the dunes and limestone gorges, is still largely intact.

## Conservation

Parts of the area have been proposed as a Game Reserve.

## References

Collar, N.J. and Stuart, S.N. (1985). *Threatened birds of Africa and related islands*. The ICBP/IUCN Red Data Book, part 1. 3rd edition. ICBP/IUCN, Cambridge, U.K. 797 pp.

Link, D.A. (1991). *Dirachma somalensis* D.A. Link sp. nov. A new species of a remarkable and highly endangered monogeneric family. *Bull. Jard. Bot. Nat. Belg.* 61: 3–13.

Thulin, M. (1990). Seven new species and one new record of *Polygala* (Polygalaceae) from Somalia. *Nordic Journal of Botany* 10: 465–475.

Thulin, M. (in press). Aspects of disjunct distributions and endemism in the arid parts of the Horn of Africa, particularly Somalia.

## Acknowledgements

This Data Sheet was prepared by Dr Mats Thulin (Department of Systematic Botany, Uppsala University, Sweden).

# GARAMBA NATIONAL PARK
## and surrounding Domaines de Chasses
### Zaïre

**Location:** Garamba National Park is located within Uele District, north-east Zaïre, on the Sudan border (Nile-Zaïre watershed) between latitudes 3°45'-4°41'N and longitudes 28°48'-30°00'E.

**Area:** 56,727 km².

**Altitude:** 710–1061 m.

**Vegetation:** Sudanian woodland, various types of savanna, papyrus marshes, riverine forests.

**Flora:** Estimated c. 1000 vascular plant species, of which c. 5% are endemic.

**Useful plants:** Timber trees, papyrus, medicinal plants.

**Other values:** Rich fauna, including large populations of elephant and giraffe.

**Threats:** Uncontrolled fires; lack of sufficient trained personnel, equipment and funds.

**Conservation:** Garamba National Park and World Heritage Site covers 49,200 km². Surrounding Domaines de Chasses (Hunting Reserves) cover 7527 km².

## Geography

Garamba National Park (Parc National de Garamba) comprises a vast undulating plateau (part of an ancient peneplain), with inselbergs (mostly of granite) and large areas of marshes, in the Uele District of north-east Zaïre. The park lies on the watershed between the River Nile and the River Zaïre, on the border between Sudan and Zaïre, between latitudes 3°45'-4°41'N and longitudes 28°48'-30°00'E. The largest rivers are the Dungu, Aka and Garamba.

The climate is tropical with a distinct wet season (March–November) and a long dry period (November–March). The mean annual rainfall is 1492 mm. Temperatures range from 15.8° to 33.5°C (Smith and Smith 1991).

## Vegetation

The most characteristic vegetation of the park is a shrub savanna or savanna woodland. The dominant grasses are *Hyparrhenia* spp. and *Loudetia arundinacea*; common shrubs and small trees include *Bridelia micrantha*, *Crossopteryx febrifuga*, *Grewia mollis*, *Hymenocardia acida*, *Nauclea latifolia*, *Stereospermum kunthianum*, *Vitex doniana* and *V. madiensis*. Fringing forests along the rivers contain *Ficus congensis*, *Irvingia smithii*, *Mitragyna stipulosa*, *Syzygium guineensis* and occasionally *Phoenix reclinata*. Some rain forest relicts exist in drier places within the fringing forests, with *Erythrophloeum suaveolens*, *Khaya grandifoliola* and *Spathodea campanulata*. The north-eastern part of the park carries Sudanian woodland dominated by *Isoberlinia doka*, with scattered *Uapaca somon*.

Other vegetation types in the park include xerophilous associations on granitic outcrops and aquatic and semi-aquatic associations along the rivers and in marshes.

## Flora

There have been no detailed studies of the flora of Garamba, except for the gymnosperms and monocotyledons (Troupin 1956). It is estimated that there are approximately 1000 vascular plant species (Mandango 1992, personal estimate), of which about 5% are endemic. The flora belongs to the Sudanian phytochorion of White (1983). Notable species include *Combretum* spp., *Hymenocardia acida*, *Khaya anthotheca*, *Kigelia africana* (the sausage tree) and *Vitex* spp.

## Useful plants

The following plants are of importance:

| Building materials | Ropes, mats, baskets |
|---|---|
| *Hallea stipulosa* | *Cyperus papyrus* |
| *Hymenocardia acida* | *Thalia welwitschii* |
| *Imperata cylindrica* | |
| *Khaya anthotheca* | **Medicinal plants** |
| *Leersia hexandra* | *Erythrophloeum guineense* |
| *Pennisetum purpureum* | *Nauclea latifolia* |
| *Terminalia mollis* | *Terminalia mollis* |
| | *Vitex doniana* |
| **Fuelwood** | |
| *Hymenocardia acida* | **Ornamental plants** |
| *Hyparrhenia diplandra* | *Spathodea campanulata* |
| *Loudetia phragmitoides* | |
| *Loudetia simplex* | |
| *Pennisetum simplex* | |

## Social and environmental values

The park contains probably the last viable natural population of the northern square-lipped or white rhinoceros (*Ceratotherium simum cottoni*), which is seriously threatened by poaching. The African elephants represent a unique population intermediate between the forest and savanna sub-species (*Loxodonta africana cyclotis* and *L. africana africana*). Like the rhinos, their numbers have been reduced as a result of poaching. Other mammals include northern savanna giraffe (*Giraffa camelopardalis congoensis*), which is found nowhere else in Zaïre, buffalo (*Syncerus caffer*), hippopotamus (*Hippopotamus amphibius*), chimpanzee (*Pan troglodytes*), olive baboon (*Papio anubis*), colobus monkeys, lion (*Panthera leo*), leopard (*P. pardus*) and several species of antelope (IUCN/UNEP 1987).

## Economic assessment

There are no figures or estimates available for the quantities or values of plants collected from the area. Long-term studies are needed.

## Threats

The main threats to the vegetation are uncontrolled burning and trampling by elephants. Since at least the 1950s, woody vegetation has been decreasing inside, and increasing outside, the National Park (Smith 1991). The reduction of cover within the National Park is probably due to a combination of increased animal density (particularly of elephants) and late burning (both accidental and deliberate, in order to increase visibility for illegal hunting). The burning attracts more animals into the park to graze on fresh grass and this, in turn, causes more damage to trees, opening up even more areas to grassland. As a result, fires can burn over a larger area (Smith 1991).

Poaching is a major threat to the large mammals. Recently, refugees from Sudan have passed through the park and have settled in Dungu. The influx of more people to the region (5000 noted by Smith 1991) could increase poaching and exploitation of plant resources.

## Conservation

Garamba was declared a National Park in 1938 and is defined in law as a "Réserve Naturelle Intégrale". It was established primarily to protect the northern white rhino and northern savanna giraffe. It is surrounded by three hunting areas (Domaines de Chasses) totalling 7527 km² (Smith 1991). They are: Domaine de Chasse Azandes (to the west of Garamba), Domaine de Chasse Mondo-Misa (to the east) and Domaine de Chasse Gangala-na-bodio (to the south). They act as buffer zones to the National Park. Limited settlement and hunting of small game for meat, using spears and other traditional

**MAP 7. GARAMBA NATIONAL PARK (CPD SITE Af49)**

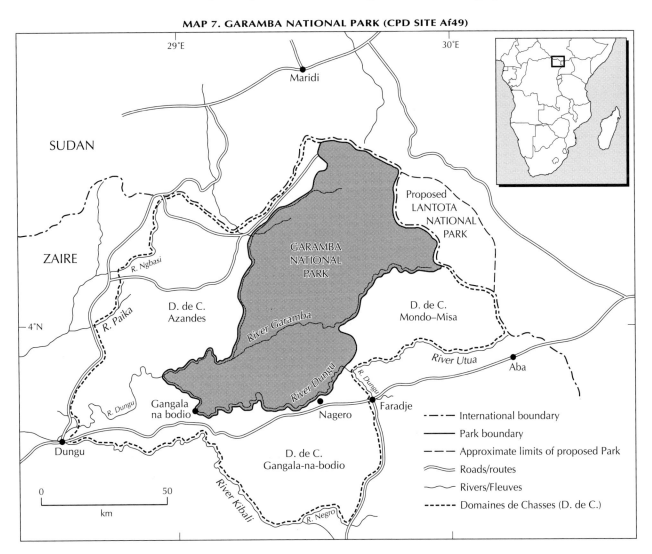

weapons (but not guns), is allowed within the reserves; however, illegal hunting also occurs within the National Park. Contiguous to Garamba, in the north-east, is the proposed Lantoto National Park (760 km²) in southern Sudan.

Garamba is the focus of a WWF project: Garamba National Park, Rhino and Ecosystem Monitoring. Fixed transects have been established to monitor vegetation changes in the National Park (Smith 1991).

## References

De Saeger, H. (1954). *Exploration du Parc National de la Garamba. Mission H. De Saeger. Introduction.* Inst. Parcs. Nat. Congo Belge, Brussels. Pp. 1–107.

IUCN/UNEP (1987). *The IUCN directory of Afrotropical protected areas.* IUCN, Gland, Switzerland and Cambridge, U.K. xix, 1034 pp.

Smith, F. and Smith, K. (1991). Garamba National Park project. Annual report 1991. Parc National de la Garamba. (Typescript.)

Smith, K. (1991). Garamba National Park, rhino and ecosystem monitoring. Progress report, January–June 1991. WWF Project 1954.01. 4 pp., map, appendices.

Troupin, G. (1956). *Flore des spermatophytes du Parc national de la Garamba. I. Gymnospermes et Monocotylédones.* Publ. Inst. Parcs Nat. Congo Belge, Brussels. 349 pp.

White, F. (1983). *The vegetation of Africa: a descriptive memoir to accompany the Unesco/AETFAT/UNSO vegetation map of Africa.* Natural Resources Research XX. Unesco, Paris. 356 pp.

## Acknowledgements

This Data Sheet was written by Professor M.A. Mandango (Chairman, Association des Botanistes du Zaïre, Kinshasa, Zaïre). Professor Paul Bamps (Jardin Botanique National de Belgique, Meise, Belgium) kindly provided additional material.

# THE KAOKOVELD
# Namibia and Angola

**Location:** North-west Namibia, extending into south-west Angola, between latitudes 17°30'–15°00'S and from the Atlantic coast to longitude c. 14°00'E.

**Area:** c. 70,000 km².

**Altitude:** 0–2000 m.

**Vegetation:** Desert vegetation, mopane savanna, escarpment vegetation.

**Flora:** c. 952 vascular plant species; at least 116 endemic or near-endemic taxa.

**Useful plants:** Recorded uses for 192 species, including plants used locally for medicinal purposes and species of religious significance.

**Other values:** Home for semi-nomadic indigenous people; spectacular scenery; desert populations of elephant, black rhino and giraffe; tourist potential.

**Threats:** Timber harvesting; over-collecting of food, medicinal and culturally important plants; fuelwood collection; clearance for cultivation; overgrazing.

**Conservation:** Most of the Angolan section is within Iona National Park (15,150 km²) and the Moçamedes Partial Reserve (4450 km²). In Namibia, only a narrow strip of coastline is protected in the Skeleton Coast National Park; the rest of Kaokoland is a Game Conservation Area.

## Geography

The Kaokoveld is a remote, mountainous region located at the northern end of the Karoo-Namib Regional Centre of Endemism. The Kaokoveld extends from the north-western corner of Namibia into south-western Angola. The southern boundary (17°30'S) is marked by the Hoanib River, the eastern boundary (c. 14°00'E) is the interior plateau of Owambo, Kunene and Huila, the western boundary is the Atlantic Ocean, and in the north, the area tails off towards the Angolan coast (15°00'S) near the port of Namibe (Moçâmedes). The Kunene River bisects the area. The greater proportion (50,000 km²) of the Kaokoveld lies within Namibia.

Topographically, the Kaokoveld can be divided into three major regions: (a) the interior highlands or escarpment zone, which reaches a maximum altitude of just over 2000 m; (b) the western or pro-Namib coastal plains; and (c) the plains of the Namib Desert proper. Although the Kaokoveld falls within the tropics, it is essentially an arid area and the distribution of plants and animals, as well as that of people, is largely determined by the availability of water. Rainfall falls predominantly in summer, from late October to early April. The rainfall along the coast is less than 100 mm per year, whereas inland, on the escarpment mountains, a mean of 350 mm per year has been recorded. Seasonal variation in rainfall is considerable.

## Vegetation

Three major vegetation zones are recognised: the Northern Namib Desert Zone; the Escarpment Zone; and the Mopane Savanna (Barbosa 1970; Giess 1971). More detailed information on the vegetation types, habitats and flora of

the Kaokoveld can be found in Barbosa (1970), De Matos (1970), Giess (1971), Malan and Owen-Smith (1974) and Jacobsen and Moss (1987).

The Northern Namib Desert Zone occurs from Namibe (Moçâmedes) in southern Angola southwards to the Huab River in Namibia. Although strictly speaking part of the Namib Desert, the Northern Namib has a different floristic composition to that of the Central and Southern Namib due to the presence of many Angolan elements (Giess 1968). Hence, it is included here as part of the Kaokoveld. The zone comprises two parts, a coastal area or littoral zone (up to 100 m a.s.l.), containing a number of mobile dune fields and a coastal plateau, and the pro-Namib (100–700 m altitude), where the sand dunes are consolidated. Large portions of the Northern Namib, especially near the coast, are covered by white sand on which vegetation is extremely sparse. The area is characterised by the following largely endemic species: *Barleria solitaria, Ectadium rotundifolium, Indigofera cunenensis, Merremia multisecta, Petalidium angustitubum, P. giesii* and *Stipagrostis ramulosa*. The coastal plateau consists largely of grassy plains (called the pro- or voor-Namib). These plains are mainly covered by *Stipagrostis* spp., although the endemic *Kaokochloa nigrirostris* also occurs in pure stands. It is on these plains that populations, or scattered individuals, of the gymnosperm *Welwitschia mirabilis* are found. The plains are interrupted by scattered rocky hills and outcrops with a variety of plants largely endemic to the area, including *Indigofera teixeirae, Sarcocaulon mossamedensis* and *Senecio alliariifolius* (N. Jacobsen, pers. comm.). The dry river courses crossing the plateau to the coast are marked by the presence of small trees or shrubs, such as *Balanites welwitschii*.

Due to the mountainous nature of the central Kaokoveld, transitions between the different vegetation types are less clearly defined than in the central and southern parts of Namibia. As a result, Giess (1971) mapped much of this area as Mopane Savanna. Portions of the area, particularly in the south should, however, be classified as the Escarpment Zone (Giess 1971). A characteristic genus of this zone is *Commiphora*, well represented by *C. africana*, *C. anacardiifolia*, *C. angolensis*, and *C. crenato-serrata*, among others. Other species typical of this vegetation type include *Cyphostemma* spp., *Euphorbia guerichiana* and *Moringa ovalifolia*.

The Mopane Savanna, as the name suggests, is dominated by *Colophospermum mopane*. In the Kaokoveld, mopane is widespread and grows in pure stands or in association with other species of savanna tree, such as *Boscia foetida*, *Euphorbia guerichiana*, *Peltophorum africanum*, *Terminalia prunoides* and many others, depending on topography and the structure of the soil. Although mostly confined to the mountainous interior, mopane does extend out onto the coastal plains along drainage lines. Other components of this savanna include *Sesamothamnus benguellensis*, which occurs in the north-west, *S. guerichii*, which is widely distributed over the western, central and southern parts of the Kaokoveld, and *Ceraria longipedunculata*, typical of the mountainous areas of the western Kaokoveld. Also well-represented is the family Acanthaceae, the following species being common: *Barleria cyanea*, *B. meeusiana*, *B. rogersii*, *Blepharis ferox*, *B. gerlindae*, *Dicliptera micranthes*, *Ecbolium clarkei*, *Lepidagathis scariosa*, *Monechma cleomoides*, *M. salsoloides*, *Petalidium* spp. and *Ruellia currorii*.

The Brandberg Massif is an isolated inselberg in northern Damaraland. The flora has many affinities to that of the Kaokoveld (see Nordenstam 1974). It forms a bridge between the Escarpment Zone flora to the south and the Kaokoveld proper to the north. It can therefore be considered a southern extension of the Kaokoveld. At least 10 of the 350 taxa recorded on the Brandberg are known to be endemic.

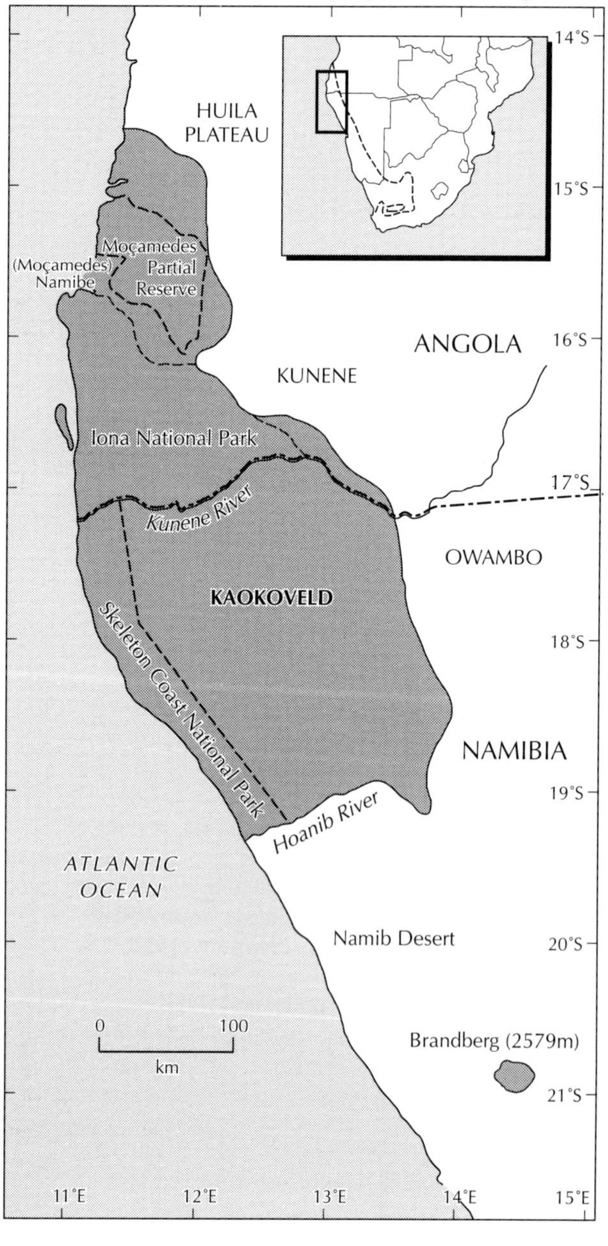

## Flora

The size of the flora is conservatively estimated to be about 952 species (G. Maggs, pers. comm.). A preliminary investigation of the flora has revealed at least 116 endemic or near-endemic taxa. The endemics appear to have few close allies. Many taxa may be very old palaeo-endemics and include taxonomically isolated, monotypic genera such as *Kaokochloa*, *Phlyctidocarpa*, and *Welwitschia*. Intense speciation appears to have occurred fairly recently, resulting in increased endemism in some groups, such as Acanthaceae, especially in the genus *Petalidium* (Nordenstam 1974).

## Useful plants

The Kaokoveld is inhabited by a small population of Herero-speaking people belonging to eight different, but closely related groups. The Hereros are pastoralists who attach great significance to plants that have grazing value for their cattle, sheep and goats. The availability of suitable grazing, together with the availability of water, determines the nomadic movements of the people in the region. Indigenous plants are also important as secondary sources of food and primary sources of traditional medicines (Malan and Owen-Smith 1974). Plant poisons are extensively used to protect stock against carnivorous predators. Sap from the palm *Hyphaene ventricosa* is used for brewing an alcoholic beverage. A number of plants have religious significance. The uses for 192 species have been recorded (Malan and Owen-Smith 1974).

## Social and environmental values

The Herero chat (*Namibornis herero*) is a restricted-range bird species which is endemic to the escarpment of northern Namibia and southern Angola. This site is at the northern limit of its range.

Desert-adapted populations of elephant, black rhino, giraffe and other wildlife occur in the region. As a result, the area has long been a focus for international conservation attention. The spectacular scenery of this wilderness area, its unusual wildlife and the presence of the semi-nomadic

**MAP 8. THE KAOKOVELD (CPD SITE Af50)**

Himba people in traditional dress have enormous tourist potential (Holmes 1992; Jacobsohn 1991–1992).

## Threats

The main threats are from overgrazing and the tapping of sap from *Hyphaene ventricosa* palms. The subsistence economy of the Kaokoveld is based primarily on semi-nomadic pastoralism. Modifications brought about by grazing have by far the greatest impact on the vegetation of the region. The development of numerous artificial watering points, removal of most predators and increase in veterinary assistance have enabled a dramatic increase in the numbers of livestock. Stabilisation of territorial boundaries, thus restricting nomadic movement, have further intensified the impact of domestic stock on the vegetation. Over-exploitation, habitat degradation and the loss of species diversity is the net result.

The tapping of palms is a cause for concern, as the tapping results in the destruction of the trees (Malan and Owen-Smith 1974).

Also of concern is an increased demand for firewood resulting in the lack of immature trees of economically important species in many parts of the Kaokoveld (Malan and Owen-Smith 1974).

Other threats are the over-collection of edible, medicinal and culturally important plants, timber harvesting and clearance of land for cultivation.

Increasing tourism has resulted in some areas being degraded by pollution, off-road driving (which destroys plants, ground-nesting birds and scars the landscape) and disturbance to local communities and wildlife (Holmes 1992).

In southern Angola there has been some diamond mining, but most mining activities have been halted by the civil war in that country. Although there are several large settlements in the Namibian portion of the Kaokoveld, all of the major urban areas are confined to the Angolan coast. Expansion of settlements and urban areas has also been limited by the Angolan civil war.

## Conservation

Most of the Angolan portion of the Kaokoveld falls into two conservation areas, namely: the Iona National Park (15,150 km²) and the Moçamedes Partial Reserve (4450 km²). Due to the current political situation, management and protection of these parks is extremely difficult. Both parks are freely used for domestic grazing (IUCN/UNEP 1987). In Namibia, only a narrow portion of coastal Kaokoveld is protected as the Skeleton Coast National Park. The rest of Kaokoland is a Game Conservation Area which, since 1983, has been patrolled by an Auxillary Game Guard network recruited from the local population (Holmes 1992). This community-based conservation scheme was expanded in 1987 into the Purros Project, which is using conservation and tourism to broaden the economic base of an impoverished community, thus positively influencing people's attitudes towards conservation (Jacobsohn 1991–1992). More formal conservation status should possibly be given to the total area westwards from the escarpment ranges of the Otjihipa and Entendeka mountains. It is important, however, that the conserved area should be large enough to facilitate multi-purpose utilisation.

## References

Barbosa, L.A.G. (1970). *Carta fitogeográfica de Angola*. Instituto de Investgação Cientifica de Angola, Luanda.

De Matos, G.C. (1970). A vegetação do Parque Nacional do Iona. *Boletim da Sociedade Broteriana (Series 2)* 44: 245–247.

Giess, W. (1968). A short report on the vegetation of the Namib coastal area from Swakopmund to Cape Frio. *Dinteria* 1: 13–29.

Giess, W. (1971). A preliminary vegetation map of South West Africa. *Dinteria* 4: 5–114.

Holmes, T. (1992). Conservation activities in Kaokoveld (north-west Namibia). *Biodiversity and Conservation* 1: 211–213.

IUCN/UNEP (1987). *IUCN directory of Afrotropical protected areas*. IUCN, Gland, Switzerland and Cambridge, U.K. xix, 1034 pp.

Jacobsen, N.H.G. and Moss, H. (1987). A contribution to the flora of the northern Namib. *Dinteria* 19: 27–68.

Jacobsohn, M. (1991-1992). Kaokoveld: making conservation work. *New Ground* 6: 2–5.

Kolberg, H., Giess, W., Müller, M.A.N. and Strohbach, B. (1992). List of Namibian plant species. *Dinteria* 22: 1–121.

Maggs, G. and Strohbach, B. (eds) (1992). Proceedings of the first National Workshop on Plant Genetic Resources. *Dinteria* 23: 1–157.

Malan, J.S. and Owen-Smith, G.L. (1974). The ethnobotany of Kaokoland. *Cimbebasia* (B)2: 131–178.

Nordenstam, B. (1974). The flora of the Brandberg. *Dinteria* 11: 3–67.

Owen-Smith, G.L. (1972). Proposals for a game reserve in the western Kaokoveld. *South African Journal of Science* 68: 29–37.

Tinley, K.L. (1971). Etosha and the Kaokoveld. *Supplement to African Wildlife* 25: 1–16.

## Acknowledgements

This Data Sheet was prepared by Craig Hilton-Taylor (National Botanical Institute, Kirstenbosch, South Africa). The author thanks Gillian Maggs and Niels Jacobsen for their help and constructive criticism and the Director of the Royal Botanic Gardens, Kew, for the use of facilities during the author's term as South African Botanical Liaison Officer. This work was funded by the National Botanical Institute, South Africa.

# WESTERN CAPE DOMAIN
# (SUCCULENT KAROO)
## Republic of South Africa and Namibia

**Location:** The Western Cape Domain (southern Namibia and western parts of the Cape Province, South Africa) occurs to the north and inland of the Cape Floristic Region; between latitudes 26°00'–32°00'S and south-west of a line drawn between Lüderitz (15°E) and Port Elizabeth (26°E).

**Area:** 111,212 km².

**Altitude:** 0–1907 m (mostly below 800 m).

**Vegetation:** Low to dwarf succulent shrubland, dominated by stem and leaf succulents and fine-leaved evergreen shrubs.

**Flora:** c. 5000 vascular plant species; 35% endemic. c. 900 on the Red Data List. Extremely rich in succulent species, particularly in the families Aizoaceae *sensu lato*, Asclepiadaceae, Crassulaceae and Euphorbiaceae. This high succulent diversity is unparalleled worldwide. There are many endemic geophytic and annual taxa.

**Useful plants:** Many ornamental plants, particularly bulbs and succulents, medicinal plants, edible plants.

**Other values:** The annual spring flower displays have great tourist potential. The area has historically been used for pastoralism. Viticulture and grain production occur in the southern, wetter areas. The region is rich in mineral resources.

**Threats:** Overgrazing and poor land management practices have lead to severe soil erosion, loss of biological diversity and desertification. Other threats include mining operations, ploughing of marginal lands, succulent collectors, alien plant invasions and urban development.

**Conservation:** <2% conserved. Urgent conservation action is required. Centres of plant diversity of greatest importance are: the Gariep Centre (Richtersveld), Kamiesberg, Western Mountain Karoo (Nieuwoudtville to Sutherland), Vanrhynsdorp Centre (Knersvlakte) and Little Karoo.

## Geography

A large portion of Southern Africa is desert or semi-desert (Meigs 1953; McGinnies, Goodman and Paylore 1968; McGinnies 1979). This arid region has traditionally been subdivided into three major areas, namely the Namib, the Kalahari and the Karoo (Leistner 1979; Werger 1986). The former is a desert in the true sense of the word (see Walter *et al.* 1986), whilst the latter two are arid to semi-arid shrublands. (Karoo is derived from the Khoi word karo meaning dry land.) Phytogeographically, this arid flora has been distinguished from the Cape flora to the south and the tropical flora to the north (Werger 1978a, b). It is generally accepted that, although the arid flora is of Palaeotropic affinity, it is a distinct regional centre of endemism, known as the Karoo-Namib Region (Werger 1978a, b, 1986; White 1983). The Karoo-Namib has been further subdivided into five ecologically homogeneous phytochoria, namely: the Namib, Namaland, Karoo and Western Cape Domains and the Southern Kalahari Subdomain (Werger 1978a). Jürgens (1991) has proposed a new approach to the phytogeographic subdivision of the region, but this new scheme has not been completely published and is not yet generally accepted. Within each of the domains a number of smaller geographically distinct areas can be recognised which have high concentrations of endemic species (Nordenstam 1969). These are usually referred to as centres of endemism. It is important to note that such centres of endemism are not necessarily centres of high plant species diversity. The Western Cape Domain has five major centres of plant endemism (the most of any of the domains), all of which also have a high species diversity. The

Western Cape Domain and its centres of diversity are, therefore, the focus of this contribution.

The boundaries of the Western Cape Domain are roughly congruent with those of the ecologically defined Succulent Karoo Biome (Rutherford and Westfall 1986) and this area is hereafter referred to as the Succulent Karoo. The Succulent Karoo covers an area of approximately 111,212 km², some 5.35% of Southern Africa. The Succulent Karoo comprises the coastal strip and the escarpment mountains, from the Lüderitz District of Namibia in the north and extending southwards to the Cape Fold Mountains which mark the edge of the Cape Floristic Region (CFR) (CPD Site Af53, see separate Data Sheet). The Worcester-Robertson Karoo and Little Karoo, lying between the Cape Fold Mountains in the CFR, are an integral part of the Succulent Karoo. The area defined is essentially that west of a line drawn between Lüderitz and Port Elizabeth and to the north and east of the CFR.

Both the geology and topography of the Succulent Karoo are diverse. Altitudes range from sea-level to 1900 m. However, most of the area is below 800 m. The most striking topographical feature is the Great Escarpment which forms the eastern border of the area. Most of the area comprises flat to gently undulating plains, such as along the western coastal platform, the Vanrhynsdorp Centre, Tanqua Karoo and parts of the Little Karoo. Rugged topography occurs in the Gariep Centre, Namaqualand, Western Mountain Karoo and Little Karoo. The Little Karoo is essentially an inter-montane plain which is interrupted by a number of sandstone inselbergs.

The geology of the Succulent Karoo is extremely complex, particularly in the far north-western corner (Haughton 1969; Visser 1986). This complexity and the variety of rock types have given rise to numerous geomorphological features. The geomorphological diversity combined with changes in soils and climate, results in environmental heterogeneity which has a profound influence on plant species diversity in the Succulent Karoo.

Along the west coast there is a narrow coastal plain covered with deep Late Tertiary, Quaternary and Recent sands. This area is the focus of extensive mining operations for diamonds washed down by the Orange River over thousands of years. The coastal dunes are also becoming the focus for heavy metal mining operations. Further inland (Gariep Centre and Namaqualand) one finds the basement rocks of the Namaqualand Complex. This complex consists of a combination of different metamorphic rocks (mainly granites and gneisses) and is represented by an inselberg landscape (for example the large granite domes of the Kamiesberg). Intermingled with this are outcrops of the Nama Sequence (Nama Group and Gariep Complex) which include sandstone, mudstone, limestone, quartzite, tillite and lava. These form either mountainous landscapes, as in the Richtersveld, or undulating plains, as on the Knersvlakte. Much of this area is of economic importance because of the occurrence of minerals like copper, zinc, lead and silver in the metasedimentary rocks of the Richtersveld; there are large deposits of gypsum (limestone) near Vanrhynsdorp.

The greater part of the Karoo lies on sediments of the Karoo System which has numerous doleritic intrusions in the form of sills or dykes. South of the Great Escarpment there is an undulating dissected landscape (Great Karoo) formed as a result of the northward erosion of the escarpment. This area is underlain by Dwyka, Ecca and Beaufort formations, comprised largely of shales and mudstones. Deposits of uranium are found in the Beaufort beds. Above the escarpment there is a vast plateau, also comprising the Dwyka, Ecca and Beaufort formations. Due to the low relief, there is little active incision by rivers and all the river valleys are deeply filled with recent aeolian sands.

In the southern and western parts of the region isolated portions of the Succulent Karoo are found amongst the Cape Fold Mountains (Little Karoo and Worcester-Robertson Karoo). These areas are underlain by the Nama, Table Mountain, Bokkeveld, Witteberg, Dwyka, Cretaceaous and Cenozoic formations and are comprised largely of sandstones, quartzites and shales. These formations have given rise to a low mountainous landscape with active incision by rivers and streams.

The dominant soils of the region are shallow calcareous lithosols and red apedal soils with high base saturation (Ellis and Lambrechts 1986). The red soils usually have a sandy topsoil, whilst the calcareous soils have a high clay content. Most of the soils of the Karoo are very stony, largely as a result of erosion of the topsoil and subsequent weathering of the underlying shales. A small portion of the Karoo, particularly in the north-west, is covered in desert pavement. The most important underlying material of the desert pavement is lime, which is in the form of hardpan calcrete, calcic horizons or rock with lime and dorbank. A large proportion of the deep, weakly structured soil is associated with unconsolidated deposits. For further details on the characteristics and nutrient status of the different soil types, readers are referred to Ellis and Lambrechts (1986).

The Succulent Karoo is confined to that area which receives most of its rainfall in the winter months. West of a line, running Spencer Bay-Viooolsdrif-Calvinia-Sutherland, more than 60% of the rain falls in winter. East of the line Swakopmund-Aus-Pofadder-Fraserburg-Prince Albert-Willowmore, more than 60% falls in summer. The area in between can thus expect rains at any time of the year, but with peaks in March and November (Weather Bureau 1957; Schulze 1984). The Succulent Karoo is thus restricted to those areas with the greatest summer aridity. The climate varies from extremely arid in the west and north-west to semi-arid in the east and is characterised by unpredictable extremes in weather. Mean annual rainfall increases from west to east and from north to south. Along the west coast, rainfall is less than 100 mm per year. Here, fog from the Atlantic Ocean plays a very important role in the maintenance of plant diversity (Werger 1986; Von Willert et al. 1992). Elsewhere, rainfall rarely exceeds 250 mm per year, except in the east and in the south near the mountains. There is considerable year to year variation in annual rainfall, particularly in the driest months. Thus, large areas are subject to periodic drought (Schulze and McGee 1978; Tyson 1978).

## Vegetation

The vegetation of the Succulent Karoo can be described as a low to dwarf (usually less than 1 m tall), open to sparse (15 to 50% canopy cover) succulent shrubland. This shrubland is dominated by stem and leaf succulents, fine-leaved evergreen shrubs and some obligately deciduous shrubs. Grasses are infrequent and are mainly annuals. There are mass flowering displays of annuals (mainly Compositae, Cruciferae and Scrophulariaceae) and geophytes (Amaryllidaceae, Iridaceae and Liliaceae sensu lato) in spring, particularly in disturbed areas. Small scattered trees (less than 3 m tall) on rocky outcrops occur in some parts of the Karoo and along river courses, where they can form woodlands.

Seven major vegetation formations known as Veld Types (VT) are recognised in the Succulent Karoo, (Acocks 1953, 1975, 1988), namely Karroid Broken Veld (VT26), Namaqualand Broken Veld (VT33), Western Mountain Karoo Veld (VT28), Succulent Karoo Veld (VT31), Strandveld (VT34), False Succulent Karoo Veld (VT39) and Mountain Renosterveld (VT43). For further information on the vegetation and ecological characteristics of the Succulent Karoo, readers are referred to Acocks (1953, 1975, 1988), Werger (1978b), White (1983), Huntley (1984), Cowling (1986), Cowling et al. (1986), Rutherford and Westfall (1986) and Cowling and Roux (1987).

## Flora

The size of the flora of the Succulent Karoo is not accurately known. Gibbs Russell (1987) calculated the size of the Succulent Karoo flora to be 2125 taxa, with 29% endemic. Le Roux (unpublished report, 1988) estimated that there were 3500 taxa in Namaqualand alone. For the whole Karoo-Namib Region, White (1983) stated that there were 3500 species. Leistner (1979) estimated that there were between 4000 and 5000 phanerograms in Southern Africa's arid ecosystems (an area which includes the entire Karoo, Kalahari and Namib Desert). Hilton-Taylor (1987) on the other hand estimated the flora (angiosperms and ferns) of the Karoo-Namib Region to exceed 7000 taxa with between 35% to 50% endemic. The total for the Succulent Karoo Biome is probably in the region of 5000 taxa, with about 35% endemic. This is, however, a best estimate; more accurate data will be available on the completion of the Namaqualand Flora (which is currently being undertaken by the Cape Nature Conservation Department and the University of Stellenbosch). There is no doubt that the Succulent Karoo has a very rich flora for a semi-arid region, especially when compared to other desert areas of the world. For example, the Sonoran Desert has a flora of c. 2440 species in an area an order of magnitude larger than the Succulent Karoo, while the Sinai Desert has 1130 species in an area 1.2 times the size of the Succulent Karoo (Cowling *et al.* 1989). How and why this diversity evolved is still open to speculation; similarly, how this diversity is maintained is largely an unanswered question.

Characteristic families include the Aizoaceae *sensu stricto* (especially the subfamilies Mesembryanthemoideae and Ruschioideae) (nomenclature follows Bittrich and Hartmann 1988), Asclepiadaceae (particularly the tribe Stapelieae), Compositae, Crassulaceae, Geraniaceae, Liliaceae *sensu lato*, Scrophulariaceae and Zygophyllaceae. There are also a number of endemic genera (e.g. *Augea, Didelta, Grielum, Nymannia* and *Tylecodon*) and genera with a high number of

species centred in the region (e.g. *Aloe, Androcymbium, Crassula, Euphorbia, Galenia, Lapeirousia, Oxalis, Pelargonium* and *Protasparagus*).

The Succulent Karoo is extremely rich in succulent plant species, particularly in the families Aizoaceae (the richest family in the Southern African flora), Aloaceae, Asclepiadaceae, Asphodelaceae, Crassulaceae, Compositae, Euphorbiaceae, Portulacaceae and Zygophyllaceae (Hilton-Taylor 1987; Van Jaarsveld 1987). Of the world's 10,000 succulent species, Van Jaarsveld (1987) estimated that 3693 (37%) occurred in South Africa, with most being found in the Succulent Karoo. This high succulent species diversity is unparalleled elsewhere in the world. This, together with the extraordinary diversity in genera and species of petaloid monocots, makes the Succulent Karoo of international importance.

## Centres of endemism

Within the Succulent Karoo there are a number of relatively small areas which have concentrations of endemic species or of closely related species. These areas have been identified in a number of phytogeographic studies on the region (Weimarck 1941; Nordenstam 1969; Werger 1978b; Hartmann 1987; Hilton-Taylor 1987, and in prep.; Jürgens 1991).

**MAP 9. WESTERN CAPE DOMAIN (SUCCULENT KAROO) (CPD SITE Af51) AND ADJACENT PHYTOCHORIA**

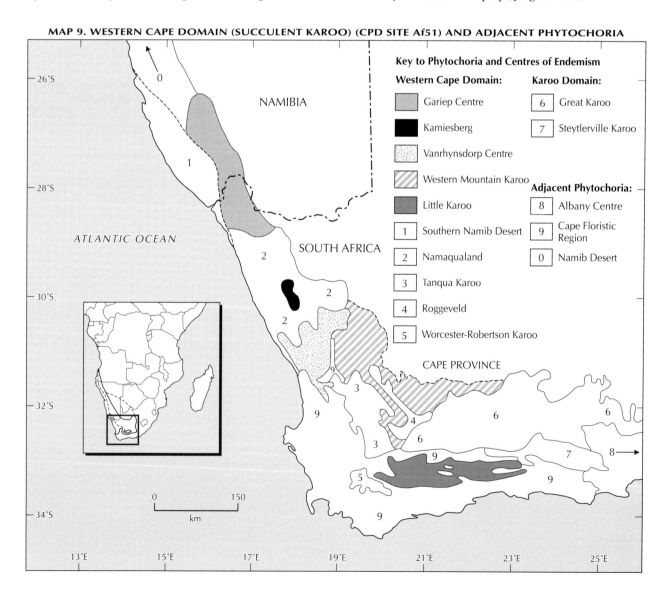

Key to Phytochoria and Centres of Endemism

**Western Cape Domain:**

- Gariep Centre
- Kamiesberg
- Vanrhynsdorp Centre
- Western Mountain Karoo
- Little Karoo
- 1 Southern Namib Desert
- 2 Namaqualand
- 3 Tanqua Karoo
- 4 Roggeveld
- 5 Worcester-Robertson Karoo

**Karoo Domain:**

- 6 Great Karoo
- 7 Steytlerville Karoo

**Adjacent Phytochoria:**

- 8 Albany Centre
- 9 Cape Floristic Region
- 0 Namib Desert

**CPD Site Af51: Succulent Karoo in the northern Gariep, with *Euphorbia dregeana* (foreground) and *Aloe dichotoma*.**
Photo: Craig Hilton-Taylor.

The accompanying map (Map 9) shows all the centres of endemism and other phytochoria within the Succulent Karoo and some of the adjacent areas. Further refinement of the boundaries will be necessary as knowledge on the floristic relationships of the areas increases. It is also not possible at this stage to give the total number of taxa or the exact number of endemics found in each centre. This is largely because of the low intensity of plant collecting in the region (Gibbs Russell *et al.* 1984) and because many of the major plant groups are in urgent need of taxonomic revision.

### Gariep Centre

The Gariep Centre is located in the south-western corner of Namibia and the north-western corner of Namaqualand, from Aus in the north to Steinkopf in the south and from the Atlantic Ocean in the west to the escarpment mountains in the east. The area defined is essentially a geographic rather than a phytogeographic one. Jürgens (1991) has recently shown that this area can be subdivided into a number of smaller units which he has provisionally called the Southern Namib District, the Western Gariep Circle, Western Richtersveld Mountains District and the Eastern Gariep District. The important distinction is the inclusion of the eastern portions of the geographically defined Gariep Centre within the Nama-Karoo Biome whereas the remainder fall within the Succulent Karoo Biome. All these units are, nevertheless, very closely linked floristically. Hence, at this stage it is probably best to consider them as forming a single large, loosely bound unit.

The Gariep Centre is mostly very mountainous, but there are sandy plains along the coast and in the inter-montane valleys. The area is bisected by the Orange River which, together with its many tributaries, acts as an important corridor for a number of taxa (see Jürgens 1991). (Gariep is derived from Garip, the Khoi-San word for the Orange River.) Rainfall may be very low (less than 50 mm per annum); however, the amount is largely dependent on local physiography. Some parts receive predominantly winter rainfall, others summer rainfall and others receive almost no rain due to rain shadow effects. Fog and coastal mists also play an important role (Werger 1986).

The Namibian portion of this centre has been classified by Giess (1971) as Desert and Succulent Steppe. This vegetation type is confined to the winter rainfall area of Namibia, which extends from Namaqualand along the Orange River to north of Lüderitz. The western parts of this area comprise extensive barren desert plains, with sand dunes akin to the Southern Namib Desert area to the north of Lüderitz. This area is probably transitional between Namaqualand to the south and the Namib Domain to the north. The rocky hills and mountains further inland, such as the Buchu Mountain and the Klinghardt Mountains, are densely covered in succulent species of many different families. This area would be classified as Succulent Karoo in terms of Acocks' Veld Types (Acocks 1953). Further inland, towards the east, the perennial vegetation cover becomes more dense. This is due in part to the rugged terrain providing a great variety of habitats and also due to the occurrence of some summer rainfall. The vegetation here is largely Namaqualand Broken Veld, with Western Mountain Karoo on the higher mountain tops. In the northern parts of the Gariep Centre, the desert areas of the Namib merge into grassland on the plains at the foot of the escarpment (essentially a transition area between the Desert Zone and the Escarpment Zone). These grass plains, known as the "Vornamib", extend northwards from near Aus to the Kunene River. The southern portion in the Gariep Centre is dominated by *Stipagrostis ciliata*, sometimes mixed with *S. obtusa*. Occasionally, pure stands of the latter may be found (Giess 1971).

The area in South Africa to the south of the Orange River bulge and to the north of the Steinkopf-Port Nolloth road, is known as the Richtersveld (Vioolsdrif and the Atlantic Ocean demarcate the eastern and western boundaries, respectively). A large portion of the mountains and interior plains are classified as the "Richtersveld Coloured Rural Area" under the administration of two local Management Boards (the Northern and Southern Richtersveld Management Boards). As a result, much of the area was, and still is, extensively used for small-stock farming, especially with goats. This pastoralism has resulted in serious over-grazing in places. After many years of negotiation, 1624 km² of land along the south bank of the Orange River was proclaimed a contractual National Park in 1991 (Van der Merwe 1991; Klinghardt 1992). The local inhabitants will still be allowed to graze some of their livestock within the park, but this is subject to a mutually agreed management plan to prevent environmental damage (Klinghardt 1992).

The coastal plain, both north and south of the Orange River, and sections along the lower Orange River are restricted diamond mining areas. Intensive and extensive mining operations have a considerable impact on the vegetation (see Threats).

No detailed scientific account of the vegetation and flora of the area has yet been published, although several extensive surveys have been made. There are, however, numerous popular articles (examples include: Van Jaarsveld 1981; Claassen 1987; Cole 1990; Williamson 1990a, b; Bailey and Rutherford 1992; Willis 1992).

Despite its many links to the Namaqualand flora, the flora of the Gariep Centre contains many endemics. Several genera of the Aizoaceae are endemic to the area, for example *Arenifera*, *Dracophilus* and *Juttadinteria*, and there are a number of endemic species of *Conophytum*, *Drosanthemum*, *Herreanthus* and *Lithops*. Some other noteworthy endemics include: *Aloe pillansii*, *A. ramosissima*, *A. pearsonii*, *Calliandra redacta*, *Pachypodium namaquanum*, *Portulacaria armiana* and *P. pygmaea*. There are also many species from the following genera which are endemic to the Gariep Centre: *Adenoglossa*, *Adromischus*, *Anacampseros*, *Cerraria*, *Crassula*, *Ectadium*, *Euphorbia*, *Monsonia*, *Pelargonium*, *Pteronia*, *Sarcocaulon*, *Trichocaulon*, *Tridentea*, *Tylecodon* and *Zygophyllum*. A preliminary attempt to catalogue all the endemics in the centre has resulted in a list of approximately 355 endemic or near-endemic taxa; there is no doubt that more will be found.

The species richness and high degree of endemism of the Gariep Centre make it an area of major conservation importance. The new Richtersveld National Park will certainly ensure protection for a number of species; however, additional conservation areas are required for adequate protection of the whole flora.

## The Kamiesberg

This centre, situated in the heart of Namaqualand, consists of granite hills and huge granite domes, separated by sandy plains. The Kamiesberg forms part of the Great Escarpment. Much of the area lies above 1200 m, with the highest peak (Rooiberg) reaching 1700 m. Temperatures are lower and rainfall is much higher than in surrounding areas, some places receiving up to 400 mm per annum. As a result, the vegetation cover is greater than in surrounding areas.

Three major vegetation types merge into one another: there are isolated pockets of Dry Mountain Fynbos on some of the higher mountains, as indicated by the presence of members of the typical fynbos families Ericaceae, Proteaceae and Restionaceae (the nearest relatives being some 100 km away on the Bokkeveld Escarpment); this merges into Mountain Renosterveld, rich in bulbous species; this, in turn, merges into Namaqualand Broken Veld, with more typical Karoo species, especially succulents.

The only published account on the flora is that of Adamson (1938). This was only a preliminary survey and is now out-dated. Rourke (1990) includes a short section on some of the endemics in the Kamiesberg; subsequent additions brings the total to 86 endemic taxa. Among the endemics are: the endangered orchid *Monadenia machrostachya*; fynbos elements, such as *Protea namaquana* and *Vexatorella alpina*; geophytes, such as *Babiana framesii* var. *kamiesbergensis*, *Galaxia kamiesmontana*, *Gladiolus kamiesbergensis* and *Tritonia kamisbergensis*; and succulents, such as *Cheiridopsis pearsonii*, *Conophytum khamiesbergense* and *Lithops naureeniae*. There are probably many more undescribed taxa endemic to the Kamiesberg (Helme 1992b).

A large portion of the central Kamiesberg is classified as a "Coloured Rural Area", known as Leliefontein, which is under the administration of a local Management Board. Much of this area is used for extensive small-stock farming, especially with karakul sheep and goats. This land was traditionally communally owned but, in 1984, when "economic units" were introduced (Steyn, unpublished paper, 1987; Archer 1990). The area was then divided up into small, fenced units and leased to farmers for commercial pastoralism, with only a small proportion being left as communal land (Archer 1990). The result has been severe over-grazing on the remaining lands held in common, as well as in the "economic units", since the farmers could no longer move their stock around seasonally to take advantage of sporadic rainfall (Helme 1992b). Subsequent legal proceedings resulted in the reinstatement of the communal land tenure system in 1988 (Archer 1990).

Apart from over-grazing, other threats to the flora include the burning of vegetation by herders to improve grazing conditions for their livestock (Helme 1992b) and the cultivation of wheat on the plains in areas of higher rainfall. No portion of the Kamiesberg falls within a conservation area, apart from a small wildflower reserve (Skilpad), purchased with funds from the South African Nature Foundation.

In view of the large number of endemics and high species diversity, a conservation area needs to be established in the Kamiesberg. This is under investigation in a joint project between the Flora Conservation Committee of the Botanical Society of South Africa and the Southern African Nature Foundation (Helme 1992b).

## Vanrhynsdorp Centre

This centre is located in the lowlands near Vanrhynsdorp, between the Groen and Olifants Rivers and between the escarpment and the sea. The region is known as the Knersvlakte and comprises sandy plains strewn with white quartz pebbles. The soils are very saline. Near the coast there are deep, red, sandy plains. Rainfall varies from 100 to 200 mm per annum. The vegetation is typically low in stature and is dominated by succulents, except in the sandy areas, where various fine-leaved shrubs or a grass (*Cladoraphis spinosa*) predominate. The area is mostly classified as Succulent Karoo Veld. In the south, the Succulent Karoo Veld merges into Strandveld, Renosterveld and fynbos. Elements from these other vegetation types increase the species richness of the Vanrhynsdorp Centre.

There are a number of endemic genera of Aizoaceae, such as *Argyroderma*, *Dactylopsis* and *Oophytum*. Other endemic species include *Euryops namaquensis*, *Leucoptera oppositifolia*, *L. subcarnosa* and some species of *Babiana*, *Bulbine*, *Othonna*, *Pelargonium*, *Senecio* and *Zygophyllum*. A preliminary count of the taxa confined to this area indicates that there are at least 150 endemics. Apart from a limited study on ecological niches (Jürgens 1986), no other detailed accounts of the vegetation have been published.

There is extensive small-stock farming; many areas, especially in the south, are seriously over-grazed and eroded. There are several mineral deposits in the area, the most important mineral being gypsum. There are large-scale open-cast mining operations for gypsum to the north of Vanrhynsdorp. There are no conservation areas in the Vanrhynsdorp Centre and the succulent-rich quartz plains of the Knersvlakte are in need of protection (Hilton-Taylor and Le Roux 1989).

## Western Mountain Karoo

This portion of the Karoo occurs on the Great Escarpment, from the Nuweveld Range above Beaufort West, westwards around the Roggeveld and northwards along the Bokkeveld Escarpment to the Hantamsberg. The inland border of this area is not clear, as the area merges into the vast interior plateau of Bushmanland and the Upper Karoo. This region represents the eastern limits of the winter rainfall zone. The higher altitude results in a cooler and wetter climate; hence many fynbos elements are present. Of interest is *Cliffortia arborea*, which grows into a small tree. This occurs on the Nuweveld Mountains above Beaufort West, on the Roggeveld near Sutherland and on the Hantamsberg above Calvinia. The lower portions of the Western Mountain Karoo are semi-succulent shrublands (Karroid Broken Veld or Succulent Karoo Veld), whilst the upper parts are non-succulent evergreen shrublands (Western Mountain Karoo Veld and *Merxmuellera* Mountain Veld), which finally merge into the suffrutescent shrublands (Arid Karoo Veld) of Bushmanland (Acocks 1953). This area is largely unexplored due to the rugged terrain.

The Hantamsberg itself is an important centre of endemism, with a number of species restricted entirely to the range. Among these strict endemics are *Diascia macrophylla*, *D. nutans*, *Hesperantha hantamensis*, *H. karroica*, *H. oligantha*, *Nemesia chrysolopha*, *Sutera divaricata* and *Zaluzianskya nemesioides*. A number of species of fynbos affinity also occur on the Roggeveld Mountains and in the Cedarberg-Nieuwoudtville area (Burgers, Nel and Pool 1987, unpublished report). The whole mountain region is phytogeographically complex, but for convenience it is here included within the Western Mountain Karoo Centre. A preliminary count for the whole complex indicates that there are at least 155 endemic taxa, a large number of which are petaloid monocots.

There are several conservation areas in this mountain complex, namely, the Niewoudtville Wild Flower Reserve, Oorlogskloof Nature Reserve, the Akkerendam Nature Reserve and the Karoo National Park. These reserves perform an important role in conserving biodiversity. The Nieuwoudtville Wild Flower Reserve, for example, which covers an area of only 115 ha, contains 300 species, of which c. 5% are endemic to the area (Snijman and Perry 1987).

## Little Karoo

The Little Karoo is enclosed by the Langeberg and Swartberg, two ranges of the Cape Fold Mountains. The western portion of the Little Karoo, sometimes referred to as the Ladismith Karoo, is separated from the eastern portion around Oudtshoorn by a large inselberg called the Rooiberg. The Rooiberg is a fynbos (Dry Mountain Fynbos)-covered mountain linking the Langeberg to the Swartberg (Levyns 1950). The western portion of the Little Karoo receives predominantly winter rainfall, whereas the eastern portion receives most of its rainfall in autumn (March) and early summer (November). The two areas, however, do not appear to be sufficiently distinct floristically to warrant their separation, although no detailed botanical survey of the area has been published. Due to orographic effects, rainfall in the Little Karoo is much higher than elsewhere in the Succulent Karoo (many places receiving more than 400 mm per annum). The effects of this are clearly evident in the dense vegetation, which is predominantly Karroid Broken Veld (Acocks 1953).

Parts of the Little Karoo are covered in Spekboomveld (Acocks 1953), in which Spekboom (*Portulacaria afra*) is dominant. Spekboomveld almost always occurs on the northern side of hills, whilst southern aspects consist either of Karroid Broken Veld or Renosterveld, depending on the geology. Spekboomveld represents a link between the Karoo and the Subtropical Thicket (Valley Bushveld) of the eastern Cape. Small scattered trees, such as *Euclea undulata*, *Pappea capensis* and *Schotia afra* occur on many of the rocky hills of the region (Bews 1921).

A striking feature of the eastern portion of the Little Karoo is the occurrence of white quartz patches reminiscent of the Knersvlakte of the Vanrhynsdorp Centre. A number of endemic succulents, such as *Gibbaeum* spp. and *Muiria hortensae*, are confined to these patches. Fine-leaved shrubs are scarce in, or absent from, these quartz patches. Much work needs to be done on the soils and dynamics of these patches to explain the distributions of the endemics, including why some endemics are absent from some of the patches.

Another dominant feature of the Little Karoo is the presence of regularly spaced circular patches or mounds (about 13 m in diameter) known as "heuweltjies" or "mima-like mounds" (Lovegrove and Siegfried 1989). These mounds are not restricted to the Little Karoo, being in fact found throughout the arid and semi-arid winter rainfall region, which includes all the Succulent Karoo and part of the Cape Floristic Region. The origin of these heuweltjies is obscure and has been the subject of much discussion (Lovegrove and Siegfried 1989; Midgley and Musil 1990; Milton and Dean 1990; Midgley and Hoffman 1991; Moore and Picker 1991; Floyd 1992). The most accepted argument is that they are of zoogenic origin and that termites (*Microhodotermes viator*) are the primary causal agents (Moore and Picker 1991). These heuweltjies, which are generally raised above the surrounding landscape, are nutrient-rich and play an important role in increasing plant species diversity through supporting a completely different set of species to surrounding areas. Succulent shrubs, such as *Euphorbia mauritanica*, woody shrubs, such as *Lycium* spp., and annual species of Aizoaceae, typical of disturbed sites, are dominant on the heuweltjies of the Little Karoo.

Succulent species are well represented throughout the Little Karoo, particularly members of the Aizoaceae, Aloaceae (*Astroloba*, *Haworthia*), Asclepiadaceae (tribe Stapelieae) and Crassulaceae. Endemic genera in the Aizoaceae include *Cerochlamys*, *Gibbaeum* and *Zeuktophyllum*, whilst *Glottiphyllum* and *Pleiospilos* have their centres of species richness within this area. No attempt has yet been made to determine the number of endemics in the area, but it is undoubtedly a major centre of plant endemism and species richness. There are probably between 200 and 300 strict endemic taxa.

Several small conservation areas are scattered throughout the Little Karoo; however, the succulent-rich quartz patches are not adequately conserved by existing reserves (Hilton-Taylor and Le Roux 1989).

## Useful plants

The Karoo flora contains many ornamental plants, particularly bulbs and succulents. Many species were first brought into cultivation during the early stages of botanical exploration in Southern Africa (Gunn and Codd 1981) and are now firmly established in the horticultural trade. For example, millions of corms of *Gladiolus* are marketed annually throughout the world both for the garden and for the cut-flower trade. Many bulbous taxa have been "improved" over the years by selective breeding and hybridisation, often to such an extent that cultivated forms of genera, such as *Freesia*, *Gladiolus*, *Ixia* and *Lachenalia*, are far removed from their wild ancestors.

Interest among South African gardeners in indigenous bulbs has been very poor. The recent publication of two books on the diversity, cultivation and propagation of South African bulbs (Du Plessis and Duncan 1989; Jeppe 1989) may help to stimulate interest. The number of species of major interest are far too numerous to list here; however, families (followed by the major genera of interest) include:

| Amaryllidaceae | *Ammocharis, Boophane, Brunsvigia, Cyrtanthus, Gethyllis, Haemanthus, Hessea, Nerine, Strumaria* |
|---|---|
| Araceae | *Zantedeschia* |
| Asphodelaceae | *Bulbine, Bulbinella, Kniphofia* |
| Colchicaceae | *Onixotis, Wurmbea* |
| Geraniaceae | *Pelargonium*, especially section *Hoarea* |
| Hyacinthaceae | *Albuca, Daubenya, Lachenalia, Neobakeria, Ornithogalum, Polyxena, Veltheimia* |
| Hypoxidaceae | *Empodium, Spiloxene* |
| Iridaceae | *Antholyza, Babiana, Barnardiella, Ferraria, Freesia, Galaxia, Geissorhiza, Gladiolus, Gynandriris, Hesperantha, Homeria, Ixia, Lapeirousia, Moraea, Romulea, Sparaxis, Syringodea, Tritonia* |
| Oxalidaceae | *Oxalis* |
| Tecophiliaceae | *Cyanella*. |

In recent years, there has been a major resurgence in interest in the cultivation of succulent plants, especially in Europe and North America. In Japan, the interest focuses particularly on diminutive species. Often the demand for some succulent taxa has far exceeded the supply available from cultivated plants and there has consequently been considerable trade in plants collected illegally from the wild. Unfortunately, many succulent taxa have restricted distributions and are naturally rare; hence the increased demand for these taxa has resulted in them becoming threatened with extinction in the wild. Several of these plants are now listed in CITES Schedules I and II (CITES Secretariat 1992).

Families and genera of interest include the following (Rowley 1978, 1987):

| Aizoaceae | *Argyroderma, Conophytum, Didymaotus, Dinteranthus, Faucaria, Fenestraria, Gibbaeum, Herreanthus, Lithops, Muiria, Oophytum, Pleiospilos, Tanquana, Titanopsis, Vanheerdea* |
|---|---|
| Aloeaceae | *Aloe, Astroloba, Gasteria, Haworthia* |
| Apocynaceae | *Pachypodium* |
| Asclepiadaceae | *Ceropegia, Duvalia, Huernia, Pectinaria, Piaranthus, Quaqua, Stapelia, Stapeliopsis, Trichocaulon, Tridentea* |
| Asteraceae | *Othonna, Senecio* |
| Crassulaceae | *Adromischus, Cotyledon, Crassula, Tylecodon* |
| Dioscoreaceae | *Dioscorea* |
| Euphorbiaceae | *Euphorbia* |
| Geraniaceae | *Pelargonium, Sarcocaulon* |
| Portulacaceae | *Anacampseros* |
| Vitaceae | *Cyphostemma*. |

Weedy genera of Aizoaceae, such as *Dorotheanthus* spp., and showy shrubs, such as *Drosanthemum* spp., are very popular as garden plants both in South Africa and overseas (Huxley, Griffiths and Levy 1992).

Very few plant taxa in the Succulent Karoo have been investigated for medicinal or nutritional values, although a number of Karoo species have medicinal, food and other socio-economic values for the inhabitants of the so-called "Coloured Rural Areas", commonly known as "Coloured Reserves", in Namaqualand (Archer 1982, 1990). These Nama inhabitants may be considered to be descendants of the Khoi pastoralists who have occupied the area for the last 2000 years (Webley, pers. comm. in Archer 1990). Although most Nama families derive their income today by working as migrant labourers, agro-pastoralism is still practised as a subsistence activity and many of the people rely on indigenous plants for subsistence (Archer 1990).

Fuelwood is the most critical plant resource, as no electricity is available in these rural areas and incomes are too low for the purchase of commercial fuels. Archer (1990) found that the major species utilised are *Acacia karoo*, *Datura stramonium*, *Euclea pseudebenus*, *Lebeckia sericea*, *Rhus incisa*, *R. pendulina*, *R. undulata* and some species of *Ruschia*. Due to increased population pressures, supplies of wood are increasingly becoming depleted and the people are having to turn to less suitable species, such as *Lebeckia sericea*, *Ozoroa dispar*, and species of *Didelta* and *Pteronia* (Archer 1990).

Although there is a tendency for rural people to forsake traditional foods for food purchased at local stores, some plants are still regularly collected. Archer (1982, 1990) has recorded more than 80 species of plant which are utilised in the Kamiesberg area. Nutritious species include *Babiana dregei*, *Cyanella hyacinthoides*, which has a high content of vitamin C, and *Moraea fugax*. The corms of all three of these species have a relatively high energy value and are potential candidates as future crop plants.

Access to primary health care in Namaqualand is limited and herbal medicines continue to play an important role. The medicinal plants are mainly used as infusions and decoctions for chest and stomach disorders and as poultices for aches, pains and open wounds. The most regularly used medicinal plants for treating influenza are *Asclepias cancellata*, *Ballota africana*, *Dodonaea angustifolia*, *Mentha longifolia*, *Rhus undulata*, *Salvia dentata* and *S. lanceolata*. *Galium tomentosum* is used to treat stomach complaints, while *Nicotiana glauca* leaves are used as a poultice for wounds. *Galenia africana* and *Melianthus pectinatus* are used to treat muscular pains and skin disorders (Archer 1990). The most sought after species are *Sceletium* sp. and *Sutherlandia frutescens*, both of which are multi-purpose medicinal plants. *Sceletium* sp. is particularly interesting, as it is psychoactive and can be used as a sedative; however, excessive use can lead to intoxication (Archer 1990). These species are certainly worth further investigation.

Archer (1990) has also shown that plants are used extensively for household purposes. The traditional beehive huts ("matjieshuise") are made from reeds (*Scirpus dioecus* and *S. inanis*), woven into mats, and placed over a framework made from dried branches of *Acacia karoo* and *Ziziphus mucronata*. Some of the older homes are constructed from the stems of *Aloe dichotoma*; however, this species is strictly protected today. Brooms are made from *Datura stramonium* and *Ischyroplepis sieberi*. The leaves of plants such as *Mesembryanthemum* species are used to remove hair from skins in traditional leatherwork, whilst the bark of *Acacia karoo* and *Rhus undulata* and the corms of *Pelargonium triste* are used to dye the leather (Archer 1990).

Unfortunately, the importance of the indigenous plant resources has largely been ignored in development plans for the Succulent Karoo. A multi-purpose approach is required in the management of the natural environment, to ensure that the rural people will continue to have access to the indigenous plants upon which they depend.

## Social and environmental values

After a good wet winter and with the onset of spring, the Succulent Karoo, in particular Namaqualand, is transformed into a kaleidoscope of orange, pink, white and yellow flowers. The Succulent Karoo has probably one of the finest displays of wildflowers to be seen anywhere in the world (Patterson 1984; Le Roux, Schelpe and Wahl 1988; Eliovson 1990) and attracts tourists from all over South

**Traditional beehive huts ("matjieshuise") made from reed mats placed on a framework of dried branches of local trees.** Photo: Craig Hilton-Taylor.

Africa and the world. The income generated from tourism provides financial and employment benefits to an essentially rural area.

The Succulent Karoo, even when not in flower, has a charm and natural beauty of its own which has inspired numerous writers and poets (see Green 1973). The large stretches of undeveloped coastline, the rocky mountains and the sandy plains have considerable aesthetic and recreational value. The Richtersveld portion of the Gariep Centre is a vast wilderness area which has excellent potential for hiking. A large portion of this area was proclaimed a contractual National Park in July 1991 (Van der Merwe 1991; Klinghardt 1992). The Orange River, along the northern boundary of the park, is extensively used for rafting and canoeing by many commercial companies and private individuals (Helme 1992a).

As mentioned previously, the Succulent Karoo is renowned as a world centre of diversity for succulent species, with the Aizoaceae, one of the world's largest succulent families, and the Crassulaceae centred here. The Succulent Karoo is also the world centre of diversity for the family Oxalidaceae and there is a high degree of endemism in many other families. Due to this high diversity, the Succulent Karoo is undoubtedly a region of international environmental value and one which requires a great deal more research and attention.

There are 19 bird species endemic to the Karoo.

## Economic assessment

Approximately 93% of the Succulent Karoo is utilised as natural grazing for commercial pastoralism (Dept van Landbou 1985a, b). The remainder of the area is used for dryland farming of wheat and barley and a small portion is under irrigation for grapes, citrus, tobacco, lucerne and various other fruit and vegetable crops (Dept van Landbou 1985a, b).

Historically, the Succulent Karoo was used for pastoralism (Webley 1986), with herders able to move over large distances in the search for suitable grazing. Today stock is restricted to relatively small farms with a mean size of 60–70 km². Some of the more wealthy farmers own two farms, for example, one in the summer rainfall area of Bushmanland and the other in the winter rainfall area of Namaqualand and they rotate their stock between the farms depending on the season. Stock today consists mostly of sheep and goats, although most farmers have a few dairy cows and occasionally some cattle. In the Little Karoo, ostrich farming is the major pastoral activity (90% of South Africa's ostrich farmers are found in this area) and there is also a fairly large dairy industry (Dept van Landbou 1985b).

Due to the low rainfall in the region, the vegetation generally has a very low carrying capacity (24 ha per large stock unit on farms with good vegetation cover and 45 ha per large stock unit on farms with poor vegetation cover; in some areas it is even as low as 9 ha per small stock unit – see Dept van Landbou 1985a; Danckwerts 1988, unpublished paper; Macdonald 1989). The condition of most of the vegetation, in terms of both cover and quality, is extremely poor and mostly well below its production potential; this is largely a result of many years of selective grazing, over-

stocking and poor management practices (Roux and Vorster 1983; Vorster and Roux 1983; Roux and Theron 1987). The low plant cover has, in turn, led to considerable soil loss through increased sheet, gully and wind erosion (Roux and Theron 1987). Danckwerts (unpublished paper, 1988) investigated the potential profitability of livestock farming in good, moderate and poor vegetation in the Succulent Karoo. He concluded that net farm income, after taking into account the costs of land development and the interest owed on the purchase price of the livestock and the land, only showed a true profit on farms with good vegetation cover and quality. Given the continued trends of vegetation deterioration, loss of diversity, soil erosion and desertification, the future of commercial pastoralism (as currently practised) in the Succulent Karoo is bleak.

It is interesting to compare the gross value of the livestock industry to that of some of the most important agricultural crops grown in the region. The figures presented here are for the years 1983–1984 and are for the North-west Agricultural Subregion, an area which covers the northern portion of the Succulent Karoo Biome (Dept van Landbou 1985a). These figures do not take into account the costs of development and production. The gross value of the stock industry was just over 19.5 million rand, whereas for wine grapes it was almost 21 million rand and for citrus 16.7 million rand (Dept van Landbou 1985a). Natural grazing contributes only 17% of the total value of agricultural production in this subregion. The reduction, or even complete elimination, of commercial pastoralism from the Namaqualand area would therefore have relatively little impact on the gross national product. Financial losses from the reduction in pastoralism in the region could easily be recouped and turned into a gain through the promotion of tourism. This profit in turn could be used for the conservation of the floristic diversity.

The situation in the Little Karoo is slightly different, as the main agricultural emphasis is on various crops and ostriches. The ostrich industry in 1983 had a gross value of nearly 22.5 million rand. However, the state of the natural vegetation in the Little Karoo is so poor that it is unable to completely support the ostrich industry and the birds have to be given supplemental feeding (Dept van Landbou 1985b).

The Succulent Karoo is very rich in mineral resources. For example, the west coast diamond fields, are amongst the richest in the world. Unfortunately, the exploitation of these minerals often results in the destruction of large areas of natural vegetation. Many of the vegetation communities associated with the mineral outcrops are unique and contain a number of endemic or near-endemic species. Mineral exploitation therefore results in the loss of diversity. It is not possible at this stage to compare the economic profits from mineral exploitation against the potential value of the plant species lost. Many of the species lost might well have ornamental, horticultural, nutritional or medicinal value.

## Threats

The main threat to the flora is agriculture, both intensive and extensive. Irrigation schemes have been established along most perennial rivers in the region, allowing large-scale intensive cultivation of grapes, citrus fruit, lucerne and vegetable crops. For example, the Olifants River scheme (with the Bulshoek and Clanwilliam Dams) had converted some 91 km² of dry land (the southern portion of the Vanrhynsdorp Centre) into arable land by 1982 (De Kock 1983, unpublished thesis). There are similar intensive schemes throughout the Worcester-Robertson Karoo and Little Karoo. There is also extensive dryland cropping in the wetter parts of the Succulent Karoo (for wheat and barley). This is not a wise practice, as the unpredictabilty of rainfall often leads to crop failure and abandoned lands. These areas take many years to become revegetated and they never revert to the plant communities characteristic of the adjoining uncultivated sites. This is particularly noticeable in Namaqualand, where by 1983 some 2269 km² had been cultivated in this way (Dept van Landbou 1985a; Macdonald 1989). Both the intensive cultivation schemes and dryland cropping make extensive use of herbicides and pesticides. The impact of these chemicals on surrounding vegetation through run-off is unknown.

Extensive agriculture, in the form of pastoralism, occurs throughout the Succulent Karoo. The resultant problems of selective overgrazing, overstocking and trampling are widespread, leading to irreversible changes in the vegetation with loss of both cover and species diversity (Roux and Vorster 1983; Vorster and Roux 1983; Hilton-Taylor and Moll 1986; Roux and Theron 1987).

There are a number of alien plant species which have become established and have subsequently invaded large parts of the Succulent Karoo (Macdonald 1989; Roux and Theron 1987). Several species of cacti have invaded the eastern portions of the Karoo (Brown and Gubb 1986; Roux and Theron 1987). Two of the major problem species were *Opuntia aurantiaca* and *O. ficus-indica*; however, biological control has limited the density and distribution of these cacti (Zimmerman, Moran and Hoffman 1986). Of greater concern are invasions by *Nicotiana glauca*, *Nerium oleander* and *Prosopis* spp. into the river beds and riparian fringes of ephemeral watercourses, particularly in the northern and central parts of the region (Brown and Gubb 1986; Roux and Theron 1987). In the southern portions of the Vanrhynsdorp Centre and in the Little Karoo, sandy areas are being invaded by *Acacia cyclops* (Brown and Gubb 1986; Roux and Theron 1987). These invasions are a threat, because they result in the loss of unique habitats and species diversity and the creation of almost mono-specific stands.

Over-seeding of natural pastures with alien species such as *Atriplex nummularia* in an attempt to raise carrying capacity is also cause for concern. Hobson (1988, unpublished report) estimated that at least 1500 km² of land throughout the Karoo are planted with *Atriplex*, which modifies the soil and surrounding environment. It is not known what effects this will have on the adjacent natural vegetation.

Mining operations, particularly open-cast mining, are a major threat to the flora of the Succulent Karoo. The 410 km stretch of coastline from Doringbaai northwards to Alexander Bay is a restricted diamond mining area under the control of five mining companies. (The entire coastline in the Namibian portion of the Succulent Karoo is also a restricted mining area, which is now being managed by Namibian conservation authorities.) In a survey on the extent of mining on the South African portion of the coast, Helme (unpublished report, 1992c) found that 270 km (65%) of the coastline had been mined and that a further 25 to 30 km were earmarked for future expansion, especially for the mining of heavy minerals. Gypsum, marble, monazite, kaolin, copper, limestone, ilmenite and titanium all occur within the Vanrhynsdorp, Namaqualand and Gariep areas. Associated with these deposits are unique habitats and numerous rare species.

Although some mining companies have established small reserves on their land and the limited public access to mining lands can act as a form of protection, exploitation of the mineral reserves inevitably leads to some loss of plant biodiversity. Attention needs to be given to the mining procedures used and, more particularly, to the rehabilitation measures taken once mining is complete.

Plant collecting is a major threat to some succulents and bulbs. Although South Africa is a signatory to CITES, large-scale trade in plants collected illegally from the wild continues. The prices fetched on overseas markets make this a very profitable business, with some species of *Haworthia*, for example, selling for between £15–25 per plant (Bruyns, pers. comm.). Until recently, the penalties imposed on those apprehended were insufficient as deterents (Hilton-Taylor and Le Roux 1989).

The effects of urbanisation are limited mostly to the Worcester-Robertson Karoo, Little Karoo and southern parts of the Vanrhynsdorp Centre. Towns in these areas have developed considerably in recent years as a consequence of increases in intensive agriculture. Natural vegetation in the Worcester-Robertson area has been reduced in extent and, as a result, the number of taxa considered to be threatened has increased markedly. The building of roads and railways has also had some impact on the flora. For example, the Sishen-Saldanha railway led to reduction in numbers and, in some cases, total elimination of several rare species in the Vanrhynsdorp Centre.

The total number of plant taxa in the Karoo currently considered to be rare or threatened is presently under review. Hall and Veldhuis (1985) reported 539 threatened plants from the whole of the Karoo, 36 of which were Vulnerable, 20 Endangered and 3 Extinct. Preliminary data now indicate that there are approximately 978 threatened taxa, 96 of which are Vulnerable, 38 Endangered and at least 13 Extinct. This represents nearly 20% of the flora. The vast majority of these taxa (35% of which are succulents) are from the Succulent Karoo, with only a few recorded from the adjoining Nama-Karoo. The rise in the number of threatened species is partly due to increased knowledge of the flora, but it is also a reflection of the increasing severity of threats.

## Conservation

The poor conservation status of the Succulent Karoo has long been a major cause for concern (Hilton-Taylor and Le Roux 1989), but, despite reviews highlighting the importance of conservation (Edwards 1974; Scheepers 1983), very little action has, until recently, been taken by governmental conservation agencies to remedy the situation, especially in the Succulent Karoo.

Hilton-Taylor and Le Roux (1989) investigated the status of conservation in the Karoo in an attempt to provide the conservation agencies with an objective list of priority areas most in need of attention. This investigation looked at the area of each of the Veld Types conserved, the area of each biogeographic region conserved and the number of rare and threatened taxa in each biogeographic region.

Hilton-Taylor and Le Roux (1989) found that only 1.2% of the Succulent Karoo was conserved in state-owned or partially state-owned conservation areas. Despite the proclamation of new conservation areas and the addition of land to existing reserves, the area conserved is still less than 2%. The figure would be higher if privately-owned conservation areas were included; these are, however, not included, as they have no long-term security.

Looking at the area of each biogeographic region conserved, Hilton-Taylor and Le Roux (1989) found that the Kamiesberg, Vanrhynsdorp Centre and Roggeveld were the areas of the highest priority for establishment of new protected areas as in all of these such areas were lacking. The next least conserved region was Namaqualand; however, Hilton-Taylor and Le Roux (1989) argued that, apart from some specific sites in the Kommaggas and Spektakel Mountains, the region was adequately conserved by the representative Goegap Nature Reserve. The Tanqua Karoo would also rate high in priority in terms of area conserved, if the degraded National Park were not included (see Hilton-Taylor and Le Roux 1989). One of the best conserved regions is the Western Mountain Karoo, with 7.7% of its total area conserved (Hilton-Taylor and Le Roux 1989).

Hilton-Taylor and Le Roux (1989) found that the Western Mountain Karoo had the highest number of threatened plant taxa per unit area, with a major concentration of these taxa in the Nieuwoudtville-Calvinia area and all mostly outside of existing conservation areas. The Kamiesberg, Worcester-Robertson Karoo, Little Karoo, Gariep Centre and Vanrhynsdorp Centre also had high numbers of threatened plant taxa per unit area.

In terms of biogeographic area conserved and the density of threatened taxa, Hilton-Taylor and Le Roux (1989) concluded that the Kamiesberg, Vanrhynsdorp Centre and Western Mountain Karoo were the areas with the highest conservation priority. This conclusion is further supported by the apparently high species diversity and the large numbers of endemics which have been recorded from these areas.

In view of the international significance of the Succulent Karoo as a major centre of plant diversity, well co-ordinated conservation action is essential (Huntley and Ellis 1984). Cowling (1986) has argued that large Biosphere Reserves are required to improve the conservation status of the area, as only with reserves larger than 150 km² will there be any possibility of re-establishing pre-settlement animal communities and grazing patterns. Although this is certainly true, indications from a preliminary analysis of the threatened plants database show that a system of smaller reserves is also necessary, if the highly restricted endemics and the high species diversity of the region are to be conserved.

There are plans for new reserves and extensions to existing reserves which will improve the overall conservation status of the Succulent Karoo (Hilton-Taylor and Le Roux 1989). All the conservation areas certainly perform an important function in that they conserve genetic diversity and help maintain seedbanks which allow for recolonisation of degraded areas. However, in view of the use of the Karoo as rangeland, the major thrust of conservation should be aimed at improved land-use management. It is only through wise utilisation that the degradation of native vegetation and the processes of soil erosion and desertification can be halted.

# References

Acocks, J.P.H. (1953). Veld types of South Africa. *Memoirs of the Botanical Survey of South Africa* 28: 1–192.

Acocks, J.P.H. (1964). Karoo vegetation in relation to the development of deserts. In Davis, D.H.S. (ed.), *Ecological studies in Southern Africa*. Junk, The Hague. Pp. 100–112.

Acocks, J.P.H. (1975). Veld Types of South Africa (2nd ed.). *Memoirs of the Botanical Survey of South Africa* 40: 1–128.

Acocks, J.P.H. (1988). Veld Types of South Africa (3rd ed.). *Memoirs of the Botanical Survey of South Africa* 57: 1–146.

Adamson, R.S. (1938). Notes on the vegetation of the Kamiesberg. *Botanical Survey of South Africa Memoir* 18: 1–25.

Archer, F.M. (1982). Voorstudie in verband met die eetbare plante van die Kamiesberge. *Journal of South African Botany* 48: 433–449.

Archer, F.M. (1990). Planning with people – ethnobotany and African uses of plants in Namaqualand (South Africa). *Mitteilungen aus dem Institüt für Allgemeine Botanik, Hamburg* 23b: 959–972.

Bailey, C. and Rutherford, M. (1992). Impressions of the Richtersveld. *Veld & Flora* 78: 21.

Bews, J.W. (1921). Some general principles of plant distribution as illustrated by the South African flora. *Annals of Botany* 35: 1–36.

Bittrich, V. and Hartmann, H.E.K. (1988). The Aizoaceae – a new approach. *Botanical Journal of the Linnean Society* 97: 239–254.

Boucher, C. and Le Roux, A. (in press). Dry coastal ecosytems: South African west coast strand vegetation. In *Ecosystems of the world 2. Dry coastal ecosystems*. Elsevier, Amsterdam.

Brown, C.J. and Gubb, A.A. (1986). Invasive alien organisms in the Namib Desert, Upper Karoo and the arid and semi-arid savannas of western Southern Africa. In Macdonald, I.A.W., Kruger, F.J. and Ferrar, A.A. (eds), *The ecology and management of biological invasions in Southern Africa*. Oxford University Press, Cape Town. Pp. 93–108.

Burgers, C.J., Nel, G. and Pool, R. (1987). Plan for nature conservation (Region A1). Recommendations for the conservation of lowland fynbos areas in the south western Cape. Unpublished report prepared for the NAKOR National Working Group for Region A1. Cape Department of Nature and Environmental Conservation, Cape Town.

CITES Secretariat (1992). *Convention on International Trade in Endangered Species of Wild Fauna and Flora*. Appendices I and II as adopted by the Conference of the Parties, valid as of 11 June 1992. CITES Secretariat, Lausanne.

Africa

Claassen, I. (1987). To save a mountain desert. *Panorama* 32: 20–27.

Cole, D.T. (1990). The Richtersveld. *Aloe* 27: 40–43.

Cowling, R.M. (1986). *A description of the Karoo Biome Project*. South African National Scientific Programmes Report, 122. CSIR, Pretoria.

Cowling, R.M., Roux, P.W. and Pieterse, A.J.H. (eds) (1986). *The Karoo Biome: a preliminary synthesis. Part 1 – Physical environment*. South African National Scientific Programmes Report, 124. CSIR, Pretoria.

Cowling, R.M., Gibbs Russell, G.E., Hoffman, M.T. and Hilton-Taylor, C. (1989). Patterns of plant species diversity in Southern Africa. In Huntley, B.J. (ed.), *Biotic diversity in Southern Africa: concepts and conservation*. Oxford University Press, Cape Town. Pp. 19–50.

Cowling, R.M. and Roux, P.W. (eds) (1987). *The Karoo Biome: a preliminary synthesis. Part 2 – Vegetation and history*. South African National Scientific Programmes Report, 142. CSIR, Pretoria.

Danckwerts, J.E. (1988). Economic and land tenureship constraints to conservation farming. Unpublished paper presented at the 4th Annual Research Meeting of the Karoo Biome Project, Springbok. Programme Abstracts.

De Kock, G.L. (1983). Aspekte van landskapverandering in die Landrosdistrikte van Clanwilliam, Vanrhynsdorp en Vredendal. Ph.D. thesis, University of Stellenbosch.

Dept van Landbou (1985a). *Landbou-ontwikkelingsprogram Noordwestesubstreek*. Dept van Landbou Winterreënstreek, Elsenburg.

Dept van Landbou (1985b). *Landbou-ontwikkelingsprogram Klein Karoosubstreek*. Dept van Landbou Winterreënstreek, Elsenburg.

Downing, B.H. (1978). Environmental consequences of agricultural expansion in South Africa since 1850. *South African Journal of Science* 74: 420–422.

Du Plessis, N. and Duncan, G. (1989). *Bulbous plants of Southern Africa. A guide to their cultivation and propagation*. Tafelberg, Cape Town.

Edwards, D. (1974). Survey to determine the adequacy of existing conserved areas in relation to vegetation types. A preliminary report. *Koedoe* 17: 2–37.

Eliovson, S. (1990). *Namaqualand in flower* (3rd ed.). Macmillan, Johannesburg.

Ellis, F. and Lambrechts, J.J.N. (1986). Soils. In Cowling, R.M., Roux, P.W. and Pieterse, A.J.H. (eds), *The Karoo Biome: a preliminary synthesis. Part I – Physical environment*. South African National Scientific Programmes, Report 124. CSIR, Pretoria. Pp. 18–38.

Floyd, G.J. (1992). Heuweltjies: nutrient factories. *Veld & Flora* 78: 31.

Gibbs Russell, G.E. (1987). Preliminary floristic analysis of the major biomes in Southern Africa. *Bothalia* 17: 213–227.

Gibbs Russell, G.E., Retief, G.E. and Smook, L. (1984). Intensity of plant collecting in Southern Africa. *Bothalia* 15: 131–138.

Giess, W. (1971). A preliminary vegetation map of South West Africa. *Dinteria* 4: 5–114.

Green, L.G. (1973). *Karoo*. Howard Timmins, Cape Town.

Gunn, M. and Codd, L.E. (1981). *Botanical exploration of Southern Africa*. Balkema, Cape Town.

Hall, A.V. and Veldhuis, H.A. (1985). *South African Red Data Book: plants – Fynbos and Karoo Biomes*. South African National Scientific Programmes Report 117. CSIR, Pretoria.

Hartmann, H.E.K. (1987). Phytogeography of the subtribe Leipoldtiinae (Mesembryanthemaceae). *Bothalia* 17: 205–212.

Haughton, S.H. (1969). *Geological history of Southern Africa*. The Geological Society of South Africa, Johannesburg.

Helme, N. (1992a). Lower Orange River conservation. *Veld & Flora* 78: 86–87.

Helme, N. (1992b). The Kamiesberg. *Veld & Flora* 78(4): The Green Pages, p. ii.

Helme, N. (1992c). The extent of diamond mining on the west coast. Unpublished report prepared for the Flora Conservation Committee of the Botanical Society of South Africa, Kirstenbosch.

Hilton-Taylor, C. (1987). Phytogeography and origins of the Karoo flora. In Cowling, R.M. and Roux, P.W. (eds), *The Karoo Biome: a preliminary synthesis. Part 2 – Vegetation and history*. South African National Scientific Programmes Report 142. CSIR, Pretoria. Pp. 70–95.

Hilton-Taylor, C. (in prep.). A phytogeographic classification of the Succulent Karoo Biome. Ph.D. thesis to be submitted to the University of Cape Town.

Hilton-Taylor, C. and Le Roux, A. (1989). Conservation status of the Fynbos and Karoo Biomes. In Huntley, B.J. (ed.), *Biotic diversity in Southern Africa: concepts and conservation*. Oxford University Press, Cape Town. Pp. 202–223.

Hilton-Taylor, C. and Moll, E.J. (1986). The Karoo – a neglected biome. *Veld & Flora* 72: 33–36.

Hobson, C.D. (1988). Micro-environments in two Oldman Saltbush *Atriplex nummularia* plantations and adjacent karoo vegetation. Unpublished paper presented at the 4th Annual Research Meeting of the Karoo Biome Project, Springbok. Programme Abstracts. Pp. 25–26.

215

Huntley, B.J. (1978). Ecosystem conservation in Southern Africa. In Werger, M.J.A. (ed.), *Biogeography and ecology of Southern Africa*. Junk, The Hague. Pp. 1333–1384.

Huntley, B.J. (1984). Characteristics of South African biomes. In Booysen, P. de V. and Tainton, N.M. (eds), *Ecological effects of fire in South African ecosystems*. Springer-Verlag, Berlin. Pp. 2–17.

Huntley, B.J. and Ellis, S. (1984). Conservation status of terrestrial ecosystems in Southern Africa. In IUCN *Proceedings of the Twenty Second Working Session, Commission on National Parks and Protected Areas*. IUCN, Gland, Switzerland. Pp. 13–22.

Huxley, A., Griffiths, M. and Levy, M. (ed.) (1992). *The new Royal Horticultural Society dictionary of gardening*. Macmillan, London.

Jeppe, B. (1989). *Spring and winter flowering bulbs of the Cape*. Oxford University Press, Cape Town.

Jürgens, N. (1986). Untersuchungen zur ökologie sukkulenter pflanzen des südlichen Afrika. *Mitteilungen aus dem Institut für Allgemeine Botanik, Hamburg* 21: 139–365.

Jürgens, N. (1991). A new approach to the Namib Region. I: Phytogeographic subdivision. *Vegetatio* 97: 21–38.

Klinghardt, G.P. (1992). The Richtersveld National Park. *Veld & Flora* 78: 20.

Leistner, O.A. (1979). Southern Africa. In Goodall, D.W. and Perry, R.A. (eds), *Arid-land ecosystems*. Cambridge University Press, Cambridge. Pp. 109–143.

Le Roux, A. (1988). Namaqualand checklist. Chief Directorate Nature and Environmental Conservation, Cape Province, Cape Town. Unpublished.

Le Roux, A., Schelpe, T. and Wahl, Z. (1988). *Namaqualand. South African Wildflower Guide 1* (2nd ed.). Botanical Society of South Africa, Kirstenbosch.

Levyns, M.R. (1950). The relations of the Cape and Karoo floras near Ladismith, Cape. *Transactions of the Royal Society of South Africa* 26: 401–424.

Lovegrove, B.G. and Siegfried, W.R. (1989). Spacing and origin(s) of Mima-like earth mounds in the Cape Province, South Africa. *South African Journal of Science* 85: 108–112.

Macdonald, I.A.W. (1989). Man's role in changing the face of Southern Africa. In Huntley, B.J. (ed.), *Biotic diversity in Southern Africa: concepts and conservation*. Oxford University Press, Cape Town. Pp. 51–77.

McGinnies, W.G. (1979). General description of desert areas. In Goodall, D.W. and Perry, R.A. (eds), *Arid-land ecosystems*. Cambridge University Press, Cambridge. Pp. 5–19.

McGinnies, W.G., Goldman, B.J. and Paylore, P. (eds) (1968). *Deserts of the world – an appraisal of research into their physical and biological environment*. University of Arizona Press, Tucson.

Meigs, P. (1953). World distribution of arid and semi-arid homoclimates. In *Review of research on arid zone hydrology. Arid Zone Programme* 1: 203–209. Unesco, Paris.

Midgley, G.F. and Hoffmann, M.T. (1991). Heuweltjies: nutrient factories. *Veld & Flora* 77: 72–75.

Midgley, G.F. and Musil, C.F. (1990). Substrate effects of zoogenic soil mounds on vegetation composition in the Worcester-Robertson valley, Cape Province. *South African Journal of Botany* 56: 158–166.

Milton, S.J. and Dean, W.R.J. (1990). Mima-like mounds in the southwestern Cape: are the origins so mysterious? *South African Journal of Science* 86: 207–208.

Moore, J.M. and Picker, M.D. (1991). Heuweltjies (earth mounds) in the Clanwilliam District, Cape Province, South Africa – 4000-year-old termite nests. *Oecologia* 86: 424–432.

Nordenstam, B. (1969). Phytogeography of the genus *Euryops* (Compositae). A contribution to the phytogeography of Southern Africa. *Opera Botanica* 23.

Patterson, F. (1984). *Namaqualand: garden of the gods*. Key Porter, Toronto.

Rourke, J.P. (1990). A new species of *Protea* (Proteaceae) from Namaqualand with comments on the Kamiesberg as a centre of endemism. *South African Journal of Botany* 56: 261–265.

Roux, P.W. and Theron, G.K. (1987). Vegetation change in the Karoo Biome. In Cowling, R.M. and Roux, P.W. (eds), *The Karoo Biome: a preliminary synthesis. Part 2 – Vegetation and history*. South African National Scientific Programmes Report 142. CSIR, Pretoria. Pp. 50–69.

Roux, P.W. and Vorster, M. (1983). Vegetation change in the Karoo. *Proceedings of the Grassland Society of Southern Africa* 18: 25–29.

Rowley, G.D. (1978). *Illustrated encyclopedia of succulents*. Salamander Books, London.

Rowley, G.D. (1987). *Cauduciform and pachycaul succulents*. Strawberry Press, California.

Rutherford, M.C. and Westfall, R.H. (1986). Biomes of Southern Africa – an objective categorization. *Memoirs of the Botanical Survey of South Africa* 54: 1–98.

Scheepers, J.C. (1983). The present status of vegetation conservation in South Africa. *Bothalia* 14: 991–995.

Schulze, B.R. (1984). *Climate of South Africa. Part 8: General survey*. 5th Ed. Government Printer, Pretoria.

Schulze, R.E. and McGee, O.S. (1978). Climatic indices and classifications in relation to the biogeography of Southern Africa. In Werger, M.J.A. (ed.), *Biogeography and ecology of Southern Africa*. Junk, The Hague. Pp. 19–52.

Scott, G. (1989). Preliminary investigation of *Cyanella hyacinthoides* (Tecophiliaceae) as an edible crop plant. *South African Journal of Botany* 55: 533–536.

Snijman, D. and Perry, P. (1987). A floristic analysis of the Nieuwoudtville Wild Flower Reserve north-western Cape. *South African Journal of Botany* 53: 445–454.

Steyn, L. (1987). Dispossession of communal land in Namaqualand. Unpublished press briefing. Surplus People Project, Cape Town.

Talkenberg, W.F.M. (1982). An investigation of the environmental impact of surface diamond mining along the arid west coast of South Africa. M.Sc. thesis, University of Cape Town.

Tyson, P.D. (1978). Rainfall changes over South Africa during the period of meteorological record. In Werger, M.J.A. (ed.), *Biogeography and ecology of Southern Africa*. Junk, The Hague. Pp. 55–70.

Van der Merwe, S. (1991). Richtersveld now finally a national park. *Custos* 20(6): 14–17.

Van Jaarsveld, E. (1981). A preliminary report on the vegetation of the Richtersveld with specific reference to the trees and shrubs of the area. *Trees in South Africa* 33: 58–84.

Van Jaarsveld, E. (1987). The succulent riches of South Africa and Namibia. *Aloe* 24: 45–92.

Visser, J.N.J. (1986). Geology. In Cowling, R.M., Roux, P.W. and Pieterse, A.J.H. (eds), *The Karoo Biome: a preliminary synthesis. Part I – Physical environment*. South African National Scientific Programmes Report 124. CSIR, Pretoria. Pp. 1–17.

Von Willert, D.J., Werger, M.J.A., Brinckmann, E., Ihlenfeldt, H.-D. and Eller, B.M. (1992). *Life strategies of succulents in deserts: with special reference to the Namib Desert*. Cambridge University Press, Cambridge, U.K.

Vorster, M. and Roux, P.W. (1983). Veld of the karoo areas. *Proceedings of the Grassland Society of Southern Africa* 18: 18–24.

Walter, H., Giess, W., Scholtz, H., Von Schwind, H., Seely, M.K. and Walter, E. (1986). The Namib Desert. In Evenari, M., Noy-Meir, I. and Goodall, D.W. (eds), *Hot deserts and arid shrublands*. Elsevier, Amsterdam. Pp. 245–282.

Weather Bureau (1957). *Climate of South Africa. Part 4: Rainfall maps*. Government Printer, Pretoria.

Webley, L.A. (1986). Pastoralist ethnoarchaeology in Namaqualand. In Hall, M. and Smith, B. (eds), *Prehistoric pastoralism in Southern Africa*. Goodwin Series 5, Cape Town. Pp. 57–61.

Weimarck, H. (1941). Phytogeographical groups, centres and intervals within the Cape flora. *Lunds Universitets Arsskrift* 37(5): 1–143.

Werger, M.J.A. (1978a). Biogeographical divisions of Southern Africa. In Werger, M.J.A. (ed.), *Biogeography and ecology of Southern Africa*. Junk, The Hague. Pp. 145–170.

Werger, M.J.A. (1978b). The Karoo-Namib Region. In Werger, M.J.A. (ed.), *Biogeography and ecology of Southern Africa*. Junk, The Hague. Pp. 231–299.

Werger, M.J.A. (1986). The Karoo and southern Kalahari. In Evenari, M., Noy-Meir, I. and Goodall, D.W. (eds), *Hot deserts and arid shrublands*. Elsevier, Amsterdam. Pp. 283–359.

White, F. (1983). *The vegetation of Africa: a descriptive memoir to accompany the Unesco/AETFAT/UNSO vegetation map of Africa*. Natural Resources Research XX. Unesco, Paris. 356 pp.

Williamson, G. (1990a). The Richtersveld, South Africa's last wilderness. *African Wildlife* 44: 26–35.

Williamson, G. (1990b). The Richtersveld, a treasure-trove of succulent plants. *Aloe* 27: 34–39.

Willis, C. (1992). Richtersveld: land of contrasts. *Veld & Flora* 78: 14–16.

Zimmerman, H.G., Moran, V.C. and Hoffman, J.H. (1986). Insect herbivores as determinants of the present distribution and abundance of invasive cacti in South Africa. In Macdonald, I.A.W., Kruger, F.J. and Ferrar, A.A. (eds), *Ecology and management of biological invasions in Southern Africa*. Oxford University Press, Cape Town. Pp. 269–274.

## Acknowledgements

This Data Sheet was prepared by Craig Hilton Taylor (National Botanical Institute, Kirstenbosch, South Africa). The author is grateful to Professor Brian J. Huntley, Professor Eugene J. Moll and Dr Tony G. Rebelo for their constructive criticism of the manuscript. Much of this text was prepared while the author was at the Botany Department of the University of Cape Town and while he was South African Botanical Liaison Officer at the Royal Botanic Gardens, Kew. The author is extremely grateful to both of these organisations for the use of their facilities. He also greatly appreciates financial support for his research received from the Foundation for Research Development of the CSIR, the South African Nature Foundation, the Conservation Committee of the South African Botanical Society and the National Botanical Institute.

# CAPE FLORISTIC REGION
## Republic of South Africa

**Location:** Cape Floristic Kingdom; southern-most tip of Africa; south of latitude 33°00'S, south-west of latitude 31°00'S and between longitudes 18°00'–25°00'E.

**Area:** 90,000 km².

**Altitude:** 0–2325 m.

**Vegetation:** Fynbos (41% of area), renoster shrubland (19%), karroid shrubland (11%), thicket (3%), Afromontane forest (1%). Some 23% of the area, mainly renoster shrubland, has been cleared for agriculture.

**Flora:** Very high diversity (8600 vascular plant species), very high species endemism (68%), high generic endemism (c. 20%), 6 endemic families (plus one family with only two extra-limital species), very many threatened species (1430 species: 17% of flora). Diversity and endemism largely confined to fynbos.

**Useful plants:** Ornamental plants, particularly bulbs, succulents and Proteaceae.

**Other values:** Water catchment area in arid sub-region, great tourist potential, viticultural and grain production area.

**Threats:** Invasive alien plants, agriculture, rapidly increasing urbanization due to a high population growth rate, fires. The lowlands are far more threatened than the mountains, owing to extensive agricultural and urban development.

**Conservation:** The majority of mountain fynbos, especially in the more species-rich west, is protected in Nature Reserves and Mountain Catchment Areas. The lowlands, particularly renoster shrubland, are very poorly protected. The entire region is to be proposed as a Biosphere Reserve.

## Geography

The Cape Floristic Region (CFR) is recognized as one of the botanical Kingdoms in the world. It encompasses the Cape Fold Mountains and their associated coastal plains and inter-montane valleys in the southern and south-western Cape Province, South Africa. Several isolated outliers also occur to the east and north-west. The CFR covers 90,000 km² and is confined to south of latitude 33°00'S, except in the north-west (west of 19°30'E) where it extends northwards to 31°00'S (Bond and Goldblatt 1984).

The CFR is topographically dominated by the Cape Fold Belt. This has two main axes of folding: east-west (Swartberg, Langeberg Mountain Ranges, confluencing in the Kouga Mountain Massif in the east) and north-south (Olifants River, Cold Bokkeveld and Cedarberg Mountain Ranges). The Cape Fold Belt is formed of hard, resistant quartzitic sandstones, forming steep-sided mountains with peaks typically 1000–2200 m above sea-level. The coastal plain is flat or undulating and lies between 200 and 300 m above sea-level. It comprises shales of the Bokkeveld or Malmesbury Groups, covered by deep Tertiary sands and, on the south coast, extensive limestone deposits (Alexandria Formation). In the extreme south-west, the Cape Fold Belt is underlain by granites of the Cape Supergroup. The Little Karoo is an inter-montane plain, 350–600 m above sea-level, underlain by Bokkeveld shales and containing some eight sandstone inselbergs varying in area from 50–500 km².

The soils of the Cape Fold Belt and Tertiary sands are extremely nutrient-poor. These contrast with the nutrient-rich shales of the plains, which now support agriculture.

The major rivers in the region flow parallel to the fold belt in the west and south-west, but transverse the fold mountains in the east. The Olifants and Berg River systems flow to the north-west and the Breede River system flows south-east. The Gouritz and Gamtoos River systems drain the regions between the fold belts and the Karoo, to the north of the CFR.

The CFR is situated in a transition zone between the circumpolar westerly system, which results in cyclonic rain in winter, and the continental sub-tropical anticyclones, which result in summer aridity in the west of the CFR and thermal rainstorms during summer in the east (Fuggle 1981). Thus, in the west, 55% of the annual rainfall occurs during the three winter months and 10% in the three summer months. On the south coast, rainfall is year-round with minor peaks in autumn and spring. Annual rainfall on the coastal plains is generally below 500 mm, inter-montane valleys occupy rain-shadows between 100–400 mm and mountains receive 1000–2500 mm (Fuggle 1981). Mean annual temperatures are 15–20°C, with an annual temperature range of about 8°C at the coast and 12°C inland. Snow occasionally occurs above 1500 m during late winter and spring, but only persists for more than a few days on south slopes. Frost occurs in inland valleys between July and August. Sea mists are fairly frequent along the west coast. Strong winds occur throughout the year. Evapotranspiration is greatest during summer, but at high altitudes this is compensated for by mists which give rise to c. 500 mm of unrecorded precipitation per year. During winter, north-westerly gales, associated with cyclones, occur. The region is also subject to gusty, desiccating katabatic winds which may raise temperatures by 10–15°C in a few hours. These "Berg" winds are associated with low pressure systems which develop with advancing cyclones and are therefore most severe in winter.

# Vegetation

There are five major vegetation types within the CFR (Moll and Bossi 1984): fynbos (36,800 km²), renoster shrubland (16,700 km²), karoo (10,100 km²), thicket (3000 km²), and Afromontane forest (1000 km²).

Fynbos and renoster shrubland are fire-climax vegetation types, burning at intervals of 4–60 and 2–15 years, respectively. Some 20,400 km² (mostly renoster shrubland of the coastal plains) have been cleared of vegetation for pastures, wheat fields and vineyards.

Fynbos is the most species-rich of the vegetation types: over 75% of CFR species occur in fynbos. These include all the endemic families and many of the endemic genera. Fynbos includes a proteoid (*Protea, Leucadendron*) overstorey (0.5–3 m), an ericaceous middlestorey (0.5–1.5 m) and a restioid (Restionaceae) understorey (0.2–1 m). Trees are typically absent.

The following 6 fynbos types are recognized, based on a structural classification (the vegetation is too rich, with too many endemics, to enable a regional floristic classification) (Campbell 1985b):

Grassy fynbos – with a high grass cover, chiefly replacing the restioid component, and occurring in the east where summer rainfall is more pronounced and soils are more fertile.

Asteraceous fynbos – with a relatively low cover comprising non-ericaceous ericoid shrubs (Asteraceae, Rhamnaceae, Thymelaeaceae), some succulents and deciduous shrubs, and with a relatively low restioid cover. It occupies the driest locations, on steeper north-facing slopes with shallow soils, and replaces renoster shrubland on shales where rainfall exceeds 600 mm.

Restioid fynbos – with a high restioid cover, few shrubs and often with an alpine stature. It occurs both in waterlogged sites and on very well drained sites at mesic, higher altitudes on skeletal soils.

Ericaceous fynbos (heathland) – with a high cover of restioids and ericaceous ericoids, combined with a low cover of emergent proteoids. It is associated with southerly aspects, in areas which have deeper, peaty soils and which receive more than 1500 mm rainfall.

Proteoid fynbos – with a high cover of 1.5–3 m tall non-resprouting proteoids, with a variable understorey. It typically occurs at lower altitudes, on deeper soils and southern slopes;

Closed-scrub fynbos – associated with rivers and streams and with tall non-proteoid shrubs and trees, but with a restioid and ericoid understorey. There is a high species turnover (approaching 100%) between substrata (sands, limestones, gravels and laterites) on the coastal forelands (Cowling *et al.* 1988).

Renoster shrubland was apparently a *Themeda triandra* grassland which, through over-grazing, was converted to shrubland during the 19th century. Today, it is dominated by Asteraceae (*Elytropappus, Eriocephalus, Pteronia, Relhania*) and other leptophyllous shrubs as well as deciduous geophytes. It is restricted to fertile shale soils with an annual precipitation of 300–600 mm. Four geographically distinct renoster shrubland types are recognized. In order of increasing grass cover these are: West Coast, Central Mountain, South West Coast and South Coast Renoster Shrubland.

Karoo vegetation is typically not considered as part of the Cape Floristic Region. Included herein are only the karroid types from within the Little Karoo, situated between the Cape Fold Mountains. Karoo replaces renoster shrubland on shale soils where annual rainfall is less than 300 mm.

Subtropical thicket and Afromontane forest are species-depauperate versions of vegetation types better represented to the north-east of the CFR (Cowling *et al.* 1988; White 1983). Both are climax vegetation types within the region, but are largely confined to high rainfall areas and localities protected from fire, although a form of thicket vegetation is typical of the immediate coastal foreland. Thicket is dominated by trees and tall shrubs including: *Cassine, Chionanthus, Euclea, Maytenus, Olea, Pterocelastrus, Rhus, Sideroxylon* and *Zygophyllum*. Afromontane forest is typical of that elsewhere in Africa.

# Flora

There are 8600 vascular plant species in the CFR, of which some 5870 species (68%) are endemic (Bond and Goldblatt 1984). It is estimated that 7000 of these species (81%) occur in fynbos vegetation. There are many species-rich genera and families. More than half of the Southern African species in the following large families (>200 species) are found in the CFR: Campanulaceae, Ericaceae, Iridaceae, Proteaceae, Restionaceae, Rutaceae and Scrophulariaceae (see Table 26, below); these account for a third of the flora. Six families are endemic to fynbos: Penaeaceae (5 genera, 25 species), Stilbaceae (5 genera, 12 species), Grubbiaceae (2 genera, 5 species), Roridulaceae (1 genus, 2 species), Geissolomataceae (1 species) and Retziaceae (1 species). An additional family, Bruniaceae (12 genera, 75 species), has only two extra-limital species.

The 10 largest genera in the CFR account for 20% of the flora. They are: *Erica* (Ericaceae: 566 species), *Aspalathus* (Fabaceae: 245), *Ruschia* (Mesembryanthemaceae: 138), *Phylica* (Rhamnaceae: 133), *Agathosma* (Rutaceae: 130), *Oxalis* (Oxalidaceae: 129), *Pelargonium* (Geraniaceae: 125), *Senecio* (Asteraceae: 113), *Cliffortia* (Rosaceae: 106) and *Muraltia* (Polygalaceae: 106).

Species richness and endemicity in the CFR is greatest in the south-west and decreases at a faster rate eastwards than northwards (Cowling, Holmes and Rebelo 1992). The centre of species richness is the Cape Hangklip region, with 1400 species in an area of 240 km² (see Table 27). Much of the high species richness of the CFR is accounted for by high beta and gamma diversities rather than high alpha diversity, as is typical of temperate floras. As a result, there are many local centres of endemism, centred on the principal mountain ranges and lowlands of fynbos, with marked turnover of species between substrata.

The Proteaceae and Restionaceae, along with the Podocarpaceae, Aponogetonaceae and Cunoniaceae, are probably Gondwanan families, showing strong connections with floras in south-western Australia and South America (Goldblatt 1978). Ericaceae and some Iridaceae show strong affinities with Europe, chiefly via the Afromontane zone, but both these families might also be Gondwanan in origin. The remaining elements may have tropical affinities. Indeed, renoster shrubland, thicket and Afromontane forest share many genera and species with vegetation types to the north-east of the CFR.

**TABLE 26. STATUS OF THE LARGEST FAMILIES (>200 SPECIES) IN THE CFR**

| Family | Total genera | Endemic genera | Total species | Endemic species | Red Data Book status | | | |
|---|---|---|---|---|---|---|---|---|
| | | | | | Ex | E+V | R | K/I |
| Asteraceae | 109 | 32 | 986 | 608 | 2 | 11 | 40 | 113 |
| Ericaceae | 22 | 17 | 688 | 666 | 5 | 26 | 48 | 59 |
| Mesembryanthemaceae | 61 | 16 | 660 | 507 | 1 | 11 | 10 | 34 |
| Fabaceae | 38 | 8 | 644 | 525 | 1 | 9 | 21 | 79 |
| Iridaceae | 39 | 8 | 612 | 485 | 5 | 46 | 90 | 101 |
| Proteaceae | 14 | 9 | 320 | 306 | 3 | 62 | 58 | 8 |
| Restionaceae | 19 | 12 | 310 | 290 | 1 | 21 | 20 | 12 |
| Scrophulariaceae | 35 | 5 | 310 | 160 | | 2 | 3 | 30 |
| Rutaceae | 14 | 6 | 259 | 242 | 2 | 20 | 52 | 29 |
| Campanulaceae | 16 | 6 | 222 | 157 | | 1 | 3 | 70 |
| Orchidaceae | 28 | 4 | 206 | 124 | | 15 | 24 | 19 |
| Cyperaceae | 26 | 5 | 203 | 124 | | | 1 | 14 |
| **Grand Total (all families)** | **955** | **193** | **8600** | **5870** | **29** | **282** | **420** | **704** |

The levels of endemicity are based on the boundaries for the CFR as determined by Bond and Goldblatt (1984). Were fynbos outliers to the north and 100 km to the east to be included, the levels of endemism for each of the Proteaceae, Restionaceae, Ericaceae and Rutaceae would approach 99%. Grand totals from Hall and Veldhuis (1985).

**MAP 10. CENTRES OF ENDEMISM IN THE CAPE FLORISTIC REGION BASED ON DISTRIBUTIONS OF THE PROTEACEAE (REBELO AND SIEGFRIED 1990)**

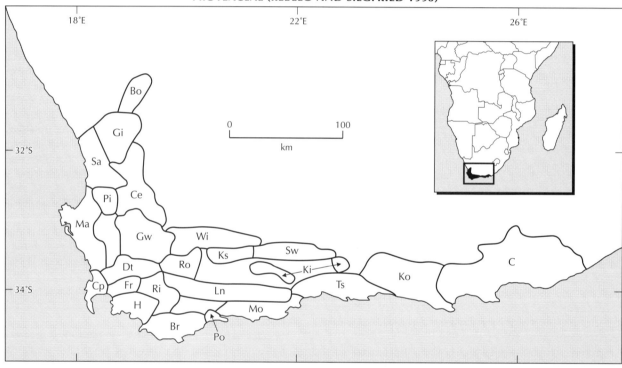

**TABLE 27. SPECIES RICHNESS AND ENDEMICITY FOR THE CENTRES OF ENDEMISM IN THE CAPE FLORISTIC REGION (REBELO AND SIEGFRIED 1990)**

| | Code | Proteaceae species | | All plant species | |
|---|---|---|---|---|---|
| | | Total | Endemic | Total | Endemic |
| **North-western Province** | | | | | |
| Cedarberg District | Ce | 63 | 7 | 1400 | 100 |
| Great Winterhoek District | Gw | 103 | 10 | | |
| Piketberg District | Pi | 33 | 2 | 630* | |
| Sandveld District: | | | | | |
| Sandveld Zone | Sa | 32 | 3 | | |
| Bokkeveld Zone | Bo | 12 | 3 | | |
| Gifberg Zone | Gi | 24 | 3 | | |
| **South-western Province** | | | | | |
| Malmesbury District | Ma | 34 | 4 | | |
| Peninsula District | Cp | 55 | 11 | 2250 | 190 |
| Riviersonderend District | Ri | 65 | 7 | | |
| Franshoek District | Fr | 102 | 3 | | |
| DuToitskloof District | Dt | 90 | 4 | | |
| Houwhoek District | H | 98 | 22 | 1400* | |
| Bredasdorp District | Br | 55 | 8 | 1750 | 140 |
| Potberg District | Po | 33 | 3 | | |
| Mosselbay District | Mo | 19 | 3 | | |

| | Code | Proteaceae species | | All plant species | |
|---|---|---|---|---|---|
| | | Total | Endemic | Total | Endemic |
| **Coastal Mountain Province** | | | | | |
| Koo Langeberg District | Kl | 58 | 3 | | |
| Langeberg District | Ln | 63 | 9 | 1100 | 140 |
| Outeniqua District | Ou | 36 | 4 | | |
| Kouga District | Ko | 30 | 2 | | |
| **South-eastern Province** | | | | | |
| Cockscomb District | C | 22 | 4 | 879 | 128 |
| **Inland Mountain Province** | | | | | |
| Swartberg District | | 57 | 13 | | |
| Swartberg Zone | Sw | 45 | 3 | | |
| KleinSwartberg Zone | Ks | 24 | 4 | | |
| Karoo Island Zone | Ki | 44 | 4 | | |
| Witteberg District | Wi | 22 | 2 | | |

\* indicates figure based on less than half the area of the centre. Areas for the centres of endemism (see Map 10) are provided in Table 30.

## Useful plants

Many species are commercially harvested from the wild and cultivated. Cut flowers, both cultivated (worldwide) and harvested from natural vegetation, include *Leucadendron*, *Leucospermum* and *Protea* (Proteaceae) and *Brunia* (Bruniaceae) (Greyling and Davis 1989). Families of fynbos plants which contain a large number of species utilized by the cut-flower trade include: Proteaceae (53 species), Ericaceae (32), Asteraceae (29), Restionaceae (27) and Bruniaceae (9) (Greyling and Davis 1989).

Genera commercially harvested from the wild, but seldom cultivated include: everlastings (*Helichrysum* in the Asteraceae), thatching (*Chondropetalum* and *Thamnochortus* in the Restionaceae), *Aloe* and *Erica*.

Crops grown commercially within the region include Rooibos tea (*Aspalathus linearis*). Species of Geraniaceae and Rutaceae have been utilized for production of oil and perfume.

Many ornamental and bulbous species have either their origin in, or part of their gene pool derived from, the CFR (Zeven and De Wet 1982). Large natural gene pools of these species still exist, including temperate races of otherwise tropical species. These are potentially important for horticulture and agriculture.

### TABLE 28. COMMERCIALLY GROWN SPECIES UTILIZED BY THE LOCAL CUT-FLOWER TRADE

| | | |
|---|---|---|
| Leucadendron | Leucospermum | Protea aurea |
| daphnoides | conocarpodendron | P. burchellii |
| L. discolor | L. cordifolium | P. compacta |
| L. floridum | L. cuneiforme | P. eximia |
| L. gandogeri | L. glabrum | P. lacticolor |
| L. laureolum | L. lineare | P. laurifolia |
| L. procerum | L. patersonii | P. longifolia |
| L. salignum | L. reflexum | P. lorifolia |
| L. strobilinum | L. spathulatum | P. magnifica |
| L. tinctum | L. tottum | P. mundii |
| L. xanthoconus | L. vestitum | P. neriifolia |
| | | P. obtusifolia |
| Serruria florida | | P. repens |
| | | P. stokoei |
| | | P. sussanae |

Source: Greyling and Davis (1989).
Note that only component species of important cultivars are listed.

### TABLE 29. PLANTS CULTIVATED IN OTHER REGIONS OF THE WORLD THAT HAVE EXTANT POPULATIONS WITHIN THE CFR

| Family | Species |
|---|---|
| Alliaceae | Tulbaghia violacea |
| Fabaceae | Aspalathus linearis |
| | Dipogon lignosus |
| Geraniaceae | Pelargonium crispum |
| | P. denticulatum |
| | P. graveolens |
| | P. odoratissimum |
| | P. tomentosum |
| Mesembryanthemaceae | Carpobrotus edulis |
| | Mesembryanthemum crystalinum |
| Poaceae | Cynodon dactylon |
| | Ehrharta calycina |
| | Hemarthria altissima |
| | Panicum maximum |
| Rutaceae | Adenandra fragrans |
| Solanaceae | Solanum aculeastrum |

Source: Zeven and De Wet 1982.

## Social and environmental values

The highest concentrations of Red Data Book species of reptiles, amphibians, butterflies and plants occur in the southwest, mainly within the greater Cape Town metropolitan area and surrounds (Hall and Ashton 1983; Rebelo 1992b).

The CFR contains 38% of Southern Africa's Red Data Book butterfly species, 35% of its RDB reptiles, 44% of its RDB amphibians and 57% of its RDB riverine fish species (Rebelo 1992b). In terms of threatened species (i.e. Extinct, Endangered or Vulnerable) the CFR contains 55, 33, 100 and 55% of the subcontinents totals for butterflies, reptiles, amphibians and riverine fish, respectively. With the exception of reptiles, more than 95% of the threatened species in these groups are endemic to the CFR.

Seven restricted-range bird species occur in the Cape Fynbos EBA, of which six are endemic to it. These birds are principally associated with the fynbos vegetation.

The mountains of the CFR are significant water catchment areas for the whole subcontinent (Hall & Ashton 1983). Although covering only 4% of the area, the mountains yield 20% of surface water run-off. The vast majority of mountain fynbos has been preserved primarily for its water catchment function. Almost 50% of the area of fynbos reserves are state-owned Mountain Catchment and a further 30% privately-owned Mountain Catchment, administered under Water Conservation Act 63 (1970).

Currently, half a million people visit Kirstenbosch National Botanical Gardens annually, with some 300,000 people using the Cable Way to the top of Table Mountain or visiting the Cape of Good Hope Nature Reserve. This makes Table Mountain the third most important tourist site in South Africa.

Over 2000 tons of wildflower material were exported in 1986 (Anon. 1989). Both the wildflower trade and the Rooibos tea industry (which is based upon the indigenous *Aspalathus linearis*) utilize fynbos vegetation.

Although the Cape was the home to the San and Khoi peoples, smallpox, wars and slavery resulted in local customs being lost or incorporated into the local European cultural traditions (Donaldson and Scott, in press). Some local herbal and medicinal traditions are recorded, but by far the majority has been lost. The large black population moving into urban regions originates from outside the CFR. There is, therefore, little traditional knowledge of the flora of the CFR. Little is known of the economic or social importance of CFR species to the "muti" (traditional medicine) trade.

## Economic assessment

There are no published figures of the economic importance of mountain catchment areas for water and recreation in the Cape Floristic Region; however, the scenic beauty of the region and its floral wealth are major tourist attractions.

The richer soils of the CFR (which once supported mainly renoster shrubland) have been converted to pasture, wheatlands and, in wetter areas, vineyards. Fynbos on shales, in areas of high rainfall, has been replaced by deciduous-fruit orchards, while karoo and fynbos vegetation alongside major rivers in the north-western CFR has been replaced by citrus orchards and vineyards. Sheep and cattle farming predominate in renoster shrubland; ostrich and goat farming occur in karoid shrublands (Anon. 1989).

Of lesser importance to the economy is the utilization of indigenous plants. Fynbos on sandy plains between the mountains in the north-western CFR has been replaced by *Aspalathus linearis* plantations. This Rooibos tea industry was worth R5.5 million in 1986 (Anon. 1989). Elsewhere, fynbos on the mountains has been converted to protea orchards, but extensive commercial harvesting from natural fynbos also occurs. The wildflower trade was estimated in 1989 to be valued at about R29 million, of which R18 million related to exports, mainly to Europe (Anon. 1989).

## Threats

Of 232 Red Data Book plant species for which data are available, 84 are threatened by invasive alien plants. Agriculture threatens 42 species, 21 species are under threat from urbanization and a further 21 species are threatened by fire regimes. Grazing/browsing, commercial and illegal collecting and mining/quarrying each threaten more than 10 species (Rebelo 1992b).

79% of coastal renoster shrubland, 49% of lowland fynbos and 24% of Afromontane forest has been lost to agriculture or afforestation. Invasive alien plants (such as *Pinus pinaster*, *Hakea* spp. and *Acacia longifolia*) infest 36% of mountain fynbos; 36% of lowland fynbos is infested by aliens, chiefly by *Acacia cyclops*, *A. saligna*, *Leptospermum laevigatum* and annual grasses, such as species of *Briza* and *Poa*. *Acacia* spp. affect 50% of thicket vegetation; *Acacia saligna* and annual grasses affect 11% of the remaining area of coastal renoster shrubland (Rebelo 1992b).

Although urban and industrial areas comprise less than 1% of the CFR area, the projected growth for the Cape Town metropolitan area is from 1.8 million in 1980 to 6.2 million in 2020. Besides the direct effects of urban development, such a large increase in the urban population is likely to lead to additional threats, such as the building of more dams to satisfy water requirements, further clearances for agriculture, greater recreational use of existing natural areas, increased levels of pollution and further pressures on wild medicinal plants. Greater Cape Town already encompasses one of the centres of lowland endemism in the CFR and surrounds the Peninsula Centre of endemism. Indeed, the Greater Cape Town metropolitan area includes the highest concentration of threatened Red Data Book plant species in the whole CFR (c. 15 Red Data Book species concentrated in 5 km² of lowland fynbos suitable for preservation in Nature Reserves) (Hall and Ashton 1983; Rebelo 1992b). A further 122 Red Data Book species occur within the city on Table Mountain (300 km²).

## Conservation

Centres of endemism in the mountains are, with the exception of arid regions, well protected in Nature Reserves and Mountain Catchment Areas (Table 30) (Rebelo and Siegfried 1990). It is estimated that 90% of the mountain flora is preserved in this network. The reserves include areas which may have been Pleistocene refugia. These areas may, therefore, be adequately buffered against natural vegetation migrations that might occur during predicted global warming (Rebelo and Siegfried 1990, 1992).

**TABLE 30. EXISTING PROTECTED AND PROPOSED PRIORITY CONSERVATION AREAS FOR THE PROTECTION OF FYNBOS VEGETATION IN THE CFR**

| | Code | Total extant area (km²) of fynbos | Proportion conserved (%) | Proportion proposed for conservation | Number of existing reserves Total | Number > 100 km² |
|---|---|---|---|---|---|---|
| **North-western Province** | | | | | | |
| Cedarberg District | Ce | 2569 | 86 | 0 | 3 | 3 |
| Great Winterhoek District | GW | 2206 | 73 | 1 | 7 | 4 |
| Piketberg District | Pi | 494 | 0 | 47 | 0 | 0 |
| Sandveld District: | | | | | | |
| Sandveld Zone | Sa | 2306 | 0 | 12 | 0 | 0 |
| Bokkeveld Zone | Bo | 850 | 6 | 0 | 1 | 0 |
| Gifberg Zone | Gi | 2370 | 0 | 0 | 0 | 0 |
| **South-western Province** | | | | | | |
| Malmesbury District | Ma | 972 | 4 | 59 | 13 | 0 |
| Peninsula District | Cp | 278 | 100 | 0 | 10 | 1 |
| Riviersonderend District | Ri | 912 | 80 | 0 | 4 | 2 |
| Franshoek District | Fr | 596 | 98 | 2 | 7 | 4 |
| DuToitskloof District | Dt | 1369 | 89 | 12 | 8 | 2 |
| Houwhoek District | H | 991 | 65 | 42 | 14 | 2 |
| Bredasdorp District | Br | 2317 | 8 | 30 | 16 | 1 |
| Potberg District | Po | 130 | 19 | 4 | 1 | 0 |
| Mosselbay District | Mo | 1549 | 2 | 0.4 | 5 | 0 |
| **Coastal Mountain Province** | | | | | | |
| Koo Langeberg District | Kl | 722 | 83 | 0 | 4 | 1 |
| Langeberg District | Ln | 1853 | 46 | 6 | 5 | 4 |
| Outeniqua District | Ou | 1619 | 96 | 12 | 35 | 5 |
| Kouga District | Ko | 6658 | 27 | 6 | 18 | 4 |
| **South-eastern Province** | | | | | | |
| Swartberg District: | | | | | | |
| Swartberg Zone | Sw | 1216 | 100 | 0 | 3 | 1 |
| KleinSwartberg Zone | Ks | 574 | 99 | 0 | 5 | 2 |
| Karoo Island Zone | Ki | 1685 | 33 | 0 | 4 | 3 |
| Witteberg District | Wi | 161 | 0 | 0 | 0 | 0 |
| **Total** | | **36,998** | **43.9%** | **11%** | | |
| Total original areas of fynbos | | 46,080 | 35.3% | 9% | | |

Source: Rebelo and Siegfried 1990. Proposed conservation areas include Mountain Catchment Areas: therefore proposed and existing conservation areas may exceed 100% in total.

Lowland areas are less well conserved; less than 3% of the lowlands are protected. Coastal renoster shrubland is particularly poorly conserved, only 0.3% being protected. In none of the four fynbos lowland centres of endemism does the area preserved approach 10% (Table 30) (Boucher 1981; Rebelo and Siegfried 1992).

The current political changes have resulted in a reduction of subsidies for local Nature Reserves and both local and provincial Nature Reserves have been deproclaimed as a consequence of the lack of funds. Additionally, it is predicted that there will be a reduction in the level of manual control of alien plant species. The flora of the CFR, therefore, faces a crisis which is exacerbated by the present political situation.

It is of paramount importance that the entire CFR be proposed a Biosphere Reserve as soon as political conditions allow.

## References

Anon. (1989). *Agriculture in South Africa*. Van Rensberg, Johannesburg.

Bond, P. and Goldblatt, P. (1984). Plants of the Cape flora: a descriptive catalogue. *Journal of South African Botany Supplement* 13.

Boucher, C. (1981). Floristic and structural features of the coastal foreland vegetation south of the Berg River, western Cape Province, South Africa. In Moll, E. (ed.), *Proceedings of a symposium on coastal lowlands of the western Cape*. University Western Cape, Bellville. Pp. 21–26.

Boucher, C. and McDonald, A.E. (1982). *An inventory of plant communities recorded in the western, southern and eastern Cape Province, South Africa up to the end of 1980*. South African National Scientific Progress Report 57. CSIR, Pretoria.

Campbell, B.M. (1985a). A classification of the mountain vegetation of the Fynbos Biome. *Memoirs of the Botanical Survey of South Africa* 50.

Campbell, B.M. (1985b). Montane vegetation structure in the Fynbos Biome: structural classification and adaptive significance of structural characters. PhD. thesis, Utrecht University.

Cowling, R.M. (ed.) (1991). *The ecology of fynbos: nutrients, fire and diversity*. Oxford University Press, Cape Town.

Cowling, R.M., Campbell, B.M., Mustart, P., McDonald, D.J., Jarman, M.L. and Moll, E.J. (1988). Vegetation classification in a floristically complex area: the Agulhas Plain. *South African Journal of Botany* 54: 290–300.

Cowling, R.M., Holmes, P.M. and Rebelo, A.G. (1992). Plant diversity and endemism. In Cowling, R.M. (ed.), *The ecology of fynbos: nutrients, fire and diversity*. Oxford University Press, Cape Town. Pp. 62–112.

Cowling, R.M., Le Maitre, D.C., McKenzie, B., Prys-Jones, R.P. and Wilgen, B.W. van (eds) (1987). *Disturbance and the dynamics of Fynbos Biome communities*. South African National Science Programmes Report 135. CSIR, Pretoria.

Day, J., Siegfried, W.R., Louw, G.N. and Jarman, M.L. (eds) (1979). *Fynbos ecology: a preliminary synthesis*. South African National Science Programmes Report 40. CSIR, Pretoria.

Day, J.A. (1983). *Mineral nutrients in Mediterranean ecosystems*. South African National Science Programmes Report 71. CSIR, Pretoria.

Donaldson, J.S. and Scott, G. (in press). Aspects of human dependence on plant diversity in the Cape Mediterranean-type ecosytem and implications for a functional approach to biodiversity. *South African Journal of Science*.

Fuggle, R.F. (1981). *Macro-climatic patterns within the Fynbos Biome*. National Programme for Environmental Science, Fynbos Biome Project, Final Report. CSIR, Pretoria.

Goldblatt, P. (1978). An analysis of the flora of Southern Africa: its characteristics, relationships and origins. *Annals of the Missouri Botanic Gardens* 65: 369–435.

Greyling, T. and Davis, G.W. (1989). *The wildflower resource: commerce, conservation and research*. Ecosystem Programmes Occasional Report Series 40. CSIR, Pretoria.

Hall, A.V. and Ashton, E.R. (1983). *Threatened plants of the Cape Peninsula*. Threatened Plants Group, University of Cape Town.

Hall, A.V. and Veldhuis, H.A. (1985). *South African Red Data Book: plants – Fynbos and Karoo Biomes*. South African National Scientific Programmes Report 117. CSIR, Pretoria.

Jarman, M.L. (1986). *Conservation priorities in lowland regions of the Fynbos Biome*. South African National Scientific Programmes Report 87. CSIR, Pretoria.

Kruger, F.J., Miller, P.M., Miller, J. and Oechel, W.C. (1985). *Simulation modelling of fynbos ecosystems: systems analysis and conceptual models*. South African National Science Programmes Report 105. CSIR, Pretoria.

Macdonald, I.A.W. and Jarman, M.L. (1984). *Invasive alien organisms in the terrestrial ecosystems of the Fynbos Biome, South Africa*. South African National Science Programmes Report 85. CSIR, Pretoria.

Macdonald, I.A.W., Jarman, M.L. and Beeston, P. (1985). *Management of invasive alien plants in the Fynbos Biome*. South African National Science Programmes Report 111. CSIR, Pretoria.

Manders, P.T. and Dicks, F.M. (1989). *A bibliography of fynbos ecology*, 2nd Ed. South African National Science Programmes Report 166. CSIR, Pretoria.

Moll, E.J. and Bossi, L. (1984). Assessment of the extent of the natural vegetation of the Fynbos Biome of South Africa. *South African Journal of Science* 80: 355–358.

Moll, E.J., Campbell, B.M., Cowling, R.M., Bossi, L., Jarman, M.L. and Boucher, C. (1984). *A description of major vegetation categories in and adjacent to the Fynbos Biome.* South African National Science Programmes Report 83. CSIR, Pretoria. Pp. 1–29.

Oliver, E.G.H., Linder, H.P. and Rourke, J.P. (1983). Geographical distribution of present-day Cape taxa and their phytogeographical significance. *Bothalia* 14: 427–440.

Pierce, S.M. (1984). *A synthesis of plant phenology in the Fynbos Biome.* South African National Science Programmes Report 88. CSIR, Pretoria.

Rebelo, A.G. (ed.) (1987). *A preliminary synthesis of pollination biology in the Cape flora.* South African National Science Programmes Report 141. CSIR, Pretoria.

Rebelo, A.G. (1992a). Preservation of biotic diversity in the Cape Floristic Region. In Cowling, R.M. (ed.), *The ecology of fynbos: nutrients, fire and diversity.* Oxford University Press, Cape Town. Pp. 309–344.

Rebelo, A.G. (1992b). The distribution and abundance of Red Data Book species in the Cape Floristic Region: threats, priorities and target species. *Transactions of the Royal Society of South Africa* 48: 55–86.

Rebelo, A.G., Cowling, R.M., Campbell, B.M. and Meadows, M. (1991). Plant communities of the Riversdale Plain. *South African Journal of Botany* 57: 186–190.

Rebelo, A.G. and Siegfried, W.R. (1990). Protection of fynbos vegetation: ideal and real-world options. *Biological Conservation* 54: 15–31.

Rebelo, A.G. and Siegfried, W.R. (1992). Where should nature reserves be located in the Cape Floristic Region, South Africa? Models for the spatial configuration of a reserve network aimed at maximizing the protection of floristic diversity. *Conservation Biology* 6: 243–252.

Rebelo, A.G. and Tansley, S.A. (1993). Using rare plant species to identify priority conservation areas in the Cape Floristic Region: the need to standardize for total species richness. *South African Journal of Science* 89: 156–161.

Simpson, M.J. (1985). A summary of the preliminary report on the wildflower industry. Unpublished report. Chief Directorate of Nature and Environmental Conservation, Cape Town.

White, F. (1983). *The vegetation of Africa: a descriptive memoir to accompany the Unesco/AETFAT/UNSO vegetation map of Africa.* Natural Resources Research XX. Unesco, Paris. 356 pp.

Zeven, A.C. and De Wet, J.M.J. (1982). *Dictionary of cultivated plants and their origin of diversity, excluding ornamentals, forest trees and lower plants.* Centre for Agricultural Publishing and Documentation, Wageningen.

## Acknowledgements

This Data Sheet was prepared by Dr Tony Rebelo (Conservation Biology Research Unit, National Botanical Institute, Kirstenbosch, South Africa).

# RONDO PLATEAU
## Tanzania

**Location:** Tanzania, Lindi District, about 40 km south-west of Lindi, between latitudes 10°00'–10°30'S and longitudes 39°00'–39°30'E.

**Area:** c. 250 km².

**Altitude:** Mostly 600–700 m, but sloping down to 300 m in the east.

**Vegetation:** Dry semi-deciduous lowland forest, woodland, thicket, secondary communities. Large parts converted to farmland and plantations.

**Flora:** Estimated 800 vascular plant species, of which >200 are strict or near-endemics; <5 strict of near-endemic genera. Many species known only from type-collections.

**Useful plants:** Timber trees (*Milicia excelsa, Pterocarpus angolensis*).

**Other values:** Rich fauna, water catchment area.

**Threats:** Logging, pole cutting, clearance for farming, burning.

**Conservation:** All indigenous forest is included within Rondo Forest Reserve, but this is not well protected.

## Geography

Rondo is a deeply dissected plateau in the coastal plains of southern Tanzania. The plateau rises slightly from east to west to reach an altitude of 600–700 m in Rondo Forest Reserve. In places, the escarpment slopes are very steep. The soils are leached white sands with very low nutrient status, derived from soft sandstones and unconsolidated sands of Jurassic or Cretaceous origin.

Rainfall is unreliable and estimated to be c. 1500 mm per annum. Rainfalls of short duration occur from November to December, while longer rains extend from February–March to April–May. Even in the rainy season, there is no surface water on the plateau and, in the dry season (May–June to October–November), most species of trees lose their leaves. Maximum temperatures reach well over 30°C at the end of the dry season, but, even at this time, the interior of the forest has a pleasant, if very humid, cooler climate.

## Vegetation

Before extensive logging in the 1940s and 1950s, this was the finest *Milicia* (*Chlorophora*) forest in East Africa. At present, about 20% of the plateau is covered with indigenous forest. Following clearance, part of the forest was converted to teak and pine plantations, but most was given over to shifting cultivation. The plantations are of very poor quality due to poor soils. No new plantings have been undertaken for the last 20 years.

The plateau-forest is extremely rich in species. Dominant or common larger trees include *Albizia adianthifolia, A. petersiana, Bombax rhodognaphalon, Cussonia zimmermannii, Dialium holtzii, Lannea antiscorbutica, Manilkara discolor, M. sulcata* (Bidgood and Vollesen 1992), *Milicia excelsa, Newtonia buchananii* and *Ricinodendrom heudelotii*. The forest is also rich in species of smaller trees, shrubs and woody climbers. There is an exceptional number of species of Rubiaceae, often dominant in the undergrowth.

Other vegetation types include *Brachystegia microphylla* thicket with *Faurea saligna* on steep slopes. This usually has a dense and rich shrub-layer comprising many of the

**CPD Site Af57: Rondo Plateau; showing the flat plateau and native vegetation covering the steep, dissected slopes.** Photo: Kaj Vollesen.

species found in the plateau forest, but it also contains a distinct floristic element of its own.

Part of the western part of the plateau is covered with *Parinari curatellifolia* woodland. It is not clear if this is a seral stage or whether it is the natural vegetation on drier parts of the plateau. There are several unusual species in the herb-layer, which seems to indicate at least a relatively well-established vegetation.

If the fallow period after cultivation is sufficiently prolonged, a very dense, almost impenetrable thicket with many species characteristic of forest undergrowth, develops. This would presumably further develop into forest if undisturbed, but in practice never happens.

## Flora

Phytogeographically, the Rondo Plateau belongs to the Zanzibar-Inhambane Region. The flora of the plateau contains relatively few strict or near-endemic genera (probably fewer than 5). Examples include *Streptosiphon* (Acanthaceae) and *Vismianthus* (Connaraceae). If genera endemic to the Zanzibar-Inhambane Region as a whole are included, the figure probably rises to around 50 (Vollesen 1992). There are numerous (probably over 200) strict or near-endemic species. If species endemic to the Zanzibar-Inhambane Region as a whole are included, this figure rises to probably over 400. The family Rubiaceae is especially well-represented.

The plateau is poorly collected. The only botanist to undertake extensive collecting was Schlieben in 1934. On a collecting trip to the plateau in 1991, at least 20 new species were collected and there is no doubt that many new plants still await discovery. Many of the species are only known from one or a few collections. The total flora of the plateau is estimated to be around 800 species.

## Useful plants

The most important plants are the timber trees *Milicia (Chlorophora) excelsa* and *Pterocarpus angolensis*, both of which are being logged selectively (and legally) by TWICO (Tanzania Wood Industries Corporation). An apparently undescribed species of *Cleistanthus* is illegally exploited for building poles in the western part of the Forest Reserve (pers. obs.).

## Social and environmental values

The forest is an important sanctuary for wildlife and is especially rich in birds. A new species of bushbaby was recently described from the area. Lions are still fairly common and elephants occasionally penetrate from the north and north-west. The plateau is an important water catchment area.

## Threats

The remaining native forest is threatened by encroaching farmland and by burning. Fires sometimes enter the forest along logging tracks, where broadleaved species of *Setaria* have become established. Once these "fire-islands" have been established, they tend to gradually enlarge, seedlings of forest trees not being able to establish themselves under the fire regime. Apart from selective legal logging within the Forest Reserve, a limited amount of illegal cutting of building poles occurs around the margins of the forest.

There has probably been agriculture on the plateau for a long time, but in recent years the population has increased dramatically and fallow periods have become shorter. This has resulted in increasing degradation of the vegetation, a process accentuated by the poor quality of the soils. A current programme to establish a permanent water supply on the plateau will probably result in a further expansion of the human population, with resulting increased pressure on the remaining forest.

## Conservation

All remaining indigenous forest is within the Rondo Forest Reserve. The Rondo Forest Station is under-staffed and unable to protect adequately the boundaries against enchroachment. It is important that at least part of the forest is given better protection.

## References

Bidgood, S. and Vollesen, K. (1992). *Bauhinia loeseneriana* reinstated, with notes on the forests of the Rondo Plateau, S.E. Tanzania. *Kew Bulletin* 47: 759–764.

Polhill, R.M. (1968). Tanzania. In Hedberg, I. and Hedberg, O. (eds), Conservation of vegetation in Africa south of the Sahara. *Acta Phytogeographica Suecica* 54: 166–178.

Vollesen, K. (1992). *Trichaulax* (Acanthaceae: Justicieae), a new genus from East Africa. *Kew Bulletin* 47: 613–618.

## Acknowledgements

This Data Sheet was prepared by Dr Kaj Vollesen (Royal Botanic Gardens, Kew).

# MAPUTALAND-PONDOLAND REGION
## South Africa, Swaziland and Mozambique

**Location:** Coastal belt extending from the Olifants-Limpopo River (24°S) in the north to just beyond the Great Kei River (33°S) in the south, bounded in the west by the Great Escarpment (below 1200 m in Transvaal and Swaziland, 1800 m in Natal Transkei and Cape Province) and in the east by the Indian Ocean.

**Area:** c. 201,640 km².

**Altitude:** 0–1800 m (mainly below 1000 m).

**Vegetation:** Very diverse, including different types of grassland, Afromontane forest, coastal forest, swamp forest, sand forest, shrub forest, valley bushveld, thornveld, semi-evergreen savanna/thicket, palm veld and rich aquatic communities (particularly in the north-east).

**Flora:** Estimated 6000–7000 species of vascular plants. Endemic/near-endemic taxa include 2 families, about 58 genera and 1222 species/infraspecific taxa. Except for the Maputaland and Pondoland Centres, endemics not always concentrated in particular areas.

**Useful plants:** Many ornamental, medicinal and food plants; many pasture species and plants used for construction craftwork and as fuel. Full potential of flora scarcely explored.

**Other values:** High landscape value; exceptionally rich fauna, including 148 endemic/near endemic bird taxa; important to the tourist industry (several major game parks), with associated benefits to the economy of the region.

**Threats:** Very densely populated over most parts (c. 15 million people) with the population rapidly increasing. Slash-and-burn shifting agriculture practised in some areas. Much of the natural vegetation has been destroyed by extensive agriculture (sugar cane, maize, bananas, tea), afforestation (pines, gums, wattles) and urban development. Most of the remaining grassland has been impoverished by intensive grazing and burning, resulting locally in serious soil erosion. Invasive alien plants and dune mining for heavy minerals also pose major threats.

**Conservation:** Several conservation areas (c. 15,138 km²; 7.5% of region), but 93% of the conserved area concentrated within the savanna vegetation in the northern parts. Maputaland Centre: almost 10% conserved; Pondoland Centre: c. 7% conserved. Most endemics restricted to grassland. which predominates in central and southern portion of the region but very little of which is conserved.

Note – This region roughly approximates to the Tongaland-Pondoland Regional Mosaic of White (1983), but EXCLUDES the area south of the Great Kei River (Eastern Cape), which is treated as a separate CPD site, namely the Albany Centre (CPD Site Af52). Also, its western border has been extended in Natal, Transkei and north-eastern Cape Province to INCLUDE those parts of White's (1983) Afromontane Region lying below the Great Escarpment. Although the Albany Centre is clearly a southward extension of the Maputaland-Pondoland Region, the presence of particularly arid Karroid and Cape floristic elements impart to it a somewhat distinct character.

The Maputaland-Pondoland Region (MPR) is floristically very diverse and complex, with endemic plants not always concentrated in particular regions. However, there are at least two clear foci of high endemism in the region, namely the Maputaland Centre (MC) and the Pondoland Centre (PC). In this Data Sheet, information is supplied either for the MPR as a whole or, where appropriate, separately for the MC and PC.

Today the politically more acceptable name for Tongaland is Maputaland. To avoid confusion it is recommended that White's formal name "Tongaland-Pondoland Regional Mosaic" be changed to "Maputaland-Pondoland Regional Mosaic".

## Geography

### Maputaland-Pondoland Region (MPR)

The delimitation of the MPR (c. 201,640 km²) is somewhat arbitrary. It extends along the Indian Ocean, from the Olifants and Limpopo rivers in the north (24°S) to just beyond the Great Kei River in the south (33°S). The western boundary is formed mainly by the Great Escarpment and is based on altitude. In the northern sector (Transvaal and Swaziland) the upper altitudinal boundary has been drawn at 1200 m and further south at 1800 m (Natal/KwaZulu, Transkei and Cape Province). In Natal, the region above 1800 m comprises the alpine region (see Data Sheet on Drakensberg Alpine Region).

The topography of the region is very diverse, consisting of dunes along the coast, low-lying plains (mainly Transvaal Lowveld and Mozambique), mountain ranges (e.g. Lebombo Mountains and Ngoye Range) and series of rugged terraces incised by deep river valleys (Natal midlands and Transkei). The landscape of the region was shaped by the rifting and break-up of east and west Gondwana and subsequent cycles of uplift and erosion (King 1982; Partridge and Maud 1987). These processes formed the Great Escarpment, which receded from the coast after the establishment of an effective drainage system. Today, this escarpment separates the elevated interior of Southern Africa from the coastal margins. The MPR is drained by several major rivers which flow mainly from west to east towards the Indian Ocean, e.g. Limpopo and numerous smaller ones.

Regional geology consists of basement granites, gneisses and schists, various sedimentary strata, lavas (basalt and dolerite intrusions) and Cretaceous, Cenozoic and Recent marine sediments (South African Committee for Stratigraphy 1980). In contrast to the orientation of the major rivers, the geological formations are aligned roughly from north to south.

The climate ranges from subtropical/tropical in the low-lying areas to more temperate with frost in winter on higher ground away from the coast. Relative humidity is generally high along the coast. Mist frequently occurs in the midlands of Natal and Transkei. Annual rainfall varies from averages of about 400 mm to more than 1200 mm and falls predominantly during summer.

Large areas of the region are very densely populated, with extensive township and urban development along the Natal coastline. Transkei and KwaZulu are some of the most densely populated rural areas in Africa, many parts having a population density of more than 100 people km². Subsistence farming is practised extensively in these areas.

### Maputaland Centre (MC)

The MC (c. 26,734 km²) is defined here as that part of southern Mozambique and north-eastern Natal bounded in

**MAP 11. MAPUTALAND-PONDOLAND REGION (CPD SITE Af59)**

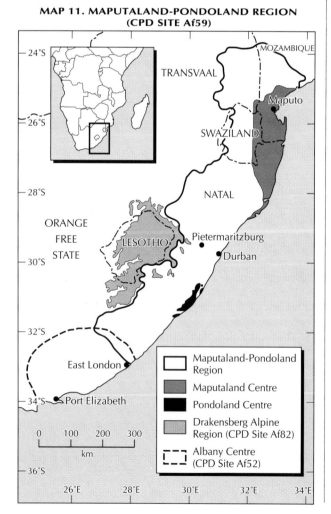

the north by the Inkomati-Limpopo River, in the east by the Indian Ocean, in the west by the western foothills of the Lebombo Mountains and in the south by the St Lucia estuary, from where it extends further along the coast down to about Mtunzini (perhaps including the transitional Ngoye Range). Biogeographically, the boundaries of the centre are clearly defined, except in the north, where demarcation is arbitrary.

With the exception of the narrow Lebombo Range, which rises to an elevation of some 600 m, the area is a nearly flat low-level coastal plain with a maximum elevation of about 150 m. A high coastal dune ridge is present along the shoreline, rising to almost 200 m above sea-level in places in Natal and said to be the tallest vegetated dunes in the world.

The Lebombo Range is formed by resistant volcanic rhyolite lavas, whereas the coastal plains consist mainly of Cretaceous to Recent marine sediments. Over most of the MC the soils are infertile, consisting of geologically recent aeolian sands. Fertile clayey alluvium occurs in the floodplains of some of the larger rivers (Bruton and Cooper 1980).

Annual rainfall averages about 1100 mm (locally over 1200 mm) along the coast, but declines progressively inland to only 600 mm on the western plains The crest of the Lebombo Range receives about 800 mm per year (Bruton and Cooper 1980).

The MC contains some extensive wetlands, particularly marshes, lakes and estuaries. Notable are Lake St Lucia (c. 350 km²), the largest estuarine system of its kind in Africa, Lake Sibaya (60–70 km²), the largest freshwater lake in Southern Africa, and the Kosi Lake System (c. 37 km²).

### Pondoland Centre (PC)

This region (c. 1880 km²) is a sharply demarcated, edaphically-related centre of endemism. It encompasses the relatively large outcrop of Natal Group sandstone (South African Committee for Stratigraphy 1980) that extends along the Indian Ocean, from the Mzimkulu River in southern Natal to the Egossa Fault (Ntsubane region) in Pondoland. Also included are the smaller outcrops of sandstone at Port St Johns (Mount Sullivan and Mount Thesiger) and Uvongo, and provisionally, the small interval of mainly Karoo sediments between the Egossa Fault and Port St Johns (Van Wyk 1990a) – henceforth referred to as the Egossa Interval.

The PC is characterized by rugged plateaus (usually 100–500 m above sea level), deeply dissected by narrow river gorges. The climate is subtropical with a mean annual temperature of about 20°C near the coast. Cool night temperatures are experienced at higher altitudes away from the coast. Average annual rainfall exceeds 1000 mm over most of the region, reaching more than 1200 mm in places. This occurs mainly during summer, although, in the southern parts, a minimum of 50 mm is expected every month of the year.

Soils are sandy, highly leached, acidic and often relatively shallow. Coastal dunes are either absent or poorly developed, whereas rocky outcrops are common.

## Vegetation

Vegetation of the MPR is very diverse. The northern, low-lying parts consist mainly of extensive savanna communities, arranged in complex patterns (Acocks 1953; Gertenbach 1983 and references therein). Unfortunately, serious depletion of vegetation and soil resources is taking place throughout the region. Overgrazing and the removal of trees for fuel are a serious problem in some tribal areas, whereas inappropriate farming practices in other parts have resulted in bush encroachment. Savanna plants are well adapted to withstand fire, a factor which is also important for the structural maintenance of this vegetation type (e.g. the density of the woody component).

Valley bushveld, a dense shrub-forest with various succulents, particularly species of *Aloe* and *Euphorbia*, is well developed in some of the hot, relatively arid inland river valleys (Acocks 1953; Edwards 1967). Most of the valley bushveld vegetation suffers from heavy overgrazing, particularly by cattle and goats.

Over most of the region and particularly in the central and southern parts, the natural vegetation is mainly grassland. Although fire is essential for maintaining the floristic diversity of these grasslands, excessive burning and severe overgrazing have seriously degraded most of this vegetation type. Extensive agriculture (sugar cane, maize, bananas, tea and other subtropical crops) and afforestation (*Acacia*, *Eucalyptus*, *Pinus*) have destroyed large tracts of grassland. The remaining grasslands are often either seriously degraded or heavily infested with alien plants (*Acacia*, *Caesalpinia*, *Chromolaena*, *Lantana*, *Rubus* and many others).

Indigenous forests are rare (less than 1% of the area) and confined to small relict patches, either along the coast (usually on dunes) or in moist fire-protected inland sites mainly on the south and south-east facing slopes of high ridges and mountains. The Indian Ocean coast belt forest of Natal and Transkei comprises riverine forest (19 km²), swamp forest (49 km²), sand forest (c. 60 km²), dune forest (c. 90 km²), coastal lowland forest (c. 390 km²) and coastal scarp forest (220 km²) (Cooper 1985; Cooper and Swart 1992). It has been estimated that in recent times over 90% of the coast lowland forest in Natal has been destroyed as a result of agriculture and afforestation (Cooper 1985). The inland forests mainly belong to (so-called) mist belt mixed *Podocarpus* forest (estimated 700 km²) and are classified as Afromontane.

### Maputaland Centre (MC)

Vegetation of the MC is exceptionally diverse. It consists of a mosaic of forest, woodland, grassland and swamps, largely determined by local edaphic conditions. The vegetation of the Natal portion of the region has been classified into at least 15 major types. These are: Lebombo forest, Lebombo Range vegetation, mixed bushveld, thicket, red-sand bushveld, floodplain vegetation, sand forest, pallid-sand bushveld, Mosi swamp vegetation, papyrus swamp, palm veld, coast grassveld, swamp forest, mangroves and dune forest (Moll 1977, 1980). On a more refined level,

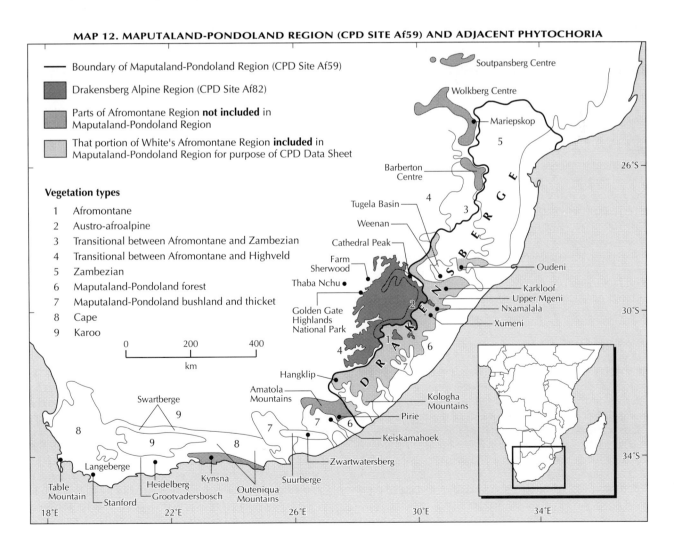

**MAP 12. MAPUTALAND-PONDOLAND REGION (CPD SITE Af59) AND ADJACENT PHYTOCHORIA**

**CPD Site Af59: Maputaland Centre, St Lucia Park. Climax coastal dune forest, with the wetlands of Lake Bangazi and Lake St Lucia beyond. The dunes exceed 70 m in height.** Photo: Roger Porter.

several other aquatic and dune forest communities have been described (Rogers 1980; Weisser 1980). Tinley (1971) recognises no less than 21 different ecosystems in the MC.

Although shifting agriculture is widely practised in the region, much of the vegetation is still in an excellent state compared to many other parts of the MPR. However, the severe exploitation of the Gwalaweni (Hlatikulu) Forest on the Lebombo Mountains is of particular concern. Large irrigation schemes on the Makatini Flats, afforestation with *Pinus* and *Eucalyptus* spp., slash and burn agriculture in some forest patches, coastal dune mining for heavy minerals and increasing pressure on the natural resources owing to a rapid population increase are all factors contributing to the devastation of this area.

### Pondoland Centre (PC)

Compared to the MC, the vegetation of the PC is less varied. It consists mainly of grassland with a few isolated forest patches confined chiefly to protected riverine gorges. Forest patches are more extensive and exposed in the south, particularly on the Karoo sediments of the Egossa Interval. Many of these forests are heavily utilized for firewood, medicinal barks and poles for domestic use. Fortunately, much of the floristically unique PC forest is situated in deep, inaccessible gorges. The PC coincides roughly with the Pondoland Coastal Plateau Sourveld, the smallest of the 70 veld types distinguished by Acocks (1953) in South Africa. Grasslands of the PC are considered the densest in Southern

Africa and are particularly vigorous, permitting a high burning frequency of two to three times per annum (Acocks 1953; Shackleton 1989). Although naturally floristically very rich, management practices of the rural population have degraded most of these grasslands, leading to a loss of floristic diversity and an increase in the unpalatable grass *Aristida junciformis*. The PC forests on sandstone are also exceptionally rich floristically (Geldenhuys 1989) and quite distinct from other forests in the MPR. Many different plant communities can be found even within a single forest (Cooper and Swart 1992). The estimated 200 km² of this forest type (Cooper and Swart 1992) are mainly located on Karoo sediments in the Egossa Interval and are not as rich in endemics as those located on sandstone. About 1 km² of swamp forest also occurs in the PC.

## Flora

Phytogeographically, the MPR is part of the Indian Ocean Coastal Belt which is both a Regional Transition Zone and a Regional Mosaic (Moll and White 1978; White 1983). The flora is a mixture of several floristic elements and communities, including tropical (particularly in the north and along the coast), Afromontane (at relatively low altitude owing to the compensating effect of increasing latitude on temperatures), Cape, Afroalpine and palaeoendemic (notably PC) elements.

The total number of vascular plant species for the MPR is estimated to be between 6000 and 7000. About 1222

**CPD Site Af59: Pondoland Centre, Fraser's Gorge, Lusikisiki District, Transkei. Sandstone cliffs, forest and grassland.** Photo: A.E. van Wyk.

species/infraspecific taxa and 58 genera of vascular plants are endemic or near-endemic to the region. In addition, several hundred species are centred in the MPR. Families rich in endemics/near-endemics are (number of species/infraspecific taxa in brackets): Asclepiadaceae (103), Compositae (102), Leguminosae-Papilionoideae (90), Liliaceae *s.l.* (71), Orchidaceae (60), Rubiaceae (57), Acanthaceae (54), Euphorbiaceae (54), Iridaceae (45), Labiateae (42) and Scrophulariaceae (41). Genera with large numbers of endemics/near-endemics (species/infraspecific taxa in brackets) include: *Aloe* (29), *Streptocarpus* (28), *Helichrysum* (25), *Senecio* (23), *Indigofera* (18), *Brachystelma* (18), *Kniphofia* (18), *Plectranthus* (18), *Euphorbia* (17), *Maytenus* (14), *Encephalartos* (13), *Pavetta* (13) and *Cyrtanthus* (11).

Maputaland Centre (MC)

Although still inadequately explored, the MC flora is very distinct from that of the rest of the MPR. An estimated 1100 species of vascular plants occur in the MC (this is probably an underestimate). Of these at least 168 species/infraspecific taxa and 4 genera (*Brachychloa*, *Ephippiocarpa*, *Helichrysopsis*, *Inhambanella*) are endemic/near-endemic to the centre. Several of the endemics are rare and known only from a few collections. The MC clearly has floristic links with the more tropical parts of Africa to the north. The centre is at the southern end of the tropics in Africa and many tropical species here reach the southernmost limits of their ranges.

Pondoland Centre (PC)

The total number of vascular plant species in the PC is about 1500. The forests and grasslands of this centre contain a rich endemic/near-endemic element of at least 118 species. This includes one monotypic family (Rhynchocalycaceae) and six monotypic genera (*Dahlgrenodendron*, *Eriosemopsis*, *Jubaeopsis*, *Pseudosalacia*, *Pseudoscolopia*, *Rhynchocalyx*). Particularly noteworthy is the presence of more than 30 species of woody endemics. Many of the PC endemics are rare and appear to be taxonomically isolated taxa on the brink of natural extinction. They show all the features of palaeoendemics and are of considerable phytogeographic interest (Van Wyk 1990a, b). The PC also contains a distinct Cape element, including the only occurrences of some taxa outside the Cape Floral Kingdom. Mixed tropical and strong Afromontane elements are also present in the region.

## Useful plants

Several million people in the MPR depend on the natural vegetation of the region for their livelihood, e.g. for the raising of livestock, food, health care, fuel and shelter. In the case of health care alone, a total number of about 900 species with specific medicinal plant usage has been recorded for the MPR (Hutchings 1989; Jansen and Mendes 1983). It is estimated that more than 80% of the local population still prefer to consult traditional practitioners as a first option. The MPR also serves as a major source of plant material for the vast herbal trade in the whole of Southern Africa (Cunningham 1990a). Studies on the active components of these medicinal plants may contribute significantly to the development of new medicines and other chemicals.

Examples of the numerous indigenous plants used as food in the MC are listed by Cunningham (1985) and Pooley (1980). Domestication of several promising food plants should be explored. Wild forms and species of the genus *Vigna* in the MPR have great potential for the improvement of cultigens of the cowpea (*V. unguiculata* subsp. *unguiculata*).

The MPR is renowned for the skilled craftsmanship of the local people. A variety of items are manufactured from plant materials. Commercialisation of these crafts has escalated in recent years, due to increased demand by tourists and curio dealers.

Although the MPR has already contributed several ornamentals (e.g. species of *Agapanthus*, *Aloe*, *Clivia*, *Cyrtanthus*, *Dierama*, *Encephalartos*, *Erythrina*, *Gladiolus*, *Kniphofia*, *Mackaya*, *Plectranthus*, *Scadoxus*, *Watsonia*), the considerable horticultural potential of the flora of the region has hardly been realized.

## Social and environmental values

The MPR has an exceptionally rich fauna (Table 31). Of the more than 472 species of birds in the MC (57% of South Africa's total), 47 subspecies are endemic/near-endemic to the centre. The MC corresponds with the southern part of the South-east African coast Endemic Bird Area (EBA). This has three endemic restricted-range birds species, which occur in a wide range of habitat types.

As with its flora, the MC is the southernmost part of the range of many components of the East African fauna. The centre is of exceptional biogeographical interest because of the sharp biogeographic transformation in the region (Poynton 1961). Other endemic/near-endemic species and infraspecific taxa (total indigenous to the centre in brackets) include 14 mammals (102 species, about 4 locally extinct), 23 reptiles (about 112 species/subspecies), 3 frogs (45 species/subspecies) and 7 freshwater fishes (67 species). The unspoiled beaches along the Maputaland coast are also a major nesting ground for marine turtles.

## TABLE 31. ENDEMISM AMONG SELECTED GROUPS OF PLANTS AND ANIMALS IN THE MAPUTALAND-PONDOLAND REGION, MAPUTALAND CENTRE AND PONDOLAND CENTRE[1]

| | Maputaland-Pondoland Region | Maputaland Centre | Pondoland Centre |
|---|---|---|---|
| Total number of vascular plants (specific & infraspecific taxa) | 6000–7000 | 1100 | 1500 |
| Endemic/near-endemic vascular plants (genera) | 58 | 4 | 6 |
| Endemic/near-endemic vascular plants (specific & infraspecific taxa) | 1222 | 168 | 118 |
| Endemic/near-endemic mammals (subspecies) | 41 | 14 | 1 |
| Endemic/near-endemic birds (subspecies) | 148 | 47 | 6 |
| Endemic/near-endemic reptiles (specific & infraspecific taxa) | 38 | 23 | 1 |
| Endemic/near-endemic frogs (specific & infraspecific taxa) | 17 | 3 | 0 |

[1] Statistics for animals based mainly on: Meester et al. (1986) [mammals]; Clancey (1980), Quickelberge (1989) [birds]; Branch (1988); FitzSimons and Broadley (1983) [reptiles]; Lambiris (1988) Passmore and Carruthers (1979) [frogs]; Bruton and Cooper (1980) [various groups]. Figures for plants based on author's own data.

With its low-lying plains, rolling hills, mountains, rugged plateaus incised by deep valleys, large rivers, estuaries and lakes, the whole of the MPR provides panoramic landscapes of breathtaking beauty. The Valley of a Thousand Hills in Natal, the Wild Coast of Transkei and the lakes and floodplains of Maputaland are well-known as some of the natural wonders of Southern Africa (Wannenburgh 1987). It is unfortunate that so much of the natural scenery has already been spoiled by severe overgrazing, afforestation, intensive sugar farming and other agricultural activities. Yet, the tourist potential of the area is still considerable. Tourism, promoted in a sensible way, can contribute significantly to the welfare of the local population.

Numerous fast-flowing rivers and streams originate in the MPR. Conservation of the natural vegetation cover of the land would help to control soil erosion (already a major problem in the region) and help to protect catchments. The MC contains three sites registered under the Ramsar Convention as wetlands of international importance, namely the St Lucia System, Kosi System and Lake Sibaya.

## Economic Assessment

Exact figures for the money generated by domestic livestock and wild game animals harvested from natural pastures in the MPR are not available, but it must amount to several hundred million Rand. Likewise statistics for the extensive medicinal plant trade are not available, but it is estimated to be tens of millions of Rand. In Natal/KwaZulu alone, Cunningham (1988) recorded over 400 indigenous plant species that are being sold as herbal medicines.

Significant income is generated by pastoralism and from the gathering of weaving materials, construction materials and wild foodstuffs in many rural parts of the MPR. Tapping palm wine from natural growing stands of *Hyphaene coriacea* and *Phoenix reclinata* is an important source of subsistence income to people in parts of the MC (Cunningham 1990b, c).

Tourism, based on the attraction of the natural environment, is a major money generator in the region. It is estimated that, in 1992, the income generated by Nature Reserves in the MPR far exceeded 300 million Rand (93 million Rand by the Kruger National Park alone). In addition, the economy of particularly rural towns benefitted greatly from the proximity of Nature Reserves and Scenic Areas.

## Threats

With a rapidly growing human population of about 15 million people and widespread poverty, illiteracy and other major socio-economic and political problems, prospects for the future survival of the vegetation and associated animal life of the MPR are very bleak indeed. Problems are aggravated by rapidly increasing urbanization; millions of people living in informal squatter settlements are exerting considerable pressure on the natural resources around cities. Durban, for example, is often considered to be the fastest or second fastest growing conurbation in the world (Nichols 1990). Growing demands for wood as fuel and building materials place heavy pressure on the small remaining forest patches in grassland areas, many of which have been completely destroyed in recent times.

Widespread overstocking and inappropriate grazing management over most of the MPR have led to the deterioration of the structure, floristic diversity and vigour of, particularly, the endemic-rich grasslands. Denudation of the land, serious soil erosion and encroachment of indigenous woody species are prevalent in many parts. For the Tugela River alone, the annual pollution by silt is over 12 million tons (Edwards 1967) and, in parts of its basin, all the topsoil has been lost, leaving a sterile landscape, devoid of vegetation. Slash and burn subsistence agriculture and excessive burning of grassland seriously threaten some of the swamps and the already very small remaining patches of forest, notably in the MC.

One of the most destructive activities to the natural vegetation of the MPR has been the establishment of extensive monocultures of sugar cane, maize and exotic trees. The remaining endemic-rich high rainfall grasslands of the MPR are quickly disappearing, as a result of large-scale afforestation with species of *Acacia*, *Eucalyptus* and *Pinus*. Afforestation is perhaps the most serious threat to biodiversity in the central and southern parts of the MPR

Africa

region, having already caused the extinction of certain species in the wild. In recent times, permits for the afforestation of hundreds of thousands of hectares of grassland have been issued, usually without any consideration being given to the floristic diversity of the affected areas.

With the exception of some of the savanna regions to the north, invasion of the natural vegetation by alien plants (more than 130 species recorded) is a major problem in the MPR (e.g. Henderson 1989). *Chromolaena odorata* forms dense monospecific thickets along the moist coastal belt of Natal, frequently smothering the margins of bush clumps and forest patches. *Acacia mearnsii* is most abundant in the mist belt grasslands, where it has been commercially planted on a vast scale. Watercourses are seriously invaded by *Acacia dealbata*, *A. mearnsii* and many others. Other major invaders are *Lantana camara*, *Psidium guajava*, *Rubus* spp. and *Solanum mauritianum*.

Heavy minerals, such as titanium, ilmenite, rutile and zircon, are being mined in the dune forests of northern Natal (MC). Current plans to expand and intensify mining activities pose a major threat to the dune forests and ecosystems of particularly the Lake St Lucia area. In the case of dune forest, indigenous vegetation established on the scars caused by these vast open-cast mines will probably take decades, if not centuries, to revert back to its original climax state. Dune mining is also a looming threat along parts of the Transkeian coastline (Cooper and Swart 1992).

With true wilderness areas becoming progressively scarcer in the MPR, the number of visitors to the few remaining unspoiled regions is rapidly increasing. The number of tourists visiting ecologically sensitive areas, such as the wetlands of the MC and the Wild Coast of Transkei, should be carefully controlled.

## Conservation

A large number of conservation areas exists in the MPR (Stuart and Stuart 1992), including the three oldest existing game conservation areas in Africa (proclaimed in 1897). These are controlled by a number of authorities, notably the Natal Parks Board, KwaZulu Bureau of Natural Resources (National Parks Board), Swaziland National Trust Commission, Transkei Department of Agriculture and Forestry (Division of Nature Conservation), and private enterprise. The combined surface area under conservation is about 151.4 km² (7.5%). Unfortunately, most of these conserved areas were not established with the primary objective of conserving plant diversity and are mainly located in the savanna vegetation of northern Natal, Swaziland and the Transvaal Lowveld (93% of the area under conservation). For example, the Kruger National Park (partly within the MPR) is not in a region with a high concentration of endemic plant species despite its large size of 19,485 km². More rare plant species are preserved in the much smaller Umtamvuna Nature Reserve (32.6 km²) than in the whole of the Kruger National Park. Other large conservation areas (mainly with savanna vegetation) in the MPR, but outside the Maputaland and Pondoland Centres, include the Umfolozi (477.5 km²), Itala (300 km²), Hlane (300 km²), Hluhluwe (230.7 km²) and Manyeleti (227.7 km²) Game Reserves.

A system whereby private landowners employ trained game guards to patrol private land is in operation, mainly in Natal. These so-called conservancies have been highly successful and today number over 100 in Natal, covering an area in excess of 8500 km² (Grobler 1990). To recognize and encourage the protection of areas and features of national significance by the private sector, the South African Department of Environmental Affairs established a National Heritage Programme in 1984. In Natal, sites covering an area of more than 150 km² have been registered under this programme. However, as with conservancies, however, the commitment is not binding on the owner of a registered site.

It has been suggested that much of the grasslands of the MPR constitutes a secondary fire-maintained vegetation type, greatly extended by the destructive activities of man (Moll and White 1978; White 1983). This view (also expressed by several other authorities) is contradicted by the fact that the overwhelming majority of the endemics in the MPR are confined to grassland. Undoubtedly, this untenable view has contributed to the present poor conservation status of grasslands, not only over most of the MPR, but also in many other parts of Southern Africa. Current evidence points to the grasslands being a long-standing component of the region's vegetation. The conservation of this severely threatened vegetation type, already completely destroyed or degraded over large areas, should receive the highest priority.

The pressure on plants for traditional medicine is immense and depredation has already resulted in the elimination or near-elimination of certain species from the natural flora in many parts of the MPR (e.g. *Siphonochilus aethiopicus*, *Warburgia salutaris*) (Cunningham 1990a). Commercial cultivation will be necessary, not only to conserve certain species (including distinct genetic forms), but also to maintain supplies and to keep prices at reasonable levels. The Silverglen Medicinal Plant Project of the Durban City Parks Department is an example of an approach to alleviate pressure on wild plants (Nichols 1990).

The challenge in conserving the great natural diversity of the MPR is to embark on an environmental strategy that integrates human development with natural resource management (Cunningham 1989). In this regard a number of institutions, perhaps most importantly the Institute of Natural Resources at Natal University, Pietermaritzburg, have initiated several important research projects in Natal and KwaZulu; a number of reports have been published. However, policy and procedural guidelines proposed by such studies mean nothing unless adopted and implemented by development agencies and nature conservation authorities.

### Maputaland Centre
Compared to the environmental deterioration that has taken place in adjacent regions, much of the vegetation in at least the Natal/KwaZulu parts of the MC is still in a pristine state. It has not been possible to establish the conservation status of the Mozambican part of the MC. In recent years the KwaZulu Bureau of Natural Resources has proclaimed large tracts of land for conservation in the MC and now controls about 740 km². Particularly significant is the involvement of the local people in the decision-making process and efforts are made to manage natural resources in ways that improve their quality of life.

In addition, the Natal Parks Board manages the Greater St Lucia Wetland Park (more than 750 km², of which 350 km² are lake surface) and Mkuze Game Reserve (340 km²). The Phinda Resource Reserve (almost 200 km²) is under private authority. Part of the Lebombo Range is included in the Mlawulu Nature Reserve (184 km²), Swaziland. The encouraging state of conservation in the MC (c. 2576 km²; almost 10% of the area, even without taking into account possible conservation areas in Mozambique) can be attributed in part to far-sighted research in the Natal/KwaZula region, good planning, promotion of the region's considerable natural assets and the commitment of the KwaZulu government and Natal Parks Board towards conservation in the region (Bruton and Cooper 1980; Tinley and Van Riet 1981). However, as population numbers increase and people exploit their resources in the face of emasculating poverty, the extraordinary biodiversity of the MC is coming under increasing pressure (Mountain 1990).

### Pondoland Centre

Conservation in the PC, in contrast to that in the MC, is still inadequate (c. 131 km²; 7%). Important existing conservation areas are the Oribi Gorge (18.4 km²) and Umtamvuna (32.6 km²) Nature Reserves in southern Natal and the Mkambati Nature Reserve (80 km²) in Transkei. A 1977 report identifying certain nature conservation priorities along the Wild Coast of Transkei has unfortunately met with little action from the Transkeian authorities (Wildlife Society of S.A. 1977). Instead, a casino was built and large areas of the PC put under sugar cane, plantations of exotic trees and maize. Some of the latter have subsequently been abandoned because of unfavourable soil conditions. In a recent report, Cooper and Swart (1992) proposed that all the Pondoland Coast forests of the MC be included in a large and consolidated conservation area or Biosphere Reserve. Because this area has the highest concentration of rare woody plant species in Southern Africa, these authors consider such an undertaking to be not only the highest conservation priority for Transkei, but indeed for the whole of Southern Africa.

## References

Acocks, J.P.H. (1953). Veld Types of South Africa. *Mem. Bot. Surv. S. Afr.* 28: 1–192. (3rd edition with updated names and illustrations published in 1988 as *Mem. Bot. Surv. S. Afr.* 57: 1–146.)

Branch, B. (1988). *Field guide to the snakes and other reptiles of Southern Africa*. Struik, Cape Town. 328 pp.

Bruton, M.N. and Cooper, K.H. (eds) (1980). *Studies on the ecology of Maputaland*. Rhodes University and Wildlife Society of S.A., Grahamstown and Durban. 560 pp.

Clancey, P.A. (ed.) (1980). *S.A.O.S. checklist of Southern African birds*. Southern African Ornithological Society, Pretoria. 325 pp.

Cooper, K.H. (1985). *The conservation status of indigenous forests in Transvaal, Natal and O.F.S., South Africa*. Wildlife Society of S.A., Durban. 108 pp.

Cooper, K.H. and Swart, W. (1992). *Transkei forest survey*. Wildlife Society of Southern Africa, Durban. 96 pp.

Cunningham, A.B. (1985). The resource value of indigenous plants to rural people in a low agricultural potential area. Ph.D. Thesis, University of Cape Town.

Cunningham, A.B. (1988). *An investigation of the herbal medicine trade in Natal/KwaZulu*. Investigational Report 29, Institute of Natural Resources, University of Natal, Pietermaritzburg. 149 pp.

Cunningham, A.B. (1989). Indigenous plant use: balancing human needs and resources. In Huntley, B.J. (ed.), *Biotic diversity in Southern Africa: concepts and conservation*. Oxford University Press, Cape Town. Pp. 93–106.

Cunningham, A.B. (1990a). People and medicines: the exploitation and conservation of traditional Zulu medicinal plants. *Mitt. Inst. Allg. Bot. Hamburg* 23b: 979–990.

Cunningham, A.B. (1990b). Income, sap yield and effects of sap tapping on palms in south-eastern Africa. *South African Journal of Botany* 56: 137–144.

Cunningham, A.B. (1990c). The regional distribution, marketing and economic value of the palm wine trade in the Ingwavuma district, Natal, South Africa. *South African Journal of Botany* 56: 191–198.

Edwards, D. (1967). A plant ecology survey of the Tugela River Basin, Natal. *Mem. Bot. Surv. S. Afr.* 36: 1–285.

FitzSimons, V.F.M. and Broadley, D.G. (1983). *FitzSimons' snakes of Southern Africa (revised edition)*. Delta Books, Johannesburg. 387 pp.

Geldenhuys, C.J. (ed.) (1989). *Biogeography of the mixed evergreen forests of Southern Africa*. Ecosystem Programmes Occasional Report 45. Foundation for Research Development, Pretoria. 208 pp.

Gertenbach, W.P.D. (1983). Landscapes of the Kruger National Park. *Koedoe* 26: 9–121.

Grobler, H. (1990). The private landowner and conservation. *Natal* (Newsletter, Natal Parks Board) 15: 1–2.

Henderson, L. (1989). Invasive alien woody plants of Natal and the north-eastern Orange Free State. *Bothalia* 19: 237–261.

Hutchings, A. (1989). A survey and analysis of traditional medicinal plants used by the Zulu, Xhosa and Sotho. *Bothalia* 19: 111–129.

Jansen, P.C.M. and Mendes, O. (1983). *Plantas medicinais seu uso tradicional em Moçambique*, 2 vols. Minerva Central, Maputo. 216 pp., 259 pp.

King, L. (1982). *The Natal monocline*. University of Natal Press, Pietermaritzburg. 134 pp.

Lambiris, A.J.L. (1988). A review of the amphibians of Natal. *Lammergeyer* 39: 1–211.

Meester, J.A.J., Rautenbach, I.L., Dippenaar, N.J., and Baker, C.M. (1986). Classification of Southern African mammals. *Transvaal Museum Monograph* 5: 1–359.

Moll, E.J. (1977). The vegetation of Maputaland – a preliminary report on the plant communities and their present and future conservation status. *Trees in South Africa* 29: 31–58.

Moll, E.J. (1980). Terrestrial plant ecology. In Bruton, M.N. and Cooper, K.H. (eds), *Studies on the ecology of Maputaland*. Rhodes University and Wildlife Society of S.A., Grahamstown and Durban. Pp. 52–68.

Moll, E.J. and White, F. (1978). The Indian Ocean Coastal Belt. In Werger, M.J.A. (ed.), *Biogeography and ecology of Southern Africa*. Monographiae Biologicae 31: 563–598. Junk, The Hague.

Mountain, A. (1990). *Paradise under pressure*. Southern Book Publishers, Johannesburg. 149 pp.

Nichols, G.R. (1990). Making the medicine plants renewable: a conservation strategy in the Durban Parks Department. *Mitt. Inst. Allg. Bot. Hamburg* 23a: 25–30.

Partridge, T.C. and Maud, R.R. (1987). Geomorphic evolution of Southern Africa since the Mesozoic. *South African Journal of Geology* 90: 179–208.

Passmore, N.I. and Carruthers, V.C. (1979). *South African frogs*. Witwatersrand University Press, Johannesburg. 270 pp.

Pooley, E.S. (1980). Some notes on the utilization of natural resources by the tribal people of Maputaland. In Bruton, M.N. and Cooper, K.H. (eds), *Studies on the ecology of Maputaland*. Rhodes University and Wildlife Society of S.A., Grahamstown and Durban. Pp. 467–479.

Poynton, J.C. (1961). Biogeography of south-east Africa. *Nature* 189: 801–803.

Quickelberge, C.D. (1989). *Birds of the Transkei*. Natural History Museum, Durban. 134 pp.

Rogers, K.H. (1980). The vegetation of the Pongola floodplain: distribution and utilization. In Bruton, M.N. and Cooper, K.H. (eds), *Studies on the ecology of Maputaland*. Rhodes University and Wildlife Society of S.A., Grahamstown and Durban. Pp. 69–77.

Shackleton, C.M. (1989). An ecological survey of a selected area of Pondoland sourveld with emphasis on its response to the management practices of burning and grazing. Unpublished report, Department of Botany, University of Transkei. 331 pp.

South African Committee for Stratigraphy (SACS) (1980). *Stratigraphy of South Africa. Part 1 (Comp. Kent, L.E.). Lithostratigraphy of the Republic of South Africa, South West Africa/Namibia and the Republics of Bophutatswana, Transkei and Venda*. Handbook of the Geological Survey of South Africa 8. Government Printer, Pretoria. 690 pp.

Stuart, C. and Stuart, T. (1992). *Guide to Southern African Game and Nature Reserves*, 2nd Ed. Struik, Cape Town. 374 pp.

Tinley, K.L. (1971). *Lake St Lucia and its peripheral sand catchment*. Wildlife Society of Southern Africa, Durban. 62 pp., map.

Tinley, K.L. and Van Riet, W.T. (1981). *Proposals towards an environmental plan for KwaZulu*. Report to the Nature Conservation Division, KwaZulu Department of Agriculture and Forestry. 242 pp.

Van Wyk, A.E. (1990a). The sandstone regions of Natal and Pondoland: remarkable centres of endemism. In Heine, K. (ed.), *Palaeoecology of Africa* 21: 243–257. Balkema, Rotterdam.

Van Wyk, A.E. (1990b). A new species of *Leucadendron* (Proteaceae) from Pondoland, with a discussion of its biogeography. *South African Journal of Botany* 56: 458–466.

Wannenburgh, A. (1987). *The natural wonder of Southern Africa*. Struik, Cape Town. 160 pp.

Weisser, P.J. (1980). The dune forest of Maputaland. In Bruton, M.N. and Cooper, K.H. (eds), *Studies on the ecology of Maputaland*. Rhodes University and Wildlife Society of S.A., Grahamstown and Durban. Pp. 78–90.

White, F. (1983). *The vegetation of Africa: a descriptive memoir to accompany the Unesco/AETFAT/UNSO vegetation map of Africa*. Natural Resources Research XX. Unesco, Paris. 356 pp.

Wildlife Society of S.A. (1977). *A preliminary survey of the Transkei coast*. Wildlife Society of Southern Africa, Linden. 48 pp., appendices.

## Acknowledgements

This Data Sheet was prepared by Professor A.E. van Wyk (Department of Botany, University of Pretoria, Republic of South Africa). The author thanks the Curator and staff of the National Herbarium (Pretoria) for assistance, Ms M. Mössmer for the calculation of statistics on endemic animals in the MPR and for critically reading and improving the manuscript.

AFROMONTANE REGIONAL CENTRE OF ENDEMISM: CPD SITE AF62

# MOUNT KENYA
## Kenya

**Location:** 193 km north-east of Nairobi and c. 480 km from the Kenyan coast, at c. 0°10'S, 37°20'E.

**Area:** 1500 km²; National Park covers 715 km².

**Altitude:** 1600–5199 m.

**Vegetation:** Afromontane moist and dry forest, bamboo forest, *Hagenia* woodland, giant heath zone, moorland, alpine vegetation with giant lobelias and tree senecios.

**Flora:** Estimated 800 vascular plant species above 2000 m; at least 10 strict endemics; c. 250 regional endemic species.

**Useful plants:** Important timber trees, medicinal plants, edible fruits.

**Other values:** Watershed for major rivers, international tourist attraction.

**Threats:** Logging, visitor pressure in peaks area.

**Conservation:** National Park covers 715 km²; Biosphere Reserve, 718 km²; Mount Kenya Forest Reserve covers 1421 km² of lower slopes.

See also Data Sheet on Afroalpine Region (East and North-east Africa) (CPD Site Af81).

## Geography

At 5199 m, Mount Kenya is the second highest peak of Africa. It is an extinct volcano, approximately 96 km wide at its base. Its lower slopes rise gently to the abrupt crags of the summit area. The highest peaks are Batian (5199 m) and Nelion (5188 m). On the lower slopes a number of subsidiary cones are present (see Jennings 1963; Coe 1967).

## Vegetation

Moist Afromontane forest occurs in areas of over 2200 mm rainfall per annum at 1600–2800 m on the north-east, east and south sides of the mountain. The dominants are *Ocotea* and *Podocarpus* Forests below 2500 m. on the west and north slopes, where the climate is much drier (875–1400 mm per annum) and dominated by *Juniperus procera* and *Olea*. Some rare forest types occur at lower altitudes. They are dry upland evergreen forest of *Croton megalocarpus*, *Brachylaena millensis* and *Calodendrum capense*, covering 42.5 km² and representing two-thirds of the total extent of this vegetation type and forest with *Celtis durandii*, *Croton sylvaticus* and *Premna maxima* on the north-east slopes between 1200–1850 m, occupying some 16 km² and the only known occurrence of this forest type.

Much of the forests on the lower slopes of Mount Kenya have been converted to agriculture or else have been selectively logged and are not included in the National Park. The total forest area on Mount Kenya (including bamboo/forest mixture) is estimated to be c. 1500 km² (Beentje, in press).

Between 2500–3000 m there is a bamboo zone, dominated by *Sinarundinaria alpina* occurring in a mosaic with *Podocarpus latifolius* at 2600–2800 m. The bamboo zone is widest on the moister aspects of the mountain. At 3000 m bamboo grades into *Hagenia-Hypericum* woodland, which in turn grades into a giant heath zone. A lower alpine or moorland zone is found at 3400–3500 m, dominated by tussock grasses and sedges (Coe 1967; Hedberg 1967).

The upper alpine zone occurs between 3800–4500 m. Some of the most spectacular plants of Mount Kenya are found here, including the giant lobelias *Lobelia keniensis* and *L. telekii* and the tree composites *Dendrosenecio deckenii* ssp. *keniensis* and *D. johnstonii* ssp. *battiscombei*. Above 4500 m there are only a few scattered vascular plants. Plants of these high altitudes adapted to an extreme climate, with a high diurnal temperature range, low moisture availability and high ultra-violet radiation (Hedberg 1964, 1968; Mabberley 1986).

A two-year project to study vegetation and ecology was initiated 1992 jointly by the Universities of Bayreuth and Tuebingen (Germany) and the University of Nairobi and Maseno University College (Kenya). Earlier collaborative research on the vegetation was undertaken between 1974–1985 by the University of Bayreuth, the Technological University of Munich and the University of Nairobi, resulting in the preparation of a vegetation map of the Afroalpine zone of Mount Kenya (Beck, Rehder and Kokwaro 1988) and a description of the Afroalpine communities (Rehder, Beck and Kokwaro 1988).

## Flora

The number of vascular plants occurring above 2000 m is estimated to be approximately 800 (H. Beentje, personal estimate). There are at least 11 strict endemic species and more than 150 near-endemics, i.e. species which also occur on one or more of: the Aberdare Mountains, Mt Kilimanjaro, Mt Elgon and the Rwenzori Mountains (White 1983; Beentje 1990). Kis (1985) lists 231 species of mosses for Mount Kenya, while the number of liverwort species is estimated to be well over 100 (Pócs 1993, *in litt.*). Endemism among the bryoflora is low, although there are a number of species with interesting disjunct distributions.

The forests of Mount Kenya are still almost unexplored botanically. However, it is estimated that they contain at least another 100 regional endemic species (i.e. species which are endemic to the Afromontane archipelago-like regional centre of endemism) (H. Beentje, personal estimate), bringing the total number of regional endemic vascular plant species on Mount Kenya to c. 250. The drier forests are relatively poor in species, but the moist forests are diverse (Beentje and Luke, in sched.), with endemic species such as *Ixora scheffleri* ssp. *keniensis, Maytenus keniensis* and *Pavetta hymenophylla*. Three species of globally rare trees are known to occur (Beentje 1988).

The bamboo zone (2500–3000 m) is relatively species-poor, except in its regeneration stages (Agnew 1985).

Between 3000–3500 m there are probably 300 vascular plant species (Robertson and Beentje, in sched.). The moorland and upper alpine zones, above 3500 m, contain 116 vascular plant species (Beentje 1987), of which four are endemic to Mount Kenya (*Calamagrostis*

*hedbergii, Dendrosenecio keniensis, D. keniophytum, Ranunculus keniensis*); over 80 are endemic to East African mountains.

## Useful plants

The forests on the lower slopes are exploited for timber. Camphorwood (*Ocotea*), Meru oak (*Vitex keniensis*), podo (*Podocarpus* spp.) and cedar (*Juniperus procera*) have been extracted on a large scale.

Of 284 woody species occurring in the forests, 26% are used for timber, 16% are used medicinally, 9% have edible fruits and 16% are used for other purposes, including for the manufacture of tool handles, glue, arrow poison and soap (Beentje, in press). There are also a number of species of cultural significance or are important for honey production. The genera *Valeriana* and *Valerianella* have been investigated by the pharmaceutical industry as possible sources of new products.

## Social and environmental values

The mountain is an important catchment reserve, with numerous minor streams supplying water to the people cultivating on the lower slopes. These streams feed into the

**CPD Site Af62: Mt Kenya, Teleki Valley, 4000 m.** *Dendrosenecio keniodendron* and low-growing *Alchemilla argyrophylla* (foreground), with *Dendrosenecio keniensis* (white rosettes) and Lewis Glacier in distance. Photo: Olov Hedberg.

Tana and Uaso Nyiro rivers, for which Mount Kenya and the Aberdares are the main catchment areas.

Both the luxury lodges on the western slopes and the mountain climbs within the national park are major tourist attractions. In 1979 the park received 10,637 visitors (IUCN/UNEP 1987), a figure which increased to c. 16,000 per annum in the latter part of the 1980s (B. Woodley 1992, *in litt.*).

Animals found in the lower forests and bamboo zone include African elephant *Loxodonta africana*, black rhinoceros (*Diceros bicornis*) and leopard (*Panthera pardus*) (the latter also in the alpine zone).

The Kenyan Mountains Endemic Bird Area (EBA) supports 7 restricted-range bird species, of which 6 have been recorded on Mount Kenya, including the threatened Hinde's pied-babbler (*Turdoides hindei*) and Abbott's starling (*Cinnyricinclus femoralis*). They are found in a variety of montane habitats, including Afromontane moist forest and moorland.

Mount Kenya has enormous potential for scientific research and environmental monitoring, particularly in the high altitude zone. It is an excellent area for studying adaptations of plants to extreme climatic conditions, including exposure to high levels of ultra-violet radiation. Palynological and meteorological studies have been undertaken.

## Economic assessment

The revenue derived from visits to the park increased from 1,080,625 Kenya shillings in 1987 to 4,994,815 Kenya shillings in 1991 (B. Woodley 1992, *in litt.*).

## Threats

Large-scale felling and the establishment of monoculture plantations of a Mexican pine (*Pinus patula*) have depleted much of the natural forest on the lower slopes. Although large-scale felling has now ceased, some small-scale felling still takes place, some of which is illegal. Since 1986, there has been a total ban on felling *Vitex keniensis*. Indigenous forests are no longer cut down for plantations.

In places, the increase in tourism has proved a threat to moorland vegetation, trampling having destroyed some of the vegetation along certain trails and resulting in muddy swathes which are subject to erosion. Litter is another concern; it attracts rodents and hyrax, which are now also feeding on giant senecios (Kokwaro and Beck 1987).

## Conservation

The zone above 3100 m has been a National Park since 1949 and includes two corridors extending into the lower zone, bringing the total area of the park to 715 km². Since 1978, 718 km² has been a Biosphere Reserve (IUCN/UNEP 1987). A five-year management and development plan is being formulated by the Kenya Wildlife Service to address such issues as research, fire management, wildlife protection, tourist impact and the need to balance

environmental protection with generation of revenue (B. Woodley 1992, *in litt.*).

The lower forests are gazetted as Mount Kenya Forest Reserve (1421 km²). It includes c. 100 km² of plantation forests. Much of the forest at lower altitudes has been selectively logged and is disturbed or secondary. An agreement has been reached between the Kenya Wildlife Service and the Forestry Department to jointly manage selected forests in Kenya (of which Mount Kenya Forest Reserve is one) to ensure that economic exploitation of forest products, tourism and recreation take place on a sustainable basis and do not jeopardise conservation values.

## References

Agnew, A.D.Q. (1985). Cyclic sequences of vegetation in the plant communities of the Aberdare Mountains, Kenya. *J. East Africa Nat. Hist. Soc. and Nat. Mus.* 75 (183): 1–12.

Beck, E., Rehder, H. and Kokwaro, J.O. (1988). *Vegetation map of Mount Kenya.* Survey of Kenya, Government Printer, Nairobi.

Beentje, H.J. (1987). Checklist of the plants of Mt Kenya above 3500 m. *Bull. Mountain Club Kenya* 83: 46–50.

Beentje, H.J. (1988). Atlas of the rare trees of Kenya. *Utafiti* 1(3): 71–121.

Beentje, H.J. (1990). Status and future of the evergreen forests of Kenya. *Mitteilungen Inst. Allg. Bot. Hamburg* 23a: 265–286. (Proceedings of the Twelfth Plenary Meeting of AETFAT, 4–10 September, 1988.)

Beentje, H.J. and Luke, Q. (in sched.). Vegetation of the moist forests of eastern Mount Kenya.

Beentje, H.J. (in press). Forests of Mount Kenya – vegetation and human uses.

Coe, M.J. (1967). *The Ecology of the alpine zone of Mount Kenya.* Junk, The Hague.

Hedberg, O. (1964). Features of Afroalpine Plant Ecology. *Acta phytogeogr. suec.* 49:1–144.

Hedberg, O. (1967). Features of Afroalpine plant ecology. *Acta Phytogeographica Suecica* 79: 177 pp.

Hedberg, O. (1968). Taxonomic and ecological studies on the Afroalpine flora of Mt Kenya. *Hochgebirgsforschung* 1: 171–194.

Hedberg, O. (1969). Growth rate of East African giant senecios. *Nature* 222: 163–164.

IUCN/UNEP (1987). *The IUCN directory of Afrotropical protected areas.* IUCN, Gland, Switzerland and Cambridge, U.K. xix, 1034 pp.

Jennings, D. (1963). Geology of Mt Kenya. In Reid, I. (ed.), *Guidebook to Mt Kenya and Kilimanjaro*. MCK, Nairobi.

Kis, G. (1985). *Mosses of south-east tropical Africa. An annotated list with distributional data*. Inst. Ecol. Bot. Hungary Acad. Sci. Vacratot. 170 pp.

Kokwaro, J.O. and Beck, E. (1987). The animal threat to Mt Kenya Afro-alpine plants. *Swara* 10: 30–31.

Mabberley, D.M. (1986). Adaptive syndromes of the Afroalpine species of *Dendrosenecio*. In *High altitude tropical biogeography*, (eds. F. Vuilleumier and M. Monasterio), pp. 81–102. Oxford University Press.

Rehder, H., Beck, E. and Kokwaro, J.O. (1988). The Afroalpine plant communities of Mt Kenya. *Phytocoenologia* 16: 433–463.

Robertson, S.A. and Beentje, H.J. (in sched.). A preliminary list of plants occurring in the area between 3000–3500 m around the Meru Mt Kenya Lodge.

White, F. (1983). *The vegetation of Africa. A descriptive memoir to accompany the Unesco/AETFAT/UNSO vegetation map of Africa*. Natural Resources Research XX. Unesco, Paris. 356 pp.

Winiger, M., Wiesmann, U. and Rheker, J.R. (eds) (1990). *Mount Kenya area. Differentiation and dynamics of a tropical mountain ecosystem*. Geographia Bernensia, African Studies, Vol. A8. Berne.

## Acknowledgements

This Data Sheet was written by Dr Henk J. Beentje (Royal Botanic Gardens, Kew, U.K.). Christine Kabuye (East African Herbarium, Nairobi, Kenya), Professor John Kokwaro (University of Nairobi, Kenya), Professor Olov Hedberg (Uppsala University, Sweden) and Bongo Woodley (Kenya Wildlife Service) provided helpful comments and additional material, while information on bryophytes was kindly supplied by Professor Tamás Pócs (Eszterhazy Teachers' College, Eger, Hungary).

## AFROMONTANE REGIONAL CENTRE OF ENDEMISM: CPD SITE AF64

# MOUNT MULANJE
# Malawi

**Location:** Southern corner of easternmost Malawi, between latitudes 15°50'–16°03'S and longitudes 35°30'–35°47'E.

**Area:** c. 500 km².

**Altitude:** 750–3002 m (summit of Sapitwa).

**Vegetation:** Woodland, evergreen forest (lowland relicts, mid-altitude and Afromontane), montane grassland, high-altitude shrubland and thicket, lithophytic communities.

**Flora:** Estimated >800 vascular plant species, including c. 30 strict endemics; some taxa at the northern limits of their ranges.

**Useful plants:** Potential for sustainable timber production (Mulanje cedar); important non-timber plant resources utilized by the local population include edible fruits and fungi, medicinal plants and plant fibres.

**Other values:** Vital watershed protection. Endemic fauna; one of Africa's key sites for threatened bird species. High landscape value, ecotourism.

**Threats:** Encroachment by subsistence farmers, cutting of streambank trees, illegal felling of cedars, indiscriminate cutting of firewood and poles, uncontrolled fires, invasive plants, tourist pressure, potentially bauxite mining.

**Conservation:** Forest Reserve, but management needs more resources. Recent initiative to develop a conservation-based management plan.

## Geography

Mulanje Mountain in south-eastern Malawi is the highest, most impressive massif in southern Tropical Africa. It lies close to the Mozambique border, between latitudes 15°50'–16°03'S and longitudes 35°30'–35°47'E. Mulanje rises spectacularly from the surrounding plains at 600–700 m to high plateaux and basins surmounted by rocky peaks. The highest point is Sapitwa (3002 m above sea-level). The mountain is uninhabited apart from scattered Forestry Department compounds and temporary sawyers' camps. The mountain is an "island" totally surrounded by subsistence cultivation and villages to the west, north and east and by tea estates along the southern border.

Dixey (1927) has described the physiography of Mulanje in detail. It consists of a cluster of plutonic intrusions of syenite, quartz-syenite and granite, which have been uplifted and faulted. There is no evidence of former volcanic activity, nor of glaciation. Bauxite deposits occur on the western side of the mountain, particularly on the Linji/Lichenya plateau. A comprehensive account of the geology of Mulanje is given by Garson and Walshaw (1969). The geological background to the age and evolution of the Mulanje Massif is summarized by Crow (1981).

The massif is about 26 × 19 km with just under 200 km² above 1800 m. It is bounded by precipitous slopes. Surmounting these steep outer cliffs is a series of discontinuous marginal plateaux at c. 1100 m above the plains. These plateaux of rolling grassland (up to 2 km wide) are developed on ferralitic lithosols and are intersected by deep, forested ravines and gullies. The rugged central area of the massif includes several large upland valleys, the largest of which is the source of the Ruo River. As with most of the rivers draining the mountain, the Ruo produces spectacular waterfalls which cascade over the edge of the massif.

The highlands of the central area are deeply fissured and boulder-strewn, culminating in numerous peaks and ridges, the majority being 2400–2700 m altitude. Sapitwa is the highest peak, attaining 3000 m. To the north, Mchese Mountain is separated from the main mass of Mulanje by a broad saddle, the Fort Lister Gap, about 2 km wide and 340 m above the Phalombe Plain. Mchese is remarkable for its dome-shaped peak rising to 2289 m and the occurrence of narrow gorges on all aspects.

In common with most of southern Africa, Malawi experiences a single rainy season, coinciding with the southern summer and extending, in the south of the country, from November to April. This is followed by the cool season through May–August, when dry weather is the norm. The hot season begins in September and culminates when the rains start in November. Through these very dry months, temperatures steadily build up, as does the smoke and dust from bush fires. The dry season is alleviated by maritime air from the Mozambique Channel bringing spells of mist, drizzle and rain to high areas and steep slopes facing south-east. This so-called "chiperone" weather can occur at any time from late May to August and may last a week or more. The effect of chiperones extends well beyond the southern foot of Mulanje and it is in this zone that the surrounding tea estates are located. At Mimosa Research Station (altitude 650 m), 5 km from the mountain, the average annual rainfall is 1626 mm with 16% falling in the dry season (i.e. May–October); on Lichenya Plateau (altitude 1875 m) the average is 2859 mm, with 19% falling in the dry season (Meteorological Department, Chileka, Malawi, 1988, pers. comm.). These rainfall figures do not take account of the frequently occurring mists at higher

## MAP 13. MOUNT MULANJE (CPD SITE Af64) AND SURROUNDING AREAS

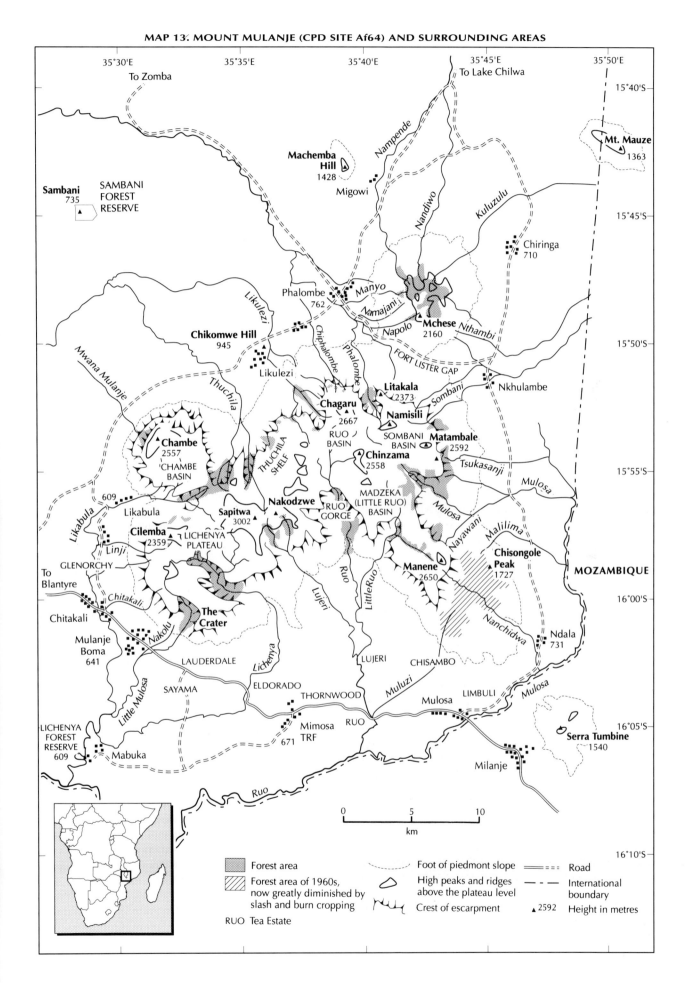

35°30'E    35°35'E    35°40'E    35°45'E    35°50'E

To Zomba

To Lake Chilwa

15°40'S

Mt. Mauze
1363

Machemba
Hill
1428

Nampende

Nandiwo

Kuluzulu

15°45'S

Migowi

Sambani
735

SAMBANI
FOREST
RESERVE

Chiringa
710

Likulezi

Phalombe
762

Manyo

Namajani

Napolo

Nthambi

Mchese
2160

Chikomwe Hill
945

Chiphalombe

Phalombe

FORT LISTER GAP

Nkhulambe

15°50'S

Likulezi

Thuchila

Litakala
(2373)

Chagaru
2667

Namisili

Sombani

RUO
BASIN

SOMBANI BASIN

Matambale
2592

Mwana Mulanje

Chambe
2557

'CHAMBE
BASIN'

THUCHILA
SHELF

Chinzama
2558

Tsukasanji

Mulosa

15°55'S

609

Likabula

Nakodzwe

RUO
GORGE

MADZEKA
(LITTLE RUO)
BASIN

Mulosa

Sapitwa
3002

Cilemba
2359

LICHENYA
PLATEAU

Mulosa

Nayawani

Malilima

Chisongole
Peak
1727

MOZAMBIQUE

Likabula

Linji

GLENORCHY

Ruo

LittleRuo

Manene
2650

To
Blantyre

Chitakali

Nakolu

The
Crater

Lujeri

Nanchidwa

Ndala
731

Chitakali

Mulanje
Boma
641

LAUDERDALE

Lichenya

LUJERI

CHISAMBO

SAYAMA

ELDORADO

THORNWOOD

Muluzi

Mulosa

LIMBULI

Mulosa

Little Mulosa

Mimosa
TRF
671

RUO

Mulosa

16°05'S

LICHENYA
FOREST
RESERVE
609

Mabuka

Serra Tumbine
1540

Milanje

Ruo

0    5    10
km

16°10'S

| | | |
|---|---|---|
| ▨ Forest area | ⌁ Foot of piedmont slope | ═══ Road |
| ▨ Forest area of 1960s, now greatly diminished by slash and burn cropping | ◇ High peaks and ridges above the plateau level | – – – International boundary |
| RUO Tea Estate | ⋀⋁⋀ Crest of escarpment | ▲2592 Height in metres |

altitudes. Furthermore, rainfall is very unreliable. There is evidence that, on occasions, the dry season has been sufficiently prolonged to result in fire penetrating far into the forests. At the other extreme, catastrophic deluges occasionally occur. For example, in March 1991, two days of heavy rain led to an avalanche on Mchese Mountain which swept away an entire village, killing 500 people and affecting adversely another 85,000 (Meteorological Department, Chileka, Malawi 1988, pers. comm.).

The mean annual temperature on the plateau falls below 15.6°C. Night frosts occur regularly between June and early September. On rare occasions, falls of snow have been reported on Sapitwa.

## Vegetation

Lowland forest (600–950 m) is dominated by *Newtonia buchananii*, with *Khaya nyasica* fringing streams in the Forest Reserve on the lower slopes of the mountain and in surrounding tea estates. The recently described lithophytic fig, *Ficus modesta*, occurs in evergreen lowland forest (Dowsett-Lemaire and White 1990). From estate correspondence (Moir 1896) and other early records (Sclater 1893), there can be no doubt that a century ago the southern foot of the mountain was covered by tall transition woodland,

**CPD Site Af64: Mt Mulanje, view from Mchese with Litakala Peak (left of centre) dominating the Phalombe Gorge. *Brachystegia* woodland and *Aloe mawii* in foreground.** Photo: Jim Chapman.

with forest in stream valleys. Such woodland is physiognomically and floristically intermediate between woodland and forest. Only on the surrounding tea estates do many large trees remain along the streams. Fringing forest persists upwards to the gorges, fanning out on the slopes or extending up onto the plateaux, where, in deep stream-hollows and along some of the main rivers and streams, particularly on the drier side of the mountain, *Widdringtonia cupressoides* (Mulanje cedar) is frequently a prominent upper canopy tree.

Miombo woodland, dominated by *Brachystegia* spp. (especially *Brachystegia spiciformis*) occurs on the foothills. Boulder-strewn woodland is the typical habitat for the Mulanje cycad, *Encephalartos gratus* (Chapman 1989). Higher up the outer slopes, Afromontane elements include *Agauria salicifolia*, *Myrica humilis*, *Philippia benguelensis* and the tree protea, *Protea petiolaris*, with patches of low canopy forest, secondary scrub and occasional outliers of *Widdringtonia cupressoides*.

Mid-altitude forest (900–1500 m) occurs at Chisongole (though reduced by slash and burn agriculture to 15 km²) and in the Crater and Ruo Gorges. The canopy reaches 35 m; frequently 90% of the trees are *Newtonia buchananii*, the main associates being *Albizia adianthifolia* (below 1000 m), *Chrysophyllum gorungosanum*, *Funtumia africana* (below 1050 m), and *Trilepisium madagascariense*. There is an abundance of epiphytes (Dowsett-Lemaire 1988). The mid-altitude forest at Chisongole originally formed a continuum with Afromontane forest from c. 1600 m to the foot of the cliffs under Manene Peak. Despite attrition, it is the largest area of forest on the mountain, although it remains seriously endangered by further encroachment by subsistence farmers.

One of the few large unfragmented blocks of Afromontane forest is on Lichenya Plateau (c. 1850 m), where there are approximately 18 km² of forest. *Olea capensis* is the most widespread emergent, apart from localised stands of *Widdringtonia cupressoides* (Dowsett-Lemaire 1988).

Mid-altitude forests contain more tree species than forests at lower and higher levels. 79 canopy and medium-sized trees have been recorded from mid-altitude forest, 63 from lowland forest and 54 from Afromontane forest. For epiphytic and lithophytic ferns and orchids, totals are: 65 (mid-altitude), 31 (lowland) and 62 (Afromontane). Excluding 7.8 km² of mid-altitude and Afromontane forest on Mchese Mountain, Afromontane forest covers 46 km², representing 73% of the total area of forest (Dowsett-Lemaire 1988). Much of the forest is fragmented in 48 widely scattered patches totalling 14.6 km². *Widdringtonia cupressoides* occurs at altitudes between 1600 and 2400 m (Sakai 1989b), where its stands represent a fire sub-climax (Topham 1936). The most extensive stands, many now decimated, are on the northern and eastern sides of the mountain and on Mchese, although stands do occur high up on the wetter south-facing slopes. Except in the most inaccessible parts of Mchese, almost every stand has suffered some exploitation since this began a century ago (Chapman 1961).

*Widdringtonia* (cedar) does not regenerate under a closed canopy. The former presence of pole stands (destroyed in the 1970s) on sites where there was evidence that mature cedar had existed earlier indicates that almost complete destruction of old forest by fire is necessary before there can be any regeneration on the same site (Chapman and White 1970). The succession, from bare ground, through forest dominated by cedar, to climax broadleaved evergreen forest, is similar to that of forests in Kenya containing pencil cedar (*Juniperus procera*) (Gardner 1926; Wimbush 1937).

Tussocky, herb-rich grassland including *Koeleria capensis* and *Digitaria maitlandii* occurs widely on the plateaux where there is normally no burning. *Festuca costata* with sporadic *Danthonia davyi* and many Cyperaceae are locally dominant along streams and in hollows. Prominent fire-break grasses include *Andropogon schirensis*, *Exotheca abyssinica*, *Loudetia simplex*, *Monocymbium ceresiiforme* and *Themeda triandra*. Occasional trees in the vicinity of rocks include *Agauria salicifolia*, *Ilex mitis*, *Philippia benguelensis* and (on Lichenya), *Syzygium cordatum*. Bracken and colourful thickets, with *Hypericum revolutum* and the endemic *Helichrysum whyteanum*, are characteristic of the grassland/forest ecotone. Low, fissured rock outcrops support *Dissotis johnstoniana*, *Plectranthus sanguineus* and dwarf shrubs such as *Anthospermum whyteanum* and *Plectranthus crassus*. Streams running through the grassland may be fringed with dense *Cliffortia linearifolia* interspersed with tree ferns (*Cyathea dregei*). On Lichenya, the bamboo *Arundinaria alpina* is locally abundant by streams. *Euphorbia mlanjeana*, a Mulanje endemic, can be seen on the precipitous rocky slopes at the entrance to Crater Gorge (Leach 1973).

Several Ericaceae occur among rocks on the lower slopes of the high peaks, including the endemic *Erica milanjiana* and the heath-like *Phylica tropica*. Also present are *Aloe arborescens* and an extraordinary grass, *Alloeochaete oreogena*, a Mulanje endemic up to 3 m tall with a trunk-like structure (Launert 1973).

The upper mountain slopes support a sparse, but ecologically interesting, vegetation. Low forest, covered in lichens and bryophytes, extends upwards in gullies and deep clefts. Except for a shrubby or dwarf form of *Widdringtonia cupressoides*, most of the trees are of species which also occur in the Afromontane forest. Higher still, this forest gives way to dense thickets of *Cliffortia* and *Ericinella*. Damp pockets are filled with *Restio mahonii*. There are patches of peat, including blanket peat, in the south-east. The tree-lily, *Xerophyta splendens*, and a Cyperaceae, *Coleochloa setifera*, are ubiquitous. Vertical cliffs provide a habitat for *Aloe mawii*, a spectacular arborescent species, and the beautiful *Scilla natalensis* (Moriarty 1975).

## Flora

Alexander Whyte's account of the vegetation of the plateau (Whyte 1892), with Rendle's description of the Mulanje cedar, drew attention a century ago to the floristic diversity and phytogeographical importance of Mount Mulanje. Subsequently, the botany of Mulanje has attracted increasing attention. So far, 630 species of vascular plants have been recorded from Mount Mulanje, though the estimated total number is expected to exceed 800 (Chapman, Seyani and Chikuni 1991). An annotated list of recent collections is being made by Strugnell, in collaboration with Chapman, Dowsett-Lemaire, and White (in prep.).

Studies of the forests of the southern/south-eastern slopes reveal 372 species of woody plants, ferns and orchids

along an altitudinal gradient of 1300 m (650–1950 m). Chorological analysis of the trees and shrubs shows that the proportion of Afromontane elements increases from 22% in lowland forest (650–950 m) to 44% in mid-altitude forest (900–1350 m in gorges and middle slopes) and to 76% in Afromontane forest (1600–1950 m on upper slopes and plateaux). The main lowland elements are Guineo-Congolian species (Dowsett-Lemaire 1988).

The forest fern flora is especially rich, with 107 species recorded to date. At least 96 families of flowering plants are represented in the flora. Compositae, Cyperaceae, Gramineae and Leguminosae rank high in terms of numbers of species. Among the Compositae the many colourful *Helichrysum* spp. are a feature of the plateau grasslands. Leguminosae, particularly *Brachystegia* spp. are prominent in the woodland on the outer slopes. Important families of forest trees include Araliaceae, Celastraceae, Cupressaceae, Ebenaceae, Euphorbiaceae, Flacourtiaceae, Meliaceae, Podocarpaceae, Proteaceae, Rosaceae, Rubiaceae (many species), Sterculiaceae and Ulmaceae. Some tree families, for example Aquifoliaceae, Canellaceae and Icacinaceae, are restricted to one species. Other families well represented in the flora are Acanthaceae (particularly in forests), Labiatae and, in grassland and on rocky terrain, Orchidaceae, Iridaceae and Liliaceae.

Since the last revision of the genus *Widdringtonia*, taxonomists have considered Mulanje cedar, the "giant" tree, and the dwarf, ecologically distinct cedar, to be contrasting forms of *W. cupressoides*, the only member of this largely Southern African genus to extend into the tropics. Elsewhere, this species seldom reaches more than 7–8 m high, but on Mulanje (at the northernmost limit of its range) it attains 30–40 m, with a bole 150–200 cm in diameter. Recent research by Anton Pauw (University of Cape Town) would suggest, however, that there are two distinct species present on Mulanje: *W. whytei*, the large tree, endemic to the massif, and *W. cupressoides*, which also occurs in the Eastern Highlands of Zimbabwe and along the Drakensberg Mountains to the Western Cape (Pauw 1992).

Other plants with Southern African affinities include *Blaeria kingaensis*, *Erica* spp., *Muraltia flanaganii*, *Phylica tropica*, *Protea caffra* subsp. *nyassae* (a Mulanje endemic) and *Vaccinium exul*.

In 1964, Wild listed 30 species which he considered to be endemic to Mount Mulanje (Wild 1964). The list included *Dasylepis burtt-davyi* (now *Rawsonia burtt-davyi*) (Dowsett-Lemaire and White 1990), the only tree species not also known elsewhere. Not all of the names applied to herbaceous taxa have been maintained, but new taxa have been discovered since. They include the grasses *Panicum nymphoides* (S. Phillips 1991, pers. comm.), three species of *Alloeochaete* (Kabuye and Renvoize 1975), a sedge, *Tetraria mlanjiensis* (B.L. Burtt 1991, pers. comm.), *Kniphofia mulanjeana* (Blackmore 1981a), *K. monticola* (Blackmore 1981b) and four species of *Streptocarpus*, namely: *S. dolichanthus* (Hilliard and Burtt 1986), *S. leptopus*, *S. milanjianus* and *S. nimbicola* (Hilliard and Burtt 1971). *S. hirtinervis* is a narrow endemic, occurring also on other mountains. However, the populations are much smaller elsewhere and at greater risk (B.L. Burtt 1991, pers. comm.).

There are many widely disjunct species in the Mulanje forest flora, including *Bridelia atroviridis*, *Buxus nyasica* (Buxaceae – known only in Malawi from Mchese and Mt Soche, 70 km to the west) (Friis 1989), *Canthium schimperanum, Cassia angolensis, Faurea racemosa* (Marner 1989), *Lasiodiscus usambarensis, Homalium dentatum, Ocotea kenyensis, Olea europaea* subsp. *africana, Pleurostylia capensis* (sub judice), *Podocarpus henkelii, Strychnos mitis, Ventilago diffusa* and *Warburgia ugandensis* (Strugnell *et al.*, in prep.).

The bryoflora of Mulanje has received little attention until recently, even though the forests contain an abundance of mosses and liverworts (Brenan *et al.* 1953, 1954). Members of the Tropical Bryology Group of the British Bryological Society made extensive collections in 1991. These are currently being worked on (M. Wigginton 1992, pers. comm.).

## Useful plants

Collection of firewood (dead branches) from miombo woodland is permitted at a small charge by the Forestry Department; however, because the surrounding countryside is today largely treeless and woodlots few and far between, the woodland is being whittled away by unauthorised cutting of trees for fuel and poles for building.

Rope is made from *Brachystegia* bark. Latex from *Diplorhynchus condylocarpon* and *Ficus natalensis* is used for bird lime. Bamboos (three species, none plentiful) are used for making grain stores and baskets. A potential exists for small-scale production of honey and beeswax from organised bee-keeping.

Trees with edible fruits include *Annona senegalensis, Azanza garckeana, Ficus* spp., *Myrianthus arboreus, Pachystela brevipes, Strychnos spinosa* and (most important) *Parinari curatellifolia* and *Uapaca kirkiana*. The fruits of *Aframomum* spp. are also eaten.

*Raphia* palm is used for a variety of purposes, while *Hyparrhenia* spp., found on the lower slopes, are an important source of thatching grass. A locally important small-scale industry making brushes from *Danthonia davyi* culms is in jeopardy through over-exploitation.

Leaves of many plants are eaten as relishes. Roots and/or bark of various trees (e.g. *Antidesma venosum, Erythrophloeum suaveolens* and *Securidaca longepedunculata*) feature in traditional medicine or ritual. Edible fungi abound in miombo woodland and are much sought after.

Introduced *Pinus patula* is an important local source of sawn timber. Charcoal from pine waste is transported for sale in the towns.

## Social and environmental values

The Mulanje cedar has recently been designated as Malawi's National Tree. The form on Mulanje and Mchese Mt grows nowhere else in the wild. For many people, the tall cedar typifies Mulanje. Brass (1953) describes these trees thus: "It (cedar) may dominate the forests in pure stands... or occur in more open order as a conspicuous super-canopy tree thrusting grey boles and lichen-draped crowns well above a mixed stand of broadleaved, evergreen trees which form the actual canopy of the forest".

The hydrological importance of the Mulanje massif has been stressed by Robertson (1985). Virtually every river and stream in the District has its source on Mulanje. Water from Mulanje is piped to surrounding villages and to those far out on the plain, thereby supplying an estimated 400,000 people (National Atlas of Malawi Co-ordinating Committee, Department of Surveys, Blantyre). The tea estates are also dependent on Mulanje for water.

Johnston-Stuart (1984), Dowsett (1985), Dowsett-Lamaire and Dowsett (1988) and Dowsett-Lamaire (1989a, b) have established the significance of the avifauna. The forests of Mount Mulanje are part of the Tanganyika-Nyasa Mountain Group Endemic Bird Area (EBA), which includes the mountains between south-eastern Kenya and northern Mozambique, and support four of the 35 restricted-range bird species of that EBA. These include the threatened white-winged apalis (*Apalis chariessa*) and Cholo alethe (*Alethe choloensis*), the latter being endemic to the mountains of southern Malawi and adjacent Mozambique. This site is considered to be a "key forest for threatened birds" (Collar and Stuart 1988).

The mountain holds the largest number of forest butterfly species in Malawi (118), of which three, *Baliochila woodi, Charaxes margaretae* and *Cymothoe melanjae* are wholly endemic and are threatened by forest destruction (Dowsett-Lemaire and Dowsett 1988).

Mulanje has possibly the last leopards in southern Malawi and an isolated, endangered population of klipspringer. The mountain is the type locality of the southern Malawi subspecies of the blue monkey (*Cercopithecus albogularis nyasae*), the yellow-spotted dassie (*Heterohyrax brucei manningi*) and the rock hyrax (*Procavia capensis johnstoni*) (Van Strien 1990). A dwarf chameleon (*Chamaeleo mlanjensis*), is endemic and is Vulnerable, possibly Endangered. Another dwarf chameleon (*Rhampholeon platyceps sensu stricto*) is known only from Mulanje and Mchese (C. Tilbury 1989, pers. comm.). Two geckos, three skinks, one rare limbless burrowing skink and two lizards are endemic to Mulanje, as are the amphibians *Rana johnstoni johnstoni* and a squeaker frog (*Artholeptis francei*). The rivers originating from Mulanje harbour endemic fishes (Dowsett-Lemaire and Dowsett 1988; Van Strien 1990).

Mulanje is attracting increasing numbers of tourists from Southern Africa and beyond, drawn by the high landscape value, stunning views and wildlife (Eastwood 1979). There are several huts on the mountain to cater for overnight stays. One of the attractions of visiting the mountain is that it is only accessible by foot: a road would be not only an environmental, but also a social disaster, as the local community rely on portering as an economic activity.

## Economic assessment

Mulanje cedar is an enormously valuable asset. Its fragrant wood is strongly resistant to termites, borers and fungal attack. Recently, the wood has been found excellent for boat-building and fisheries officials have urged that remaining supplies be reserved for new boats for the Lake Malawi fishing industry, which is so important to the national economy (May 1984).

The forests and woodlands of Mulanje are vital for watershed protection. Had woodland and streambank trees on the lower slopes of Mchese Mountain still been intact, it is likely that the effects of a major and devastating avalanche in March 1991 would have been less severe.

Ecotourism provides a vital economic activity for local people.

## Threats

Despite Forest Reserve status, the vegetation and flora of Mulanje are threatened through clearing of forest and woodland for subsistence farming, uncontrolled firewood collection and pole cutting, cutting of streambank trees, illegal felling of cedars, wild fires and the spread of invasive plants.

Most destructive is the deforestation on the southern and south-eastern slopes. In the early 1980s, hundreds of hectares of *Newtonia* forest were destroyed to grow maize. None of the wood was salvaged for timber and little as firewood. Dowsett-Lemaire and Dowsett (1988) estimate that, between 1974 and 1984, the forest at Chisongole was reduced from c. 38 km² to 25 km². Forest and miombo woodland clearance continues. The forest up to 1600 m, including all mid-altitude forest, has been destroyed. A replanting programme, funded through the World Bank and using *Eucalyptus*, has resulted in fresh clearings in the submontane forest.

The problem of encroachment is compounded by a rapidly expanding local population and an influx of refugees from Mozambique. Most of the cultivable land along the southern foot of the mountain is occupied by tea estates.

Until alternative sources of fuelwood and poles for building are available, the illegal cutting of trees for firewood will continue. Illicit charcoal burning has become a serious threat in miombo woodland. The preferred trees are *Burkea africana*, *Faurea saligna*, *Heteropyxis natalensis*, *Pterocarpus rotundifolius* and *Uapaca kirkiana*. Streambank trees are protected by law. Nonetheless, licences have regularly been issued to cut mahogany, *Khaya nyasica* and *Adina microcephala* within the Forest Reserve.

Fire affects the whole mountain and attempts to control it are is based on a system of fire-breaks and patch-burning. Although fire is part of the natural system and essential to maintain ecological diversity, widespread fires started by poachers are especially harmful particularly late in the dry season and have caused extensive damage to the forests and, on the outer slopes, to populations of the endemic *Euphorbia mlanjeana* (Leach 1973) and the near-endemic cycad *Encephalartos gratus*.

The spread of Mexican Pine, *Pinus patula*, in the high-altitude grassland is a serious threat. Trial plots were planted at Sombani and on the Chambe saddle in the early 1940s and plantations established on Chambe in the 1950s. The intention was to use the pine as a temporary nurse for the frost-tender cedar (Willan 1950s). Policy changed and pine, as well as Mexican cypress (*Cupressus lusitanica*) came to be seen as valuable in their own right. *P. patula* has now spread through natural seed dispersal to every major plateau except Madzeka (Little Ruo), even invading Afromontane thicket on, for example, Chambe Peak and Namisile. So far, it has appeared on Mchese Mountain. It is most abundant in scrub which has developed as a result of cessation of early burning of the plateau grasslands. Pine competes with cedar regeneration on the edge of cedar stands and, because it is more vigorous, becomes dominant (Edwards 1982). A determined eradication programme was carried out in 1987/1988 (Sakai 1989c). This entailed cutting down or uprooting trees and burning all cones. The work was not completed and Sombani and Chambe areas remained uncleared. By 1991, pines were re-appearing on the other plateaux (Jenkins 1991).

Himalayan Raspberry, *Rubus ellipticus*, is another serious invasive species. First observed on the mountain in 1946 (Brenan 1953, 1954), it is now firmly established on forest edges and is one of the most vigorous pioneers of fire-protected grassland (Edwards 1982).

Wasteful exploitation and lax controls (Sakai 1989b) have so reduced a potentially sustainable resource that Mulanje cedar must now be regarded as Endangered (Read 1991, pers. comm.). The trees are pitsawn in the forest and the timber headloaded down the mountain. No sizeable stand remains unexploited and many former stands have been entirely destroyed.

Bauxite deposits were discovered on Mulanje in 1924. There are at least 20 million tons of ore. Exploitation of these deposits remains a potentially serious threat.

The increasing number of tourists already poses problems; present facilities were never intended to service so many people.

As a result of forest clearance, Mount Mulanje can no longer be relied upon to provide an abundant year-round supply of clean water.

## Conservation

Mulanje was gazetted a Forest Reserve in 1927. This was intended mainly to ensure that the Forestry Department had permanent rights to exploit cedar. Subsequently, the boundary has been adjusted on numerous occasions because of continuing encroachment by cultivators on the lower slopes. Only a resettlement programme will avert the eventual conversion of Chisongole forest to cultivation plots and gum (*Eucalyptus*) plantations. Woodlots close to villages are essential to alleviate the problems of illegal firewood collection.

Cedar is so valuable that only the greatest vigilance can prevent organized theft of prime trees, particularly from the more remote corners of the mountain. A programme of re-planting cedar is urgently required (Sakai 1989b). A wilderness area, with entry restricted to biological monitoring, is essential. Mchese Mt is the logical choice for its location.

An initiative to develop an integrated conservation and management plan was advanced by the National Herbarium and Botanic Gardens of Malawi in 1991. The initiative brings together government departments, institutions, organizations (e.g. Wildlife Society of Malawi) and individuals concerned with conservation, to set up a working group to develop the plan. The long term objectives are "... to formulate and implement broad spectrum conservation measures in which plants, animals, water and other resources will be integrated on a sustainable utilization basis ... illegal tree felling, bush fires, hunting and other human activities which degrade the environment will be put under control" (Seyani 1991).

## References

Blackmore, S. (1981a). *Kniphofia mulanjeana* (Liliaceae), a new species from Malawi. *Kew Bulletin* 35: 793–795.

Blackmore, S. (1981b). *Kniphofia monticola* (Liliaceae), a new species from Malawi. *Nordic Journal of Botany* 1: 481–483.

Brass, L.J. (1953). Vegetation of Nyasaland: report on the Vernay Nyasaland Expedition of 1946. *Memoirs of the New York Botanical Garden* 8: 161–190.

Brenan, J.P.M. et al. (1953, 1954). Plants collected by the Vernay Nyasaland Expedition of 1946. *Memoirs of the New York Botanical Garden* 8(3–5), 9(1).

Burtt, B.L. (1986). A new species of *Helichrysum* (Compositae) from Malawi. *Notes from the Royal Botanic Garden, Edinburgh* 43: 233.

Chapman, J.D. (1961). Some notes on the taxonomy, distribution, ecology and economic importance of *Widdringtonia* with particular reference to *W. whytei*. *Kirkia* 1: 138–154.

Chapman, J.D. (1962). *Vegetation of the Mlanje Mountains Nyasaland*. Government Printer, Zomba.

Chapman, J.D. (1989). *Encephalartos gratus*: living fossils of Mulanje Mountain, Malawi. *Nyala* 14: 2.

Chapman, J.D., Seyani, J.H. and Chikuni, A.C. (1991). The Mulanje Mountain in Malawi – a national and world heritage resource worth conserving. Paper presented at the XIIIth AETFAT Congress, Zomba, Malawi, April 1991.

Chapman, J.D. and White, F. (1970). *The evergreen forests of Malawi*. Commonwealth Forestry Institute, Oxford.

Collar, N.J. and Stuart, S.N. (1988). *Key forests for threatened birds in Africa*. ICPB Monograph No. 3. International Council for Bird Preservation, Cambridge in collaboration with the IUCN Species Survival Commission, Gland, Switzerland. 102 pp.

Crowe, M.J. (1981). *Age and evolution of the Mulanje massif*. Geological Survey of Malawi. Report MJC/23.

Dixey, F. (1927). The Mlanje Mountains of Nyasaland. *Geogr. Rev.* 17: 611–626.

Dowsett, R.J. (1985). The conservation of tropical birds in central and southern Africa. In Diamond, A.W. and Lovejoy, T.E. (eds), *Conservation of tropical forest birds*. ICBP Technical Publication 4. International Council for Bird Preservation, Cambridge. Pp. 197–212.

Dowsett-Lemaire, F. (1988). The forest vegetation of Mt. Mulanje (Malawi): a floristic and chorological study along an altitudinal gradient (650–1950 m). *Bull. Jard. Bot. Nat. Belg.* 58: 77–107.

Dowsett-Lemaire, F. (1989a). Ecological and biogeographical aspects of forest bird communities in Malawi. *Scopus* 13: 1–80.

Dowsett-Lemaire, F. (1989b). Vegetation and birds of evergreen forests of southern Malawi with particular reference to mid-altitude forests. *Nyala* 14: 29–37.

Dowsett-Lemaire, F. and Dowsett, R.J. (1988). Threats to the evergreen forest of southern Malawi. *Oryx* 22: 158–162.

Dowsett-Lemaire, F. and White, F. (1990). New and noteworthy plants from the evergreen forests of Malawi. *Bull. Jard. Bot. Nat. Belg.* 60: 73–110.

Eastwood, F. (1979). *Guide to the Mulanje massif*. ABC Press, Cape Town. 147 pp.

Edwards, I. (1982). Plant invaders on Mulanje Mountain. *Nyala* 8: 89–94.

Friis, I. (1989). A synopsis of the Buxaceae in Africa south of the Sahara. *Kew Bulletin* 44: 293–299.

Gardner, H.M. (1926). East African pencil cedar. *Empire Forestry Journal* 5: 39–53.

Garson, M.S. and Walshaw, R.D. (1969). *The geology of the Mlanje area*. Geological Survey Department Bulletin No. 21. Government Printer, Zomba.

Hilliard, O.M. and Burtt, B.L. (1971). *Streptocarpus: an African plant study*. Pietermaritzburg-University of Natal Press.

Hilliard, O.M. and Burtt, B.L. (1986). Studies in the Gesneriaceae of the Old World: XLIX – additions and amendments to *Streptocarpus*. *Notes from the Royal Botanic Garden, Edinburgh* 43: 230–231.

Jenkins, P. (1991). Unpublished report to Dr Seyani, National Herbarium and Botanic Gardens of Malawi, Zomba.

Johnston-Stewart, N.G.B. (1984). Evergreen forest birds in the southern third of Malawi. *Nyala* 10: 99–119.

Kabuye, C.H.S. and Renvoize, S.A. (1975). The genus *Alloeochaete*, Tribe Danthonieae (Gramineae). *Kew Bulletin* 30: 569–577.

La Croix, I.F., La Croix, E.A.S., La Croix, T.M., Hutson, J.A. and Johnston-Stewart, N.G.B. (1983). *Malawi orchids 1: Epiphytic orchids*. National Fauna Preservation Society of Malawi.

Launert, F. (1973). The genus *Alloeochaete* (Gramineae). *Garcia de Orta, Ser. Bot., Lisboa*, 1(1–2): 91–92.

Leach, L.C. (1973). *Euphorbia* species from the *Flora Zambesiaca* area. *Journal of South African Botany* 39: 3–8.

Marner, S.K. (1989). New and noteworthy species of *Faurea* (Proteaceae) from the evergreen forests of Malawi and elsewhere. *Bull. Jar. Bot. Nat. Belg.* 59: 427–431.

May, E.D. (1984). Learning about our new "National Tree of Malawi". *Daily Times* (Blantyre) (June 1984).

McClounie, J. (1896). Cedar tree of Mount Mulanje (*Widdringtonia whytei*, Rendle.). Despatch from Commissioner Johnston to the Marquess of Salisbury. *Kew Bulletin* DXXXVII: 216–217.

Moir, J.W. (1896). Lauderdale, Mlanje. The coffee-bush and its food. *Central African Planter* (August 1896): 237–240.

Moriarty, A.W. (1975). *Wild flowers of Malawi*. Purnell, Cape Town. 166 pp.

Pauw, A. (1992). *A revision of the genus Widdringtonia Endl. (Cupressaceae) occurring in Malawi, Mozambique, Zimbabwe and the Transvaal (South Africa)*. Honours thesis, Department of Botany, University of Cape Town. (Unpublished.)

Robertson, L.H. (1985). *The importance of the protection of forest catchments with special reference to Mulanje Mountain*. Water Department, Lilongwe. (Unpublished report.)

Sakai, I. (1989a). *A report on the deforestation on the outer slopes of Mt. Mulanje*. Forestry Research Report No. 89005. Forestry Research Institute of Malawi, Zomba.

Sakai, I. (1989b). *A report on the Mulanje cedar resources and the present crisis*. Forestry Research Record No. 65. Forestry Research Institute of Malawi, Zomba.

Sakai, I. (1989c). *The problem of Pinus patula on Mulanje Mountain*. Forestry Research Report No. 89006. Forestry Research Institute of Malawi, Zomba.

Sclater, B.L. (1893). Routes and distances in southern Nyasaland. *Geogr. J.* 2: 415.

Seyani, J.H. (1991). Re: preparatory meeting of the proposed project for the integrated conservation and management of Mulanje Mountain. National Herbarium and Botanic Gardens of Malawi, Zomba.

Strugnell, A., Chapman, J.D., Dowsett-Lemaire, F. and White, F. (in prep.). Recent plant collections made on Mt. Mulanje, Malawi: an annotated check-list. *Occasional Papers from the Oxford Herbaria* No. 5.

Topham, P. (1936). Some forest types in Nyasaland. In Burtt-Davy, J. and Hoyle, A.C. (eds), *Check lists of the forest trees and shrubs of the British Empire, No. 2*. Nyasaland Protectorate Imperial Forestry Institute, Oxford.

Van Strien, N. (1990). Notable vertebrates of Mulanje Mt. *Nyala* 14: 45.

White, F. (1983). *The vegetation of Africa: a descriptive memoir to accompany the Unesco/AETFAT/UNSO vegetation map of Africa*. Natural Resources Research XX. Unesco, Paris. 356 pp.

Whyte, A. (1892). Botany of Milanji in Nyassa-Land. *Kew Bulletin* CCXLIV: 121–124.

Wild, H. (1964). The endemic species of the Chimanimani Mountains and their significance: appendix 1. Mlanje endemics. *Kirkia* 4: 157.

Willan, R.G.M. (1950s). *A working plan for the Mulanje cedar forests*. Government Archives, Zomba, Malawi.

Wimbush, S.H. (1937). Natural succession in the pencil cedar forests of Kenya Colony. *Empire Forestry Journal* 16: 49–53.

## Acknowledgements

This Data Sheet was prepared by J.D. Chapman. The author wishes to thank the National Geographic Society for its generous support of fieldwork and the Malawi Forestry Department and the National Herbarium and Botanic Gardens of Malawi for their assistance.

# EAST USAMBARA MOUNTAINS
## Tanzania

**Location:** Tanga Region, north-east Tanzania; between latitudes 4°48'–5°13'S and longitudes 38°32'–38°48'E.

**Area:** Forest area: 231 km², but this figure excludes some areas not covered by the Amani Forest Inventory and Planning Project (perhaps an additional 50 km² of forest).

**Altitude:** c. 150–1506 m.

**Vegetation:** Lowland semi-deciduous forest, evergreen submontane forest, derived communities.

**Flora:** 1921 vascular plant taxa recorded so far, high number of near-endemics, a few endemics, many threatened species.

**Useful plants:** Timber and pole species, horticultural plants (*Saintpaulia* and *Streptocarpus* spp., medicinal plants, fat from *Allanblackia* seeds, wild coffee relatives, latex-producing trees.

**Other values:** Watershed protection, many animal endemics and near-endemics, including a rich bird fauna, potential for tourism.

**Threats:** Logging, pole-cutting, forest clearance for agriculture, invasive species, climatic change.

**Conservation:** 25 Catchment Forest Reserves, forest reserve management plan, conservation work outside reserves, including soil erosion control and tree-planting. Proposed Nature Reserves require legal establishment.

## Geography

The East Usambaras are a group of low mountains close to the coast (40 km) in north-eastern Tanzania. They include a main range 40 km long and 10 km wide, rising abruptly from the lowlands at 150–300 m and bound on all sides by steep escarpments which level off at 900–1050 m onto a deeply dissected plateau, which is most extensive in the south. The highest peaks are on the edges of the plateau and include Nilo (1506 m) in the north. To the east of the main range there are three isolated mountains, from north to south, Mtai (1060 m), Mhinduro (1033 m) and Mlinga (1069 m); all rise abruptly from the lowlands and have only limited areas of more level ground at higher altitudes.

Geologically the rocks of the East Usambaras are mainly gneisses belonging to the Precambrian Usagaran system. Uplift of the mountains by block-faulting is ancient, certainly earlier than 25 million years and possibly more than 100 million years (Sampson and Wright 1964). The East Usambaras form part of a chain of mountains in eastern Tanzania, including, from North to South, Meru, Kilimanjaro, North Pare, South Pare, West Usambaras, East Usambaras, Nguu, Nguru, Ukaguru, Uluguru, Uzungwa (and others). Except for volcanic Meru and Kilimanjaro, these mountains are composed of Precambrian rocks and are old; the non-volcanic mountains have been termed the Eastern Arc Mountains and the forests on them the Eastern Arc forests (Lovett in Hamilton and Bensted Smith 1989).

The soils are clays or clay-loams, red or otherwise brightly coloured, usually deep and freely draining and with nutrients concentrated in a humus-coloured darker topsoil not more than 20 cm deep. There is a marked change in soil type at 850–900 m (Hamilton and Bensted Smith 1989), believed related to the frequent presence of persistant cloud above this altitude (especially in the rainy seasons and

probably more so in the past than now). Higher altitude soils are acidic to very acidic (pH 3.5–5.5) and are exceptionally well leached and impoverished of nutrients below a thin upper organic-rich stratum. Lower altitude soils are richer in cations and much less acidic. Both soil types have a low cation exchange capacity and the higher altitude soils are unsuitable for sustained agriculture unless a reasonable amount of organic matter can be retained in the topsoil.

The climate is monsoonal, with a main rainy season in March to May and further rains in October–December. There tends to be occasional precipitation even during the dry seasons. The driest month at Amani (altitude 910 m, in southern part of main range) receives an average of 76 mm (F.D. Dowsett *et al.* in Hamilton and Bensted Smith 1989). There are major variations in climate associated with altitude, aspect and local topography. Rainfall is greatest at higher altitudes and to the south-east. Mean annual rainfall in the lowlands around the mountains varies from c. 1000–1300 mm to the south and east, to less than 600 m in the north. On the plateau of the main range, there is a decline from over 2000 mm in the south to 1650 mm in the north. Abundant epiphytic lichens and bryophytes show that isolated steep summits and some escarpment edges have unusually humid micro-climates.

The pattern of temperature change with altitude is different from that in central Africa (Moreau 1934, 1935; Hamilton and Bensted Smith 1989). Temperatures in the lowlands are essentially normal, though slightly depressed (related to proximity to the sea). However, at higher altitudes mean maximum daily temperatures are 4–5°C lower than experienced at equivalent altitudes in inland Africa. The cause of these depressed maximum temperatures is probably common persistence of day-time cloud (especially in the past).

# Vegetation

The East Usambaras were probably once more or less entirely forested (except in the dry lowlands to the north) and it is the forests which are of special biological value and conservation concern. A 1986/87 inventory by the Forest Division and FINNIDA revealed c. 231 km² of forest remaining. Of this total c. 81 km² occurred on very steep slopes. Only c. 30 km² consists of intact, more or less undisturbed forest.

Floristic and vegetation surveys were carried out by Forestry Division/FINNIDA and IUCN in 1986/87 (Forestry Division 1987; Hamilton and Bensted Smith 1989). These show that altitude is the biggest determinant of forest composition, which changes gradually with increasing altitude. These is some indication that equivalent changes in floristic composition tend to occur at altitudes 150 m higher in the north-west, compared to the south, related to the drier northern climate.

It is convenient to divide the forests into two main types, lowland semi-deciduous and submontane evergreen forest; the altitudinal boundary between them can be taken as lying at about 850 m. The following descriptions are based on profile diagram studies carried out in Kwamgumi and Kwamsambia Forest Reserves, at altitudes of 210–260 m and 920–980 m respectively.

The lowland forests are generally of lower stature than the submontane forests. Three tree strata are typically present. The upper layer consists of scattered emergents to 35 m tall, with *Antiaris toxicaria*, *Ficus sur*, *Milicia excelsa* and

**CPD Site Af71: East Usambara Mountains, showing interior of submontane forest at 810 m altitude. The large tree is *Milicia excelsa* (iroko), an important timber species.** Photo: Alan C. Hamilton.

*Rhodognaphalon schumannianum*. Common trees in the second tree layer (15–25 m) include *Blighia unijugata*, *Celtis* spp., including *C. mildbraedii*, *Diospyros squarrosa*, *Funtumia africana* and *Pachystela msolo*. The lowermost tree stratum contains *Craterogyne kameruniana*, *Leptonychia usambarensis* and *Tabernaemontana* sp. Forest floor vegetation varies considerably, related to tree falls among other factors. Denser forest can contain abundant *Culcasia* and *Dorstenia*, while *Olyra latifolia* is found in more open places.

The submontane forests can be exceptionally tall and luxuriant, with the largest trees reaching 65 m in favourable sites. Trunks tend to be straight and soaring and up to four, usually ill-defined layers, of woody plants can be found. There is notable catenary variation in floristic composition. The largest trees (often over 40 m tall) include *Beilschmiedia kweo*, *Cephalosphaera usambarensis*, *Isoberlinia scheffleri*, *Maranthes goetzenii*, *Newtonia buchananii*, *Ocotea usambarensis* (on ridges) and *Parinari excelsa*. The second tree layer (20–30 m) often contains *Allanblackia stuhlmannii*, *Englerodendron usambarense*, *Greenwayodendron suaveolens* and *Strombosia scheffleri*: crowns in this and the third stratum tend to be narrow. The third stratum (10–20 m) includes many small individuals of trees which grow taller and also *Drypetes gerrardii* and various species of *Uvariodendron*. The lowermost tree/shrub layer (1–10 m) contains *Alchornea hirtella* and species of *Memecylon* and Rubiaceae. The herbaceous stratum contains *Blotiella stipitata* under dense forest and *Culcasia* and *Clidemia hirta* (introduced), *Dracaena steudneri* and others in more open places.

A TWINSPAN classification of the Forest Division/ FINNIDA inventory data resulted in an arbitrary floristic classification of the forests into nine types. The most interesting results were demonstration that lowland forest varies considerably in floristic composition with, for example, Kwamsambia Forest Reserve on the main range being different from Marimba Forest to the east of the main range (*Funtumia africana*, *Leptonychia usambarensis*, *Tabernaemontana* spp. and *Pachystela msolo* being much more common in the former and *Grewia goetzeana* in the latter) and that submontane forests on the south end of the main range are considerably richer in species (including near-endemics) than those further north.

Rocky summits on the East Usambaras tend to have unusual vegetation, often with Afromontane species growing at exceptionally low altitudes. Each summit seems to have its own peculiar combination of Afromontane elements. *Rapanea melanophloeos* is on Lutindi and Mtai summits, *Agauria salicifolia* is on Mtai and *Podocarpus latifolius* on Mlinga.

The boundary been lowland and submontane forests on the East Usambara (c. 850 m) is c. 550 m lower than the equivalent biological boundary in western Uganda. This altitudinal difference corresponds to the temperature differences between the two areas, suggesting a likely causal factor.

# Flora

The flora of the East Usambaras consists of 1921 indigenous vascular plant taxa, 64 (3.3%) of which are strict endemics, with an additional 41 taxa known elsewhere only from the West Usambaras. There are 160 naturalized taxa. 464 species of bryophytes are known from the Usambaras (Pócs

1990), of which 30 are strict endemics. A further 11 species are near-endemics, while 29 bryophyte species exhibit "Lemurian" disjunct distributions (i.e. they grow widespread in Madagascar or neighbouring Indian Ocean islands, but occur only sporadically in East Africa).

According to Hamilton and Bensted Smith (1989), there are 217 tree species (reaching >10 m height) known from the East Usambara forests, of which 71 (33%) can be classified as lowland, 104 (48%) as submontane, 20 (9%) as both lowland and submontane and 22 (10%) as being too poorly known in terms of distribution to be classified. Using a broader definition of a tree (>5 m tall), Iversen (1991) recognized 684 taxa indigenous to either one or both of the East and West Usambaras, of which 42 are strict endemics and 153 near-endemic (i.e. found only in a few other sites).

In terms of wider distribution, the species can be classified (on the basis of current, often limited, knowledge) into strict endemics (found only in the East Usambaras), near-endemics (on one or more of the other Eastern Arc mountains), East African coastal species (found in other, mainly lowland, forests along the East African coast, especially in Kenya and/or Tanzania) and widely distributed African species (nearly all in the main Guineo-Congolian forests in West and Central Africa or, for higher altitude species, in other mountainous areas). The numbers of East Usambara species which fall into each of these four categories are: strict endemics 11 (5%), near-endemics 42 (19%), East African coastal species 31 (14%), widely distributed African species 131 (60%) and unclassified 2 (1%). [Note – these figures are probably too low. For example, Iversen (1991) gives a total of 16, not 11, for the strict endemic category]. The large percentages of both lowland (42%) and submontane (37%) species which are found only in the East African coastal forests (including the Eastern Arc Mountains) and not further west in Africa testifies to the long floristic isolation of these two forest areas.

The floristic distinction of the East African coastal forests is emphasised by White (1983), who classifies them into the Zanzibar-Inhambane floristic area, distinct from the main Guineo-Congolian floristic area. However, rather misleadingly, he places some of the East Usambara forests into the Afromontane floristic region; in fact "true" Afromontane species are very marginally represented, mainly a few trees on isolated rocky summits.

Although only a relatively few species of trees are strict endemics, conservation of the East Usambara forests is a high botanical priority, because of the presence of a large number of lowland and submontane species which are found elsewhere only very locally and where they are often highly endangered. This applies to both lowland and submontane forests. Particular valuable features of the East Usambaras are the comparatively extensive areas of both lowland and submontane forests, the latter related to the flattening out of the main range into a plateau at a particularly favourable altitude. Comparisons of the relative importance of the East Usambaras with other Eastern Arc mountains in terms of floristic richness and endemism are hampered by very incomplete information from the other mountains.

## Useful plants

Ruffo and Ruffo *et al.* in Hamilton and Bensted Smith (1989) have described the uses of plants on the East Usambaras for a wide variety of purposes. There are many very valuable timber species, including *Cephalosphaera usambarensis* and two mahoganies, *Entandrophragma excelsum* and *Khaya nyasica*. A large number of species yield building poles. Ropes and twine are made from a number of climbers, including *Adenia* sp., *Landolphia kirkii*, *Tiliacora funifera* and *Triclisia sacleuxii*.

At least 15 species of trees and climbers yield edible fruits. The seeds of *Allanblachia stuhlmannii* contain an edible oil used locally and also traded elsewhere. 21 species of plants give dyes. There are two species of wild coffees.

A survey of medicinal plant usage provided a list of 185 species used to treat 63 different diseases or conditions (Ruffo, Mwasha and Mmari 1989). 63 of these are forest plants, the highest use of forest plants (up to 67%) being found in more remote areas where older traditions may have survived.

The East Usambaras contain a number of ornamental species, many not yet cultivated. The most famous are *Saintpaulia* (African violet) and *Streptocarpus*, found mainly in shaded, usually forested sites, especially near rocky summits. The East Usambaras (including nearby Mt Tongwe) contain 8 species of *Saintpaulia*, more than anywhere else in the world.

## Social and environmental values

The mountains are of major catchment importance, especially in providing tributaries to the River Sigi, which drains much of the main range and also parts of Mts Mhinduro and Mlinga. The southern escarpments and southern plateau area of the main range, where rainfall is relatively high, are especially significant and it is important to keep as much forest here as possible to conserve water supplies. The River Sigi is impounded by Mabayani Dam, 15 km from the coast and from where water is extracted for Tanga Town. Water supplies are just sufficient at present, but could become critically reduced with further forest clearance.

The East Usambara forests have many endemic animals (Rodgers and Homewood 1982; Hamilton and Bensted Smith 1989). For example, there are 41 species of millipedes (here major macro-decomposers), many of which are endemic. In some groups of molluscs, up to 75% of species are endemic. 15 of the 30 species of amphibians and reptiles of the West and East Usambaras are endemics; 7 are known only from the East Usambaras.

The Usambaras Mountains include sections of two Endemic Bird Areas (EBAs). The submontane forests are part of the Tanganyika-Nyasa Mountain Group EBA, which includes the mountains between south-eastern Kenya and northern Mozambique, and support 16 of the 35 restricted-range bird species of that EBA. These include 9 threatened species, 2 of which are endemic to the Usambaras, namely the Nduk eagle-owl (*Bubo vosseleri*) and the Usambara akalat (*Sheppardia montana*). The lowland semi-deciduous forests are included in the Kenyan and Tanzanian coastal forests EBA. Six out of the 10 restricted-range bird species of that EBA have been recorded on the lower slopes of the Usambaras, including the threatened Sokoke scops-owl (*Otus ireneae*). This site is considered to be a "key forest for threatened birds" (Collar and Stuart 1988).

The Usambara Mountains were included as a "Threatened Community" in the IUCN Invertebrate Red Data Book (Wells, Pyle and Collins 1983).

# Threats

Although people have been living in the East Usambara forests for at least 2000 years (Schmidt in Hamilton and Bensted Smith 1989) it is probable that the amount of forest destruction during recent decades is on a scale never previously witnessed. German colonisation resulted in expropriation of much of the mountain range as estates, but forest clearance was relatively minor. The Germans also established a botanic garden at Amani, in 1902, for testing economic trees and crops. Coming under British rule in 1916, some of the old German estates were made forest reserves, while there was some expansion in tea-planting, involving forest clearance. The timber industry remained rather unimportant before the 1960s.

Since national independence in 1961, there has been a move towards more immediate utilization of the natural resources of the East Usambaras. This has involved greatly increased sawmilling and pit-sawing. A big growth in population has resulted in expansion of small-scale agriculture and there has been degradation or destruction of substantial areas of forest, especially outside forest reserves. The logging problem has been greatly compounded by ill-conceived foreign aid to a local nationalised sawmill and associated assistance for the production of two inadequate forest management plans, which virtually completely ignored any biological or environmental values and failed to adequately take into account the need for logging operations to be sustainable. After much criticism, an improved management plan for the forest reserves was produced in 1987 and industrial logging in forest reserves ceased in the same year. However, industrial logging has remained active in some areas outside forest reserves, where there has also continued to be much pit-sawing.

Cardamom cultivation started to become a big business in the 1960s, affecting c. 35 km² of forest by 1986/7. Cultivation involves clearing forest undergrowth and smaller trees, with the establishment of the cardamom under a canopy formed by the remaining large trees. The soil is exhausted after 8 years and the crop abandoned. Usually, the forest is destroyed as a result of further tree deaths or replacement by other crops. This is therefore a non-sustainable use of the forest environment.

The forests contain numerous animal traps, set mainly to catch bushpig and duiker. With the exception perhaps of pig, larger animals are now uncommon.

The forests are very unusual, perhaps unique among continental tropical forests in that they are subject to serious invasion by a number of exotic tree species, most of which are escapes from the Amani Botanical Garden. The most serious threats are posed by *Maesopsis eminii* (a Guineo-Congilean Species) and *Melia azadarach*. The *Maesopsis* case has been studied by Binggeli, Macfadyen and others (in Hamilton and Bensted Smith 1989; see also Binggeli and Hamilton 1993). Work on forest dynamics has established that *Maesopsis* invades gaps in natural (unlogged) forest, grows aggressively and could form up to 50% of the forest canopy in 200 years time. *Maesopsis* also changes the characteristics of the lower vegetation layers and of the soil. The lower vegetation beneath *Maesopsis* includes many pioneer tree species and weedy shrubs (many also introduced), but few individuals of species of more mature natural forest. The soil lacks the humus layer found in natural forest and contains a very different soil fauna. *Maesopsis*

**CPD Site Af71: East Usambara Mountains, showing clearance of submontane forest for agriculture near Amani.**
Photo: Alan C. Hamilton.

forest has an open canopy and a much more desiccating microclimate than natural forest.

There is evidence that the climate of the East Usambaras has changed since about 1970, with less mist, less predictable rain, (tending to be concentrated in sharp episodes) and higher temperatures. These changes could be due partly to local deforestation. There has also been a tendency for a greater number of very dry years, with occasional very wet years; these changes are regional and can only be marginally due to deforestation on the East Usambaras. Some biological changes, which may be related to climatic changes, include an ability to grow certain crops, including citrus, at altitudes where this was formerly impossible, reduced growth of epiphytes and an exceptionally high number of recent tree falls in natural forest.

## Conservation

By the 1950s, 25 Forest Reserves had been established, building on the few created earlier by the Germans. These reserves are now Catchment Forest Reserves administered by the Forest Division. Although there has been some agricultural encroachment in Forest Reserves, most of their borders have been respected. However, the still fairly extensive forest outside the reserves is vulnerable and continues to be destroyed.

Following criticisms of management plans written in the 1980s, a tree inventory of the forests was carried out in 1986/87 by the Forest Division assisted by FINNIDA. A NORAD-funded IUCN project was carried out over the same period to assist with production of a new management plan. This plan appeared in 1987 and a new Forest Division/FINNIDA project was launched in 1991 for implementation. Apart from other prescriptions, the plan calls for creation of a fairly extensive Nature Reserve, covering both lowland and submontane forest, at the south end of the main range and a small Nature Reserve on the summit of Mt Mlinga.

In 1987, an EEC-funded environmental conservation and agricultural development project was launched by the Tanzanian Government and IUCN. Nurseries have been established to supply seedlings for forest reserve boundary marking, enrichment planting in the forest and for the use of villagers. There is a current (1991) ban on logging in the Forest Reserves. Management techniques for regulating pit-sawing on Public Land are being evaluated by IUCN. Contour farming has been introduced and encouragement given to grow more perennial crops.

Despite these various efforts, forests on the East Usambaras remain very vulnerable, situated as they are in an area of high rainfall and high population density.

## References

Binggeli, P. and Hamilton, A.C. (1993). Biological invasion by *Maesopsis eminii* in the East Usambara forests, Tanzania. *Opera Botanica* 121: 229–235.

Collar, N.J. and Stuart, S.N. (1988). *Key forests for threatened birds in Africa.* ICPB Monograph No. 3. International Council for Bird Preservation, Cambridge in collaboration with the IUCN Species Survival Commission, Gland, Switzerland. 102 pp.

Forestry Division (1987). *East Usambara forests and forestry: results of the forest inventory and management plan.* Forestry Division, Tanzania and FINNMAP/Sylvestria, Finland.

Hamilton, A.C. and Bensted Smith, R. (eds) (1989). *Forest conservation in the East Usambara Mountains, Tanzania.* IUCN, Gland, Switzerland and Cambridge, U.K. 392 pp.

Hedberg, I. and Persson, E. (eds) (1990). *Research for conservation of Tanzanian catchment forests.* Proceedings from a workshop held in Morogoro, Tanzania, 13–17 March 1989. Uppsala University, Sweden. 176 pp.

Iversen, S.T. (1991). The Usambara Mountains, NE Tanzania: phytogeography of the vascular plant flora. *Acta Universitatis Upsaliensis Symbolae Botanicae Upsalienses* 29: 234 pp.

Moreau, R.E. (1934). A contribution to tropical African bird-ecology. *Journal of Animal Ecology* 3: 41–69.

Moreau, R.E. (1935). A synecological study of Usambara, Tanganyika Territory, with particular reference to birds. *Journal of Ecology* 23: 1–43.

Pócs, T. (1990). Geography and ecology of Usambara's bryophytes. In Hedberg, I. and Persson, E. (eds), *Research for conservation of Tanzanian catchment forests.* Proceedings from a workshop held in Morogoro, Tanzania, 13–17 March 1989. Uppsala University, Sweden.

Rodgers, W.A. and Homewood, K.M. (1982). Species richness and endemism in the Usambara mountain forests, Tanzania. *Biological Journal of the Linnean Society* 18: 197–242.

Ruffo, C.K., Mwasha, I.V. and Mmari, C. (1989). The use of medicinal plants in the east Usambaras. In Hamilton, A.C. and Bensted Smith, R. (eds), *Forest conservation in the East Usambara Mountains, Tanzania.* IUCN, Gland, Switzerland and Cambridge, U.K. Pp. 195–206.

Samson, D.N. and Wright, A.E. (1964). The geology of the Uluguru Mountains. *Bulletin of the Geological Survey of Tanzania*, No.37.

Wells, S.M., Pyle, R.M. and Collins, N.M. (comps) (1983). *The IUCN Invertebrate Red Data Book.* IUCN, Gland, Switzerland and Cambridge, U.K. Pp. 561–566.

White, F. (1983). *The vegetation of Africa: a descriptive memoir to accompany the Unesco/AETFAT/UNSO vegetation map of Africa.* Natural Resources Research XX. Unesco, Paris. 356 pp.

## Acknowledgements

This Data Sheet was compiled by Dr Alan C. Hamilton (WWF) with grateful thanks to Dr Inga Hedberg, Professor Olov Hedberg and Dr Svein Iversen (Uppsala University, Sweden), and to Douglas Sheil (IUCN, Nairobi, Kenya) for their comments on an earlier draft. Professor Tamás Pócs (Eszterhazy Teachers' College, Eger, Hungary) kindly supplied information on bryophytes.

# AFROALPINE REGION
## East and North-east Tropical Africa

---

**Location:** The upper parts of high mountains along the Great Rift Valley in east and north-east Africa, between latitudes 6°S–14°N and longitudes 25°–40°E.

**Area:** A number of widely disjunct Afroalpine enclaves with an estimated total area of c. 3500 km². Many Afroalpine species occur also at lower levels on the mountains.

**Altitude:** Main area above 3500–3800 m, but the floristic demarcation at the lower altitude limit is not sharp.

**Vegetation:** Moist *Dendrosenecio* forest, *Dendrosenecio* woodland, *Helichrysum* scrub, *Alchemilla* scrub, tussock grassland, *Carex* bog.

**Flora:** c. 300–350 vascular plant species; phytogeographically outstanding due to its richness in regional and local endemics (>80%) and the striking ecological adaptations of the flora to the tropical-alpine climate.

**Useful plants:** No direct use of Afroalpine plants for food or medicine has been documented, but Afroalpine vegetation is locally used for cattle grazing and browsing and for fuel.

**Other values:** Contributes to watershed protection of important catchment areas; tourist attraction.

**Threats:** Increasing tourist pressure in some areas, firewood collection of slow-growing trees, occasional fires.

**Conservation:** National Parks cover some of the most important enclaves, but often need added resources. Some Afroalpine areas are entirely unprotected.

---

## Geography

The Afroalpine belt consists of a number of widely disjunct enclaves on the upper parts of mostly volcanic high mountains along the Rift Valleys of Eastern Africa. The most important of these mountains in East Africa are Kilimanjaro (5890 m; Tanzania), Mt Kenya (5199 m; Kenya – CPD Site Af62, and treated in more detail in a separate Data Sheet), Rwenzori (5119 m; Uganda/Zaïre – CPD Site Af77), Mt Meru (4566 m; Tanzania), Virunga Volcanoes (Karisimbi – 4507 m; Uganda/Rwanda/Zaïre – CPD Site Af78), Mt Elgon (4315 m; Kenya/Uganda – CPD Site Af63) and the Aberdare Mts (3900 m; Kenya). The major Afroalpine sites in Ethiopia are the Simen Mts (4550 m; CPD Site Af61), Bale Mts (4321 m; CPD Site Af60), Mt Guna (4225 m), Mt Guge (4200 m), Mt Abune Yosef (4190 m), Mt Kaka (4190 m), Choke Mts (4113 m), Mangestu Mts (4072 m), Mt Bada (4036 m) and Mt Abuye Meda (4012 m). (For summaries of CPD sites, see the entries in the Regional Overview.)

The flora of the Afroalpine belt is not sharply delimited from that of the ericaceous belt at lower altitudes; some Afroalpine species even occur in the mountain forest belt. Most of the mountains concerned have steep and sharply eroded summit areas, but Elgon consists of a wide caldera and, in the Bale Mts, there is a flat Afroalpine area of more than 100 km².

Temperatures in the Afroalpine belt show small seasonal variations, but there are large diurnal changes, with "summer every day and winter every night". Mean annual temperatures and low enough to allow glacier formation on three of the mountains (Kilimanjaro, Mt Kenya and Rwenzori). The wetness of the climate differs greatly between mountains, the extremes being the almost permanently moist Afroalpine climate of Rwenzori and the desert-like conditions of Mt Meru and parts

of Kilimanjaro. Soils also vary considerably according to differences in parent rock, slope gradient and moisture. Bogs occur in areas with high precipitation and impeded drainage, especially on Rwenzori, Elgon and Mt Kenya. Permanent human settlements are absent from the Afroalpine belt, except in parts of the Simen Mountains in Ethiopia. (For further details see Hedberg 1951, 1964a, b.)

## Vegetation

The five most important vegetation types of the Afroalpine belt are: *Dendrosenecio* woodland, *Helichrysum* scrub, *Alchemilla* scrub, tussock grassland and *Carex* bog and related wetland communities. The development of these types varies according to moisture, from the dense *Dendrosenecio* forest and tall *Helichrysum stuhlmannii* scrub of Rwenzori to the scattered *Dendrosenecio* groves and dry *Helichrysum citrispinum* scrub of Kilimanjaro and some Ethiopian mountains. Brief descriptions of plant communities on the East African mountains are given in Hedberg (1964b). The Afroalpine vegetation provides good examples of vicarious plant communities, as in *Alchemilla* scrub, described by Hedberg (1964b). Detailed comparison suggests that the constituent species of these communities have dispersed, one by one, between the mountains, and that the vicarious plant communities have developed independently on each of the mountains concerned (Hedberg 1970).

## Flora

The Afroalpine flora of Tropical East Africa is now reasonably well known, although that of Ethiopia remains less well explored (Hedberg 1957). Phytogeographical data for Ethiopia may therefore require considerable modification in future.

One of the most striking features of the Afroalpine flora is its poverty in species – not more than 300–350 vascular plant taxa are known to occur regularly in the Afroalpine belt of at least one high mountain (and hence qualify as true Afroalpines). Most Afroalpine species occur also at lower levels and several have their closest relatives in the much richer Afromontane flora.

However, this poverty in species cannot detract from the scientific interest of the Afroalpine flora, one of the most characteristic features of which is high degree of endemism – more than 80% of the species and four of the genera are endemic to the high mountains of East Africa, including Ethiopia (Hedberg 1961). This suggests that the Afroalpine

archipelago of mountain enclaves has long been isolated from other mountain areas. Equally impressive is the number of geographically vicarious taxa, indicating that the enclaves themselves have long been isolated from each other. The number of local endemics seems to increase with the age of a mountain (Table 32).

It is interesting to compare the number of species held in common by different pairs of mountains (Table 33). The values in the table demonstrate that the greater the distance between mountains, the smaller the number of shared species. It is also noteworthy that "two-mountain endemics", with one of their occurrences on the Bale Mountains may have their second occurrence on any one of a number of other mountains, for example on Mt Kenya (e.g. *Myosotis keniensis*), Elgon (e.g. *Trifolium elgonense* and *Swertia uniflora*) or Rwenzori (e.g. *Poa ruwenzoriensis*). This,

**MAP 14. MOUNTAINS OF EAST AND NORTH-EAST AFRICA SHOWING LOCATION OF AFROALPINE AREAS**

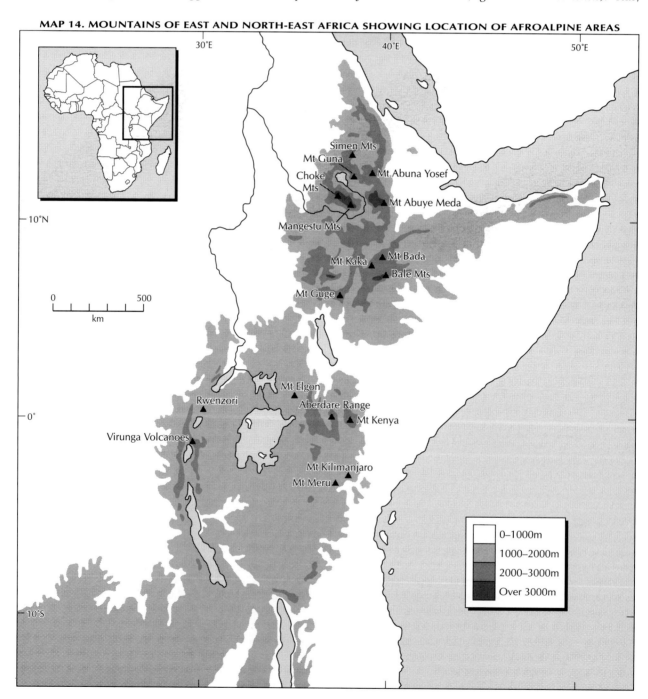

together with existence of vicarious plant communities, suggests that inter-mountain dispersal has occurred through "mountain hopping" rather than by overland migration (Hedberg 1969a in press).

**TABLE 32. NUMBER OF AFROALPINE VASCULAR PLANT TAXA AND NUMBER OF LOCAL (ONE-MOUNTAIN) AFROALPINE ENDEMICS IN VARIOUS EAST AFRICAN MOUNTAIN AREAS, COMPARED TO THE APPROXIMATE AGES OF THE MOUNTAINS (HEDBERG 1992)**

| Area | Approximate age (million years) | Number of Afroalpine taxa | Number of local endemics |
|---|---|---|---|
| Elgon | 15–23 | 182 | 16 |
| Mt Kenya | 2–3.5 | 166 | 9 |
| Southern Ethiopia |  | 162 | 9 |
| Aberdare Mts | 5–6.5 | 146 | 6 |
| Kilimanjaro | 0.2–1.1 | 137 | 6 |
| Northern Ethiopia |  | 129 | 5 |
| Rwenzori Mts | 1–12 | 98 | 14 |
| Virunga Volcanoes | 0.1–2.7 | 96 | 5 |
| Mt Meru | 0.1–0.2 | 77 | 2 |

**TABLE 33. NUMBER OF AFROALPINE VASCULAR PLANT TAXA COMMON TO PAIRS OF MOUNTAINS. THE NUMBER OF LOCAL ENDEMICS, AS WELL AS THE TOTAL NUMBER OF AFROALPINES ON EACH MOUNTAIN, ARE ALSO INDICATED (HEDBERG 1992)**

|  | SE | El | Ab | Ke | Ki | Me | Vi | Rw | Endemics | All spp. |
|---|---|---|---|---|---|---|---|---|---|---|
| NE | 92 | 87 | 70 | 77 | 65 | 31 | 52 | 43 | 5 | 129 |
| SE |  | 106 | 89 | 93 | 80 | 45 | 58 | 54 | 9 | 162 |
| El |  |  | 122 | 135 | 111 | 62 | 79 | 71 | 16 | 182 |
| Ab |  |  |  | 126 | 100 | 60 | 67 | 62 | 6 | 137 |
| Ke |  |  |  |  | 115 | 64 | 77 | 66 | 9 | 166 |
| Ki |  |  |  |  |  | 69 | 67 | 62 | 6 | 137 |
| Me |  |  |  |  |  |  | 41 | 32 | 2 | 77 |
| Vi |  |  |  |  |  |  |  | 68 | 5 | 96 |
| Rw |  |  |  |  |  |  |  |  | 14 | 95 |

Number of species

**Key:** NE – Northern Ethiopia, SE – Southern Ethiopia, El – Mt Elgon, Ab – Aberdare Mts, Ke – Mt Kenya, Ki – Mt Kilimanjaro, Me – Mt Meru, Vi – Virunga Mts, Rw – Rwenzori Mts.

**TABLE 34. FLORA ELEMENTS OF THE AFROALPINE FLORA OF EAST AFRICA (HEDBERG 1986)**

| Element | Number of taxa | Percent |
|---|---|---|
| Endemic Afromontane element | 82 | 32 |
| South African element | 25 | 10 |
| Southern Hemisphere temperate element | 6 | 2 |
| Northern Hemisphere temperate element | 34 | 13 |
| Mediterranean element | 18 | 7 |
| Himalayan element | 8 | 3 |
| Pantemperate element | 87 | 33 |
| **Total** | **260** | **100** |

Table 34 shows the complexity of the Afroalpine flora's derivation. The Afroalpine species from East Africa, which belong to each of the various elements, are enumerated in Hedberg (1986).

Yet another striking feature of the Afroalpine flora is the conspicuous adaptations of its species to the tropical-alpine environment. This has resulted in the evolution of some distinct life-forms, described in detail in Hedberg (1964 a, b). Comparison of these Afroalpine life-forms to those of the páramo in the South American Andes demonstrates a classical case of parallel ecological adaptation in two very different floras (Hedberg and Hedberg 1979; Balslev and Mena 1986).

## Useful plants

Since human habitation is absent or rare in the Afroalpine belt, little seems to be known of the use of wild plants for food and medicine. Much of the vegetation is used for grazing and browsing in the Simen area, where there is also agriculture up to 3800 m altitude, resulting in accelerated erosion. Some Afroalpine trees have been used for fuel – thus, in the Bale Mountains, groves of *Philippia trimera* ssp. *abyssinica* seem to be regularly exploited for this purpose. Stems of *Dendrosenecio* have been used as fuel on some of the East African mountains.

## Social and environmental values

In spite of its harsh night climate, the Afroalpine environment has a great potential for tourism, offering a cool climate in the tropics, magnificent views of glaciers at the Equator and exciting possibilities for climbers. Advanced rock climbing is available, e.g. on Mt Kenya, Kilimanjaro, and Rwenzori, while the caldera of Elgon offers a camping site with natural hot and cold running water. The amazing life-forms of giant senecios and giant lobelias offer "botanical big game".

The Afroalpine region corresponds with the higher-altitude sections of several EBAs, namely the South Ethiopian highlands EBA, which supports four restricted-range bird species, the Albertine Rift mountains (39 species), the Kenyan mountains EBA (8 species) and the northern part of the Tanganyika-Nyasa Mountain Group EBA (35 species). Many of the restricted-range species of these EBAs range into the Afroalpine belt from habitats at lower altitudes, but few are restricted to it. Among the rare fauna in the Afroalpine zone are walia ibex (*Capra ibex waliae*), gelada baboon (*Theropithecus gelada*) and Simen fox (*Canis simensis*) in the Simen Mountains, while mountain nyala (*Tragelephas buxtoni*) occur in the Bale Mountains.

Afroalpine vegetation, together with that of the ericaceous and montane forest belts, covers some of the most important catchments of eastern Africa, the conservation of which is of fundamental importance for the water economy of the countries concerned.

## Threats

The largest threat to the Afroalpine ecosystem comes from human impact, through extraction of firewood, over-grazing and over-browsing by cattle and burning. The tourist impact above Naro Moru and in Teleki Valley on Mt Kenya has caused severe erosion in the Afroalpine bogs, while careless deposition of waste has occasionally caused problems. It is therefore important to restrict tourist movement, as far as possible, to definite tracks and it might be advisable to improve tracks passing through bogs by plank gangways. Campaigns should be undertaken to ensure that all tourists carry their own fuel, avoid burning of slow-growing high-altitude woody plants and remove all litter.

The growth rates of most Afroalpine plants means that vegetation only recovers from damage very slowly. The annual growth of a *Dendrosenecio* stem is only about 25 mm (Hedberg 1969b); hence, these plants must never be exploited for firewood.

## Conservation

Considerable parts of the Afroalpine belt are already covered by National Parks and Nature Reserves. Thus, parts of Mt Elgon (Kenya), Rwenzori (Uganda/Zaïre) are within National Parks. The Virungas are partly protected within Virunga National Park (Zaïre) and Mghinga Gorilla National Park (Uganda). Management in these areas sometimes needs further resources and further areas should be strictly protected. Management plans have been elaborated for the Simen National Park (Hurni 1986) and for the Bale Mountains (Hillman 1986). Similar plans might usefully be elaborated for other Afroalpine areas.

It must be remembered that the Afroalpine ecosystem cannot survive alone – there are numerous biological interrelations between the Afroalpine belt and vegetation belts at lower altitudes. Therefore, long-term conservation of the Afroalpine flora and its environment requires integrated planning and catchment conservation. Earlier conservation efforts have been jeopardized in some countries by wars and civil unrest (see, for example, Gebre-Michael, Hundessa and Hillman 1992).

## References

Balslev, H. and Mena, P. (1986). Comparación entre la Vegetación de los Páramos y el Cinturón Afroalpino. *Reports from the Botanical Institute, University of Aarhus* No. 12.

Gebre-Michael, T., Hundessa, J. and Hillman, J.C. (1992). The effects of war on World Heritage Sites and protected areas in Ethiopia. In Thorsell, J. and Sawyer, J. (eds), *World Heritage twenty years later*. IUCN, Gland, Switzerland and Cambridge, U.K. Pp. 143–150.

Hedberg, I. and Hedberg, O. (1979). Tropical-alpine life-forms of vascular plants. *Oikos* 33: 297–307.

Hedberg, O. (1951). Vegetation belts of the East African mountains. *Svensk Bot. Tidskr.* 45: 140–202.

Hedberg, O. (1957). Afroalpine vascular plants. A taxonomic revision. *Symb. Bot. Uppsal.* 15: 1–411.

Hedberg, O. (1961). The phytogeographical position of the Afroalpine flora. *Rec. Adv. Botany (Toronto)* 1: 914–919.

Hedberg, O. (1964a). Etudes écologiques de la flore afroalpine. *Bull. Soc. Roy. Bot. Belgique* 97: 5–18.

Hedberg, O. (1964b). Features of Afroalpine plant ecology. *Acta Phytogeographica Suecica* 49: 1–144.

Hedberg, O. (1969a). Evolution and speciation in a tropical high mountain flora. *Biol. J. Linn. Soc.* 1: 135–148.

Hedberg, O. (1969b). Growth rate of East African giant senecios. *Nature* 222: 163–164.

Hedberg, O. (1970). Evolution of the Afroalpine flora. *Biotropica* 2: 16–23.

Hedberg, O. (1986). Origins of the Afroalpine flora. In Vuilleumier, F. and Monansterio, M. (eds), *High altitude tropical biogeography*. Oxford University Press, Oxford. Pp. 443–468.

Hedberg, O. (1992). Afroalpine vegetation compared to páramo: convergent adaptations and divergent differentiation. In Balslev, H. and Luteyn, J.L. (eds), *Páramo*. Academic Press, London. Pp. 15–29.

Hedberg, O. (in press). Afroalpine centres of biodiversity and endemism. *Proceedings of the XIIIth AETFAT Congress, Zomba, Malawi, 1991.*

Hillman, J.C. (1986). *Bale Mountains National Park: management plan*. Wildlife Conservation Organization, Addis Abeba. 250 pp.

Hurni, H. (1986). *Management plan. Simien National Park and surrounding rural area*. Unesco World Heritage Committee and Wildlife Conservtion Organization, Ethiopia.

White, F. (1978). The Afromontane region. In Werger, M.J.A. (ed.), *Biogeography and ecology of Southern Africa*. Junk, The Hague. Pp. 463–513.

## Acknowledgements

This Data Sheet was written by Professor Olov Hedberg (Department of Systematic Botany, Uppsala University, Sweden).

# DRAKENSBERG ALPINE REGION
## Lesotho and South Africa

**Location:** The major portion of this region lies in the mountain area of Lesotho, with extensions into South Africa. The region lies mostly between latitudes 28°30'–31°20'S and longitudes 27°00'–29°40'E.

**Area:** c. 40,000 km².

**Altitude:** c. 1800–3482 m (summit of Thabana Ntlenyana, Lesotho).

**Vegetation:** Chiefly subalpine and alpine grassland, shrubland (heathland), with scrub and savanna at lower altitudes. The vegetation of the alpine belt (above 2750 m) may be regarded as tundra. Extensive wetlands occur in this belt (c. 5% of the area).

**Flora:** >1750 vascular plant species recorded in the Natal Drakensberg. Hilliard and Burtt (1987) give 394 endemics in the southern Natal Drakensberg out of 1375 species, i.e. c. 30% endemism.

**Useful plants:** Vegetation widely used as grazing for domestic stock and indigenous animals. Dwarf shrubland plants used locally as fuel in Lesotho. Grasses and sedges used for thatching and the production of rope, hats and sleeping mats. Many plants are used in traditional medicine.

**Other values:** Important water catchment; the Lesotho Highlands Water Project will be entirely dependent on this water source. The foothills of the Natal Drakensberg are popular tourist attractions and there is potential elsewhere.

**Threats:** In Lesotho, extreme overstocking of grazing animals, severe soil erosion, invasive exotic plants and clearance for crops in an area poorly suited to arable agriculture; fewer threats in Natal.

**Conservation:** 2193.6 km² of region (3% in Lesotho and 97% in the Natal Drakensberg) are protected as Nature Reserves, National Parks and Wilderness Areas. Cross-border management schemes are desirable. Much greater protection is needed in Lesotho.

This region has been variously termed the Eastern Mountain Region (Phillips 1917), the Austro-afroalpine Region (Van Zinderen Bakker and Werger 1974), the Afroalpine Region (Killick 1978), the Austral Domain of the Afroalpine Region (M.J.A. Werger 1976, pers. comm.), Altimontane vegetation, in part (White 1983) and the Southern Eastern Mountain Region Mosaic (Hilliard and Burtt 1987). It is treated here as the Drakensberg Alpine Region to distinguish it from the Afroalpine Region of East and North-east Africa (Af81, see separate Data Sheet). The location of the region is shown in Map 12 included in the Data Sheet on the Maputaland-Pondoland region (CPD Site Af59).

## Geography

The major part of the region lies on the high plateau of Lesotho, bounded by the Drakensberg escarpment to the east and south and extending into South Africa (mainly Natal) and Transkei as spurs of the Little Berg There are outliers to the north and south. The Low Berg, a north-easterly extension of the Natal Drakensberg, also belongs to the region. The entire region covers an area of c. 40,000 km² and lies between altitudes of 1800 and 3482 m (Thabana Ntlenyana in Lesotho, the highest mountain in Southern Africa).

The principal rivers are the Orange/Senqu River, flowing westwards to the Atlantic Ocean, and the Tugela River, flowing eastwards to the Indian Ocean. Other rivers include the Mkomazi, Mzimkhulu, Mzimvubu and Bashee Rivers.

Most of the region is formed of basaltic lavas of the Drakensberg or Lesotho Formation, with sheer cliffs 460 m high. An area south of Thaba-Ntsu consists of Clarens sandstone, attaining an altitude of 2500 m. Soils are thin on the summit plateau, but deep on the Little Berg. During summer, the soils on the summit plateau are waterlogged. During winter, the soil is subjected to freezing every night and thawing every day in exposed sites.

The climate is broadly classified as temperate with summer rainfall. The mean temperature of the warmest month is below 22°C. The climate of the alpine belt is severe, with temperatures ranging from cool to hot in summer, and cold to freezing in winter. The highest temperature recorded at Letseng-la-Terai (3050 m) is 31°C (January 1972) and the lowest -20°C (June 1967). Snow in winter can lie for periods of up to six months, especially on southern slopes. Mean annual rainfall varies from 633.9 mm in the Oxbow area to 1609 mm at the Organ Pipes Pass. On the Little Berg, the highest temperature recorded at Cathedral Peak is 32°C and the lowest -4.5°C, with frost being almost a daily occurrence in winter. Mean annual rainfall varies from 1418 to 2017 mm, depending on altitude. Winds on the summit and the Little Berg are important ecologically.

Fire, both natural and man-induced, is a potent environmental factor in the whole region.

## Vegetation

The vegetation of the region can be classified into alpine (c. 2800–3500 m) and subalpine (1800–2800 m) belts (Killick 1963, 1978). The vegetation of the alpine belt may be designated as tundra and consists of climax heath communities forming a dwarf shrubland, limited in extent and dominated mainly by low woody species of *Erica* (*E. dominans* and *E. glaphyra*) and *Helichrysum* (*H. trilineatum*) interspersed with extensive grasslands dominated by *Festuca caprina, Merxmuellera disticha* and *Pentaschistis oreodoxa*. Wetlands cover some 5% of the belt. There are also lithophilous communities. The vegetation reflects the severity of the climate and most of the plants exhibit xeromorphic characters.

The vegetation of the subalpine belt on the Little Berg consists mainly of bunch grassland (chiefly *Themeda triandra* grassland), temperate grasslands (dominated by *Bromus speciosus, Festuca costata* or *Pentaschistis tysonii*), tall grassland (dominated by *Cymbopogon validus, Hyparrhenia dregeana* or *Miscanthus capensis*), *Rendlia altera* grassland and *Merxmuellera macowanii* grassland. Woody communities include *Cliffortia linearifolia* scrub, *Buddleja salviifolia* scrub, *Protea* savanna and the climax community of the belt, subalpine tall shrubland (fynbos), dominated by *Erica ebracteata, E. evansii, Passerina drakensbergensis, Widdringtonia nodiflora* and others. In addition, there are aquatic, hygrophilous, rock outcrop and cliff communities, as well as large areas of bracken (*Pteridium aquilinum*). In Lesotho, the grasslands of the subalpine belt are dominated by *Festuca caprina* or *Themeda triandra*, depending upon altitude and aspect.

## Flora

The exact number of plant species in the Drakensberg Alpine Region is unknown, but, according to the PRECIS database, there are 2046 plant species in the Natal Drakensberg, i.e. from Mont aux Sources in the north to Bushman's Pass in the south. This number includes 1677 angiosperms, 5 gymnosperms, 72 pteridophytes and 292 bryophytes (lichens are abundant, but have not been collected intensively). For the Afroalpine Region as a whole, i.e. including the central plateau of Lesotho, the number is probably higher.

In the angiosperms, Phillips (1917) lists 91 families, 466 genera and 1551 species for the Eastern Mountain Region. The largest families are Scrophulariaceae, Iridaceae, Cyperaceae, Asclepiadaceae and Ericaceae. The largest genera are *Helichrysum, Senecio, Erica, Disa, Selago, Crassula, Argyrolobium, Moraea, Thesium* and *Hypoxis* (Hilliard and Burtt 1987).

According to Hilliard and Burtt (1987) there are 394 angiosperm species, subspecies and varieties endemic to the region, i.e. c. 30% of 1375 species recorded in the southern Natal Drakensberg. In the Red Data Book (Hall *et al.*, 1980), 6 species are listed as Vulnerable and 24 as Rare.

## Useful plants

The vegetation is extensively grazed by domestic and indigenous animals. Domestic animals represent This is obviously a vital resource, particularly in Lesotho, where wool and mohair are important export products and where personal wealth is determined by the number of stock owned.

Dwarf shrubland plants in the alpine belt, such as *Eumorphia sericea, Erica dominans, E. glaphyra*, and *Helichrysum trilineatum* are used as fuel by the local inhabitants. The invasive Karoo plant, *Chrysocoma ciliata*, is also used for fuel. These shrubs burn readily even when

**CPD Site Af82: Drakensberg Alpine Region.** *Erica dominans* **dwarf shrubland south of Mont aux Sources in the alpine belt of Lesotho. Such large stands of this community are not common in the alpine belt.** Photo: Donald Killick.

green, probably because of contents of high oil or resin. Such a source of fuel is clearly valuable in a region which is treeless, but harvesting should be undertaken in a way which is sustainable.

Tall grasses, such as species of *Hyparrhenia* and *Merxmuellera*, are used for thatching. Other grasses, such as species of *Agrostis*, *Arundinella*, *Eragrostis*, *Festuca* and *Merxmuellera* are used for a variety of purposes, for example for the manufacture of rope, string, hats, brooms, palisades, basket and sieves. The sedge, *Scirpus ficinioides*, is widely used in Lesotho and Natal for making sleeping mats.

Numerous plants are used for medicinal purposes. Jacot Guillarmod (1971) lists nearly 300 species which are used in Lesotho (lowland and mountain regions) as medicines. With increasing emphasis on traditional medicine, these plants are assuming considerable importance.

## Social and environmental values

Two restricted-range bird species are endemic to the alpine habitats of the Drakensberg Mountains and two more to the subalpine grasslands, the threatened Rudd's lark (*Heteromirafra ruddi*) and Botha's lark (*Spizocorys fringillaris*). Other, more widespread threatened bird species which occur in this region are southern bald ibis (*Geronticus calvus*), Cape vulture (*Gyps coprotheres*), yellow-breasted pipit (*Anthus chloris*) and wintering lesser kestrel (*Falco naumanni*).

The high watershed areas of the alpine belt are important water sources, both for the immediate region and for the region and downstream. The Lesotho Highland Water Project will be entirely dependent on this water source.

With its natural grandeur and scenic beauty, the mountain area of Lesotho has a great potential for outdoor recreation and tourism. It is expected that the construction of dams during the Lesotho Highland Water Project will result in a vastly improved infrastructure of roads, power and communications, which will undoubtedly assist in the development of tourism.

As with the Lesotho side of the Drakensberg escarpment, that part of the escarpment in Natal and Transkei is also important for water catchment. Fortunately, most of the Little Berg, except for the KwaZulu and Transkei components, is protected and well managed. A result of this protection is that both the vegetation and fauna are in outstanding condition, so that the area admirably serves visitors to the many tourist hotels located in the intervening valleys.

## Economic assessment

The economic value and potential of the region lies chiefly in its water resources and tourism. It is estimated that the royalties accruing to Lesotho as a result of the water supplied to South Africa through the Lesotho Highlands Water Project will (at 1988 values) amount to c. US$38 million per annum by the year 2020. The Project will also supply hydroelectricity to Lesotho.

As far as the Natal Drakensberg is concerned, it is estimated that the value of water produced from the entire Drakensberg catchment area amounts to c. US$929 million per annum (Bainbridge 1987).

The Drakensberg is the premier inland centre for outdoor recreation and tourism in Natal, but no figures for revenue are available.

## Threats

Terrestrial and wetland vegetation in the alpine belt of Lesotho suffers from extreme overstocking of livestock (carrying capacity exceeded by an estimated 300%). This results in serious soil erosion. Huge areas, estimated by Van Zinderen Bakker (1981) to exceed 50% of the pasturage, have been invaded by the unpalatable shrubs *Chrysocoma ciliata* and *Helichrysum trilineatum*. The valuable pasture grass, *Themeda triandra*, has been significantly reduced in quantity. A further result of overstocking is destabilization of water supplies and increased silt loads, both factors which are highly detrimental to the Lesotho Highlands Water Project.

Another serious threat is posed by the cultivation of crops in areas not suitable for arable agriculture. According to the USDA system of land capability classification as applied to the Maluti/Drakensberg Conservation Programme study area (typical of the alpine belt), none of the land is regarded as arable (Bainbridge, Motsamai and Weaver 1991).

## Conservation

At present 2193.6 km² of the region (97% in Natal and 3% in Lesotho) are protected natural areas, comprising Nature Reserves, National Parks and Wilderness Areas (Bainbridge 1987). Protection in Natal is probably adequate, but in Lesotho it is desirable that a much greater area of the alpine and subalpine belts be conserved. It would be ideal if new protected areas could be combined with the existing protected natural areas in Lesotho and the Natal Drakensberg to form a single binational conservation area. This enlarged conservation area could then possibly qualify for designation as a Biosphere Reserve or World Heritage Site.

It is essential that an acceptable management plan be applied to the whole of the high plateau of Lesotho, with particular reference to the problems of overstocking and cultivation in unsuitable areas.

## References

Bainbridge, W.R. (1987). The Drakensberg/Maluti Mountain System: an area of conservation importance to southern Africa. In Joint Planning Team Representatives, R.S.A., *Proposals for a reconnaissance survey of the alpine areas of the Maluti Mountains, Lesotho*. pp. 1–22.

Bainbridge, W.R., Motsamai, B. and Weaver, L.C. (eds) (1991). *Report of the Drakensberg/Maluti Conservation Programme*. Natal Parks Board, Pietermaritzburg. 55 pp.

Hall, A.V., De Winter, M., De Winter, B. and Van Oosterhout, S.A.M. (1980). *Threatened plants of Southern Africa*. South African National Scientific Programmes Report No. 45. 244 pp.

Hilliard, O.M. and Burtt, B.L. (1987). *The botany of the southern Natal Drakensberg*. National Botanic Gardens, Cape Town. 253 pp.

Jacot Guillarmod, A. (1971). *Flora of Lesotho*. Cramer, Lehre. 474 pp.

Killick, D.J.B. (1963). An account of the vegetation of the Cathedral Peak area of the Natal Drakensberg. *Memoirs of the Botanical Survey of South Africa* 34: 1–178.

Killick, D.J.B. (1978). The afro-alpine region. In Werger, M.J.A. (ed.), *Biogeography and ecology of Southern Africa*. Junk, The Hague. Pp. 515–542.

Phillips, E.P. (1917). A contribution to the flora of the Leribe Plateau and environs. *Annals of the South African Museum* 16: 1–379.

Van Zinderen Bakker, E.M. (snr) (1981). The high mountains of Lesotho – a botanical paradise. *Veld & Flora* 67: 106–108.

Van Zinderen Bakker, E.M. (snr) and Werger, M.J. (1974). Environment, vegetation and phytogeography of the high-altitude bogs of Lesotho. *Vegetatio* 29: 37–49.

White, F. (1983). *The vegetation of Africa: a descriptive memoir to accompany the Unesco/AETFAT/UNSO vegetation map of Africa*. Natural Resources Research XX. Unesco, Paris. 356 pp.

## Acknowledgements

This Data Sheet was prepared by Dr D.J.B. Killick (c/o National Botanical Institute, Pretoria, South Africa).

# HIGH ATLAS
## Morocco

**Location:** Central High Atlas Massif between Jbel Toubkal, to the south of Marrakech, and Jbel Ayachi, near Midelt, between latitudes 31°05'–32°41'N and longitudes 4°43'–7°57'W.

**Area:** c. 7000 km².

**Altitude:** 1000–4165 m (summit of Jbel Toubkal).

**Vegetation:** Forest covers 28% of the High Atlas; trees include *Cedrus atlantica*, *Juniperus thurifera*, *Pinus halepensis* and *Quercus ilex* 30% of the High Atlas is in the alpine zone and includes meadows (pozzines) with various scrub communities comprising *Adenocarpus*, *Genista* and *Retama*. Over 30% of the High Atlas consists of eroded rock, alpine pseudo-steppe, dwarf spiny scrub of *Bupleurum spinosum* and scree. The remainder of the area consists of high summits, including bare rock and permanent snow or glaciers.

**Flora:** Nearly 1000 vascular plant species have been recorded; 160 species are endemic to the high mountain zone. Nearly a third of the 600–650 endemic species in Morocco are found in the High Atlas.

**Useful plants:** Timber trees, including *Cedrus atlantica*, *Juglans regia*, *Juniperus thurifera*. Shrubs, such as *Adenocarpus anagyrifolius*, *Genista florida* subsp. *maroccana* and *Retama dasycarpa*, are used as fuelwood.

**Other values:** Highest summits of North Africa; important recreational region; cultural heritage of the Berber people; globally threatened mammals and birds.

**Threats:** Population pressure, leading to cultivation of vast areas for summer cereals in areas formerly covered by spiny shrubland; grazing pressure. Over-exploitation of timber trees and fuelwood species.

**Conservation:** 2 National Parks (IUCN Management Category: V): Toubkal (360 km²) and Haut Atlas Oriental (500 km²) (which is currently being gazetted). Takherkhort Faunal Reserve (IUCN Management Category: IV) covers 12.3 km² within Toubkhal National Park.

## Geography

The Atlas Mountains extend for over 2000 km along the northern part of Morocco and into Tunisia. The main ranges are: the Anti-Atlas (which reach 2359 m) in the south-west part of the range; the High Atlas (Haut Atlas) which reach 4165 m at the summit of Jbel Toubkal; the Middle Atlas (or Moyen Atlas) reaching 3190 m to the north of the High Atlas; and the Saharan Atlas (maximum altitude: 2066 m) in the north-eastern part of the chain. In Tunisia, the Atlas Mountains reach 1544 m at Jebel Chambi. The Atlas have a great influence on the climate of Morocco, forming a barrier between the arid Saharan region to the south and east and the mild northern and western zones.

The main centre of plant diversity is the Central High Atlas Massif. Within this, the area between Jbel Toubkal, to the south of Marrakech, and Jbel Ayachi near Midelt is the most species-rich. The area under consideration extends for over 350 km and ranges from a few kilometres to 20 km wide.

Toubkal National Park is situated at the western end of the High Atlas. The park is about 110 km to the west of the provincial capital, Ouarzazate, and 70 km south of Marrakech (Eaux et Forêts 1980). The nearest town is Oukaimeden, about 3 km north of the park. The park encircles the massif of Toubkal and the associated heights of Angour (3614 m), Anrhemir (3893 m) and Ouanoukrim (4000 m), all of which are part of the High Atlas. The southern (Saharan) slopes of Toubkhal National Park are particularly abrupt, with glacial valleys cutting into the mountainside (e.g. at Tifnoute). Ifni Lake (35 ha), which occurs within the park, is a high-

mountain oligotrophic lake, formed as a result of damming by landslides. It has a maximum depth of 65 m and a mean depth of 20 to 30 m and is regarded as an unique example of its type in the Maghreb (Morgan 1982).

The area is rich in minerals and contains numerous types of metamorphic rocks, as well as limestones and other sedimentary formations.

There is a range of bioclimatic zones, from Mediterranean sub-humid to alpine. The highest peaks retain some areas of permanent snow.

The Atlas Mountains are inhabited by Berber people who retain their traditional transhumance lifestyle. Terrace agriculture is also practised (Eaux et Forêts 1980). There are numerous small Berber villages throughout the massif, as at El Azib-n-Tinzar, while lower altitudes are permanently settled (e.g. the Oirikia Valley).

## Vegetation

The vegetation of the High Atlas is influenced by altitude and the proximities of the Atlantic Ocean and Sahara Desert. Forests cover 28% of the High Atlas. In the Toubkal and Midelt regions, forests occupy 5–15% of the land area (Eaux et Forêts 1980). Much of the forest has been degraded. The northern, humid slopes are covered by maquis and woodland of holm oak (*Quercus ilex*) and aleppo pine (*Pinus halepensis*), with an understorey of *Juniperus* spp. Atlantic cedar (*Cedrus atlantica*) was formerly abundant on the northern slopes between 1500–2800 m, and occasionally up to 3000 m. Cedar is now reduced to relict stands following a long history of over-exploitation. Important natural stands of cedar occur at Midelt and Tounfite. Of Morocco's 1318 km² of cedar forests, 542 km² occurs in the forestry province of Khenifra within the Centre Sud, Haut and Middle Atlas region.

The south-facing slopes of the massif, which are more arid than those of the north, are less wooded. Junipers dominate and alternate with more open areas supporting wormwood (*Artemisia* spp.) scrub and *Stipa* grasses. Among the shrub genera represented are *Arbutus*, *Cytisus*, *Erica*, *Retama* and *Ziziphus*. River valleys support a rich flora dominated by oleander (*Nerium oleander*), with *Crataegus monogyna*, *C. laciniata*, *Ficus carica*, *Populus nigra*, *P. alba*, *Quercus ilex*, *Q. faginea*, *Salix* spp., *Juglans regia* and *Vitis vinifera* also present.

At higher altitudes, the forest is dominated by junipers and eventually gives way to alpine meadows, pseudo-steppe, scree slopes and alpine cushion-vegetation. The alpine zone has a harsh climate and includes communities of mosses and lichens on screes and rocks and dwarf *Bupleurum spinosum* scrub and grasses on more gentle slopes.

Lakes Ifni and Tislit have diverse aquatic floras (Morgan 1982).

Much of the land at low altitudes is given over to intensive cultivation, whilst pasture is generally predominant above 1500 m.

## Flora

Nearly 1000 vascular plant species have been recorded from the High Atlas. This represents about 27% of the total flora of Morocco. The high mountains are rich in boreo-alpine relicts. About one-third of Morocco's 600–650 endemic vascular plant species occur in the High Atlas (Heywood 1991). At least 160 endemics are restricted to the high mountain zone.

The alpine zone is a refuge for numerous endemic plants and contains a number of relict European Tertiary species, such as *Arabis josiae*, *Campanula maroccana*, *Cirsium chrysacanthum*, *Erodium atlanticum*, *Euphrasia minima*, *Genista florida* subsp. *maroccana*, *Medicago suffruticosa* subsp. *maroccana*, *Narcissus watieri* and *Prunus prostrata* (Dresch and De Lepiney 1938; Eaux et Forêts 1980).

Many taxa have very restricted distributions (point endemics) and are represented by a small number of individuals. Among those whose status is Rare on a global scale are (Mathez, Quézel, and Raynaud 1985): *Agropyron embergeri*, *Alyssum flahaultianum*, *Carum asinorum*, *Epilobium psilotum*, *Erodium atlanticum*, *Gentiana tornezyana*, *Phagnalon iminouakense*, *Potentilla guillermondii* and *Saxifraga luizetana*.

Many species are represented by endemic variants which are particularly vulnerable. They include: *Achnatherum argentea* subsp. *mesatlantica*, *Aconitum lycoctonum* var. *atlanticum*, *Carex leporina* subsp. *atlasica* and *Gentiana verna* subsp. *penetii*.

Species which are locally threatened, but which are found elsewhere in the Palaearctic include: *Botrychium lunaria*, *Gentianella tenella*, *Meum athamanticum*, *Polygonum bistorta* and *Polystichum lonchitis*.

## Useful plants

Important timber trees include *Cedrus atlantica*, *Juniperus thurifera*, *Pinus halepensis* and (of less importance) *Quercus ilex*. Cedar, in particular, has been heavily exploited for a very long period of time. Its wood is still highly valued as a construction timber for palaces and mosques, and is also now used in the construction of hotels. Its leaves are a valuable supply of fodder. Walnut (*Juglans regia*) and poplars (*Populus alba* and *P. nigra*) are used by the local population for fuel, timber, food and fodder. *Adenocarpus anagyrifolius*, *Genista florida* subsp. *maroccana* and *Retama dasycarpa* are used as fuelwood.

Common grasses, important fodder plants, include *Dactylis glomerata* and *Festuca arundinacea* (Bounejmate 1991).

## Social and environmental values

Apart from the flora, the fauna, geology, landscape and cultural heritage of the High Atlas are of regional and global importance.

The invertebrate fauna includes numerous Ponto-Mediterranean and restricted-range species of butterflies such as Moroccan orange tip (*Anthocharis belia*), sooty orange tip (*Zegris eupheme meridionalis*), Provence hairstreak (*Tomares ballus*), purple-shot copper (*Heoles alciphron*) and mountain argus (*Aricia artaxerxes*). Endemic species include Moroccan copper (*Thersamonia phoebud*), Martin's blue (*Plebejus martini*) and the Atlas blue (*Plebicula atlantica*). An indigenous subspecies of trout, *Salmo trutta macrostigma*, is present in mountain streams up to 2000 m. The isolated trout of Lac Ifni may well be a separate species with close affinities to *S. pallaryi* (Eaux et Forêts 1980).

Mammals recorded include the globally threatened Cuvier's gazelle (*Gazella cuvieri*), Barbary macaque (*Macaca sylvanus*), hyaena (*Hyaena hyaena barbara*) and a population of some 400 Barbary sheep (*Ammotragus lervia*). Leopards (*Panthera pardus*) are occasionally recorded.

The number of tourists who visit the High Atlas is small. The main tourist centre is in the north-west around Toubkal and the settlement of Oukaimeden. This area is frequented mainly by skiers and mountaineers.

## Economic assessment

The mainstays of the regional economy are small-scale hay and cereal cultivation, agriculture and livestock rearing. However, tourism, in the form of ski resorts, trekking and horse-riding tours, is becoming increasingly important.

## Threats

Timber exploitation has occurred for thousands of years. Cedar forests have been reduced to such an extent that most remaining populations contain individuals which are of inferior quality compared to those which occurred in the past. *Juniperus thurifera* has been heavily exploited throughout the Atlas. The reduction in tree cover has led locally to severe soil erosion (Benabid 1991).

The High Atlas flora is at great risk from over-grazing by livestock. Intensive grazing has occurred throughout Morocco since the 10th–12th centuries, but has become even more intense during the latter part of this century.

Even within Toubkal National Park, excessive over-grazing and illegal timber and wood extraction take place. Livestock herds are allowed to roam freely during the spring, following winter rains and snow, and this results in a great deal of damage to the pastures. Proposals to restrict livestock numbers have not been successful so far (Eaux et Forêts 1980). Pressure from tourism, especially around the ski-resort of Oukaimeden, combined with a lack of management infrastructure, may also be having a detrimental effect on the ecology of the park. Surveillance and coordination of management by local forestry wardens is rarely undertaken and the management policies outlined when the park was first established have not been fully implemented (Posner 1987).

## Conservation

About 12.5% of the High Atlas is protected, or is in the process of being protected, within Nature Reserves or National Parks. All forested areas are legally protected as State Forest under Ministry of Agriculture regulations. Protection categories include Protection Forest, Conservation Forest, National Park and Nature Reserve. Protection Forest includes woodland being maintained by the Water and Forest Service (Service des Eaux et Forêts), established to prevent erosion and soil degradation on steep slopes.

There are two National Parks (IUCN Management Category: V), namely: Toubkal National Park (360 km², including the Takherkhort Faunal Reserve of 12.3 km²) and Haut Atlas Oriental National Park (500 km²). The latter is in the process of gazettement. It will contain the most important protected stands of Atlantic cedar in Morocco.

Toubkal National Park was created to give protection to natural resources in the High Atlas region and especially to the flora and fauna. When it was established, it was envisaged that the park would consist of a research area, with access and multi-use zones. This system of zoning has not yet been implemented. However, there is restricted access to Takherkhort reserve, established to protect the threatened Barbary sheep and its ecosystem; the reserve is marked by a boundary fence or markers; hunting, livestock grazing and wood collecting are forbidden.

The boundaries of Toubkhal National Park are to be redefined in the near future to exclude degraded habitats and wardening is to be made more effective to reduce the adverse effects of livestock grazing. It has been proposed that grazing be prohibited between 1 November and 1 July of each year on the alpine pastures. Originally, a proposed area of 30 km² was recommended to be set aside for scientific research, with prohibitions on livestock grazing and herding, and the lighting of fires. However, there has been some resistance from local people. Currently, controlled fishing, agriculture, forestry, mineral extraction and hunting are permitted.

Protection is minimal over much of the rest of the High Atlas, including in the State Forests. However, there is some traditional community protection in tribal grazing areas (guich and agdal commonlands), such as on the Agdal escarpment between Imilchil and Aghbala.

There is now growing support for conservation in Morocco. The main voluntary organisation is the Association for Protection of the Environment (Association Marocaine pour la Protection de l'Environnement – ASMAPE), established in 1986. There is an active group of volunteers in the Marrakech area which undertake species counts.

The Laboratoire d'Ecologie Végétale de la Faculté des Sciences de Marrakech is undertaking field studies on *Juniperus thurifera* on the Oukaimeden Massif, south of Marrakech (Gauquelin and Savoie 1991).

## References

Beaubrun, P. and Thevenot, M. (1982). *Etude et protection des zones humides aux Maroc, rôle de l'Institut Scientifique de Rabat*. Deuxième reunion technique régionale sur les zones humides de l'ouest Africain, Nouhadibou, 9–14 December 1982.

Benabid, A. (1991). La préservation de la forêt au Maroc. In Rejdali, M. and Heywood, V.H. (eds), *Conservation des ressources végétales*. Editions Actes, Rabat, Morocco. Pp. 97–104.

Bousquet, B. (1991). *Guide des parcs nationaux d'Afrique: Afrique du nord, Afrique de l'ouest*. Delachaux and Niestlé, Paris. 368 pp.

Bounejmate, M. (1991). Utilisation du potentiel génétique des espèces fourragères et pastorales de la flore Marocaine. In Rejdali, M. and Heywood, V.H. (eds), *Conservation des ressources végétales*. Editions Actes, Rabat, Morocco. Pp. 73–80.

Brosset, A. (1957). Contribution à l'étude des oiseaux de l'Oukaimeden et l'Angour (Haut Atlas). *Alauda* 25: 43–50.

Dresch, J. and De Lepiney, J. (1938). *Le massif du Toubkal*. Service du Tourisme, Rabat, Morocco. 233 pp.

Drucker, G.R.F. (1986). Protected areas in Morocco. Unpublished report. Sussex, U.K.

Drucker, G.R.F. (1987). *Directory of the protected areas of North Africa* (draft). Protected Areas Data Unit, IUCN Conservation Monitoring Centre, Cambridge and Kew, U.K.

Du Puy, A.R. (1986). La conservation de la nature au Maroc. *Le Courrier de la Nature* 104: 21–29.

Duvall, L. (1988). *The status of biological resources in Morocco, constraints, and options for conserving biological diversity*. Government of the United States of America and the U.S. Agency for International Development. 58 pp.

Eaux et Forêts (undated). *Aperçu sur le Maroc forestier*. Ministère de l'Agriculture et de la Réforme Agraire, Royaume du Maroc. 55 pp.

Eaux et Forêts (undated). *La mise en place de réserves et de parcs nationaux pour le sauvegarde des espèces menacées de disparition*. Ministère de l'Agriculture et de la Réforme Agraire, Royaume du Maroc.

Eaux et Forêts (1980). *Sur le Parc National du Toubkal. Fiche de la Direction des Eaux et Forêts*. Ministère de l'Agriculture et de la Réforme Agraire, Rabat. 6 pp.

Eaux et Forêts (1991). *Rapport sur les aires protégées au Maroc*. Paper presented at the Third Man and Biosphere Meeting on Biosphere Reserves in the Mediterranean and the First IUCN-CNPPA Workshop on Protected Areas in the North Africa-Middle East Region, 14–19 October 1991, Tunis. 18 pp.

Emberger, L. (1936). The flora and vegetation of the High Atlas. *The New Flora and Sylva* (London) 5: 77–82.

Emberger, L. and Maire, R. (1941). *Catalogue des plantes du Maroc*. Alger Minerve and Mém. H. S. Soc. Sc. Nat. Maroc.

FAO (1983). *Aménagement des parcs nationaux, Maroc. Rapport de la mission*. FAO, Rome. 27 pp.

Galland, N. (1984). Recherches sur l'origine de la flore orophile du Maroc. Thèse Fac. Sciences, Univ. Neuchatel.

Gattefossé, J. (1952). Contributions à la connaissance de la flore du Maroc. *Bull. Soc. Sci. Nat. Maroc* 32: 53–59.

Gauquelin, T. and Savoie, J.M. (1991). L'écologie et la régénération du Genevrier Turifère (*Juniperus thurifera* L.) dans le Haut-Atlas de Marrakech (Maroc). In Rejdali, M. and Heywood, V.H. (eds), *Conservation des ressources végétales*. Editions Actes, Rabat, Morocco. Pp. 157–158.

Heywood, V.H. (1991). Assessment of the state of the flora of west Mediterranean Basin. In Rejdali, M. and Heywood, V.H. (eds), *Conservation des ressources végétales*. Editions Actes, Rabat, Morocco. Pp. 9–17.

Hooker, J.P. and Bull, J. (1878). *Journal of a tour of Morocco and the Great Atlas*. London.

Ibn Tatou, M. and Fennane, M. (1991). Aperçu historique et état actuel des connaissances sur la flore vasculaire du Maroc. In Rejdali, M. and Heywood, V.H. (eds), *Conservation des ressources végétales*. Editions Actes, Rabat, Morocco. Pp. 35–45.

IUCN Threatened Plants Committee Secretariat (1980). *First preliminary draft of the list of rare, threatened and endemic plants for the countries of North Africa and the Middle East*. Mimeo. IUCN, Kew, U.K. 170 pp.

Jahandiez, E. and Maire, R. (1931-1934). *Catalogue des plantes du Maroc*, 3 volumes. Minerva, Alger, Algeria.

Mahnouj, M. (1991). Rapport sur l'état de la conservation de la nature au Maroc. Presented at the Third Man and Biosphere Meeting on Biosphere Reserves in the Mediterranean, 14–19 October 1991, Tunis. Division de Recherches et d'Expérimentations Forestières, Direction des Eaux et Forêts et de la Conservation des Sols, Rabat, Morocco. 18 pp.

Maire, R. (1952-1980). *Flore d'Afrique du nord*, 16 volumes. Lechevalier, Paris.

Mathez, J., Quézel, P. and Raynaud, C. (1985). The Maghreb countries. In Gomez-Campo, C. (ed.), *Plant conservation in the Mediterranean area*. Junk, Dordrecht. Pp. 141–157.

M'Hirit, Z.O. (1990). *Evaluation des ressources forestières Marocaines, 1990*. Unpublished document prepared by the Division de Recherches et d'Expérimentation Forestières du Maroc.

Morgan, N.C. (1982). An ecological survey of standing waters in north west Africa. III. Site descriptions for Morocco. *Biological Conservation* 24: 161–182.

Posner, S.D. (1987). Toubkal National Park past, present and possibilities for the future. Unpublished report for the U.S. Peace Corps.

Quézel, P. (1957). *Peuplement végétal des hautes montagnes de l'Afrique du nord*. Lechevalier, Paris.

Sauvage, C. (1959). Au sujet de quelques plantes rares ou menacées de la flore du Maroc. *IUCN 7th Technical Meeting, Athens* 5: 156–157.

SOMAD (1989). La forêt Marocaine, droit, economie, ecologie. La Société Marocaine pour le Droit de l'Environnement, Editions Afrique Orient, Morocco. 200 pp.

Thevenot, M. (1987). Parc nationaux, réserves et autres sites protégés au Maroc. Unpublished report.

Thomas, C.D. and Mallorie, H.C. (1985). Rarity, species richness and conservation: butterflies of the Atlas Mountains in Morocco. *Biological Conservation* 33: 95–117.

## Acknowledgements

This Data Sheet was prepared by Graham R.F. Drucker (World Conservation Monitoring Centre, Cambridge, U.K.).

# REGIONAL OVERVIEW: INDIAN OCEAN ISLANDS

---

**Total land area:** 594,200 km².

**Population (1992):** 14,500,000.

**Number of islands:** 12 main islands, >100 smaller islets.

**Maximum altitude:** 3069 m (summit of Piton des Neiges, Réunion).

**Natural vegetation:** Varied, although originally the islands were mostly covered by tropical lowland and montane forests, with dry deciduous forest and thicket and palm savanna in drier areas.

**Number of vascular plants:** c. 11,000 species.

**Number of endemic species:** c. 9000 species.

**Vascular plant families:** c. 180 families.

**Number of endemic families:** 9.

**Number of genera:** c. 1500.

**Number of endemic genera:** c. 350.

---

The islands treated in this Regional Overview are those of the south-western Indian Ocean, namely: Comoros, Madagascar, Mauritius, Réunion, Rodrigues and Seychelles. For Pemba and Zanzibar, see the Regional Overview on Africa. Islands in other parts of the Indian Ocean are treated elsewhere. For Socotra, see South West Asia and the Middle East; for Sri Lanka, Maldives and the Andaman and Nicobar Islands, see Indian Subcontinent; for Christmas Island (Indian Ocean), see Australia and New Zealand.

## Introduction

The islands of the south-western Indian Ocean below the Equator and above the Tropic of Capricorn, and between longitudes 40°–70°E, cover some 594,200 km² and include about 11,000 vascular plant species, of which more than 80% are endemic to the region.

The jewel in the crown, and the largest island in the region, is Madagascar, which has about 10,000 vascular plant species, of which about 81% are endemic to Madagascar (see Data Sheet on Madagascar, IO1). However, smaller island groups in the region also harbour many endemic species. To the east of Madagascar lie the Mascarene islands, comprising three main islands: Mauritius and Rodrigues (both part of the Republic of Mauritius) and Réunion (a French *Département*). The Comoros are located to the north-west of Madagascar and are divided into two political entities: Mayotte (a French *collectivité territoriale*) and the independent Republic of the Comoros, which includes Moheli, Anjouan and Grande Comore. The Republic of Seychelles, north of Madagascar and closest to the Equator, has as major islands Mahé, Praslin, La Digue and Silhouette. In addition, over 100 smaller and floristically important islands occur in this region.

The islands are geologically very different. Madagascar was once part of Gondwanaland, but has been isolated for a very long time, perhaps having broken from Africa as long as 165 million years ago. The main islands of the Seychelles are also of very old continental granitic origin, although the western islands, including Aldabra and the Amirantes, are more recent coralline atolls. Comoros and the Mascarene islands are all of volcanic origin and have never been attached to any continental landmass. Two of the islands (Grande Comore and Réunion) still have active volcanoes.

All these Indian Ocean islands are for the most part tropical, although areas at higher elevations can receive frost. Snow is almost unknown, although occasional snowfalls occur in parts of Madagascar. Madagascar, being a minicontinent, also experiences the highest temperatures. The hottest summer temperatures (close to 40°C) are in the west, north and south. On the smaller islands, the hottest summer temperatures hover around 30°C (occasionally reaching 32°C). Humidity can be 100%. Generally the east coasts of the islands are much more humid than the west coasts. There are seasonal variations in rainfall, with islands close to the Equator having the least seasonal variation. Rainfall can be less than 350 mm per year in the driest areas of Madagascar, and over 8000 mm per year in certain parts of Réunion. In general, the higher the rainfall, the more diverse the flora; however, when rainfall exceeds 5000 mm per annum, the number of species per unit area usually decreases.

All the islands are densely populated; Mauritius has one of the highest population densities in the world (see Table 35). Population growth has slowed dramatically on the most densely populated islands in recent years (notably on Mauritius and Seychelles), but the growth rate is still high on Madagascar and Comoros. The latter two countries are economically poorer than Mauritius and Seychelles.

**TABLE 35. POPULATION STATISTICS FOR THE MAJOR INDIAN OCEAN ISLANDS**

| Island | Land area (km²) | Population (1992) | People /km² | Population growth |
|---|---|---|---|---|
| Madagascar | 587,000 | 12.2 million | 21 | 3.8% |
| Mauritius and Rodrigues | 1969 | 1.1 million | 559 | 0.8% |
| Réunion | 2512 | 607,000 | 242 | 1.9% |
| Seychelles | 455 | 69,000 | 152 | 0.9% |
| Comoros | 2171 | 477,000 | 220 | 3.5% |

Sources: PC Globe (1992); Population Reference Bureau 1992.

While there is no evidence of human occupation on Madagascar earlier than 2500 years ago (Jenkins 1987), human occupation of both Madagascar and Comoros is generally cited as beginning around the 5th century. The smaller islands were more recently colonized: the first permanent settlers on the Mascarenes arrived in 1598, and the first permanent colony on Seychelles was established as late as 1770.

## Vegetation

The native vegetation of all the Indian Ocean islands is seriously endangered due to the extensive conversion of land to agricultural use. Much of the remaining natural vegetation is seriously threatened by invasive introduced species. Prior to human colonization, the islands were probably mostly forested, the forest type changing with altitude and rainfall gradients. Today, however, more than 75% of Madagascar has no significant native woody plant cover (Jenkins 1987), and in Mauritius only about 2% of the island is still under native, although in many cases degraded, vegetation. The situation is not much better in the Seychelles where only patches of native vegetation remain, the majority of the land being covered by introduced species. Likewise, the Comoros have been very damaged and many species introduced. Excluding Madagascar, Réunion probably has some of the best tracts of native forests, although they are still being exploited and are threatened by invasive species.

All the islands have tropical evergreen montane wet forest. This is the most species-rich vegetation type in the islands. It comprises species which belong to mostly the same families throughout the islands. However, there are great differences at the generic, and especially specific, levels as a result of isolation of the islands (both in distance and in time).

Drier forests and thickets, and heath vegetation, also occur on many of the islands. Forests on rockier substrates or higher altitudes tend to be shrubby, with many woody Asteraceae and "heath" species, including Ericaceae (*Philippia*) as well as Rhamnaceae. The ground flora includes many species of ferns as well as herbaceous Urticaceae, Lobeliaceae and Orchidaceae. Many species of ephiphytic orchids and ferns occur in moist areas.

The vegetation type most affected by human colonization has been primary evergreen (for the most part lowland) forest, since this is where most people live and have cleared areas for cultivation. Hardly any lowland forest remains in the Mascarenes, and much of that on Madagascar has been cleared or degraded. In addition, the montane forests once found on the Central Plateau in Madagascar, where the population density is now very high, have been virtually totally destroyed. The lowlands in the Seychelles are mostly covered by secondary forests and coconut plantations.

Grande Comore, the largest island of the Comoro group, has lost virtually all of its lowland forest below 600 m (J.-J. Floret, pers. comm.). The local people cultivate bananas under the forest, clearing away all the undergrowth. There is also intense pressure for firewood. The forests are being affected by invasive species, the main ones being *Psidium cattleianum* and *Syzygium jambos*. Moheli is apparently the least modified, having a low population density. On the other hand, Anjouan is the most degraded, with very high population pressure and widespread cultivation. There is a large cirque in the centre of the island, and the forest around the crater lake is considered sacred and therefore respected. Mayotte still has some lowland forest in the south. Although it has been exploited and modified, it could be saved if action is taken now. Of interest is that *Litsea glutinosa* is invasive on this island but not on the others (J.-J. Floret, pers. comm.).

Mangroves are found on most of the major islands, although they are absent from Rodrigues and rare on Réunion and Comoros. Lowland "palm savannas", originally found on the smaller islands, are now practically extinct, with only a few degraded examples remaining. The extinction of all the giant tortoises (*Geochelone* spp.) (each of the small main islands originally having one or two strictly endemic species) may have played a role in this. The only giant tortoise remaining in the Indian Ocean is that from Aldabra (now renamed *Aldabrachelys elephantina*), which has since been introduced to all the other islands.

South Madagascar has a very striking dry *Alluaudia* forest which is still largely intact (Jenkins 1987), probably because the extensive areas of limestone on which it grows are unsuitable for agriculture. This vegetation type, with the highest level of endemism in the entire Indian Ocean, is unique.

On Madagascar, the endemic *Ravenala madagascariensis* (Strelitziaceae) is a dominant component of secondary lowland forest. This species has been introduced to all the other islands in the south-western Indian Ocean, where it is invasive and forms monotypic thickets. On these islands, it is unlikely that natural succession will replace the introduced *Ravenala* forests.

The vegetation on the islands of the south-western Indian Ocean is highly threatened. If no further conservation action is taken, many species will become extinct within the next 50 years.

For details of the vegetation of individual islands and island groups selected as centres of plant diversity and endemism, see the Data Sheets IO1–IO3.

## Flora

There is no complete Flora for the whole region. However, a number of institutions are actively engaged in study and research on the flora. They include the universities of Antananarivo and Toliara, the National Botanic Garden at Tsimbazaza and FOFIFA (the Forestry Herbarium) in Madagascar, the Missouri Botanical Garden in the U.S.A., Muséum national d'histoire naturelle in France, and the Royal Botanic Gardens, Kew in the U.K.

Much more work is needed before an accurate assessment can be given on the plant diversity of Madagascar. However, the floras of some of the smaller islands are better known. The *Flore des Mascareignes* is nearing completion and a Flora for the Seychelles is underway. The completion of both of these projects is urgent. In addition, the flora of Comoros needs to be better studied and its plant conservation priorities assessed. As a result of the incomplete coverage of taxonomic treatments, only very approximate regional analyses can be given.

It is estimated that there are very approximately 11,000 flowering plant species in the region, a figure that will probably be increased once further research is undertaken (see Table 36). Over 80% are endemic to the region, including 9 described endemic plant families, although 4–5 of these may eventually be reduced to synonymy in future taxonomic treatments.

### TABLE 36. FLOWERING PLANTS OF THE INDIAN OCEAN

| | Species | Families | Genera | Endemic genera | % Species endemism |
|---|---|---|---|---|---|
| Madagascar | 10,000 | 160–181 | 1289(?) | 260(?) | 80% |
| Mascarenes[a] | 955* | 108 | 323 | 38 | 73%* |
| Comoros[b] | 416(?) | 136(?) | ? | ? | 33%(?) |
| Seychelles[c] | 250 | 93 | 170 | 12 | 35%(?) |

Sources: [a] Strahm (1993). (* refers to flowering plant species, subspecies and varieties.) [b] Voeltzkow (1917). [c] Robertson (1989).

There are a large number of endemic genera, particularly on Madagascar, the Mascarenes and the Seychelles (see Table 37). More taxonomic work is needed before a precise figure for the total number of endemic genera can be given, but it is estimated that some 350 genera are endemic to the region.

### TABLE 37. NUMBER OF ENDEMIC GENERA ON ISLANDS IN THE INDIAN OCEAN

| Island or group of islands | Number of endemic genera |
|---|---|
| Mauritius | 8 |
| Réunion | 7 |
| Rodrigues | 6 |
| Mascarenes (+1 genus also in Seychelles) | 16 |
| Seychelles | 12 |
| Madagascar | 260? |
| Comoros | ? |
| Madagascar and other islands | c. 40 |
| **Total** | **350** |

Major families with forest trees and shrubs present on several islands include Sapotaceae, Ebenaceae (*Diospyros*), Rubiaceae, Flacourtiaceae, Myrtaceae (*Syzygium, Eugenia*), Burseraceae (*Canarium*), Myrsinaceae (*Badula, Oncostemon*), Clusiaceae, Lauraceae, Melastomataceae, Anacardiaceae, Loganiaceae (*Nuxia*), Combretaceae (*Terminalia*), Araliaceae and Monimiaceae (*Tambourissa*). Other significant families include Euphorbiaceae, Sterculiaceae (*Dombeya*), Cunoniaceae (*Weinmannia*), Sapindaceae, Pittosporaceae, Erythroxylaceae, Celastraceae (*Elaeodendron, Maytenus*) and others. Palms form (or formed) a dominant element in many vegetation types, and *Pandanus* thickets are especially common in marshy areas. Of interest is the high diversity of palm species, including many endemic genera, particularly when compared to Africa where palm diversity is low.

Most of the flora of the Indian Ocean Islands has affinities with those of Africa and Madagascar. However, a small percentage of the flora is more closely related to that of Asia. This is probably the result of a relictual Asian element in the flora arising from past contact between the land masses of Madagascar and Seychelles with that of Asia. In addition, the flora of the east coast of Madagascar has weaker African affinities than that of the west coast. This is probably due to speciation among relict species present on the island.

A few species are more closely related to Australian than to African species. For example, *Elaeocarpus integrifolius*, a Mauritius endemic, appears to be more closely related to *Elaeocarpus* in Australia than to those in Madagascar (M.J. Coode, pers. comm.). The endemic *Acacia heterophylla* on Réunion is very closely related to *A. koa*, endemic to Hawaii, and their common ancestor was probably Australian. However, these cases are the exception rather than the rule, and most affinities point to either relict or African sources as the basis on which the highly endemic Indian Ocean flora has evolved. Long distance dispersal of species from the east to west, even though this is the way that the ocean currents move, was probably much less common than species arriving from the nearest large landmass, Africa.

## Useful plants

### Medicinal plants

Plants are used medicinally on all the islands and are sold on medicinal plant stalls in markets. There are well over 200 native and introduced medicinal plant species growing and used on the islands. Medicinal plant lists have been compiled by Bouton 1857, 1864; Daruty 1886; Wong Ting Fook 1980; Adjanohoun *et al.* 1982, 1983; and Jenkins 1987. The best known medicinal plant species used internationally is *Catharanthus roseus* (Madagascan periwinkle), used to treat certain types of infantile leukaemia and Hodgkinson's disease. Other endemic species probably have important properties; some sampling and testing has taken place on all the Indian Ocean islands.

### Timber trees

The most economically important species in the past were the extremely slow-growing, fine hardwood timbers. The original black ebony of commerce, *Diospyros tessellaria*, is endemic to Mauritius and was heavily exploited by the Dutch until large trees became too rare to make harvesting economically feasible. Timber was also exploited from Madagascar and other islands, but for the most part the trees that remain are too inaccessible for commercial purposes. With over-exploitation having occurred in the past, timber is no longer a major regional economic asset. On Réunion, however, the endemic *Acacia heterophylla* and some Sapotaceae (*Mimusops, Labourdonnaissia*) and Combretaceae (*Terminalia*) are managed for timber production, with large areas covered by virtual monocultures of *Acacia*. The harvesting cycle is at least 80 years, so at present these forests are not commercially viable. A detailed evaluation of the forests of Réunion and recommendations for their conservation and sustainable utilization are given in Doumenge and Renard (1989).

## Tree ferns

Tree ferns (*Cyathea* spp.) are one of the most widely used group of plants on islands with sufficient rainfall for their growth. Tree ferns are cut down to make either plant pots, or to provide supports for orchid culture. Widespread exploitation has caused the disappearance of tree ferns in many areas of Mauritius, and their use in Madagascar and Réunion will probably not be sustainable either.

## Palms and pandans

Palms which have edible meristems ("hearts"), such as (in the Mascarenes) *Dictyosperma* and *Acanthophoenix*, are virtually extinct in the wild as a result of over-exploitation and habitat loss. However, these species are widely cultivated to supply the rapidly growing tourist market. Palm hearts could be developed as an important economic resource on an international scale.

Palms have also been important as building materials in the past, and their leaves are still used for thatch. The huge fruits of the "Coco de mer" or "Coco fesse" (*Lodoicea maldivica*) are sold to tourists on Seychelles, providing revenue to the local economy, as well as providing a tourist attraction. The leaves of some other species (particularly *Pandanus*) are used on all the islands as material for baskets, hats and other artefacts. These are sold for local use as well as to tourists.

## Crop relatives

Over 50 endemic species of *Coffea*, reputably low in caffeine (although also low in taste), grow on the islands of the Indian Ocean (mainly Madagascar). These species could serve as valuable sources of genetic material for developing new cultivars of coffee, particularly new varieties with low caffeine-content in their beans.

Many wild species of plants are eaten locally (particularly on Madagascar). Some may be worthy of being introduced to the international market, and may therefore be of greater importance to the regional economy.

## Ornamental plants

There is a large number of species of ornamental value. Some, such as the "crown of thorns" (*Euphorbia millii*), an endemic to Madagascar, are now sold throughout the world as popular house plants. In addition, many species of orchids and succulents are highly sought after by specialist collectors. Collecting poses a threat to some species when plants are taken directly from the wild.

## Plants of cultural value

Many native plant species, particularly those on Madagascar, which has had a longer history of human habitation, play an important cultural role.

## Environmental values

The environmental and economic benefits of maintaining native plant cover to halt the massive soil erosion taking place (particularly on Madagascar) cannot be calculated. In addition, natural vegetation is of great value in maintaining the great attraction of the islands. Tourism is a major industry on many of the islands in the region, and specialist natural history tours are increasing in popularity. If the economies of the islands are to continue to benefit from such tourism, the native flora and vegetation, which provide the habitats for many endemic and rare animals, needs to be protected.

## Factors causing loss of biodiversity

The major causes of loss of biodiversity on the islands today are poverty and population pressure, habitat destruction and the introduction of alien plant species to the islands.

## Population pressure

Poverty is a major problem. People must eat and find fuel to cook their food. As a result, the poorer areas on all the islands suffer from widespread degradation, as wood is cut for fuel, and land is cleared for cultivation to feed the ever-increasing population. Where people have been able to buy food and gas cookers, the pressure on land and wood resources has declined dramatically. However, the standard of living for the majority of people in Madagascar (one of the poorest countries in the world) is not expected to rise significantly for many years, by which time most of the forests will have been cut for fuelwood or cleared for agriculture. In the short-term, protection of the remaining forests is urgently required along with the provision of alternative resources for local people, while the raising of living standards is the only way of ensuring long-term conservation of the remaining forests.

## Habitat destruction

Natural vegetation continues to be cleared for agriculture. Slash and burn methods adopted on Madagascar are particularly destructive. Green and Sussman (1990) calculated that between the years of 1950 and 1985 the rate of deforestation in the eastern rain forests of Madagascar alone amounted to 1110 km$^2$ per year.

On Mauritius, the building of a military/weather station and the installation of electricity lines have recently impinged on the small area of remaining native vegetation on the island. Trees are also cut to facilitate the customary "hunt" (of introduced deer).

Large-scale clearance of native forest is taking place in Réunion to build roads, as well as to "regenerate" native forest to produce more timber from *Acacia heterophylla*. A detailed study of the status of the forests of Réunion is given in Doumenge and Renard (1989).

## Over-collecting

The over-exploitation of tree ferns, edible palms and ornamental plants has already been referred to above. Some plants known to be effective medicinally have also been heavily exploited, sometimes to the point of extinction. For example, *Senecio lamarckianus* on Mauritius, was unknown in the wild for many years (probably due to over-collecting).

Plants which are perceived to be, or known to be, of medicinal value should be cultivated where posssible and made available to local people to ease the pressure on wild plants.

## Introduced animals

Introduced animals have been particularly detrimental to native vegetation on the smaller islands. Apart from giant tortoises (now extinct), there were no large native herbivores on these islands prior to their introduction by man, and the native plants had evolved few defenses against browsing and trampling. As a result, deer, pigs, monkeys, rabbits and rats have all had devastating effects on native vegetation. The tenrec (*Tenrec ecaudatus*), which is endemic to Madagascar, has also been introduced to the smaller islands where it causes significant damage to native vegetation.

Fortunately, there have been fewer introductions of large animals to Madagascar, and the damage has been less. The introduction of deer to Madagascar would be a great threat to the vegetation.

## Invasive plants

Plant introductions have been disastrous on all the islands (see, for example, the Data Sheets on Madagascar, the Mascarenes and Seychelles, sites IO1–IO3). Different islands have their own problem species, but perhaps the most widespread problem is *Psidium cattleianum* (Chinese or strawberry guava). This species, originally from Brazil, grows well in moist forest and forms dense thickets in any disturbed area. It also penetrates undisturbed areas, profiting from any gaps in the forest, replacing native pioneer species and preventing natural succession. In Madagascar, this species has been less invasive to date than on the smaller islands. However, it is likely to become a greater problem in the future as more areas are available for its spread. Large areas at Ranomafana are completely covered by guava thickets, and guava will spread into native forest when given the chance (W. Strahm, pers. obs.). Unfortunately, guava is highly appreciated by the local population for its fruit, so while complete destruction through biological control is desirable in terms of conserving the native vegetation, much education will be needed to convince people that guava is a detrimental, rather than a beneficial, species.

Many other alien species have completely transformed the vegetation of the Indian Ocean islands in a very short time. Without further conservation measures, the islands will one day form a homogeneous flora of only a few species. Alien species, therefore, are the single largest threat to the maintenance of biodiversity on the smaller islands; natural regeneration having virtually stopped or having been extremely curtailed. Once the long-lived canopy trees finally die, only alien species will be present to take their place. Only by undertaking intensive management in nature reserves will this problem be able to be combatted.

## Conservation

To date, three World Heritage Sites have been declared in the region: Aldabra Island, the Vallée du Mai on the island of Praslin, Seychelles and the Tsingy de Bemaraha National Park of Madagascar.

Mauritius and Rodrigues still have important areas of unique vegetation that are not officially protected as Nature Reserves (e.g. the Magenta and Chamarel valleys in Mauritius, and the south-east facing valleys of Rodrigues). These should be protected as the last remnants of forests long since disappeared over much of the island.

Réunion has a very inadequate coverage of protected areas, with only one Strict Nature Reserve covering just 68 ha. (Larger areas are classified under less strict protection categories, but there is no legal long-term commitment to the protection of these other areas.)

There is a growing environmental awareness on Seychelles and the protected area network covers a number of important sites (see Data Sheet on Seychelles, CPD Site IO3). Many partially protected areas should gain official reserve status for their long-term protection.

The protected area coverage on Madagascar is good, although more needs to be added in order to conserve an adequate representation of the incredibly rich biodiversity on the island (see Data Sheet on Madagascar, CPD Site IO1). Unfortunately, many areas are protected in name only and are under threat, due to a lack of infrastructure for guarding and managing the areas, and the lack of alternatives for local people for harvesting wood or growing crops. The problem of introduced species also needs to be addressed.

The protected area network of the region needs to be increased in order to ensure that all of the native species can be found in one or more protected sites. At present, however, endemic species are found both within and outside of protected areas. Many endemic species occur, for example, on one cliff or in one valley. This means that the network of protected areas needs to include some small sites, as well as reserves covering larger areas. Given proper management, native species can be conserved in relatively small areas, but reserve management, particularly on the smaller islands, will need to be intensive if the endemic species are to survive and the alien species controlled.

Programmes aimed at eradicating alien animals on some of the smaller islands have been successful (e.g. rabbits from Round Island) (Merton *et al.* 1989), and the number of these programmes needs to be increased. Research into the biological control of invasive weed species needs to be undertaken, and manual weeding of undesirable species needs to be effected in the short-term.

*Ex situ* plant cultivation has a very important role to play in the conservation of the native flora, particularly for those species which have been reduced to such low numbers that they will not survive in the long-term unless they receive intensive care which botanic gardens can provide. Efforts to conserve any remaining genetic diversity and bulk up numbers must often be made *ex situ*, with the long-term goal being the reintroduction of the plants to protected and properly managed areas in the wild.

*Ex situ* cultivation can also bulk up commercially desirable (and often rare) species in order to eliminate demand on wild populations. However, some benefits or alternative forms of income must accrue to local populations, or else the temptation to harvest and illegally sell wild plants of commercial importance will continue.

Finally, *ex situ* cultivation is an important tool for education, both for the local population, which needs to conserve their biological diversity, as well as for developed countries, which are often the users of such biological diversity. Programmes are needed to demonstrate sustainable use of plant resources.

An important opportunity for conservation is the increase in tourism to the islands. Increased efforts to ensure that tourism benefits local people, and does not destroy the natural resources on which it is based, need to be put into place.

## Centres of plant diversity and endemism

Since the main islands have a range of vegetation types and a high percentage of endemic species, each are considered as important centres of plant diversity and endemism.

### IO1. Madagascar

– see Data Sheet.

Madagascar is treated here as one regional CPD. However, it is important to note that many individual sites within Madagascar deserve Data Sheet treatment in their own right. The sheet includes summaries on a number of outstanding sites of botanical importance but the current extent of botanical knowledge precludes selection of individual CPD sites at present.

### IO2. Mascarene Islands, including Mauritius, Rodrigues and Réunion

– see Data Sheet.

### IO3. Seychelles (granitic islands)

– see Data Sheet.

### IO4. Comoros

Lack of information on Comoros prevented the selection and treatment of this island group as a Data Sheet site. Voeltzkow (1917) gave a figure of 416 vascular plant species, of which about 33% are endemic.

## References

Adjanohoun, E.J., Aké Assi, L., Ahmed, Ali, Eymé, J., Guinko, S., Kayonga, A., Keita, A. and Lebras, M. (1982). *Contribution aux études ethnobotaniques et floristiques aux Comores*. ACCT, Paris, France. 217 pp.

Adjanohoun, E.J., Aké Assi, L., Eymé, J., Gassita, J.N., Goudoté, E., Guého, J., Ip, F.S.L., Jackaria, D., Kalachand, S.K.K., Keita, A., Koudogbo, B., Landreau, D., Owadally, A.W. and Soopramanien, A. (1983). *Contribution aux études ethnobotaniques et floristiques à Maurice (Iles Maurice et Rodrigues)*. ACCT, Paris, France. 214 pp.

Bouton, L.S. (1857). Medicinal plants growing or cultivated in the island of Mauritius. *Trans. Roy. Soc. Arts Sci. Mauritius new ser.* 1: 1–177.

Bouton, L.S. (1864). *Plantes médicinales de Maurice*. 2nd Ed. Port Louis, Mauritius. 147 pp.

Daruty, C. (1886). *Plantes médicinales de l'Ile Maurice et des pays intertropicaux*. Mauritius. 137 pp.

Doumenge, C. and Renard, Y. (1989). *La Conservation des Ecosystèmes forestiers de l'Ile de la Réunion*. UICN, Gland, Switzerland and Cambridge, U.K. viii, 95 pp.

Green, G.M. and Sussman, R.W. (1990). Deforestation history of the eastern rain forests of Madagascar from satellite images. *Science* 248: 212–215.

Jenkins, M.D. (ed.) (1987). *Madagascar, an environmental profile*. IUCN Conservation Monitoring Centre, Cambridge, U.K. 374 pp.

Merton, D.V., Atkinson, I.A.E., Strahm, W., Jones, C., Empson, R.A., Mungroo, Y., Dulloo, E. and Lewis, R. (1989). *A management plan for the restoration of Round Island Mauritius*. JWPT and Ministry of Agriculture, Fisheries and Natural Resources, Mauritius. 46 pp.

PC Globe (1992). *PC Globe software 5.0*. Tempe, Arizona, U.S.A.

Robertson, S.A. (1989). *Flowering plants of Seychelles*. Royal Botanic Gardens, Kew. 327 pp.

Strahm, W. (1989). *Plant Red Data Book for Rodrigues*. Koeltz Scientific Books, Konigstein, Germany. 241 pp.

Strahm, W.A. (1993). The conservation and restoration of the flora of Mauritius and Rodrigues. Ph.D thesis, Reading University, U.K.

Voeltzkow, A. (1917). Flora und Fauna der Comoren. In *Reise in Ostafrika din den Jahren 1903–1905. Wiss. Ergeb.* 3(5): 429–480.

Wong Ting Fook, W.T.H. (1980). *The medicinal plants of Mauritius*. ENDA (Environment and Development Action in the Third World) Doc. 10: 35 pp.

# MADAGASCAR

---

**Location:** Western Indian Ocean, between latitudes 11°57'–25°35'S and longitudes 43°14'–50°27'E.

**Area:** 587,000 km², including a number of small islands, the largest of which are Nosy Be and Nosy Boraha each of which covers c. 200 km².

**Altitude:** 0–2876 m.

**Vegetation:** Physiognomic formations diverse, but predominantly forests and thicket, falling into 17 major vegetation types. Primary plant communities are generally dominated by endemic species; exotic species and non-endemics predominate in secondary vegetation.

**Flora:** c. 9345 native vascular plant species described so far, of which c. 81% are endemic to Madagascar. Total vascular flora likely to exceed 10,000 species. 2 major phytogeographic regions: East Malagasy Region and West Malagasy Region. Affinities primarily with Eastern and Southern Africa, secondarily West Malesia.

**Useful plants:** Medicinal plants, fibres, timber, edible leaves, seeds and fruits, ornamental plants, crop relatives, rich in unresearched genetic resources.

**Other values:** Watershed protection, scenic value for tourism, cultural and religious importance, soil conservation, habitat for rich endemic fauna.

**Threats:** Development pressure, fire, clearance for agriculture, grazing pressure, mining, uncontrolled felling of timber, plant collecting for horticulture (primarily export of succulents), charcoal production, invasive exotic species, erosion.

**Conservation:** 38 protected areas, incl. 5 National Parks, 11 Strict Nature Reserves and 23 Special Reserves, covering 11,252 km² (c. 1.9% of land area), 158 areas of classified forest with partial protection (total area: 26,710 km², c. 4.6% of land area). 2 Biosphere Reserves; 1 World Heritage Site (1520 km²). 23 additional areas currently proposed for protection. Little reliable information available on conservation status of individual plants. Some plant species are protected by CITES regulations.

---

Madagascar is treated here as one regional CPD area; however, it is important to note that many individual sites within Madagascar deserve Data Sheet treatment in their own right and that virtually every sizeable tract of native vegetation will contain at least some endemic plants. The account below includes summary information on a number of outstanding sites of botanical importance but the current extent of botanical knowledge precludes selection of individual CPD sites at present. It is hoped that further identification and documentation of important plant sites will be forthcoming in the future.

## Geography

Madagascar is situated in the Western Indian Ocean, between latitudes 11°57' and 25°35'S and between longitudes 43°14' and 50°27'E. It is approximately 1600 km long and 580 km across at its widest point. It is the fourth largest island in the world (after Greenland, New Guinea and Borneo), with a total area of approximately 587,000 km². In addition to the main island, there are a number of small islands which are parts of the Malagasy Republic and are included in this account. The largest of these islands are Nosy Be and Nosy Boraha which each cover approximately 200 km².

Madagascar is separated from Africa by the Mozambique Channel, which is approximately 400 km wide (frequently mis-stated in the literature as 300 km) at its narrowest point between Tanjona Vilanandro (Cap Saint André) in north-west

Madagascar and Cape Saint Vincent in northern Mozambique. Madagascar was originally part of the ancient Gondwanan continent situated adjacent to what is now Tanzania and Kenya, and is believed to have moved south-eastwards relative to the African mainland to its present position (Paulian 1984).

The physical relief of Madagascar is complex, but is dominated by the following features (Bastian 1967; Jenkins 1987):

1. A central highland ranging in altitude from approximately 500–1500 m extends nearly the whole length of Madagascar. It is formed by a metamorphic Pre-Cambrian basement which has been extensively uplifted, faulted and eroded. Although it is often referred to as the central or high plateau, in many areas its topography is highly dissected and it often forms an undulating hilly landscape. Soils on the central highlands are predominantly lateritic clays. The highlands slope downwards gradually from east to west and narrow towards the north and the south. They are drained mainly by rivers flowing to the west coast.

2. To the east of the central highlands the land slopes abruptly down to the east coast to form a steep continuous, or in some places, stepped escarpment, which is drained by numerous short, fast-flowing rivers. The escarpment is primarily formed, like the central highlands, from the Pre-Cambrian basement, but areas of volcanic and granitic formations and some recent alluvial deposits give rise to

271

## MAP 15. CPD SITE IO1: MADAGASCAR, SHOWING PHYTOGEOGRAPHIC DIVISIONS AND PROTECTED AREAS

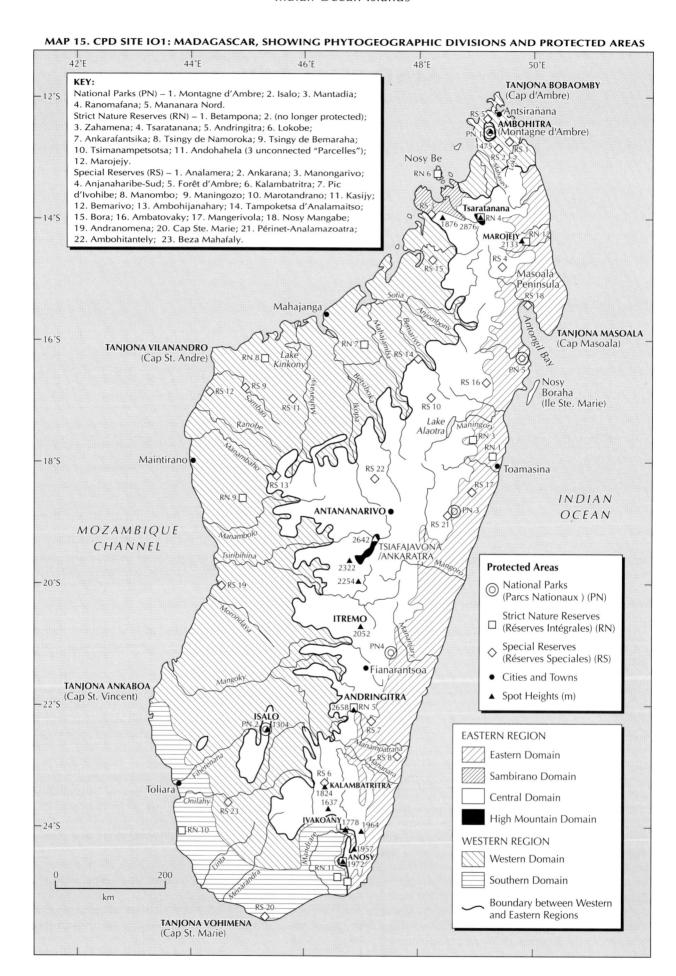

**KEY:**
National Parks (PN) – 1. Montagne d'Ambre; 2. Isalo; 3. Mantadia;
4. Ranomafana; 5. Mananara Nord.
Strict Nature Reserves (RN) – 1. Betampona; 2. (no longer protected);
3. Zahamena; 4. Tsaratanana; 5. Andringitra; 6. Lokobe;
7. Ankarafantsika; 8. Tsingy de Namoroka; 9. Tsingy de Bemaraha;
10. Tsimanampetsotsa; 11. Andohahela (3 unconnected "Parcelles");
12. Marojejy.
Special Reserves (RS) – 1. Analamera; 2. Ankarana; 3. Manongarivo;
4. Anjanaharibe-Sud; 5. Forêt d'Ambre; 6. Kalambatritra; 7. Pic
d'Ivohibe; 8. Manombo; 9. Maningozy; 10. Marotandrano; 11. Kasijy;
12. Bemarivo; 13. Ambohijanahary; 14. Tampoketsa d'Analamaitso;
15. Bora; 16. Ambatovaky; 17. Mangerivola; 18. Nosy Mangabe;
19. Andranomena; 20. Cap Ste. Marie; 21. Périnet-Analamazoatra;
22. Ambohitantely; 23. Beza Mahafaly.

**Protected Areas**

◎ National Parks (Parcs Nationaux ) (PN)

□ Strict Nature Reserves (Réserves Intégrales) (RN)

◇ Special Reserves (Réserves Speciales) (RS)

● Cities and Towns

▲ Spot Heights (m)

**EASTERN REGION**

Eastern Domain

Sambirano Domain

Central Domain

High Mountain Domain

**WESTERN REGION**

Western Domain

Southern Domain

Boundary between Western and Eastern Regions

a greater variety of soils. Most of the east coast is remarkably straight and runs parallel to the escarpment. In the north-east the escarpment is not so evident and the coastline is more rugged, in this region the Masoala Peninsula and the Bay of Antongil form very distinctive features.

3. To the west of the central highlands the land continues to slope gradually to the west coast. Below about 500 m altitude the metamorphic basement is replaced by a continuous zone of sedimentary formations. Much of this sedimentary zone belongs to the Karoo system dating from the Lower Jurassic to the Cretaceous periods. The zone extends from the north to the south of Madagascar and includes areas of marine deposits which form extensive limestone reefs which have been subjected to karst processes (referred to as "tsingy"). Soils within this western sedimentary zone are diverse, they are frequently sandy and include decalcified clays derived from the limestone karsts. However, lateritic clay is never found. The major rivers draining from the central highlands through the western zone often form extensive deltas.

4. Mountains rise above the undulating plateau within the central highland region. They comprise volcanic formations of various ages, granites and quartzitic outcrops. The principal ranges are as follows: the Tsaratanana Massif, with the highest peak in Madagascar, which reaches 2876 m above sea-level, and the associated Marojejy and Manongarivo Massifs; the Ankaratra Range, in the centre, near the capital, Antananarivo, which reaches 2642 m; the Andringitra Massif, further south, which reaches 2658 m; and, in the south-east, a series of lower mountains, including the Anosy and Ivakoany Ranges and Kalambatritra Mountain, which rises to nearly 2000 m.

Numerous lakes occur in Madagascar; 18 exceed 10 km² in area (Keiner 1963). The largest, Lake Alaotra, is situated at 750 m altitude on a step in the eastern escarpment and covers about 220 km². Most of the other lakes occur within the western sedimentary zone at low altitude.

There is a wide range of climatic conditions in Madagascar (Donque 1975; Jenkins 1987). Rainfall shows a double gradient, generally decreasing in annual total from the east to the west, and from the north to the south (the extreme north is an exception to this rule), while increasing in seasonality in the same directions, with heavy cyclonic rain storms during summer months. Typically, the east coast and eastern escarpment receives rain throughout the year and the total rainfall generally exceeds 2000 mm per annum. Between Toamasina (Tamatave) and Maroantsetra, and on the Masoala Peninsula, annual rainfall may exceed 3500 mm. The rest of Madagascar has a marked dry winter season, lasting from April or May until October or November. Total rainfall ranges from about 2200 mm in the Sambirano basin and on Nosy Be in the north-west, to about 1000 mm around Antsiranana (Diego-Suarez) in the extreme north, and to under 350 mm per annum in the south-west coastal zone between the city of Toliara (Tuléar) and Tanjon' I Vohimena (Cap Sainte-Marie). Much of the central highlands and west coast receives between 750–1500 mm per annum. In the semi-arid south-west the rainfall is erratic and prolonged periods of drought may occur. Typical sub-equatorial to tropical temperatures

are experienced in Madagascar, with altitude having a significant effect. The average lapse rate is around 0.6°C for every 100 m increase in altitude. Frost is sometimes experienced at localities over 1500 m altitude, although snow has only been recorded very rarely. While the proximity of the Indian Ocean and the high rainfall exerts a cooling effect on the eastern escarpment, the warm Mozambique Channel has little effect on the west coast where the highest temperatures are recorded.

Madagascar's population in 1992 was estimated to be 12.2 million (PC Globe 1992); the growth rate is currently estimated at 3.8% per annum (Population Reference Bureau 1992). The distribution of the population is very uneven. There are more than 100 people/km² on the east coast, approximately 60 people/km² in the central highlands, and only 5/km² on the west coast. Antananarivo, the capital, has over 1 million inhabitants, but overall about 80% of Madagascar's population live in rural areas.

## Vegetation

The natural vegetation of Madagascar is very varied, reflecting variations in topography, geology, soils and climate. Seventeen broad vegetation types are recognised. Within each of these there are many distinct plant communities, but no systematic classification at community level is available due to inadequate basic research for most parts of the island.

The original vegetation of Madagascar is believed to have been predominantly evergreen or deciduous forest or deciduous, spiny, succulent thicket, with rupicolous shrublands occurring locally on various types of rock outcrops, and with montane bushland and thicket occurring on the highest mountains. However, much of the original vegetation has been destroyed or seriously degraded and is now replaced by grasslands or secondary forest. Primary vegetation types and their resultant secondary formations are discussed below. The treatment largely follows that of Koechlin, Guillaumet and Morat (1974) and White (1983).

**Primary lowland rain forest** occurs below about 800 m altitude on the eastern escarpment and the Sambirano basin, and on Nosy Be in the north-west, where annual rainfall exceeds 2000 mm. The forest canopy is relatively low (25–30 m) compared to forests in climatically similar parts of the world. Large emergent trees are absent and nearly all species are evergreen. Primary lowland rain forest is very species-rich and no single species dominates. Common canopy species include many members of the families Anacardiaceae, Araliaceae, Euphorbiaceae, Flacourtiaceae, Loganiaceae, Malpighiaceae, Myrtaceae, Rubiaceae, Sapindaceae and species of *Canarium, Cryptocarya, Cynometra, Dalbergia, Diospyros, Mammea, Symphonia, Ocotea, Sloania* and *Tambourissa*, together with *Dilobeia thouarsii*. The lower canopy is well-developed and there are many epiphytes, including ferns and species of Melastomataceae and Orchidaceae. Palms are well represented in all strata.

Degradation of primary lowland rain forest results in secondary forest, secondary grasslands, or intermediate scrub formations where invasive exotic woody species predominate. Secondary lowland forest ("savoka") is very poor in indigenous species. Of these, species of *Canarium, Croton, Macaranga, Dombeya*, and *Harungana madagascariensis, Ochlandra capitata, Psiadia altissima* and *Ravenala madagascariensis*

**CPD Site IO1: Madagascar, showing "deciduous thicket" in the Southern Domain of the Western Region, in Andohahela Reserve (Parcelle 2) near Amboasary, altitude c. 100 m, with *Alluaudia ascendens* and *A. procera* (tall, poorly-branched trees), together with *Euphorbia stenoclada*, *Aloe divaricata* and (in the foreground) *Xerophyta* sp.** Photo: Peter B. Phillipson.

are of widespread occurrence. Shrubby species of *Philippia* (Ericaceae) dominate degraded vegetation on leached coastal sand dunes. Secondary grasslands are also very poor in species, with *Aristida similis* usually dominating. *Psidium* spp. are the predominant invasive exotic trees.

**Moist montane forest** is transitional between lowland rain forest and sclerophyllous montane forests. It occurs above 800 m on the upper part of the eastern escarpment, on lower and more humid areas of the central highlands that still support primary vegetation, and on the mountains of the north. Moist montane forest is predominantly evergreen and generally shorter (20–25 m high) than lowland forest, but is similar in composition. Members of the Myrsinaceae, bamboos and species of *Grewia*, *Pandanus*, *Vernonia* and *Weinmannia*. are additional important canopy components. The herb layer is well-developed and contains many temperate elements. Epiphytes are very prolific and diverse. Where it has been replaced by secondary vegetation, transitional grassland communities occur.

**Sclerophyllous montane forest** occurs generally between 1300 and 2300 m altitude. It is predominantly evergreen and is shorter (10–12 m high) than forest types at lower altitudes. Canopy components commonly include members of the families Araliaceae, Compositae, Ericaceae, Rubiaceae and

Verbenaceae, and species of *Dombeya*, *Faurea*, *Nuxia*, *Ocotea*, *Oncostemum*, *Podocarpus*, *Symphonia*, *Vaccinium* and *Weinmannia*, together with *Aphloia theiformis* and *Ilex mitis*. The understorey is not particularly well-developed. Among epiphytes, lichens and bryophytes predominate. The forest is very susceptible to destruction by fire and is replaced by floristically impoverished secondary grasslands of two types, namely: "tanety" grasslands, between 1200–1500 m altitude, which are mostly dominated by *Aristida rufescens*; and "tampoketsa" grasslands, at higher altitudes, which are dominated by the Malagasy endemic *Loudetia simplex* subsp. *stipoides*.

**Montane bushland and thicket** generally occurs above the sclerophyllous forest (of which it is a depauperate derivative) at more than 2000 m altitude. It consists of a single stratum of short (6 m high) woody shrubs and occasional emergent individual trees. The shrubs are evergreen and have small sclerophyllous leaves. Members of the Compositae and Rubiaceae, and species of *Philippia* predominate. There are many species of emergent trees, including many which are found in sclerophyllous montane forest. Palms are generally absent. Secondary grasslands have replaced much of the bushland and thicket but include a higher diversity of species than other grassland types in Madagascar, and include both Malagasy endemic and "African" high-altitude species of Gramineae.

**Tapia forest**, dominated by *Uapaca bojeri*, occurs on the warmer and drier western slopes of the central highlands at altitudes between 800 and 1600 m. The forest is evergreen, 10–12 m high and lacks a dense canopy. Commonly occurring trees include members of the Anacardiaceae, Compositae, Rubiaceae and Sarcolaenaceae, together with species of *Weinmannia*, and *Asteropeia densiflora*, *Dodonaea madagascariensis*, *Faurea forficuliflora* and *Schefflera bojeri*. Tapia forest probably originally covered a very large area of central Madagascar, but most has been replaced by extensive secondary grasslands and localised intermediate woodlands. The grasslands are floristically poor. At higher altitudes *Loudetia simplex* subsp. *stipoides* and other species of the tampoketsa are found, while at lower altitudes *Hyparrhenia rufa* and *Heteropogon contortus* are increasingly dominant. In secondary woodlands, the fire tolerant *Uapaca bojeri* persists while most of the other woody species are destroyed.

**Dry deciduous forest** is the primary vegetation throughout most of the western part of Madagascar below about 800 m in altitude. In the wet Sambirano region it is replaced by lowland rain forest, while in the semi-arid south it is replaced by deciduous thicket. Deciduous forest may be subdivided on the basis of substrate, which strongly influences species composition. Generally, however, the forests have a canopy of 12–15 m, with tall (25 m) individual emergents. Commonly occurring trees include species of *Adansonia*, *Albizia*, *Cryptocarya*, *Dalbergia*, *Delonix*, *Protorhus* and *Stereospermum*. *Tamarindus indica* is especially prominent on sandy soils. Lianas, particularly Asclepiadaceae, and shrubs are common. Herbs and epiphytes (including mosses and lichens) are very few.

Most of the deciduous forest has been destroyed and is replaced by secondary grassland or wooded grassland. The dominant grasses include species of *Aristida*, *Loudetia* and *Hyparrhenia*, and *Heteropogon contortus*, *Hyperthelia dissoluta*, *Panicum maximum* and *Themeda quadrivalvis*.

***Bismarckia nobilis*** **in grassland near Isalo National Park in the south-western part of the central plateau of Madagascar, at c. 800 m. This area is transitional between the Central Domain of the Eastern Region and the Western Domain of the Western Region.** Photo: Peter B. Phillipson.

The commonest trees are tolerant of annual burning. In areas were fires are less frequent, other herbaceous and sub-shrubby species may be present, mainly species of Leguminosae. In some areas trees up to 12 m high are present; the vegetation in these cases has been referred to as "savanna".

**Deciduous thicket** occurs in the semi-arid south-west. Thickets are commonly from 3 to 6 m high, sometimes with emergent trees reaching about 10 m or more high. Succulent and spinescent plants, particularly members of the family Didiereaceae, which is essentially endemic to the thicket, and *Euphorbia* spp. are common and conspicuous components both in the thicket layer and sometimes as emergents. Other important thicket components include species of *Acacia, Aloe, Commiphora, Dichrostachys, Grewia, Kalanchoe, Megistostegium, Pachypodium, Terminalia* and *Uncarina*. Emergents also include species of *Adansonia, Delonix* and *Ficus, Gyrocarpus americanus* and *Tetrapterocarpon geayi*. Lianas are numerous, including many Asclepiadaceae, while epiphytes and the ground layer are generally sparse. Deciduous thicket has been replaced by secondary grasslands and wooded grasslands over much of its natural area of distribution.

**Rupicolous shrublands** occur on rock outcrops of various types throughout Madagascar, although it is in the central highlands that they are most common. They consist of shrubby species, generally not exceeding 2 m high, rooted in the rock crevices or in shallow mats of soil on more level surfaces. The plants are subjected to fluctuating moisture, high winds and temperature extremes due to shallow soils and exposed situations. Species tolerating these conditions show a variety of xeromorphic growth forms. Common components include: leaf succulents, such as species of Orchidaceae, *Aloe* and *Kalanchoe*; stem and root succulent shrubs, such as species of *Cynanchum* and *Tetradenia*; spinescent and succulent species of *Euphorbia*; revivescent plants, such as *Myrothamnus moschatus* and numerous ferns; species of *Xerophyta*; and tufted grasses and sedges of various genera. At higher altitudes, bryophytes and lichens are common.

**Mangroves** occur in many parts of Madagascar (Jenkins 1987; Rabesandratana 1984), mainly around the river mouths and bays of the west coast. They are estimated to cover a total of between 2176 km² (Koechlin, Guillaumet and Morat 1974) and 3300 km² (Keiner 1972) (c. 0.4–0.6% of the land area). The predominant species are typical of mangroves found elsewhere in the Indian Ocean.

See Harcourt (1992) for a recent map of lowland, montane and mangrove forests at scale 1:4,000,000.

## Flora

Madagascar has an extraordinarily rich flora and a very high level of endemism. Various estimates of the size of the flora and the level of species endemism can be found in the literature. These are mostly extrapolations of figures given by Humbert (1959) who counted 7900 known species of flowering plants, of which 6400 (81%) were regarded as endemic to Madagascar. He estimated that the total angiosperm flora would probably amount to about 10,000 species. Based on data in the Missouri Botanical Garden and other databases, approximately 1170 endemic species were described from Madagascar, between 1959 to 1992. A reliable estimate of the number of additional non-endemic species recorded during this period is not readily accessible; however, assuming a proportional increase in records of non-endemic species, these might amount to approximately 275. Thus, in 1993, the known flora of Madagascar probably totals about 9345 species, of which 7570 (81%) are believed to be endemic.

It is clear that in many families large numbers of species still remain to be collected and described. For example, current work on Labiatae suggests that in some genera only about 25% of the species represented in herbaria have been described (unpublished work and Hedge pers. comm.), while recent botanical exploration in many areas of Madagascar is generating many new discoveries. For example, recent fieldwork has discovered 30–40 previously unrecorded species of palms (all of which are endemics) (H. Beentje 1993, pers. comm.). To some extent, new discoveries may be balanced by the reduction of narrowly delimited species as synonyms under more broadly defined species; however, it seems likely

that the total number of species will eventually exceed Humbert's (1959) estimate of 10,000.

Reliable modern estimates of numbers of genera and generic endemism are lacking. Perrier de la Bâthie (1936) refers to 1289 genera of which approximately 20% were endemic. However, many more genera have been described subsequently and many others have been lost in synonymy. The level of endemism is particularly high in some families. For example, of the 115 described species of palms, 111 are endemic to Madagascar. (13 of the 21 palm genera known so far from Madagascar are endemic, but major taxonomic changes are expected following recent discoveries) (H. Beentje 1993, pers. comm.). Of the 160 to 181 families of seed plants currently recognised (estimates are dependent upon the taxonomic system being followed), the following four are regarded as endemic (following Cronquist 1981): Didiereaceae, Didymelaceae, Sarcolaenaceae, Sphaerosepalaceae. The following families are recognised as endemic by some authorities, but they are included in more widespread families (indicated in parentheses) by Cronquist: Asteropeiaceae (Theaceae), Diegodendraceae (Ochnaceae), Humbertiaceae (Convolvulaceae), Melanophyllaceae (Cornaceae), Physenaceae (probably Capparidaceae).

Based on floristic and ecological data, Madagascar can be divided into two major phytogeographic regions, which can be subdivided into a number of floristic domains.

**Scenery in the Isalo National Park in the south-western part of the central plateau of Madagascar, at c. 1200 m, showing "tapia" trees (*Uapaca bojeri*) and evergreen forest patches in the valleys. Rupicolous shrublands, including many endemic xeromorphic shrubs and succulents, occur on exposed rock outcrops. Photo: Peter B. Phillipson.**

**TABLE 39. PROTECTED AREAS IN THE SEYCHELLES (EXCLUDING FOREST RESERVES)**

| Name of area | IUCN management category | Area (ha) |
|---|---|---|
| **National Parks** | | |
| Morne Seychellois | VIII | 3045 |
| Praslin | II | 675 |
| (In addition, there are 5 **Marine National Parks**) | | |
| **Special Nature Reserves** | | |
| Aldabra | I | 35,000 |
| Aride Island | I | 70 |
| Cousin Island | I | 28 |
| La Digue Veuve | I | 8 |
| **Nature Reserves** | | |
| Beacon Island | VI | ? |
| Booby or Ile aux Fous | VI | ? |
| Boudeuse | VI | ? |
| Etoile | VI | ? |
| Ile au Vache Marine | VI | ? |
| King Ross | VI | ? |
| Les Mamelles | VI | ? |
| Vallée de Mai | IV | 18 |
| **Protected Areas** | | |
| African Banks | ? | ? |
| Ile Cocos | ? | ? |
| **World Heritage Sites** | | |
| Aldabra Atoll | X | 35,000 |
| Vallée de Mai | X | 18 |

Source: World Conservation Monitoring Centre protected areas database (1993).

Aldabra was inscribed as a World Heritage site in 1982, mainly for the importance of its whole ecosystem, including giant land tortoises and important bird colonies. The Vallée de Mai Nature Reserve (see below) was inscribed as a World Heritage Site in 1983.

## Important botanical sites

Botanically interesting sites have been documented by Jeffrey (1968). The most important (with a few additions) are:

❖ The **Vallée de Mai Nature Reserve** and World Heritage Site covers an area of 18 ha within Praslin National Park. It contains *Lodoicea maldivica* forest.
❖ Lowland rain forest and glacis vegetation sites
  *Mahé*
    **Bernica Hill** (c. 15 ha), within Morne Seychellois National Park, includes glacis vegetation with *Medusagyne oppositifolia*.
    **Mt Sebert** (c. 20 ha), glacis vegetation with *Medusagyne oppositifolia*.
    **La Réserve** (c. 10 ha), *Deckenia nobilis* palm forest.
  *Silhouette*
    **Rocky slopes from Pt Grand Barbe to Coco dans trou** (c. 2 km$^2$), including large granite outcrops. Coastal *Calophyllum* forest, mixed with *Deckenia* and *Mimusops* glacis vegetation.
    **La Réserve** (c. 15 ha), from Grebau to Pt La Varangue. *Mimusops-Intsia-Carissa* forest and glacis vegetation.
  *Curieuse*
    **Central area** (c. 50 ha), of *Lodoicea-Dillenia* forest. (The whole island is part of Curieuse Marine National Park.)
  *Félicité*
    **Small areas above Baie Chagrin and at Anse Songe**, with *Mimusops-Intsia* forest and *Calophyllum-Terminalia* forest (c. 10 ha).

❖ Mountain mist forest sites
  *Mahé*
    **Morne Seychellois National Park** (3.5 km$^2$). Central ridges and peaks from about 550–900 m, covering an area of c. 2 km$^2$, especially Mt Jasmin, Mt Coton, Morne Seychellois and slopes to Congo Rouge and Morne Blanc. Includes *Northea-Glionnetia-Rapanea* forest with *Nepenthes* and epiphytic bryophytes.
    **Mt Capucins** (c. 25 ha), *Northea* forest.
  *Silhouette*
    **Mt Dauban** crest to Grand Congoman, from about 500–750 m, covering c. 50 ha. Includes *Northea-Glionnetia-Rapanea* forest with *Nepenthes*.
❖ Mountain rain forest site
    **Dans Mapou** (upper valley of Anse Mondon river at about 500 m, of area c. 25 ha). *Pisonia sechellarum* forest with *Amaracarpus*, *Psychotria silhouettae* and epiphytic *Schefflera* and *Piper* (a type of vegetation known only from one sheltered valley, and discovered in 1983).

Not all of these places have official reserve status yet. They are, nevertheless, under the supervision of the National Parks Commission.

A special feature of the conservation programme is the management of *Lodoicea*; many have been planted, especially in the Vallée de Mai. A priority is to ensure that as large a population as possible of the native trees is maintained.

The Seychelles has a botanic garden, Mahé Botanical Gardens, which should be encouraged to propagate the islands' threatened species.

## References

Anon. (1971). *Conservation policy in the Seychelles*. Government Printer, Union Vale, Mahé. 10 pp.

Baker, J.G. (1877). *Flora of Mauritius and the Seychelles*. Reeve, London. 557 pp.

Christensen, C. (1912). On the ferns of the Seychelles and the Aldabra group. *Trans. Linn. Soc. Lond. 2nd Ser. Zool.* 15: 407–422.

Dickison, W.C. (1990). The morphology and relationships of *Medusagyne*. *Pl. Syst. Evol.* 171: 27–55.

FAO (1988). *An interim report on the state of forest resources in the developing countries*. FAO, Rome.

Fosberg, F.R. and Renvoize, S.A. (1980). The flora of Aldabra and neighbouring islands. *Kew Bulletin Additional Series* 7: 1–353.

Friedmann, F. (1986). *Flowers and trees of Seychelles*. Delroisse, Boulogne. 196 pp.

Friedmann, F. (1993). Flore des Seychelles (Première partie: Dicotylédones). (Unpublished.)

Harcourt, C. (1992). Indian Ocean islands. In Sayer, J.A., Harcourt, C.S. and Collins, N.M. (eds), *The conservation atlas of tropical forests: Africa*. Macmillan. Pp. 206–213.

Horne, J. (1875). Report on the Seychelles islands. *Transactions of the Royal Society of Arts and Science, Mauritius* 9: 52.

Jeffrey, C. (1968). Seychelles. In Hedberg, I. and Hedberg O. (eds), *Conservation of vegetation in Africa south of the Sahara*. Acta Phytogeogrica Suecica 54, Uppsala. Pp. 275–279.

Lionnet, G. (1972). *The Seychelles*. David and Charles, Newton Abbot. 200 pp.

Miller, J.A. and Mudie, J.D. (1961). Potassium-argon age determination on granite from the island of Mahé in the Seychelles archipelago. *Nature* 192: 1174–1175.

PC Globe (1992). *PC Globe software 5.0*. Tempe, Arizona, U.S.A.

Procter, J. (1984). Vegetation of the granitic islands of the Seychelles. In Stoddart, D.R. (ed.), *Biogeography and ecology of the Seychelles islands*. Junk Publishers, The Hague. Pp. 209–220.

Robertson, S.A. (1989). *Flowering plants of the Seychelles (an annotated checklist of angiosperms and gymnosperms with line drawings)*. Royal Botanic Gardens, Kew. 327 pp.

Stoddart, D.R. (1984). Impact of man in the Seychelles. In Stoddart, D.R. (ed.), *Biogeography and ecology of the Seychelles islands*. Junk Publishers, The Hague. Pp. 641–654.

Summerhayes, V.S. (1931). An enumeration of the angiosperms of the Seychelles. *Trans. Linn. Soc. Lond. 2nd Ser. Zool.* 19: 261–299.

Taylor, J.D., Braithwaite, C.J.R., Peake, J.F. and Arnold, F.N. (1979). Terrestrial faunas and habitats of Aldabra during the late Pleistocene. *Phil. Trans. R. Soc. Lond. B.* 286: 47–66.

Vercoutre, A.T. (1913). Le Silphium des anciens est bien un palmier (*Lodoicea sechellarum* Labill.). *Rev. Gen. Bot.* 25: 31–37.

Walsh, R.P.D. (1984). Climate of the Seychelles. In Stoddart, D.R. (ed.), *Biogeography and ecology of the Seychelles islands*. Junk Publishers, The Hague. Pp. 39–62.

## Acknowledgements

This Data Sheet was prepared by Dr Francis Friedmann (Muséum national d'Histoire naturelle, Paris).

# REGIONAL OVERVIEW: SOUTH WEST ASIA AND THE MIDDLE EAST

LOUTFY BOULOS, ANTHONY G. MILLER AND ROBERT R. MILL

**Total land area:** c. 7,078,670 km².

**Population (1990):** 201,600,000.

**Altitude:** -392 m (Dead Sea) to c. 7000 m (Hindu Kush).

**Natural vegetation:** Large parts of the region are sand and rock deserts with sparse dwarf shrubland, or virtually no plant cover in hyper-arid areas. Forest, woodland, steppe, semi-desert and extensive halophytic shrublands, mixed dwarf shrub and herbaceous communities, including thorn-cushion (tragacanthic) communities; Mediterranean areas with maquis, phrygana and broadleaved sclerophyllous woodland.

**Number of vascular plants:** c. 23,000 species.

**Number of regional endemics:** c. 7100 species.

**Vascular plant families:** 219.

**Number of endemic families:** 0 (1 near-endemic family – Dirachmaceae).

**Number of genera:** 2107.

**Number of endemic genera:** 125.

**Important plant families:** Boraginaceae, Caryophyllaceae, Chenopodiaceae, Compositae, Cruciferae, Gramineae, Labiatae, Leguminosae, Liliaceae, Rosaceae.

Sources: Population from United Nations Population Division (World Resources Institute 1992); flora statistics based on Davis, Mill and Kit Tan (1988); Hedge and Wendelbo (1970, 1978); Miller and Nyberg (1991); Shmida (1984); and Zohary (1973).

## Introduction

South West Asia and the Middle East include Asiatic Turkey (Anatolia), Syria, Lebanon, Israel, Jordan, the Sinai Peninsula, Iraq, Iran and the southernmost part of Azerbaijan, the countries of the Arabian Peninsula (including the Socotran Archipelago which is politically part of Yemen) and Afghanistan. The region (as here defined) is bounded in the west by the Suez Canal and Mediterranean Sea, in the north by the southern coast of the Black Sea and the southern states of the former Soviet Union, in the south by the Gulf of Aden and the Arabian Sea, and in the east by Pakistan.

The region is topographically diverse, ranging from high mountains (with peaks exceeding 5000 m in the Elburz and 7000 m in the Hindu Kush) to the lowest point in the world (-392 m at the Dead Sea); and from the fertile alluvial lowlands of Iraq to the almost rainless sand-seas of the Rub' al-Khali in Arabia. One of the most spectacular features of the region is the Syro-African Rift Valley which includes, in its Asiatic part, the Beqa'a Valley in Lebanon, the Dead Sea depression, the Gulf of Aqaba and the Red Sea. Its rifting was accompanied by volcanic activity, which resulted in the formation of extensive lava fields in the eastern part of the Arabian Peninsula. Some of the world's major oil fields are found in the region.

## Geology

For much of its geological past South West Asia was covered by the Tethys Sea, on whose floors thick layers of sedimentary rocks were formed. Relatively recently, in geological terms, these sedimentary rocks were uplifted to form the extensive mountain chains which now dominate the region. The main events are summarised below.

At the beginning of the Mesozoic (c. 245 million years BP) Africa and Asia were part of the super-continent of Pangaea and the region now covered by South West Asia was inundated by the Tethys Sea. Later, during the Triassic (245–208 million years BP) the southern continent of Gondwana broke away from Pangaea and the Tethys Sea spread westwards completely separating Gondwana from the remaining part of Pangaea (now Eurasia). Following the breakup of Gondwana during the Cretaceous (144–66 million years BP), the African Plate (with Arabia attached) began to drift northwards towards Eurasia until, during the Miocene (20–14 million years BP), the two continents met in a series of collisions which resulted in the formation of a series of mountain chains extending from the Alps to the Zagros Mountains. During the same period, the Himalayas were formed by the collision of the Indian Plate and Eurasia. The Mediterranean, Black, Caspian and Aral seas are isolated remnants of the Tethys Sea. The final event of importance was the rifting of the Red Sea some 15 million years BP separating the Arabian Plate from Africa.

The collision of fragments of Gondwana with Eurasia during the Cenozoic was of major importance, not only in shaping the present topography of South West Asia, but also in allowing the Palaeotropical floras from the south to come into contact with the Holarctic floras to the north.

There are two principal geological provinces:

1. **The Arabian Shield**

   This consists of a platform of Pre-Cambrian crystalline rocks and represents a northerly offshoot of the old African Plate. It comprises most of the Arabian Peninsula, Jordan, Syria and southern Iraq. Since the Pre-Cambrian, the Arabian Shield has been more or less stable, subjected only to gentle orogenic movement. Ancient rocks of the shield (over 600 million years BP) are exposed in western Saudi Arabia, but elsewhere are covered by a thick sequence of continental and shallow-water shelf sediments, along with deep marine rocks deposited during the Phanerozoic, when the region was inundated by the Tethys Sea. Aeolian sands cover large parts of the north, east and south of the Arabian Peninsula.

2. **The Irano-Anatolian Folded Zone**

   This represents the southern part of the Eurasian Plate. Sedimentary rocks (deposited in the Tethys Sea) have been deeply folded into a series of mountain chains running in an arc across Turkey, northern Iraq, Iran and northern Oman to Afghanistan. These mountains are part of the great chain of mountains formed during the Cenozoic and which extend along the southern margin of Eurasia, from the Atlas Mountains and European Alps, in the west, to the Himalayas in the east.

## Climate

The climate of South West Asia is extremely diverse, ranging from cool temperate to tropical. Typical Mediterranean conditions are mainly restricted to littoral belts, while the greater part of the area has a continental climate. Winter rains prevail, with the exception of a few regions, such as southern Arabia, southern Iran and the Pontic and Hyrcanian areas of northern Turkey and Iran, which have summer rains. Some hyper-arid regions, such as the Rub' Al-Khali in Saudi Arabia, may receive no rain for several consecutive years. The highest rainfall recorded in the Pontic and Hyrcanian areas is over 2000 mm per annum. The extreme south of the region has a monsoonal climate with rains associated with the south-west (summer) and north-east (winter) monsoons. The easternmost part of Afghanistan, bordering on Kashmir, is also influenced by the south-west monsoon, especially at higher altitudes.

Temperature regimes show great variation over the region. Some areas in the east and south have cloudless summer days, with long hours of sunshine, resulting in low relative humidity and high evaporation rates. Maximum day temperatures in these areas can reach over 50°C, much higher than those at the Equator and among the hottest on Earth. On the other hand, extreme minima (below -50°C) are recorded in some mountains and northern areas. In many parts of the region, such as in parts of south-east Turkey and Arabia, the diurnal temperature range is enormous, sometimes as much as 30°C.

## Vegetation

Since much of the region is arid, drought-resistant vegetation predominates. Large parts of the region are covered with sand and rock deserts which support sparse dwarf shrubland, but plant cover is almost totally absent in some extremely arid areas. Woodland is rare in desert areas, although *Prosopis cineraria* woodland occurs in southern Arabia. Shrubland and drought-deciduous woodland are common at low altitudes in semi-deserts and mountains in the south of the region, whilst at higher altitudes, drought-resistant evergreen woodland is found.

The mountains and steppes of the northern and central parts of the region have a wide variety of vegetation, including evergreen needle-leaved forest, cold-deciduous forest, evergreen and deciduous woodlands, steppe, semi-desert shrubland, halophytic shrubland and large areas of mixed dwarf shrub and herbaceous communities. Thorn-cushion (tragacanthic) communities, usually with *Astragalus* and *Acantholimon* spp., are characteristic of subalpine zones over much of the region.

At low altitudes bordering the Mediterranean are maquis, phrygana and broadleaved sclerophyllous woodland containing *Quercus* spp., *Pistacia* spp., *Laurus nobilis* and *Olea europaea*. Evergreen coniferous forests, dominated by *Pinus* spp., *Abies cilicica* and (in the south) *Cedrus libani*, occur at higher altitudes (above 1000 m). Areas of high-rainfall along the Black Sea and Caspian coasts support cold-deciduous, broadleaved forests including species of *Fagus*, *Acer*, *Carpinus* and *Tilia*. Sino-Himalayan shrubs and trees extend into eastern Afghanistan (e.g. *Cedrus deodara*, *Picea smithiana*).

Extensive areas of halophytic shrubland are found on the salt flats in the eastern part of the Arabian Peninsula, central Iran and in small pockets in the north of the region (such as at Tuz Gölü in Anatolia – CPD Site SWA13). These shrublands are dominated by members of the Chenopodiaceae, such as species of *Arthrocnemum*, *Halocnemum*, *Halopeplus*, *Salsola* and *Suaeda*.

Small patches of mangrove are found along the coasts of the Red Sea, Arabian Gulf and Indian Ocean.

Early civilization began in the "Fertile Crescent" – the plains and valleys drained by the Tigris and Euphrates rivers in what is now Iraq. The region is one of the areas where agriculture first developed about 10,000 years ago. Early farmers domesticated plants and started the process of clearance and modification of natural vegetation in order to grow crops. Over large parts of the region (such as central Anatolia, south-western Arabia and the maquis around the Mediterranean) thousands of years of man's activities have profoundly altered the vegetation. As a result, few "natural" landscapes remain; the original vegetation can only be inferred from small remnants. Some of the least altered landscapes are in the mountains of Turkey, Iran and Afghanistan, the salt flats of Iran and the deserts of Arabia.

## Flora

The region includes c. 23,000 species of vascular plants, of which c. 7100 are endemic to the region. Although there are no endemic families, the Dirachmaceae is a near-endemic, one species being found on Socotra and another in Somalia.

Some 2107 genera are recorded, of which c. 125 are endemic. The most important (largest) are: *Acantholimon*, *Achillea*, *Alcea*, *Allium*, *Anthemis*, *Artemisia*, *Astragalus*,

*Campanula, Centaurea, Cousinia, Delphinium, Echinops, Euphorbia, Ferula, Galium, Iris, Nepeta, Onobrychis, Origanum, Paracaryum, Phlomis, Potentilla, Quercus, Salsola, Salvia, Sideritis, Silene, Stachys, Tamarix, Trifolium* and *Verbascum.*

### TABLE 40. FLORISTIC RICHNESS AND ENDEMISM IN SOUTH WEST ASIAN COUNTRIES

| Country or region | Vascular plant species | Endemic species | % Species endemism |
|---|---|---|---|
| Afghanistan | 4000 | 800 | 20.0 |
| Bahrain | 248 | 0 | 0.0 |
| Iran | 8000 | 1400 | 17.5 |
| Iraq | 3000 | 190 | 6.3 |
| Israel | 2225 | 165 | 7.4 |
| Jordan | 2100 | 145 | 7.3 |
| Kuwait | 282 | 0 | 0.0 |
| Lebanon | 2600 | 311 | 12.0 |
| Oman | 1200 | 73 | 6.1 |
| Qatar | 306 | 0 | 0.0 |
| Saudi Arabia | 2028 | 34 | 1.7 |
| Sinai (Egypt) | 984 | 30 | 3.1 |
| Syria | 3100 | 395 | 13.0 |
| Turkey | 8650 | 2675 | 30.9 |
| United Arab Emirates | 340 | 0 | 0.0 |
| Yemen* (N) | 1650 | 58 | 3.5 |
| Yemen* (S) | 1180 | 77 | 6.5 |
| Socotra (Yemen) | 815 | 230–267 | 28.2–32.7 |

*Yemen was unified in 1991; figures for North Yemen (Yemen Arab Republic), South Yemen (People's Democratic Republic of Yemen) and Socotra are kept separate for convenience.

South West Asia is at a phytogeographical crossroads where two great floristic kingdoms meet: the Holarctic and the Palaeotropical. All the major phytochoria found in South West Asia extend into surrounding regions or are, indeed, centred outside the region. The two major phytochoria are: the Irano-Turanian Regional Centre of Endemism and the Sahara-Sindian Regional Zone. There are also significant areas of the Mediterranean Regional Centre of Endemism in the north-west of the region and the Somali-Masai Regional Centre of Endemism in southern Arabia. There are small penetrations of the Afromontane Regional Centre of Endemism (in south-western Arabia), the Sino-Himalayan Region (in south-east Afghanistan) and the Hyrcano-Euxine Province of the Euro-Siberian Region (along the Black Sea coast of Turkey and the Caspian coast of Iran).

### TABLE 41. FLORISTIC RICHNESS AND ENDEMISM IN SOUTH WEST ASIAN PHYTOCHORIA

| Phytochorion | Area (km²) | Vascular plant species | Endemic species | % Species endemism | Endemic genera |
|---|---|---|---|---|---|
| Irano-Turanian | 2,400,000 | 17,000 | 5100 | 30 | 80 |
| Mediterranean | 175,000 | 3–4000 | 600–800 | 20 | 3–4 |
| Somali-Masai | 375,000 | 1800 | 500 | 28 | 16 |
| Sahara-Sindian | 3,600,000 | 1500 | 100 | 7 | 6 |
| Afromontane | 60,000 | 400 | 55 | 14 | 1 |
| Euro-Siberian | 160,000 | 4000 | 500 | 12 | 5 |
| Sino-Himalayan | 30,000 | 1200 | 50 | 4 | ?0 |

Note: All figures are estimates and relate to the range of the phytochoria within South West Asia and the Middle East. Arrangement here is by number of endemic species. Further details on each phytochorion are provided later in this chapter.

## Useful plants

South West Asia and the Middle East have provided mankind with food, fibre, oil and other economic plants for thousands of years. Examples of the most important indigenous economic plants are listed below.

**Food plants**

| | | |
|---|---|---|
| Amygdalus communis | almond | seeds |
| Beta vulgaris | beet | edible root |
| Castanea sativa | sweet chestnut | edible nut |
| Ceratonia siliqua | carob | edible fruit |
| Cicer arietinum | chickpea | pulse |
| Corylus avellana | hazel | edible nut |
| Corylus colurna | hazel | edible nut |
| Corylus maxima | hazel | edible nut |
| Cydonia vulgaris | quince | edible fruit |
| Ficus carica | fig | edible fruit |
| Ficus sycomorus | sycamore fig | edible fruit |
| Hordeum spp. | barley | grain |
| Juglans regia | walnut | edible nut |
| Lens culinaris | lentil | pulse |
| Olea europaea | olive | edible oil |
| Phoenix dactylifera | date palm | edible fruit |
| Pistacia vera | pistacio | edible nut |
| Prunus armeniaca | apricot | edible fruit |
| Prunus avium | sweet cherry | edible fruit |
| Punica granatum | pomegranate | edible fruit |
| Secale cereale | rye | grain |
| Trigonella foenum-graecum | fenugreek | pulse |
| Triticum spp. | wheats | grain |
| Vicia faba | broad bean | pulse |

**Fibre plants**

| | | |
|---|---|---|
| Linum usitatissimum | flax | textile fibre |

**Oil plants**

| | | |
|---|---|---|
| Carthamus tinctorius | safflower | edible oil |
| Linum usitatissimum | flax | painting oil |
| Olea europaea | olive | edible oil |

**Gums and resins**

| | | |
|---|---|---|
| Astragalus gummifer | tragacanth | gum |
| Boswellia sacra | frankincense | oleo-gum-resin |
| Cistus creticus | ladanum | resin |
| Commiphora spp. | myrrh | oleo-gum-resin |
| Dorema ammoniacum | gum ammoniacum | resin |
| Liquidambar orientalis | storax | balsam |
| Pinus spp. | pine | resin |
| Pistacia lentiscus | mastic | resin |

**Timber trees**

Abies spp.
Acacia spp.
Carpinus betulus
Castanea sativa
Cedrus spp.
Cupressus sempervirens
Fagus orientalis
Juglans regia
Juniperus spp.
Olea europaea
Pinus spp.
Quercus spp.
Ziziphus spina-christi

**Medicinal plants**

Many plants from the region are of medicinal value; some of the most important are:

Achillea fragrantissima
Achillea santolina
Alhagi graecorum
Aloe perryi
Ammi spp.
Anagyris foetida
Anastatica hierochuntica
Artemisia herba-alba
Artemisia judaica
Cannabis sativa
Calotropis procera
Cassia senna
Citrullus colocynthis
Crocus sativus
Cymbopogon proximus
Datura stramonium
Digitalis spp.
Ephedra alata
Eryngium campestre
Ferula asa-foetida
Foeniculum vulgare
Glossostemon bruguieri
Glycyrrhiza spp.

## USEFUL PLANTS ...continued

Haplophyllum tuberculatum
Hyoscyamus spp.
Juniperus phoenicea
Lavandula dentata
Marrubium spp.
Mentha pulegium
Myrtus communis
Ocimum kilimandscharicum
Otostegia fruticosa
Papaver somniferum
Peganum harmala
Retama raetam
Rhamnus spp.
Rhus tripartita
Ricinus communis
Ruta chalepensis
Salvia fruticosa
Symphytum spp.
Teucrium polium
Thymus spp.
Tribulus terrestris
Urginea maritima
Verbascum sinuatum
Verbena officinalis
Ziziphus jujuba

**Dyes**
Alkanna tinctoria
Anchusa italica
Anthemis tinctoria
Arnebia spp.
Asperugo procumbens
Chrozophora tinctoria
Echium italicum
Indigofera spp.
Isatis tinctoria
Lawsonia alba
Lawsonia inermis
Rubia tinctoria

**Essential oils, perfumes, herbs**
Achillea spp.
Artemisia spp.
Lavandula stoechas
Moringa peregrina
Origanum spp.
Rosmarinus officinalis
Satureja spp.
Sideritis spp.
Thymus spp.

**Plants of horticultural value**
Many plants from the region are of horticultural value, especially
bulbous plants; some of the most important are:
Allium spp.
Aloe spp.
Asparagus spp.
Asphodeline spp.
Asphodelus spp.
Begonia socotrana
Bellevalia spp.
Caralluma spp.
Chionodoxa spp.
Colchicum spp.
Crocus spp.
Cyclamen spp.
Dionysia spp.
Exacum affine
Fritillaria spp.
Gagea spp.
Galanthus spp.
Gladiolus spp.
Iris spp.
Ixiolirion tataricum
Lilium spp.
Muscari spp.
Narcissus spp.
Ophrys spp.
Orchis spp.
Ornithogalum spp.
Pancratium spp.
Rosa persica
Scilla spp.
Sternbergia spp.
Tulipa spp.

# Factors causing loss of biodiversity

Much of the region is either desert or under threat of desertification caused by overgrazing on fragile rangelands, poor agricultural practices, inappropriate irrigation practices resulting in the salinization or alkalization of agricultural land, and the clearance of woodland for fuelwood, timber and charcoal production. This is not a recent process in South West Asia; the "Fertile Crescent", between the Tigris and Euphrates rivers, which 4000 years ago was the cradle of civilisation, is now (in many parts) virtually a desert. The process of desertification in most areas seems to be accelerating.

## Population growth

In 1990, the population of the region was estimated to be approximately 201.6 million (World Resources Institute 1992) and is estimated to double within the next 20 to 30 years. Table 42 provides population statistics for each country in the region.

Many factors responsible for the loss of plant biodiversity in the region are directly or indirectly related to population growth. Population increase brings further pressures on the land for increased food production, urban development and dam construction. For example, in Turkey there are plans to construct a dam in the upper reaches of the Tigris and Euphrates rivers. This will not only drown a large, floristically interesting region, but the irrigation water from the reservoirs will inevitably change the composition of the flora over a wide area.

Other important demographic trends throughout the region are the movement of rural populations to urban centres and the disappearance of traditional nomadic lifestyles. In the countries of the Arabian Gulf, immigrant workers make up a significant proportion of the population (e.g. 75% in Qatar and 50% in Saudi Arabia). In other countries, large numbers of people work abroad. For example, prior to the Gulf War 1.5 million Yemenis worked in Saudi Arabia and the Gulf States. However, since 1990 compulsory repatriation has caused major problems. Thus, the influx of people forced to return to Yemen has placed increased pressure on woodlands there, as many people have resorted to gathering wood for fuel and charcoal. In Israel, the annual growth rate has risen to 5.8% since 1990, mainly as a result of immigration.

## Overgrazing

Overgrazing by goats, sheep, cattle and camels is one of the principal causes of desertification in the region. The problem is particularly acute in Saudi Arabia and the Gulf States where traditional nomadic lifestyles and pastoral practices have broken down. Water is now supplied to herds by tankers, and stock is transported by trucks to areas where vegetation has appeared after rain.

## Agriculture

Changing agricultural practices throughout the region are resulting in important wetland sites being drained (e.g. the Hula Swamps in the Rift Valley of northern Israel). Expansion of the area under cultivation, along with the effects of

**TABLE 42. SIZE AND GROWTH OF POPULATION IN SOUTH WEST ASIAN COUNTRIES**

| Country | Area (km²) | Population (millions)[a] | Population density (#/km²) | Annual growth rate[b] (1985–1990) (%) | Estimated population in 2025[b] (millions) |
|---|---|---|---|---|---|
| Afghanistan | 636,267 | 16.56 (1990) | 26.0 | 2.63 | 40.48 |
| Bahrain | 661 | 0.48 (1990) | 726.2 | 3.67 | 1.00 |
| Iran | 1,648,000 | 53.90 (1988) | 32.7 | 2.74 | 113.83 |
| Iraq | 438,446 | 17.80 (1990) | 40.6 | 3.48 | 49.99 |
| Israel | 20,750 | 4.98 (1991) | 240.0 | 1.66 | 6.91 |
| Jordan | 97,668 | 3.17 (1990) | 32.5 | 3.25 | 9.88 |
| Kuwait | 24,281 | 2.04 (1990) | 84.0 | 3.40 | 3.78 |
| Lebanon | 10,400 | 3.00 (1989) | 288.5 | 0.25 | 4.70 |
| Oman | 271,950 | 2.10 (1991) | 7.7 | 3.79 | 4.75 |
| Qatar | 11,437 | 0.37 (1987) | 32.4 | 4.16 | 0.86 |
| Saudi Arabia | 2,401,554 | 14.00 (1990) | 5.8 | 3.96 | 44.75 |
| Syria | 185,170 | 11.30 (1988) | 61.0 | 3.61 | 34.08 |
| Turkey | 779,452 | 56.40 (1990) | 72.4 | 2.08 | 87.70 |
| UAE | 75,150 | 1.80 (1990) | 24.0 | 3.26 | 2.65 |
| Yemen | 477,540 | 12.00 (1990) | 25.1 | 3.42 | 34.57 |

Sources:
[a] Hunter (1992).
[b] World Resources Institute (1992).

increasing use of herbicides, pesticides and fertilisers, is becoming a serious problem in many areas (e.g. on the Çukurova Plain in Turkey). The abandonment of traditional rangeland management in Arabia is leading to serious overgrazing; in Yemen the migration of rural workers to the rich Gulf States has led to the virtual abandonment of the sophisticated systems of terracing in mountain areas, resulting in serious soil erosion on steep slopes. Deep ploughing on the Anatolian plateau is causing a reduction in the abundance of formerly common species. Large areas of prime rangeland in Arabia have been ploughed to grow cereals and other crops.

## Fuelwood harvesting

Wood and charcoal are the main energy sources throughout large parts of the region. There is now a severe fuelwood shortage in many places, particularly in some highland areas, such as south-western Arabia and north-eastern Afghanistan. In Afghanistan, the few remaining forested areas are being rapidly destroyed to meet the fuel requirements of large towns (World Conservation Monitoring Centre 1988). The demand, particularly for charcoal, by urban populations has led to rapid deforestation around towns and cities.

## Logging

The forests of South West Asia have been exploited for timber for millennia. For instance, the lowland forests of the East Mediterranean were largely cleared in ancient times and the forests of Afghanistan in medieval times. It is estimated that the Levantine forests barely cover 5% of their original area. In many areas there is uncontrolled logging, for instance on Jabal an Nusayriyah in Syria. Logging is a particular problem in high rainfall areas, such as north-east Anatolia, where high rainfall on steep mountain slopes causes severe soil erosion.

## Plantation forestry

Plantations are changing the character of the vegetation in some areas. For instance, in order to avert predicted wood and cellulose shortages next century, there are plans to afforest 3000 km² per year over a 10-year period in east Anatolia at the expense of steppe vegetation.

## Plant collecting

In Turkey, commercial gathering of bulbs and corms for the horticultural trade is having a significant effect on wild populations. The main genera collected are *Chionodoxa*, *Crocus*, *Colchicum*, *Cyclamen*, *Galanthus*, *Lilium* and *Scilla*. In some areas entire populations have disappeared. In an effort to control over-harvesting, annual quotas are fixed by the Turkish Government for the numbers of bulbs of certain taxa which may be exported.

In Sinai (Egypt), Jordan and the Arabian Peninsula medicinal herbs are extensively collected for local use and often for commercial purposes, including the export of dried plants. There are hardly any practical steps taken by the local authorities to control this growing activity, although some laws have been recently passed in most of these countries to protect the vegetation in many areas.

## Tourism

Tourist development, particularly along the Mediterranean coastal plains, is having an increasingly serious effect on the vegetation. Tourism in the Mediterranean areas of south-western Turkey, for example, increased dramatically in the 1980s. Much of the associated development was uncontrolled and had little regard for the environment. For example, hotels were built in the Kuçuk Menderes river delta, one of the most endangered wetlands on the west Turkish coast.

The Isaurian and Cilician Taurus (CPD Site SWA15, in part, see Data Sheet) are less threatened than parts of south-west Turkey; however, development of the coastal and delta areas is beginning even here. Ulu Dağ (CPD Site SWA20) (Turkey's first National Park) is protected at present, but any increase in the present levels of tourist use could be detrimental to the flora.

In the Levant, tourist development at Latakia threatens the coastal forest which has an unusual assemblage of species which are highly localized on ophiolitic rock formations.

## Other factors

Over the last few decades, the region has unfortunately suffered from the effects of warfare. Most recently, large parts of the Persian Gulf were affected by oil pollution, while fragile desert soils have been adversely affected by military manoeuvres. In Iraq and Iran, important wetlands have been damaged by military activities, while warfare in Afghanistan has led to the destruction of many forests.

## Conservation

Traditional forms of land management in the region have often ensured the protection of natural resources. For example, traditional Islamic beliefs include respect for nature, while under Jewish law certain trees should not be destroyed. Traditional forms of protected areas such as "hema", in Saudi Arabia, and "mahmeya", in Syria, may have their origins over 2000 years ago, pre-dating Islam, and result from an ancient recognition of the need to conserve scarce and valuable natural resources.

### TABLE 43. PROTECTION SYSTEMS* IN SOUTH WEST ASIAN COUNTRIES

| Country | Number of protected sites >10 km² | Combined area protected* | % of country protected |
|---|---|---|---|
| Afghanistan | 5 | 1834 | 0.29 |
| Bahrain | 0 | 0 | 0.00 |
| Iran | 60 | 75,290 | 4.59 |
| Iraq | 0 | 0 | 0.00 |
| Israel | 20 | 2000 | 9.64 |
| Jordan | 8 | 1004 | 1.03 |
| Kuwait | 1 | 300 | 1.24 |
| Lebanon | 1 | 35 | 0.34 |
| Oman | 6 | 28,633 | 14.21 |
| Qatar | 0 | 0 | 0.00 |
| Saudi Arabia | 10 | 208,556 | 8.68 |
| Syria | 0 | 0 | 0.00 |
| Turkey | 32 | 5570 | 0.71 |
| UAE | 0 | 0 | 0.00 |
| Yemen | 0 | 0 | 0.00 |

Note that the figures presented here refer only to those areas which cover **10 km² or more** and are in IUCN Management Categories I–VIII. It is very important to note that, in some cases, figures include sites which are only partially protected. The combined area protected and percentage of country protected are summations of individual areas and do not take into account areas which may have overlapping boundaries. In some cases, therefore, the figures imply a greater area protected than is really the case. A further important consideration is that many protected areas have been established primarily for their fauna and do not necessarily protect the best areas for plants.

* Source: World Conservation Monitoring Centre (1992).

In recent times, many of the traditional forms of resource management have been abandoned. Today, very little of the region is under effective protection; many important ecosystems are wholly unprotected and under threat. According to Lean, Hinrichsen and Markham (1990), less than 1% of the land in most countries of South West Asia is included in legally protected areas, and in many countries of the region, protected areas exist only on paper, with little or no enforcement of legal protection on the ground. For instance, the coastal strip of Olimpos Beydağları National Park in Turkey has recently been sacrificed to hotel development.

Israel probably has the most effective conservation measures in South West Asia. Numerous species are protected by law. However, even here protected areas are sometimes turned over to agricultural or military use as a result of strategic pressures.

Protected area legislation in Iraq and Syria seems to be on the way; certain areas have been set aside in Syria (e.g. to protect the *Cedrus* forest on Jebal an Nusayriyah), while in Iraq a few conservation areas have been recommended in the Tigris/Euphrates marshes. There are effectively no protected areas in Yemen, but a network has been recommended by UNEP/IUCN. Bahrain, Qatar and United Arab Emirates also lack any protected areas which cover more than 10 km² and which meet IUCN management criteria.

A number of protected areas were planned in Afghanistan, but as yet there is no protective legislation (World Conservation Monitoring Centre 1988). Political unrest brought an abrupt halt to conservation activities in 1979 and no up to date information is available.

A review of the protected areas system and conservation legislation throughout the region is given in IUCN (1992). Table 43 provides a summary of protected area coverage.

## Centres of plant diversity and endemism

The most species-rich and endemic-rich areas for plants are listed below. The list has been developed by staff at the Royal Botanic Garden, Edinburgh, in conjunction with Professor Loutfy Boulos (University of Kuwait) and from advice received from numerous collaborators in the region (see Acknowledgements). 11 areas have been selected for Data Sheet treatment. They contain, or are estimated to contain, more than 1000 vascular plant species, of which more than 100 are endemic to that site or phytogeographic region. Exceptions to this rule are Socotra, which has slightly less than 1000 vascular plant species, but qualifies for Data Sheet treatment on account of its high level of plant endemism, and the Touran Protected Area Biosphere Reserve which has approximately 800 vascular plant species but includes most of the endemics of the Central Iranian deserts.

The distribution of Data Sheet sites broadly reflects the diversity of flora and vegetation within each phytogeographic region (see Table 44 below); in general, phytochoria with large numbers of species and endemics (such as the Irano-Turanian and Mediterranean Regional Centres of Endemism) are allocated proportionately more Data Sheets than phytochoria with fewer species and endemics.

## TABLE 44. NUMBER OF CPD SITES SELECTED FOR EACH PHYTOCHORION

| Phytochorion | Vascular plant species | Endemic species | % Species endemism | No. of CPD sites | No. of Data Sheets |
|---|---|---|---|---|---|
| Irano-Turanian | 17,000 | 5100 | 30 | 7 | 3 |
| Mediterranean | 3–4000 | 600–800 | 20 | 3 | 3 |
| Somali-Masai | 1800 | 500 | 28 | 4 | 2 |
| Sahara-Sindian | 1500 | 100 | 7 | 2 | 0 |
| Afromontane | 400 | 55 | 14 | 1 | 1 |
| Euro-Siberian | 4000 | 500 | 12 | 3 | 2 |
| Sino-Himalayan | 1200 | 50 | 4 | 1 | 0 |

Note: Flora figures are estimates and relate to the range of the phytochoria in South West Asia and Middle East. Arrangement here is by number of endemic species. Further details on each phytochorion are provided later in this chapter.

## TABLE 45. LIST OF SOUTH WEST ASIAN SITES IDENTIFIED AS CENTRES OF PLANT DIVERSITY AND ENDEMISM

The list of sites is arranged below according to the sequence adopted in the Regional Overview. Sites selected for Data Sheet treatment appear in bold.

**SOMALI-MASAI REGIONAL CENTRE OF ENDEMISM**
SWA1.   **Dhofar Fog Oasis** (Oman, Yemen)
SWA2.   Hadramaut (Yemen)
SWA3.   Jebal Areys (Yemen)
SWA4.   **Socotra** (Yemen)

**AFROMONTANE REGIONAL CENTRE OF ENDEMISM**
SWA5.   **Highlands of South-western Arabia** (Saudi Arabia, Yemen)

**SAHARA-SINDIAN REGIONAL ZONE**
SWA6.   Southern Sinai and Northern Hijaz (Egypt, Saudi Arabia)
SWA7.   Harrat Al-Harrah (Saudi Arabia)

**IRANO-TURANIAN REGIONAL CENTRE OF ENDEMISM**
SWA8.   Bamian Ghorat (Afghanistan)
SWA9.   North-east Afghanistan (Afghanistan)
SWA10. **Touran Protected Area Biosphere Reserve** (Iran)
SWA11. Zagros Mountains (Iran)

SWA12. **Anti-Taurus Mountains and Upper Euphrates** (Turkey)
SWA13. Tuz Gölü (Turkey)
SWA14. **Mountains of South-east Turkey, North-west Iran and Northern Iraq** (Turkey, Iran, Iraq)

**MEDITERRANEAN REGIONAL CENTRE OF ENDEMISM**
SWA15. **Isaurian, Lycaonian and Cilician Taurus** (Turkey)
SWA16. **South-west Anatolia** (Turkey)
SWA17. **Levantine Uplands** (Turkey, Syria, Lebanon, Israel, Jordan)

**EURO-SIBERIAN REGION**
SWA18. **Hyrcanian forests** (Iran, Azerbaijan)
SWA19. **North-east Anatolia** (Turkey)
SWA20. Ulu Dağ (Turkey)

**SINO-HIMALAYAN REGION**
SWA21. Safed Koh (Afghanistan)

The list below is arranged alphabetically by country for cross-reference purposes. Sites selected for Data Sheet treatment appear in bold. Numbers refer to site numbers used in the Regional Overview.

**AFGHANISTAN**
SWA8.   Bamian Ghorat
SWA9.   North-east Afghanistan
SWA21. Safed Koh

**AZERBAIJAN**
SWA18. **Hyrcanian forests**

**EGYPT**
SWA6.   Southern Sinai and Northern Hijaz

**IRAN**
SWA10. **Touran Protected Area Biosphere Reserve**
SWA11. Zagros Mountains
SWA14. **Mountains of South-east Turkey, North-west Iran and Northern Iraq**
SWA18. **Hyrcanian forests**

**IRAQ**
SWA14. **Mountains of South-east Turkey, North-west Iran and Northern Iraq**

**ISRAEL**
SWA17. **Levantine Uplands**

**JORDAN**
SWA17. **Levantine Uplands**

**LEBANON**
SWA17. **Levantine Uplands**

**OMAN**
SWA1.   **Dhofar Fog Oasis**

**SAUDI ARABIA**
SWA5.   **Highlands of South-western Arabia**
SWA6.   Southern Sinai and Northern Hijaz
SWA7.   Harrat Al-Harrah

**SYRIA**
SWA17. **Levantine Uplands**

**TURKEY**
SWA12. **Anti-Taurus Mountains and Upper Euphrates**
SWA13. Tuz Gölü
SWA14. **Mountains of South-east Turkey, North-west Iran and Northern Iraq**
SWA15. **Isaurian, Lycaonian and Cilician Taurus**
SWA16. **South-west Anatolia**
SWA17. **Levantine Uplands**
SWA19. **North-east Anatolia**
SWA20. Ulu Dağ

**YEMEN**
SWA1.   **Dhofar Fog Oasis**
SWA2.   Hadramaut
SWA3.   Jebal Areys
SWA4.   **Socotra**
SWA5.   **Highlands of South-western Arabia**

## MAP 16. CENTRES OF PLANT DIVERSITY AND ENDEMISM: SOUTH WEST ASIA AND THE MIDDLE EAST

The map shows the locations of the CPD Data Sheet sites for the region superimposed on the main phytogeographical areas or phytochoria.

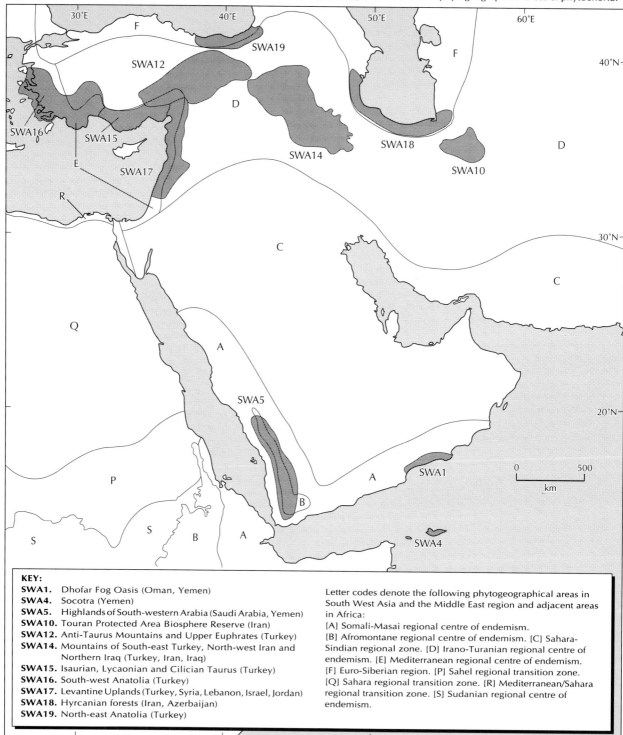

**KEY:**

**SWA1.** Dhofar Fog Oasis (Oman, Yemen)
**SWA4.** Socotra (Yemen)
**SWA5.** Highlands of South-western Arabia (Saudi Arabia, Yemen)
**SWA10.** Touran Protected Area Biosphere Reserve (Iran)
**SWA12.** Anti-Taurus Mountains and Upper Euphrates (Turkey)
**SWA14.** Mountains of South-east Turkey, North-west Iran and Northern Iraq (Turkey, Iran, Iraq)
**SWA15.** Isaurian, Lycaonian and Cilician Taurus (Turkey)
**SWA16.** South-west Anatolia (Turkey)
**SWA17.** Levantine Uplands (Turkey, Syria, Lebanon, Israel, Jordan)
**SWA18.** Hyrcanian forests (Iran, Azerbaijan)
**SWA19.** North-east Anatolia (Turkey)

Letter codes denote the following phytogeographical areas in South West Asia and the Middle East region and adjacent areas in Africa:

[A] Somali-Masai regional centre of endemism.
[B] Afromontane regional centre of endemism. [C] Sahara-Sindian regional zone. [D] Irano-Turanian regional centre of endemism. [E] Mediterranean regional centre of endemism. [F] Euro-Siberian region. [P] Sahel regional transition zone. [Q] Sahara regional transition zone. [R] Mediterranean/Sahara regional transition zone. [S] Sudanian regional centre of endemism.

# SOMALI-MASAI REGIONAL CENTRE OF ENDEMISM

This region occupies a large part of tropical North-east and East Africa extending across the Red Sea into South West Asia where it is restricted to the south of the Arabian Peninsula and Socotra. To the north (and inland) it is bounded by the deserts of the Sahara Regional Transitional Zone and at higher altitudes, above about 1500 m, it grades into Afromontane vegetation. Within South West Asia it covers an area of c. 375,000 km².

## Climate

The climate is arid to semi-arid with a mean annual rainfall of 100–500 mm; some coastal areas are much drier. Rainfall is bi-seasonal (summer and winter) with the summer rain in most areas heavier and more predictable. Precipitation from fog plays an important role in the development of the vegetation in some areas (e.g. Dhofar, CPD Site SWA1 – see Data Sheet on Dhofar Fog Oasis), where it can increase the effective precipitation by several hundred percent.

## Flora

This is undoubtedly the floristically richest region in Arabia. Endemism is particularly high in certain succulent genera (e.g. *Aloe, Caralluma* and *Euphorbia*). About one third (c. 250 spp.) of the species and nine genera are endemic to the Socotran archipelago.

| | |
|---|---|
| Number of vascular species: | 1800 |
| Number of endemic species: | 500 |
| Regional endemism: | 28% |
| Endemic families: | 1 (near-endemic) |
| Endemic genera: | 16 (14 Socotra) |

Note: The above figures refer only to the part of the region lying in South West Asia. Many species extend into Somalia and beyond.

## Main vegetation types

The most common vegetation type is open deciduous shrubland dominated by *Acacia* and *Commiphora* spp. and with many succulents, such as species of *Aloe, Caralluma* and some *Euphorbia*, often 3–4 m high and sometimes forming dense thickets. Riparian woodland (usually with *Ficus* spp.) develops along larger wadis. Evergreen shrubland occurs on hills and lower slopes of mountains. This vegetation is often transitional with Afromontane vegetation at higher altitudes. In Dhofar, a unique fog-woodland, dominated by *Anogeissus dhofarica*, occurs on the seaward slopes of mountains (see Data Sheet on Dhofar Fog Oasis, CPD Site SWA1). Large areas are covered with semi-desert grassland and, as in North-east Africa, this is probably derived from degraded deciduous bushland.

## Species of economic importance

| | | |
|---|---|---|
| *Aloe* spp. | aloe | glucosides |
| *Boswellia sacra* | frankincense | oleo-gum-resins |
| *Catha edulis* | qat | stimulant, narcotic |
| *Commiphora* spp. | myrrh | oleo-gum-resins |
| *Gossypium* spp. | cotton | fibre |
| *Hordeum* spp. | barley | cereal |
| *Medicago sativa* | alfalfa | forage |
| *Panicum* spp. | millet | cereal |
| *Sorghum bicolor* | sorghum | cereal |
| *Triticum* spp. | wheats | cereal |

## Factors causing loss of biodiversity

Overgrazing by goats and camels, and to a lesser extent cattle, is the main agent responsible for the loss of the original vegetation. In recent years, overgrazing has been exacerbated by increased stocking rates associated with new wells being sunk for drinking water, improved veterinary services and a breakdown in traditional (and more environmentally sympathetic) pastoral practices. Both human and livestock populations have increased in recent years.

Fuelwood cutting and timber harvesting for building have also been important factors responsible for the removal woody vegetation over much of the area.

## Conservation

Apart from Asir National Park (4150 km²) in Saudi Arabia, there are no protected areas covering the region. Protected areas are planned in southern Oman.

## Centres of plant diversity and endemism

### Oman, Yemen

### SWA1. Dhofar Fog Oasis

– see Data Sheet.

### Yemen

### SWA2. Hadramaut

Area: c. 30,000 km². Covers part of the Hadramaut and Mahra Governorates comprising, for the most part, an inhospitable limestone plateau deeply dissected by large wadis. Altitude: mostly c. 1000 m, attaining 2220 m.
❖ Flora: Botanically the least-known area of the Arabian Peninsula and possibly the least explored region in South West Asia. Almost 40 endemic species are recorded from the region, most are poorly known.
❖ Conservation: No legal protection.

### SWA3. Jebal Areys

An isolated, frequently fog-covered, volcanic massif, 150 km east of Aden on the southern coast of Yemen. Area: 1700 km². Altitude: 0–1705 m.
❖ Vegetation: Semi-desert grassland at lower altitudes, deciduous shrubland above, and succulent shrubland dominated by *Euphorbia balsamifera* on upper, seaward, fog-affected slopes.
❖ Flora: 15 endemics, including the extraordinary leafless succulent *Kleinia deflersii*.
❖ Conservation: No legal protection.

### SWA4. Socotra

– see Data Sheet.

## AFROMONTANE REGIONAL CENTRE OF ENDEMISM

This region is described by White (1983) as an archipelago-like centre of endemism. It consists of scattered "islands" of vegetation on high mountains throughout Africa. In South West Asia, Afromontane vegetation is found only on the mountains of south-western Arabia in Saudi Arabia and Yemen at altitudes above 2000 m. It covers an area of c. 60,000 km². White and Léonard (1991) note that the southern Arabian Afromontane flora is extremely impoverished compared to that of Africa. Of the 12 tree species which may collectively be used to identify Afromontane forests in Africa, only *Nuxia congesta* is found in Arabia. In Arabia, Afromontane vegetation merges into Somali-Masai vegetation at lower altitudes.

## Climate

The rainfall (300–500 mm per annum rising to c. 1000 mm in the wettest areas) is bi-seasonal, falling in March and from July to September. The mean monthly temperature is over 20°C in summer and about 10°C. Frosts are frequent in winter.

## Flora

| | |
|---|---|
| **Number of vascular species:** | 400 |
| **Number of endemic species:** | 55 |
| **Regional endemism:** | 14% |
| **Endemic families:** | 0 |
| **Endemic genera:** | 1 |

Note: The above figures refer only to the part of the region lying in South West Asia.

## Main vegetation types

Virtually no Afromontane vegetation has survived undisturbed, and most has gone following thousands of years of clearance for agriculture. In the Asir Mountains of Saudi Arabia well-developed *Juniperus procera* woodland remains intact. In Yemen, the vegetation probably consisted of evergreen bushland and thicket with *Acacia origena*, *Hypericum revolutum*, *Buddleja polystachya*, *Erica arborea*, *Rosa abyssinica* and *Nuxia congesta*.

## Species of economic importance

| | | |
|---|---|---|
| *Catha edulis* | qat | stimulant, narcotic |
| *Sorghum* spp. | sorghum | cereal |
| *Ziziphus spina-christi* | sidr | browse, timber, edible fruits |

## Conservation

In Saudi Arabia the Asir National Park (4150 km²), established in 1981, is managed by the General Department for National Parks in the Ministry of Agriculture and Water. There are no protected areas in Yemen but several sites in the highlands have been recommended for protection by UNEP/IUCN.

## Factors causing loss of biodiversity

Little natural vegetation has escaped clearance for cultivation. That which remains is threatened by uncontrolled cutting of wood for fuel, timber and charcoal production, and by severe overgrazing. Recently, lack of maintenance of field terraces has led to severe soil erosion.

## Centres of plant diversity and endemism

### Saudi Arabia, Yemen

### SWA5. Highlands of South-western Arabia

– see Data Sheet.

## SAHARA-SINDIAN REGIONAL ZONE

This vast region extends from north-west Africa to the deserts of Sind in Pakistan and north-west India; in South West Asia it covers some 3,600,000 km². It is a region of very low rainfall (usually below 100 mm per annum) with some areas receiving no rain for many successive years. The topography includes sand seas, gravel and stony plains, exposed rock surfaces, mountains and sabkha (saline flats). The vegetation is sparse.

## Flora

| | |
|---|---|
| **Number of vascular species:** | c. 1500 |
| **Number of endemic species:** | c. 100 |
| **Regional endemism:** | 7% |
| **Endemic families:** | 0 |
| **Endemic genera:** | 6 |

Note: The above figures refer only to the part of the region in South West Asia.

This is the largest region but floristically the poorest phytochorion in South West Asia, with low levels of both specific and generic endemism. For example, in the 500,000 km² of the Rub' al-Khali in southern Arabia there are only 37 species, of which one is endemic. Many of the species of the Sahara-Sindian Regional Zone occur over very wide ranges and extend both to the east and west of the region; endemics mostly occur in the mountains.

## Species of economic importance

| | | |
|---|---|---|
| *Phoenix dactylifera* | date palm | dates |
| *Prosopis cineraria* | Arabian mesquite | timber, browse |
| *Tamarix* spp. | tamarisk | timber |
| *Ziziphus spina-christi* | sidr | timber, edible fruits, browse |

## Factors causing loss of biodiversity

Much of the region is arid or hyper-arid, or under threat of desertification caused by severe overgrazing by sheep, goats and camels. Inappropriate irrigation has resulted in salinization or alkalization of agricultural land. Woodlands are under severe threat from fuelwood cutting, timber harvesting and the production of charcoal. Some rangeland is used for irrigated cereal and fodder production.

## Conservation

No overall assessment of protection status is available. Where areas have been fenced in the Arabian Peninsula, the recovery of vegetation has been spectacular.

## Centres of plant diversity and endemism

### Egypt (Sinai), Saudi Arabia

### SWA6. Southern Sinai and Northern Hijaz

Area: 16,000 km².
❖ Flora: c. 700 vascular plant species, of which c. 35 are endemic; 1 endemic genus. The flora includes Mediterranean, Irano-Turanian and Saharo-Sindian elements. Jabal Dibbagh, in north-west Saudi Arabia, is probably the richest area for endemics in extra-tropical Arabia outside Oman.
❖ Conservation: No legal protection in Saudi Arabia, but some areas protected in Sinai.

### Saudi Arabia

### SWA7. Harrat Al-Harrah

An important desert area in northern Saudi Arabia consisting largely of black lava flows. Area: 45,000 km².
❖ Flora: c. 300 vascular plant species. No endemics are known.
❖ Conservation: 13,000 km² are in a Protected Area administered by the National Commission for Wildlife Conservation and Development of Saudi Arabia.

## IRANO-TURANIAN REGIONAL CENTRE OF ENDEMISM

The Irano-Turanian covers 2,400,000 km², extending eastwards from Anatolia (Asiatic Turkey) to include most of Syria, Iran and north-east Afghanistan, northern Iraq and parts of Lebanon, Jordan and Israel. Outside South West Asia, it extends northwards into Central Asia (including most of Kazakhstan) and eastwards to the Tien Shan and Altai mountain chains (see Regional Overview on Central and Northern Asia). It is topographically very diverse, including deserts, low plains, high plateaux and high mountains.

## Climate

Most of the region experiences severely cold winters (mean 7.5°C to -5°C, with extremes dropping to -30°C to -40°C) and hot, dry summers (mean 20–30°C, reaching 45°C). Rainfall varies from 100 mm to over 1000 mm, most falling in winter and spring.

## Flora

| | |
|---|---|
| Number of vascular species: | 17,000 |
| Number of endemic species: | 5100 |
| Regional endemism: | 30% |
| Endemic families: | 0 |
| Endemic genera: | 80 |

Note: The above figures refer only to the part of the region lying in South West Asia.

The Irano-Turanian is one of the richest centres of speciation in the Holarctic Kingdom (Frey and Probst 1986) and it is floristically the richest area in South West Asia. The flora is dominated by several genera with large numbers of species, including *Astragalus* (c. 1400 spp.), *Cousinia* (c. 660 spp.), *Acantholimon* (c. 120 spp.) and *Centaurea* (c. 260 spp.), all with at least 60% of their species endemic to the region. The mountains of north-east Afghanistan, Iran and Iraq constitute an important centre of speciation for many Irano-Turanian genera.

## Main vegetation types

Drought-tolerant vegetation formations dominate the region. On the mountains there are extensive areas of evergreen needle-leaved forest, mixed evergreen forest, deciduous forest and evergreen and deciduous woodlands. Open woodland, dwarf shrubland and herbaceous formations dominate the plains. There are significant areas of halophytic shrubland, particularly in central Iran. Thorn-cushion (tragacanthic) formations are characteristic of subalpine zones.

## Species of economic importance

The region is an important centre of origin of many cultivated plants. Numerous primitive strains are still in cultivation. Amongst the most important of these are cereals, including species and land races of *Aegilops*, *Hordeum*, *Secale* and *Triticum*. The region is particularly rich in Leguminosae, with many genera important for fodder and pulses (e.g. *Astragalus*, *Cicer*, *Lathyrus*, *Pisum*, *Trifolium* and *Vicia*). Examples of useful plants include:

| | | |
|---|---|---|
| Amygdalus communis | almond | edible nut |
| Cicer arietinum | chickpea | pulse |
| Hordeum vulgare | barley | cereal |
| Ficus carica | fig | edible fruit |
| Lens culinaris | lentil | pulse |
| Linum usitatissimum | flax | oil and textile fibre |
| Pistacia vera | pistachio | edible nut |
| Secale cereale | rye | cereal |
| Triticum aestivum | wheat | cereal |

## Factors causing loss of biodiversity

Overgrazing by sheep and goats; cutting of trees for timber, fuelwood and charcoal production; dam building.

## Conservation

There are many small or modest-sized protected areas, particularly in Iran and Turkey. Many protected areas have been established for game, rather than for plant conservation.

## Centres of plant diversity and endemism

### Afghanistan

For a discussion of endemism in Afghanistan, see Hedge and Wendelbo (1970). The following areas are floristically rich and contain numerous endemics:

### SWA8. Bamian Ghorat

This area represents an isolated extension of the flora of north-east Afghanistan and adjacent Central Asia and apparently includes a large number of endemics. However, no detailed information is currently available.

### SWA9. North-east Afghanistan

The mountains of north-east Afghanistan are among the most floristically rich areas in South West Asia. Wendelbo (1971) and Hedge and Wendelbo (1970) point out that many Irano-Turanian genera (e.g. *Eremurus*, *Eremostachys* and *Acantholimon*) have important centres of species diversity in north-east Afghanistan and adjacent areas of Central Asia. Kamelin (1965) lists 58 endemic genera (from 14 families) in adjacent Central Asia; this region contains an extension of that flora. According to Hedge and Wendelbo (1970), it is doubtful if any area of comparable size in temperate Asia exhibits a higher degree of endemism.

### Iran

For a discussion of endemism in Iran, see Hedge and Wendelbo (1978).

### SWA10. Touran Protected Area Biosphere Reserve

– see Data Sheet.

### SWA11. Zagros Mountains

A complex system of parallel mountain ridges divided by deep intermontane valleys extending south-east from near the Turkish border for over 1000 km, in an arc between 100 and 200 km wide, to near Bandar Abbas in southern Iran. Limestones predominate, often in folded beds of great thickness. The climate is continental with hot summers and cold winters. Rainfall occurs mainly in winter (often as snow, which can lie for several months on the higher slopes in the north). Rainfall is markedly less on the eastern side of the mountains and also declines gradually to the south. Altitude: the highest point is Kuh-i-Dinar (4276 m) and there are many peaks above 3000 m.

❖ Vegetation: Drought-tolerant vegetation predominates, with evergreen needle-leaved forest, mixed evergreen forest, deciduous forest and evergreen and deciduous woodlands with *Quercus* spp., *Pistacia* spp. and rosaceous shrubs. Thorn-cushion (tragacanthic) formations are found in the subalpine zone.

❖ Flora: No detailed figures available, but considered to be one of the richest areas in the Irano-Turanian Regional Centre of Endemism. Several endemic genera are known, including *Acanthocardamum*, *Pseudofortuynia*, *Straussiella* and *Zerdana* (all Cruciferae).

❖ Threats: Overgrazing, fuelwood cutting, charcoal production and uncontrolled removal of timber.

❖ Conservation: A number of protected areas have been established. However, no information is available on their present status.

### Turkey

### SWA12. Anti-Taurus Mountains and Upper Euphrates

– see Data Sheet.

### SWA13. Tuz Gölü

A vast inland salt lake about 130 km south-east of Ankara. Area: fluctuates considerably in extent, both seasonally and from year to year, but is on average about 1100 km². Altitude: 905 m. The lake itself is very shallow, being only 30–60 cm deep in some seasons.

❖ Vegetation: *Artemisia fragrans* steppe surrounds the outermost saline zone of *Salsola inermis*, *Limonium iconium*, *Cynodon dactylon* and *Aeluropus lagopoides*. The inner saline zone includes almost pure stands of *Halocnemum strobilaceum*. *Frankenia hirsuta/Limonium iconium* association occurs on gentle slopes; *Petrosimonia birandii* on mud near the lake margin; and *Puccinellia distans/Limonium gmelinii*, together with *Juncus maritimus*, *Limonium globuliferum* and *Salicornia europaea*, in areas of seasonally flooded sandy clay soils (Birand 1960; Zohary 1973).

❖ Flora: 12 vascular plant taxa are endemic to Tuz Gölü, including *Kalidiopsis wagenitzii* (an endemic genus). Several more taxa are near-endemics found also in saltmarshes around Bor and Aksaray. Chenopodiaceae and Plumbaginaceae are well represented in the flora. There are at least 35 species of the former, including 6 endemics (2 being monotypic endemic genera) and 14 species of the latter family (3 endemics).

❖ Threats: Relatively safe; summer droughts and seasonal waterlogging makes most of the basin unfavourable for agriculture. However, extensive drainage schemes on the plains have seriously reduced, and in many cases eliminated, entire wetland ecosystems.

❖ Conservation: No legal protection, but proposed as a protected area (Green and Drucker 1990).

## Turkey, Iran, Iraq

### SWA14. Mountains of South-east Turkey, North-west Iran and Northern Iraq

– see Data Sheet.

## MEDITERRANEAN REGIONAL CENTRE OF ENDEMISM

The Mediterranean region comprises a narrow belt along the Mediterranean Sea, from the west and south coasts of Turkey southwards to Israel, and covers c. 175,000 km². It consists of a coastal plain beyond which are mountains attaining 3000 m or more. In Turkey, the boundary between the Mediterranean region and the Irano-Turanian to the east is poorly defined, whereas in Lebanon, Syria and Israel the boundary between the two regions is clearly demarcated. There are small enclaves of Mediterranean vegetation along the Black Sea coast.

## Climate

The climate of the Mediterranean region is characterised by mild, wet winters and warm, dry summers.

## Flora

| | |
|---|---|
| Number of vascular species: | 3–4000 |
| Number of endemic species: | 600–800 |
| Regional endemism: | c. 20% |
| Endemic families: | 0 |
| Endemic genera: | 3–4 |

Note: The above figures refer only to the part of the region lying in South West Asia.

The region is strongly influenced by adjacent Irano-Turanian vegetation. It is particularly rich in annuals, which may represent up to 50% of the total number of species. There are many neo-endemics and relatively few palaeo-endemics.

## Main vegetation types

At lower altitudes (up to c. 1000 m) maquis, phrygana and broadleaved sclerophyllous woodland with *Quercus* spp., *Pistacia* spp., *Laurus nobilis* and *Olea europaea* predominates. Evergreen coniferous forests, dominated by *Pinus nigra*, *P. brutia* and *P. halepensis*, with *Abies cilicica* and *Cedrus libani* in the southern part of the region, occur above 1000 m altitude.

## Species of economic importance

| | | |
|---|---|---|
| *Amygdalus communis* | almond | edible nut |
| *Citrus sinensis* | orange | edible fruit |
| *Citrus* spp. | grapefruit, lemon, mandarin | edible fruit |
| *Ficus carica* | fig | edible fruit |
| *Juglans regia* | walnut | edible nut |
| *Olea europaea* | olive | edible oil, timber |
| *Prunus armeniaca* | apricot | edible fruit |
| *Triticum* spp. | wheats | cereal |
| *Vitis vinifera* | grapevine | wine |

There are also many legumes, including species of *Cicer*, *Lens*, *Medicago*, *Phaseolus*, *Pisum* and *Vicia*.

## Factors causing loss of biodiversity

Logging and clearance of forests for agriculture; overgrazing by sheep and goats; draining of wetlands for agriculture; commercial collecting of ornamental bulbs and corms for export; urbanisation; uncontrolled tourist development, especially along the coast.

## Centres of plant diversity and endemism

### Turkey

### SWA15. Isaurian, Lycaonian and Cilician Taurus

– see Data Sheet.

### SWA16. South-west Anatolia

– see Data Sheet.

### Turkey, Syria, Lebanon, Israel, Jordan

### SWA17. Levantine Uplands

– see Data Sheet.

## EURO-SIBERIAN REGION

In South-West Asia, this region is represented by the Hyrcano-Euxine Province of northern Turkey (Euxine subprovince) and northern Iran (Hyrcanian subprovince). It covers an area of c. 160,000 km².

## Climate

The region experiences warm, wet summers (rainfall 600–2600 mm per annum) and mild winters.

## Flora

| | |
|---|---|
| **Number of vascular species:** | c. 4000 |
| **Number of endemic species:** | c. 500 |
| **Regional endemism:** | c. 12.5% |
| **Endemic families:** | 0 |
| **Endemic genera:** | c. 5 |

Note: The above figures refer only to the part of the region lying in South West Asia.

Species endemism is lower than in the adjacent Irano-Turanian region but there are some significant relict Arcto-Tertiary and Indo-Malesian taxa for which the region was a refuge during the ice-ages (Frey and Probst 1986).

## Main vegetation types

Broadleaved deciduous forests, with conifers (*Abies* spp., *Picea* spp. and *Pinus* spp.) at higher altitudes in the Euxine subprovince, but significantly absent from the Hyrcanian subprovince. Characteristic genera include *Acer*, *Carpinus*, *Fagus*, *Pterocarya*, *Quercus*, *Tilia*, *Ulmus* and *Zelkova*. The endemic genus *Parrotia* is an important component of the Hyrcanian forest vegetation.

## Species of economic importance

Cherries (*Cerasus* spp.), hazelnuts (*Corylus avellana*); timber trees (e.g. *Carpinus* spp., *Castanea sativa*, *Fagus orientalis* and *Quercus* spp.); ornamental bulbous species (*Cyclamen*, *Galanthus*, *Lilium* and *Scilla*).

## Factors causing loss of biodiversity

Uncontrolled and illegal logging; clearance of forests for agriculture; commercial collection of ornamental bulbs and corms for export.

## Centres of plant diversity and endemism

### Iran, Azerbaijan

### SWA18. Hyrcanian forests

– see Data Sheet.

### Turkey

### SWA19. North-east Anatolia

– see Data Sheet.

### SWA20. Ulu Dağ

A range of mountains about 10–15 km south-east of Bursa in north-west Anatolia. It is a somewhat isolated outcrop in the western part of the Pontic Mountains, which reach their greatest heights in North-east Anatolia (CPD Site SWA19, see Data Sheet). The lower slopes of Ulu Dağ are of schists and gneiss, but the upper part of the massif (above 2200 m) is hard crystalline limestone. Altitude: up to 2543 m.

❖ Vegetation: Dense beech (*Fagus orientalis*) forest on lower slopes between 600–1400 m; fir (*Abies bornmuelleriana*) forest up to the tree line (c. 2000 m). Calcareous summit vegetation includes rock and scree communities with *Phaeopappus drabifolius*, *Anthemis carpathica*, *Achillea multifida*, *Saxifraga adscendens*, *S. exarata*, *Veronica gentianoides* and the endemics *Aubrieta olympica* and *Lamium veronicifolium* (Quézel and Pamukçuoğlu 1970).

  Grazed meadows and subalpine moorland includes sclerophyllous grasses (e.g. *Bellardiochloa violacea*), *Astragalus* spp. and shrubby labiates. Moorland, dominated by *Juniperus nana*, occurs on metamorphic slopes; calcareous alpine meadows include *Genista lydia* and *Hypericum* spp. *Nardus stricta* grassland includes a disjunct population of *Bruckenthalia spiculiflora* (whose main centre of distribution is in the Balkans).

❖ Flora: c. 30 vascular plant species and several infraspecific taxa are endemic to Ulu Dağ. Several more taxa are near-endemics, occurring on Ulu Dağ and one or more other mountains of western Anatolia. Other species show a disjunction between their main centres on the eastern Pontic Range of north-east Anatolia and an outlier on Ulu Dağ. Many Euro-Siberian species found on Ulu Dağ occur nowhere else in Anatolia. The mountain is therefore of considerable phytogeographical interest.

❖ Threats: Expansion of the present level of tourism, especially that associated with the ski resort, and mining activities (copper, coal and tungsten are, or have been, mined on the slopes of the mountain).

❖ Conservation: The mountain and its environs were designated in 1961 as Turkey's first National Park, covering 113 km².

## SINO-HIMALAYAN REGION

Within South West Asia, the Sino-Himalayan Region is represented by a relatively small area (c. 30,000 km²) in the extreme east in the Nuristan and Laghman regions of eastern Afghanistan (bordering Jammu and Kashmir), a tract of rugged mountains and hillsides dissected by streams in deep valleys. The area is sparsely populated.

## Climate

The region is the only part of South West Asia to be influenced by the south-west monsoon; the area also receives winter rains.

## Flora

| | |
|---|---|
| **Number of vascular species:** | c. 1200 |
| **Number of endemic species:** | c. 50 |
| **Regional endemism:** | c. 4% |
| **Endemic families:** | 0 |
| **Endemic genera:** | 0 – few |

Note: The above figures refer only to the part of the region lying in South West Asia.

## Main vegetation types

Sclerophyllous evergreen woodland at lowest levels; a broad belt of mixed *Quercus*, *Pyrus pashia* and *Parrotiopsis* forest between 1300–2000 m; above this *Quercus semecarpifolia* occurs with *Taxus wallichiana*, *Syringa emodi*; *Pinus gerardiana* (xerophytic) occurs between 2100–2500 m; *Cedrus deodara* occurs between 2500–3100 m; *Picea smithiana* and *Abies* spp., with *Pseudomertensia edelbergii* (Boraginaceae) and *Lilium polyphyllum* common in Kashmir at the highest levels where rainfall is greatest. Above the tree-line, subalpine thickets of *Juniperus* occur. Himalayan, species-rich, alpine meadows are found above c. 5000 m, containing many alpines common in Kashmir, including *Saussurea* spp., *Saxifraga flagellaris*, *Paraquilegia anemonoides*, *Ermannia himalayensis*, and others.

## Species of economic importance

The area has several important timber species, such as *Cedrus deodara* and other conifers.

## Factors causing loss of biodiversity

Uncontrolled exploitation of woodland for timber and fuelwood.

## Centres of plant diversity and endemism

### Afghanistan

### SWA21. Safed Koh

This area represents the westernmost extension of the Sino-Himalayan area. It is a relatively small mountainous area rising to 4761 m on Mt Sikaram with relatively high (450–800 mm) summer monsoonal rainfall.

❖ Vegetation: Cedar (*Cedrus deodara*) forest between 2500–3100 m in areas with 450–650 mm rainfall, replaced by *Juniperus seravschanica* in drier areas. Mixed forest, with *Picea smithiana*, *Abies wallichiana* and *Quercus semecarpifolia*, between 2900–3300 m, in high rainfall (>800 mm) areas. For a more detailed description of the vegetation, see Freitag (1971).

❖ Flora: The flora has affinities with that of the Himalayas (see Regional Overview on the Indian Subcontinent). Endemics include *Primula edelbergi*, *Rhododendron afghanicum* and *R. collettianum*.

❖ Threats: The coniferous woodlands of this area are unique in Afghanistan and are seriously threatened by uncontrolled felling.

❖ Conservation: No information is available on the present status of this area.

## References

Ali, S.I. and Qaiser, M. (1985). A phytogeographical analysis of the phanerogams of Pakistan and Kashmir. *Proc. Roy. Soc. Edinburgh* 89B: 89–101.

Birand, H. (1960). Erste Vegetations-Untersuchungen in der Zentralanatolischen Steppe. *Bot. Jahrb.* 79: 256–296.

Boulos, L. (1985). The Middle East. In Goodin, J.R. and Northington, D.K. (eds), *Plant resources of arid and semi-arid lands*. Academic Press. Pp. 129–185.

Brenan, J.P.M. (1978). Some aspects of the phytogeography of tropical Africa. *Ann. Missouri Bot. Gard.* 65: 437–478.

Danin, A. (1985). Flora and vegetation of Sinai. *Proc. Roy. Soc. Edinburgh* 89B: 159–168.

Davis, P.H. (1971). Distribution patterns in Anatolia with particular reference to endemism. In Davis, P.H., Harper, P.C. and Hedge I.C. (eds), *Plant life of South West Asia*. Botanical Society of Edinburgh. Pp. 15–27.

Davis, P.H. (ed.) (1965-1985). *Flora of Turkey and the East Aegean Islands*. Edinburgh University Press, Edinburgh. (9 vols and Supplement; for latter see Davis, Mill and Tan 1988.)

Davis, P.H., Harper, P.C. and Hedge, I.C. (eds) (1971). *Plant life of South West Asia*. Botanical Society of Edinburgh. 335 pp.

Davis, P.H., Mill, R.R. and Kit Tan (1988). *Flora of Turkey and the East Aegean Islands*, Vol. 10 (Supplement). Edinburgh University Press, Edinburgh.

Freitag, H. (1971). Studies in the natural vegetation of Afghanistan. In Davis, P.H., Harper, P.C. and Hedge, I.C. (eds), *Plant life of South West Asia*. Botanical Society of Edinburgh. Pp. 89–106.

Freitag, H. (1985). Notes on the distribution, climate and flora of the sand deserts of Iran and Afghanistan. *Proc. Roy. Soc. Edinburgh* 89B: 135–146.

Frey, W. and Probst, W. (1986). A synopsis of the vegetation of Iran. *Beih. Tübinger Atlas Vorderen Orient*. A24: 9–43.

Green, M.J.B. and Drucker, G.R.F. (1990). Current status of protected areas and threatened mammal species in the Saharo-Gobian region. World Conservation Monitoring Centre, Cambridge, U.K. (Unpublished report.)

Hedge, I.C. and Wendelbo, P. (1970). Some remarks on endemism in Afghanistan. *Israel J. Botany* 19: 401–417.

Hedge, I.C. and Wendelbo, P. (1978). Patterns of distribution and endemism in Iran. *Notes Roy. Bot. Gard. Edinburgh* 36: 441–464.

Hedge, I.C. (1985). Plant life of South West Asia. *Proc. Roy. Soc. Edinburgh* 8B: 1–322.

Hunter, B. (ed.) (1992). *The statesman's year-book, statistical and historical annual of the states of the world for the year 1992-1993*. Macmillan, London. 1702 pp.

IUCN (1992). *Protected areas of the world: a review of national systems. Volume 2: Palaearctic.* IUCN, Gland, Switzerland and Cambridge, U.K. xxviii, 556 pp. (Prepared by the World Conservation Monitoring Centre.)

Johnstone, P. (1986). *Operation world*, 4th ed. Bromley, Kent.

Kamelin, R.V. (1965). Generic endemism of the flora of Central Asia. *Bot. Zhurn.* 50: 1702–1710.

Lean, G., Hinrichsen, D. and Markham, A. (1990). *Atlas of the environment.* London. 192 pp.

Léonard, J. (1988, 1989, 1992). Contribution à l'étude de la flore et de la végétation des deserts d'Iran, Fasc. 8, 9 and 10.

Mandaville, J.P. (1984). Studies in the flora of Arabia: XI. Some historical and geographical aspects of a principal floristic frontier. *Notes Roy. Bot. Gard. Edinburgh* 42: 1–15.

Mandaville, J.P. (1986). Plant life in the Rub' al Khali, the Empty Quarter, south-central Arabia. *Proc. Roy. Soc. Edinburgh* 89B: 146–157.

Miller, A.G. and Nyberg, J.A. (1991). Patterns of endemism in Arabia. *Flora et Vegetatio Mundi* 9: 263–279.

Müller-Hohenstein, K. and Al-Hubaishi, A. (1984). *An introduction to the vegetation of Yemen.* GTZ, Eschborn. 209 pp.

Quézel, P. and Pamukçuoğlu (1970). Végétation des hautes montagnes d'Anatolie Nord-Occidentale. *Israel J. Botany* 19: 348–400.

Rappenhoner, D. (1989). *Resource conservation and desertification control in the Near East.* Bayreuth. 294 pp.

Shmida, A. (1984). Endemism in the flora of Israel. *Bot. Jahrb. Syst.* 104: 537–567.

Takhtajan, A. (1986). *Floristic regions of the world.* University of California Press, Berkeley. 522 pp.

Wendelbo, P. (1971). Some distributional patterns within the *Flora Iranica* area. In Davis, P.H., Harper, P.C. and Hedge, I.C. (eds), *Plant life of South West Asia.* Botanical Society of Edinburgh. Pp. 29–41.

White, F. (1983). *The vegetation of Africa: a descriptive memoir to accompany the Unesco/AETFAT/UNSO vegetation map of Africa.* Natural Resources Research XX. Unesco, Paris. 356 pp.

White, F. and Léonard, J. (1991). Phytogeographical links between Africa and Southwest Asia. *Flora et Vegetatio Mundi* 9: 229–246.

World Conservation Monitoring Centre (1988). Directory of protected areas, Afghanistan, draft. WCMC Protected Areas Data Unit, Cambridge, U.K. (Unpublished draft document.)

World Resources Institute (1992). *World resources 1992–93: a guide to the global environment.* Oxford University Press, New York. 385 pp. (Prepared in collaboration with UNEP and UNDP.)

Zohary, M. (1971). The phytogeographical foundations of the Middle East. In Davis, P.H., Harper, P.C. and Hedge, I.C. (eds), *Plant life of South West Asia.* Botanical Society of Edinburgh. Pp. 43–52.

Zohary, M. (1973). *Geobotanical foundations of the Middle East*, 2 vols. Fischer, Stuttgart, and Swets and Zeitlinger, Amsterdam. 739 pp.

## Acknowledgements

The preparation of this text has involved input from a number of individuals. Professor Loutfy Boulos (University of Kuwait) and Mr A.G. Miller (Royal Botanic Garden, Edinburgh) prepared the bulk of the text during 1991–1992. Dr Robert Mill provided information on Tuz Gölü and Ulu Dağ, and with Mr Ian Hedge and Dr David Chamberlain (Royal Botanic Garden, Edinburgh), Professor H. Freitag (University of Kassel, Germany) and Professor J. Léonard (Nationale Plantentuin van België, Meise, Belgium) provided valuable comments on an earlier draft. Mrs Sheila Collenette and Dr Shaukat Chaudhary (National Herbarium, Riyadh, Saudi Arabia) kindly read through and commented on the sections on Saudia Arabia. Grateful thanks are also extended to Dr Kerim Alpinar (Istanbul Üniversitesi Eczacilik Fakültesi, Istanbul) who co-ordinated the activities of Turkish botanists in supplying information on sites in Turkey, and to Dr David G. Mann (Deputy Regius Keeper, Royal Botanic Garden, Edinburgh) who co-ordinated the preparation of the text at the Royal Botanic Garden, and who hosted several meetings between collaborators in the work.

# DHOFAR FOG OASIS
## Oman and Yemen

**Location:** Fog-affected escarpment mountains of southern Arabia and surrounding desert (the Nejd), including the eastern part of the Mahra Governorate of the Republic of Yemen and part of the Southern Region of the Sultanate of Oman, between longitudes 52°15'–56°00'E and latitudes 16°30'–17°00'N.

**Area:** 30,000 km².

**Altitude:** 0–2100 m.

**Vegetation:** Dry deciduous shrubland on the seaward-facing escarpment, semi-deciduous thicket and grassland at higher altitudes. Northern dip-slopes have open desert shrubland giving way to open desert.

**Flora:** c. 900 vascular plant species, of which c. 60 are endemic. 2 endemic genera.

**Useful plants:** *Boswellia sacra* (frankincense); a wide range of plants traditionally used by the indigenous population. Many species provide fodder and browse for cattle, camels and goats.

**Other values:** Watershed protection, potential tourist attraction.

**Threats:** Breakdown of traditional socio-economic system; overgrazing by goats, cattle and camels; population increase; indiscriminate use of 4-wheel-drive vehicles.

**Conservation:** Protected areas planned but as yet no protection. Vegetation under serious threat.

## Geography

The area comprises the fog-affected escarpment mountains of southern Arabia and surrounding desert (the Nejd), including the eastern part of the Mahra Governorate of the Republic of Yemen and part of the Southern Region of the Sultanate of Oman, between longitudes 52°15'–56°00'E and latitudes 16°30'–17°00'N. It is bordered in the south by the Arabian Sea and to the north, east and west by desert steppe.

The most remarkable feature of the area is the escarpment mountains which are blanketed in thick fogs during the summer months, allowing the formation of a narrow band of dense woodland on the seaward-facing slopes, in stark contrast to the desolation of the surrounding desert. The mountains extend some 320 km from near Damqawt in Yemen to Ras Hasik in Oman. They consist of three ranges: Jebel Qamar in the west, Jebel Qara in the centre, and Jebel Samhan in the east. The tops of the mountains consist of a relatively flat plateau averaging 800–900 m altitude on Jebel Qamar and Jebel Qara, and rising to over 2100 m on Jebel Samhan. To the south, the mountains fall in steep escarpments and are dissected by large, steep-sided wadis (water courses) which reach the Arabian Sea. In the north they give way to gravel hills and desert along their entire length. Along the coast lies a plain varying from >1 km to 12 km in width. Soils on the coastal plain are mainly alluvial, with areas of sand and compacted gravels, whilst mountain soils are mostly shallow, silty clays. Bare rocks occur over large areas.

The mountains are mainly lower Tertiary and Cretaceous limestone overlying a basement complex of Pre-Cambrian rocks. The latter are exposed in a few places and consist of schists, gneisses and granite. There are no permanent rivers in the area, but in the south, along the base of the escarpment mountains, and along the desert's edge to the

north, are a series of spring-fed pools. Pools also persist into the dry season in some of the larger wadi beds.

Dhofar lies in the monsoon belt. For three months each year from mid-June to mid-September the area comes under the influence of the south-west monsoon. During these months, there is an upwelling of cold water off the Dhofar coast. This rapidly cools the moist winds to dew-point, causing dense fog to build up against the seaward-facing escarpments. The fog, where it spills over the summit ridges, rapidly dissipates as it is blown inland. Rainfall data are scarce. The mean annual rainfall on the coast is about 100 mm and that on the mountains between 200–400 mm. However, the latter figure is increased by several hundred percent by drip-precipitation from fog moisture. The quantities of fog-precipitation recorded in Dhofar are among the highest readings from any part of the world. Outside the months of the south-west monsoon, storms and cyclones bring heavy rainfall on average about once every three years.

On the coastal plain, the highest temperatures occur in May and June with a mean of 32°C. During the south-west monsoon, because of cloud cover, the temperature drops and relative humidity reaches 90–97%. The temperature rises again when the monsoon lifts in September. Lowest temperatures are recorded in January and February with means of 27–28°C; frosts are rarely recorded in the mountains (Shaw Reade *et al.* 1980).

The mountains are inhabited by tribal people, the Jabali, who are mainly cattle herders. Goats, sheep and camels are kept mainly on the drier coastal plain and surrounding semi-desert ranges. The tribes of the desert are Harsusi, Mahri and Arabic-speaking bedouin who lead a nomadic or semi-nomadic existence.

Long isolation of the area and war has retarded economic development in the mountains. However, since the end of the 1975 war, the Omani part of the region has undergone rapid economic development. This has resulted in many changes, including the construction of a road network, the sinking of bore holes on the summit plateau and vastly improved medical and veterinary services. Improved medical services have led to a massive increase in the population, now estimated to be increasing at the rate of 6.1% per annum.

## Vegetation

The vegetation forms a series of zones from the coastal plains to the desert in the north (Miller and Morris 1988). Dense deciduous woodland, dominated by the endemic tree *Anogeissus dhofarica*, together with *Acacia senegal* and *Commiphora* spp., occurs on seaward-facing slopes. At higher altitudes this is replaced by semi-deciduous thicket, with *Olea europaea*, *Dodonaea viscosa*, *Carissa edulis* and *Rhus somalensis*. Summit plateaux are covered by grassland and scattered trees of *Ficus vasta*, *F. sycomorus* and patches of evergreen thicket.

Further north, and away from the influence of fog, grassland is replaced by a belt of low succulent shrubland dominated by *Euphorbia balsamifera*. Beyond this, the vegetation becomes rapidly sparser, with a zone of open desert-woodland, dominated by scattered trees of *Boswellia sacra*, and eventually giving way to open desert.

## Flora

About 900 vascular plant species have been recorded from the area, of which c. 60 are endemic, including the 2 endemic genera *Dhofaria* and *Cibirhiza* (Miller and Morris 1988).

The area falls within the Somali-Masai Regional Centre of Endemism (White 1983). The largest families are Gramineae, Leguminosae and Compositae. Families which are richest in endemics are: Compositae, Labiatae, Asclepiadaceae and Euphorbiaceae (Miller and Nyberg 1991). Some of the commonest trees and shrubs in the escarpment woodlands are endemic (e.g. *Anogeissus dhofarica*, *Euphorbia smithii*, *Jatropha dhofarica* and *Blepharispermum hirtum*). The majority of endemics are known from the semi-desert zone intermediate between the mountains and desert.

## Useful plants

In former times many plants were of great importance to economy of the area (Miller and Morris 1988). The most important is *Boswellia sacra*, from which the oleo-gum-resin "frankincense" is obtained. At present, frankincense is extracted on a small scale, mainly for local use, but in ancient times was an important export which brought great wealth to the region. In addition, *Aloe dhufarensis* and *A. inermis* were important medicinally; *Dracaena serrulata* and *Nannorrhops ritchieana* provided fibre for rope; *Euphorbia balsamifera* for fodder,

**CPD Site SWA1: Dhofar Fog Oasis; monsoon woodland dominated by the endemic *Anogeissus dhofarica* on the Jebal Qamar.** Photo: Anthony G. Miller.

chewing-gum and as an adhesive; and *Anogeissus dhofarica* was valued for its timber and for dyeing fabrics. Some species have also been important sources of food, e.g. *Cibirhiza dhofarensis* and *Raphionacme arabica*, endemics highly prized for their edible tubers.

## Social and environmental values

Dhofar is among the most notable areas for wildlife in the Arabian Peninsula. On the drier mountains (e.g. Jebel Samhan), leopard and ibex are still present, though in small numbers. The green woodlands of Dhofar are famed throughout Arabia. A tourist industry is beginning; there is considerable potential for its expansion.

Natural vegetation in the mountains plays a vital role in intercepting water from the moisture-laden winds of the south-west monsoon. The constant dripping of water from trees keeps woodland soils moist. This is in contrast to areas cleared of vegetation, such as the coastal plain, where little natural vegetation is left to intercept moisture. Precipitation derived from fog moisture is important in maintaining dense vegetation cover on steep escarpment slopes, which in turn protects thin mountain soils from being eroded by heavy rain storms which occur sporadically in the region.

Low plants and seedlings receive little precipitation unless they are under the canopy of a tree or shrub. This means it is difficult to re-establish vegetation in areas which have been cleared.

## Threats

The main threat to the vegetation is from overgrazing by cattle, goats and camels. Livestock herds have dramatically increased because of improved veterinary services, the availability of cheap fodder and the sinking of deep bore holes in areas where no water was previously available. The effects of serious overgrazing are already apparent in many areas. Summit grasslands are now invaded by unpalatable species and their productivity has been dramatically reduced. A breakdown in traditional grazing practices is rapidly accelerating this decline.

Cutting of wood for fodder, timber and firewood is also a serious problem. In some areas, particularly on the coastal plains and foothills, the vegetation has been almost completely destroyed.

Indiscriminate driving of 4-wheel-drive vehicles on the coastal plain and in the mountains has had a severe effect on the vegetation.

The population growth rate is now running at 6.1% per annum, a rapid expansion in the population which inevitably makes environmental problems more acute. It is difficult to predict how the vegetation of this unique area could survive without swift and decisive action for its protection.

The above comments refer to the situation in Oman. Little is known about the small area of wet woodland in Yemen, but there is some evidence suggesting a less critical situation there.

## Conservation

A Royal Decree in 1979 allows the setting up of National Parks and Nature Reserves in Oman. They are administered by the Ministry of Regional Municipalities and Environment and by the Office of the Adviser for Conservation of the Environment, Diwan of Royal Court. No major protected areas have so far been established in Dhofar. There is a small Bird Sanctuary on the coastal plain at Khor Salalah which protects some of the coastal vegetation.

In 1984, proposals for a national wildlife and conservation programme in Oman were formulated by IUCN. This provides for a number of protected areas, several for Dhofar, including Jebel Qamar (58,000 km²), Jebel Semhan (346,000 km²), and the coast east of Dhofar (Green and Drucker 1990).

In Yemen, there is no legislation for protected areas although various agencies have been set up, including a Conservation Section in the Department of Forestry, Ministry of Agriculture, and a National Environment Council which has responsibility for the protection and conservation of nature (Green and Drucker 1990).

## References

Bruyns, P. (1988). Studies in the Flora of Arabia, XXI: *Cibirhiza*, a new genus of Asclepiadaceae from Oman. *Notes Roy. Bot. Gard. Edinburgh* 45: 51–54.

Green, M.J.B. and Drucker, G.R.F. (1990). Current status of protected areas and threatened mammal species in the Saharo-Gobian region. World Conservation Monitoring Centre, Cambridge, U.K. (Unpublished report.)

Miller, A.G. (1988). Studies in the Flora of Arabia, XXII: *Dhofaria*, a new genus of Capparaceae from Oman. *Notes Roy. Bot. Gard. Edinburgh* 45: 45–60.

Miller, A.G. and Morris, M. (1988). *Plants of Dhofar – the Southern Region of Oman, traditional, economic and medicinal uses.* Office for Conservation of the Environment, Oman. 360 pp.

Miller, A.G. and Nyberg, J.A. (1991). Patterns of endemism in Arabia. *Flora et Vegetatio Mundi* 9: 263–279.

Schwartz, O. (1939). Flora des tropischen Arabien. *Mitt. Inst. Allg. Bot. Hamb.* 10: 1–393.

Shaw Reade, S.N. et al. (eds) (1980). The vegetation of Dhofar. In Scientific results of the Oman Flora and Fauna Survey 1977 (Dhofar). *Journal of Oman Studies Special Report* No. 2: 59–86.

White, F. (1983). *The vegetation of Africa: a descriptive memoir to accompany the Unesco/AETFAT/UNSO vegetation map of Africa.* Natural Resources Research XX. Unesco, Paris. 356 pp.

## Acknowledgements

This Data Sheet was written by Mr A.G. Miller (Royal Botanic Garden, Edinburgh), with thanks to Mr R. Daly and Mr I. McLeish (Office for Conservation of the Environment, Muscat, Oman), and to Mrs S. Collenette and Dr Shaukat Chaudhary (National Herbarium, Riyadh, Saudi Arabia) for their comments on an earlier draft.

# SOCOTRA
## Yemen

**Location:** The Socotra Archipelago consists of four islands: Socotra, 'Abd al Kuri, Semhah and Darsa in the northern part of the Indian Ocean, east of Somalia between latitudes 12°06'–12°42'N and longitudes 52°03'–54°32'E.

**Area:** Socotra, 3625 km²; 'Abd al Kuri, Semhah and Darsa in total cover less than 400 km².

**Altitude:** 0–1519 m on Socotra, 850 m on 'Abd al Kuri, 779 m on Semhah and 357 m on Darsa.

**Vegetation:** Semi-desert and dry-deciduous shrubland on coastal plains and lower slopes of mountains; semi-deciduous thicket and grassland at higher altitudes. Tree succulents are a dominant part of the vegetation, particularly on lower slopes of mountains.

**Flora:** c. 815 vascular plant species recorded, of which c. 230–260 are endemic; 9 endemic genera, 1 near-endemic family (Dirachmaceae).

**Useful plants:** Gums and resins historically important but now of little commercial significance (e.g. *Dracaena cinnabari*, *Aloe perryi*, *Boswellia* spp., *Commiphora* spp.). Many plants provide important fodder for goats, sheep and cattle.

**Other values:** Watershed protection, potential tourist attraction.

**Threats:** Overgrazing by goats, timber cutting, fuelwood cutting, charcoal production.

**Conservation:** No legal protection at present; traditional restraints on cutting wood.

## Geography

The Socotra Archipelago is situated in the northern part of the Indian Ocean between latitudes 12°06'–12°42'N and longitudes 52°03'–54°32'E. 'Abd al Kuri lies c. 80 km due east of Cape Guardafui in Somalia and Socotra is c. 380 km south of Ras Fartak on the mainland of Arabia. The archipelago contains four islands: Socotra, 'Abd al Kuri, Semhah and Darsa. The islands are separated from one another by relatively shallow seas and from mainland Africa by a deep trench of several hundred fathoms (Forbes 1903). They are administered as part of the Aden Governorate of the Republic of Yemen.

The island of Socotra covers 3625 km² and is about 40 by 120 km. 'Abd al Kuri, Semhah and Darsa are much smaller and cover in total less than 400 km².

The population of Socotra is variously estimated between 20,000 and 80,000 but is probably much nearer the lower figure. According to the only available figures (from 1967) the population of 'Abd al Kuri is 200, Semhah 40 and Darsa uninhabited (Thabet 1982). On Socotra, the transhumant indigenous population of the interior are subsistent farmers and pastoralists, while coastal dwellers engage mostly in fishing and trade.

Socotra has lagged seriously behind Yemen mainland in economic development. No port facilities exist and ships have to be unloaded onto lighters, and there are only two commercial flights a week from Aden. Moreover, transport to and from Socotra virtually ceases during summer because of the south-west monsoon. There are no metalled roads and electricity is only available for a few hours a day in Hadiboh. There are no effective medical facilities; malaria, tuberculosis and bilharzia are common and infant mortality is high (50%).

Socotra is composed of a basement complex of igneous and metamorphic rocks of Pre-Cambrian age overlain by sedimentary rocks (mainly limestone and sandstones) of Cretaceous and Eocene age. The main outcrop of the basement rocks is in the Haggier Mountains in the north-west of the island; there is an extensive limestone plateau extending across most of the island.

Topographically the island may be divided into 3 zones:

### 1. Coastal Plains

These vary considerably in width and are about 5 km at their widest. The largest unbroken stretch is the Nogad Plain in the south, a stretch of c. 60 km averaging 4 km in width. In other parts of the island the shorter stretches are broken by rocky headlands and by the cliffs of the limestone plateau. The soils of the plains are alluvial, mainly of compacted gravels, stones and coarse sands, some areas with sand dunes, particularly on the Nogad Plain. No permanent streams cross the plains, although they do reach the sea when in flood.

### 2. Limestone Plateau

This extends across a large part of the island, averaging 300–700 m in altitude and reaching 816 m at its highest point in the west. The plateau drops in steep, often almost vertical escarpments either to the coastal plain or directly to the sea. The summit consists of rolling hills, but in some areas it is broken by well-vegetated cliffs and gullies. The plateau is dissected by a number of deep valleys and in the west there is a large, dry and poorly vegetated drainage basin, the Zahr. Soils are poorly developed but fine, grey clays accumulate in hollows and rock crevices.

### 3. Haggier Mountains

These are in the north-west of Socotra and are perhaps the most spectacular feature on the island. They rise in a series of dramatic pinnacles, the highest of which, Mashanig, reaches 1519 m. Deep and fertile red soils have accumulated in the valleys and on the gentler slopes.

The climate of Socotra is monsoonal, strongly influenced by south-west and north-east monsoons. The south-west monsoon blows from April until October, bringing hot dry winds (often averaging 70 mph) from Africa. Life on Socotra during these months is very harsh, with scarce precipitation and extreme desiccating conditions brought by the dry winds which also have a significant effect on the development of the vegetation.

In November the south-west winds are replaced by the north-east winter monsoon; this dominates until March when the winds are lighter, bringing most of the annual precipitation.

Mean annual temperatures on the coastal plain vary from 17°–26°C (minimum) and 27°–37°C (maximum) (Thabet 1982). It is considerably cooler in the mountains, but no exact figures are available. Frost is not reported. Rainfall is sporadic and in some years the coastal areas receive none. Mean annual rainfall on the plain is around 150 mm; the mountains probably receive about 1000 mm. Most rain falls in the winter. The mountains are frequently shrouded in clouds and heavy dews are common.

## Vegetation

In general, the islands are sparsely vegetated and dominated by xeromorphic life-forms. The development of the vegetation is strongly influenced by the desiccating winds which sweep the islands in summer. As a result, only sheltered valleys and high mountain areas support relatively luxuriant vegetation. The most distinctive vegetation of the island is the succulent shrubland, dominated by tree succulents such as *Dendrosicyos socotranus*, *Adenium obesum* ssp. *sokotranum* and *Euphorbia arbuscula*. This occurs mainly on the coastal foothills of the mountains and the limestone escarpments. The exposed summits of the limestone plateau are covered with sparse shrubland or low woody-herb communities with more luxuriant vegetation developing on cliffs and in gullies. The coastal plains are largely semi-desert, with open shrubland, or are, in some areas, more or less devoid of vegetation.

Four main types of vegetation can be recognised:

### 1. Open deciduous shrubland of coastal plains and low inland hills
This shrubland is dominated by the endemic *Croton socotranus*. It is generally below 1.5 m high, with scattered emergent trees (*Euphorbia arbuscula*, *Dendrosicyos socotranus* and *Ziziphus spina-christi*) and low cushion-shrubs. A good cover of grasses and herbs develops after rain.

### 2. Open deciduous shrubland of lower slopes of mountains, limestone plateau and escarpments
This shrubland is much richer in species than the previous type and is the most widespread vegetation on the island. In some areas, particularly on seaward facing escarpments, it is dominated by succulent trees giving the vegetation the distinctive and rather bizarre aspect for which Socotra is famed. *Croton socotranus* and *Jatropha unicostata* are the main shrubs present. There are also many emergent trees, such as *Dendrosicyos*, *Sterculia africana* var. *socotrana*, *Boswellia* spp. and *Commiphora* spp.

### 3. Submontane, semi-deciduous thicket
This vegetation type is frequent in areas on the limestone plateau and on the middle slopes of the granite mountains. It is dominated by *Rhus thyrsiflora*, *Buxus hildebrandtii*, *Carphalea obovata* and *Croton* spp. and very rich in the number of species.

### 4. Mosaic of dense thicket, low shrubland, grassland and rock vegetation
This mosaic vegetation occurs over the higher slopes of the granite mountains and on rock pinnacles. The thicket is dominated by *Rhus thyrsiflora*, *Cephalocroton socotranus* and *Allophylus rhoidiphyllus*, with emergent *Dracaena cinnabari*. It is very dense and forms an almost impenetrable barrier around the base of the granite pinnacles. The thicket merges above into a low shrubland dominated by *Hypericum* spp. On gentler slopes, the vegetation has been cleared to provide pastures for cattle. Open rock faces are covered with lichens and low cushion plants, including several endemic *Helichrysum* spp. and *Nirarathamnos asarifolius* (an endemic monotypic genus of Umbelliferae).

## Flora

About 815 vascular plant species are recorded from Socotra, of which 230–260 are endemic (28–32% species endemism). The endemics include 10 species which are restricted to 'Abd al Kuri (Miller 1991). White (1983) comments that Socotra ranks as a local centre of endemism within the Somali-Masai Regional Centre of Endemism.

There are 9 endemic genera: *Ballochia* and *Trichocalyx* (Acanthaceae), *Duvaliandra* and *Socotranthus* (Asclepiadaceae), *Haya* (Caryophyllaceae), *Lachnocapsa* (Cruciferae), *Dendrosicyos* (Cucurbitaceae), *Placoda* (Rubiaceae) and *Nirarathamnos* (Umbelliferae). The family Dirachmaceae is a near-endemic (recently a second species in the family has been found in Somalia). Families with the highest number of endemic species are: Compositae (26), Acanthaceae (24), Euphorbiaceae (21), Labiatae (20) and Asclepiadaceae (11).

Since the pioneering botanical expeditions of Isaac Bayley Balfour in 1880 (Balfour 1888) and Georg Schweinfurth in 1881, Socotra has been famed for its botanical curiosities (Guarino, Miller, Baazara and Obadi 1990). These include: *Dendrosicyos socotranus* – the only arborescent species in the Cucurbitaceae, somewhat resembling a small baobab; *Dorstenia gigas* (Moraceae) – another swollen-trunked species; *Punica protopunica* – related to the pomegranate (*P. granatum*) but with smaller and less palatable fruits and the only other species in Punicaceae; *Dirachma socotrana* – one of only two species in the Dirachmaceae; *Begonia socotrana* (Begoniaceae) – the hybrid parent of winter-flowering begonias and one of several plants of horticultural importance found on the island; and *Dracaena cinnabari* (Liliaceae) – the Dragon's Blood tree, a Tertiary relict with related species in southern Arabia, north-east Africa and the Canary Islands.

Endemic species are found throughout the island and in all vegetation types. The most abundant plants on the island (*Croton socotranus* and *Jatropha unicostata*) and most of the characteristic species, including almost all of the common shrubs and trees, are endemic. The richest areas for endemics are the **limestone plateau** and the **Haggier Mountains**.

## Useful plants

Socotra was famed in the ancient world as the source of several important plant products, including Dragon's Blood (the resin of *Dracaena cinnabari*), Socotrine aloes (from *Aloe perryi*), and various other gums and resins (mainly from *Boswellia* and *Commiphora* spp.). Nowadays only small amounts continue to be exported (mainly to Aden) and the commercial exploitation of the vegetation is limited to certain resins and gums for local sale. However, plants still have an important place in the life of the island and most islanders have an intimate knowledge of their uses (Miller 1990).

In addition to gums and resins, the vegetation provides a variety of miscellaneous products for the islanders. Plant extracts are used in tanning, dyeing, as insecticides, rope manufacture, cosmetic preparations and as medicines. The better woods are used in the manufacture of a variety of implements. Important woods for building include: *Arthrocarpum gracile*, *Ormocarpum caeruleum*, *Maerua socotrana*, *Grewia* spp., *Cordia* spp. and *Croton* spp. The most important sources of gums and resins are *Commiphora parvifolia*, *C. socotrana*, *Boswellia ameero* and *Dracaena cinnabari*. *Cephalocroton socotranus* (drahmam) provides an important aromatic wood for burning.

In the past, various plants were important sources of food, but are of less importance now with increasing availability of government-subsidised basic foodstuffs.

However, certain wild fruits and roots are well-liked and are gathered for local consumption and sale. The most important of these are the tubers of *Dioscorea lanata*.

## Social and environmental values

There is no industry on the island and, with the exception of the coastal fisheries, no economically exploitable resources. Local people practice subsistence farming with small-scale production, for local consumption, of dates, cow peas, finger millet and sweet potatoes. However, the harsh climate on Socotra restricts cultivation to certain areas. It is impossible for the small areas under cultivation to support the population. By far the most important part of the local economy is the production of livestock. Consequently, the vegetation on which the livestock graze is vitally important. Plants are also used for fuel, building materials, medicines and food.

The natural vegetation plays an important role in watershed protection. As a result of Socotra's steep topography and short run-off to the sea, the removal of vegetation cover from the upper slopes of the mountains would result in accelerated soil erosion and the loss of surface water through increased run-off rates.

Of the 110 bird species which have been recorded on Socotra (31 species of which are known or thought to breed on the island) 6 species are endemic. There are at least 12 endemic subspecies of land birds.

**CPD Site SWA4: Socotra; granite pinnacles (Jebal Fieri) of the Haggier Mountains in north-east Socotra with endemic dragon's blood tree (*Dracaena cinnabari*) and other endemic woody vegetation. Photo: Anthony G. Miller.**

The unique flora and bizarre vegetation of Socotra, together with its dramatic landscape would perhaps provide a tourist potential. At present the lack of facilities make the likelihood of a tourist industry rather remote. However, there could be scope for small-scale tourism in the future.

## Threats

The main threats to the vegetation are from overgrazing and the cutting of wood for timber and fuel. At present there are no signs that the vegetation is being seriously over-exploited. However, various development projects have recently been formulated for the island. Plans include the development of water resources, sinking of new wells, building of new roads and provision of port facilities. This development activity is likely to significantly affect the socio-economic balance on the island and could have serious environmental side-effects.

The most important factor in the continued survival of the vegetation is the number of livestock. At present, herd numbers are limited by scarce fodder and water during the dry season and frequent droughts. Improved supplies of water and the possibility of importing cheap supplementary feed could enable livestock to survive such droughts. The present fragile equilibrium between livestock, man and vegetation would consequently be destroyed. In the areas around the larger coastal settlements signs of overgrazing are already apparent.

Wood is used on the island for fuel and building purposes. Imported wood is expensive and often difficult to obtain. This places further pressure on indigenous trees. Traditional practices and government rules exist to control the cutting of live trees but enforcement is inconsistent. The rapid growth of some coastal settlements and the lack of available alternatives for building material and fuel present obvious threats to the vegetation.

## Conservation

At present the Government of Yemen has no official conservation policy for Socotra. However, traditional practices on the island include, for instance, restrictions on cutting live wood and livestock management which prevents overgrazing. Any management plan for the islands should seek to encourage these practices. At a local level many islanders recognise the importance of the vegetation to support their way of life and there is an awareness, at least among the local authorities on the island, that Socotra's plants are special and of international interest. There is a strong feeling at the local level and within government that some conservation policy is needed.

The Conservation Unit in the Forestry Section of the Ministry of Agriculture and Agrarian Reform, based on the mainland at El-Kod near Aden, is the agency responsible for conservation. Possible desirable developments in conservation on Socotra are:

**CPD Site SWA4: Socotra, Nogad Plain, with the endemic cucumber tree (*Dendrosicyos socotrana*).**
**Photo: Anthony G. Miller.**

1. Survey and monitoring of vegetation and further collection of information on traditional plant uses and management practices.

2. Seed collection for long-term storage.

3. Setting up a nursery and arboretum on Socotra.

4. Distribution of live plants to the people of Socotra and, via El-Kod, to interested institutions worldwide. The Socotri have a tradition of transplanting, to their settlements, young plants of useful trees. This is a practice which should be encouraged by making such plants available for free distribution from the nursery.

5. Setting up of exclosures. These should initially be established to study natural regeneration, in areas thought to be suffering from over-exploitation. For example, *Croton socotranus*, the commonest shrub on the coastal plains, is a major source of wood for building and burning. It is important to assess whether this is declining or whether it is regenerating sufficiently to meet the local demand for wood. The apparent lack of regeneration of *Dendrosicyos socotranus* on the coastal plain should also be studied.

6. Production and dissemination of educational and publicity material to schools and Local Defence Councils. At the minimum, a leaflet on the important plants for the general public and a field guide to the flora is needed.

7. Research into whether range improvement should be carried out in selected areas without negative environmental repercussions (e.g. in existing grassland enclosures for cattle).

## References

Balfour, I.B. (1888). Botany of Socotra. *Trans Roy. Soc. Edinburgh* 31: 1–446.

Botting, D.S. (1958). *Island of dragon's blood*. Hodder and Stoughton, London.

Cronk, Q.C.B. (1985). Socotra (PDRY) – a conservation strategy for sustainable development. Report of WWF Project 3324. Unpublished.

Cronk, Q.C.B. (1986). Botanical survey of Socotra for conservation and plant genetic resources. *WWF Conservation Yearbook 1985/1986*: 516–517.

Forbes, H.O. (ed.) (1903). *The natural history of Socotra and Abd-el-Kuri*. Liverpool. 598 pp.

Guarino, L., Miller, A.G., Baazara, M. and Obadi, N. (1990). Socotra: the island of bliss revisited. *Diversity* 6(3–4): 28–31.

Gwynne, M.D. (1968). Socotra. In Hedberg, I. and Hedberg, O. (eds), Conservation of vegetation in Africa south of the Sahara. *Acta Phytogeographica Suecica* 54: 179–185.

Lavranos, J. (1971). The island of Abd-al-Kuri and its peculiar *Euphorbia*. *Cactus and Succulent Journal of America* 43: 109–111.

Miller, A.G. (1990). South Yemen – Socotra, conservation of flora and vegetation. Report of WWF Project 3339. Unpublished.

Miller, A.G. (1991). Checklist of Socotra. Unpublished.

Miller, A.G., Guarino, L., Baazara, M. and Obadi, N. (1991). *Dirachma socotrana* – back from the brink. *Oryx* 25(4): 229–232.

Popov, G.B. (1957). The vegetation of Socotra. *J. Linn. Soc. Bot.* 55: 706–720.

Radcliffe-Smith, A., et al. (1971). New or noteworthy species from Socotra and Abd al Kuri. *Hooker's Icones Plantarum* 7(4): 3673–3700.

Thabet, A.R. (1982). Report of the Faculty of Scientific Education Mission to Socotra, 1982. Unpublished.

Vierhapper, F. (1907). Beiträge zur Kenntnis der Flora Südarabiens und der Inseln Sokotra, Sémha und 'Abd el Kuri. *Denkschr. Kaiserl. Akad. Wiss. Wien math.-nat. Kl.* 71: 321–490.

Wettstein, R. (1906). Sokotra. In Karsten, G. and Schenck, H. (eds), *Vegetationsbilder* 3(5): t. 25–30.

White, F. (1983). *The vegetation of Africa: a descriptive memoir to accompany the Unesco/AETFAT/UNSO vegetation map of Africa*. Natural Resources Research XX. Unesco, Paris. 356 pp.

## Acknowledgements

This Data Sheet was written by Mr A.G. Miller (Royal Botanic Garden, Edinburgh) and Mr L. Guarino (IBPGR, Rome).

# HIGHLANDS OF SOUTH-WESTERN ARABIA
## Saudi Arabia and Yemen

---

**Location:** The highlands of South-western Arabia above 200 m, including part of the Asir Mountains of Saudi Arabia, between latitudes 13°13'–18°18'N and longitudes 42°00'–45°40'E.

**Area:** 70,000 km².

**Altitude:** 200–3760 m (summit of Jebal Nabi Schwaib).

**Vegetation:** *Acacia-Commiphora* deciduous bushland and thicket from 200 m to c. 2000 m altitude; evergreen bushland and thicket and *Juniperus* woodland, above c. 2000 m.

**Flora:** c. 2000 vascular plant species, of which c. 170 are endemic. 2 endemic genera. Below c. 2000 m altitude, the flora belongs to the Somali-Masai Regional Centre of Endemism; above c. 2000 m to the Afromontane Archipelago-like Regional Centre of Endemism.

**Useful plants:** *Catha edulis*, stimulant; land-races of barley, wheat and sorghum; *Commiphora* spp. (myrrh). *Coffea arabica* (coffee) introduced from Ethiopia.

**Other values:** Watershed protection; source of timber, charcoal and fuelwood; grazing and browse for cattle, goats, sheep and camels.

**Threats:** Destruction of terraces leading to soil erosion; uncontrolled cutting of wood for fuel, timber and charcoal; overgrazing.

**Conservation:** Saudi Arabia – Asir National Park (4150 km²); protected areas proposed in Yemen.

---

## Geography

The area as defined here covers approximately 70,000 km² and comprises the highlands of South-western Arabia (above 200 m), including part of the Asir Mountains of Saudi Arabia and most of the highlands of the Yemen. It extends north to Jebal Sawdah (18°18'N 42°20'E), south to Turbah (13°13'N 44° 07'E) and east to Mukayras (45°40'E). Excluded are the coastal plain (the Tehama) and the inner desert regions.

The main topographical feature of the area is the escarpment mountains which run in a north-south direction overlooking the Red Sea. They rise in a series of dramatic steps to several peaks over 3000 m altitude (including the highest point in Arabia, Jebal Nabi Schwaib, at 3760 m). East of the escarpment mountains is the high plateau. Still further eastwards the mountains drop, rather more gently than in the west, to the sands of the "Rub' al-Khali", the Great Sand Desert, which covers the interior of southern Arabia.

The mountains are composed mainly of marine sediments (limestones, sandstones and shale) of Jurassic, Cretaceous and lower Tertiary age overlying a basement complex of Pre-Cambrian granites, gneisses and quartzites. Volcanic activity has resulted in extensive areas of lava flows, particularly on the high plateau. Perennial streams are found in the mountains, but they become lost in the sands of the coastal plain before they reach the sea.

Yemen lies in the monsoon belt, influenced by north-east and south-west monsoons. Most rain is in the form of heavy thunderstorms during the summer, with peaks in April/May and July/August. There is a pronounced dry period during the winter. There is considerable variation in rainfall across the region depending on altitude and aspect.

The coastal plain is relatively dry with less than 200 mm annual rainfall. The escarpment mountains receive 600–800 mm, rising to over 1000 mm in the wettest areas. The high plateau receives 300–500 mm, dropping rapidly to below 100 mm in the east. On most days, and particularly during the rainy season, clouds build up against the escarpments at an altitude of between 2000–2500 m (the "coffee zone"). Highest temperatures occur in summer, with means of 20–25°C in the highlands and 30°C on the coastal plain and interior. The highlands are cold in winter with a mean temperature of 10°C. Frosts occur above 2000 m. Snow occasionally falls on the higher peaks (Rappenhöner 1989).

Only 12% of the population live in towns, the remainder in small villages scattered throughout the countryside (Rappenhöner 1989). Traditionally the mainstay of the economy has been agriculture. High productivity depended on an elaborate system of terraced fields, irrigated by a sophisticated rainfall harvesting system which has been maintained for over two thousand years on the steep, semi-arid mountain slopes.

## Vegetation

Large areas of Yemen were formerly covered in forest and woodland (Hepper and Wood 1979; Al-Hubaishsi and Müller-Hohenstein 1984) but agricultural activities over thousands of years have resulted in little of the original vegetation remaining. In the escarpment mountains, patches of woodland survive only in deep valleys and in one or two places (between 500–1500 m) on steeper slopes of the more inaccessible outer escarpment mountains (e.g. Jebal Bura' and Jebel Melhan). On the high plateau, virtually no woodland remains, except in the Asir Mountains of Saudi Arabia, where well-developed *Juniperus procera* woodland remains intact. An outline of the vegetation may be described from the few patches which survive.

Below 2000 m, the most widespread formation is *Acacia-Commiphora* deciduous bushland and thicket, with *Grewia* spp. and various succulents. Above about 2000 m, this is replaced by evergreen bushland and thicket characterised by *Barbeya oleoides, Carissa edulis, Dodonea viscosa, Euclea schimperi* and arborescent *Euphorbia* spp. Afromontane species, such as *Acacia origena, Hypericum revolutum, Buddleja polystachya* and *Nuxia congesta* occur at higher altitudes.

## Flora

About 2000 vascular plant species are known, of which about 170 are endemic. There are 2 endemic genera (*Saltia* and *Centaurothamnus*) (Miller and Nyberg 1991). The largest families are Gramineae, Leguminosae, Compositae and Labiatae. Succulents contribute an important feature of the vegetation and, in general, endemism among succulents in all families is very high. Asclepiadaceae is the most endemic-rich family, due largely to *Caralluma*, while the high percentage of endemics in Euphorbiaceae and Liliaceae is due to the large numbers of succulents in *Euphorbia* and *Aloe*, respectively.

The flora of South-western Arabia has strong affinities with that of adjacent parts of Africa. White (1983) considers areas below 1500–2000 m an extension of the Somali-Masai Regional Centre of Endemism and areas above this to be an impoverished outlier of the Afromontane Archipelago-like Regional Centre of Endemism.

Several areas are noteworthy for their vegetation or floristic richness:

❖ *Juniperus* woodland in the Asir Mountains;
❖ escarpment woodland on Jebel Bura' and Jebel Melhan;
❖ high-rainfall mountains near Ibb, which have several characteristic taxa occurring mainly above 2800 m, including *Kniphofia sumarae*, the only extra-African species of this largely South African genus, and *Helichrysum arwae*, the closest relatives of which occur in South Africa on the Drakensberg;
❖ the Hujariyah, a mountainous region south of Taiz, in the extreme south of the area, is floristically perhaps the richest in Arabia. In the 100 km grid square on which it is centred, 99 of the 357 endemics of mainland Arabia can be found. There are also 8 endemics restricted to the Hujariyah itself, including the spectacular *Crotalaria squamigera, Kickxia woodii, Blepharispermum yemenense* and *Centaurea yemense*.

## Useful plants

Agriculture has been the major human activity in the highlands of South-western Arabia for thousands of years. Land-races of several crop plants, including wheat, barley and sorghum are still cultivated and represent an important genetic resource.

In the past, South-western Arabia was one of the sources of myrrh, a gum-resin obtained from some *Commiphora* species. There is still a flourishing trade in the holy cities of Saudi Arabia for myrrh and the "balm of Gilead". However, there is no record of myrrh being collected in Yemen in recent years.

Many tree species are exploited for timber, charcoal and firewood. According to a World Bank study, 16 million kg of wood for firewood and timber and 5 million kg of wood for charcoal are consumed daily in northern Yemen (Rappenhöner 1989). A study carried out in the Haraz region of Yemen revealed that in 1985, 900,000 tonnes of wood were being traded annually in the region, of which 90% was firewood. Despite most families in the main towns using butane for cooking, the demand for fuelwood has doubled in the last 20 years as a result of population growth (current growth rate: 2.5% per annum) and increasing income (Rappenhöner 1989).

*Catha edulis* (qat) is widely cultivated in the highlands. The leaves are chewed as a mild stimulant and it is of major social and economic importance. *Coffea arabica* (coffee) although introduced from Ethiopia, was first cultivated in Yemen.

## Social and environmental values

Agriculture is the mainstay of the economy of the highlands. The extensive system of terraces and ingenious water-harvesting systems are highly productive allowing two crops on 200–400 mm of rainfall a year. The terrace system is extremely effective in preventing soil erosion on the steep mountain slopes. However, the system is labour-intensive and relies upon a high degree of social organisation.

There is potential for increasing tourism in the highlands. The spectacular mountains, with their picturesque villages and terraced slopes, are of outstanding landscape appeal. Certain areas of natural vegetation are especially attractive. For instance, the succulent shrubland in the Taiz area, dominated by arborescent *Euphorbia* spp., and the *Juniperus* woodland in the Asir Mountains, are of exceptional interest.

A total of 7 restricted-range land bird species are endemic to the Arabian Mountains Endemic Bird Area. An additional 6 species are largely confined to this region. As the major landmass connecting the African and Eurasian continents, Saudi Arabia has a pivotal role for many migrating species: vast numbers of passerines and near passerines pass through the country during spring and autumn *en route* between sub-Saharan Africa and the Palaearctic, and the Azir Mountains no doubt provide good refuelling habitat. Yemen is also an important flyway, especially for birds of prey that make the sea crossing at Bab al-Mandab, the narrowest point between the Arabian Peninsula and Africa.

## Threats

The main threats in the highlands are soil erosion, uncontrolled cutting of fuelwood and timber, and overgrazing. Since the mid-1970's, up to one third of the adult male population has worked abroad in the oil-rich Gulf countries. This, together with a general movement of the rural population to the towns, has resulted in poor maintenance of the terraced field systems. As a result, torrential rain in the mountains rapidly causes severe soil erosion on the steep mountain slopes (Rappenhöner 1989).

The remaining areas of woodland on the lower slopes of the escarpment mountains are rapidly being destroyed by cutting for timber, firewood and charcoal. This exploitation has intensified over the last few years through the availability of 4-wheel-drive vehicles and the greatly improved road network which now allows easy access to wood markets in the main towns from the previously inaccessible mountain woodlands.

More recently, and particularly since the Gulf War, the demand for labour in the Gulf countries has decreased. Workers have returned to find a stagnant economy and have turned to wood-cutting as a ready means of income. This has placed more pressure on the remaining woodland.

Large increases in livestock herds and the breakdown of rangeland management have led to severe overgrazing in many areas.

## Conservation

No areas of nature conservation value are protected by law in Yemen, but a network of reserves has been recommended by UNEP/IUCN. This includes several sites in the highlands, such as Al Mahwit woodlands, Jebel Bura' valley woodlands, Jebel an Nabi Shu'ayb and Taiz woodlands and the Shibam/Kawkaban escarpment.

In Saudi Arabia, the Asir National Park (4150 km²) was established in 1981 and is managed by the General Department for National Parks in the Ministry of Agriculture and Water. The National Commission for Wildlife Conservation and Development has responsibility for managing new protected areas (Green and Drucker 1990).

## References

Al-Hubaishsi, A. and Müller-Hohenstein, K. (1984). *An introduction to the vegetation of the Yemen*. Eschborn.

Collenette, S. (1985). *An illustrated guide to the flowers of Saudi Arabia*. Scorpion, Essex, U.K. 514 pp.

Green, M.J.B. and Drucker, G.R.F. (1990). Current status of protected areas and threatened mammal species in the Saharo-Gobian region. World Conservation Monitoring Centre, Cambridge, U.K. (Unpublished report.)

Hepper, F.N. and Wood, J.R.I. (1979). Were there forests in Yemen? *Proceedings of the Seminar for Arabian Studies* 9: 65–71.

König, P. (1986). Vegetation und Flora im südwestlichen Saudi-Arabien (Asir, Tihama). *Diss. Bot.* 101: 257 pp.

König, P. (1986). Zonation in the mountainous region of south-western Saudi Arabia. In Kurschner, H. (ed.), Contributions to the vegetation of Southwest Asia. *Beih. Tübinger Atlas Vord. Orient.* A24: 137–166.

Miller, A.G. and Nyberg, J.A. (1991). Patterns of endemism in Arabia. *Flora et Vegetatio Mundi* 9: 263–279.

Rappenhöner, D. (ed.) (1989). *Resource conservation and desertification control in the Near East*. Report of the International Training Course, 1988, in Germany and Jordan. Bayreuth.

Schwartz, O. (1939). Flora des tropischen Arabien. *Mitt. Inst. Allg. Bot. Hamb.* 10: 1–393.

White, F. (1983). *The vegetation of Africa: a descriptive memoir to accompany the Unesco/AETFAT/UNSO vegetation map of Africa*. Natural Resources Research XX. Unesco, Paris. 356 pp.

White, F. and Léonard, J. (1991). Phytogeographical links between Africa and Southwest Asia. *Flora et Vegetatio Mundi* 9: 229–246.

## Acknowledgements

This Data Sheet was prepared by Mr A.G. Miller (Royal Botanic Garden, Edinburgh), with thanks to Mrs S. Collenette and Dr Shaukat Chaudhary (National Herbarium, Riyadh, Saudi Arabia) for their comments on an earlier draft.

# TOURAN PROTECTED AREA BIOSPHERE RESERVE
## Iran

**Location:** North-east central Iran, in the provinces Semnan and adjacent Khorasan, between latitudes 36°30'–34°45'N and longitudes 55°00'–57°00'E.

**Area:** 18,604 km².

**Altitude:** 690–2281 m.

**Vegetation:** Temperate Irano-Turanian semi-desert vegetation, rich psammophytic and halophytic vegetation.

**Flora:** Estimated 1000 vascular plant species, including most of the c. 150 endemics of the Central Iranian deserts.

**Useful plants:** Many herbaceous plants have been used in the past for medicine and food; most woody species still exploited for firewood and charcoal.

**Other values:** Probably the most complete desert fauna in Iran, including Persian wild ass, goitered and Jebeer gazelles, Alborz red sheep, cheetah and leopard; arid landforms; potential tourism.

**Threats:** Overgrazing by sheep and goats; firewood cutting.

**Conservation:** Touran Protected Area established in 1971; designated a Man and Biosphere Reserve (10,000 km²) in 1976. Protection measures need to be enforced. A reduction in size is being considered.

## Geography

Touran Protected Area (18,604 km²) is situated in the north-eastern corner of Semnan province and in adjacent Khorasan in north-east central Iran. The area includes a comprehensive range of arid region landforms. The southern part of the reserve includes the north-eastern corner of the Great Kavir, the largest salt desert (playa) in the world. Its totally unvegetated surface is covered by white, coloured or black polygonal salt crusts during most of the year, but turns to an impassable salt swamp after rains and the influx of water during winter and spring.

The Kal-e-Shur River bisects the Touran from north to south. For 30 km it follows a narrow valley, but meanders further north through immense alluvial flats composed of salty clay. Parallel to the marshy Kavir border arise three high mountain ranges, the Shotor Kuh (2281 m), the Kuh-e-Molhadu (2411 m), the Kuh-e-Peighambar (2265 m) and many smaller ranges and isolated hills. They consist of hard Cretaceous limestones and ophiolites, and andesite. The more resistant limestone ranges have extremely steep slopes and deeply cut gorges. Smaller hilly areas consist of highly eroded Neogene clay deposits and tuff.

Wide basins are filled with graded sediments arranged in alluvial fans. Most are located between 750 and 1400 m, but smaller playas and takyr plains occur at different altitudes. Sand sheets covering the bahada (dasht) plains are common. At the eastern border of the Touran are the northernmost sand dunes in Iran. This sand sea consists of partly active dunes covering an area of c. 1100 km², at an altitude of 900–1250 m.

The climate is characterized by hot and dry summers alternating with cold winters, which often bring a short snow cover of up to 15 cm on the higher plains. Mean annual temperature varies from about 20°C at the edge of the Kavir, to 15–20°C on most plains, and 10–15°C in the higher mountains. Mean monthly temperatures at lower altitudes vary from 5–10°C in January to 30–35°C in July. Daily maxima of 45°C have often been measured in July and August.

Annual rainfall is low and highly variable. Low altitudes receive less than 100 mm. Only the higher mountains might get 150–250 mm. Flash floods follow rare storms.

## Vegetation

A preliminary map of the natural vegetation of the Touran Protected Area at a scale of 1:400,000 has been produced by Freitag (1977, 1980). Five main plant communities and 17 smaller units are distinguished, but many communities of restricted distribution, such as those of rock crevices, gorges and around springs, are not sufficiently large to be mapped at this scale.

Most of the area is covered by semi-desert vegetation in which the average plant cover is between 5–40% during the optimum period of growth (spring). In most communities, therophytes and geophytes with a very short period of annual growth are accompanied by drought-resisting dwarf-shrubs and shrubs. Of the latter, many are succulent or else shed their leaves completely or succesively when soil moisture is diminishing.

Trees are only found in the most sheltered places in the mountains and habitats near to groundwater. Halophytic and psammophytic communities are widespread. Halophytic vegetation covers the seasonally marshy margin of the Great Kavir, the greater part of the Kal-e-Shur valley and other seasonally flooded clayey soils. The composition and diversity of halophytic communities depends on water supply and salinity. For example, communities dominated by *Tamarix* (of which there are 6 species) are restricted to habitats with permanent water supply, whereas the most salt-tolerant communities are dominated by *Halocnemum strobilaceum*. Other communities are dominated by *Halostachys caspica, Kalidium caspium, Petrosimonia glauca, Reaumuria fruticosa, R. oxiana* and *Seidlitzia rosmarinus*.

Xero-halophytic plant communities occur mainly on gypsiferous marl deposits and on tuff. In the latter case, they often consist exclusively of annual chenopod species, such as *Atriplex moneta* and *Gamanthus gamocarpus*. On marls, communities with some woody species occur. They are either dominated by *Anabasis calcarea, A. eriopoda, Salsola aucheri*, or *Cousinia neurocentra*.

There are several types of psammophytic vegetation. Most undisturbed types have a high percentage of shrubs.

The sand sea itself is covered by a complex of *Stipagrostis karelinii/Smirnowia turkestanica* community on mobile dune crests, and *Salsola richteri/Calligonum microcarpum* on stabilized lower slopes and in depressions. Fixed low sands at the margin of the sand sea support the most luxuriant type of semi-desert vegetation, which is dominated by *Calligonum leucocladum*. *Haloxylon persicum* is an important component of most types of sandy semi-deserts.

Dasht plains (bahada) from 750–1300 m are dominated by species-rich open semi-desert shrublands of *Zygophyllum eurypterum*, on sandy to gravelly alluvium, and by *Haloxylon ammodendron*, on silty and slightly saline basin deposits.

On coarse-textured and rocky pediments they grade into a variety of dwarf-shrubland communities, dominated by *Salsola kerneri* or *Amygdalus lycioides*. Runnels and washes are bordered by dense thickets of *Pteropyrum aucheri*.

The vegetation of limestone ridges is very diverse and varies according to altitude, aspect and soil. On rocky slopes at lower altitudes, the vegetation is very sparse and consists of an *Artemisia aucheri/Atraphaxis spinosa* community which may include scattered small trees of *Pistacia khinjuk* and *P. atlantica*. Locally, in sheltered gorges, the latter form open woodlands with *Ficus joannis*. Above c. 1800 m (or on north-facing, exposed slopes above 1400 m) spiny cushion shrublands, dominated by *Astragalus pachyacanthus* occur, while in summit regions subalpine *Onobrychis cornuta* communities occur. Scree-covered slopes have a dense *Artemisia sieberi/Krascheninnikovia ceratoides* vegetation, often rich in perennial herbs.

## Flora

Despite the severe semi-arid climate, the Touran Protected Area is a remarkable centre of plant diversity. The first provisional plant list of the area (Rechinger 1977) listed only 288 species. Subsequent fieldwork by Freitag in 1976 and 1978 (which provides the basis for much of the present account) has increased the number of vascular plants

**CPD Site SWA10: Touran Protected Area Biosphere Reserve;** *Salsola richteri/Calligonum* **community on sand dunes in the foreground and** *Haloxylon ammodendron* **community in silty, temporarily inundated basins in central-north Shotorkuh at 1100 m altitude. Photo: H. Freitag.**

recorded to about 800. It is estimated that the area contains about 1000 vascular plant species in total.

Among the 62 vascular plant families represented in the area, the following have the highest number of species: Asteraceae 105, Brassicaceae 71, Chenopodiaceae 68 and Poaceae 62. The highest species diversity is found in the genera *Astragalus* (with 32 species in the area), *Salsola* (18 species) and *Heliotropium* (12 species).

Most of the flora belongs to the Irano-Turanian phytochorion. Many are endemic to central or eastern Iran, including the most spectacular succulent *Anabasis calcarea* found on gypsiferous marl deposits, the taxonomically-isolated shrub *Salsola abarghuensis* which occurs on wet salt-marshes, and the shrub *Astragalus kavirense* found on sand dunes. Many other species are at their southern or northern limit of distribution.

The floristic richness of the Touran is due to several factors. The Touran is located at the centre of the Irano-Turanian phytochorion and contains a complete set of semi-arid landforms, from sand dunes and playas to bahadas, pediments and slopes. As well having a wide altitudinal range, the Touran has a diverse geology providing many localized edaphic conditions. These factors combine to provide a diverse range of habitats. A further factor is that the region has experienced comparatively low human impact.

## Useful plants

Many species of desert shrubs have been used for many centuries as sources of firewood and for charcoal production. *Haloxylon* is particularly suitable, having very dense wood which has been used as fuel in copper smelting. Indeed, numerous slag sites, probably dating from the Sassanian period (225–650 AD) occur amongst stands of *Haloxylon ammodendron*.

Semi-desert vegetation of the plains serves as pasture for goats, sheep and camels in spring. The shortage of watering places has kept grazing pressure comparatively low except around villages.

In the past, some geophytes, such as *Scorzonera* spp., have been used as sources of food. Many plant species, particularly *Artemisia* spp. and *Ferula* spp. are used for medicinal purposes.

## Social and environmental values

Touran Protected Area probably has the most complete semi-desert fauna in Iran, although population numbers are much reduced. There are many species of rodents, and among the large mammals are Persian wild ass (*Equus hemionus*), goitered gazelle (*Gazella subgutturosa*), Jebeer gazelle (*G. dorcas*), Alborz red sheep (*Ovis ammon orientalis*), cheetah (*Acinonyx jubatus*), leopard (*Panthera pardus*), wolf (*Canis lupus*), golden jackal (*Canis aureus*), several species of foxes, marbled polecat (*Vormela peregusna*), striped hyaena (*Hyaena hyaena*) and the cats *Felis catus*, *F. margarita*, *F. manul* and *Lynx caracal*.

The landscape, flora, fauna, geology and the traditional methods of agriculture and pastoralism still practiced, all contribute to the attraction of the area.

An integrated study of desert ecosystems began in 1975. It aims to determine methods of management to ensure sustainable use of natural resources which would benefit the local population. So far only few results have been published and the work has been interrupted by political events.

## Economic assessment

The region could be developed as a temperate counterpart of the savanna reserves of East Africa, in which tourism could bring major economic benefits to the local people.

The area is very sparsely populated. In 1977 the population was around 16,000, but considerable depopulation has occurred during the last twenty years. The mainstay of the economy is traditional small-scale agriculture, little influenced by modern technology, which is based on irrigation with run-off from the limestone ranges and water from qanats. Wheat, millet, tobacco, turnips, alfalfa, sesame and poppy are grown, all except poppy for local consumption.

Transhumant pastoralism during the period from November to May plays an important role in the local economy. The number of sheep, goat and camels in the area may reach 150,000 temporarily. However, significant overgrazing occurs only locally.

## Threats

During the last decade, shrubs have almost completely disappeared around villages and in some remote areas as a result of over-cutting of wood for fuel. Over-stocking of grazing animals has led to floristic impoverishment of rangelands in some areas. Large desert mammals are threatened by a resumption of hunting and by the increasing numbers of livestock which compete for pasture and water resources.

## Conservation

Touran Protected Area was established in 1971 and was formally declared a Man and Biosphere Reserve in 1976. It is divided into a Wildlife Refuge (IUCN Management Category: I) of area 5650 km², a Protected Area (IUCN Management Category: V) of area 12,954 km² and areas around settlements which have no legal protection. The Biosphere Reserve covers a total area of 10,000 km².

Hunting, charcoal-burning and the cutting of shrubs and brushwood were effectively controlled by guardians, and grazing was regulated in the past. However, during the Islamic Revolution these protective measures were curtailed. Today the area is still listed as a Protected Area under the supervision of the Department of Environment, but a reduction in its size is being considered and protection measures are no longer enforced.

An extension of the area to include the large sand sea at the eastern border of the Touran is strongly recommended, along with the reintroduction of conservation measures and the continuation of studies to determine optimum levels of resource use.

# References

Akhani, H. and Ghorbanli, M. (1993). A contribution to the halophytic vegetation and flora of Iran. In Lieth, H. and Al Masoom, A. (eds), *Towards the rational use of high salinity tolerant plants.* Kluwer, Dordrecht. Pp. 35–44.

Breckle, S.-W. (1983). The temperate deserts and semi-deserts of Afghanistan and Iran. In Goodall, D.W. (ed.), *Ecosystems of the World 5.* Elsevier, Amsterdam. Pp. 271–319.

Brown, R.E. (1977). Rodent ecology in the Touran Protected Area. (Unpublished manuscript.)

Ehlers, E. (1980). *Iran. Grundzüge einer geographischen Landeskunde.* Wissenschaftliche Buchgesellschaft, Darmstadt. 596 pp.

Firouz, E. and Harrington, F.A. (1976). Iran: concepts of biotic community reservation. *IUCN Publications New Series* 34: 147–169.

Freitag, H. (1977). Vegetation. In Spooner, B. *et al.* (eds), *Case study on desertification – Iran: Touran.* Department of the Environment, Tehran. Pp. 18–20, 29–33, 86–89.

Freitag, H. (1980). Vegetation. In Biswas, M.R. and Biswas, A.K. (eds), *Desertification.* Environmental Sciences and Applications, Vol. 12. Pergamon Press, Oxford. Pp. 188–190, 196–199, 243–245.

Freitag, H. (1983). *Astragalus kavirensis,* eine neue Art von *Astragalus* sect. *Ammodendron* (Leguminosae) aus dem Iran. *Willdenowia* 13: 133–136.

Freitag, H. (1986). Notes on the distribution, climate and flora of the sand deserts of Iran and Afghanistan. *Proc. Roy. Soc. Edinburgh* 89B: 135–146.

Freitag, H. (1992). The flora of the Touran Protected Area. (Unpublished.)

Freitag, H. and Podlech, D. (1980). Zwei neue *Astragalus*-Arten aus dem Touran-Schutzgebiet im Iran. *Mitt. Bot. Staatssamml. München* 16(Beih.): 7–10.

Gehrke, U. and Mehner, H. (eds) (1975). *Iran. Natur, Bevölkerung, Geschichte, Kultur, Staat, Wirtschaft.* Erdmann, Tübingen/Basel. 471 pp.

Harrington, F.A. (1976). Fauna of the Touran Protected Area. (Unpublished manuscript.)

Harrington, F.A. (ed.) (1976). Iran: wildlife research as a base for management. *IUCN Publications New Series* 34: 114–132.

Harrington, F.A. (1977). *A guide to the mammals of Iran.* Department of the Environment, Tehran. 89 pp.

Krinsley, D.B. (1970). *A geomorphological and palaeo-climatological study of the playas of Iran.* U.S. Government Printing Office, Washington, D.C. 486 pp.

Léonard, J. (1981-1992). *Contribution à l'étude de la flore et de le végétation des déserts d'Iran.* Jardin botanique national de Belgique, Meise. (10 parts.)

Moore, P.D. and Bhadresa, R. (1978). Population structure, biomass and pattern in a semi-desert shrub, *Zygophyllum eurypterum,* in the Touran Biosphere Reserve of north-eastern Iran. *J. Applied Ecology* 15: 837–845.

Rechinger, K.-H. (ed.) (1966- ). *Flora Iranica. Flora des iranischen Hochlandes und der umrahmenden Gebirge,* Vols 1–171. Akademische Drück- und Verlagsanstalt, Graz.

Rechinger, K.-H. (1977). Plants of the Touran Protected Area, Iran. *Iran. J. Bot.* 1: 155–180.

Spooner, B. et al. (eds) (1977). *Case study on desertification – Iran: Touran.* Department of the Environment, Tehran. 97 pp.

Spooner, B. et al. (1980). The Turan Programme. In Biswas, M.R. and Biswas, A.K. (eds), *Desertification.* Environmental Sciences and Applications, Vol. 12. Pergamon Press, Oxford. Pp. 181–251.

Spooner, B. and Horne, L. (eds) (1980). Cultural and ecological perspectives from the Turan Program, Iran. *Expedition* 22(4): special issue.

Weise, O.E. (1970). Morphodynamics and morphogenesis of pediments in the deserts of Iran. *Geogr. J.* 143: 450–462.

Zohary, M. (1973). *Geobotanical foundations of the Middle East,* 2 vols. Fischer, Stuttgart, and Swets and Zeitlinger, Amsterdam. 739 pp.

## Acknowledgements

This Data Sheet was prepared by Professor Dr. H. Freitag (Department of Botany, University of Kassel, Germany).

IRANO-TURANIAN REGIONAL CENTRE OF ENDEMISM: CPD SITE SWA12

# ANTI-TAURUS MOUNTAINS AND UPPER EUPHRATES
## Turkey

---

**Location:** Eastern Anatolia. The Anti-Taurus Mountains extend north-east from near Pozantı (Adana vilayet) to near Darende (Malatya). The Upper Euphrates plain lies to the east of the Anti-Taurus ranges and includes all, or part of, the provinces of Elazığ, Erzincan, Bingöl, Tuncelı, Adıyaman and Malatya.

**Area:** c. 60,000 km².

**Altitude:** 700–3734 m (summit of Ala Dağ).

**Vegetation:** Mainly Irano-Turanian, with some East Mediterranean montane vegetation, especially in southern parts of Anti-Taurus. Steppe, coppiced oakwoods (especially in east), open park-like forest (remnants of more continuous climax vegetation).

**Flora:** c. 3200 vascular plant species, of which 725 are endemic to Turkey, 82 endemic to Anti-Taurus, c. 165 endemic to Upper Euphrates, c. 390 confined to the "Anatolian Diagonal" (a remarkable floristic demarcation running NE/SW from near Bayburt through Munzur Dağları to the Anti-Taurus; many species in Turkey occur only to the west or east of this discontinuity).

**Useful plants:** *Juglans regia* (source of walnuts), *Rubia* spp., *Isatis* spp. (dye plants); *Gypsophila* spp. (roots used medicinally by local people, also exported); *Salvia* spp. (herbal infusions).

**Other values:** Important gene pool for Old World cereal crops (the area is on the northern borders of the "Fertile Crescent"). Archaeological sites; tourist potential.

**Threats:** Dam construction and large-scale irrigation schemes, deep ploughing of steppe, re-afforestation, plant collecting.

**Conservation:** Munzur Vadısı Milli Parkı (National Park, area: 428 km²) (IUCN Management Category: II) protects part of the valley of the Munzur Çay, but very little of the Munzur Dağları with its rich endemic flora. Designation of more protected areas urgently required.

---

## Geography

The region under consideration lies in eastern Inner Anatolia (Turkey) and comprises parts of the following Turkish vilayets (provinces), from south to north: Adana (north-east part, including the Ala Dağları); Niğde (extreme south-east part, i.e. the western slopes of Ala Dağları); Maraş (north of the town of Maraş); Adıyaman (northern part, the area around Kahta); Malatya; Elazığ; Erzincan; Bingöl; Tuncelı; and Sivas (south-east part, centred on Gürün).

## Anti-Taurus Mountains

The Anti-Taurus Mountains lie in the provinces of Adana, Maraş, southern Kayserı and extreme south-east Niğde. The mountains extend north-east from near Pozantı in northern Adana to near Darende in Malatya. They comprise a number of peaks and ranges, including (from south-west to north-east) the Ala Dağları (of which the highest peak is Ala Dağ itself, at 3734 m altitude), Bakır Dağ (2071 m), Höbek Dağ (2374 m), Isik Dağ (2957 m), Binboğa Dağları (2917 m) and Berıt Dağ (3014 m). An important outlier is Ahir Dağ (2301 m), north of Maraş, which connects the Anti-Taurus with the northern part of the Amanus Mountains (Nur Dağları).

North-east of Elbıstan and Darende the main mountain mass divides into two great ranges: (1) the southern Güneydoğu Toroslar, which form a wide arc between the Tigris and Euphrates valleys from near Malatya as far east as Bitlis in South-east Anatolia, marking the northern edge of the Arabian platform; they are mostly above 2500 m (e.g. Nurıhak Dağ, 2548 m, and the Malatya Dağları, reaching 2583 m); (2) the

Munzur Silsilesı, or Mercan Dağları, which run north-east from near Kemaliye, on the Euphrates, to near Erzincan, with several peaks between 2950–3462 m altitude. North of Erzincan, this branch of the eastern Taurus joins the southern foothills of the North-east Anatolian Pontus Mountains (see Data Sheet on North-east Anatolia, CPD Site SWA19), in what is a notorious earthquake zone.

## Upper Euphrates

This consists of the high plateau lying to the east of the Anti-Taurus and Munzur Dağ, comprising the provinces of Malatya (except the western part, which forms part of the Anti-Taurus), Adıyaman, Elazığ, Erzincan and Tuncelı, together with small parts of western Bingöl and southern Gümüşhane. Most of the land is between 800–1500 m above sea-level, but some mountain ranges exceed 2000 m a.s.l. There are some natural lakes (e.g. Hazar Göl, a crater lake near Elazığ) and a network of large artificial lakes and dams (barajı).

The principal drainage systems of the above two areas are those of the two great rivers Firat (Euphrates) and Dicle Nehri (Tigris) and their many tributaries, which flow into the Persian Gulf. The Ceyhan Nehri and its tributaries drain the south-western part of the area, and flow into the Mediterranean at the Gulf of Iskenderun.

The area has a varied mixture of ancient massifs, folded sedimentary rocks and recent igneous intrusions. The Ala Dağları are Cretaceous limestone, the Tahtali Dağları are of Palaeozoic age, while Munzur Dağları is of hard Mesozoic limestone. The more southerly system is composed of a series of Palaeozoic blocks. Between the two main ranges is a very broken terrain of high plateaux and minor mountain ranges, with some fairly level pockets of land around Elazığ and Malatya. There are extensive outcrops of ophiolitic rocks, especially east of the Munzur Dağları, and also large areas of basaltic igneous rocks. The area is seismically active.

The climate over most of the area is continental. Average annual rainfall is between 350–500 mm, most occurring in spring. Winters can be bitterly cold (0 to -5°C during the day, -4 to -13°C at night) and often there are heavy snowfalls (Takahashi and Arakawa 1981). Summers are hot (28–30°C by day, dropping sharply at night).

## Vegetation

The vegetation is Irano-Turanian in character, with some East Mediterranean montane elements on the southern mountain ranges. There are two principal vegetation types: large areas of deciduous scrub and open, park-like forest (probably the remnants of previously more continuous forest) and tree-less steppe. The latter occurs around Malatya and from Erzincan eastwards towards Erzurum.

Phytogeographically, the Anti-Taurus is an extension inland of the Mediterranean flora. Further away from the coast, Mediterranean type forests are replaced by steppe forest. Zohary (1973) pointed out that Malatya is at a critical phytogeographical boundary between Xero-Euxinian steppe forests to the west and north, and the Irano-Turanian steppe forests of the Kurdo-Zagrosian type to the south and east. West of Malatya, the forests are co-dominated by *Quercus cerris* and *Q. pubescens* (Xero-Euxinian species), with various arborescent Rosaceae, such as *Crataegus laciniata* and *Pyrus laciniata*, which form "wild orchards". East of Malatya, towards Elazığ, the vegetation is Kurdo-Zagrosian oak forest, dominated by *Q. brantii*, *Q. libani* and *Q. boissieri*, in which steppe vegetation (including tragacanthic species such as *Astragalus* spp., *Gundelia tournefortii*, *Noaea mucronata* and *Salvia cryptantha*) occurs in clearings.

*Artemisia fragrans* steppe is one of the most common vegetation types at lower elevations. Associated species include *Verbascum glomeratum*, *Cousinia birandii*, *Euphorbia macroclada*, *Medicago murex*, *Phlomis nissolii* and many species of Boraginaceae, Caryophyllaceae, Compositae, Gramineae, Labiatae and Leguminosae. An unusual type of steppe vegetation, dominated by broadleaved species, is found on the higher plateaux. Typical species include: *Achillea vermicularis*, *Ajuga chia*, *Helianthemum nummularium*, *Malcolmia africana* and *Marrubium parviflorum*.

The vegetation of the Munzur Dağları is exceedingly rich and contains many endemics (see FLORA, below). Chasmophytes are frequent.

## Flora

Although there have been few floristic and vegetation studies in the area (cf. Ekim and Güner 1986), it is clear that this is one of the richest parts of Anatolia. About 3200 vascular plant species are known to occur, of which at least 725 species are endemic to Turkey. The Anti-Taurus Mountains have at least 82 endemic species. These include: *Thlaspi crassum*, *Astragalus stridii*, *Ononis sessilifolia*, *Centaurea chrysantha* and *Veronica*

*tauricola* (all on Ala Dağ); *Aethionema papillosum*, *Alyssum haussknechtii*, *Astragalus ramicaudex*, *Pastinaca glandulosa*, *Achillea armenorum*, *Paracaryum reuteri*, *Scrophularia byssopifolia*, *Salvia haussknechtii* and *Asphodeline peshmeniana* (on Berıt Dağ); *Thlaspi rosulare*, *Bornmuellera glabrescens*, *Centaurea aladaghense* and *Veronica hispidula* subsp. *ixodes* (on Masmeneu Dağ); and *Graellsia davisiana* and *Doronicum haussknechtii* (on Binboğa Dağ, with the latter also on Berıt Dağ).

Several endemics occur in low-lying areas in the Elbistan/Darende region, including *Paronychia cataonica*, *Centaurea cariensiformis* and *C. fimbriata*. The distribution of some endemic species extends to the northern part of the Amanus Mountains, e.g. *Silene inclinata*, *Kundmannia syriaca* and *Verbascum infidelium*.

About 165 vascular plant species are endemic to the Upper Euphrates area. They include 3 species each of *Isatis*, *Barbarea* and *Reseda*; 6 species of *Gypsophila*; 8 species of *Stachys*; 9 species of *Galium*; nearly a dozen species of *Astragalus*; and 16 species of *Verbascum*. A number of species are endemic to Munzur Dağları; examples include *Ranunculus munzurensis*, *Aethionema munzurense*, *Paronychia kurdica* subsp. *montis-munzur*, *Vicia glareosa*, *Eryngium ilex*, *Campanula munzurensis*, *Omphalodes davisiana*, *Scrophularia subaequiloba*, *Stachys munzurdagensis*, *Origanum munzurense* and *Carex eriocarpa*. Several of these species are of isolated taxonomic position and therefore of considerable evolutionary and floristic interest. A few endemics, principally of the Anti-Taurus, extend to mountains further east in the Upper Euphrates area, e.g. *Achillea magnifica*, *Astragalus elbistanicus*, *Paronychia kemaliya* and *Thesium tauricolum*. *Uechtritzia armena*, endemic to Sipikör Dağ, is the only member of the Compositae tribe Mutisieae in Turkey. The genus *Uechtritzia* is ditypic; the only other species, *U. kokanica*, occurs on the Tien Shan and Pamir Alai. The Turkish species is presumably a relict.

Other notable centres of endemism include the area around Kemaliye, Keşiş Dağ, Harput and Hazar Göl, the area around Pülümür and Sipikör Dağ. Several gypsicolous endemics occur in the Erzincan area, e.g. *Gypsophila lepidioides* and *Reseda tomentosa*. Some endemics, including the taxonomically very isolated *Scrophularia lepidota*, extend into neighbouring Sivas.

Davis (1965, 1971) noted that there is a remarkable floristic break through the middle of Inner Anatolia, which he termed the "Anatolian Diagonal". This runs from the southern foothills of the Pontus Mountains near Bayburt, south-west through Munzur Dağ to the Anti-Taurus, where it divides. One branch leads to the Cilician Taurus, the other to the Amanus Mountains. A high proportion of plant species in Turkey occur either only west of the line or only to the east of it. About 390 species have distributions more or less confined to the Diagonal, but only 15 of these extend along its full length (Ekim and Güner 1986). Examples of taxa more or less confined to the Diagonal include the endemic monotypic genus *Neotchihatchewia* (*N. isatidea*) and *Graellsia davisiana*.

The origins of the Diagonal are the subject of several hypotheses. Davis (1971) put forward the hypothesis that its origins are palaeogeographical: land to the west of the line (now the Central Anatolian steppe) was mainly land during the Miocene, while land to the east was submerged beneath the sea until northern Anatolia came into contact with the

Caucasus, leading to the ultimate formation of the mountainous plateau of East Anatolia. Sonnenfeld (1974), however, believed that during Miocene times there was a large water channel which extended diagonally north-east from the present Gulf of Iskenderun towards Sivas, then east-north-east through Erzurum, Armenia and Nakhichevan to the present Caspian Sea, and that this effectively separated the western Anatolian Peninsula plateau from the Turkish eastern highland plateau and Armenian Highlands. It is likely that this water channel may have been a barrier to the migration of plant species across it, and the mountains uplifted along it during the Alpine orogeny would also have acted as a barrier to the dispersal of species adapted to lower elevations on either side. Ekim and Güner (1986) believe that ecological and climatic factors are more important than palaeogeographical ones as an explanation for the floristic demarcation.

## Useful plants

Vegetable dyes are extracted from species of *Isatis, Rubia* and from *Juglans regia*, as well as from numerous other sources known only to the local inhabitants. These are used to dye the wool in the manufacture of Turkish carpets.

*Salvia* spp. are used to make herbal infusions. The roots of *Gypsophila* spp. are medicinal and quantities are exported as well as consumed locally.

The area is on the northern fringe of the "Fertile Crescent" and is an important gene pool of Old World cereal crop relatives (e.g. *Triticum* spp., *Aegilops* spp.) and other species of local and global agricultural importance.

## Social and environmental values

The Euphrates (Firat) and Tigris (Dicle), which flow through the region, and some of whose headwaters rise in it (on the Munzur Dağları), have been two of the world's most important rivers since ancient times. The valley of the Munzur Çay, especially near Ovacik, is very lush and supports an important local dairying industry. However, much of the rest of the region is very infertile. Some parts, notably the Tuncelı area, are among the most economically undeveloped areas in the whole of Turkey.

The area has potential for tourism; there are several important archaeological sites, notably the magnificent Commagenian rock carvings at the summit of Nemrut Dağ which date back to c. 60 BC.

## Threats

By far the greatest potential threat to the flora of the region is the on-going programme to dam the Euphrates and Tigris rivers. Apart from submerging areas of floristic interest, the resultant large-scale irrigation schemes will be a threat to many species adapted to the present water regime. Many formerly common species are already becoming scarce due to intensive agriculture and deep ploughing methods introduced in the last few decades. Ultimately, the programme of dam construction will provide water for irrigation throughout the southern part of the area and the whole of Mesopotamia (an important centre of genetic diversity of crop plants).

In order to avert a predicted severe shortage of wood and cellulose in the next century, the Elaziğ Forest Regional Directorate is aiming to re-afforest 3000 km² per annum in the region. Such large-scale re-afforestation will completely change the character of the vegetation of much of East Anatolia and will destroy the habitat of many steppe species.

Other threats include erosion as a result of the increasing number of climbing expeditions to the Ala Dağları and, to a lesser extent, the Munzur Dağları. Plant collecting is a threat in some areas, especially in the Ala Dağları, Demirkazık and the Narpız Gorge.

## Conservation

The only National Park in the area is the Munzur Vadısı Milli Parkı (428 km²). This protects a wide stretch of the valley of the Munzur Çay from Tuncelı north to just beyond the southern boundary of Erzincan vilayet. However, very little of the Munzur Dağları, with its rich endemic flora, is included in the park. Designation of more protected areas throughout the region is urgently required.

## References

Davis, P.H. (ed.) (1965-1985). *Flora of Turkey and the East Aegean Islands.* Edinburgh University Press, Edinburgh. (9 vols and Supplement; for latter see Davis, Mill and Tan 1988.)

Davis, P.H. (1971). Distribution patterns in Anatolia with particular reference to endemism. In Davis, P.H., Harper, P.C. and Hedge, I.C. (eds), *Plant life of South-West Asia.* Botanical Society of Edinburgh. Pp. 15–27.

Davis, P.H., Mill, R.R. and Kit Tan (1988). *Flora of Turkey and the East Aegean Islands*, Vol. 10 (Supplement). Edinburgh University Press, Edinburgh.

Ekim, T. and Güner, A. (1986). The Anatolian Diagonal: fact or fiction? *Proc. Roy. Soc. Edinburgh* 89B: 69–77.

Sonnenfeld, P. (1974). The Upper Miocene evaporite basins in the Mediterranean region – a study in paleo-oceanography. *Geol. Rundschen* 63: 1133–1172. [Reprinted in 1981 as Pp. 276–315 in Sonnenfeld, P. (ed.), *Tethys: the ancestral Mediterranean.* Benchmark Papers in Geology 53. Hutchinson Ross, Stroudsburg, Pennsylvania.]

Takahashi, K. and Arakawa, H. (eds) (1981). *World survey of climatology. Vol. 9. Climates of southern and western Asia.* Elsevier, Amsterdam.

Zohary, M. (1973). *Geobotanical foundations of the Middle East*, 2 vols. Fischer, Stuttgart, and Swets and Zeitlinger, Amsterdam. 739 pp.

## Acknowledgements

This Data Sheet was written by Dr Robert R. Mill (Royal Botanic Garden, Edinburgh).

# MOUNTAINS OF SOUTH-EAST TURKEY, NORTH-WEST IRAN AND NORTHERN IRAQ
## Turkey, Iran and Iraq

**Location:** North-west Iran (provinces of Kordestan and Āžarbāyān-e Gharbi); northern Iraq (governorates of Dihōk, Arbil and Sulaymānīyah; S.E. Anatolia, Turkey (vilayets of Bitlis, Hakkari, Siirt and Van).

**Area:** 147,332 km² (Iran, 63,848 km²; Iraq, 37,284 km²; Turkey, 46,200 km²).

**Altitude:** c. 1400–4168 m (summit of Reşko Tepe).

**Vegetation:** Irano-Turanian oak forest at lower altitudes, now mostly destroyed except for isolated stands; "yellow umbellifer" mountain steppe zone between 2200–2700 m; thorn-cushion zone of spiny *Astragalus* and A*cantholimon* spp.; *Cousinia* and *Cirsium* spp. between 2700–3300 m; alpine zone of more Euro-Siberian character with *Myosotis* and *Primula* spp. above 3300 m; alpine grassland; scree and rock vegetation on highest summits.

**Flora:** c. 2500 vascular plant species, of which c. 500 endemic to the region. 1750 species in S.E. Anatolia, of which 100 endemic to S.E. Anatolia, 200 endemic to Turkey and 225 endemic to S.E. Anatolia and adjacent Iraq/ Iran; 100 species endemic to Iraq alone; figure for Iran not known.

**Useful plants:** Centre of diversity for almond, hawthorn and pears; gum tragacanth obtained from several species of *Astragalus*, some of which yield gum of commercial quality.

**Other values:** Remote and rugged nature of terrain could, under more stable political conditions, offer potential for mountaineering and ecotourism. Rich fauna includes brown bear.

**Threats:** Few; afforestation may endanger some areas of steppe vegetation; further clearance of oak woods could endanger endemic species, such as *Pelargonium quercetorum*. The Tigris irrigation scheme (2 dams to open by 1994 in Siirt region) is a serious threat to the natural vegetation of Siirt.

**Conservation:** Turkey: Tatvan Forest Recreation Area, Süphandağı Game Reserve; Cilo-Sat Dağları and Nemrut Crater proposed, Hakkari Dağları and Lake Van recommended. Iraq: no protected areas legislation and no protected areas in the region. Iran: Lake Uromiyeh National Park (4636 km²).

## Geography

This mountainous region (frequently referred to as Kurdistan or the Kurdish Mountains) comprises the Turkish vilayets of Bitlis, Hakkari and Siirt, together with the part of the province of Van lying south of Van Gölü (hereafter referred to as South-east Anatolia); northern Iraq, from the Turkish border south to about Kirkuk and east to the Iran border, and including the governorates of Dihōk, Arbil and Sulaymānīyah; and north-west Iran (provinces of Kordestan and Āžarbāyān-e Gharbi). For convenience, the part of Van province lying north of Lake Van is also included, although floristically it has more in common with the Armenian Highlands of the former Soviet Union. The region thus defined has an area of 147,332 km², of which 63,848 km² is in Iran, 37,284 km² in Iraq and 46,200 km² in Turkey. This Data Sheet deals mainly with those mountains lying in South-east Anatolia, as they are botanically the best known.

The dominant feature of the northernmost part of South-east Anatolia is Van Gölü, the largest lake in Turkey. It is a vast inland sea, 120 km long and up to 80 km wide, with an area of 3173 km² and lying at an altitude of 1720 m. Immediately to the north of the lake are several volcanoes of Quaternary age, including Nemrut Dağ (2935 m, with 5 lakes in its 8 km-wide crater) and Süphan Dağ (4434 m). Basaltic lava-flows cover much of the area to the north.

To the south of Van Gölü the land rapidly rises from the Armenian High Plateau. Only about 30 km south of the lake shore, the Kavuşşahap Dağları rise to several peaks of

3000–3500 m. From Çatak, another main range, the Hakkari Dağları, runs south-east to Şemdinli and Yüksekova near the Iranian frontier. The Cilo Dağları forms part of this complex. Its highest peak, Reşko Tepe (4168 m), is the highest mountain in South-east Anatolia, and in the region under consideration. It has a large glacier on its northern side.

Near Yüksekova, several spurs run east (Mor Dağı, 3809 m), north-east (Doğanı Dağ and Hirabit Dağ, up to 3550 m) and south-west (Tanintanini Dağları, 3055–3375 m). The mountains of Siirt are lower, the main ranges being the Yazlıca Dağları, of which the principal peak is Herakol Dağ (2812 m).

A complex of mountains occurs on the Iran-Turkey frontier, of which the highest is Kuh-e Zaki (3079 m) in the extreme north-west of Iran. The main ranges in Iraq are the Chiyā-i Marmarūt (2000 m), the Chiyā-i Matiñ or Ser Amadîya (2000–2500 m), and the Ser Kirawa (3650 m) on the Turkish frontier.

The whole region is drained principally by the Great Zab River and its tributaries. The Siirt region in south-east Turkey is drained by the Tigris (called in Turkey the Dicle) and many tributaries such as the Botan Çay.

The population of the region is about 5 million (Iran: 2.19 million, 1982 estimate; Iraq: 1.48 million, 1977 estimate; Turkey: 1.33 million, 1980 estimate) and consists mainly of ethnic Kurds. Other minority groups or languages in northern Iraq include Assyrians and the Yezidis, or Dasnayi. For a long period, South-east Anatolia has been under martial law and is only very rarely open to foreign visitors, except for transit purposes. Some Armenians still live in northern Iran. In 1981, 14,000 Uzbek and Kirghiz Turkish refugees from Afghanistan were resettled in the Lake Van area by the Turkish Government (Dubin and Lucas 1989). More recently, there have been two waves of Kurdish refugees entering South-east Anatolia and have, at least temporarily, resettled there. Some have moved back to Iraq, but many remain.

Communications in these wild, remote regions are difficult and living conditions extremely harsh. Roads are few and hazardous, especially in winter when many passes are closed for months. The only railway runs to Tatvan on the west side of the lake. Van also has an airport; there are also four airports in northern Iran.

The climate is severe. The mean winter (October/ November–April) temperature in the mountains is -20°C; in summer (May/June–September) most land below 2500 m has mean temperatures of about 20°C, but on the mountains temperatures are of the order of 8–12°C. Maxima may reach 50°C in sheltered valleys, 30–40°C being more typical. The diurnal range often exceeds 20°C and can be as much as 35°C. Rainfall is moderate on the mountains (800–1000 mm), but only 400–550 mm at lower altitudes. Spring and autumn are very brief.

## Vegetation

Forest occurs on the slopes of sheltered valleys, and includes *Quercus libani* intermixed with scattered trees of *Acer, Rhamnus, Pistacia* and *Sorbus* (Davis 1956). Extensive *Quercus infectoria* scrub occurs between Pelli Dağ and Tatvan, near Van Gölü. Much of the oak forest, which was formerly continuous, is now degraded or destroyed, especially below 1400 m in Iraq and Iran. The oak forest can be divided into lower, middle and higher zones dominated respectively by *Q. aegilops, Q. aegilops/Q. infectoria* and *Q. infectoria/Q. libani*. Associated shrubs and trees include *Celtis tournefortii, Rhamnus kurdica, Lonicera arborea* and *Crataegus* spp. (including several endemics). The herb flora includes *Phlomis kurdica, Gundelia tournefortii, Prangos pabularia, Ferulago stellata, Poa bulbosa, Geranium tuberosum, Anemone coronaria, Orchis anatolica* and many others (Townsend and Guest 1966– ).

Mountain steppe, dominated by tall, yellow-flowered umbellifers belonging to *Ferula, Prangos* and other genera, occurs between 2200–2700 m. Other plants of this community include *Papaver pseudo-orientale*, the ancestor of the large red oriental poppies of horticulture.

A thorn-cushion community of Irano-Turanian character, dominated by tragacanthic species of *Astragalus* and species of *Onobrychis* and *Acantholimon*, occurs from 2700–3000/3300 m. Many thistle-like species belonging to *Cousinia* and *Cirsium* are characteristic of the thorn-cushion zone, as are spiny umbellifers such as *Eryngium* spp. Herbs such as *Stachys lavandulifolia, Helichrysum* spp. and *Achillea vermicularis* are also typical.

At still higher altitudes, on limestone screes, species such as *Pisum formosum, Gentiana verna, Primula auriculata* and *P. elatior* subsp. *pallasii* and various Cruciferae occur. This alpine flora is more Euro-Siberian in character than the *Astragalus* zone. Other plants typical of the alpine zone in Iraq include *Myosotis alpestris, Silene odontopetala, Physoptychis gnaphalodes, Arabis caucasica,*

*Artemisia splendens, Galium pallasii, Scutellaria orientalis, Lamium tomentosum, Prunus brachypetala* and bulbs such as *Gagea* spp. and *Fritillaria* spp.

A small area (100 km²) of *Pinus brutia* forest occurs near the villages of Zawita and Atrush (near Amadîya) in Dihōk governorate (northern Iraq) on limestone crags. The herb flora includes *Fumana arabica, Thymbra spicata, Hypericum scabrum* and *Sideritis kurdica* – all species or genera with an East Mediterranean rather than Irano-Turanian affinity (Townsend and Guest 1966– ).

## Flora

Of the three Flora projects covering the region, only *Flora of Turkey* (Davis 1965–1985; Davis, Mill and Kit Tan 1988) is complete. *Flora Iranica* (Rechinger 1963– ), which covers the mountains of Iran and northern Iraq, is substantially complete, but one of the most pertinent parts, dealing with the huge thorn-cushion genus *Astragalus*, has yet to be published. *Flora of Iraq* (Townsend and Guest 1966– ) is only half completed. Further exploration of the whole area is needed, but little has been possible for the last 20 years.

The flora of the region is estimated to contain 2500 vascular plant species, of which about 500 are endemic. Some 1750 species have been recorded from South-east Anatolia; 200 of these are endemic to Turkey and over 100 are endemic to South-east Anatolia. A further 125 species are endemic to South-east Anatolia and the adjacent mountains in Iran and Iraq. Many other species occur in Iran and Iraq but not Turkey.

Examples of species endemic to the whole region include *Consolida anthoroidea, Peltariopsis planisiliqua, Alcea kurdica, Linum persicum, Pelargonium quercetorum* (a relict species of this mainly South African genus, inhabiting oak woods in Hakkari and northern Iraq), *Astragalus siliquosus* (and several other members of the genus), *Rosularia rechingeri, Ferula stellata, F. bernardi, Doronicum hakkiaricum*, 5 species of *Centaurea, Campanula persica, Omphalodes luciliae* subsp. *kurdica* (disjunct from the Cilician and Greek subspecies and the most south-easterly taxon in the genus), *Veronica davisii, Lamium tomentosum* (with 3 varieties) and *Allium anacoleum*. Taxa endemic to South-east Anatolia include *Ranunculus crateris* (on Nemrut Dağ), *Isatis spateola, Thesium oreogetum* and *Fritillaria minima* (on the isolated 3475 m peak of Artos Dağ which is composed of crystalline limestone), *Gypsophila graminifolia, Paronychia saxatilis, Astragalus bashkalensis, Acantholimon spirizianum* var. *spirizianum* and *Allium microspathum* (on Ispiriz Dağ, 3587 m, the lower and upper slopes of which are marble, with a broad band of serpentine in between), *Gypsophila hakkiarica, Vicia splendens, Lathyrus satdaghensis, Senecio davisii, Centaurea longifimbriata* and *Solenanthus formosus* (on Sat Dağ), and *Draba thylacocarpa, Eryngium bornmuelleri, Cephalaria hakkiarica, Cirsium hakkiaricum, Serratula hakkiarica, Scorzonera mirabilis, Crepis hakkarica* and *Dionysia teucrioides* (on the Cilo Dağ massif).

Zohary (1950) lists 190 species endemic to Iraq, of which over 100 are confined to the Iraqi mountains treated here. They include *Noaea kurdica, Bellevalia kurdistanica, Umbilicus kurdicus, Nigella assyriaca, Hypericum haussknechtii, Grammosciadium longilobum, Symphytum kurdicum, Stachys kotschyi, Cousinia handelii* and *Dianthus kurdicus.*

## Useful plants

The region is a centre of diversity for pears (*Pyrus* spp.), almonds (*Amygdalus* spp.) and hawthorns (*Crataegus* spp.). Among the several endemic taxa are *Amygdalus kotschyi, A. carduchorum, Crataegus davisii, Pyrus hakkiarica* and *P. salicifolia* var. *serrulata*. The extent to which these might be useful in plant breeding has yet to be determined; they could be useful in introducing frost hardiness.

Numerous species of tragacanthic *Astragalus* species occur; some, such as *A. gummifer*, are a source of gum tragacanth. *A. gummifer* is relatively rare; *A. adscendens* is reported to yield the best gum in Iraq, while *A. gossypinus* produces gum of commercial quality which is sold in Baghdad.

## Social and environmental values

This mountainous region has been described by the few mountaineers and alpinists who have been able to visit it as the most dramatic range between the Alps and the Hindu Kush. There is considerable potential for ecotourism when political conditions become more stable. The region has a rich fauna including brown bear.

## Threats

The remoteness of the region and its poor communications, the sparse population and the inhospitable climate all combine to make the region unattractive for large-scale development. Local people practice a nomadic pastoral form of agriculture, moving their herds to alpine pastures (yayla) during the brief summer period. The landscape is largely unspoilt (apart from forest clearance over thousands of years) and given continuance of the present political situation, is likely to remain so. There is a possible threat in South-east Anatolia from the increased number of refugees from Iraq and Afghanistan. Otherwise, the main threat is from overgrazing (not nearly as severe here as in Mediterranean Turkey) and further degradation of the forest. An ambitious plan to afforest huge tracts of eastern Anatolia (at the rate of 3000 km² per year over a 10-year period) would restore much of the former forest flora but it would be at the expense of steppe vegetation. However, this threat is likely to affect eastern Anatolia, rather than South-east Anatolia which is so much more mountainous.

Siirt lies within the area likely to be under threat from a programme to dam the Tigris and create a series of reservoirs to irrigate the area. Of these, two (the Îlisu Baraj, south of Siirt, and the Cizre Baraj, west of Cizre) are planned to open in 1994. The potentially very severe threat to the natural vegetation posed by this scheme is discussed in detail in the Data Sheet on the Anti-Taurus Mountains and Upper Euphrates (CPD Site SWA12).

## Conservation

Apart from the Tatvan Forest Recreation Area and the Süphandağı Game Reserve, there are no protected areas in South-east Anatolia. Cilo-Sat Dağları and Nemrut Crater have been proposed as protected areas. Van Gölü, Hakkari Dağları and Nemrut Crater Lake have been recommended as reserves. Iraq has no protected areas legislation; some conservation areas have been recommended, but all are wetland areas in the Tigris/Euphrates marshes, with none of the mountains being selected. In Iran, Uromiyeh Lake National Park covers an area of 4636 km².

## References

Davis, P.H. (1956). Lake Van and Turkish Kurdistan: a botanical journey. *Geographical Journal* 122: 156–165.

Davis, P.H. (ed.) (1965-1985). *Flora of Turkey and the East Aegean Islands*. Edinburgh University Press, Edinburgh. (9 vols and Supplement; for latter see Davis, Mill and Tan 1988.)

Davis, P.H., Mill, R.R. and Kit Tan (1988). *Flora of Turkey and the East Aegean Islands*, Vol. 10 (Supplement). Edinburgh University Press, Edinburgh.

Dubin, M. and Lucas, E. (1989). *Trekking in Turkey*. Melbourne and Berkeley.

Lynch, H.J.B. (1901). *Armenia*, Vol. 2. London.

Rechinger, K.H. (ed.) (1963- ). *Flora Iranica*. Graz, Austria.

Townsend, C.C. and Guest, E. (1966- ). *Flora of Iraq*. Parts 1–4, 8,9. Baghdad.

Zohary, M. (1950). *The flora of Iraq and its phytogeographical subdivision*. Baghdad.

## Acknowledgements

This Data Sheet was prepared by Dr Robert R. Mill (Royal Botanic Garden, Edinburgh).

# ISAURIAN, LYCAONIAN AND CILICIAN TAURUS
## Turkey

**Location:** The area comprises the eastern part of the Taurus Mountains in East Antalya, İçel, southern Adana and southern Konya, between latitudes 36°01'–37°20'N and longitudes 31°27'–36°00'E.

**Area:** c. 45,120 km².

**Altitude:** 0–3524 m (Bolkar Dağları). Much of the land is above 2500 m.

**Vegetation:** Maquis and phrygana at low altitudes; oak and pine forest, and some stands of *Cedrus libani*, at middle altitudes (much now destroyed); alpine pasture, mountain steppe (including thorn-cushion plants) and scree communities at higher altitudes. Littoral dune communities between Mersin and Silifke; halophytes and remnants of alluvial forest in Silifke Valley; wetland vegetation on Göksu Delta and Çukurova.

**Flora:** At least 2500 vascular plant species, of which at least 235 are endemic to the area; c. 520 species are endemic to Turkey. 1 endemic genus (*Sartoria*, Leguminosae: threatened, possibly extinct); 2 genera (*Thurya*, Caryophyllaceae; *Leucocyclus*, Compositae) endemic to this area and the Anti-Taurus Mountains and Amanus Range.

**Useful plants:** Fruit and nut trees (e.g. fig, walnut, pomegranate, hazel, all of which are native and cultivated). *Glycyrrhiza glabra* (roots used as syrup); *Elymus farctus, Ipomoea stolonifera* and other dune-stabilizers; ornamental bulbs.

**Other values:** Göksu Valley is one of the most important wetlands in the whole of the Mediterranean; remaining natural lagoons of Çukurova extremely important for waterfowl.

**Threats:** Intensive agriculture, commercial collection of ornamental bulbs, dune communities threatened by sand mining, exotic plant species and tourist pressure; potential threat of pollution from oil refinery and motorway.

**Conservation:** 1 small National Park (Tasari Milli Parkı) on Bolkar Dağları; 1 Bird Sanctuary on Çukurova; Kargı Game Reserve (30 km²). Many important ecosystems wholly unprotected and threatened.

## Geography

The area comprises the eastern end of the Taurus Mountains (Toros Dağı) and associated coastline, from Manavgat (Antalya) to Ceyhan (Adana) near the northern extremity of Iskenderun Bay and the Amanus Range. It lies between latitudes 36°01'–37°20'N and longitudes 31°27'–36°00'E and covers a total area of about 45,120 km². It comprises the following:

- the eastern part of Antalya vilayet (c. 6400 km²);
- the whole of İçel (15,853 km²);
- the southern low-lying part of Adana (c. 14,500 km²), the northern part being part of the Anti-Taurus Mountains (CPD Site SWA12, see Data Sheet) and the easternmost part being the north-western part of the Amanus Mountains (see Data Sheet on the Levantine Uplands, CPD Site SWA17);
- the mountainous southern tip of the province of Konya (Lycaonian Taurus: c. 5900 km²);
- and the part of Aydos Dağ and Bolkar Dağları in south-east Konya (c. 2470 km²).

The Taurus Range runs in a broad arc along the Mediterranean coast of Turkey to the east of South-west Anatolia (CPD Site SWA16, see Data Sheet). The north-facing slopes, mostly in Konya, form the Lycaonian Taurus. The Isaurian Taurus is separated from the Cilician Taurus by the Göksu Gorge. The main range of the Cilician Taurus, the Bolkar Dağları (highest point: 3524 m), ends in the north-

east in another very deep gorge, the summit of which is the famous Gülek Boğazı (Cilician Gates).

Much of the coastline is very steep. Exceptionally difficult terrain is encountered from Gazipaşa to Silifke (the Cilicia Trachea or "Rough Cilicia"). East of Mersin lies the broad expanse of the Çukurova or Cilician Plain, a flood plain of two great rivers, the Ceyhan and Seyhan. The headwaters of these rivers rise respectively in the northern Amanus and the Anti-Taurus Mountains. To the west of Çukurova the only streams of note are the Gök Su and the Lamas Çay.

Much of Isauria and Cilicia is limestone. There are extensive areas of soft chalk near Ermenek and Mut. Above Bolkar Maden, in the Cilician Taurus, there are outcrops of diorite. There are also considerable areas of shale, slate and basic igneous rocks (Davis 1965).

The climate is Mediterranean, but hotter in summer than further west. Nevertheless, the onset of spring flowering is retarded by cold winds blowing south from the Anatolian Plateau. This results in spring beginning later here than in Lebanon or the Peloponnese of Greece (Davis 1965). Rainfall is very variable from year to year with plant life sometimes suffering extreme drought conditions. In coastal Isauria and Cilicia, annual rainfall figures for various sites are: Silifke – 632 mm; Tarsus – 677 mm; Adana – 703 mm; Mut (further inland in the Gök Su valley) – 448 mm (Kürschner 1984). In the Cilician Taurus, mean annual rainfall varies from 743–783 mm (at Pozantı) to 1095 mm (at Karsantı); most rainfall occurs during winter and spring. The summer months (June–August) are very dry with only 16–37 mm rainfall during the period.

Mean maximum temperatures at Pozantı, near the Cilician Gates, range from about 9°C in January to 31°C in August (the hottest month). The minimum temperature in January is about -11°C, with a mean minimum of -5°C. Mean temperatures at the coast range from 2–41°C (at Silifke), while the range at Adana is -8 to 45°C (Kürschner 1984).

Adana is by far the largest city. A huge development project is underway which will provide homes for an additional one million people by the year 2000 (Demirsar 1990). A coastal road (often very steep and hazardous) runs from Antalya to Ceyhan. Three important trunk roads traverse the Taurus Mountains (one of which follows the route taken by Alexander the Great's army) and a relief motorway is being built, parallel to existing roads, from the Cilician Gates to Tarsus and then east to Gaziantep. There are few other roads apart from these. There is a civil airport and a military airfield in the vicinity of Adana.

## Vegetation

The vegetation is East Mediterranean in character, with numerous Irano-Turanian elements at higher altitudes (particularly on the Bolkar Dağları) and where overgrazing has allowed a more steppic type of vegetation to develop.

Typical trees include *Abies cilicica* and *Cedrus libani*. Indeed, there are probably more cedars of Lebanon in southern Turkey than are left in Lebanon. As in South West Anatolia, maquis or (where modified) phrygana predominates at lower levels. Deciduous (*Quercus pubescens*) and coniferous (*Pinus nigra*) forests are the climax forest types up to the tree-line, which in the Cilician Taurus is at about 1800–2000 m. *Juniperus foetidissima* and/ or *J. excelsa* occur at the limit of tree growth.

Above the tree-line (in the alpine zone) there are steppic communities and widespread perennial thorn-cushion plants, including numerous species of *Astragalus*, interspersed by tall herbs such as *Asphodeline taurica*.

Alluvial *Tamarix smyrniensis/Populus euphratica* forest was formerly present along all the major rivers and deltas. It persists only in the valley of the Göksu Nehri.

## Flora

At least 2500 species of vascular plants are known to occur in the region; the total number of species may be considerably higher as much of the area remains poorly known botanically. About 520 vascular plant species are Turkish endemics; some 235 of these are endemic to Isauria and/or Cilicia. These include many species of Labiatae (in genera such as *Lamium, Marrubium, Micromeria, Phlomis, Sideritis, Teucrium* and *Thymus*) and Boraginaceae (especially *Alkanna* spp.). Many of these plants contain chemicals (ethereal oils in the Labiatae, pyrrolizidine alkaloids in the Boraginaceae) which make them resistant to grazing.

The area of soft chalk between Ermenek, Mut, Karaman and Silifke supports a very distinctive vegetation with a large number of narrow endemics (well over 40 species). These include cavernicolous species such as *Erodium pelargoniiflorum, Arenaria speluncarum, Teucrium cavernarum, Poa speluncarum* (also found at Lamas Çay), *Omphalodes ripleyana* (also found in the Pisidian Taurus)

and other taxa, including *Silene ermenekensis, Pimpinella isaurica, Cousinia davisiana, Campanula leucosiphon, Alkanna saxicola, A. hispida, Verbascum isauricum, Origanum leptocladum* and *Inula sarana*.

Along the coast between Mersin and Silifke is one of several important littoral dune areas in Turkey. Between Anamur and Mersin, lime-rich littoral dunes occupy an area of 51 km², the largest being the Silifke Dune (50 km²), about one-sixth the total area of dunes in Turkey. The dunes have been studied phytosociologically by Uslu (1977). They contain Euro-Siberian enclaves, including such trees as *Pterocarya fraxinifolia, Taxus baccata, Cornus mas, C. sanguinea* subsp. *australis* and *Sorbus torminalis*, and herbs such as *Lapsana communis, Dorycnium graecum* and *Rubus canescens*. (Most of these species do not occur on the dunes themselves, but along associated watercourses.)

Geyik Dağ, and Ak Dağ immediately to the south of it, have several notable endemics. These include the monotypic legume genus *Sartoria*; *S. hedysaroides* is still only known from the original specimen collected by Heldreich on Geyik Dağ almost 150 years ago, and may already be extinct. Another endemic genus, *Thurya* (Caryophyllaceae) occurs in the Cilician Taurus as well as in the Anti-Taurus and Amanus Mountains. Other species endemic to Geyik Dağ or the nearby Ak Dağ include: *Arenaria isaurica, Gypsophila serpylloides, Dorycnium sanguineum, Doronicum cacaliifolium, Verbascum flavipannosum, Origanum bilgeri, Euphorbia davisii* and *Poa pseudobulbosa*.

There is a large number of *Verbascum* spp., many of which are narrow endemics in the Gülnar, Gilindire (Aydıncık/Kelenderis), Ermenek and Karaman areas.

The Cilician Taurus, especially the Bolkar Dağlari and the area near the Cilician Gates, is another local centre of endemism, including such species as *Helianthemum strickeri, Dianthus lactiflorus, Linum empetrifolium, Heracleum pastinaca, Valerianella bolkarica, Achillea monocephala, Verbascum cilicicum, Aristolochia cilicica, Allium alpinarii* and *Asplenium reuteri*. The monotypic endemic genus *Leucocyclus* (Compositae) is represented by *L. formosus* subsp. *formosus*, which also occurs in Pisidia. *Kitaibela balansae* (Malvaceae) is only known from the Cilician Gates; the only other species of the genus, *K. vitifolia*, is endemic to former Yugoslavia (Webb 1968).

Endemics are also found on the plain of Çukurova. Endemics here include *Beta adanensis, Reseda balansae, Linum anisocalyx, Trigonella halophila, Bellevalia modesta* and *Bromus psammophilus*. These are all threatened as a result of the large-scale changes in land use since the middle of the 20th century.

In the Silifke Valley there is a halophytic community which includes *Halocnemum strobilaceum, Arthrocnemum glaucum* and *Limonium gmelini* (Uslu 1977).

Where disturbance to maquis has given rise to a more steppic type of vegetation, there are numerous Irano-Turanian species, including *Trigonella* spp., *Helianthemum kotschyanum* and *Lotus halophilus*.

## Useful plants

Walnut, fig, pomegranate and hazel are indigenous species which are also cultivated in the region. *Nerium oleander, Populus euphratica* and *Vitex agnus-castus* are used for firewood (Uslu 1977). The roots of *Glycyrrhiza glabra* are used to make syrup, and together with *Pancratium maritimum, Eryngium maritimum, Polygonum equisetiforme, Ipomoea stolonifera* and *Elymus farctus* (*Agropyron junceum*), has been recommended for stabilizing dunes (Uslu 1977).

Species in the Labiatae genera of *Thymus* and *Sideritis* contain oils and other chemicals which are used in the perfume industry and to make herb teas. Such species are also valuable in preventing soil erosion and helping rehabilitation of degraded areas (Kürschner 1984).

The roots of *Alkanna* spp. contain a purple or red dye. The endemic beet, *Beta adanensis* may yield useful genetic material for sugar beet breeding.

There are many species of bulbs of horticultural importance, including *Anemone blanda, Cyclamen cilicium, Eranthis hyemalis* and *Galanthus elwesii*. These are subjected to commercial collection from the wild (see THREATS, below).

Sclerophyllous oak forest has been exploited for firewood and charcoal for such a long time that it is now difficult to find any natural forest in good condition. Deciduous oak forest has also been cleared except for isolated stands, because the excellent soil it favours is valued for agriculture.

The leaves of *Ononis natrix* were formerly used for roofing of houses (Uslu 1977).

## Social and environmental values

The Göksu River delta near Silifke is one of the most important wetlands in the Middle East (see CONSERVATION, below). It is the only breeding ground for the purple gallinule, *Porphyrio porphyrio*; other rare breeding birds include marbled teal, white-breasted kingfisher and graceful warbler. The area is also very important for wintering waterfowl (Yazgan, Magnin and Demirsar 1990). Two species of marine turtles (loggerhead and green) also breed here.

The plain of Çukurova has mostly been drained since the early 1950s and is now mostly under intensive agriculture. It is one of the most important cotton growing regions of Turkey and supports an expanding textile industry. There are still extensive areas of lagoons and freshwater marshes, and these support one of the largest Mediterranean breeding populations of Kentish plover and many black francolin and marbled teal. It is also a stop-over point on the migration route of the white pelican (Yazgan, Magnin and Demirsar 1990).

## Threats

Remnants of natural vegetation of the Çukurova are threatened by the continued expansion of intensive agriculture and by pollution from pesticides, fertilisers, herbicides and other agrochemicals. Oil spillage from refineries in the Gulf of Iskenderun, east of the delta, is a potential threat. When completed, the motorway linking the Cilician Gates with Adana and the east of Turkey will lead to greatly increased levels of pollution from vehicle exhausts and dust. This could be a threat to the survival of several endemics occurring near the Cilician Gates.

Sand from the Silifke dune system is used by local farmers to improve the texture of clayey soil. Wind erosion of the dunes is also apparent, and there is a threat from over-trampling if the tourist industry expands significantly. Much

of the Çukurova dune system has been planted with exotic species (e.g. *Eucalyptus* spp. and exotic *Pinus* spp.) to stabilize the dunes, in spite of recommendations to use native species. The use of exotics is a further threat to the native flora. Coastal endemics must be considered threatened, particularly those on the Çukurova and near developing holiday villages. In addition, *Glycyrrhiza glabra*, which otherwise helps to stabilize dunes, is uprooted in order to make a syrup.

Many bulbs in the region are subject to commercial collection for export. The Ministry of Agriculture and Rural Affairs reported the following export quotas in 1992: *Anemone blanda* (8,000,000), *Cyclamen cilicium* (350,000), *Eranthis hyemalis* (8,000,000) and *Galanthus elwesii* (6,000,000). Most, but probably not all, are collected from the wild within the area under consideration.

The slopes of Cilicia Trachea have been transformed under a government agriculture scheme into banana plantations, olive groves and citrus and fig orchards. Clearance of pine forest changes the quality of the soil (the humus fraction decreases to about 3%); soil erosion and wind transport of topsoil increase markedly after forest clearance (Kürschner 1984).

As yet, tourism in the region is less of a threat than along the western Mediterranean and Aegean coasts (see Data Sheet on South-west Anatolia, CPD Site SWA16). However, the Göksu Delta and its rich wildlife are threatened by the uncontrolled development of holiday villages, and there are hotel developments at Anamur and Mersin, and another holiday village at Kızkalesi. Further developments in the delta region include the construction of fish and shrimp farms.

## Conservation

There is one small National Park, the Tasari Milli Parkı, in the Cilician Taurus above Silifke. Akyatan Gölü, near Karataş, the largest lagoon on the Çukurova, is a Bird Sanctuary. There is a 30 km² Game Reserve at Kargı (Green and Drucker 1990). Göksu Delta Special Protection Area covers 130 km² (IUCN Management Category: IV).

There is a need to conserve more areas in the region, especially the Göksu Valley and associated chalk area, and parts of the Bolkar Dağları.

## References

Davis, P.H. (ed.) (1965-1985). *Flora of Turkey and the East Aegean Islands*. Edinburgh University Press, Edinburgh. (9 vols and Supplement; for latter see Davis, Mill and Tan 1988.)

Davis, P.H., Mill, R.R. and Kit Tan (1988). *Flora of Turkey and the East Aegean Islands*, Vol. 10 (Supplement). Edinburgh University Press, Edinburgh.

Demirsar, M. (ed.) (1990). *Insight guide to Turkish coast*. Apa Publications, Hong Kong.

Green, M.J.B. and Drucker, G.R.F. (1990). Current status of protected areas and threatened mammal species in the Saharo-Gobian region. World Conservation Monitoring Centre, Cambridge, U.K. (Unpublished report.)

Kürschner, H. (1984). *Der östliche Orta Toroslar (Mittlerer Taurus) und angrenzende Gebiete. Eine formationskundliche Darstellung der Vegetation Südöst-Anatoliens.* Wiesbaden. 146 pp.

Uslu, T. (1977). A plant ecological and sociological research on the dune and maquis vegetation between Mersin and Silifke. *Comm. Fac. Sci. Univ. Ankara Sér. C2: Bot.* 21 (Suppl. 1): 1–60.

Webb, D.A. (1968). *Kitaibela.* In Tutin, T.G. *et al., Flora Europaea* 2: 249. Cambridge University Press, Cambridge, U.K.

Yazgan, N., Magnin, G. and Demirsar, M. (1990). Coastal wildlife and environmental issues. In Demirsar, M. (ed.), *Insight guide to Turkish coast.* Apa Publications, Hong Kong. Pp. 102–107.

## Acknowledgements

This Data Sheet was written by Dr Robert R. Mill (Royal Botanic Garden, Edinburgh). Colleagues at the Society for the Protection of Nature, Istanbul, provided many helpful comments on an earlier draft.

MEDITERRANEAN REGIONAL CENTRE OF ENDEMISM: CPD SITE SWA16

# SOUTH-WEST ANATOLIA
## Turkey

**Location:** The area comprises the Turkish vilayets of Aydın, Burdur, Denizli, Isparta, Izmir, Manisa and Muğla, together with West and Central Antalya (as far east, on the coast, as Manavgat). It lies between latitudes 36°05'–39°24'N and longitudes 26°11'–31°27'E.

**Area:** 75,680 km².

**Altitude:** 0–3070 m (summit of Ak Dağ).

**Vegetation:** Mainly maquis or (where degraded) phrygana at low altitudes (below 1200 m); forest mostly above 1200 m, or at lower altitudes on steep cliffs and in other places which have not been greatly disturbed. Dominant trees include oaks, hornbeam, pines and carob. Maquis shrubs include *Lavandula* and *Cistus* spp.

**Flora:** At least 3365 vascular plant species, of which 675 are endemic to Turkey, and a further 30 species are near-endemics which are also found on adjacent Greek islands. 2 endemic genera: *Dorystoechas* (Labiatae) and *Nephelochloa* (Gramineae). 3 other endemic Turkish genera extend into the region. Many endemic species of Labiatae, Liliaceae, Compositae, Caryophyllaceae; many geophytes.

**Useful plants:** Timber trees (e.g. cedar of Lebanon, *Cedrus libani*); food plants (e.g. carob, *Ceratonia siliqua*); oriental sweet gum (*Liquidambar orientalis*), source of oriental storax; *Sideritis* spp. used locally to make teas.

**Other values:** Flood plain wetlands of international importance as breeding grounds for a wide variety of birds, including Dalmatian pelican. Breeding areas of endangered turtles and monk seal populations along coast.

**Threats:** Rapidly expanding tourist industry along Aegean and Lycian coasts; pollution from heavy industry and other sources, near Izmir and Dalaman; overgrazing by goats; clearance of maquis for agriculture; draining of wetlands; over-collection of bulbs and other plants for local use and export.

**Conservation:** Several National Parks and Protected Zones; 5 Biogenetic Reserves (covering c. 264.5 km²). Security of protected areas threatened by conflicting demands and pressures of industry and tourism.

## Geography

The area as defined here comprises the whole of the seven south-western Turkish vilayets (provinces) of Aydın, Manisa, Izmir, Denizli, Muğla, Burdur and Isparta, together with the western part of Antalya, as far east as Manavgat. It lies between latitudes 36°05'–39°24'N and longitudes 26°11'–31°27'E. The provinces have a combined area of 75,680 km² (Aydın – 8007 km²; Burdur – 6887 km²; Denizli – 11,868 km²; Isparta – 8933 km²; Izmir – 11,973 km²; Manisa – 13,810 km²; together with about 14,200 km² of Antalya). The remainder of Antalya forms part of the Isaurian Taurus (see Data Sheet on the Isaurian, Lycaonian and Cilician Taurus, CPD Site SWA15).

South-west Anatolia has very varied geology. In the west, chalk occurs at low altitudes, while high peaks consist of basic igneous rocks, mica schists (especially in the Ödemiş area), granite and limestone. Much of Caria, especially Sandras Dağ and the Marmaris Peninsula, is serpentine; this forms outcrops both here, at the western extremity of the Taurus Range, and again at the eastern extremity (Ala Dağ, Masmutli Dağ and Acimam Yayları: see Data Sheet on the Isaurian, Lycaonian and Cilician Taurus, CPD Site SWA15), and also in north-west Syria (see Data Sheet on the Levantine Uplands, CPD Site SWA17), but nowhere in between (Quézel 1973). The Bey Dağları (Lycian Taurus), west of Antalya, consists of hard limestone (Davis 1965). The western part, in particular, is subject to earthquakes and there are hot springs in several places, including Çeşme (Izmir) and Pamukkale (Denizli).

The coastline is very indented, with many spectacular gulfs and coves. There are five major peninsulas on the Aegean coast: the Çeşme Peninsula, west of Izmir; the Dilek Peninsula, opposite Samos; the Bodrum Peninsula, opposite Kos; the very narrow Reşadiye (or Datça) Peninsula; and the nearby Marmaris (or Daraçya) Peninsula, extending south-west towards Rodhos. All main offshore islands, except those in the Gulf of Izmir and Kekova Adası south-west of Kale (Antalya), belong to Greece. The Kastellorizo group of islets near Kaş are also administered by Greece.

There are many complex mountain ranges, mostly running east-west or north-east/south-west. Although they are not as high as mountains further east, individual peaks are sufficiently high and isolated to have significant numbers of endemics. The main peaks are Boz Dağ (1407 m), Aydın Dağ (1142 m), Oyuklu Dağ (1367 m), Sandras Dağ (2294 m), Eren Tepe (2421 m), Baba Dağ (1969 m), Honaz Dağ (2571 m), Elmalı Dağ (2505 m), Çiçek Dağ (2239 m), Dedegöl Dağları (highest peak, 2992 m) and Ak Dağ in the Bey Dağları (3070 m). The mountains plunge steeply into the sea along virtually the entire coastline. Exceptions are the low-lying ground surrounding Izmir; the flood plains of the Küçük Menderes and Büyük Menderes rivers in the Ödemiş/Meryemana and Aydın/Priene areas, respectively; the Dalaman area; and the coastal plain of Pamphylia bordering Antalya Körfezi, east of Antalya near Manavgat. There are several large inland lakes in the Burdur/Isparta area including Beyşehir Gölu, Eğridir Gölu and Burdur Gölu, as well as Bafa Gölu on the Carian coast.

The climate is typically Mediterranean, with mild wet winters and long, hot, arid summers. Temperatures are less extreme on the Aegean coast than on the Mediterranean coast. At Izmir, temperatures range from 8°C in January to 27°C in July, while at Antalya the corresponding minima and maxima are 12°C and 36°C. On the western side, inland temperatures are only slightly cooler in winter than on the coast, but the Lycian Taurus is much colder in winter (down to about -4°C in January). Annual rainfall over most of the region is 500–800 mm, but the Datça Peninsula and the coastal ranges from Marmaris to Finike, receive over 1000 mm, and locally up to 1500 mm. Most of the rainfall occurs in winter. The coastal regions are the wettest parts in winter but, conversely, they are the most arid in summer, when they receive almost no rain at all, while the Lycian Mountains (the wettest area in summer) receive 40–60 mm rainfall in summer.

The population was estimated in 1980 at 5,197,800 (about one-eighth of the total population of Turkey: Aydın – 652,488; Burdur – 235,009; Denizli – 603,338; Isparta – 350,116; Izmir – 1,976,763; Manisa – 941,941; Muğla – 438,145; the population of the whole of Antalya was 748,706). In ancient times the area was the home of many indigenous peoples (Arzawans, Leleges, Luwians, Lydians, Lycians, Carians). The present population is mostly Turkish, with some Jewish and other ethnic minorities in Izmir, the largest city.

The road network is fairly extensive and is undergoing rapid development in some districts. There are several harbours and ports, including Datça, Bodrum, Marmaris, Izmir, Kuşadasi, Fethiye, Kaş, Finike, Kemer and Antalya. There are major airports at Izmir and Dalaman, the latter a very recent development catering for charter holiday traffic. Another tourist airport is being built at Güllük near Bodrum (Demirsar 1990).

## Vegetation

The region belongs mostly to the East Mediterranean floristic province, which extends from Italy to Lebanon (Takhtajan 1986). Below 1200 m, the principal vegetation is maquis dominated by evergreen shrubs, such as *Cistus creticus*, *C. salviifolius*, *Erica verticillata* and *Pistacia lentiscus*. Phrygana develops where maquis has been degraded; *Lavandula stoechas*, *Thymbra spicata*, *Smilax excelsa* and *Nerium oleander* are the main species of phrygana. Forests occur above 1200 m altitude, and at lower altitudes in places where the vegetation has not been greatly modified (e.g. on some of the steeper cliffs). Dominant trees include *Carpinus betulus*, *Celtis australis*, *Ceratonia siliqua*, *Pinus brutia*, *Quercus coccifera*, *Q. libani* and *Q. haas*. Above 1200 m, *Pinus nigra* subsp. *pallasiana* is often the most abundant tree. Elmalı has a small forest of *Cedrus libani*. *Juniperus excelsa* often forms the tree-line (Davis 1965). Quézel (1973) noted that throughout the Taurus, slopes facing the Mediterranean were almost totally forested (or had the potential to be so), while north-facing slopes are much drier and their flora resembles that of the Anatolian steppe.

*Pinus pinea* is extremely localised as a native in Turkey, being largely or wholly confined to the coastal strip between Antalya and Manavgat where it is the dominant tree on the sand dunes in the area. Unfortunately, these are severely threatened by tourism development, including those at Belek, the finest stands of all.

Serpentine rocks (ophiolites and diorites) support a distinct calcifuge vegetation characterised by species such as *Asplenium cuneifolium*, *A. septentrionale*, *Cheilanthes marantae*, *Cystopteris fragilis* and *Sedum dasyphyllum*. Sandras Dağ, which largely comprises serpentine and other ophiolithic rocks, is covered with *Pinus nigra* forest up to 2100 m (although this is fragmented above 1900 m). It has an exceedingly rich herb flora at middle and upper altitudes, with many narrow and localised endemics. Typical species of Sandras Dağ include *Viola sandrasea* and *Potentilla calycina* (both of which have disjunct distributions, occurring as distinct subspecies on Sandras Dağ and the eastern outcrops of Ala Dağ), *Ebenus pisidicus* and *Rosularia serpentinica*. Species growing on serpentine screes at higher altitudes include *Rumex scutatus*, *Senecio sandrasicus* and *Spodiopogon pogonanthus*. Ak Dağ, in Lycia, has abundant cedar forests up to 2000 m, and very degraded *Juniperus excelsa* scrub up to 2300 m on north- and east-facing slopes.

Associations found on calcareous rocks in the Lycian Taurus include:

1. *Verbascum pestalozzae/Polylophium thalictroides* association, e.g. on the north slope of Teke Dağ, from 1500–2000 m. Characteristic species are suffrutescent chamaephytes, e.g. *Verbascum pestalozzae*, *Asyneuma lycium* (a rare endemic), *Nepeta phyllochlamys*, *Aethionema polygaloides*, *Anthemis anatolica* and *Salvia caespitosa*.

2. *Agropyron divaricatum/Aurinia rupestris* association, e.g. on Ak Dağ between 1600–2500 m. Typical species include *Asyneuma linifolium*, *Aurinia rupestris*, *Elymus lazicus* subsp. *divaricatus* (*Agropyron divaricatum*), *Micromeria juliana* var. *myrtifolia* and *Rosularia pestalozzae*.

3. *Aubrieta canescens/Scrophularia depauperata* association, which replaces the above association on Ak Dağ above 2700 m. Dominant species are *Aubrieta canescens*, *Scrophularia depauperata*, *Arenaria uninervia*, *Asperula lycia*, *Sideritis perfoliata* and *Veronica quezelii*.

Calcareous screes (e.g. on Ak Dağ) include *Ferula lycia*, *Heldreichia bourgaei*, *Heracleum massicyticum*, *Nepeta lycia* and *Scrophularia uniflora* among their flora.

Much of the Taurus is covered with grazed, xeric alpine meadows dominated by chamaephytes and caespitose hemicryptophytes, belonging to families such as Boraginaceae, Caryophyllaceae, Cruciferae, Labiatae and Scrophulariaceae. Thorn cushion plants are well represented, e.g. *Acantholimon echinus* and *Minuartia juniperina*.

Some typical associations of these "grazed lawns" include:

1. *Tanacetion praeteriti* association, localised on Tahtali Dağ and Bey Dağ and including *Anthemis rosea*, *Astragalus paecilanthus*, *Dianthus eretmopetalus*, *Odontites aucheri* and *Tanacetum praeteritum*.

2. *Agropyron-Stachyon* association, which covers much of the western central Taurus east of Antalya and extends to the Isaurian and Cilician Taurus. *Elymus tauri* (*Agropyron tauri*), *Arenaria acerosa*, *Asphodeline taurica*, *Silene supina* and *Stachys lavandulifolia* are some of the typical species present.

3. *Alyssum propinquum* and *A. masmenaeum*, with species of the *Tanacetion*, occur on serpentine rocks of Sandras Dağ.

The summit vegetation of the Lycian Taurus includes such species as *Alopecurus lanatus*, *Asperula lycia*, *Dianthus brevicaulis*, *Paronychia lycia*, *Lamium cymbalariifolium*, *L. microphyllum*, *Ranunculus brevifolius* and *Thesium tauricolum*. The two *Lamium* species are vicarious endemics, *L. cymbalariifolium* being confined to Sandras Dağ and *L. microphyllum* to Honaz Dağ (Denizli); both are closely allied to another narrow endemic, *L. veronicifolium* found on Ulu Dağ (CPD Site SWA20). *Centaurea urvillei*, *Eryngium spinosissimum*, *Onobrychis cornuta* and *Saponaria chlorifolia* form a distinct association on calcareous moraines.

## Flora

Over 3365 vascular plant species are known to occur in the region, of which 675 species are endemic to Turkey. Two genera are endemic to South-west Anatolia (*Dorystoechas* and *Nephelochloa*), while 3 other Turkish endemic genera, *Leucocyclus*, *Microsciadium* and *Olymposciadium* extend into the region. On the flood plain of the Dalaman Çay, there is a remarkable, periodically flooded, *Liquidambar orientalis* forest (the main area of which covers c. 63 km²) (Huş 1949). This species occurs only in West Anatolia (at several sites in the Dalaman/Marmaris area, also near Çine and Kalkan, and further inland near Burdur) and on the neighbouring Greek island of Rodhos. It is a Boreal-Tertiary relict, closely related to *L. styraciflua* of western North America. Associated species include *Periploca graeca*, *Platanus orientalis*, *Vitis vinifera*, *Alisma plantago-aquatica* and *Lysimachia vulgaris* (Yaltirik 1973).

The Bey Dağları has some endemics, while the range extending from Tahtalı Dağ to Bereketli Dağ has a high number of palaeoendemics. These include a remarkable shrubby labiate, *Dorystoechas hastata*, together with *Asyneuma lycium*, *Globularia davisiana*, *Verbascum davisianum* and many endemic species of *Sideritis*, *Phlomis*, *Micromeria* and *Origanum*. All 3 Turkish endemic species of *Chionodoxa* occur in the region (one extends as far as Ala Dağ in the Anti-Taurus Mountains, CPD Site SWA12 – see Data Sheet).

Endemics are fewer in the west than in the south of the region; however, nearly every peak, including Manisa Dağ, Honaz Dağ and Boz Dağ, has at least one or two (and often a dozen or more) endemic species. Sandras Dağ has a high number of serpentine endemics, while the Elmali area is another notable centre of endemism.

## Useful plants

*Liquidambar orientalis* (oriental sweet gum) is the source of oriental storax, referred to in the Bible as "balm". Many species of *Sideritis* sect. *Empedoclea* are used locally to make herb teas. Other herbs, e.g. *Origanum* spp., are of culinary and/or medicinal importance. *Chionodoxa*, *Crocus*, *Galanthus*, *Lilium*, *Scilla* and other bulbs are of horticultural value and large quantities are exported.

Important populations of timber trees, such as *Cedrus libani*, occur in the region. Carob (*Ceratonia siliqua*) is a source of food.

## Social and environmental values

The maquis is used by local people as a source of plant dyes for clothing and Turkish carpets, animal fodder and as a source of wood for fuel. The amenable climate and the exceptionally fertile soil along the coast allows a wide variety of food and cash crops to be grown. Until recently, Turkey was one of only seven countries wholly self-sufficient in food, but population growth and poor agricultural management probably means that this is no longer the case.

The wetland areas on the Kuçuk Menderes and Büyük Menderes flood plains, the Çamaltı Tuzlası swamps along the north-western part of Izmir Bay, and Bafa Gölü, are all of paramount international importance for the richness of their bird fauna. Çamaltı Tuzlası has over 180 breeding or wintering species, while the Büyük Menderes is a major breeding ground for the Dalmatian pelican, an endangered species, of which there are only about 2000 pairs remaining throughout its range. The wetland system of Köyceğiz Lake and Dalyan (near Fethiye) is particularly important for the wide range of habitats present. Part of this site, Iztuzu Beach, is a major breeding ground for loggerhead turtles (Yazgan, Magnin and Demirsar 1990).

South-west Anatolia has been settled since Stone Age times and contains an immense number of archaeological sites of major importance.

## Threats

Tourism is expanding rapidly and is now a major threat to the coast and peninsulas. By 1988 there were 40 holiday villages along the Aegean and Mediterranean coasts. Another 60 village resorts are under construction (Erten 1990). The Lycian coast is termed "The Honolulu of Turkey" and many previously small fishing villages have been developed into bustling holiday towns. Much of the development has been uncontrolled with little or no thought to the effect on the environment. The Küçük Menderes River delta between Izmir and Ephesus is one of the most endangered wetland areas on the western Turkish coast. Twelve hotels have already been built there; more are under construction. The building of roads will allow access and development in inland areas.

The Çamaltı Tuzlası Bird Sanctuary, and an area near Dalaman which is not protected, is affected by pollution from heavy industries in Izmir Bay. Dalaman Çay is polluted by waste from the Seka paper plant, a threat to the health of humans and to the survival of breeding turtles.

The main threats in the mountains are overgrazing by goats and the clearance of native vegetation for agriculture. Such clearances affect the soil moisture balance, resulting in spring floods and extreme summer drought. Some lakes, including Söğüt Göl in Antalya, have been drained or have dried up, thereby causing the loss of significant populations of aquatic plants and associated fauna.

Afforestation of lowland sites on limestone and serpentine is a threat to the rich ground flora of these developed on these substrates. Of particular concern is the threat to the flora of serpentine and related rocks of the Datça Peninsula, including rare and local species, such as *Colchicum lingulatum*, *Fritillaria forbesii*, *Muscari macrocarpum*, *Linum arboreum*, *Eryngium thorifolium* and *Phoenix theophrasti*. The native open woodlands around Marmaris, which support a rich ground flora, are threatened by afforestation with *Pinus brutia*.

Large quantities of ornamental bulbs and corms are commercially collected for export. This has seriously depleted populations of *Cyclamen* (including the localised *C. mirabile*), *Sternbergia* (including illegal collection of *S. candida*) and *Lilium candidum*. Orchids (the tubers of which are used to make salep, a milk-based drink said to have aphrodisiac properties) are also uprooted.

## Conservation

Five Biogenetic Reserves were established in the area between 1978 and 1981 (Taylor-Saçlioğlu 1987):

❖ Termessos Scrub Flora Biogenetic Reserve (67 km², Antalya);
❖ Köprülü Canyon Cypress Forest Biogenetic Reserve (4.4 km², Antalya, near the Isaurian Taurus);
❖ Dilek Peninsula Flora Biogenetic Reserve (109 km², Aydın, currently being extended as a National Park to 360 km²);
❖ Köyceğiz Forest Biogenetic Reserve (30 ha, Muğla);
❖ Kasnak Forest Oak Biogenetic Reserve (83.8 km², Isparta).

The cedar forest of Elmalı is a Protected Area. The Köyceğiz-Dalyan wetlands are designated a Special Protection Area of 11.5 km² (IUCN Management Category: IV). A large area of eastern Lycia between Kumluca and Antalya, including Tahtali Dağ with its numerous endemics, now comprises the Olimpos-Beydağları Sahil Milli Parkı (698 km²) (National Park, IUCN Management Category: II). Unfortunately, this has not prevented development. The National Park originally extended to the beach to protect one of the last remaining breeding sites (30–60 animals) of the monk seal in the Mediterranean. The coastal strip was, however, sacrificed for hotel development.

## References

Davis, P.H. (ed.) (1965-1985). *Flora of Turkey and the East Aegean Islands*. Edinburgh University Press, Edinburgh. (9 vols and Supplement; for latter see Davis, Mill and Tan 1988.)

Davis, P.H. and Henderson, D.M. (1984). *Lilium*. In Davis, P.H. (ed.), *Flora of Turkey*, Vol. 8. Edinburgh University Press, Edinburgh. Pp. 279–284.

Davis, P.H., Mill, R.R. and Kit Tan (1988). *Flora of Turkey and the East Aegean Islands*, Vol. 10 (Supplement). Edinburgh University Press, Edinburgh.

Demiriz, H. and Baytop, A. (1985). The Anatolian Peninsula. In Gómez-Campo, C. (ed.), *Plant conservation in the Mediterranean area*. Geobotany Series 7. Dr W. Junk, Dordrecht. Pp. 113–121.

Demirsar, M. (ed.) (1990). *Insight guide to Turkish coast*. Apa Publications, Hong Kong.

Erten, S.Ü. (1990). Holiday villages. In Demirsar, M. (ed.), *Insight guide to Turkish coast*. Apa Publications, Hong Kong. Pp. 96–97.

Huş, S. (1949). Suğla Ağacının (*Liquidambar orientalis* Mill.) ormancılık bakımından önemi ve sığla yağının kimyasal arastırılması. *Orman Genel Müdürlüğü Yayınları* (Istanbul), no. 83.

Quézel, P. (1973). Contribution à l'étude phytosociologique du massif du Taurus. *Phytocoenologia* 1: 131–222.

Takhtajan, A. (1986). *Floristic regions of the world*. University of California Press, Berkeley. 522 pp.

Taylor-Saçlioğlu, V. (1987 transl.) *Biological diversity in Turkey*. Environmental Problems Foundation of Turkey, Ankara.

Yaltirik, F. (1973). The floristic composition of major forests in Turkey. *Kazdağı Göknarı ve Türkiye Florasi Uluslarası Simpozyomu Bildirileri (Proceedings of the International Symposium on Abies equi-trojani and Turkish Flora), Istanbul, 22–28 October 1973*. Pp. 179–194.

Yazgan, N., Magnin, G. and Demirsar, M. (1990). Coastal wildlife and environmental issues. In Demirsar, M. (ed.), *Insight guide to Turkish Coast*. Apa Publications, Hong Kong. Pp. 102–107.

## Acknowledgements

This Data Sheet was written by Dr Robert R. Mill (Royal Botanic Garden, Edinburgh).

# THE LEVANTINE UPLANDS
## Turkey, Syria, Lebanon, Israel and Jordan

**Location:** The area comprises southern Turkey (the Hatay), north-west Syria (Jabal an Nusayriyah and associated hills) including Latakia, the whole of Lebanon and parts of northernmost Israel and Jordan, as far south as Mount Carmel, approximately between latitudes 32°45'–37°35'N and longitudes 34°58'–37°00'E.

**Area:** 96,675 km².

**Altitude:** 0–3083 m (summit of Qornet-es-Saouda).

**Vegetation:** *Quercus calliprinos* forest and scrub, *Abies cilicica* forest, *Cedrus libani* forest; only 5% of original forest cover remaining. *Juniperus* scrub, subalpine tragacanthic communities and alpine vegetation. Degraded vegetation includes maquis, garigue and batha.

**Flora:** c. 4160 vascular plant species in 146 families and c. 950 genera. About 635 endemic species (c. 14%); endemism higher in north than in south. 7 genera endemic within the area, of which *Lycochloa* is endemic to Lebanon; all are monotypic.

**Useful plants:** Many species used locally as sources of food, fodder, pasture, vegetable dyes, essential and edible oils. Timber trees (e.g. Cilician fir, cedar of Lebanon) formerly extremely important.

**Other values:** Part of the "Fertile Crescent" – soils very fertile in some places and used for agriculture, citriculture; tourism.

**Threats:** Uncontrolled logging, intensive agriculture, urbanization, coastal tourist developments at Latakia, over-harvesting of some species to extract essential oils.

**Conservation:** No protected areas covering that part of the region in Lebanon or Turkey; few in Syria, more in Israel but all small. Some species, e.g. all Orchidaceae, protected in Israel.

## Geography

The Levantine Uplands consist of two mountain chains running parallel to the eastern shore of the Mediterranean Sea and separating the latter from the Syrian Desert (Bridges 1990). The area under consideration comprises the mountains of southernmost Turkey (the Hatay), western Syria, Lebanon and small parts of northern Israel and Jordan, together with associated coasts and valleys. The region lies between longitudes 36°15'–37°00'E at latitude 37°30'N and between 34°58'–36°00'E at latitude 32°45'N.

The western chain of mountains has its northernmost point at Ahir Dağ, north of Maraş in Turkey. It connects with the Taurus and Amanus Mountains. Principal peaks include Daz Dağ (2240 m), Karlik Tepe (1420 m), Kizil Dağ (1795 m) and Musa Dağ (1281 m). The valley of the Orontes River (Asi Nehri) in Turkey separates the Amanus Mountains from the Jabal an Nusayriyah, most of which are in north-western Syria. To the south lies Jabal Lubnan, or the Lebanon Mountains. These are more lofty than the Jabal an Nusayriyah and include numerous peaks of over 2000 m, the highest being Qornet-es-Saouda (3083 m, the highest peak in Lebanon).

In Israel and south Lebanon, with a westernmost extremity in Sinai, there is a chain of low hills and mountains reaching 1208 m at Har Meron (Jabal Jarmak) in Galilee. The Galilee Hills (included in the region as here defined) are separated from those of Samaria (which lie outside the region) by a wide alluvial plain (Emek Yizreel). Mount Carmel is the most southerly point of the area included in this Data Sheet. The hills of Samaria and Judaea and the whole of the ranges in Jordan (Gilead, Moav, Edom, Ammon) are excluded, as floristically they have more in common with the Saharo-Arabian flora than that of the Mediterranean or Irano-Turanian regions.

The eastern chain of mountains commences in the north as low hills extending from Kapuşam in Turkey, south to Sof Dağ and Kurd Dağ on the Syrian border, through minor ranges and a broad basaltic plain in the Syrian Desert, to the much higher Anti-Lebanon Mountains (Jabal Lubnan ash Sharq), which reach 2729 m at Jabal el Atneine. The Anti-Lebanon Mountains run parallel to the Lebanon Mountains, from which they are separated by the Beqaa Valley. A small gap separates the southernmost peaks of the Anti-Lebanon from Mount Hermon (Jabal ech Cheikh, 2814 m), which dominates the Damascus Plateau and forms the boundary between Syria and Lebanon. Its southern foothills are the Golan Heights.

Between the two major chains of hills and mountains which comprise the Levantine Uplands is a northern extension of the East African Rift Valley, running through Wadi Arava, the Dead Sea, the Jordan Valley and Lake Tiberias, to 'Emeq Hula (the Hula Plain) on the Israel/Syria/Lebanon border. North of the Hula Plain, the Rift Valley turns slightly northeast, crosses the boundary between Syria and Turkey and then turns west across the flood plain of Amik to enter the Mediterranean at Samandağ.

Most of the mountains are calcareous. Soils are typically "brown mediterranean" or red "terra rossa". The Jurassic, Cretaceous and Eocene limestones of the Jebel Akra and northern Jabal an Nusayriyah weather into a jaggedly dissected terrain with sharp ridges and crests, locally known as "Lapiaz". Black rendzina soils are common here (Nahal 1962).

Chalky marls occur in the Rift Valley and near Latakia. Peridotite and serpentine rocks occur only around Baer-Bassit in north-west Syria and in several outcrops in the

Amanus Mountains. These form part of a Miocene reef marking the boundary of a shallow "Levantine sea" in the area of the Gulf of Iskenderun underlain by evaporites (Sonnenfeld 1974). They are similar in age and character to the ophiolitic rocks of the Troodos Mountains (Cyprus) (CPD Site Eu18 – see Data Sheet) and parts of the Cilician Taurus (see Data Sheet on the Isaurian, Lycaonian and Cilician Taurus – CPD Site SWA15) which form part of the same system.

The climate throughout the territory is Mediterranean but, especially on the leeward side of the mountains, is transitional to that prevailing in the Syrian and Arabian Deserts. Along the coastal plain, summers are humid and warm and winters very mild. The mountains are cooler and have such a pleasant climate in summer that numerous small tourist resorts have developed. The highest rainfall (c. 1700 mm per annum) occurs in parts of the Amanus range above 1750 m (Akman 1973a), compared with 740 mm for Beirut and up to 1400 mm on the western slopes of the Syrian ranges (Takahashi and Arakawa 1981). The eastern chain is in the rainshadow, with 200–1000 mm rainfall in Lebanon and rather less in Syria. Summer temperatures (July) mostly range from 21–37°C, the coolest places being the middle and upper slopes of the Amanus Mountains and the hottest being inland depressions, such as the Ghab and the Beqaa Valley. In early and late summer, the hot dry *khamsin* wind sometimes blows from the Arabian Desert, bringing extremely hot conditions for short periods.

The population of the Hatay region of Turkey is c.856,000; western Syria has a population of c. 6,300,000 (c. 56% of the total Syrian population); while Lebanon's population is 3,000,000 (Hunter 1992).

## Vegetation

The vegetation is primarily Oro-Mediterranean in character. On the coastal plain, geophytes are an important component of the vegetation. They include *Iris* spp., *Narcissus tazetta*, *Pancratium maritimum* and *Tulipa* spp.

A mosaic of vegetation types occurs in the hills and mountains. Only 5% of the original forest cover remains; much has been cleared or degraded to maquis, garigue and batha (a low, very degraded type of garigue comprising shrubs on average not more than 50 cm high, as opposed to 1 m for garigue).

Climax vegetation types that were once widespread in the region are (Zohary 1973): *Ceratonia siliqua/Myrtus communis* thermophilous community, restricted to the lowest zone (200–300 m) of the western slopes of southern Lebanon; *Quercus calliprinos/Pistacia palaestina* association, formerly widespread throughout the area below 1000 m, but much now cleared; *Pinus halepensis* forest in southern Lebanon; *Pinus brutia* forest in the northern parts of the region up to 1200–1500 m; *Cupressus sempervirens* evergreen maquis; *Pinus pinea* forest in central and southern Lebanon between 350–1200 m, mainly on sandstone (*Rhododendron ponticum* occurs as a relict of this vegetation); *Quercus boissieri/ Q. cerris* forest in the Anti-Lebanon Mountains and west-facing slopes of Jabal an Nusayriyah; *Cedrus libani* forest, mainly between 1600–2000 m (of which there are relictual stands in Lebanon, e.g. at Bisharra, Cedres, Ehden, Haddeth and Jebel Qarnuta; and on the east-facing slopes of Jabal an Nusayriyah in north-western Syria); *Abies cilicica* forest on

cooler and wetter north- and west-facing slopes, especially those of Jabal an Nusayriyah; *Juniperus excelsa* on drier slopes facing the steppes and deserts; subalpine tragacanthic community of cushion-like dwarf shrubs and associated herbs, found above the tree-line in northern Lebanon and Syria in particular; alpine vegetation between 2500–3000 m (less species-rich than the subalpine tragacanthic community).

The principal lowland secondary communities in the mountains are garigue and batha, both dominated by *Sarcopoterium spinosum*. Typical associated species include *Cistus creticus, Rhamnus palaestinus, Salvia triloba, Teucrium polium, Andropogon distachyus, Dactylis glomerata* and *Hyparrhenia hirta*.

Calcareous sandstone near the coastline of Israel supports *Limonium sinuatum, Lotus creticus, Trifolium palaestinum* and other psammophytes, including some endemics. In contrast, the dry southern and eastern slopes of the Anti-Lebanon and Lebanon mountains and Mt Hermon, support batha and garigue with many Irano-Turanian elements of the adjacent Syrian Desert, e.g. *Asphodelus microcarpus, Astragalus sanctus, Gundelia tournefortii, Heliotropium rotundifolium* and *Kickxia aegyptiaca*. On Mount Carmel there is an unusual localised *Genista fasselata* association, with *Cistus creticus, C. salviifolius, Phlomis viscosa* and *Salvia hierosolymitana*.

Bare rocks and outcrops below 1000 m are colonised by various lithophytes such as *Ballota saxatilis, Micromeria fruticosa, Stachys palaestina* and *Varthemia montanum*, often in association with *Cyclamen persicum, Onosma* spp. and *Umbilicus intermedius*. The growth of thick rootstocks of *Varthemia montanum* and *Onosma* spp. breaks up rocks and thereby helps to restore soil cover.

The Amanus Mountains are important phytogeographically as they lie at the southern end of the "Anatolian Diagonal" (see Data Sheet on Anti-Taurus Mountains and Upper Euphrates – CPD Site SWA12) and can be considered its southern extension into Syria and Lebanon. They also provide a migration route for species along Lebanon mountain ranges, the Taurus range, and also along the mountain chains in south-east Turkey and the northern Syrian Desert. They contain several southern enclaves of Euxine or Euro-Siberian vegetation, including species such as *Acer platanoides, Alnus incana, Ostrya carpinifolia, Tilia argentea, Ulmus glabra* (Euro-Siberian elements) and *Fagus orientalis, Ilex colchica, Juglans regia, Rhododendron ponticum* and *Staphylea pinnata* (Euxine elements) and many species of woodland herbs (Akman 1973). It is thought that these enclaves are relicts of a vegetation which migrated southwards during the cooler, pluvial periods of the Pleistocene, and which has persisted because of the locally high rainfall. Many species are at their southernmost limits, such as *Acer campestre, Alnus incana, Asperula odorata, Atropa belladonna, Fragaria vesca* and *Lathraea squamaria*. Smaller enclaves occur around Silinfah and Nabi Matta on the Jabal an Nusayriyah, to which *Cerasus mahaleb, Corylus avellana, Daphne oleoides, Inula conyza* and *Sorbus torminalis* extend (Nahal 1962).

Pioneer communities of abandoned fields and olive groves are dominated by annuals, often with brightly coloured flowers: the "lilies of the field". These include *Adonis* spp., *Chrysanthemum coronarium, Nigella arvensis* and *Papaver* spp., and are often associated with such geophytes as *Anemone coronaria, Crocus* spp., *Cyclamen* spp., *Iris* spp., *Ixiolirion tataricum* and *Tulipa* spp. These make abandoned cultivated areas a mass of brilliant colours in the peak flowering season. Many of the species are pan-Mediterranean, others are restricted to the east Mediterranean, while a few are endemic to the area under consideration.

For more detailed treatments of the vegetation of the region, see Mouterde (1966–1982) and Zohary (1973). Nahal (1962) treats the vegetation of the Jabal an Nusayriyah in more detail, while Akman (1973b, c) covers the Amanus Mountains. The vegetation of Israel and Jordan is covered by Zohary (1962).

## Flora

About 4160 vascular plant species have been recorded from the area under consideration (of nearly 5000 species occurring in the whole of Lebanon, Syria, Jordan, Israel and the Amanus Mountains). These are distributed among 146 families and about 950 genera. About 3300 species are dicotyledons, of which 534 (16%) are endemic, 818 species are monocotyledons, of which 101 (14%) are endemic, 14 species are gymnosperms (0 endemic) and 41 species are pteridophytes (0 endemic). (Note that these figures apply to the area covered by this Data Sheet; figures in Table 46 below refer to the *entire* area of each territory.)

There are no endemic families, but 7 genera are endemic to the area under consideration. They are *Astoma*, *Chaetosciadium* and *Synelcosciadium* (all Umbelliferae), *Mosheovia* (Scrophulariaceae), *Postia* (Compositae), *Pilgerochloa* and *Lycochloa* (Gramineae). The latter is narrowly endemic to Lebanon; all the genera are monotypic.

Species endemism is higher in the north of the region than in the south.

### TABLE 46. TOTAL PLANT SPECIES IN THE AMANUS MOUNTAINS, LEBANON, SYRIA, ISRAEL AND JORDAN

| | Total species | Broad endemics | Narrow endemics | Total endemics | % Endemism |
|---|---|---|---|---|---|
| Amanus | c. 2400 | 128 | 139 | 267 | 12 |
| Lebanon | c. 2600 | 221 | 90 | 311 | 12 |
| Syria | c. 3100 | 250 | 145 | 395 | 13 |
| Israel | c. 2225 | 130 | 35 | 165 | 7.4 |
| Jordan | c. 2100 | 99 | 46 | 145 | 7.3 |

Broad endemics are defined here as species which are restricted to two or more of the territories treated in this Data Sheet (but including parts of those territories outside the Data Sheet area); narrow endemics are those species which occur in only a single territory (including parts of those territories outside the Data Sheet area).

All the Jordanian endemics, and many of the Israeli ones, grow in localities outside the area covered here. The high endemism in Syria is also in large part accounted for by species endemic to Irano-Turanian steppe and tragacanthic communities in the Syrian Desert and its associated hills, excluded from this treatment.

The Amanus, though a very small part of the area, is notable for its very high number of narrow endemics – more than half of the total – including *Alkanna amana*, *Allium karamanoglui*, *Crocus adanensis*, *Erodium amanum*, *Fritillaria haradjianii*, *Gypsophila arsusianum*, *Hypericum monadenum*, several *Isatis* spp., *Origanum brevidens*, *Ornithogalum sorgerae*, numerous species (or microspecies) of *Thlaspi*, 7 species of *Verbascum* and many others.

*Leucocyclus formosus* subsp. *amanicus*, *Alyssum cassium*, *A. haradjianii*, *Anthemis cassia*, *Chamaecytisus cassius*, *Peucedanum haradjianii*, *Stachys petrokosmos* and *Thlaspi microstylum* are endemic to the serpentine

formations of Mt Cassius and nearby parts of the Amanus Mountains. Species of *Alyssum* and *Thlaspi* are nickel-accumulators restricted to serpentine.

Species endemic to both the Lebanon and Anti-Lebanon ranges (some extending into the Amanus) include: *Berberis libanotica*, *Centaurea libanotica*, *Convolvulus libanoticus*, *Elymus libanoticus*, *Eremopoa capillaris*, *Gypsophila mollis*, *Lamium ehrenbergii* and *Romulea nivalis*. Endemics of the Lebanon range include *Alchemilla diademata*, *Allium sannineum*, *Hieracium kneissaeum*, *Ranunculus schweinfurthii* and *Tripleurospermum sannineum* (all on the Jabal Knisse and/or Jabal Sannine massifs), and *Astragalus kornet-es-saudae* and *Lepidium culminicolum*, both on Qornet-es-Saouda, the highest peak of Lebanon. Anti-Lebanon endemics include *Ajuga chasmophila*, *Allium zebdanense*, *Centaurea longispina*, *Erodium gaillardotii* and *Iris antilibanotica*. A few species, such as *Iris nusairiensis* and *Stachys nusairiensis*, are endemic to Jabal an Nusayriyah.

Littoral and coastal communities, from Amanus and Latakia southwards, have a number of endemic species, including *Aegilops sharonensis*, *Anthemis tripolitana*, *Ballota philistaea*, *Convolvulus secundus*, *Ornithogalum densum*, *Rumex occultans*, *Silene modesta* and two species of *Trifolium*.

There are close connections between the floras of the East Mediterranean mountains, Cilician Taurus and Cyprus, as a result of Cyprus being joined to the mainland in the recent geological past. Many species, some near-endemic, extend to the Cilician Taurus, Cyprus or both, but have their main centre of distribution in the Levant. They include *Thlaspi densiflorum* (Cyprus and Cilicia), *Anthriscus lamprocarpa*, *Erodium cedrorum* and *Glycyrrhiza flavescens* (Cilicia), and *Convolvulus coelesyriacus*, *Euphorbia cassia* and *Scrophularia peyronii* (Cyprus). *Genista fasselata* only occurs on Mount Carmel (Israel) and the Troodos Mountains (Cyprus).

The flora of the region is included in the following: Post (1896, 1931–1933), Davis (1965–1985), Zohary (1966, 1972), Mouterde (1966–1982), Akman (1973a) and Feinbrun-Dothan (1978, 1986).

## Useful plants

A large number of plant species are of, or have had, some economic value. *Arum* spp., *Campanula rapunculus*, *Chenopodium* spp., *Diplotaxis acris*, *Sisymbrium irio*, *Gundelia tournefortii*, *Lactuca cretica* and *Silybum marianum* are used as greens and salads; *Capparis spinosa*, *Laurus nobilis*, *Capparis spinosa*, *Origanum syriacum*, *Satureja thymbra* and *Teucrium* spp. as condiments or spices; and the tubers or bulbs of *Allium ampeloprasum*, *Astoma seselifolium*, *Crocus hyemalis*, *Erodium hirtum* and *Hordeum bulbosum* as root vegetables.

Edible fruits include *Arbutus andrachne*, *Prunus ursina*, *Rubus sanctus* and many legumes. *Sinapis alba*, *S. arvensis* and various other crucifers, as well as *Olea europaea* and *Ricinus communis* are, or were, sources of edible oils. Essential oils are extracted from many shrubby labiates belonging to *Calamintha*, *Lavandula*, *Micromeria*, *Origanum*, *Salvia*, *Thymbra* and *Thymus* and are used in the perfume industry.

*Alkanna tinctoria*, *Echium italicum*, *Phelypaea lutea* and *Reseda luteola* were used formerly as sources of vegetable dyes; their use has now largely been supplanted by synthetic dyes.

Numerous species are sold in markets as folk medicines, e.g. *Alkanna strigosa*, *Calamintha incana*, *Cynoglossum creticum*, *Leontice leontopetalum*, *Origanum syriacum*, *Teucrium polium*, *Thymelaea hirsuta*, *Datura stramonium*, *Foeniculum vulgare*, *Glycyrrhiza glabra* and *Nerium oleander*.

Many species of grasses have been valued as pasture for sheep and cattle since ancient times; many legumes, including *Astragalus* spp., *Lathyrus* spp. and *Vicia* spp., are important for fodder.

Beekeeping is important to the local economy of these countries; good sources of honey are provided by *Sinapis* spp. and other crucifers, *Trifolium* spp., *Amygdalus communis*, *Centaurea* spp., *Daucus* spp., *Coridothymus capitatus*, *Inula viscosa* and *Prosopis farctus*.

Many native species are of ornamental value. Important species for the cut flower trade include *Anemone coronaria*, *Narcissus tazetta*, *Cistus villosus*, *Lavandula stoechas* and *Paeonia corallina*.

The forests of the region supplied earlier civilizations with timber for shipbuilding and the construction of palaces, temples and other buildings. Over centuries, the forests of Amanus, Lebanon and Syria were cut and the timber exported. Much valuable timber was used for locomotive fuel and for railway sleepers during the World Wars (Zohary 1962; Chouchani, Khoueani and Quézel 1974).

## Social and environmental values

The mountains of the Levant act as a climatic barrier, being both responsible for the existence of the Syrian Desert to the east (because of their rain shadow effect) and preventing the spread of the desert westward to the Mediterranean. The Orontes gap has a profound effect on the phytogeography of the mountains of Iraqi Kurdistan as it allows rain-bearing winds to cross the Syrian Desert and so allows the development of an East Mediterranean type of flora on those mountains; some species are disjunct between the Levantine Uplands and Iraqi Kurdistan as a result (Zohary 1973).

Many small mountain resorts, including skiing resorts, have been developed in the Levantine Uplands but the long-running wars in the region have prevented the tourist industry from attracting people from outside the immediate area. Recently, however, large-scale tourist developments have begun on the coast near Latakia.

Trees have had religious significance among the local people for millennia and they were previously used as meeting places where open air judiciary courts were held.

## Threats

Remaining forests represent barely 5% of the original cover as a result of centuries of clearance for agriculture and over-exploitation for timber. These same processes are a threat to that which remains. Uncontrolled logging has almost totally eliminated some climax forest types. For example, *Quercus calliprinos* forest formerly covered the whole of the Jabal an Nusayriyah between 200 and 800 m, but only small remnants now remain around sacred sites in Mazars. Cedar forests have also been decimated. In former times, regeneration of the forests took place during periods of lower demand for timber; however, intensive modern methods often do not allow forest regeneration.

The Levantine Uplands form part of the "Fertile Crescent" and for centuries forest, garigue and maquis have been converted to arable land. This process has been exacerbated by the influx of refugees and immigrants, resulting in more pressure on the land for settlements and food production. Even such common species as *Anemone coronaria* and *Papaver rhoeas* are declining in numbers due to modern intensive agricultural methods, while the expansion of citrus cultivation is a threat to many coastal plant communities in Israel, Lebanon and Syria.

Urbanization along the coast is a threat to remaining local carob and olive trees (Pons and Quézel 1985). Many bulbous plants (including endemics) are threatened by deep-ploughing and over-collection (for their medicinal or ornamental value).

Important wetland sites are seriously threatened by large-scale drainage schemes. Some, such as the Hula swamps (which were among the largest representative samples of Near Eastern hydrophytic vegetation) (Boulos 1985), have already suffered damage, or have been totally destroyed. Three-quarters of a list of 26 plants now considered extinct in Israel are wetland species (Dafni and Agami 1976) and many local populations of other aquatic plants and animals are threatened.

Tourist developments are a threat to remaining coastal forest at Latakia (Boulos 1985). This forest is peculiar to the local ophiolitic rocks and not found elsewhere in the Levant. It is important that some is conserved.

Over-harvesting of species providing essential oils, such as *Origanum onites* and *Laurus nobilis*, is a threat to the sustainability of these resources.

## Conservation

Nahal (1962) has made a passionate plea for the conservation of all climax forest types. Protected areas within the the Levantine Uplands and current legislation in each country are given below.

### Israel

*Protected areas* – Gilboa NR: 728 km²; Hermon River NR: 81 km²; Hula Swamp NR: 310 km²; Mount Hermon NR: 186 km²; *Sternbergia clusiana* NR: 56 km²; Mount Carmel Nature Park; Har Meron Reserve.

Israel has some of the most effective conservation measures and protected areas legislation in the Middle East. The latter includes the Forest Ordinance of 1926 and the National Parks and Nature Reserves Authority Law 1963. Numerous plant species are protected by law, including all Orchidaceae, many species of *Iris*, *Cyclamen coum*, *C. persicum* and *Centaurea crocodylium*. However, most of the Levantine Uplands fall outside Israel's jurisdiction. Increasing economic and strategic pressures could threaten the security of existing reserves (Green and Drucker 1990).

### Syria

*Protected areas* – Ghabo Lake Protected Area: 320 km²; Qutinna Lake (Buhayrat Qattinah) Protected Area: 6000 km².

There is no protected areas legislation. The Ministry of Agriculture Directorate of Forests and Afforestation has designated a significant amount of protected forest and is at present setting up *Cedrus* forest reserves in the Jabal an Nusayriyah (Green and Drucker 1990).

## Lebanon

*Protected areas* – None known in the area under consideration. It is also not known if there are any conservation measures to protect remaining cedar stands and other habitats deemed worthy of conservation.

## Turkey

*Protected areas* – No protected areas exist, or are currently proposed, in the area under consideration although Pleistocene relict forests of the Amanus Mountains deserve protection.

Protected areas legislation exists in the form of the National Park law No. 2873/1983 and the Environment Law 2872/1983. National Park legislation was first implemented in 1985 but is only partly effective owing to a lack of measures for effectively preventing damaging activities.

## References

Akman, Y. (1973a). Contribution à l'étude de la flore des montagnes de l'Amanus, I–III. *Comm. Fac. Sci. Univ. Ankara* 17C: 1–19, 21–42, 43–70.

Akman, Y. (1973b). Aperçu préliminaire sur les conditions phyto-écologiques de la chaine de l'Amanus dans la Région du Hatay, I. *Comm. Fac. Sci. Univ. Ankara* 17C: 75–98.

Akman, Y. (1973c). Aperçu préliminaire sur les conditions phyto-écologiques de la chaine de l'Amanus dans la Région du Hatay, III. *Comm. Fac. Sci. Univ. Ankara* 17C: 137–163.

Boulos, L. (1985). The arid eastern and south eastern Mediterranean region. In Gómez-Campo, C. (ed.), *Plant conservation in the Mediterranean area*. Elsevier, Amsterdam. Pp. 123–140.

Bridges, E.M. (1990). *World geomorphology*. Cambridge University Press, Cambridge, U.K.

Chouchani, B., Khoueani, A. and Quézel, P. (1974). À propos de quelques groupements forestiers du Liban. *Biol. Écol. Médit.* 1: 63–77.

Dafni, A. and Agami, M. (1976). Extinct plants of Israel. *Biological Conservation* 10: 49–52.

Davis, P.H. (ed.) (1965-1985). *Flora of Turkey and the East Aegean Islands*. Edinburgh University Press, Edinburgh. (9 vols and Supplement; for latter see Davis, Mill and Tan 1988.)

Davis, P.H., Mill, R.R. and Kit Tan (1988). *Flora of Turkey and the East Aegean Islands*, Vol. 10 (Supplement). Edinburgh University Press, Edinburgh.

Demiriz, H. and Baytop, T. (1985). The Anatolian Peninsula. In Gómez-Campo, C. (ed.), *Plant conservation in the Mediterranean area*. Elsevier, Amsterdam. Pp. 113–121.

Feinbrun-Dothan, N. (1978). *Flora Palaestina*, vol 3. Israel Academy of Sciences and Humanities, Jerusalem.

Feinbrun-Dothan, N. (1986). *Flora Palaestina*, vol 4. Israel Academy of Sciences and Humanities, Jerusalem.

Green, M.J. and Drucker, G.F. (1990). Current status of protected areas and threatened mammal species in the Saharo-Gobian region. World Conservation Monitoring Centre, Cambridge, U.K. (Unpublished report.)

Hunter, B. (ed.) (1992). *The statesman's year-book, statistical and historical annual of the states of the world for the year 1992–1993*. Macmillan, London. 1702 pp.

Mouterde, P. (1966-1982). *Nouvelle Flore du Liban et de la Syrie*. Dar El-Machreq, Beirut. (Vol. 1, 1966; vol. 2, 1970; vol. 3 in parts, ed. A. Charpin and W. Greuter: part 1 – 1978, part 2 – 1979, part 3 – 1980, part 4 – 1982).

Nahal, I. (1962). Contribution à l'étude de la végétation dans la Baer-Bassit et de Djebel Alaouite de Syrie. *Webbia* 16(2): 477–641.

Pons, A. and Quézel, P. (1985). The history of the flora and vegetation and past and present human disturbance in the Mediterranean region. In Gómez-Campo, C. (ed.), *Plant conservation in the Mediterranean area*. Elsevier, Amsterdam. Pp. 25–43.

Post, G. (1896). *Flora of Syria, Palestine and Sinai*. Ed. 1. Beirut. (Ed. 2 revised by J.E. Dinsmore, 1931–1933, American Press, Beirut.)

Sonnenfeld, P. (1974). The Upper Miocene evaporite basins in the Mediterranean region: a study in paleo-oceanography. *Geol. Rundschen* 63: 1133–1172. [Reprinted in 1981 as Pp. 276–315 in Sonnenfeld, P. (ed.), *Tethys: the ancestral Mediterranean*. Benchmark Papers in Geology 53. Hutchinson Ross, Stroudsburg, Pennsylvania.]

Takahashi, K. and Arakawa, H. (eds) (1981). *World survey of climatology. Vol. 9. Climates of southern and western Asia*. Elsevier, Amsterdam.

Zohary, M. (1962). *The plant life of Palestine: Israel and Jordan*. Ronald Press, New York. 262 pp.

Zohary, M. (1966). *Flora Palaestina*, vol. 1. Israel Academy of Sciences and Humanities, Jerusalem.

Zohary, M. (1972). *Flora Palaestina*, vol. 2. Israel Academy of Sciences and Humanities, Jerusalem.

Zohary, M. (1973). *Geobotanical foundations of the Middle East*, 2 vols. Fischer, Stuttgart, and Swets and Zeitlinger, Amsterdam. 739 pp.

## Acknowledgements

This Data Sheet was written by Dr Robert R. Mill (Royal Botanic Garden, Edinburgh).

# HYRCANIAN FORESTS
# Iran and Azerbaijan

**Location:** Extending in an arc along the southern shore of the Caspian Sea from the Talysh region of Azerbaijan (at longitude 48°E) to Gorgan in Iran (at longitude 56°E) and between latitudes 38°55'N in Azerbaijan and 35°05'N in Iran.

**Area:** c. 50,000 km².

**Altitude:** 0–2500 m.

**Vegetation:** Broadleaved deciduous forest, in appearance very similar to the forest of the Black Sea coast in northern Turkey; shrublands.

**Flora:** No available estimate for size of flora; 4 endemic monotypic genera known.

**Useful plants:** Timber trees, including species of *Carpinus, Fagus, Fraxinus* and *Quercus*; ornamental species, such as *Parrotia persica* and *Zelkova carpinifolia*.

**Threats:** Large areas of forest have been cleared for agriculture (particularly on the coastal plain) and for timber. Some areas of the coastal plain invaded by a "spiny maquis" of exotic species.

**Conservation:** Several protected areas but no information available on their current status.

## Geography

The Hyrcanian forests extend in an arc along the southern shore of the Caspian Sea from the Talysh region of Azerbaijan (at longitude 48°E) to Gorgan in Iran (at longitude 56°E) and between latitudes 38°55'N in Azerbaijan and 35°05'N in Iran. The area covers approximately 50,000 km², most of which is within the Iranian provinces of Gilan and Mazanderan. The area, as here defined, comprises the southern coastal plain of the Caspian Sea, the eastern slopes of the Talysh Mountains (Talyshskiye Gory) of north-western Iran and south-eastern Azerbaijan and the northern slopes of the Elburz Mountains in Iran, up to about 2500 m. Above this altitude the vegetation is floristically transitional with the vegetation of the Irano-Turanian Regional Centre of Endemism.

The Elburz Mountains are an extensive system of folded mountains with ridges running in a predominantly east/west direction. The ridges are between 2000–4000 m altitude and reach 5766 m on the volcanic peak of Mount Damavand (which lies outside the area under consideration). At one time there were extensive areas of swamps along the coastal plain, but these have now been drained for agriculture. Along the coast are areas of shingle and sandy soils, behind which are salt marshes and coastal lagoons.

The climate is warm, with wet summers (rainfall 600–2600 mm per annum) and mild winters. The coastal plain and lower mountain slopes have a typical oceanic climate not unlike that of the Atlantic coast of Europe, whilst at higher altitudes (above 500 m) winter temperatures drop sharply and are similar to those of cold temperate zones (Zohary 1973). Rainfall decreases from west to east in the region.

The area is a major agricultural region. Rice, tobacco and cotton are the most important crops.

## Vegetation

The dominant vegetation is mesic, broadleaved deciduous forest. At lower altitudes this takes on the appearance of jungle, while at higher altitudes almost pure stands of *Fagus orientalis* dominate the forest. These lush forests are in sharp contrast, and clearly delimited, from the xeric vegetation of the dry southern slopes of the Elburz Mountains which belong to the Irano-Turanian Regional Centre of Endemism.

In many areas, the Hyrcanian forests have been extensively felled and the floristic composition of that which remains has been much altered. This makes it difficult to reconstruct the original altitudinal zonation of the vegetation. Zohary (1973) recognises four main units within the region. These are summarised below.

### Alluvial forest

Alluvial forest, dominated by *Salix* spp., *Populus canescens, Pterocarya fraxinifolia, Alnus subcordata* and *A. barbata*, once occupied moist lands and river banks of the alluvial plains in the coastal belt. Apart from a few remnants it has been cleared for agriculture.

### Broadleaved deciduous forest

This occupies drier habitats from sea-level to c. 1000 m. Dominants are *Quercus castaneifolia* with *Carpinus betulus, Fraxinus excelsior, Ulmus campestris, Acer insigne, Parrotia persica, Zelkova carpinifolia, Diospyros lotus, Alnus subcordata, Albizia julibrissin* and *Juglans regia*. There are many climbers and low shrubs, giving the forest a jungle-like appearance. Much of the forest has been cleared for agriculture; that which remains is much-degraded. A "spiny maquis" of *Gleditsia caspica, Mespilus germanica* and *Punica granatum* has invaded many areas.

### Beech forest

The zone from 1200–2000 m is occupied by almost pure beech forest dominated by *Fagus orientalis*. Other common tree species include *Quercus castaneifolia, Parrotia persica, Carpinus orientalis, Acer insigne, Ulmus glabra, Tilia rubra* and, occasionally, *Taxus baccata*.

### Low forest or shrubland

This occurs in climatically less favourable sites and on thin soils between 1800–2500 m. Dominant species include *Quercus macranthera*, with *Cotoneaster racemiflora, Sorbus boissieri, S. graeca, Crataegus pentagyna, C. microphylla* and *Pyrus boissieriana*.

As well as these main forest types, Zohary (1973) also recognises two relict forest types. The first, dominated by *Cupressus sempervirens* var. *horizontalis*, with *Cotoneaster racemiflora* and *Acer turcomanicum*, occurs in a few scattered areas in the Elburz Mountains. The second, dominated by *Thuja orientalis*, with *Quercus castaneifolia, Pyrus boissierana, Crataegus monogyna* and *Acer turcomanicum*, is found in the east near Astrabad in Gorgan.

On the north slopes of the Elburz Mountains the timber-line occurs at about 2500 m. Above this there is a narrow band of low shrubland dominated by *Juniperus communis*, with *Berberis* spp., *Daphne* spp. and *Rosa* spp. This gives way to dwarf tragacanthic shrubland at higher altitudes. This zone is transitional between the Euro-Siberian and Irano-Turanian regions. The tragacanthic shrubland is typically Irano-Turanian in composition and the herbaceous vegetation is dominated by typically Euro-Siberian genera, such as *Rumex, Oxyria, Corydalis, Anemone* and *Androsace*.

There are variations in the composition and altitude of forest zones from west to east, corresponding to a gradient of increasing wetness. In the centre and west, the timber-line is about 2500 m, whereas in the east it drops to about 1000 m.

## Flora

The vegetation of the area belongs to the Hyrcano-Euxine province of the Euro-Siberian Region. This is well illustrated by the importance of several boreal tree genera (including *Acer, Carpinus, Fagus, Quercus, Tilia* and *Ulmus*) in the forests of the region.

There is no available accurate estimate for the size of the flora or for the number of endemics in the region. Hedge and Wendelbo (1978) record 4 endemic monotypic genera: *Amblyocarpum* (Compositae) from Talysh; *Alyssopsis* (Cruciferae) from the upper forest regions; *Parrotia* (Hamamelidaceae) from the forests of northern Iran; *Phuopsis* (Rubiaceae) from Gilan and Talysh. The most distinctive of these is *Parrotia*, a widespread and important constituent of forest vegetation from sea-level to 1240 m. It forms trees up to 20 m tall. It is most closely related to the north-west Himalayan genus *Parrotiopsis*. Both genera are monotypic and have affinities with North American, rather than Asiatic, members of the family.

According to Gauba (1954–1955), at least 50 species of trees and 60 of shrubs are found in the area. There is also a rich herb flora. Hedge and Wendelbo (1978) note that there are a number of striking woody endemics in the region, including *Gleditsia caspica, Quercus castaneifolia, Ilex spinigera* and *Buxus hyrcana*. Zohary (1973) states that a considerable number of the herbaceous species forming the ground cover in the Hyrcanian forests are endemic or near-endemic. Hedge and Wendelbo (1978) point out that there are few examples of distinctive specific endemics amongst the herbs of the lowland and montane forests, whereas the number of endemics clearly increases in *Fagus orientalis/Quercus macranthera* forest at higher altitudes.

The forests of the Hyrcanian and Euxinian subprovinces share many species in common; however, there are some important differences. Several genera, which are important constituents in the Euxinian forests of northern Turkey are absent from the Hyrcanian forests. They include the genera *Pinus, Abies, Picea* and *Rhododendron*.

## Useful plants

A number of important timber trees occur in the Hyrcanian forests, including: *Alnus subcordata, Carpinus betulus, C. orientalis, Cupressus sempervirens* var. *horizontalis, Fagus orientalis, Fraxinus excelsior, Juglans regia, Quercus castaneifolia* and *Ulmus glabra*. Other indigenous trees are important ornamental species of value in horticulture. They include *Parrotia persica* and *Zelkova carpinifolia*.

## Threats

The main threats to the forests are from clearance for agriculture and uncontrolled logging. Degradation of woodland by selective felling is a serious problem and results in the invasion of exotic species. On the coastal plain, there are important wetlands; the few areas of coastal forests remaining are in need of protection.

## Conservation

A number of protected areas have been established in the area, but no information is available on their present status.

## References

Gauba, E. (1954-1955). Ein Besuch der Karpischen Wälder Nordpersiens. *Ann. naturh. Mus. Wien* 60: 60–76.

Hedge, I.C. and Wendelbo, P. (1978). Patterns of distribution and endemism in Iran. *Notes Roy. Bot. Gard. Edinburgh* 36: 441–464.

Zohary, M. (1973). *Geobotanical foundations of the Middle East*, 2 vols. Fischer, Stuttgart, and Swets and Zeitlinger, Amsterdam. 739 pp.

## Acknowledgements

This Data Sheet was written by Mr A.G. Miller (Royal Botanic Garden, Edinburgh).

# NORTH-EAST ANATOLIA
## Turkey

**Location:** The area comprises the Turkish vilayets (provinces) of Giresun, Trabzon, Rize and Çoruh in north-east Turkey, together with that part of the Pontus Mountains in the vilayet of Gümüşhane. It is bordered on the north by the Black Sea coast, to the west by the Melet River (vilayet of Ordu) and to the east by Gruziya (Georgia), between latitudes 39°02'–41°32'N and longitudes 37°57'–42°37'E.

**Area:** c. 33,200 km².

**Altitude:** 0–3932 m (summit of Kaçkar Dağ). Many peaks are over 3000 m.

**Vegetation:** Euxine forest, varying from coastal humid subtropical forest to fir forest; *Rhododendron* scrub and scree vegetation above tree-line; acid peat communities.

**Flora:** At least 2460 vascular plant species, of which c. 300 (12%) are endemic to Turkey and a much higher percentage endemic to North-east Anatolia and adjacent parts of Gruziya.

**Useful plants:** Fruit trees (e.g. *Prunus* spp.), nut trees (e.g. *Corylus* spp.), timber trees.

**Other values:** Watershed protection, climate maintenance, rich fauna (including bear, ibex, wolf and many species of butterfly), tourism.

**Threats:** Logging, clearance for agriculture, commercial collection of bulbs, peat cutting, mining, depopulation resulting in decline of traditional management practices in alpine pastures.

**Conservation:** 1 National Park (Altindere Vadisi Milli Parkı).

## Geography

North-east Anatolia (sometimes referred to as Lazistan) comprises the Turkish vilayets of Giresun, Trabzon, Rize, Çoruh and Gümüşhane in north-eastern Turkey, between latitudes 39°02'–41°32'N and longitudes 37°57'–42°37'E. All except Gümüşhane are bordered to the north by the Black Sea (Kara Deniz) coast. Giresun, the most westerly vilayet, is bounded on the west by Ordu vilayet. The eastern boundary is formed by the border with the Republic of Gruziya (Georgia). The Turkish provinces have a combined area of 33,202 km² (Giresun – 6934 km²; Trabzon – 4685 km²; Rize – 3920 km²; Çoruh – 7436 km²; Gümüşhane – 10,227 km²).

The population of North-east Anatolia was estimated in 1980 at 2,076,574 (Giresun – 480,083; Trabzon – 731,045; Rize – 361,258; Çoruh – 228,997; Gümüşhane – 275,191). Most of the population are Turks or of mixed descent. However, the five coastal towns of Pazar, Ardeşen, Findikli, Arhavi and Hopa are the home of the Laz people. About 20 km inland of Pazar is the village of Çamlihemşin, in the environs of which live another Georgian people, the Hemşinli.

Urbanisation of the very narrow coastal strip has been rapid in recent decades. A modern highway isolates the coastal towns from the sea. Apart from this, and the international route from Trabzon via Gümüşhane and the inner plateau to Iran, roads are few and poorly surfaced, and are constrained by the topography to run north-south. There are airports at Trabzon and Rize, while Bulancak, Görele, Vakfikebir, Trabzon, Şürmene, Rize, Pazar and Hopa have port facilities.

The ranges of the Giresun Dağları and Karadeniz Dağları (the eastern portion of the Pontus Mountains) have many peaks of over 3000 m and reach their highest point at Kaçkar Dağ (3932m), south-east of Çamlihemşin. This part of the range is sometimes referred to as the Pontic Alps, or the Little Caucasus. Other important ranges include the Yalnizçam Dağları, south-east of Artvin (with a number of peaks between 2413–3050 m), Alaca Dağ and Şavval Tepe (both above Murgul) and the Soğanli Dağları (3193–3353 m) which more or less forms the boundary between North-east Anatolia and the East Anatolian high plateau. The region is connected to the high plateau, and thus to the rest of mainland Asia, by a few high passes (geçidi). The most important of these are the Zigana Geçidi, the Soğanli Geçidi, the Ovitdağı Geçidi and the Scuruca Geçidi. These have been used for centuries by silk merchants and other travellers from the Far East.

Most of the rock is basic igneous but many of the highest jagged peaks are of granite (Davis 1965). There are also outcrops of cyanite and granodiorite in the Kaçkar Range; these are rock types rarely found in Turkey. The mountains show signs of fairly extensive past glaciation and there are still some small glaciers on the highest peaks of the Kaçkar Dağları (Dubin and Lucas 1989). There are over 100 small alpine lakes in the mountains. To the north of the main chain, many streams and torrents flow in deep parallel south-north gorges which contain numerous waterfalls. The coastline of the Black Sea is very steep. To the south, the range falls steeply to the inner Anatolian plateau. A fault line parallel to the mountain chain is occupied by the Çoruh Nehri, by far the major river of the region. This cuts through the mountains in a spectacular gorge near Artvin before flowing into the Black Sea at Batum (in Gruziya).

The climate is unique in Turkey for its very high all-year-round rainfall and mist precipitation. Most of the region receives over 1000 mm, while between Rize and Hopa the annual rainfall is more than 2000 mm. Rainfall is much higher below the tree line than above; in summer, alpine valleys may be scorched by the sun while the valleys below are shrouded in mist. Only for a short period, between late August and early October, do the mists on the seaward slopes of the Pontus Mountains disappear daily for any length of time. The coastal climate is mild, with mean temperatures ranging from about 4°C in winter to about 23°C in summer; on the peaks of the main mountain ranges the temperature range is more extreme, from -16°C in winter to 12°C in summer. At least at lower levels, the climate has much in common with that of Atlantic Europe and this is of phytogeographical significance.

## Vegetation

The climax vegetation is lush Euxine subtropical cloud forest. At lower altitudes this is deciduous, with some evergreen shrubs. The main trees are *Castanea sativa*, *Carpinus betulus*, *Acer cappadocicum* and *Diospyros lotus*. At higher altitudes, conifers are more abundant and eventually predominate. Species include *Picea orientalis* and *Abies nordmanniana*. Other characteristic species which do not extend further west in Turkey than North-east Anatolia are *Betula medwedewii*, *B. browicziana* (endemic), *Alnus barbata* and *Quercus pontica*. At still higher altitudes, several *Rhododendron* species (one endemic) occur in narrow, altitudinally delimited belts with occasional hybridisation occurring at contact zones (e.g. *R.* × *sochadzeae*).

Herbs include the monotypic endemic genera *Pachyphragma* (Cruciferae) and *Chamaesciadium* (Umbelliferae), together with numerous species of *Galanthus*, *Scilla* and other bulbs of horticultural value.

Quézel, Barbéro and Akman (1980) have studied the vegetation of the whole of northern Anatolia (including the area discussed here) in great detail. The vegetation of North-east Anatolia has much in common with the more westerly parts of the Pontus Mountains, but there are also numerous unique features. They divide the vegetation into two broad types, Mediterranean and Euxine, which are further subdivided into various phytosociological groupings and associations.

### Mediterranean vegetation

Mediterranean vegetation is restricted to a narrow, interrupted coastal strip, and to what Quézel, Barbéro and Akman (1980) term the "intra-Pontic" valleys. The latter run transversely between the mountain ranges which make up the Pontus chain. The Mediterranean enclaves in these valleys are all at altitudes not exceeding 600–700 m and occur mainly in the western part of the Pontus Mountains.

Undisturbed coastal Mediterranean vegetation consists of sclerophyllous shrubs and typical Mediterranean trees, such as *Carpinus orientalis*, *Phillyrea media* and *Arbutus andrachne*; characteristic herbaceous species include *Dorycnium pentaphyllum* subsp. *herbaceum* and *Scutellaria albida*. Degradation of Mediterranean vegetation results in maquis comprising *Cistus creticus*, *C. salviifolius*, *Juniperus oxycedrus*, *Arbutus andrachne* and associated herbs and grasses, such as *Origanum vulgare* and *Aira caryophyllea*.

### Euxine vegetation

The most important associations are those Euxine forest and shrub climaxes found below 1300 m (types 1–4, below). Above c. 1300–1400 m, chestnut and hornbeam forests are replaced by vast, mostly well-preserved beech, fir and pine forests (types 5–7). In the north-easternmost sector, at higher altitudes these give way to *Rhododendron* scrub.

#### 1. Hornbeam forest
Hornbeam (*Carpinus orientalis*) forest occurs on seaward slopes at 300–400 m on north- and east-facing slopes, and at 400–600 m on south- and west-facing slopes. The flora includes many Mediterranean elements, such as *Erica arborea*, *Ruscus aculeatus*, *Vitis vinifera* and *Cistus salviifolius*. *Laurus nobilis*, *Oplismenus undulatifolius*, *Buxus sempervirens* and *Vinca minor* occur locally.

#### 2. Chestnut forest
Sweet chestnut (*Castanea sativa*) forest occurs from (100–) 200–1000 m, especially in sparsely populated districts. Chestnuts mostly occur as pure stands, but the ground flora is very rich and includes *Campanula alliariifolia*, *Cicerbita bourgaei*, *Lilium szovitsianum*, *Rhamnus imeretinus* and the fern *Pteris cretica*. In more thermophilous habitats, *Carpinus orientalis* is sometimes present along with *Omphalodes cappadocica*, *Hedera colchica* and *Iris lazica*.

#### 3. Maritime pine forest
Pine (*Pinus sylvestris*) forests are very localised (near Of) from near sea-level to c. 400 m altitude. *Epimedium pinnatum* subsp. *colchicum*, *Festuca gigantea*, *Hyalopoa pontica*, *Carex latifolia* and numerous ferns, including *Osmunda regalis*, *Blechnum spicant* and *Dryopteris* spp. are characteristic herbs.

#### 4. Alder woodland
Alder (*Alnus barbata*) occurs on damp soils in the chestnut forest zone between 300–1300 m altitude. Typical species include *Cardamine lazica*, *C. raphanifolia*, *Chrysosplenium dubium* and *Thelypteris limbosperma*. Some species normally found in poplar woods also occur (such as *Gentiana asclepiadea* and *Rhynchocorys elephas*). Some alder woods in the vicinity of Rize are floristically distinct.

#### 5. Beech forest
Beech (*Fagus orientalis*) forest occurs above 1300–1400 m on andesite substrates, especially from Erbaa to Ünye. Beech forms more or less pure, dense stands, with individual trees reaching 30 m or more. The herb layer includes *Veronica magna*, *Arum orientale*, *Vicia lutea*, *Asperula odorata*, *Neottia nidus-avis*, *Cardamine bulbifera* and *Scrophularia scopolii*. Mixed beech/fir forests occur above the chestnut belt south of Giresun, and especially around Hamsiköy.

#### 6. Fir forest
Fir (*Picea orientalis*) forest occurs above 1500–1600 m, above the mixed beech/fir belt. East of the Melet River, as far as the border with Gruziya (and beyond), there are vast fir forests (of which c. 2000 km² occurs within North-east Anatolia). These forests include many relict species, such as *Epigaea gaultherioides*, *Rhodothamnus sessilifolius*, *Betula*

*medwedewii, Rhamnus imeretinus, Osmanthus decorus, Rhododendron caucasica, R. ungernii* and *R. smirnowii. Paris incompleta, Ranunculus buschei, Arenaria rotundifolia, Cyclamen coum* var. *caucasicum* and *Oxalis floribunda* are frequent associates. There is a very rich bryophyte flora.

### 7. Montane pine forest

Montane pine (*Pinus sylvestris*) forest occurs between 1700–2100 m, especially near Giresun and Trabzon. These forests are snow-covered for 6–7 months of the year. Species present include *Vaccinium myrtillus*, Pyrolaceae spp. (e.g. *Moneses uniflora, Orthilia secunda* and *Pyrola rotundifolia*), *Scilla monanthos* and many hawkweeds (*Hieracium* spp.).

On high passes, especially around Zigana (Trabzon), there are three very floristically rich associations of coniferous forest. These are:

i)   *Picea orientalis/Telekia speciosa* association on north-facing slopes. According to Quézel, Barbéro and Akman (1980) the wealth of flowers during July is an unforgettable sight. Species include *Senecio lazicus, Symphytum asperum, S. savvalense* and *Cirsium pseudopersonata*.

ii)  *Pinus sylvestris/Lilium ciliatum* association on south-facing slopes. Typical species include *Lilium ciliatum, Euphorbia djimilensis, Vicia freyniana* and *Melampyrum arvense*.

iii) *Pinus sylvestris/Daphne glomerata* association between 1700–2100 m on north-facing slopes. Species include *Geum coccineum, Leucorchis albida, Polygala alpestris* and other subalpine species. At high altitudes in the Pontus Mountains are deep acid peat communities resembling blanket bogs. These are extremely localized in Turkey and support a flora which comprises species otherwise very rare in Turkey. These include *Carex lasiocarpa, C. magellanica* subsp. *irrigua, Drosera intermedia, D. rotundifolia, Eriophorum angustifolium, E. vaginatum* and *Rhynchospora alba*.

Tall herbs, such as *Geranium sylvaticum, Aruncus sylvester, Impatiens noli-tangere* and *Campanula latifolia* are common to all three associations.

## Flora

At least 2460 species of vascular plants are known to occur in the region, of which approximately 300 (12%) are endemic to Turkey. About 160 species are only known from North-east Anatolia. Endemic species occur all along the Euxine phytogeographical province in Turkey bordering the Black Sea; however, there is a sudden increase in their frequency east of the Melet River (near Ordu). Beyond Turkey, the flora of adjacent parts of Gruziya, especially Abkhaziya and Adzhariya, also contains many endemics. At least 130 species are endemic to the combined area of North-east Anatolia and Gruziya.

Species endemic to North-east Anatolia include *Ranunculus tempskyanus, Papaver lateritium, Silene scythicina, Doronicum tobeyi,* 7 species of *Centaurea,* 24 species of *Hieracium, Symphytum savvalense, Symphyandra*

*lazica, Cyclamen parviflorum, Lamium sulfureum, Lilium ciliatum* and *Crocus aerius.* An entire section of *Campanula,* Section *Symphyandriformes,* is endemic to the region.

Centres of endemism in North-east Anatolia include the Cimil region, Çoruh Gorge and the mountains above Artvin and its outlying villages.

Many species are relicts and evidently descendants of the ancient Boreal-Tertiary flora that once covered a large part of temperate Eurasia. Examples include *Epigaea gaultherioides* (endemic to Gruziya and North-east Anatolia), *Rhodothamnus sessilifolius* (the only other species of the genus occurs in the eastern Alps), *Rhamphicarpa medwedewii* (the nearest relative of which occurs in East Africa and western India), and 4 species in the *Lilium ponticum* group (whose nearest allies are in eastern Asia) (Davis 1971).

Of the 97 pteridophyte taxa occurring in Turkey, 64 occur in North-east Anatolia and 28 of these are apparently found nowhere else in Turkey. Several of these, such as *Hymenophyllum tunbrigense* and *Dryopteris aemula,* are Atlantic species for which North-east Anatolia and adjacent parts of Caucasia form an eastern refuge far from their main centre of distribution (Fraser-Jenkins 1974).

The Euxine flora of the mountains of North-east Anatolia has some affinities to that of the Pyrenees (Davis 1971). North-east Anatolia is also home to species such as *Cynoglossum imeretinum* and *Duchesnea indica,* whose nearest localities, or nearest relatives, are in the Himalaya and Afghanistan. *Rhamphicarpa medwedewii* (Scrophulariaceae) occurs only in North-east Anatolia and Gruziya; all the other species of the genus are tropical African or Australasian. There is a strong Far Eastern element in the native (and introduced) flora of the region.

The area in the vicinity of Bayburt, in the rain shadow of the Pontic range, marks the northern end of the "Anatolian Diagonal", which forms an important floristic demarcation in Anatolia (Davis 1971; Ekim and Güner 1986). The Diagonal is discussed in more detail in the Data Sheet on the Anti-Taurus Mountains and Upper Euphrates (SWA12).

The only complete Flora of the entire Colchic region is that of Albov (1895) although the Turkish part is comprehensively treated in Davis (1965–1985) and in Davis, Mill and Tan (1988). Floras are in progress for Abkhaziya and Gruziya. A detailed account of the East Asiatic elements in Adzhariya is given by Ponert (1977).

## Useful plants

Useful plants include cherries (*Cerasus* spp.) (after which Giresun takes its name) and nut trees. Hazel nuts are an important crop: *Corylus avellana* is native, while *C. maxima* has been cultivated in the region for more than 400 years and has become naturalised. Sweet chestnut (*Castanea sativa*) is one of the most important timber trees of Anatolia.

Horticulturally important plants include many species of bulbs and tubers. Among those of particular importance are species of *Scilla, Galanthus, Lilium* and *Cyclamen.*

*Tanacetum coccineum* subsp. *chamaemelifolium* (endemic to North-east Anatolia and Gruziya) is an important source of pyrethrum, while *Poncirus trifoliatus* is used as a graft stock for citrus trees and as a hedge plant (Davis, Mill and Tan 1988).

## Social and environmental values

The region is of outstanding natural beauty and includes lush vegetation of moss-covered trees, forested valleys and mountain slopes, and numerous fast-flowing streams. This makes the area attractive for a variety of outdoor pursuits, including white-water canoeing, fishing and walking. The area abounds with butterflies in spring and summer, and remote ranges are the home of ibex, wolf, bear, deer and various birds of prey. There are extensive tea plantations and citrus orchards as well as many reminders of the area's cultural past.

The native wildlife and vegetation of North-east Anatolia and adjacent Caucasia, as well as the plantations, depend on the maintenance of the existing climate with its high rainfall and moderate temperatures. Both climate and native vegetation are mutually inter-dependent; were the dense forests to disappear, the intensity of the rainfall would cause massive landslips, erosion and loss of soil fertility because of the extreme steepness of the valleys. Rainfall patterns would be affected by forest clearance and lower slopes could become drier as a result.

## Threats

The main threats are logging and clearance of forest for agriculture. However, the steepness of the terrain limits intensive agriculture, so North-east Anatolia is less threatened than the inner plateau region of Turkey and the Mediterranean areas in the south and west. Mining is a potential threat; the area around Artvin is currently being prospected by many mining companies.

Commercial collection of bulbs and tubers for export is a threat to some species of *Scilla*, *Galanthus*, *Lilium* and *Cyclamen*. In 1992, the Turkish Ministry of Agriculture and Rural Affairs permitted the export of 150,000 bulbs of *Cyclamen coum*, 2,000,000 of *Galanthus ikariae* and 6357 of *Lilium ciliatum*.

North-east Anatolia is the only region in Turkey where emigration to cities and small family sizes are resulting in a net loss of population. Fewer people return each year to the yayla (alpine pasture) of high mountains where centuries of traditional management have resulted in species-rich hay meadows. These are increasingly at risk due to neglect. Peat cutting (by the yayla communities) is a serious, but localized, threat to the acid peat flora.

The Kaçkar Mountains are increasingly visited by Turkish and foreign trekkers and climbers. If tourism were to increase significantly there could be problems of erosion in areas most often visited.

## Conservation

There is only one National Park (Altindere Vadisi Milli Parkı) in the region. None of the eastern valleys and mountains of the Little Caucasus are protected in any way.

## References

Albov, N. (1895). *Prodromus Florae Colchicae*. Tiflis and Geneva.

Davis, P.H. (ed.) (1965-1985). *Flora of Turkey and the East Aegean Islands*. Edinburgh University Press, Edinburgh. (9 vols and Supplement; for latter see Davis, Mill and Tan 1988.)

Davis, P.H. (1971). Distribution patterns in Anatolia with particular reference to endemism. In Davis, P.H., Harper, P.C. and Hedge, I.C. (eds), *Plant life of South-West Asia*. Botanical Society of Edinburgh. Pp. 15–27.

Davis, P.H., Mill, R.R. and Kit Tan (1988). *Flora of Turkey and the East Aegean Islands*, Vol. 10 (Supplement). Edinburgh University Press, Edinburgh.

Dubin, M. and Lucas, E. (1989). *Trekking in Turkey*. Melbourne and Berkeley.

Ekim, T. and Güner, A. (1986). The Anatolian Diagonal: fact or fiction? *Proc. Roy. Soc. Edinburgh* 89B: 69–77.

Fraser-Jenkins, C.R. (1974). The distribution of *Dryopteris aemula* and its discovery in the Canaries and Turkey. *Fern Gazette (U.K.)* 11: 54.

Ponert, J. (1977). Ergasiophygophytes and xenophytes of East Asiatic origin in Adjaria. A stimulus to new terminology, especially for ergasiophygophytes. *Folia Geobot. Phytotax. (Praha)*: 12: 9–22.

Quézel, P., Barbéro, M. and Akman, Y. (1980). Contribution à l'étude de la végétation forestière d'Anatolie septentrionale. *Phytocoenologia* 8: 365–519.

## Acknowledgements

This Data Sheet was written by Dr Robert R. Mill (Royal Botanic Garden, Edinburgh). Colleagues at the Society for the Protection of Nature, Istanbul, provided many helpful comments on an earlier draft.

# APPENDIX 1
## DEFINITIONS OF SOME TERMS AND CATEGORIES

## 1. IUCN Conservation (Red Data Book Categories)

Conservation categories are given in the text for some threatened species where this information was readily available. The IUCN categories are given a capital letter to distinguish them from general usage of the terms.

### A. Threatened Categories

**Extinct (Ex)**
Taxa which are no longer known to exist in the wild after repeated searches of their type localities and other known or likely places.

**Endangered (E)**
Taxa in danger of extinction and whose survival is unlikely if the causal factors continue operating.

Included are taxa whose numbers have been reduced to a critical level or whose habitats have been so drastically reduced that they are deemed to be in immediate danger of extinction.

**Vulnerable (V)**
Taxa believed likely to move into the Endangered category in the near future if the causal factors continue operating.

Included are taxa of which most or all the populations are *decreasing* because of over-exploitation, extensive habitat or other environmental disturbance; taxa with populations that have been seriously *depleted* and whose ultimate security is not yet assured; and taxa with populations that are still abundant but are *under threat* from serious adverse factors throughout their range.

**Rare (R)**
Taxa with small world populations that are not at present Endangered or Vulnerable, but are at risk.

These taxa are usually localized within restricted geographical areas or habitats or are thinly scattered over a more extensive range.

**Indeterminate (I)**
Taxa *known* to be Extinct, Endangered, Vulnerable, or Rare but there is not enough information to say which of the four categories is appropriate.

### B. Unknown Categories

**Status Unknown (?)**
No information is available with which to assign a conservation category. [Note that this category was not used in CPD, but is included here for completeness.]

**Insufficiently Known (K)**
Taxa that are suspected but not definitely known to belong to any of the above categories, following assessment, because of lack of information.

### C. Not Threatened Category

**Safe (nt)**
Neither rare nor threatened.

## 2. Categories and Management Objectives of Protected Areas

IUCN Management Categories for protected areas are given in the text where this information was readily available. In some cases, nationally designated areas (such as some National Parks) do not meet the criteria required to be assigned an IUCN Management Category. However, the omission of an IUCN category in the CPD text does not imply that the area concerned has not been assigned a management category.

### Category I: Scientific Reserve/Strict Nature Reserve

To protect nature and maintain natural processes in an undisturbed state in order to have ecologically representative examples of the natural environment available for scientific study, environmental monitoring, education, and for the maintenance of genetic resources in a dynamic and evolutionary state.

### Category II: National Park

To protect natural and scenic areas of national or international significance for scientific, educational and recreational use.

### Category III: Natural Monument/ Natural Landmark

To protect and preserve nationally significant natural features because of their special interest or unique characteristics.

### Category IV: Managed Nature Reserve/Wildlife Sanctuary

To assure the natural conditions necessary to protect nationally significant species, groups of species, biotic communities, or physical features of the environment where these require specific human manipulation for their perpetuation.

### Category V: Protected Landscape or Seascape

To maintain nationally significant natural landscapes which are characteristic of the harmonious interaction of man and land while providing opportunities for public enjoyment through recreation and tourism within normal life style and economic activity of these areas.

## Category VI: Resource Reserve

To protect resources of the area for future use and prevent or contain development activities that could affect the resource pending the establishment of objectives which are based upon appropriate knowledge and planning.

## Category VII: Natural Biotic Area/ Anthropological Reserve

To allow the way of life of societies living in harmony with the environment to continue undisturbed by modern technology.

## Category VIII: Multiple-Use Management Area/Managed Resource Area

To provide for the sustained production of water, timber, wildlife, pasture, and outdoor recreation, with the conservation of nature primarily oriented to the support of economic activities (although specific zones may also be designed within these areas to achieve specific conservation objectives).

## Category IX: Biosphere Reserve

These are part of an international scientific programme, the Unesco Man and the Biosphere (MAB) Programme, which is aimed at developing a reserve network representative of the world's ecosystems to fulfil a range of objectives, including research, monitoring, training and demonstration, as well as conservation roles. In most cases the human component is vital to the functioning of the Biosphere Reserve.

## Category X: World Heritage Site

The *Convention Concerning the Protection of the World Cultural and Natural Heritage* (which was adopted in Paris in 1972 and came into force in December 1975) provides for the designation of areas of "outstanding universal value" as World Heritage Sites, with the principal aim of fostering international cooperation in safeguarding these important sites. Sites, which must be nominated by the signatory nation responsible, are evaluated for their world heritage quality before being declared by the World Heritage Committee. Article 2 of the Convention considers as natural heritage: natural features consisting of physical and biological formations or groups of such formations, which are of outstanding universal value from the aesthetic or scientific point of view; geological or physiographical formations and precisely delineated areas which constitute habitat of threatened species of animals or plants of outstanding universal value; and natural sites or precisely delineated areas of outstanding universal value from the point of view of science, conservation or natural beauty. Criteria for inclusion in the list are published by Unesco.

The definitions above are abridged from:

IUCN (1990). *1990 United Nations list of national parks and protected areas*. IUCN, Gland, Switzerland and Cambridge, U.K. 284 pp.

McNeely, J.A. and Miller, K.R. (eds) (1984). *National parks, conservation, and development. The role of protected areas in sustaining society*. Smithsonian Institution Press, Washington, D.C. Pp. 47–53.

## 3. Endemic Bird Areas (EBAs)

Analysis of the patterns of bird distribution by BirdLife International shows that species of birds with restricted ranges tend to occur together in places which are often islands or isolated patches of a particular habitat, especially montane and other tropical forests. Boundaries of these natural groupings have been identified and the areas thus defined have been called Endemic Bird Areas (EBAs). They number 221 and embrace 2484 bird species, which is the vast majority (95%) of all restricted-range birds (which are those species with known breeding ranges below 50,000 km$^2$). The presence of restricted-range bird species in CPD sites is noted in the Data Sheets.

For more information and a full list of EBAs, the reader is referred to the following:

ICBP (1992). *Putting biodiversity on the map: priority areas for global conservation*. International Council for Bird Preservation, Cambridge, U.K. 90 pp.

Stattersfield, A.J., Crosby, M.J., Long, A.J. and Wege, D.C. (in prep.). *A global directory of Endemic Bird Areas*. BirdLife International, Cambridge, U.K.

# APPENDIX 2
## LIST OF ACRONYMS AND ABBREVIATIONS

**ACT** – Australian Capital Territory

**AETFAT** – Association pour l'Etude Taxonomique de la Flore d'Afrique Tropicale

**ANCON** – Asociación Nacional para la Conservación de la Naturaleza (Paraguay)

**ASBOZA** – Association des Botanistes du Zaïre

**BIOTROP** – Southeast Asian Regional Centre for Tropical Biology

**BP** – Before present (years)

**CDF** – Charles Darwin Foundation

**CECON** – Centro de Estudios Conservacionistas, Universidad de San Carlos (Guatemala)

**CENARGEN** – Centro Nacional de Pesquisas de Recursos Genéticos e Biotecnologia (Brazil)

**CEPEC** – Centro de Pesquisas de Cacau (Brazil)

**CIPRA** – International Commission for the Protection of the Alps

**CITES** – Convention on International Trade in Endangered Species of Wild Fauna and Flora

**CMC** – IUCN Conservation Monitoring Centre (now WCMC)

**CNPPA** – Commission on National Parks and Protected Areas (IUCN)

**COA** – Corporación Colombiana para la Amazonia (Colombia)

**CODEFF** – Comité Nacional Pro Defensa de la Fauna y Flora (Chile)

**CONAF** – Corporación Nacional Forestal (Chile)

**CPD** – Centres of Plant Diversity

**CSIRO** – Commonwealth Scientific Industrial Research Organisation, Australia

**CTFT** – Centre Technique Forestier Tropical (Paris)

**CUMAT** – Centro de Investigaciones de la Capacidad de Uso Mayor de la Tierra (Bolivia)

**DANIDA** – Ministry of Foreign Affairs, Department of International Development

**dbh** – Diameter at breast height

**DoT** – Department of Transmigration (Indonesia)

**EBA** – Endemic Bird Areas

**ECAN** – Environmentally Critical Areas Network (Philippines)

**ECE** – Economic Commission for Europe (UN)

**ECOCIENCIA** – Fundación Ecuatoriana de Estudios Ecológicos (Ecuador)

**EEC** – European Economic Community

**EIA** – Environmental impact statement

**ELC** – Environment Liaison Centre

**EMBRAPA** – Empresa Brasileira de Pesquisa Agropecuária

**ESCAP** – Economic and Social Commission for Asia and the Pacific (UN)

**FAO** – Food and Agriculture Organisation of the United Nations

**FELDA** – Federal Land Development Authority (Malaysia)

**FINNIDA** – Finnish International Development Agency

**FRIM** – Forest Research Institute, Malaysia

**GEMS** – Global Environment Monitoring System (UNEP)

**GNPS** – Galápagos National Park Service

**GRID** – Global Resources Information Database (UNEP/GEMS)

**GTZ** – Deutsche Gesellschaft für Technische Zusammenarbeit

**HIID** – Harvard Institute for International Development

**IBGE** – Instituto Brasileiro de Geografia Estaqtistica (Brazil)

**IBP** – International Biological Programme

**IBPGR** – International Board for Plant Genetic Resources

**ICBP** – International Council for Bird Preservation (now BirdLife International)

**IIED** – International Institute for Environment and Development

**INBio** – Instituto Nacional de Biodiversidad de Costa Rica

**INDERENA** – Instituto Nacional de los Recursos Naturales y del Ambiente (Colombia)

**INPA** – Instituto Nacional de Pesquisas da Amazônica (Brazil)

**IPT** – Asian Wetland Bureau

**ITTA** – International Tropical Timber Agreement

**ITTO** – International Tropical Timber Organisation

**IUCN** – International Union for Conservation of Nature and Natural Resources – The World Conservation Union

**IUFRO** – International Union of Forestry Research Organisations

**MAB** – Man and the Biosphere Programme (Unesco)

**MOPAWI** – Mosquitia Pawisa (Honduras)

**NCS** – National Conservation Strategy

**NGO** – Non-governmental organization

**ODA** – Overseas Development Administration (UK)

**ORSTOM** – Institut Français de Recherche Scientifique pour le Developpement en Cooperation

**POSSCEF** – Project on Study Survey and Conservation of Endangered Species of Flora (India)

**Ramsar Convention** – Convention on Wetlands of International Importance Especially as Waterfowl Habitat

**RePPProt** – Regional Physical Planning Programme for Transmigration (Indonesia)

**SEDUE** – Subsecretaría de Ecología, Dirección de Flora y Fauna Silvestres (Mexico)

**SIDA** – Swedish International Development Authority

**SPREP** – South Pacific Regional Environment Programme

**SSC** – Species Survival Commission (IUCN)

**TFAP** – Tropical Forestry Action Plan

**TPU** – Threatened Plants Unit (formerly of IUCN, now of WCMC)

**UN** – United Nations

**UNCTAD** – United Nations Conference on Trade and Development

**UNDP** – United National Development Programme

**UNEP** – United Nations Environment Programme

**Unesco** – United Nations Educational, Scientific and Cultural Organisation

**UNIDO** – United Nations Industrial Development Organisation

**UNSO** – United Nations Sudano-Sahelian Office

**US-AID** – US Agency for International Development

**USDA** – United States Department of Agriculture

**WCED** – World Commission on Environment and Development

**WCMC** – World Conservation Monitoring Centre

**WCS** – World Conservation Strategy

**WRI** – World Resources Institute

**WWF** – World Wide Fund for Nature

# INDEX